Frank Grant Johnson

Johnson's Natural Philosophy, and Key to Philosophical Charts

Illustrated with 500 cuts; being reduced photographic copies of all the diagrams contained in the author's philosophical series of indestructible school charts

Frank Grant Johnson

Johnson's Natural Philosophy, and Key to Philosophical Charts
Illustrated with 500 cuts; being reduced photographic copies of all the diagrams contained in the author's philosophical series of indestructible school charts

ISBN/EAN: 9783337068745

Printed in Europe, USA, Canada, Australia, Japan

Cover: Foto ©Thomas Meinert / pixelio.de

More available books at **www.hansebooks.com**

JOHNSON'S

NATURAL PHILOSOPHY,

AND

KEY TO PHILOSOPHICAL CHARTS.

ILLUSTRATED WITH 500 CUTS; BEING REDUCED PHOTOGRAPHIC COPIES OF ALL THE DIAGRAMS CONTAINED IN THE AUTHOR'S PHILOSOPHICAL SERIES OF INDESTRUCTIBLE SCHOOL CHARTS.

FOR THE USE OF

SCHOOLS AND FAMILIES,

BY

FRANK G. JOHNSON, A.M., M.D.

NEW YORK:
J. W. Schermerhorn & Co.,
1872.

PREFACE.

The rapid diffusion of scientific knowledge, and the continually widening field of its application to the useful pursuits of life, have created an increased demand for new and improved means of teaching the various branches of Natural Philosophy. But no want is more generally felt, especially in common-schools and academies, than the necessity of Philosophical Diagrams, in the form of *Wall Charts*, to supply the absence of the expensive Philosophical Apparatus.

To supply this want is the purpose of the Philosophical Series of the compiler's *Indestructible School Charts;* to accompany and explain which, and provide a suitable text-book for schools and academies, are the objects of this volume.

Before describing these, reference is here made to a Series of Charts prepared to supply this need, by the same compiler, in 1856; being a set of ten Philosophical Charts, 3 by 4 feet, embracing about two hundred diagrams, a large edition of which was readily sold; but, in consequence of the engravings being destroyed by fire, no subsequent editions were issued.

To show the purpose of these Charts and the favor with which they were received at the time of their publication, we give the opinions of a few of the most distinguished men of the age:

From Benjamin Silliman, LL.D., Prof. Emeritus in Yale College.

Dr. Johnson's Philosophical Charts are well worthy of the attention of all teachers and learners of the different branches of Natural Philosophy, to which they relate.

The diagrams, drawn in colored or contrasted lines upon a black ground, are perfectly distinct and intelligible, and the large size and handsome mounting of the Charts give them a striking and attractive appearance.

To teachers without apparatus, they must be an invaluable acquisition, and a very useful one to those who *have* the instruments.

Such illustrations, as they speak to the mind through the eye, admit of indefinite extension to every branch of Natural Science. BENJ. SILLIMAN.

From Rev. Francis Wayland, D.D., LL.D., formerly Pres. of Brown University.

I have carefully examined Dr. Johnson's Philosophical Charts, and think them well adapted to the purposes for which they are intended. They will afford important aid to instructors in academies and schools where Philosophical Instruments are not furnished to perform illustrative experiments. In many cases they will also be of service even in addition to any ordinary apparatus.

FRANCIS WAYLAND.

Providence, R. I., Feb. 8th, 1856.

PREFACE.

From the Hon. Theodore Frelinghuysen, Pres. Rutgers College, New Jersey, formerly Chancellor of New York University.

Dr. Johnson's "Philosophical Charts," designed for the use of schools and academies, furnish an admirable substitute for the far more expensive apparatus. These Charts, hung on the walls of the school-room—in all of which I hope to see them—will spread before the scholar a palpable illustration of the great laws in Natural Philosophy. He will learn much of God, from the works of his hand and the ordinances of his appointment.

The small volume that accompanies them, and a little explanation from the teacher, will render the Charts one of the most useful means of instruction.

THEODORE FRELINGHUYSEN.

From the Hon. Horace Mann, President Antioch College, Ohio, formerly Secretary Board of Education of Massachusetts.

* * * * * * In schools where there is not the Philosophical Apparatus, these beautiful "Charts" will be an excellent substitute for it; and I shall be glad to show and to commend them to such persons as can best introduce them into schools, and especially to such as shall go forth from our institution to become school-teachers.

HORACE MANN.

These Charts were made on paper, and mounted on cloth and rollers, in the usual manner.

They were executed in *white lines*, by printing the background black; which, it is admitted, is the most desirable method, as it renders the diagrams more *conspicuous, yet easier for the eye.* The difficulty of printing a clean and pure black on so large a surface, however, made it impossible to execute them with desirable neatness and perfection. This difficulty has, finally, been overcome.

There are several serious objections to the usual method of making Charts and Maps on paper, and then mounting them on cloth and rollers, which it is desirable to avoid:

1st. As already stated, it is next to impossible to print a large black ground, and so give the diagram *in white*, or light-colored lines.

2d. Cloth and paper, pasted together, do not work well. In *damp* weather the *cloth shrinks* and the *paper swells*, and vice versa in *dry* weather. This draws the chart out of a true plane, renders the surface wavy, and prevents it from hanging flat on the wall.

3d. The tape-binding, sewed or pasted on the edges, and the sticks nailed on at top and bottom, render the Chart clumsy and awkward to handle, as well as liable to need repairs.

4th. The cloth and paper, and the paste between them, make the Chart so stiff, that if it be rolled up in *damp* and unrolled in *dry* weather, it is impossible to make it hang flat on the wall.

5th. The varnish employed to improve and protect the surface soon cracks and crumbles off.

6th. They soon appear dingy and show age.

7th. The paste employed in mounting often tempts the rats and mice to test what virtue there is in schooling for *them*, to the entire destruction of the Charts on the first investigation.

8th. Charts thus made are not sufficiently durable for school purposes.

To obviate all these objections, the compiler has invented and adopted a method of producing what he terms INDESTRUCTIBLE SCHOOL-CHARTS.

The method of making these Charts is entirely new. There is neither paper, ink, printing-press, tape, rollers, nor varnish, employed in their manufacture. They are printed by hand in pure white lines, with imperishable oil-colors, on enamelled jet-black cloth.

They are as smooth as glass, as soft and pliable as silk, and hang perfectly flat on the wall. They are as durable as a stone schoolhouse; they can be employed as table-covers, scrubbed with soap and water for years, and *then* be employed as Charts. *The background is jet-black, and far superior to any ink-printing.* Black and white are not the only colors that may be employed; for any desirable color can be used for either background or diagrams.

Each Chart is surrounded with a highly-colored border, giving it a remarkably neat and lively appearance.

The mounting consists of an oval stick inclosed in a hem of the Chart at top and bottom, thus avoiding *paste, binding, nails, and clumsy rollers.*

The *Philosophical Series* consists of ten Charts, each 33 by 54 inches, and is intended to much more than supply the place of the series above alluded to, embracing, instead of about two hundred diagrams, over five hundred, on the various branches of *Natural Philosophy*, as taught in schools; each diagram being carefully drawn, and standing out in bold white lines on a jet-black surface, constituting, we are confident, the *most complete, most durable, and cheapest substitute for the Philosophical Apparatus ever published.*

These Charts are to Natural Philosophy what blackboards are to mathematics, and what maps are to geography.

Every drawing is made simple as possible, without omitting any part necessary to give a clear illustration of the essential law or principle to be explained.

Each diagram is numbered, and provided with designating letters sufficiently large and bold to be seen across the recitation-room.

The entire set of ten is arranged, if desired, on a Sliding Chart-Rack, in such a manner that the whole set will occupy but about *four* feet in width of wall-room, yet either one of the set can be brought to view as readily as a leaf can be turned in a book.

These Charts are *especially* designed to supply the wants of our common-schools and academies which are not provided with the apparatus, which they have come greatly to need, but are generally unable to purchase. In many parts of the country, the *majority* of district-schools are no longer " common-schools," merely, where is taught only spelling, reading, and writing, together with the primary branches, arithmetic, geography, and grammar; but they have come to be academies, where, at least, so much of the natural sciences is taught as is contained in the ordinary school-manuals on Natural Philosophy; *thus creating a general and ever-increasing necessity for a work of this kind as a cheap and adequate substitute for the Philosophical Apparatus.*

With a set of these Charts in the schoolroom the teacher can awaken in his pupils the liveliest interest for the study of Natural Philosophy, and fix in their minds more lasting impressions of general principles than by any other means, in the same time and with equal effort.

While the intelligent teacher will be able to make invaluable use of them, with whatever text-book he may have in his school, or even without any text-book, yet, to render the Charts more useful to the cause of education, this volume, instead of being limited to an explanation of the diagrams of the Charts, embraces an enunciation and demonstration of more general laws and principles relating to the various departments of Natural Philosophy than are usually contained in school-manuals on this branch of education.

The *average* number of cuts or diagrams in text-books on this subject falls considerably below three hundred, while these Charts contain *five hundred* (counting two for one in a few instances, where they are combined to save space), all of which are contained in this volume; and, in order to have them appear as much like the Charts as possible, they are made quite large, in white lines on black ground, and copied by photography; hence they are reduced *fac-similes* of the Chart-diagrams.

The plan of numbering the paragraphs has been adopted for convenience of reference.

Physics, or, as more generally termed, *Natural Philosophy*, embracing several sciences, as Mechanics, Hydrostatics, Pneumatics, Acoustics, Heat, Optics, Magnetism, Electricity, Astronomy, etc., many volumes would be required to contain all that is known relating to the various branches of the subject. Hence, within the narrow limits of a text-book, only the leading or fundamental principles can be set forth. The field is so large, and the variety from which to select so great, that compilers of school-manuals, differing in their views respecting the relative practical importance of the different parts of the subject, have produced a variety of compendiums, which, however, treating of the eternal laws, can differ only in size, arrangement and classification of subjects, judiciousness of selection, aptness of illustration, precision and clearness of statement, and embracing important new discoveries.

In these respects, the relative merits of various schoolbooks on Natural Philosophy will be most justly estimated in the schoolroom by the practical teacher and earnest student.

TO THE TEACHER.

To make this book as comprehensive as possible, without rendering it too large for school purposes, the practical illustrations, under the general principles, have not been multiplied. Besides, it is not the best plan for the compiler of text-books, after having clearly enunciated and demonstrated a general principle, to go on and point out all its practical illustrations and applications; for, by so doing, he deprives the teacher and student of the opportunity to exercise their ingenuity in performing this part of the work. The instructor should impress upon the mind of the learner the importance of forming the *habit* of observing the operations of Nature that are always occurring about him, and to exercise his mind by referring them to the laws or general principles by which they are explained.

The teacher can make use of the *Charts* in various ways. He may use the pointer himself, or have the pupil use it. A good plan is to have the scholar exercise himself by demonstrating, with the pointer, diagrams contained in previous lessons, which he will be able to do with success and advantage, having witnessed the teacher's previous demonstrations; or the pupil may do the same with the advance lesson *before* listening to the instructor's explanation.

It is of the utmost importance that the scholar acquire the habit of oral demonstration, as it is by this practice that the teacher is enabled to know what the scholar's difficulties are—to ascertain what he *understands*, and what he *does not*, a quick appreciation of which is one of the greatest secrets of successful teaching. By frequent demonstrations, the learner, at the same time, cultivates the power of expressing and communicating to others what he has acquired. Besides, it is by demonstrating that definite and thorough knowledge is obtained.

The pupil should be frequently exercised, also, in reviewing, in order to impress the *idea* on the memory; for, to *learn*, and *forget* as readily, is of but little use.

Habitual demonstrating and constant reviewing are indispensable to the highest degree of success in the art of teaching; and these Charts are particularly adapted to facilitate both of these exercises.

Once in the schoolroom, they are constantly before the learner, and at the command of the instructor, instead of being *locked up* and *out of sight*, as is usually the case with the apparatus. They can be seen, too, at greater distance, and by greater numbers at a time. Besides, many things are well delineated by the Charts that could not be shown at all in the schoolroom with the apparatus.

TO THE TEACHER.

NECESSITY AND USEFULNESS OF MAPS AND CHARTS.

No institutions of the age are of more importance than those of common education; of these none hold a more essential rank than the "Common-Schools." In these the *first habits* of study are formed, and the rudimentary and fundamental principles of knowledge and science are acquired; and every experienced teacher understands the importance of forming correct *habits* of study, and the still greater necessity of acquiring a *lucid and thorough understanding of the elementary principles*, in order to comprehend the more intricate and complicated principles of science, that constitute an endless study for all subsequent lifetime. Hence, whatever promotes the success of such institutions, or facilitates the art of teaching, must be deserving of attention, and worthy the necessary means of acquisition. When the scanty supply, the almost entire absence, of aids and helps—save a bundle of birch rods and a huge oak ruler—which constituted the assistance of the teacher a few years ago, is contrasted with the many facilities with which the instructor is, or may be, surrounded at the present day, every one who has a child to be educated, or feels himself at all interested in the general education of his fellow-beings, will be at once pleased and surprised to behold how great and rapid has been the improvement achieved in this important question of educational progress.

Among the many means which, for the past few years, have been brought to aid in this most essential art of life, that of teaching, the most serviceable and popular is that of *representing to the eye* what before *was only demonstrated to the ear*.

How limited would be our knowledge of Language, Geometry, Algebra, and Arithmetic, for instance, without their *visible* symbols. And with them how great is our progress in these branches, and how extensive is their application in the development of other sciences, and the useful pursuits of life. Imagine the slow and tedious process of teaching Mathematics to a young mind through the *ear*, without representing the same to the *eye* by means of *figures, letters*, and *diagrams*. But by these symbols, with slate and blackboard, he gives to these *invisible*, and, as it were, imaginary things, *dimensions, localities*, and *names*, so that he may be able to *see* them, and seeing, *grasp* them, while the mind's eye contemplates them at leisure. Music could not rise to the dignity of a regular art until musical notes were invented, which rendered it possible to express harmonies of sound to the *eye*. If the mind may be so greatly aided by ocular signs, when there is no natural relation between them and the objects they represent, as in letters, numerals, figures, and musical notes, how much more must its power be increased, when the symbols and drawings assume the pictorial character, and become, in a manner, *actual imitations* of the things to be considered.

Visible diagrams are most useful where definite and exact properties and relations are to be communicated to the mind, as in natural science.

Whenever the object consists of such fixed elements and qualities as are capable of delineation, but are not themselves tangible, pictorial illustrations of some kind become indispensable, as in Geometry, Trigonometry, and other higher mathematics. In communicating descriptions of physical objects, which, in their extent and complexity, are beyond the scope of direct vision, as in Geography, Geology, and Astronomy, illustrations and delineations are indispensable. With what success could Geography be taught or comprehended by written and oral description without the aid of *maps?* A mere *glance*, however, of the *eye*, at geographical maps and astronomical charts, will give a more correct appreciation of the position and magnitude of oceans, continents, rivers, mountains, states, counties, and towns, also of suns, planets, comets, and stars, than it were possible to obtain by reading *volumes* of *written* description. A person, for instance, by spending only *one hour* in viewing a well-executed *panorama* of the Mississippi river and its scenery, will obtain a more *correct* and *lasting* impression of the same, than by perusing an elaborate and well-written description for weeks and months. An entire volume, and a course of lectures descriptive of a large city, would fail to equal one good cosmoramic view, requiring but *five minutes'* contemplation.

It would seem impossible in these times to acquire a respectable knowledge of Anatomy, Physiology, and Surgery, without the aid of the numberless and elaborate illustrations thickly interspersed throughout every recent book on these subjects.

The study of History, too, is greatly facilitated by charts and diagrams. The study of Natural History would be impossible without the assistance of pictorial representations; but with the help of these, a specimen of every class, species, and variety of man, beast, bird, fish, reptile, and insect, from every quarter of the globe, can be brought into the study or schoolroom to be contemplated by the learner at his leisure.

When objects to be considered are too minute to admit of immediate observance, or in their nature are wholly invisible, invaluable assistance is rendered by pictorial descriptions, as in microscopic science and chemistry.

Again, in the Mechanic Arts and Architecture, how important is the aid derived by means of delineations. If it were attempted to give a full description of a modern steam-engine, or a watch, or a complicated printing-press, by addressing the imagination and perceptive faculties orally, without any kind of illustrative diagrams, *volumes* would be required to impart little more than a vague idea of these objects; on the other hand, a mere *glance* of the *eye*, at the diagrams and pictorial illustrations of these complicated machines, will enable even younger minds to obtain quite a clear understanding of their construction and operation.

Moral sentiments, too, cannot possibly by any other method be half so immovably impressed upon the mind as by means of pictures. Henry Ward Beecher says he used to look at the picture of the "boy stealing apples" till he fairly wore out that leaf of his spelling-book. All children will read "Æsop's Fables" *with the pictures*, while hardly any will read them without the illustrations. Grown persons as well as children will have their attention excited when *real* objects are brought before them, and in the absence of real objects, good pictures will interest them equally; and this is for the reason that their *understanding* is so much *aided by them* as to receive *gratification*, and yield the *ready* pleasure of KNOWING. But in oral and written descriptions alone, the *mental effort* required to *comprehend* overpowers *curiosity*, which renders it a task to give attention, and thus destroys the pleasure of study. In conversation on common subjects, even, do we not almost *instinctively* catch up pen or pencil, and represent to the *eye* what we are attempting to describe to the *ear?* And this is because we can make ourselves so much more easily and distinctly apprehended.

Books, which but few years ago were made in solid pages of reading matter, presenting a dull, monotonous appearance, are now relieved and enlivened by a thousand interesting illustrations, each page inviting the learner and claiming his attention with some lucid and instructive picture. Many subjects which before were considered dry and uninteresting, and even beyond the capacity of ordinary minds, and therefore seldom pursued by them, or, if so, with an obscureness that amounted to a waste of time, have now come to be so clearly explained, by means of this picture-making art, as to be brought within the comprehension of the most ordinary minds; thus causing the natural sciences, especially, to be more generally read and appreciated than were possible by any other method.

The superiority of the *eye* over all other senses, as a means of education, is undeniable, for it has been demonstrated beyond a question. No other system of teaching renders the acquisition of knowledge—especially scientific knowledge—so pleasant and agreeable to the learner. With appropriate diagrams and drawings, properly demonstrated, scholars will become *fascinated* in studying those principles and sciences which before they dreaded, and pronounced tedious and irksome, and tried their utmost to avoid. This method not only makes study a *pleasure*, both to teacher and pupil, but it greatly economizes their time and labor, and produces in the learner the habit of *demonstrating ;* giving the acquired knowledge of general principles an exactness and fixedness in the mind which enables him, in after-life, to make a ready and practical application of his education.

In short, Authors, Lecturers, and Teachers, in almost every branch of learning, have found, by the infallible test of experience, that they may POUR knowledge, in large measures, through the *eye*, and impress it *indelibly* on the mind. Otherwise, why have books on all subjects come to be so filled up with pictures? There is hardly a work now, on the natural sciences, at least, but what contains hundreds of illustrations. Pictures are no longer made solely for the *amusement of children*. Books treating of the most intricate sciences, even, have come to be, emphatically, " *Picture-Books*."

Already many books may be *read* by their pictures. *Less reading matter* and *more pictures* is fast becoming the motto in book-making.

Of the various methods of pictorial illustrations, that of maps and charts, on a large scale, for the use of teachers and lecturers, is the most serviceable, as it enables the instructor to make his demonstrations to a whole class, school, or public audience of thousands, even, with the same time and effort required to give the same explanation to one learner alone. Especially useful and necessary are such maps and charts in common-schools and academies, where the learners are *beginners*, and consequently their powers of abstraction as yet undeveloped. Even the " A, B, C's " and " a-b ab's," addition and multiplication tables, etc., are now extensively printed in the form of charts, and at once placed before the whole school or class, and are thus taught with a *hundredfold* greater success than by the old method of calling up one youngster at a time and pointing with a pin at a dozen small, obscure, half-obliterated letters, and telling him " *that* is A, *that* is B, *that* is C," etc., then, shutting the book, sending him to fold his hands for the next two or three hours, to gaze at nothing but the *blank walls*. If the assistance rendered by charts be so great in teaching these mere *symbols* and simplest rudiments, how much greater must be their utility in teaching those *general principles* which constitute the basis of several *important sciences*, as in the study of Natural Philosophy.

Natural Philosophy, as treated in schoolbooks, being composed of a description of the *fundamental* and leading principles of several sciences, as Mechanics, Acoustics, Optics, Electricity, Astronomy, etc., becomes, therefore, the common branch of education most generally pursued by scholars after acquiring a degree of proficiency in the more purely rudimentary branches. Natural Philosophy, too, being of an abstract nature, especially to beginners and young minds, it is of the greatest necessity that its leading principles be represented to the *eye* of the learner in the most lucid and simple form possible, that he may receive a *clear, strong,* and *lasting* impression of the important principles that make up this most essential branch of common education. Natural Philosophy is so almost universally applicable, in one or another form, to the useful pursuits of life, that every scholar should pursue it and engraft its principles deep in his mind, before he set out on his practical life in earnest. If any one study is to be more thoroughly demonstrated and mastered than another, it should be this. But it is the opinion of all teachers, that without the aid of appropriate *apparatus* or *drawings*, Natural Philosophy, especially, can be taught with but little success. To draw the necessary diagrams on the blackboard, from day to day, requires too much of the teacher's *time*, and so much of his patience and skill that he seldom draws them at all; and, if he *draw* them, they are erased from the board the next half-hour: and to obtain the real, necessary philosophical apparatus, is too expensive to be generally afforded. Of common-schools and academies, hardly one in a thousand can afford the apparatus. Many thousand dollars would be required to purchase all the apparatus represented by these charts; yet these will serve all the *general purposes* of a complete set of apparatus, and in some respects answer better, and are not so expensive but that *every* school may obtain them.

BROOKLYN, N. Y., January 1, 1872.

CONTENTS.

INTRODUCTION.

MATTER, FORCE, MOTION, AND MECHANICS.

CHAPTER I.

(CHART NO. 1.)

[References are to paragraphs, not to pages.]

Definitions and Preliminary Principles—Matter—Different kinds of matter—Simple elements, 1—Changes in matter, *chemical* or *physical*, 2—*Imponderables:* light, heat, and electricity, 3—Atoms, or ultimate constitution of matter, 4—Molecules, 5—The properties of matter are *general* or *specific*, 6—Physical and chemical properties of matter, 7—Physics, or Natural Philosophy, and Chemistry, 8.

CHAPTER II.

Definitions and General Properties of Matter—ESSENTIAL PROPERTIES OF MATTER: magnitude or extension, 9—Impenetrability, 10—SECONDARY OR ACCESSORY PROPERTIES OF MATTER: divisibility, 11—Compressibility, 12—Expansibility, 13—Porosity—Physical pores—Sensible pores, 14—Mobility—Motion and rest are relative and absolute, 15—Inertia—Inertia and momentum (or motion), equally inherent conditions of matter, 16—Indestructibility, 17—ATTRACTION: Attraction of gravitation—Terrestrial attraction—Cohesion—Adhesion—Affinity, 18—VARIETIES OF MOTION: Translation and direct motion, 19—FORCES, 20—Momentum, 21—Cohesion and repulsion, 22—Relation of cohesion and repulsion in the three states of matter, 23—Structure in solids—The formative force of matter—Crystalline and organic forms, 24.

The Characteristic Properties of Solids—Crystalline form, 25—ELASTICITY: Tension—Flexure—Torsion, 26—Resistance to fracture, 27—Hardness, 28—Malleability, 29—Ductility, 30—Flexibility and pliability, 31—Brittleness, 32—Hardening and annealing, 33—Welding, 34.

CHAPTER III.

ATTRACTION.

Molecular Attraction—Fig. 1, Interstices between atoms and molecules of matter, 35—Fig. 2, Cohesive attraction, 36—Fig. 3, Adhesive attraction, 37—Fig. 4, Phenomena of capillarity, 38.

Gravitation—Weight, 39—Fig. 5, Centre of gravity of bodies—Equilibrium of bodies, *stable, unstable,* and *neutral,* 40—Fig. 6, Method of finding the centre of gravity, 41—Fig. 7, Neutral and unstable equilibrium, 42—Fig. 8, Stability of bodies, 43—Fig. 9, Relative stability of cubes and pyramids, 44—Fig. 10, Centre of gravity of vehicles, 45—Fig. 11, Centre of gravity in man, 46—Fig. 12, Law of intensity of gravity—Tabular statement of the law, 47.

Conditions affecting Gravity—Gravity affected by altitude, 48—Gravity affected by depression below level of the sea, 49—Gravity affected by shape of the earth, 50—Gravity affected by the earth's rotation, 51—Earth drawn toward falling bodies, 52—Direction of gravity—*Up* and *down*, relative terms, 53.

CHAPTER IV.

Motion and Force—MOTION: Variety of motions—Uniform, accelerated, and retarded motion—FORCES: Definition of force—Unit of force—Direction and intensity of forces—Equilibrium of forces—Measure of force stated in *four propositions*, 54—**Fig. 13**, Laws of falling and rising bodies—Tabular statement—Finding the velocity of rising and falling bodies, 55—**Fig. 14**, Accelerated velocity illustrated by flow of liquids, 56—**Fig. 15**, Reflected motion, 57—**Fig. 16**, Resultant motion—Compound and resultant forces—Parallelogram of velocities, motions, and forces—Composition and resolution of forces, 58—**Fig. 17**, Action of wind on sails of vessels, 59—**Fig. 18**, Compensating pendulum, 60—**Fig. 19**, Laws of oscillation of the pendulum—General propositions—Scientific uses of the pendulum, 61—**Fig. 20**, Motion of projectiles, vertically *upward, downward*, and in *other* directions—Greatest horizontal range of projectiles, 62—**Fig. 21**, Perpetual revolution, 63—**Fig. 22**, Falling of projectiles thrown from horizontal guns, 64—**Fig. 23**, Action and reaction are equal, 65.

CHAPTER V.
MECHANICAL POWERS.

Levers—Definition of *machine, motor, power, weight*, etc.—Equilibrium of *force* and *resistance*—**Fig. 24**, Lever of the *first class*—Conditions of equilibrium with all levers—Formulæ for finding the *power, weight*, and *arms*—Example, 66—**Fig. 25**, Lever of the *second class*—Example, 67—**Fig. 26**, Lever of the *third class*—Example, 68—**Fig. 27**, Compound lever—Formulæ—Example—Samples of the different levers, 69—**Fig. 28**, Limbs of animals levers of the third class, 70.
Wheel and Axle—**Fig. 29**, The wheel and axle—Formulæ for calculating the different parts—Example, 71—**Fig. 30**, Simple windlass a modification of wheel and axle, 72—**Fig. 31**, Chinese differential windlass, 73—**Fig. 32**, Compound wheel and axle—Formulæ for calculating the parts—Example, 74.
Pulleys—**Fig. 33**, Simple fixed pulley—The law of the pulley—Use of the simple pulley—Example, 75—**Fig. 34**, Simple movable pulley—Formulæ—Example, 76—**Fig. 35**, Movable and immovable pulley—Formulæ—Example, 77—**Fig. 36**, A system of pulleys with more than one cord—Formulæ—Example, 78—**Fig. 37**, Compound pulleys with two or more movable pulleys—Formulæ—Example, 79—**Fig. 38**, Compound pulleys with one movable pulley—Formulæ—Example, 80—**Fig. 39**, A system of pulleys with more than one rope and three cords to each pulley—Formulæ—Example, 81—**Fig. 40**, A system of pulleys with two ropes, having one fixed and two movable pulleys—Example, 82.
Inclined Plane—**Fig. 41**, Inclined plane—Conditions of equilibrium—Formulæ—Example, 83—**Fig. 42**, The screw a modification of the inclined plane—Formulæ—Example, 84—**Fig. 43**, The wedge a modification of the inclined plane—Conditions of equilibrium—Formulæ, 85—**Fig. 44**, Endless screw—Combination of the five mechanical powers—Formulæ—Example, 86.

CHAPTER VI.
(CHART NO. 2.)
HYDROSTATICS.

Distinguishing properties of Solids, Fluids, and Gases—Attraction and repulsion—Rigidity of bodies caused by preponderance of cohesion—Fluidity caused by equilibrium between cohesion and repulsion—Gaseous condition, caused by preponderance of repulsion—Definition, 87—Mobility of liquids—Cause of different degrees of mobility—Heat increases mobility—Ultimate atoms of gaseous bodies as hard as those of solids, 88—Compressibility of liquids, 89—Cohesion in liquids, 90—Repulsion in gases, 91.

Pressure of Liquids—**Fig. 1**, Liquids transmit pressure equally in all directions—Pressure at every point perpendicular to the surface, 92—**Fig. 2**, Pressure of liquid not in proportion to its quantity but to its height, 93—**Fig. 3**, Equilibrium of liquids in communicating vessels, 94—Artesian wells, 95—**Fig. 4**, The water-level, 96—**Fig. 5**, The spirit-level, 97—**Fig. 6**, Tendency of liquids to seek a level shown by aqueducts, 98—**Fig. 7**, Intermitting springs, 99—**Fig. 8**, Upward pressure of liquids equal to downward pressure at the same depth—Buoyant effort of fluids, 100—**Fig. 9**, Downward pressure of liquids independent of shape and capacity of containing vessel, 101—Equilibrium of liquids of different densities, 102—**Fig. 10**, Pressure of a liquid is in proportion to its height and the area of its base, 103—**Fig. 11**, Pressure of liquids on the sides of a vessel, 104—The total pressure upon the walls of a vessel, 105—The total pressure on the bottom and sides of a vessel, 106—**Fig. 12**, Hydrostatic paradox, 107—**Fig. 13**, Practical use of the principle that liquids transmit pressure in all directions alike—Formulæ, 108—**Fig. 14**, Hydrostatic press—Formulæ—Example, 109—**Fig. 15**, Bursting a cask with hydrostatic pressure, 110—**Fig. 16**, Hydrostatic bellows, 111—**Fig. 17**, Hydrostatic pressure in mountains, 112—**Fig. 18**, Submerged bodies not pressed in all directions equally—Upward pressure the buoyant effort of the fluid, 113.

Specific Gravity—Specific gravity, what it is, and how found, 114—**Fig. 19**, Method of finding specific gravity of solids—Rule for solids heavier than water—Rule for solids lighter than water—Rule for liquids—Examples, 115—**Fig. 20**, Specific gravity of liquids, continued — Hydrometer — Example, 116 — **Fig. 21**, Liquids of unequal densities seek different levels in the same vessel, 117—**Fig. 22**, Principles of flotation—The plane of flotation—A toy illustrating flotation, 118.

CHAPTER VII.
(CHART NO. 2.)
PNEUMATICS.

General Principles—Definitions—Gases—Vapors—Tension, 119—Gases are simple or compound—Expansion, 120—Mechanical condition of gases, 121.

Atmospheric Air—**Fig. 23**, The atmospheric air an aërial ocean enveloping the earth—Inequalities of the earth's surface, 122—Height of the atmosphere—Its weight and elasticity in equilibrium, 123—Composition of the atmosphere—Its adaptation to animal life and combustion—Compensatory relation of animal respiration and vegetation, 124—**Fig. 24**, Impenetrability of gases, 125—**Fig. 25**, Pressure or weight of the atmosphere—Its pressure equal in all directions—Amount of its pressure on the human body—All physical pores filled with it, 126—**Fig. 26**, Compression and expansion of the atmosphere, 127—**Fig. 27**, Air-pump, receiver, and vacuum, 128—(Fig. 27), Various phenomena in vacuo: no combustion; no flight; no life; no "suction;" no resistance, 129—**Fig. 28**, Pressure of air equal in all directions, shown by hollow hemispheres, 130—**Fig. 29**, Expansion fountain, 131—**Fig. 30**, Atmospheric pressure variable at the same place—Equilibrium of hydrostatic and atmospheric pressures, 132 — Atmospheric pressure sustains different liquids at different heights: their heights being inversely as their specific gravities—Example—Water and mercury, 133.

The Barometer—**Fig. 31**, The Barometer and its uses, 134—Height of the mercury at different elevations, 135—Barometer as a weather-glass—Rules for reading the changes of the barometer, 136—Diurnal variations of the barometer, 137—**Fig. 32,** The wheel-barometer, 138—**Fig. 33,** Density of the atmosphere at different altitudes, 139—**Fig. 34,** Balloons, 140—**Fig. 35,** Diving-bells, 141—**Fig. 36,** Atmospheric pressure shown by inverted tumbler of water, 142—**Fig. 37,** Atmospheric pressure shown by currents of air, 143—**Fig. 38,** Atmospheric pressure shown by tubes and water, 144—**Fig. 39,** Vacuum fountain, illustrating atmospheric pressure, 145—**Fig. 40,** Animal respiration dependent upon atmospheric pressure, 146—**Fig. 41,** Mariotte's Law relating to the elastic force of gases, 147—**Fig. 42,** Condenser and condensed air, 148—**Fig. 43,** Condensed air fountain, 149—**Fig. 44,** Air-gun, 150.

CHAPTER VIII.
(CHART NO. 3.)
HYDRAULICS.

General Principles—Definitions, 151—Shape of orifices, 152—Friction between liquids and solids, 153—**Fig. 1,** Velocity and gravity—Projected streams subject to the same laws as other projectiles, 154—**Fig. 2,** Velocity of discharge—Tabular statement, 155—**Fig. 3,** Flowing of rivers, 156—**Fig. 4,** Finding the velocity of rivers, 157.

Water as Motive Power—Water as motive power, 158—**Fig. 5,** Overshot water-wheel, 159—**Fig. 6,** Breast water-wheel, 160—**Fig. 7,** Undershot water-wheel, 161—**Fig. 8,** Turbine water-wheel, 162—**Fig. 9,** Reaction and centrifugal machine, or Barker's mill, 163.

Machines for Elevating Water—Variety of water elevators, 164—**Fig. 10,** Lifting wheel, 165—**Fig. 11,** Wheel and buckets, or Persian wheel, 166—**Fig. 12,** Endless chain of pots, 167—**Fig. 13,** Chain-pump, 168—**Fig. 14,** First invented centrifugal pump, 169—**Fig. 15,** The T-centrifugal pump, 170—**Fig. 16,** Archimedes' screw, 171—**Fig. 17,** Hydraulic ram, 172.

Suction Pumps—**Fig. 18,** The principle of suction pumps, 173—**Fig. 19,** Proof of atmospheric pressure in pumps, 174—**Fig. 20,** Double cylinder rotary pump, 175—**Fig. 21,** Single cylinder rotary pump, 176—**Fig. 22,** Double cog-wheel rotary pump, 177—**Fig. 23,** Bellows suction pump, 178—**Fig. 24,** Diaphragm suction pump, 179—**Fig. 25,** Plunger suction and force pump, 180—**Fig. 26,** Single cylinder suction pump, 181—**Fig. 27,** Suction and force pump, 182—**Fig. 28,** Double acting suction and force pump, 183—**Fig. 29,** Single-acting suction and force pump, 184—**Fig. 30,** Double-acting suction and force pump, with only two valves, 185—**Fig. 31,** Fire-engine, or two cylinder force pump, 186—**Fig. 32,** Stomach pump, 187.

Syphons, Fountains, etc.—**Fig. 33,** The syphon dependent on atmospheric pressure, 188—Intermittent springs, 189—**Fig. 34,** Sharp angles obstruct flow of liquids—Shown by syphons, 190—**Fig. 35,** Conveying water over hills with syphons, 191—**Fig. 36,** Syphon for the chemical laboratory, 192—**Fig. 37,** Loss of effective head in public water-works, 193—Lateral pressure of liquids diminished by their motion, 194—Fountains, and vertical jets of water, 195—**Fig. 38,** Hiero's fountain, 196—**Fig. 39,** Intermittent fountains—Importance of water—Importance of hydraulic and hydro-pneumatic machines, 197.

CHAPTER IX.
(CHART NO. 4.)
HEAT AND STEAM-ENGINE.

Preliminary General Principles Relating to Heat—Definitions, 198—Heat and cold relative terms, 199—Temperature, 200—Nature of heat—Emission theory—Undulatory theory, 201—GENERAL EFFECTS OF HEAT; it expands bodies; is a source

CONTENTS. 15

of mechanical energy; it determines the distribution of animals and plants; it more or less controls chemical affinity, and limits vital forces, 202—Equilibrium and transference of heat, 203—Luminous and obscure heat, 204.

Sources of Heat—PHYSICAL SOURCES OF HEAT: Solar radiation, 205—Quantity of heat emitted by the sun, 206—Extremes of natural temperature, 207—Terrestrial radiation, 208—Atmospheric electricity, 209—CHEMICAL SOURCES OF HEAT, 210—Combustion, 211—MECHANICAL SOURCES OF HEAT: Friction—Compression—Percussion, 212—PHYSIOLOGICAL SOURCES OF HEAT: Animal and vegetable, 213—Difference between quantity and intensity of heat, 214.

EXPANSION.

Solids—Fig. 1, Linear expansion of solids—Pyrometers—Laws of expansion, 215—Coefficient of expansion, lineal and cubic, 216—Fig. 2, Cubic expansion of solids, 217—Relation between linear and cubic expansion, 218—Amount of expansion of solids absolute and relative—Table of expansion of solids, 219.

Liquids—Fig. 3, Expansion of liquids, 220—The amount of expansion of liquids, 221—Fig. 3, Different liquids expand differently for the same increase of temperature—Table of expansion of liquids, 222—Water at certain temperatures an exception to the laws of contraction and expansion, 223—Beneficial effects of unequal expansion of water, 224—Freezing of water in small tubes, 225.

Gases—Fig. 4, Expansion of gases, 226—The general laws of expansion of gases by heat, 227—Relation between compressibility and expansibility, 228—Density of gases, 229.

Specific Heat—Fig. 5, Calorimetry, 230—Specific heat or caloric capacity, 231—Unit of heat, or thermal unit, 232—Standard of specific heat—Table of specific heat of different substances, 233—Effects of specific heat of water on climate, 234—Specific heat of gases, 235—Fig. 6, Compression of air and other gases diminishes their capacity for heat, 236—*Two-sevenths* of the heat applied to warming houses is consumed in expanding the air, 237—Specific heat affected by change of state—Table of specific heat of different states of bodies, 238.

COMMUNICATION OF HEAT.

Heat is communicated by *conduction, convection,* and *radiation,* 229.

Conduction of Heat—SOLIDS: Conduction of heat—Conductors and non-conductors, 240—Different solids conduct heat differently, 241—Fig. 7, Determination of the conductibility of solids—Table of conductibility of solids, 242—Musical tones caused by conduction, 243—Conductibility varies with molecular arrangement, 244—Fig. 8, Conduction the principle of the safety-lamp of Davy, 245—LIQUIDS: Conductibility of liquids, 246—Fig. 9, Heat in liquids not equalized by conduction, 247—Fig. 10, Non-conductibility of liquids shown by experiments with water and ice, 248—GASES: Conductibility of gases, 249—Relative conductibility of moist and dry air, 250—Relative conductibility of solids, liquids, and gases of the same temperature, 251—The philosophy of clothing, 252.

Convection of Heat—LIQUIDS: Convection of liquids, 253—Ocean currents—The Gulf Stream, 254—Fig. 11, Heating buildings by convection of fluids in pipes, 255—GASES: Convection of Gases, 256—Heating buildings by steam, 257—The atmosphere an immense steam heating apparatus, 258—Relation of air to the earth same as glass to a hot-house, 259.

Winds—Definition, 260—KINDS OF WIND: Regular, Variable, Periodical, Hurricanes, Tornadoes, 261—Fig. 12, Cause of wind—Trade winds, 262—Variable winds, 263—Land and sea-breezes, 264—Hurricanes or cyclones, 265—Tornadoes or whirlwinds—Water-spouts, 266—Physical properties of winds: hot, dry, moist, etc., 267—Table of general direction or frequency of different winds, 268—Fig. 13, Anemometers—Pressure of winds, 269—Velocity of winds—Table of velocity and force of wind, 270.

Measure of Temperature—*Thermometers,* 271—**Fig. 14,** *Mercurial thermometers:* Fahrenheit, Centigrade, Réaumur, 272—Rule of conversion of thermometric scales—Example, 273—**Fig. 15,** Method of making a thermometer, 274—Standard points of the thermometer, 275—**Fig. 16,** Method of graduating thermometers—Fixing the *freezing* point, 276—**Fig. 17,** Fixing the *boiling* point of thermometers, 277—Tests of thermometers, 278—Sensibility of a thermometer, 279—Limits of the mercurial thermometer—Pyrometers, 280—Spirit thermometers—Air thermometers, 281—**Fig. 18,** Self-registering thermometers, 282—**Fig. 19,** Differential thermometers, 283.

Radiation of Heat—Radiation of heat, 284—Cooling by radiation, 285—Intensity of radiation—Laws of radiation, 286—Radiant heat is partially absorbed by the medium through which it passes, 287—Radiation in vacuo, 288—Universal radiation and constant mutual exchange of heat between bodies, 289.

ACTION OF DIFFERENT BODIES UPON HEAT.

Surface Action—Incident heat absorbed and reflected, 290—**Fig. 20,** Laws which govern reflection of heat—Angles and planes of incidence and reflection, 291—**Fig. 21,** Reflection of heat from concave mirrors, 292—Reflective power of different substances, 293—Determination of reflective power, 294—**Fig. 22,** Absorptive power—Relative absorptive power of different substances—Absorptive power of colors, 295—Emission or radiating power of different substances, 296—Causes which modify the *reflective, absorbent,* and *emission* powers of bodies; as polish, density, direction of rays, source of heat and color, 297.

Diathermancy—Refraction—Polarization—Transmission of radiant heat, 298—Causes which modify the diathermanic power of bodies, 299—Diathermancy of the air, 300—**Fig. 23,** Refraction of heat, 301—Polarization of heat, 302.

CHANGE OF STATE OF BODIES BY THE ACTION OF HEAT.

Latent Heat—Liquefaction and Solidification—Latent heat of fusion, 303—Liquefaction and solidification, or melting and freezing—The laws of liquefaction and solidification—Table of melting points of different substances—Decomposition by heat—Refractory bodies, 304—Peculiarities in the fusion of certain solids, 305—Melting and freezing always gradual—Melting is a cooling, and freezing, a warming process, 306—Why ice does not acquire great thickness, 307—*Latent heat, irregular expansion,* and *high specific heat* of water graduate the changes of the seasons, 308—Freezing mixtures, 309—Crystallization, 310.

Vaporization—Definitions—Vaporization, 311—Volatile liquids and fixed liquids, 312—Latent heat of evaporation, 313—Latent heat of steam, 314—Latent and sensible heat of steam at different temperatures, 315.

Ebullition or Boiling—**Fig. 24,** Ebullition, 316—Laws that govern the phenomena of ebullition, 317—*Causes that modify the boiling point of liquids*—**Fig. 25,** Variation of pressure varies the boiling point—Water boiled by application of cold, 318—Useful applications of boiling water under diminished pressure—Boiling point affected by altitude—**Fig. 26,** Franklin's pulse-glass, 319—Boiling point affected by solution of solids in the liquid, 320—Nature of the vessel varies the boiling point, 321.

Evaporation—Evaporation, 322—**Fig. 27,** Evaporation in a vacuum—Laws of evaporation—Limit of tension, 323—**Fig. 28,** Evaporation under pressure, 324—Heat increases and cold decreases the tension of vapors, 325—Causes that accelerate evaporation are pressure, increase of surface, dryness of air, and circulation of air, 326.

Condensation—Causes of condensation are chemical action, pressure, and diminution of temperature, 327—Dew-point, 328.

Steam—**Fig. 29,** Pressure exerted by steam or heated vapor, 329—**Fig. 30,** Candle-bombs, illustrating the explosion of steam-boilers, 330—Spheroidal state of liquids—Causes of the spheroidal state of liquids, 331—**Fig. 31,** Condensation of steam, 332—**Fig. 32,** Illustration of the principle of the low-pressure engine, 333—**Fig. 33,**

High-pressure steam—Boiling point under high pressure—Table of boiling point of water at different atmospheric pressures, 334.

Frost-Bearer—Rain, Snow, etc.—Fig. 34, Freezing by evaporation—The Cryophorus, or frost-bearer, 335—Rain, 336—Snow, 337—Hail, 338—**Fig. 35,** Rain-gauge, 339—Distribution of rain, 340—Days of rain—Table of rainy days in different latitudes, 341—Annual depth of rain in different places, 342—**Fig. 36,** Hygrometer, or moisture-measurer—Dew-point varies with the moisture in the air, 343.

Combustion—Fig. 37, Combustion and structure of flame—Elements of organic bodies—Elements of combustibility—Carbon and hydrogen burn differently—Hydro-carbons the best illuminators, 344.

Steam-Engines—Origin of the steam-engine, 345—**Fig. 38,** The Eolipile, 346—Improvements in steam-engines, 347—Reciprocating and rotary motions of engines, 348—**Fig. 39,** The high-pressure engine, 349—**Fig. 40,** The eccentric—Its importance, 350—**Fig. 41,** Steam-boiler, and operation of steam-valves, 351—Condensation in steam-engines, 352—**Fig. 42,** Stuffing-boxes, 353—**Fig. 43,** The low-pressure or condensing engine—Its operation—The governor—The fly-wheel, etc., 354 (see frontispiece).

CHAPTER X.

(CHART NO. 5.)

OPTICS.

General Properties of Light—Optics—Light, 355—Nature of Light—*Theories:* Corpuscular, or emission theory—Wave, or undulatory theory, 356—Sources of light, 357—Similarity of light and heat, 358—Relation of different bodies to light—Luminous and non-luminous bodies—Transparent, translucent, and opaque bodies, 359—A medium—Propagation of light in a homogeneous medium, 360—Absorption of light, 361—**Fig. 1,** Rays, pencils, and beams of light, 362—**Fig. 2,** Visible bodies emit light from every point, 363—Properties of light, Absorption, Dispersion, Reflection, and Refraction, 364.

CATOPTRICS, OR REFLECTION OF LIGHT.

Reflectors—Mirrors—Specula—Reflectors, 365—Mirrors and specula, 366—Forms of reflectors, 367—Laws of reflection of light, 368—Direction in which objects are seen, 369.

Reflection at Plane Surfaces—Fig. 3, Reflection of diverging rays, 370—**Fig. 4,** Reflection of converging rays, 371—**Fig. 5,** Reflection of parallel rays, 372—**Fig. 6,** Convex, plane, and concave mirrors, 373—**Fig. 7,** Intensity of light reflected at different angles, and from different surfaces, 374—**Fig. 8,** Images formed by plane reflectors—Virtual image, 375—**Fig. 9,** Multiplicity of images, 376—Kaleidoscope, 377—**Fig. 10,** Deception by several mirrors—Seeing through a brick, 378—**Fig. 11,** Plane mirrors may reflect objects double their own length, 379—**Fig. 12,** The mariner's sextant, 380.

Reflection at Curved Surfaces—Fig. 13, Convex spherical mirrors illustrated by plane mirrors, 381—**Fig. 14,** Convex spherical mirrors, 382—Apparent size of objects, 383—**Fig. 15,** Formation of images by convex reflectors, 384—Images formed by convex mirrors are smaller the nearer the object approaches the mirror, and vice versa (Fig. 15), 385—**Fig. 16,** Concave reflectors the reverse of convex reflectors, 386—**Fig. 17,** Formation of images by concave reflectors, 387—**Fig. 18,** Foci of concave mirrors, for parallel and convergent rays—Converging rays and virtual focus (Fig. 18), 388—**Fig. 19,** Foci of concave mirrors for divergent rays—Properties of conjugate foci, 389—Secondary axes—Oblique pencils, 390—**Fig. 20,** Spherical aberration of reflectors—Caustics, 391—**Fig. 21,** Parabolic reflectors, 392—**Fig. 22,** Formation of images by concave mirrors when the object is beyond the centre of curvature, 393.

Dioptrics, or Refraction of Light—Fig. 23, Definitions, 394—Laws of refraction, 395—Causes of refraction, 396—Fig. 24, Refraction by parallel strata of different media, 397—Fig. 25, Refraction and internal reflection—Double reflection of mirrors, 398—Fig. 26, Refraction and total reflection, 399—Fig. 27, Effects of refraction on the rising and setting of the heavenly bodies, 400—Fig. 28, Refraction by dense media spreads out the light, 401—Fig. 29, Mirage, 402—Fig. 30, Looming, 403—Fig. 31, The depth of water rendered apparently less by refraction, 404.
Prisms and Lenses—Fig. 32, Different kinds of prisms and lenses—Convergent and divergent, 405—Fig. 33, Refraction by prisms—Finding the direction of the refracted and emergent rays—Effects of a plane-glass, 406—Fig. 34, The course of light through a sphere of glass or spherical lens, 407—Fig. 35, Action of convex lenses on light—Definitions, 408—Fig. 36, Conjugate foci, 409—Fig. 37, Conjugate foci, continued, 410—Fig. 38, Analogous effects of prisms and double convex lenses, 411—Fig. 39, Longitudinal spherical aberration of lenses—Determining the foci of lenses—Plano-convex lenses, 412—Fig. 40, Formation of images by convex lenses when the object is twice the focal distance, 413—Fig. 41, Formation of images, when the object is more or less than twice the focal distance, 414—Fig. 42, Formation of images when the object is at less than the focal distance, 415—Fig. 43, Light-houses, 416—Fig. 44, Effects of concave lenses on diverging, parallel, and converging rays, 417—Fig. 45, Formation of images by concave lenses, 418.
Chromatics and Decomposition of Light—Fig. 46, Solar spectrum—Primary colors, 419—Properties of the solar spectrum (Fig. 46), 420—Complementary colors, 421—Analysis of colors by absorption, 422—Fig. 47, Union of two primary colors to produce a secondary color, 423—Fig. 48, Composition of the several colors of the solar spectrum, 424—Refraction and dispersion of the solar spectrum (Fig. 48), 425—Dark lines in the solar spectrum (Fig. 48), 426—Lines in light vary with different sources of light, 427—Fixed lines in the spectra of different colored flames, 428—Color of opaque bodies, 429—Color of transparent bodies, 430—Recomposition of light, 431.
The Rainbow—Figs. 49 and 50, Rainbows—primary and secondary, 432—Fig. 51, How we see all the colors of the rainbow from one position, 433—Fig. 52, See 431—Fig. 53, The arch of the rainbow—Width of the bows and the space between them, 434—Fig. 54, See 431.

CHAPTER XI.
(CHART NO. 6.)

OPTICS, CONTINUED, AND OPTICAL INSTRUMENTS.

Rainbows further Explained—Chromatic Aberration—Fig. 1, Effects of a drop of water upon parallel rays of light, 435—Fog-bows, Halos, and Coronas, 436—Fig. 2, Chromatic aberration, 437—Fig. 3, Achromatic combination of lenses, 438—Fig. 4, Recomposition of light by means of reversed prisms (see 431).
Vision—Fig. 5, The camera obscura, 439—The eye a camera obscura, 440—Fig. 6, Method of adjusting the pupil of the eye, 441—Fig. 7, Means of adjusting and holding the eye, 442—Fig. 8, *Structure of the interior of the eye:* Sclerotic coat—Cornea—Choroid coat—Retina—Optic nerve—Crystalline lens—Aqueous humor—Vitreous humor, 443—Lachrymal, or tear gland, and eye-lid, 444—Fig. 9, Adjustability of the eye to different distances, 445—Optical axis, 446—Optic angle, 447—Angle of vision (Fig. 8), 448—Inversion of images formed in the eye, 449—Why we see objects erect, their images being inverted, 450—The brightness of the ocular image, 451—Fig. 10, Indistinct vision—Sufficiency of illumination, 452—Fig. 11, How to see objects close to the eye, 453—Fig. 12, Upon what brilliancy of vision depends, 454—Limit of distinct vision, 455—Fig. 13, Visual rays must be nearly parallel, 456—Size of the image on the retina, 457—Fig. 14, Near-sightedness—Long-Sightedness, 458—Fig. 15, Near-sightedness and long-sightedness caused by defective form of the eyeball, 459—Long-sightedness of old persons, 460—Conditions of distinct vision,

461—Sensibility of the retina, 462—Color-blindness, 463—Effect of different colors on vision, 464—Effects of background—Irradiation, 465—Estimation of distance and magnitude of objects, 466—Why with two eyes we see objects single, 467—Double vision, 468—Binocular vision, 469—Duration of impression upon the retina, 470—Optic toys, 471—Time required to produce visual impressions, 472—Sensations of light excited by other causes than light, 473.

Optical Instruments—Variety, and principal uses of optical instruments, 474—Spectacles, 475.

Microscopes—The simple microscope—Magnifying power of lenses, 476—**Fig. 16**, Compound microscope, 477—**Fig. 17**, Magic lantern, 478—**Fig. 18**, Solar microscope, 479—Polyrama, and dissolving views, 480—**Fig. 19**, Opera-glass, 481—Night-glasses, 482.

Camera Obscura—**Fig. 20**, The camera obscura, as employed for tracing landscapes, etc., 483—**Fig. 21**, Another form of the camera obscura, 484—The camera lucida, 485—Daguerreotyping, 486—Photography, 487.

Telescopes—The different kinds of telescopes, 488—**Fig. 22**, The refracting astronomical telescope, 489—**Fig. 23**, The terrestrial telescope, 490—**Fig. 24**, Herschel's reflecting telescope, 491—**Fig. 25**, The Gregorian telescope, 492—**Fig. 26**, The improved Newtonian reflecting telescope, 493—Lord Rosse's reflecting telescope, 494—**Fig. 27**, The telestereoscope, 495—**Fig. 28**, The stereoscope, 496—**Fig. 29**, The principles of the stereoscope, 497—**Figs. 30 and 31**, The stereomonoscope, 498.

WAVE THEORY OF LIGHT.

Interference, Diffraction, etc.—**Fig. 32**, Waves of light, 499—**Fig. 33**, Direction of vibrations and waves of light, 500—Brilliancy dependent on amplitude of waves, 501—Color dependent on length of waves, 502—**Fig. 34**, Interference of light, 503—**Fig. 35**, Non-interference of light, 504—**Fig. 36**, Demonstration of interference of light, 505—Laws of interference and non-interference of light, 506—**Fig. 37**, Interference colors, 507—**Figs. 38 and 39**, Determining the length of waves of light, 508—Length of waves or undulations of light—Table for the different colors, 509—The cause of the waves of light, 510—**Fig. 40**, Diffraction fringes caused by interference, 511.

Polarization of Light—Poles in physics, 512—**Fig. 41**, Transmission of luminous waves, 513—**Fig. 42**, Action of tourmaline on ordinary light, 514—**Fig. 43**, Polariscope—Polarization by reflection, 515—Plane polarization, 516—Waves in any number of planes resolved to two planes, 517—Partial polarization, 518—Double refraction, 519—Polarization by double refraction, 520—Useful application of polarized light, 521.

Shadows—**Fig. 44**, Shadows of bodies larger than the illuminating body, 522—**Fig. 45**, Shadows of bodies smaller than the illuminating body, 523—Umbra and penumbra (Fig. 45), 524—**Fig. 46**, Density of shadows, 525.

Velocity and Intensity of Light—**Fig. 47**, Velocity of light, 526—**Fig. 48**, Intensity of light, 527—**Fig. 49**, Photometers: Ritchie's—Rumford's—Silliman's—Bunsen's, 528—**Fig. 50**, Intensity of light at different distances, 529.

CHAPTER XII.
(CHART NO. 7.)
ACOUSTICS.

Production and Propagation of Sound—Definition, 530—Sonorous or sounding bodies, 531—Mediums, 532—Sound a sensation, 533—Different sounds, 534—Sonorous difference of bodies, 535—Time is required for the transmission of sound, 536—Calculation of distances by sound, 537—Velocity of all sounds the same, 538—Velocity of sound in air, 539—Velocity of sound in different gases and vapors, 540—Velocity of sound in liquids, 541—Velocity of sound in solids, 542—Time required to distinguish sounds, 543.

Reflection of Sound—Fig. 1, Reflection of sound at right angles, 544—Fig. 2, Sound reflected at oblique angles, 545—Circular waves reflected from a plane, 546—Echoes, 547—Fig. 3, Multiple echoes—Echoes modify the tones of sound, 548—Resonance, 549—Fig. 4, Sound reflected in a sphere, 550—Fig. 5, Sound propagated from foci of ellipses, 551—Whispering galleries, 552—Audience rooms, 553—Fig. 6, Reflection of waves by parabolic curves, 554.

Intensity of Sound—Intensity of sound, 555—Causes which modify the intensity of sound, 556—Intensity of sound in tubes, 557—Fig. 7, The ear-trumpet, 558—Fig. 8, Speaking-trumpet, 559—Fig. 9, Vibrations of sonorous bodies illustrated by the Jews-harp, 560—Fig. 10, Sound waves caused by striking a bell, 561—Fig. 11, Cause of vibrations in sonorous bodies illustrated by a bell, 562—Fig. 12, Harmonicon, 563.

Interference of Sound—Fig. 13, Interference of sound, 564—Combination of waves in liquids, 565—Fig. 14, Interference in an ellipse, 566—Waves of condensation and rarefaction, 567—Interference of sound waves—Co-existence of sonorous waves, 568—Undulation of solids, 569.

Vibration of Cords—Fig. 15, Elasticity of cords and wires developed by tension, 570—Fig. 16, Nodal points of vibrating cords—Figs. 17 and 18, Two or more nodal points in one string, 571—Laws of the vibration of cords, 572—Fig. 19, Verification of the laws of vibration—The Sonometer—Fig. 20, Interference of sound illustrated by two vibrating cords—Fig. 21, Interference of sound further illustrated, 573—Fig. 22, Sounds caused by the burning of hydrogen, 574—Fig. 23, Sound not propagated in a vacuum, 575.

Vibration of Rods and Plates—Vibration of rods, 576—Means of vibrating plates, 577—Nodal lines of plates, 578—Determination of nodal lines of plates, 579—Figs. 24, 25, 26, 27, 28, 29, Nodal points, figures, and lines, 580—Fig. 30, Refraction of sound, 581—Laws of refraction of sound, 582.

Sound from Pipes—Sound from pipes, 583—Fig. 31, Pipes with fixed mouth-pieces, 584—Reed pipes, 585—Fig. 32, Arrangement of reeds, 586—The organs of voice a reed instrument, 587.

Musical Sounds—Difference between musical sounds and noises, 588—Qualities of sound, 589—Limits of perceptible sounds, 590—Unison, 591—Melody—Chord—Harmony, 592—The principal harmonies, 593—The most pleasing harmonies, 594—The limit of harmonies, 595—The musical, or diatonic scale—Gamut, 596—Formation of the musical scale—Absolute number of vibrations corresponding to each note, 597.

CHAPTER XIII.
(CHART NO. 7.)
MAGNETISM.

General Properties of Magnets—Definition, 598—Lodestone, or natural magnets, 599—Fig. 33, Magnetic manifestations of lodestone, 600—Fig. 34, The armature, 601—Fig. 35, A fully-mounted lodestone magnet, 602—Artificial magnets, 603—Fig. 36, Method of making an artificial magnet with lodestone, 604—Fig. 37, Distribution of force in magnets, 605—The law of distribution of attraction, 606—The force of magnetic attraction at different distances, 607—Effect of heat on magnets, 608—Fig. 38, Various forms of magnets, 609—Fig. 39, Compound horse-shoe magnet, 610.

Charging Magnets—Methods of charging magnets, 611—Fig. 40, Method of charging horse-shoe magnets, 612—Fig. 41, Method of magnetizing straight bars, 613—Fig. 42, Both poles must co-exist in every magnet, 614—Magnetic and magnetized bodies, 615.

Magnetic Induction—Fig. 43, Induction—Magnetism by contact, 616—Fig. 44, Magnetic Induction illustrated by a series of rings, 617—Fig. 45, Arrangement of poles in a star-shaped body, 618—Fig. 46, Production of two sets of poles in one bar by induction, 619—**Fig. 47,** Induction without contact, 620—**Fig. 48,** Magnets do not part with their own power, 621—**Fig. 49,** Unlike poles neutralize each other, 622—**Fig. 50,** Neutralization shown by the Y-magnet, 623—**Fig. 51,** The inductive power of the earth's magnetism, 624.

Hypothesis and Laws of Magnetism—Fig. 52, Hypothesis of two magnetic fluids, 625—Laws of attraction and repulsion, 626—The coercitive force, 627—**Fig. 53,** *Magnetic curves* rendered apparent to the eye, 628—**Fig. 54,** Curves with two magnets and unlike poles, 629— **Fig. 55,** Curves with two magnets and similar poles, 630—Magnetic attraction not intercepted, 631—Preservation of magnets, 632.

Terrestrial Magnetism—The earth as a magnet, 633—**Fig. 56,** The astatic needle, 634—**Fig. 57,** Magnetic needle, 635—Directive force of magnets—The directive force simply rotates the magnet, or needle, 636—Magnetic meridian, 637—*Variations of the needle*—Declination, 638—Daily, annual, and other variations of the needle, 639—Inclination or dip of the needle, 640—**Fig. 58,** Action of the earth illustrated by the action of a magnet, 641—**Fig. 59,** Dipping needle, 642—**Fig. 60,** Position of the dipping needle in different parts of the earth, 643—**Fig. 61,** The mariner's compass, 644—Table for correcting the variations of the compass—Discovery of the compass —Magnetic intensity, 645—The inductive power of the earth's magnetism, 646—Utilization of magnetism, 647.

CHAPTER XIV.
(CHART NO. 8.)

ELECTRICITY.

STATICAL OR FRICTIONAL ELECTRICITY.

Fundamental Principles—Definitions, 648—Discovery of electricity, 649—The sources of electricity, 650—**Fig. 1,** Electrical effects, 651—Electroscope—Electrical pendulum, 652—**Fig. 2,** Vitreous and resinous, or positive and negative electricities, 653—The theory of two fluids, 654—The single fluid hypothesis—The term fluid, 655 —**Fig. 3,** Attraction and repulsion, 656—Laws of electrical attraction and repulsion, 657—Conductors of electricity, 658—Insulators, 659—The earth is the great reservoir, 660—Method of electrifying bodies, 661—Electrical tension, 662—**Fig. 4,** Electricity accumulates only on the outer surfaces of bodies—**Fig. 5,** The same fact shown in a different way, 663—Proof-plane, 664—**Fig. 6,** Distribution dependent on form, 665— The power of points, 666 —The loss of electricity in excited bodies, 667.

Induction of Electricity—Fig. 7, Bodies electrified by induction, 668—**Fig. 8,** The two fluids separated and obtained by induction—Laws of electrical induction, 669— **Fig. 9,** Dielectrics—Explanation of induction, 670—Attraction and repulsion of light bodies explained, 671—ELECTROMETERS: Electroscope, 672—**Fig. 10,** The quadrant electrometer, 673—**Fig. 11,** The gold-leaf electrometer, 674—Method of using the gold-leaf electrometer, 675.

Electrical Machines—Figs. 12 and 13, The electrophorus, 676—**Fig. 14,** The cylinder electrical machine, 677—**Fig. 15,** The plate electrical machine, 678—Use of the electrical machines, 679—Measure of the quantity of electricity in the machine, 680—Precautions in using the machines, 681—**Fig. 16,** The hydro-electric machine, 682—Other sources of electrical excitement, 683.

Experiments Illustrating Electrical Attraction and Repulsion—The insulating stool—Electrical spark—Electrical shock, 684—**Fig. 17,** Electrical puppets, 685 —**Fig. 18,** The electrical chime, 686—**Fig. 19,** The electrical wheel, 687—**Fig. 20,** The electrical blow-pipe, 688—**Fig. 21,** The electrical egg, produced by passing electricity through a vacuum, 689.

Accumulation of Electricity—Latent or disguised electricity, 690—The electrical condenser, 691—**Fig. 22,** The Leyden jar, 692—**Fig. 23,** Charging the Leyden jar, 693—Limit of the charge in a condenser, 694—DISCHARGING THE JAR: Disruptive discharge, 694—Insensible or gradual discharge—Discharge by small and sudden discharges—Instantaneous discharge, 695—DISCHARGERS (Fig. 22): The discharging rod, or hand discharger, 696—**Fig. 24,** The universal discharger, 697—Electricity in the Leyden jar resides on the glass, 698—**Fig. 25,** The electric battery, 699—**Fig. 26,** The electric spark, 700—The color of the electric spark, 701—**Fig. 27,** Difference between the positive and negative spark, 702—**Fig. 28,** The electrical square, 703.

Effects of Accumulated Electricity—EFFECTS OF THE ELECTRIC DISCHARGE, 704—Physiological effects, 705—Heating power of electricity, 706—The mechanical effects of electricity, 707—The chemical effects of statical electricity, 708.

Atmospheric Electricity—Franklin's experiment with a kite, 709—Free electricity in the atmosphere, 710—Causes of atmospheric electricity, 711—Thunder storms—Origin of thunder clouds, 712—Thunder, 713—Lightning, 714—CLASSES OF LIGHTNING: Zigzag, or chain lightning—Sheet lightning—Heat lightning—Volcanic lightning, 715—Velocity of lightning, 716—The return shock, 717—**Fig. 29,** Lightning-rods—Other means of safety—Liability of being struck by lightning, 718—Aurora borealis, 719—**Fig. 30,** Slow discharge of a Leyden jar—A beautiful toy, 720.

CHAPTER XV.
DYNAMICAL ELECTRICITY.
FUNDAMENTAL PRINCIPLES.

Fundamental Principles—Galvanism, 721—**Fig. 31,** Galvani's discovery and experiments, 722—Galvani's explanation, 723—Volta's theory of contact—Volta's discovery, 724—The electro-chemical theory, 725—**Fig. 32,** Simple Voltaic couple, 726—**Fig. 33,** The Voltaic pile or battery, 727—Varieties of Voltaic piles, 728—Polarity of the pile, 729—Electrical currents of the pile, 730—Electro-positive and electro-negative, 731—The difference between *quantity* and *intensity*, 732—Quantity increases with surface, intensity with number of pairs, 733—Amalgamated zinc, 734.

Batteries—Smee's battery, 735—**Fig. 34,** Sulphate of copper battery, 736—**Fig. 35,** Bohnenberger's *electroscope*, 737—**Fig. 36,** Grove's nitric acid battery, 738—**Fig. 37,** Carbon battery, 739—**Fig. 38,** Batteries of two or more couples, 740—The electromotive force, 741.—Resistance to the current, 742—Laws determining the force of a Voltaic current, 743—Difference between static and dynamic electricity, 744.

Applications of Voltaic or Galvanic Electricity—THE EFFECTS OF THE VOLTAIC BATTERY, 745—*Physical effects:* **Fig. 39,** Illuminating effects, 746—**Fig. 40,** The Voltaic arch, 747—**Fig. 41,** The oval form of the arch, 748—**Fig. 42,** The shape of the electrodes, 749—Properties of the electric light, 750—**Fig. 43,** Heating effects—Deflagration, 751—*Chemical effects:* Decomposition, 752—**Fig. 44,** Method of electrotyping—Preparing the mould—Method of depositing the metal on the mould, 753—Electro-gilding and electro-plating, 754—**Fig. 45,** Voltaic decomposition of water, 755—**Fig. 46,** Decomposition of salts, 756—Quantity of electricity required to produce chemical action is enormous, 757—*Physiological effects* of the Voltaic current, 758.

CHAPTER XVI.
ELECTRO-DYNAMICS.

Electro-magnetism—Relation between magnetism and electricity, 759—Ersted's discovery, 760—**Fig. 47,** Action of an electric current upon a magnet or needle, 761—**Fig. 48,** Galvanometers, or multipliers, 762—The directive action of the earth, 763—**Fig. 49,** The astatic needle, 764—The electro-magnetic force is lateral and tangential to the electric current, 765—Ampère's electro-magnetic theory, 766—**Fig. 50,** Mutual action of electric currents, 767—**Fig. 51,** Attraction of currents, 768—**Fig. 52,** Action of magnets upon currents, 769—**Fig. 53,** A single helix, 770—**Fig. 54,** A double helix, 771—**Fig. 55,** Magnetizing by the helix and electrical current, 772—**Fig. 56,** Electro-magnets, 773—Bodies suspended without contact, 774—Utilization of electro-magnetic force, 775.

The Electric Telegraph—First experiments in electrical telegraphing, 776—**Fig. 57,**

Morse's recording telegraph—The receiving or recording instrument—The alphabet—The instrument for transmitting the message—House's telegraph, or printing telegraph, 777—The earth's circuit—Insulators, 778.

Electro-dynamic Induction—Magneto-electricity—Thermo-electricity, etc. —**Fig. 58**, The revolving electro-magnet, 779—**Fig. 59**, Cause of the earth's magnetism, 780—**Fig. 60**, Magneto-electricity, 781—Magneto-electric Machines, 782—**Figures 61 and 62**, *Diamagnetism*, 783—INDUCTION BY CURRENTS: **Fig. 63**, Currents induced by other currents, 784—**Fig. 64**, Induced currents of different orders, 785—The properties of induced currents, 786—**Fig. 65**, *Thermo-electricity*, 787—**Fig. 66**, The thermo-electric revolving arch, 788.

Organic Electricity—Animal electricity, 789—Electrical animals, 790—Electricity of plants, 791.

CHAPTER XVII.
(CHART NO. 9.)
ASTRONOMY.

Definitions, Introductory Observations, and Theories—Astronomy, 792—GENERAL DIVISIONS OF THE SUBJECT: Descriptive astronomy—Physical astronomy—Practical astronomy, 793—Different classes of heavenly bodies, 794—Extent of space, 795—Magnitude of heavenly bodies, 796—The number of heavenly bodies, 797—Distances between heavenly bodies, 798—The orbital motions of heavenly bodies, 799—The velocity of heavenly bodies, 800—Early observations of astronomical phenomena, 801 — Ptolemy's great system, 802 — Copernicus' theory, 803—Kepler's discoveries and laws, 804—Galileo's discoveries, 805—Newton's discovery, 806.

The Solar System—CLASSIFICATION—**Fig. 1**, The solar system—*Planets*, primaries and secondaries—Interior and exterior planets—Comets—Solar bodies, 807—**Fig. 2**, Relative magnitude of the planets, 808—**Fig. 3**, Approximate relative distances of the planets, 809—Impossibility of delineating the solar system—Solar system represented by real objects—Representation of the motion of the planets, 810.

The Sun—Influence of the sun, 811—Magnitude of the sun, 812—The distance of the sun from the earth, 813—Telescopic view of the sun—Dark spots—Motions of the sun, 814.

The Primary Planets—Periodic revolutions, 815—Velocity of the planets, 816—Diurnal revolution of the planets, 817—Magnitude of the planets, 818—Relative magnitude of the planets, 819—The distances of the planets from the sun, 820—Density of the planets, 821—Attraction of the planets, 822—Light and heat of the planets, 823—The ASTEROIDS—Table of the asteroids, 824.

The Secondary Planets or Satellites—Compound motion of the satellites, 825—The earth's satellite or moon, 826—Jupiter's satellites (Figs. 1 and 3)—Their diameters, distances, and periodic times, 827—Saturn's satellites (Figs. 1, 3, and 9)—Their distances and periodic times, 828—Uranus' satellites (Figs. 1 and 3)—Their distances and periodic times, 829—Neptune's satellite (Figs. 1 and 3)—Its distance and periodic time, 830.

Comets—Nature of comets, 831—Orbits and velocity of comets (Fig. 1), 832—Periodic times of comets, 833—The number of comets, 834—The direction of motions of comets, 835.

A few particulars relating to the telescopic views of the primary planets, 836.

Orbits, Eccentricity of Orbits, etc.—**Fig. 4**, Orbits are elliptical, 837—The eccentricity of a planet's orbit—The eccentricity of the different orbits, 838—Aphelion and Perihelion, 839—The radius vector (Fig. 4), 840—The radius vector passes over equal areas in equal times, 841—**Fig. 5**, Circular motion, 842—Centripetal and centrifugal forces, 843—Why the planets do not fall to the sun, 844—Centre of gravity and motion of the solar system, 845—Planes of orbits, 846—**Fig. 6**, The ecliptic, 847—Obliquity of the ecliptic, 848—Inclination of orbits of planets to the plane of the ecliptic (Fig. 6), 849—**Fig. 7**, The figure or form of the planets, 850—**Fig. 8**, Venus as morning and evening star, 851—**Figures 9 and 10**, Saturn's rings, 852—**Fig. 11**, Distances of the satellites from their primaries, 853—**Fig. 12**, Solar and sidereal time, 854.

The Moon—Its Path, Phases, etc.—Fig. 13, The moon's path around the sun, 855—Sidereal and synodic revolution of the moon, 856—The rotation of the moon on her axis, 857—The moon's librations in latitude and longitude, 858—**Fig. 14**, The actual path of the moon—The motion of the moon is never retrograde, 859—**Fig. 15**, The moon's orbit always concave toward the sun, 860—View of the earth from the moon, 861—**Fig. 16**, The moon's phases—Importance of the phases and motions of the moon, 862—Why the dark side of the moon is visible near conjunction, 863—Other particulars relating to the moon, 864.

CHAPTER XVIII.
(CHART NO. 10.)
ASTRONOMY.
ZODIAC, SEASONS, ECLIPSES, TIDES, FIXED STARS, ETC.

The Zodiac and Philosophy of Seasons—Fig. 1, The zodiac, 865—The signs or constellations of the zodiac, 866—Day and night (Fig. 1), 867—Causes of the seasons, (Fig. 1), 868—The earth at the solstitial points (Fig. 1), 869—The earth at the equinoctial points (Fig. 1), 870—The sun's declination, 871 and 931—Constellations of the zodiac (Fig. 1), 872—The sun's apparent motion in the ecliptic (Fig. 1), 873—Division of the signs, 874—The recession of the equinoxes or precession of the constellations, 875—Longitude in the heavens, 876—**Fig. 2**, Intersection of the ecliptic and equinoctial, 877—Polar inclination and seasons of the different planets, 878.

The Philosophy of Transits, etc.—Transits—Nodes, 879—**Fig. 3**, Transits of Mercury, 880—The calculation of transits and eclipses, 881—**Fig. 4**, Mercury's oscillation, 882—**Fig. 5**, Inclination of the moon's orbit to the plane of the ecliptic, 883—View of the moon at the poles and at the equator, 884.

Parallax of the Heavenly Bodies, Conjunction, etc.—Fig. 6, Annual parallax, or parallax of the stars, 885—**Fig. 7**, Diurnal parallax, 886—The effect of parallax on bodies, 887—The principles of parallax of great importance, 888—**Fig. 8**, Convexity of the Earth's surface, how shown, 889—**Fig. 9**, Conjunction and opposition of planets, 890—Direct, stationary, and retrograde motion of planets (Fig. 9), 891—The transit of Venus, an important event, 892—Transits of Venus from 1639 to 2012— **Fig. 10**, The periodic revolution of the sun, 893.

CHAPTER XIX.

Philosophy of Eclipses—Shadows of solar bodies, 894—Interest felt in eclipses, 895—Position of sun, earth, and moon when eclipses occur, 896—Eclipses are either total, partial, or annular, 897—**Fig. 11**, The direction in which eclipses come on, 898—Total eclipse of the moon, and partial eclipse of the sun (Fig. 11), 899—Dimensions of the earth and moon's shadows, 900—**Fig. 12**, Total and annular eclipses of the sun, 901—Duration of eclipses, 902—The general effects of a total eclipse of the sun, 903—The number of eclipses in any one year, 904—**Fig. 13**, Why eclipses are not more frequent, 905—Retrograde motion of the moon's nodes, 906—**Fig. 14**, The solar and lunar ecliptic limits, 907—Why there are more solar than lunar eclipses, 908—Eclipses or occultation of the stars, 909—Eclipses of Jupiter's moons, 910—Eclipses of Saturn's moons, 911.

CHAPTER XX.

Philosophy of the Tides—Motion of the water of the earth, 912—The tides are not uniform, 913—The principal cause of the tides, 914—**Fig. 15**, Influence of the earth upon its waters, 915—**Fig. 16**, A single tide-wave, 916—**Fig. 17**, The two tide-waves, 917—**Fig. 18**, Lagging of the tide-wave behind the moon, 918—**Fig. 19**, Influence of the sun upon tides, 919—**Fig. 20**, Causes of the opposite tide-wave, 920 —The secondary cause of the opposite tide-wave (Fig. 20), 921—Relative influence of the sun and moon on the tides, 922—**Fig. 21**, Spring and neap tides, 923 —Variations in the spring tides (Fig. 21), 924—Tides affected by declination, 925— OTHER CAUSES AFFECTING TIDES: The winds affect the tides, 926—The conformation of the land affects tides, 927—The average elevation of tides, 928—The different heights of water in different oceans and seas, 929—*Atmospherical tides*, 930.

Sun's Declination, Zones, and Temperature—Fig. 22, The declination of the sun differently illustrated, 931—The zones—The torrid zone—The frigid zones—The temperate zones, 932—When the sun shines on the poles (Fig. 22), 933—The effect of the sun's declination on temperature, 934.

Terrestrial and Celestial Globes—LATITUDE AND LONGITUDE: **Fig. 23**, Celestial and terrestrial latitude, 935—Celestial and terrestrial longitude, 936—The terrestrial globe, 937—THE CELESTIAL GLOBE (Fig. 23),—The celestial poles—The plane of a meridian—The right ascension of a body—The angle of right ascension—Circles of celestial latitude—The angles of longitude—The celestial horizon—The sensible horizon—Vertical circles—The meridian—The prime vertical circle—Zenith distance —The azimuth—Amplitude, 938—Nutation of the earth's axis (Fig. 23), 939.

The Fixed Stars—Motion of the stars, 940—Variable or periodical stars, 941—Temporary or "new and lost" stars, 942—Double stars, 943—Binary systems, 944—Clusters of stars, 945—Nebulæ, 946—*Classes of Nebulæ*: 1, Resolved; 2, Resolvable; 3, Stellar; 4, Irresolvable; 5, Planetary, 947—The milky way an annular nebula, 948—The number of stars, 949—The term Universe, 950—Our Cluster or Firmament, 951.

INTRODUCTION.

CLASSIFICATION OF THE SCIENCES.

A *law* is a necessary relation between *cause and effect;* universal experience having shown that *like causes* always produce *like effects.*

General Science is a knowledge of the laws of the Universe.

A *special science* consists of the collection, classification, and explanation of all the known laws and leading truths relating to some definite subject. For example: the Science of Astronomy is made up of the collection, classification, and explanation of all the known laws and leading truths which relate to the heavenly or celestial bodies.

Knowledge which relates to Mind is called *Science of Mind,* or METAPHYSICS; and is subdivided into *Intellectual Science, Moral Science,* Science of Logic, etc.

Knowledge which relates to the Material Universe is called *Physical Science,* or *Natural Philosophy;* which is subdivided into *Science of Organized Matter,* or PHYSIOLOGY, and *Science of Unorganized Matter,* or GENERAL PHYSICS.

Physiology treats of matter as modified by the force or principle of *vitality,* and is further divided into two branches: *Animal Physiology,* or ZOÖLOGY, and *Vegetable Physiology,* or BOTANY.

Unorganized matter is divided into two classes, *Celestial* and *Terrestrial.* Hence General Physics treats of celestial bodies (including the earth as a whole), called *Astronomy,* and terrestrial bodies, called *Terrestrial Physics.*

Terrestrial Physics is again subdivided into two branches, called *Physics* (or *Natural Philosophy*) and *Chemistry.* The former treats of the general properties of *bodies;* the latter treats of the *ultimate particles of bodies* and their laws of combination.

For a further explanation of the relation between the science of *Chemistry* and that of *Physics* (or Natural Philosophy), see paragraphs 2, 6, 7, and 8.

HANDBOOK

OF

NATURAL PHILOSOPHY.

CHAPTER I.

(CHART NO. 1.)

MATTER, FORCE, MOTION, AND MECHANICS.

Definitions and Preliminary Principles.

1. **Matter.**—Matter is the general name of everything that occupies space, and which, in an infinite variety of forms, is the object of sense. It is only through the agency of our five senses that we become conscious of the existence of any matter, even of our own bodies.

A *body* is a definite and limited portion of matter, be it a world, or a particle of dust.

Different kinds of matter, as iron, granite, or water, are called *substances*. Though there are a vast number of different substances, there have been found, by chemical analysis, as yet, only about sixty-four different kinds of matter, termed *elements*,—some ten or twelve, only, of these making up the great bulk of all we see.

Some bodies or substances consist of a single element, as oxygen, carbon, iron, sulphur, gold, etc.; others of two or more elements, as water, consisting of two (hydrogen and oxygen), and oil, three; crystallized common salt, four; crystallized alum, five; pure white of eggs, six.

2. **Changes in matter, chemical or physical.**—The peculiar attraction which draws and unites together the ultimate atoms of different simple elements is termed *chemical affinity*. The simple elements, when united by this affinity, become entirely changed in their physical properties; for instance, oxygen, which is a gas, and the best supporter of combustion, and hydrogen, also a gas, and the most inflammable and lightest element. when *chemically* combined, instead of remaining gases (or forming a new gas) and affording a substance for rapid combustion with intense heat, as might be expected, are so modified by the chemical affinity which unites them, that water, a dense and unelastic liquid which extinguishes fire, is the result. And though the specific identity of these two elements is wholly destroyed by this chemical union, yet the ultimate atoms are *not* changed. Such changes, destructive of *specific identity*, are called *chemical changes*.

Changes which do not destroy specific identity are termed *physical changes;* as when an iron bar acquires magnetism from loadstone, or when a glass tube becomes electrical, by being rubbed with silk; or, as in the case of water, which, being deprived of a portion of its heat, becomes a solid, or, by an increase of heat, is changed to steam or vapor, when again it returns to the earth, as dew, mist, rain, hail, or snow, and so back to its liquid form. But water, through all these changes of state and position, is still the same substance, having lost none of its properties.

3. **Light, heat, and electricity.**—These may be considered *agents* or *forces* connected with or growing out of the changes of matter, physical or chemical, or both. Or, as most generally believed, they may depend on the existence of certain hypothetical fluids, or on the vibrations of an assumed ethereal medium.

As these fluids, forces, or agents, are without weight and other sensible properties of grosser or denser matter, they are termed *imponderables*. These, as it were, are the life and spirit of matter.

4. **Atoms.**—There is a difference of opinion about the ultimate constitution of matter. The general belief is, that matter is formed of *ultimate particles*, which are movable, solid, impenetrable, and so hard as never to wear or break in pieces; having a certain definite size, figure, and weight, which they retain unchangeable through all their various combinations. These are called *atoms*,—signifying that which cannot be divided. Their sizes, in different elements, are supposed to vary, though the largest of them are *inconceivably small;* and their forms may be very various, though considered to be generally globular.

5. **Molecules.**—The term molecule (a little mass) is more commonly applied to what, in chemistry, are termed divisible atoms; that is, to a group of two or more atoms of different elements; as, for instance, a molecule of water is composed of at least two atoms, one of oxygen and one of hydrogen, forming a chemical compound.

However small the various ultimate atoms are, their oval form affords space around about and between them; while *molecules* are supposed to touch each other, if at all, only at a few points, thus affording interspaces larger than their own bulk, which accounts for the two general properties of matter, termed *compressibility* and *expansibility*.

6. **The properties of matter are general or specific.**— Gold, for example, occupies space and possesses weight, so also does all matter, whether solid, liquid, or gaseous; hence these properties are general. But its color, lustre, crystalline form, and other peculiarities that distinguish it from other substances, are *specific properties*.

7. **Physical and chemical properties of matter.**—The chemical and physical *changes* of matter (2) above described, correspond to its chemical and physical *properties*. The specific properties of gold depend solely upon its physical qualities. Density, lustre, color, form, malleability, and its high point of fusion, are all qualities of gold which can never be lost without an essential change of its nature, and are, therefore, termed *physical* properties. Exposed, however, to the action of chlorine and certain other agents, gold loses its specific identity, and becomes, as it were, a new substance, while the same change passes equally upon the agent by whose efficiency the transmutation is effected, thus destroying the essential specific identity of both substances. *These* changes are the result of *chemical affinity*, which depends upon the *chemical properties* of matter.

8. **Physics, or Natural Philosophy, and Chemistry.**—The foregoing fundamental distinctions between the physical and chemical *changes*, and between the physical and chemical *properties* of matter, show the distinction between *Natural Philosophy* and the science of *Chemistry ;* but as all substances possess both physical and chemical properties, it is evident that a thorough acquaintance with either of these branches of knowledge involves some familiarity with the other.

The object, then, of Natural Philosophy, or Physics, is the investigation of the general properties of unorganized bodies, and of their action on each other.

CHAPTER II.

DEFINITIONS AND GENERAL PROPERTIES OF MATTER.

The essential properties of matter.—These are *magnitude*, or *extension*, and *impenetrability*.

9. **By magnitude, or extension,** is meant the property which every body possesses of occupying a portion of space. The amount of space occupied is termed its volume. Every body, however small, has three dimensions—length, breadth, and thickness.

10. **By impenetrability** is meant that property of matter which renders it impossible for two separate bodies to occupy the same space at the same time. Some bodies, like air, may be compressed almost indefinitely, but the power required to do it, becomes the evidence and the measure of its impenetrability. A nail driven into wood, or a stone dropped into water, or a ball thrown through the air, are instances of displacement, and not penetrability.

Secondary or accessory properties of matter.—These are Divisibility, Compressibility, Expansibility, Porosity, Mobility, Inertia, Indestructibility, and Attraction.

11. **Divisibility.**—By divisibility of matter is meant that a body may be divided into two parts, and that these parts may again be divided into other parts, and so on, until the parts become infinitesimally small. Suppose a bit of marble (carbonate of lime) to be thus divided, and when the smallest imaginable particle has been reached, it can be still further divided by chemical decomposition into three elements: first into *carbonic acid* and lime; then the former of these into carbon and oxygen, and the latter into calcium and oxygen.

Some idea of the extreme divisibility of matter may be obtained by the fact that a single grain of musk will scent a large hall for many years and lose no appreciable part of its weight. Again, many kinds of animalcules, as well adapted to life as the largest beasts, are so small that hundreds of thousands might swim side by side through the eye of a small needle; yet each of these is a fully organized being. How minute, then, must be the particles of the elements that chemically combine to make the compound substances out of which their organs are built up!

12. **Compressibility.**—Compressibility is owing to porosity of matter. Diminution of volume in solids, by mechanical means, and by loss of heat, is a fact well known. Even columns and arches of stone, supporting heavy loads, are found to sensibly diminish by pressure alone. Metals are compressed by hammering. Compressibility of liquids and gases will be alluded to under the head of hydrostatics and pneumatics.

13. **Expansibility.**—Expansibility and contraction of all bodies by change of temperature (heat and cold) is a fact sufficiently familiar. Upon this property of matter is based the construction of instruments for reading changes of temperature. This subject will be again referred to under the head of heat.

14. **Porosity—Physical Pores.**—The facts connected with the compressibility of matter and its change of form by heat, indicate that the ultimate atoms (assumed to be unchangeable, 4) are not in contact (see Fig. 1). The spaces between them are called *physical pores*, on the existence of which depends the property of *porosity*. These molecular or physical pores are no more sensible to our organs than the atoms themselves, and are permeable only to light, heat, and electricity.

Sensible pores.—It is important to distinguish the molecular pores, just described, from those sensible openings which give to certain substances the property generally known as porosity. The pores of organic bodies, as of wood, skin, and tissues, are only capillary openings, or canals for the circulation of fluids.

15. **Mobility.**—By mobility is meant the susceptibility of being set in motion. Motion is recognized only by comparing the moving body with some other body at *rest*. Motion and rest are *absolute* or *relative*. For instance, a person walking on the deck of a moving ship appears to change his place in reference to objects on the deck, while all these objects are in motion with himself; hence his motion is only *relative;* but if the ship is at rest, then his motion (referring to these objects about him) is *absolute*. All the motion on the earth's surface is relative, for the reason that the globe itself has at least two motions; one around its axis and the other around the sun.

Rest is *absolute* when the body really occupies the same point in space, and *relative* when it remains the same apparent distance from surrounding objects which are *not*, but which appear to be, at rest. For example, a ship sailing up a river at the rate of five miles an hour, while the water flows at the same rate in the opposite direction, will appear, to persons on its deck and on the river-banks, to be at rest.

Strictly, there is *no* absolute rest. There is not an *atom* of matter in absolute rest throughout the boundless expanse of space. The earth, and all the other planets, and all their satellites, revolve around their own centres; and the moons around the planets; and all these around the sun; and the sun, with all these planets and moons, together with other solar systems, around some more central sun; and, probably, so on, systems around systems, in masses, and at distances from each other, and with velocities that astound the human mind, and exhibit to our senses the infinite power and wisdom of God.

16. **Inertia.**—No particle of matter, in a state of rest, possesses within itself the power of putting itself in *motion ;* or, if it be moving, to bring itself to a state of *rest*. A body, to be put in motion, therefore, must be acted upon by some external cause; or, conversely, if it be in motion, it cannot cease to move on in an unchanging direction and with an unchanging velocity, without the application of some opposing force. This passive property of matter is termed *inertia*.

It is not so apparent that bodies in motion will not of themselves come to a state of rest, as that, being at rest, they will not of themselves move. This is because the motion of all bodies on the earth is continually opposed by friction and the resistance of the atmosphere, which, in a longer or shorter time, will bring them to a state of rest. This is proved by the fact that moving bodies, as a top or pendulum, will not so readily come to a state of rest in a vacuum as in the air; and by the fact that the same body, as, for example, a revolving wheel with large or small bearings, under otherwise the same circumstances, will continue longer in motion the more friction is diminished. The planets, however, not being influenced by these or other obstructions, afford examples, and the only examples, of constant motion.

17. **Indestructibility.**—By this is meant that matter cannot be annihilated. Organized bodies, animal and vegetable, can be reduced to inorganic substances; and compound substances to simple elements; and simple elements to various forms, from solid to fluid, and from fluid to gaseous; but the ultimate *atoms* cannot be changed or destroyed (4). *They* remain forever the same. For example: A ton of coal, by the force of heat, may be decomposed and reduced to a few pounds of ashes, and the balance of its weight to large volumes of smoke and invisible gas, but the aggregate weight of the products will equal the weight of the coal. Not one of the *atoms* that composed the coal is *changed, lost,* or *destroyed*. This is the case through all the ceaseless motions and infinite variety of forms which matter, acted upon by the *forces* of nature, is made to pass.

18. Attraction.—There are several kinds of attraction, namely, *gravitation, cohesion, adhesion, capillarity, affinity,* and *magnetic* and *electric* attraction.

Attraction of gravitation is that force or form of attraction by which all *bodies*, at *sensible distances*, tend to approach each other. By this force every atom of matter in the universe attracts every other atom.

Terrestrial gravitation is that manifestation of gravitation which draws all bodies on the earth toward its centre.

Attraction which takes place only at insensible distances is termed *molecular attraction*. Of this there are four kinds:

1st. *Cohesion*, which binds together the atoms and molecules (4) of matter. It is this force which binds together the atoms of iron, and holds together the molecules of water, to form bodies or masses.

2d. *Adhesion*, which exists between unlike atoms or particles of matter, when in simple contact with each other.

3d. *Capillarity*, which exists between liquids and tubes, or sensible pores of matter.

4th. *Affinity*, which unites atoms of unlike substances into compounds, possessing new and distinct properties (1 and 2).

Magnetic and electric attraction will be alluded to hereafter.

19. Varieties of motion.—1st, *Translation*, or *direct motion*, in which all the points of a body move parallel to each other; 2d, *rotation*, as of a wheel on an axis, where the different parts of a body move at the same time in different directions; 3d, *a combination* of translation and rotation, as in the motions of the planets.

20. Forces.—By *force*, as used in mechanics, is meant any cause producing, or modifying, motion. In this sense all known forces have their origin in three causes: 1st, *gravitation* (or the mutual attraction of bodies for each other); 2d, the unknown cause of the phenomena of *light, heat,* and *electricity*; and, 3d, *life*, or the mysterious agency producing motion of animals.

21. Momentum.—The momentum of a body is its amount of motion, or its tendency to continue in motion, and it is equal to the mass or weight of the body multiplied by its velocity.

22. Cohesion and repulsion.—These are two *opposing* principles or forces inherent in the atoms and molecules of matter, termed *molecular forces.* These are either *attractive* or *repulsive*, drawing the particles of bodies toward each other, or tending to separate them. Though this attractive force (termed cohesion) draws the particles *toward* each other, it is not supposed they come into actual contact, being prevented from doing so by their mutual repulsion. It is this that accounts for the insensible or physical pores (14), existing between the atoms and molecules of all matter.

23. Relation of cohesion and repulsion in the three states of matter.—Matter exists in three states : the *solid, liquid,* and *gaseous.* In *solids* the attractive force greatly overpowers the repulsive, holding the particles in a relatively fixed position at certain distances from each other. Heat will increase the power of repulsion, and cold (decrease of heat) will diminish it; hence, by varying the heat of a body its size can be sensibly varied, which is the result of altering the distance, and size of the pores, between the particles.

In liquids or inelastic fluids these two forces are in perfect equilibrium, which leaves the particles to move with perfect freedom among themselves (88 and 90).

In gases or elastic fluids the repulsive force holds sway, which causes the body to dilate, unless confined by external force (91). Liquids and gases as well as solids are contracted and expanded by variations of heat.

24. By structure in solids is meant relative disposition of their atoms and molecules or their groups. This structure may be either symmetrical or regular, as in living beings and crystals; or amorphous, as in most rocks and many other substances.

There is a *formative force or principle* pervading or inherent in all matter, disposing or arranging its atoms and molecules and their groups in definite forms. In the organic—vegetable and animal—kingdoms this force or principle is termed vitality; and forms thus produced are mostly bounded by curved lines and surfaces. In the inorganic or lifeless world, different formative forces or principles govern the arrangement of particles; forming, under favorable circumstances, bodies which are angular and bounded by plane faces. Such bodies are termed crystals; and their geometrical forms, thus produced, are analogous to the more complicated forms found in animal and vegetable life. The formative principle in inorganic bodies is easily or often interrupted, which accounts for so many irregular forms of crystals.

DEFINITIONS AND PROPERTIES OF MATTER. 37

THE CHARACTERISTIC PROPERTIES OF SOLIDS:

Some of these depend upon the atomic structure of the material; as, Crystalline form, Elasticity, Resistance, and Hardness; and others upon a permanent change in the arrangement of the molecules; as, Malleability, Ductility, Temper, etc.

25. Crystalline form.—The molecules of certain substances, when left free to move among themselves, by means either of solution, fusion, sublimation, or electrical or chemical decomposition, will be acted upon by the force of crystallogenic attraction, and thereby be united into solids or masses of certain definite and uniform shapes, termed crystals—each substance yielding its own peculiar form.

26. Elasticity.—This is that property of matter which disposes it to resume its original form or shape after having been bent or compressed by some external force. It is not so much a distinct property of matter as it is a phenomenon of attractive and repulsive forces. Different bodies possess this property in very different degrees.

When elasticity takes place in the direction of the length of the body, as a wire, it is termed *elasticity of tension and compression;* when in a direction transversely to the body, as in the case of a bent beam, it is termed *elasticity of flexure;* and when a body is twisted by a force applied at one end while the other extremity is fixed, it is called *elasticity of torsion.*

The *limit of elasticity* of any body (whatever be its substance) is reached when, if the applied force ceases to act, the body will fail to come back to its original position. If the force acts beyond the limit of elasticity, the molecules are forced into new relations with each other, and the body is said to have been *forced.*

27. Resistance to fracture, or tenacity, is that property which resists separation of the particles longitudinally or transversely, and gives strength to materials, and depends upon the force of cohesive attraction, which varies greatly in different substances, according to the nature of the atoms or molecules composing them.

28. Hardness is that property in virtue of which the particles of bodies resist impression, or the action of any force that tends to change their form. Hence, a body whose particles can be easily changed in their relative position, by slight forces, is said to be soft; therefore, softness is the opposite of hardness. Hardness does not imply density; for example, lead is more dense but softer than iron.

29. Malleability is the property of being wrought under the hammer, and belongs to many of the metals in an eminent degree; and upon it largely depends their utility. The most malleable, in order of softness, are lead, tin, gold, zinc, silver, copper, platinum, and iron. But gold may be beaten thinner than any other metal. It can be hammered so thin that the thickness of a million leaves will be less than an inch.

30. Ductility is the property in virtue of which a substance admits of being drawn into wire, which is not altogether unlike malleability; yet there is a marked difference, as shown by the fact that the most malleable are not the most ductile substances. Tin and lead are highly malleable but not ductile, as they cannot be drawn into fine wire; while gold is both very malleable and ductile; having been drawn into wire so fine that one ounce of it would extend fifty miles.

31. Flexibility and pliability are those properties which permit considerable motion between the particles of a body without their passing beyond the reach of their power of cohesive attraction. Bodies of this kind are not easily *broken*. These properties differ from elasticity in that, that elastic bodies, within their limits of elasticity, resume their original form, while with flexible bodies the original form is not resumed.

32. Brittleness is the property which renders bodies easily broken into fragments. It is the characteristic of most hard substances. In a brittle body the attractive force between the atoms or molecules exists within such narrow limits, that a very slight change of position, or increase of distance among them, is sufficient to overcome it, and the body breaks.

33. Hardening and annealing.—Some bodies, as steel and iron, by being brought to a high temperature and then suddenly cooled, by plunging into cold water, oil, or mercury, will become very hard. This is called *tempering*, and the hardness is supposed to be caused by thus producing a slight change in the relative position of the atoms or molecules of the substance. Some substances, as bronze, are hardened by being hammered, and others, as zinc and iron, by being rolled.

It is singular, however, that heating and sudden cooling should harden some substances, as steel, while other substances, as copper, will be softened by the same process. This, probably, is owing to the fact that heat and cold do not produce the same changes in the relative position of the atoms in the one substance that they do in the other.

34. **Welding** is the process of uniting the atoms of substances, as iron to iron or iron to steel, by cohesive attraction, which is accomplished by hammering them together when at a high temperature, which brings the particles so close together that they are brought within the reach of their cohesive force.

CHAPTER III.

ATTRACTION.

Molecular Attraction.

35. **Figure 1.—Interstices between atoms and molecules of matter.**—The three different sized balls or spheres in the diagram, may represent *bodies* of matter, as cannon-balls, bullets, and shot, or as apples, plums, and currants; or they may represent *atoms* or *molecules* (4) of matter, which vary in size, as those of water, salt, and sugar.

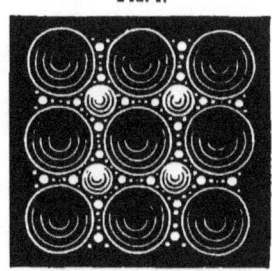

Fig. 1.

If a vessel be filled as full as possible with water, considerable salt may be put into the vessel without disturbing the water, and then a quantity of sugar can be introduced without displacing the water, which may be accounted for by supposing the molecules of these various substances to be spherical and of different sizes, and, probably, not in absolute contact (22), as shown in the figure.

36. **Figure 2.—Cohesive attraction.**—Cohesion is the force of attraction which holds atoms and molecules of the same bodies together; as, for example, a mass of stone, iron, or wood.

This figure represents two hemispheres of lead, with their flat surfaces made very smooth, and joined together by firmly rubbing one against the other.

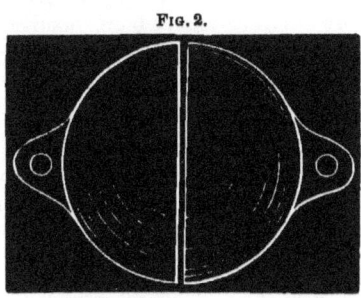

Fig. 2.

If cords be fastened to the side projections and an effort made to separate these hemispheres, it will be found that more than fifteen pounds of force to the square inch of the surface between them (which represents the atmospheric pressure) is required to draw them asunder; thus proving they are held together by cohesive attraction. Other smooth substances present the same phenomena, but with different degrees of intensity. Cohesion can be shown independent of atmospheric pressure, by separating the hemispheres in the vacuum of an air-pump.

37. **Figure 3.—Adhesive attraction.**—This force of attraction is that which holds the molecules of dissimilar bodies together, and is termed *adhesion*. It is adhesion that holds wood, glue, and paint together, and causes liquids to adhere to solids.

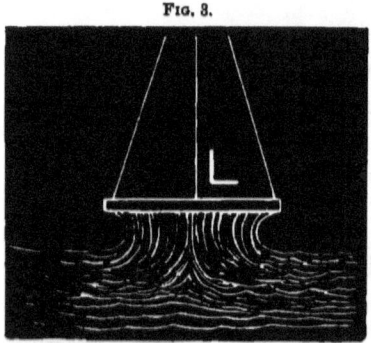

FIG. 3.

Let L be a disk of glass or metal, counterpoised by a scale-pan, and so adjusted that the disk will just touch the surface of the liquid; then place in the scale-pan just sufficient weight to separate the disk from the liquid, and this will indicate the measure of adhesion between them.

The experiment will also indicate the force of *cohesion* among the particles of liquid, which is somewhat less than the adhesion between the liquid and solid; for, were it not less, then none of the liquid would adhere to the disk and thus be separated from itself, and the disk would come up dry. The force of cohesion is not the same in all liquids; that of alcohol and turpentine being but little more than half as intense as that of water.

38. **Figure 4.—A few phenomena of capillarity.**—Capillary forces are molecular forces exerted between liquids and tubes, or liquids and sensible pores of bodies (14).

If tubes of small bore, open at both ends, are placed vertically in water, the liquid will rise both in the tubes and on the outside, as shown at H and J; rising higher within as the tubes are smaller, as seen at J. If the tube is over half an inch in diameter the effect is hardly observable. If mercury is employed (which does not wet the glass) there is a depression of the surface of the liquid, both within and without the tube, as exhibited at Y; and this becomes greater as the tubes are smaller. In a greased tube water is similarly depressed.

These phenomena are independent of atmospheric pressure; taking place equally in a vacuum or compressed air. They vary, however, with the material of the tube and with the nature of the liquid.

The attraction and repulsion observed between light bodies floating on liquids is due to capillarity. The floating bodies are drawn near to each other, either when both are or are not moistened, as at L and P, and repelled if the liquid wets only one of them, as at R. At L, both

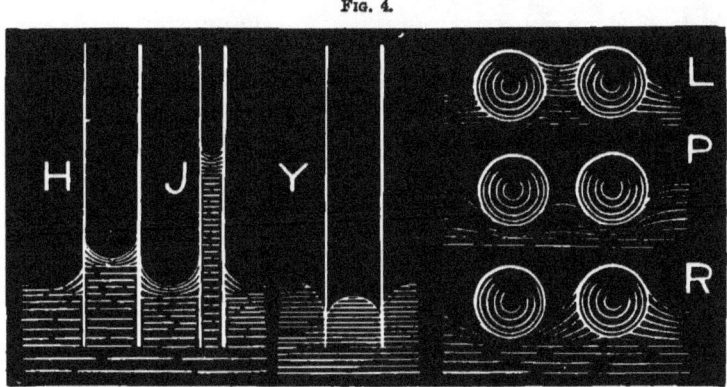

FIG. 4.

balls being moistened, the liquid rises (by capillarity) higher between than on the outside of them, which acts as a loaded cord to *draw* them together; while at P, both balls being dry, the water is depressed lower between than outside of them, which causes them to be *crowded* together. At R, one ball being wet and the other dry, causes the water to rise around one and to be depressed around the other, which effects, combined, build up an inclined plane between them, and thus they are kept apart, as shown in the figure.

Gravitation.

39. **Gravitation.**—The attraction of cohesion, as has been shown, unites particles of matter into masses or bodies, and the attraction of gravitation tends to draw these masses together to form bodies of greater dimensions.

Weight.—The fall of a body to the earth, and its downward pressure upon the earth's surface, are due to the force of gravity; and the amount of this pressure is called the *weight* of the body.

40. **Figure 5.—Centre of gravity of bodies.**—The centre of gravity of a body is that point through which the direction of the weight always passes, and this point coincides with the centre of inertia. The figure shows that when two or more bodies are connected

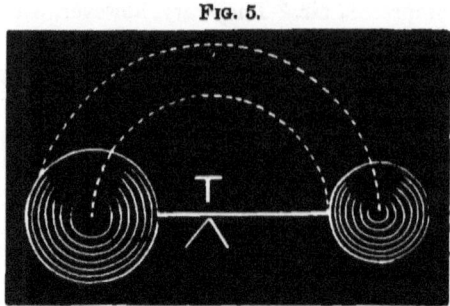

Fig. 5.

together, they may be regarded as one body, having but one centre of gravity. If the fulcrum, T, supports the centre of gravity of the two bodies, they will remain at rest; and this point, if the bodies are of equal weight, will be in the middle of the line which unites them (measuring from the separate centres of gravity); but if they be of unequal weight, the centre of gravity will be as much nearer the heavier body, as the heavier exceeds the lighter one in weight.

A prop that supports the centre of gravity supports the whole body, which may be applied directly *at* the centre of gravity, or immediately *above* or *below* it, on the line that points to the earth's centre of gravity.

A body is in a *state of equilibrium* when its weight is completely counteracted by supporting the centre of gravity.

There are three kinds of equilibrium; *stable*, *unstable*, and *neutral*.

A body is in *stable* equilibrium when, on being slightly disturbed from its state of rest, it tends, of itself, to return to that state. A rocking-chair is a case of this kind.

A body is in *unstable* equilibrium when, on being slightly disturbed from its state of rest, it does not tend to return to that state, but continues to depart from that state more and more.

A body is in a *neutral* equilibrium when, on being slightly disturbed, it has no tendency either to return to its former state or to depart further from it. The last two kinds of equilibrium are illustrated by Fig. 7 (42.)

41. **Figure 6.—Method of finding the centre of gravity**

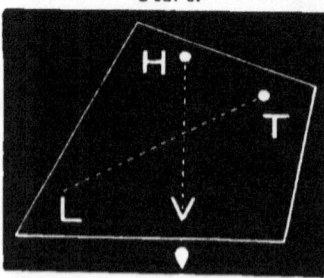

Fig. 6.

of irregular shaped bodies. Let the object be freely suspended from some point, as H, and the centre of gravity will fall into the vertical line HV (marked by plummet and line). If now the body be freely suspended from some other point, as T, the centre of gravity will again fall into the vertical line, which (being marked by the plumb-line TL), will be found to cross the line HV; therefore,

ATTRACTION.

the centre of gravity will be at the intersection of these two lines, for it cannot be in both lines at any other point.

42. **Figure 7.—Neutral and unstable equilibrium illustrated** with a wheel or ball on a horizontal and inclined plane.

If the plumb-line from the centre of the wheel or ball (which is the centre of gravity) be drawn, it will pass through the base or point on which it rests on the horizontal plane N, which supports the body from moving. This will be the case whichever side up the ball may be, or on whatever point of the plane it may be placed, affording an illustration of *neutral* equilibrium.

FIG. 7.

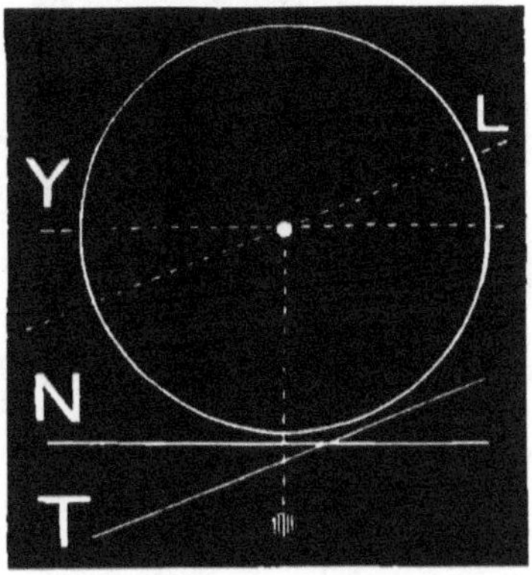

If the horizontal plane be removed, and the ball allowed to bear upon the inclined plane T, the point of contact is back, or at one side of the plumb-line, which deprives the centre of gravity of its vertical support; therefore, in search of support it will begin to fall, and continue to descend in the direction of the dotted line L, which is parallel to the inclined plane.

This figure also shows that the reason why a wheel or ball is so easily moved over a horizontal plane is, because the centre of gravity is not elevated by the movement. If the ball be rolled along the plane N, the centre of gravity will pass along the dotted horizontal line Y, which neither rises nor falls.

43. **Figure 8.—Stability of bodies depends upon the position of the centre of gravity.**—Suppose the diagram to represent a cube of wood, iron, or stone, with its centre of gravity indicated by the dot at the centre.

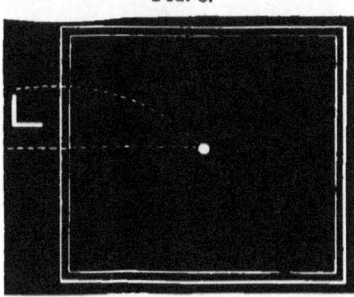

FIG. 8.

Place one foot of the dividers at the lower left hand corner of the cube and the other at the centre of gravity, and draw the curved dotted line, and with a rule draw the straight dotted horizontal line; and the distance between these two lines, at their intersection with the surface of the block, will equal the vertical distance that the centre of gravity, or the weight of the body, must be elevated in order to overturn the block.

44. **Figure 9.—Relative stability of cubes and pyramids.**—Let the altitude and base of the pyramid be the same as those of the above cube, with the centre of gravity indicated by a dot, which is at one-third of the distance from the base to the apex. The space L, it will be seen, between the two dotted lines, is much greater than in the previous figure; showing that, as the centre of gravity in the pyramid is nearer the base than in the cube, the weight requires to be elevated a greater vertical distance in order to be passed over the edge of the base; hence the pyramid has greater stability than the cube.

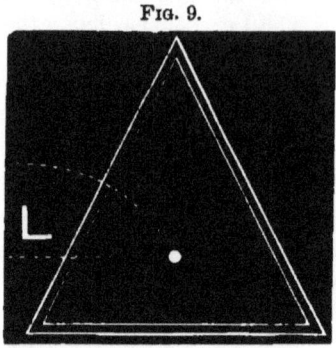

FIG. 9.

The stability of *any* body, at rest, of given bulk and weight, depends upon how far the centre of gravity must be elevated in order to pass it over the edge of its base nearest to the vertical line passing through its centre of gravity.

45. **Figure 10.—Centre of gravity of vehicles.**—Suppose the vehicle, freighted with lead, to be moving across an inclined plane, and the centre of gravity to be at L; then the line of direction, shown by the arrow on the right, would fall within the base; that is, between the wheels of the vehicle, in which case it would not be overturned. · If the vehicle were loaded with such material as would bring the centre of gravity at N, it would *not* be overturned, as the line of direction, shown by the middle arrow, still falls between the wheels; but if the wagon were so freighted as to bring the centre of gravity at T, it *would* be overturned, because then the line of direction would fall *without* the wheels or base, as shown by the arrow on the left.

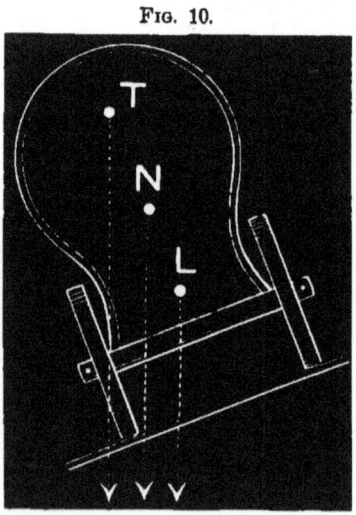

FIG. 10.

ATTRACTION. 45

46. **Figure 11.—Centre of gravity in man.**—The centre of gravity in man being between his hips, the line of direction, if he stands erect, will fall within his base, that is, between his feet. But if he carries a burden he will lean in the opposite direction from it, in order to bring the resultant centre of gravity of himself and burden into the vertical line passing down between his feet, as shown by the dotted arrow; otherwise the line of direction would fall without the base, that is, outside of his feet, and it would be impossible to prevent himself from falling.

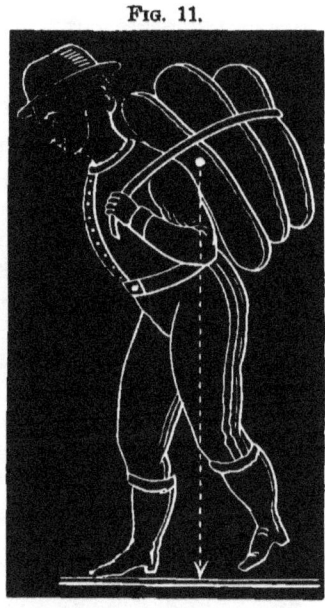

Fig. 11.

47. **Figure 12.—Law of intensity of gravity.**—*The force of gravity varies directly in proportion to the quantity of matter contained in bodies, and inversely as the square of the distance between them,* measuring from their centres of gravity.

Let the diverging lines, in the diagram, represent lines of attraction, then the small parallelogram formed between them at the earth's surface may represent the force of gravity at this point, which equals 1; and its distance from the centre of the earth equals 1. If further on, at a distance equal to 2, another parallelogram be constructed between these diverging lines, it will be four times as large as the small one, shown by the dotted division lines; and if at a distance equal to 3 a parallelogram be drawn, it will be nine times as large, and so on. Now, as there is only a given amount of attraction between these diverging lines, it follows that its intensity *diminishes* as the space between these lines *increases;* and, as 1, 4, and 9 are, respectively, the squares of 1, 2, and 3, this space increases in the same ratio as the square of the distance (from the earth's centre of gravity) increases.

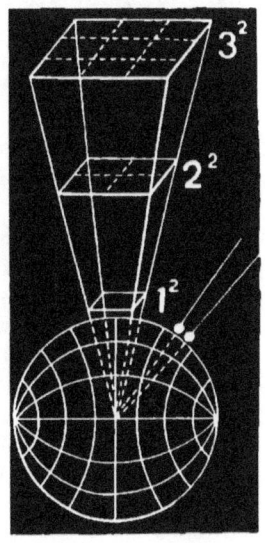

Fig. 12.

This law is stated in a tabular form thus:

Distances	1	2	3	4	5	6	7	8	9	10	11	12	etc.
Intensity of attraction	1	$\frac{1}{4}$	$\frac{1}{9}$	$\frac{1}{16}$	$\frac{1}{25}$	$\frac{1}{36}$	$\frac{1}{49}$	$\frac{1}{64}$	$\frac{1}{81}$	$\frac{1}{100}$	$\frac{1}{121}$	$\frac{1}{144}$	etc.

Conditions Affecting Terrestrial Gravity.

48. Gravity affected by altitude.—In accordance with this law of attraction, if a body at 4,000 miles from the centre of the earth (which would be at its surface) weighs 1 pound, at 8,000 miles (that is, 4,000 from the surface) it would weigh $\frac{1}{4}$ of a pound, and at 12,000 miles $\frac{1}{9}$ of a pound, and so on. Hence, bodies weigh slightly less on mountains than at the level of the sea.

49. Gravity affected by depression below level of the sea.—In passing from the surface to the centre of the earth the weight decreases also—not, however, as the *square* of the distance, but *directly* as the distance increases; for, at the centre of the earth, the weight or gravity of a body would be nothing, as the distance from the centre of gravity is nothing. And, in this case, the body would be attracted by the earth equally in all directions. A body, therefore, that weighs a pound at the surface, would weigh only half a pound if it could be placed half way from the surface to the centre of the earth. Hence, bodies will slightly decrease in weight as they are placed in deep excavations below the level of the sea.

50. Gravity affected by shape of the earth.—Owing to the flattening of the earth at the poles, a body at the equator will be 13 miles further from the centre of gravity of the earth than when it is at either pole. Hence, it will weigh less at the equator than at the poles; and, for this cause alone, the difference in weight would be about $\frac{1}{585}$. But it is found that the actual difference is $\frac{1}{194}$ of the equatorial weight: that is, a body weighing, at the equator, 194 pounds, would weigh, at the poles, 195 pounds; showing that this great difference must be accounted for by some other cause; which is the centrifugal force resulting from the rotation of the earth.

51. Gravity affected by the earth's rotation.—The centrifugal force (caused by the rotation of the earth on its axis), which is nothing at the poles and regularly increases toward the equator, where it is greatest, in the same ratio *diminishes* the weight of bodies on the earth's surface. If the earth were to revolve seventeen times faster than it now does (or once in 1 h. 24 m. 25 s.), the centrifugal force would balance the force of gravity, and bodies at the equator would have no sensible weight; while at the poles the weight of bodies would remain the same. If the earth were to revolve in less time than about

1 h. 24 m., the oceans would be thrown off at the equator, like water from a grindstone, and loose bodies would fly into space above the earth's surface.

52. **Earth drawn toward falling bodies.**—A body falling through space to the earth also draws the earth through space toward itself. The mass of the earth, however, being so much greater than any of its detached bodies, and the relative distances that the earth and the detached bodies move being inversely as their masses, of course, the earth's motion would be incalculably small, but mathematically a fact.

53. **Direction of gravity.**—The direction in which gravity acts corresponds to straight lines, drawn from the earth's centre of gravity, and perpendicular to the earth's surface. The two small balls and lines on the right of the diagram (Fig. 12) may represent two plumb-lines, which, by gravity, are attracted toward the centre of gravity of the earth, as seen by the continued dotted lines; thus showing that plumb-lines, though sensibly parallel, are not mathematically so; and hence, proving that the walls of a building, for instance, laid up by plumb-lines, are not exactly vertically parallel with each other.

Up and down, relative terms.—As the law of direction of gravity holds good on all sides of the earth alike, it shows that *up* and *down* are only relative terms—*up* meaning *away from* the earth, and *down* signifying *toward* it; so that the direction *up* to *us* would be *down* to our *antipodes;* or antipodes pointing one *up* and one *down* would point in the same absolute direction.

CHAPTER IV.

MOTION AND FORCE.

54. **Motion and force.**—There are three varieties of motion: *translation*, or *direct motion; motion of rotation;* and a *combination* of translation and rotation (see 15 and 19). Besides these there are *uniform motion; accelerated motion;* and *retarded motion.*

A body has *uniform motion* when it moves over equal spaces in equal times.

A body has *uniformly accelerated motion* when its velocity increases by a constant quantity in a given time.

A body has *uniformly retarded motion* when its velocity diminishes by a constant quantity in a given time.

The increase of velocity in a second is called the *acceleration;* and the decrease in a second the *retardation.*

Force.—For definition and origin of force, see 20. In determining a force there must be taken into consideration: 1st, the *point of application;* 2d, the *direction;* 3d, the *intensity* or *energy* with which the force acts.

Forces are represented by lines; and any given length of line may be taken as the *unit of force;* hence, the direction of a line will represent the *direction* in which the force acts; and its length, the *magnitude* or *intensity* of the force.

Statics is the science of equilibrium; and *dynamics* treats of the motions which forces produce.

Equal forces acting in opposite directions, the body upon which they act, as also the forces themselves, are said to be in *equilibrium.*

The direction in which a force is applied determines the direction in which the body receiving the force will move, or of the resultant pressure if the body is not free to move.

Measure of forces.—The following propositions will express the effects of different forces:

1. Two constant forces are to each other as the masses to which, in equal times, they impart equal velocities.
2. Two constant forces are to each other as the velocities which they impress, during the same time, upon two equal masses.
3. Two constant forces are to each other as the products of the masses, by the velocities which they impart to these masses in the same time.
4. The measure of a force is the product of the mass moved by the acceleration, or velocity, imparted in a unit of time.

The *momentum* of a body is equal to its mass or weight multiplied by its velocity.

55. **Figure 13.—Laws of falling and rising bodies.**—The main line in the diagram, for convenience, is divided into four equal parts, H, N, L, and R, of 16 feet each, to represent the track of a falling or rising body during two seconds of time.

It has been found by experiment that a body starting from a state of rest will fall 16 feet the first second, and that its velocity at the starting point is nothing, and at the end of the second it is equal to 32 feet per second, showing that the average is just half the accelerated

MOTION AND FORCE.

velocity. At the end of the next second it will have acquired another acceleration of 32 feet, which, added to the first acceleration, makes 64 feet.

The body S, therefore, would fall through the space H the first second, and its acquired velocity of 32 feet would carry it the next second over the lines N and L, and the force of gravity would (of itself) carry it over the line K; hence, it would fall during the 1st second 16 feet, and during the 2d second 32 feet + 16 feet = 48 feet; and during the 3d second 64 feet + 16 feet = 80 feet, and during the 4th second 96 feet + 16 feet = 112 feet; and so on.

Fig. 18.

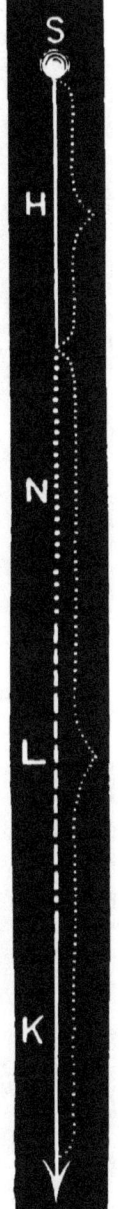

Or, thus stated, it would fall during the

1st second 16 feet   = 16   = 16 feet.
2d   "   32 + 16   = 32 + 16 = 48 "
3d   "   32 + 32 + 16   = 64 + 16 = 80 "
4th   "   32 + 32 + 32 + 16 = 96 + 16 = 112 "

Or, by adding, we have the space passed over in the

1st second   -   -   16 feet. | 3d second   -   -   144 feet.
2d   "   -   -   64 " | 4th   "   -   -   256 "

It will be seen that these spaces are to each other as the squares of the time; that is,

1^2 is to 2^2 as 16 is to 64.
1^2 is to 3^2 as 16 is to 144.
1^2 is to 4^2 as 16 is to 256, or,

2^2 is to 3^2 as 64 is to 144.
3^2 is to 4^2 as 144 is to 256; and so on.

Or, in tabular form:

The intervals being	1	2	3	4	5	6	7	8	9	10	etc.
The spaces described each interval	1	3	5	7	9	11	13	15	17	19	
And the whole space will be	1	4	9	16	25	36	49	64	81	100	

As the motion of a body is uniformly accelerated when falling to the earth, so it is uniformly retarded when rising from the earth, passing over spaces *decreasing* each interval as the square of the time.

50 MATTER, FORCE, MOTION, AND MECHANICS.

Fig. 14.

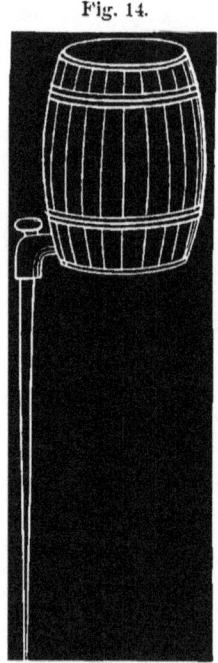

To find the velocity of a falling body at the end of any second, multiply 32 feet by the number of seconds it has been falling.

To find the velocity of a rising body at any particular second, multiply the seconds it has been rising by 32 feet, and subtract this from the velocity it had at starting.

Bodies also acquire the same velocity in falling the same perpendicular distance from a state of rest, whatever path they may take, as on an inclined plane, or on a pendulum-rod, etc.

56. **Figure 14.—Accelerated velocity of falling bodies** illustrated by the flow of thick liquids.—Suppose the material flowing from the faucet to be some thick, tenacious liquid, as molasses or syrup; and though, at the faucet, the stream be an inch or more in diameter, it will, if it fall far, dwindle away to a fine thread-like stream; but as no more of the liquid can pass in any one part of the stream than another, it proves that the liquid moves with greater velocity the farther it falls.

57. **Figure 15.—Reflected motion.**—It is a law of moving bodies, set in motion by a single force, to move forward in a straight line until some other force or impediment, acting in a different direction, changes their course.

Fig. 15.

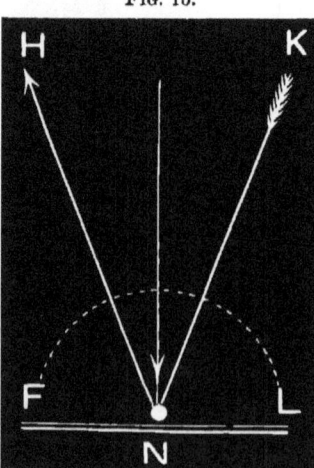

Suppose FL to be a floor, made of marble or some other elastic substance, and N an ivory or some kind of an elastic ball, thrown toward the floor in the direction of the line KN; it will be reflected in the direction of NH, making the angles KNL and HNF equal. If the ball be thrown down the perpendicular line, which is called the *normal*, it will rebound in the same direction. The angle formed by the normal and KN is termed the *angle of incidence*, and that formed by

MOTION AND FORCE. 51

the normal and N II is the *angle of reflection,* and these angles are always equal.

58. Figure 16.—Resultant motion.—This is produced by two or more forces, termed *components,* acting in different directions on the same body at the same time.

When several forces act on a body they may be arranged in three ways, according to their direction. The forces may act,
1st. All in one direction;
2d. In exactly opposite directions; or,
3d. At some angle.

In the *first* case, the resultant is the sum of all the forces, and the direction is unaltered.

In the *second* case, the resultant is the difference of the forces, and takes the direction of the greater. If they be equal, no motion is produced.

In the *third* case, a resultant is found to *two* of the forces by the parallelogram of forces, according to the following law, namely: by any number of forces acting together for a given time, a body is brought to the same place as if each of the forces had acted on the body separately and successively for an equal time.

Fig. 16.

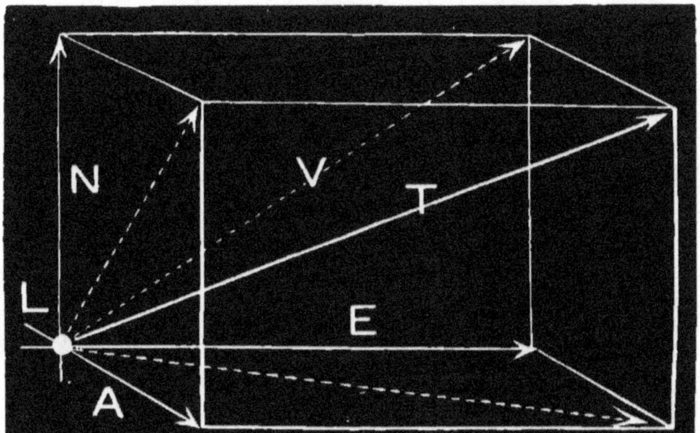

If a force act on the ball L in the direction of and equal to the line N, it will pass over this line; but if there be simultaneously applied to the ball another force, in the direction of and equal to the line E, it will pass over the dotted diagonal line V; and, by the joint action of the two forces it will be moved over the line V in the same time that the first force would impel it over the line N, and the second force over the line E, or, which is the same, over their opposite parallel lines. If, in addition to these two forces, a third force be simultaneously applied, equal to and in the direction of the line A, the ball will be driven over the heavy line T; or, if it be impelled by the resultant V and the force represented by A; or, if it be impelled by the resultant of A and N and the resultant of N and E.

These forces act at right angles to each other, but the same law holds good, whatever be the angles.

In the same manner a resultant may be found for any number of motive forces, by compounding them two by two successively.

This is called the *composition of forces*. By reversing the operation a single force may be divided into two or more forces, the sum of which is equal to the one force. This is called *resolution of forces*.

Curvilinear motion will be illustrated hereafter (842).

59. **Figure 27.—Action of wind on sails of vessels.—** Many practical examples of the resolution of forces might be given, but the sailing of a boat in a direction different from the wind affords a familiar illustration of these principles.

FIG. 17.

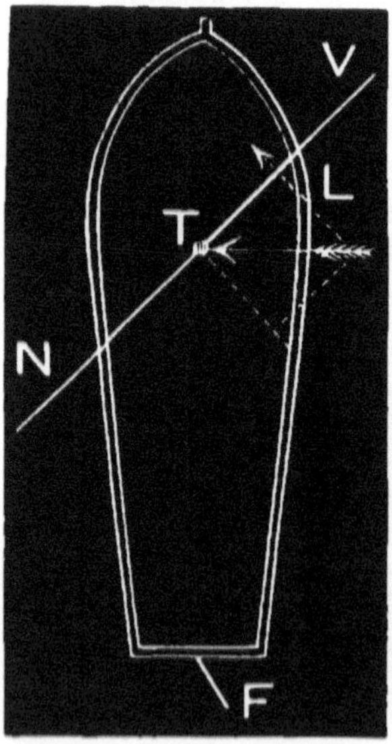

Let the arrow, crossing the deck of the vessel at right angles to the keel, represent the force and direction of the wind; then resolve this force into two others, by forming the dotted parallelogram, and the force of the wind which falls upon the sail NV at right angles to its surface will be represented by the dotted arrow L.

If this force be resolved into two others, it will be seen what amount of force is applied to the vessel in the direction of her keel. By the rudder, F, the boat is kept in the proper direction to receive the wind upon the sail to the best advantage with reference to the desired course.

To apply these principles to the best advantage, it is necessary that the boat be so modelled as to advance as freely as possible through the water in the direction of the keel, while it offers great resistance to lateral motion. It is for this reason that sailing-vessels are provided with keels and centre-boards.

The Pendulum.

60. **Figure 18.—Compensating pendulum.**—A pendulum clock, to run with accuracy, requires that the pendulum remain always the same length; but, as heat expands and cold contracts it, it varies with the temperature (215). To overcome this variation is the object of the compensating or gridiron pendulum.

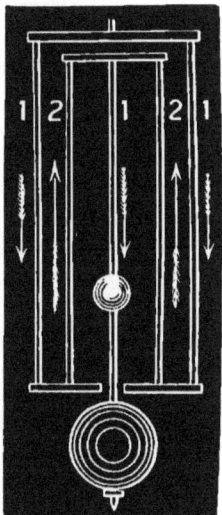

Fig. 18.

The central and two outer rods, marked 1, are steel; the two intermediate rods, marked 2, are brass. If the two outer rods expand, say an eighth of an inch, the pendulum will be lowered this much; and as the central rod will expand the same, it will be lowered *two*-eighths of an inch. As the expansion of brass is twice that of steel, the rods, marked 2, will *elevate* the pendulum, by their expansion, two-eighths of an inch; and thus the expansion or contraction of the brass just neutralizes that of the steel rods, as indicated by the arrows.

Variations in the vibration of the pendulum are effected, at will, by depressing or elevating the pendulum-ball by means of a screw and nut at the bottom, or by moving the small ball on the central rod.

61. **Figure 19.—Laws of oscillation of the pendulum.**—Let the pendulum be suspended at A; then, when it is in the position N it is in equilibrium, as the action of gravity, which acts vertically, is resisted by the tension of the string or rod. If the ball be drawn aside to T, and then allowed to swing, gravity acts to draw it back again to N, where it will move with the same velocity as though it had fallen through the vertical height from

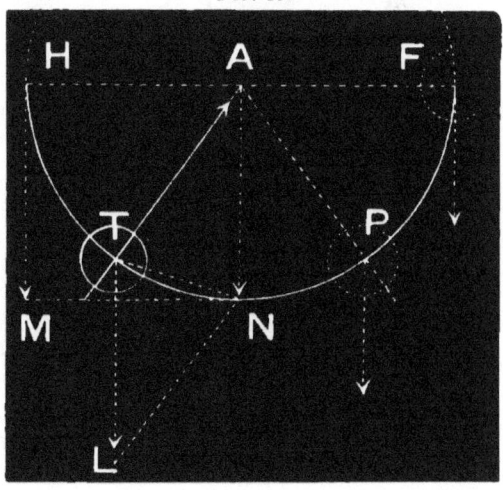

Fig. 19.

T to the dotted line MN. In consequence of its inertia and acquired velocity, it will pass on to the position of P. From T to N gravity acts as an accelerating force, but from N to P as a retarding force. Were it not for the resistance of the air, NP would rigorously equal NT.

Let AT represent the tension of the rod, and TL the force of gravity, then construct the parallelogram TANL, and TN will represent the force with which the ball is drawn to the vertical line passing through the point of suspension, which continually diminishes as it approaches this line, until, finally, it becomes nothing; when the lines TA and TL will form a straight line, and the forces which they represent will act in opposition.

Laws of oscillation.—For pendulums of unequal lengths, the times of oscillation are proportional to the square roots of their lengths.

For the same pendulum the time of oscillation is independent of the amplitude, provided the amplitude be small.

For the same pendulum at different places, the times of oscillation are inversely as the square roots of the force of gravity at those places.

Scientific uses of the pendulum.—The pendulum is employed to measure time and regulate the movements of clocks. And as its oscillation is caused by the force of gravity, its movements are affected by whatever affects this force; hence, it is a most valuable scientific instrument in the investigation and application of principles relating to gravity, latitude, altitude, shape and motion of the earth, etc.

Projectiles.

62. **Figure 20.—Motion of projectiles.**—Projectiles are bodies thrown into the air by some momentary force, therefore they are subject to two forces: viz., the projectile force, which is momentary, and gravity, which is constant.

If the body is projected vertically upward or vertically downward, see the laws of rising and falling bodies, Fig. 13, (55); but the space traversed, and also the velocity, are resultants of the sum of the two forces.

If the direction of the projectile is not perpendicular, then the path of the projectile must be a curve.

In the figure suppose the *length* of the narrow parallelograms to be the distance the projectile would travel in each second, and their *width* (16 feet, Fig. 13), the distance the projectile would fall in one second

MOTION AND FORCE. 55

by the force of gravity. If now a cannon ball be projected from A (the gun ranging at the angle of 45°), it would be driven, by the projectile force alone, the *first* second, along the straight line toward the point L, to F, but, by the force of gravity alone (55), it would fall to the lowest corner of the first parallelogram; hence the two forces, acting together, would drive it along the curved line in the first

Fig. 20.

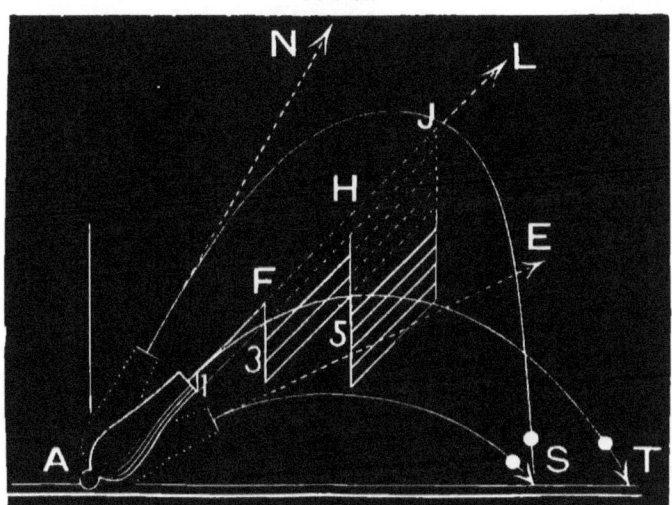

parallelogram. During the *second* second the projectile force, acting alone, would drive the ball from F to H, but during the *second* second gravity would (by the law of falling bodies) draw it down the width of three parallelograms, to the bottom of the line 3; hence, it will pass along the curved line crossing these three parallelograms. During the *third* second the projectile force, acting alone, would drive the ball from H to J, and gravity would depress it over the width of five of the parallelograms, to the bottom of the line 5; hence, it will pass along the curved line traversing these five parallelograms; and so on, until the ball falls on the horizontal line at T.

It will reach T in the same time that the projectile force (uninfluenced by gravity) would drive it along the line FJ to a point where this line would intersect a perpendicular erected at T, which would be the same time required for a ball to fall (by gravity) from this intersection to T.

The greatest possible horizontal range, with a given velocity of projection, is obtained by placing the gun at the angle of 45° with the

56   MATTER, FORCE, MOTION, AND MECHANICS.

horizon; in which case the greatest height attained is one-fourth of the range.

For any range equally above or below 45°, the horizontal range will be equally diminished; that is, the horizontal range will be the same for 40° and 50°, and the same for 30° and 60°; as shown by the other two curves in the diagram.

63. **Figure 21.—Perpetual revolution.**—Suppose the sphere to represent the earth, with a tower reaching above the atmosphere

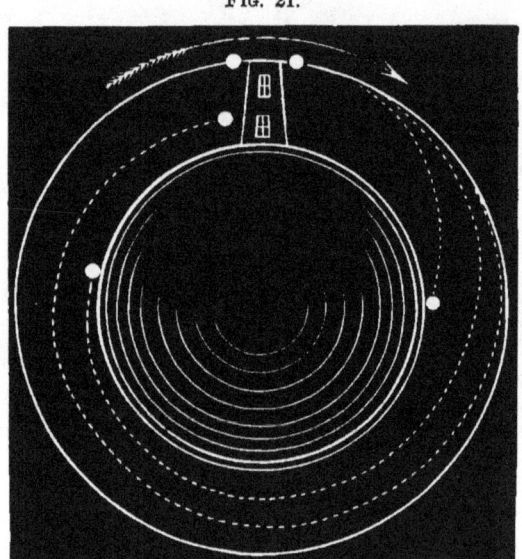

FIG. 21.

(say fifty miles high), from which to project a cannon-ball. A ball shot from a cannon at this elevation, not being resisted by the air, might be driven eighty miles or more; and, with sufficient projectile force, a ball might be driven completely around the earth to the point of starting, as shown in the diagram; in which case it would continue to revolve perpetually around the earth, same as the moon.

64. **Figure 22.—Falling of projectiles thrown from horizontal guns.**—A ball horizontally projected from an elevated gun will reach the ground in the same time that it would fall vertically from the same elevation, whatever be the projectile velocity.

Suppose the cannon to be elevated at such a height that a ball falling vertically from its mouth would be just three seconds in reaching

MOTION AND FORCE. 57

the ground, by the action of gravity, and the range of the gun to be exactly horizontal.

Suppose a ball to be projected from the gun, and to reach N in one second, then the horizontal line N1 will intersect the vertical line L3 at the point to where an unshot ball would fall by gravity, at the end of the *first* second. During the second second, suppose the projected

FIG. 22.

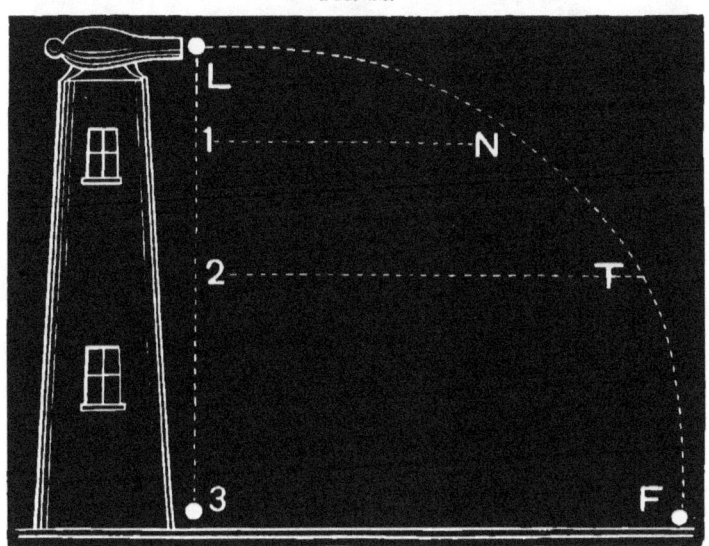

ball to pass from N to T, then the horizontal line T2 will intersect the vertical line at the point to where the unshot ball would fall at the close of the *second* second. During the third second, suppose the projected ball to pass from T to F, then draw the horizontal line F3 (which coincides with the earth), and it will intersect the vertical line at the point to where the unshot ball would fall at the close of the *third* second; hence, the projected ball reaches the earth in the same time that the unshot ball falls vertically from the mouth of the cannon to the earth.

65. **Figure 23.—Action and reaction are equal,** or force and resistance are equal.—This is shown by a series of ivory or other elastic balls suspended by cords. If the ball 1 be drawn from the perpendicular, and then allowed to fall so as to strike the one next to it, the motion of the falling ball will be communicated through the whole series from one to the other, without moving any but the last. This is owing to the fact that the *reaction* of 2 is just equal to the *action* of 1; and that the reaction of 3 is just equal to the action (communicated from 1) of 2; and so on, until the motion 1 arrives at 6, which, having nothing to act upon, is itself put in motion and thrown off to L. It

FIG. 23.

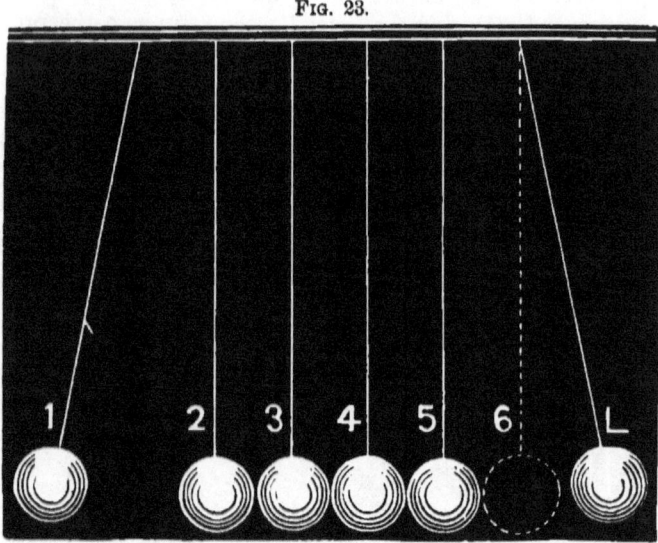

is, therefore, *reaction* which causes all the intermediate balls to remain at rest.

If 1 and 2 be drawn aside and allowed to fall together, then 5 and 6 will be thrown off. In these experiments elastic balls must be employed.

The law, that action and reaction are equal, is often overlooked by inventors who strive to produce a perpetual motion.

CHAPTER V.

MECHANICAL POWERS.

66. **Machine, motor, power, weight, etc.**—A machine is any contrivance that transmits the action of force. A force employed to move a machine is a *motor*.

The moving force in a machine is called *the power;* the place of its appliance, *the point of application;* the line in which this point tends to move, *the direction of the power;* the resistance to be overcome, *the weight;* and the part of the machine immediately applied to the resistance is the *working point*.

Forces (or what is the same, forces and resistances) in equilibrium must be to each other inversely as their velocities, and *inversely as the spaces which they describe.*

Levers.

Figure 24.—Lever of the first class.—A lever, in use, implies an inflexible bar, fulcrum, power, and resistance. *Weight* is substituted for resistance in these illustrations.

In the first class, the fulcrum is between the power and weight, as shown in the diagram, dividing the lever into a long and short arm.

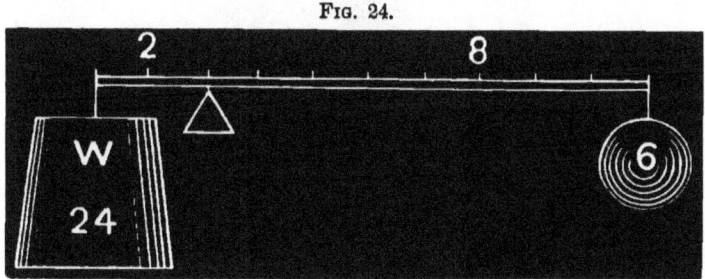

FIG. 24.

The relative length of these arms is shown by *figures*, and also by a corresponding number of equal *spaces*, marked on the lever; and the relation between the power and weight is indicated by figures—the ball being the power.

The conditions of equilibrium with all levers are these: *the weight and power are to each other inversely as their distances from the fulcrum;* or, power multiplied into its arm (its distance from the fulcrum) equals the weight multiplied into its arm; or, as shown in the diagram, $6 \times 8 = 24 \times 2$; or, P. (power) is to W. (weight) as short arm is to long arm. Hence, the weight, short arm, power, or long arm, in all levers may be found, respectively, by the following formulæ:

$$\frac{\text{long arm} \times \text{P.}}{\text{short arm}} = \text{W., or } \frac{8 \times 6}{2} = 24;$$

$$\frac{\text{long arm} \times \text{P.}}{\text{W.}} = \text{short arm, or } \frac{8 \times 6}{24} = 2;$$

$$\frac{\text{short arm} \times \text{W.}}{\text{long arm}} = \text{P., or } \frac{2 \times 24}{8} = 6;$$

$$\frac{\text{short arm} \times \text{W.}}{\text{P.}} = \text{long arm, or } \frac{2 \times 24}{6} = 8.$$

These rules apply to each of the other simple levers.

67. **Figure 25.—Lever of the second class.**—In this lever the weight is between the fulcrum and power, which affords greater

FIG. 25.

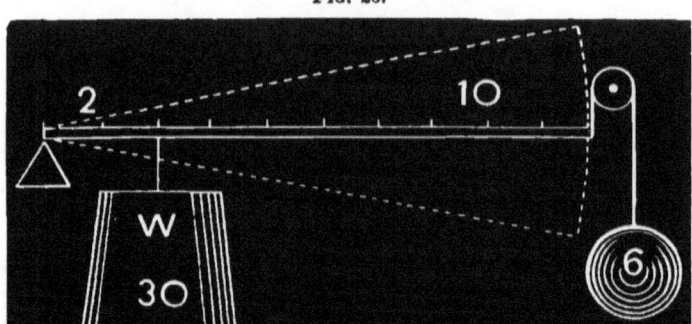

leverage with a lever of the same length; as it will be seen that all the ten spaces, instead of eight, come between the power and fulcrum, which gives the power a fifth greater advantage over the weight than in the former case; or $6 \times 10 = 30 \times 2$; thus making the weight 30 instead of 24.

The dotted lines show that the space through which the weight passes is to the space through which the power passes as the power is to the weight; and as the short arm is to the long arm.

FIG. 26.

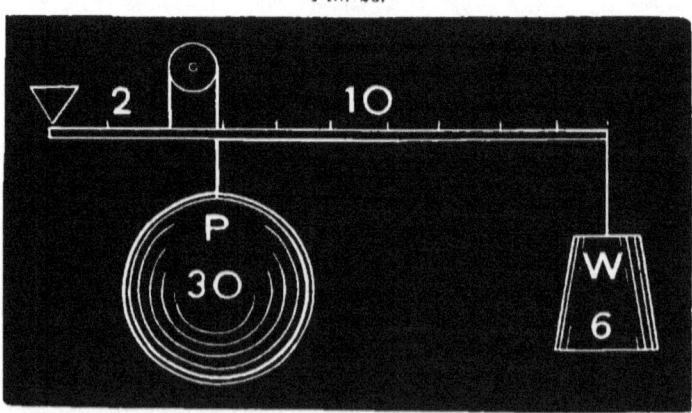

68. **Figure 26.—Lever of the third class.**—In this lever the power comes between the fulcrum and weight, which brings the

MECHANICAL POWERS. 61

weight on the long instead of the short arm, thus decreasing the motion of the power at the expense of the leverage; the weight having the advantage of the whole length of the lever, and the power only one fifth of it; or $30 \times 2 = 6 \times 10$; thus making the weight 6 and the power 30.

In this case the long arm (that to which the power is usually applied) becomes the short arm, and the short arm becomes the long arm, which must be kept in mind when applying the rules previously given.

69. **Figure 27.—Compound levers.**—A compound lever consists of two or more simple levers. The one here exhibited consists of three simple levers of the first class.

FIG. 27.

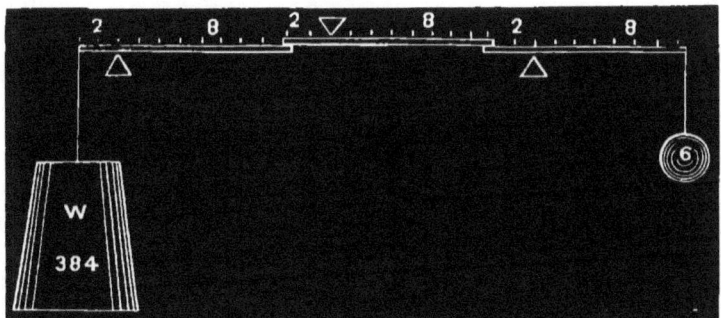

The conditions of equilibrium in such a system are, that the product of all the long arms multiplied by the power must equal the product of all the short arms multiplied by the weight; or $8 \times 8 \times 8 \times 6 = 2 \times 2 \times 2 \times 384$. Or the weight of the 1st lever (beginning next to the power) becomes the power of the 2d lever, and the weight of the 2d lever becomes the power of the 3d, and so on. Hence we have:

$$\frac{P \times \text{long arm}}{\text{short arm}} = \text{1st W., and}$$

$$\frac{\text{1st W.} \times \text{2d long arm}}{\text{2d short arm}} = \text{2d W., and}$$

$$\frac{\text{2d W.} \times \text{3d long arm}}{\text{3d short arm}} = \text{3d W., and so on. Or,}$$

$$\frac{6 \times 8}{2} = 24, \text{ and } \frac{24 \times 8}{2} = 96, \text{ and } \frac{96 \times 8}{2} = 384.$$

Among the examples of levers of the first class, in practical use, may be mentioned the crowbar, scissors, pincers, snuffers, hand-truck, scales, steelyards, etc.

Levers of the second class are not so common. The crowbar, however, is often employed as a lever of this class, and nut-crackers afford another example.

Regarding the practical use of levers of the third class, see Fig. 28 (70).

Examples of compound levers are found in various platform scales.

70. **Figure 28.—Limbs of animals, levers of the third class.**—Many of the bones of animals (including man) are levers of the third class, moved by the contraction and expansion of muscles, which are the power; and the great extent and alacrity of motion given to the limbs of animals are owing to the fact that the muscles are attached to the bones near the fulcrums; as illustrated by the human arm in the diagram. Let the bone of the forearm be the lever; the ball and forearm itself, the weight; the lower end of the bone HY, the fulcrum; and the muscle IL, the power. If now the forearm and ball be raised, without moving the elbow, it is evident that the muscle must exert a force as much greater than the weight of the forearm and ball, as the distance from the elbow to the hand is greater than that from the elbow to the point of attachment of the muscle; and therefore the rapidity and extent of motion of the hand will be correspondingly greater than that of the contraction of the muscle. If the leverage be as 12 to 1, and the weight 50 pounds, the muscle will exert a force of 600 pounds.

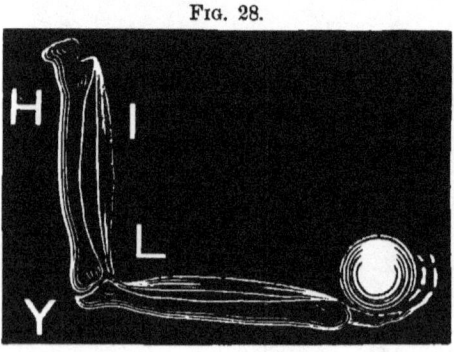

FIG. 28.

The Wheel and Axle.

71. **Figure 29.—The wheel and axle.**—This machine is a modification of the lever of the first class, and, being constant in its action, it is sometimes called the perpetual lever. It consists of a cylinder, termed the *axle*, connected with a *wheel* of much greater diameter. The power is applied to the circumference of the wheel (usually by means of an endless rope), and the weight is attached to a rope wound around the axle. Draw from the centre, or fulcrum, the long arm of the lever, equal to the radius of the wheel, and the short

FIG. 29.

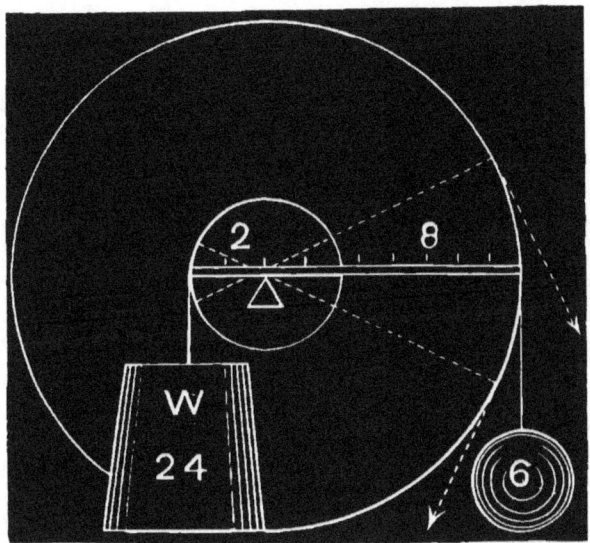

arm, equal to the radius of the axle, as shown; then, as the conditions of equilibrium, we shall have, of course,

W × radius of the axle = P × radius of the wheel; or,

$$24 \times 2 :: 6 \times 8.$$

P. is to W. as *radius of axle* is to *radius of wheel;* or,

$$6 : 24 :: 2 : 8.$$

The power and weight are inversely as their velocities.

$$\frac{\text{Wheel radius} \times \text{P.}}{\text{axle radius}} = \text{W., or } \frac{8 \times 6}{2} = 24;$$

$$\frac{\text{wheel radius} \times \text{P.}}{\text{W.}} = \text{axle radius, or } \frac{8 \times 6}{24} = 2;$$

$$\frac{\text{axle radius} \times \text{W.}}{\text{wheel radius}} = \text{P., or } \frac{2 \times 24}{8} = 6;$$

$$\frac{\text{axle radius} \times \text{W.}}{\text{P.}} = \text{wheel radius, or } \frac{2 \times 24}{6} = 8.$$

The dotted lines may show that the entire wheel and axle are made up of an indefinite number of simple levers; each, in its turn, coming

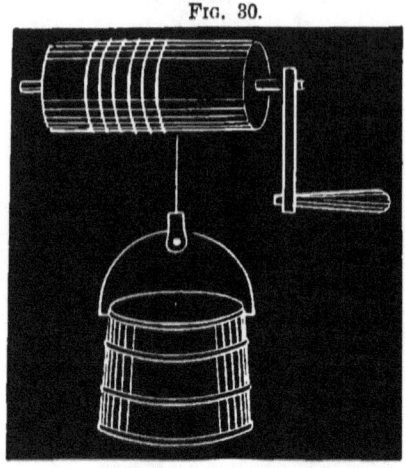

Fig. 30.

around to the horizontal line, and revolving around the fulcrum.

The capstan, employed on ships for raising the anchor, is a modification of the wheel and axle.

72. **Figure 30.—Simple windlass a modification of wheel and axle.**—The axle, in this case, is revolved by means of a handle, termed the winch, or crank, which is equivalent to a pin driven into one of the spokes of the wheel. The conditions of equilibrium are, that the

W. × axle radius = P. × length of the crank.

73. **Figure 31.—Chinese differential windlass or double axle.**—In this machine it will be perceived that the axle consists of two parts of unequal diameters, and that the rope winds around them

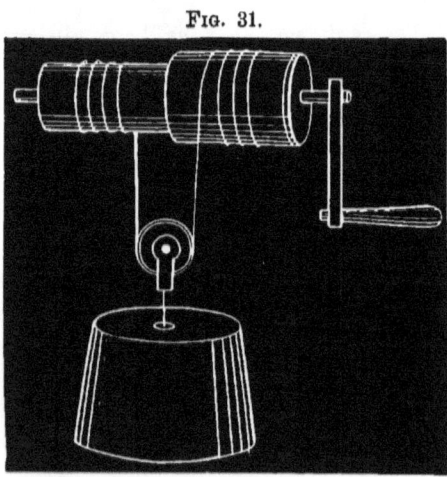

Fig. 31.

in different directions; therefore, every turn of the windlass or handle winds up a portion of the rope equal to the circumference of the one, but unwinds a portion equal to the circumference of the other; and if the two be nearly equal, the weight has but a slight motion; and, consequently, the power has great advantage over it. If the weight rise 1 inch while the power at the handle describes 100 inches, 1 pound will balance 100 attached to the rope.

Hence the conditions of equilibrium are, that the power multiplied by the circumference described by the handle, equals the weight multiplied by the distance it moves.

By this device *space* and *time* are conveniently exchanged for *power*. Differential pulleys, worked by an endless chain, are arranged on the same principle.

74. **Figure 32.—Compound wheel and axle.**—In the figure suppose the small circles (the axles) to be cog-wheels, working into cogs on the circumferences of the large wheels, and the horizontal

FIG. 32.

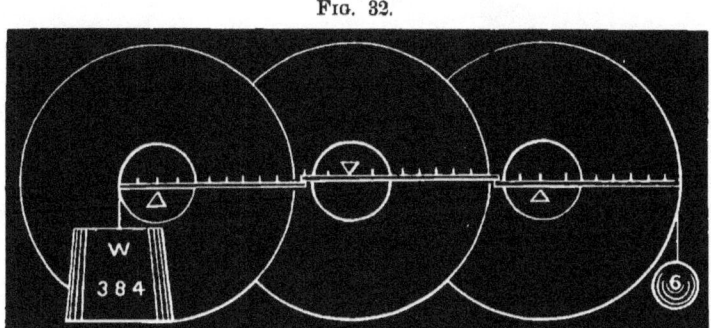

diameters to be three simple levers of the same dimensions of that in Fig. 29 (71); then it will be seen that the conditions of equilibrium are the same as those of the compound lever, Fig. 27 (69):

Product wheel radii × P. = product axle radii × W. Or, 8 × 8 × 8 × 6 = 2 × 2 × 2 × 384. Or (beginning next to power),

$$\frac{\text{1st wheel radius} \times \text{P.}}{\text{1st axle radius}} = \text{1st W., and}$$

$$\frac{\text{2d wheel radius} \times \text{1st W.}}{\text{2d axle radius}} = \text{2d W., and}$$

$$\frac{\text{3d wheel radius} \times \text{2 W.}}{\text{3d axle radius}} = \text{3d W., and so on. Or}$$

$$\frac{8 \times 6}{2} = 24, \text{ and } \frac{8 \times 24}{2} = 96, \text{ and } \frac{8 \times 96}{2} = 384.$$

Pulleys.

75. **Figure 33.—Simple fixed or immovable pulley.**— It is the *law* of the pulley that a cord or rope, when stretched, must have the same strain upon it throughout its length.

The two vertical cords passing over the fixed pulley at the top of the diagram, sustain an equal strain. Allowing nothing for friction and rigidity of rope, the power just equals the weight; or, 6 = 6.

The horizontal diameter of the pulley is a lever of the first class, with its fulcrum at its centre, the cords being attached at the ends of its equal arms T and L; hence we have, as conditions of equilibrium, the W × T (its arm) = P × L (its arm).

The pulley may be considered as made up of an indefinite number of such levers, revolving around their fulcrum. Therefore, the only advantages of this pulley are to change the direction of force and apply it at a distance from its source.

The object of the pulley at the bottom is to again change the direction of the force. The cross-bar and arrows represent a whiffletree and parts of traces of a harness.

FIG. 33.

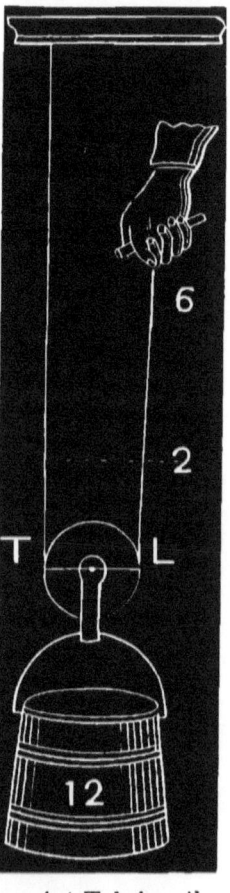

FIG. 34.

76. Figure 34.—Simple movable pulley.— In this pulley one end of the cord is attached to a rigid beam, and the other end is controlled by the power; therefore, it is evident that the beam sustains half the weight and the power the other half; for the pulley acts as a lever of the second class, whose arms are to each other as 1 is to 2; the point T being the fulcrum; TL, the long arm, or the leverage of the power; and the distance from T to axis of pulley, the short arm, or leverage of the weight. Now, as the long arm is the *diameter*, and the short one the *radius* of the pulley, equilibrium will obtain when the power is equal to one-half the weight. Or, P is to W as the diameter of pulley is to radius of pulley; hence

MECHANICAL POWERS. 67

P : W = 1 : 2—or, in numbers, 6 : 12 = 1 : 2; or $P = \dfrac{W}{2}$, and

W = P × 2—or, in numbers, $6 = \dfrac{12}{2}$, and 12 = 6 × 2.

The power moves twice as fast as the weight.

77. **Figure 35.—Movable and immovable pulley.**—This is a combination of the two pulleys previously described; and, as the

FIG. 35.   FIG. 36.

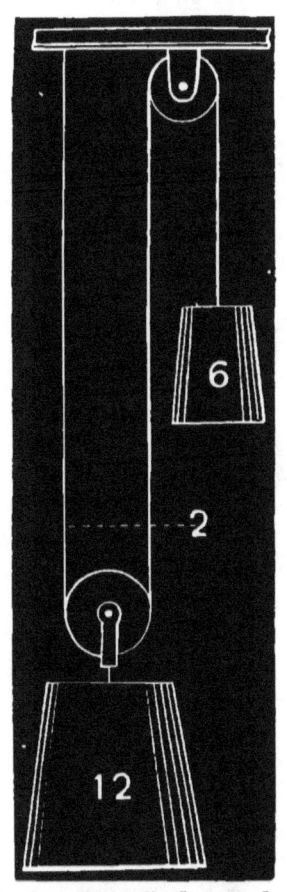
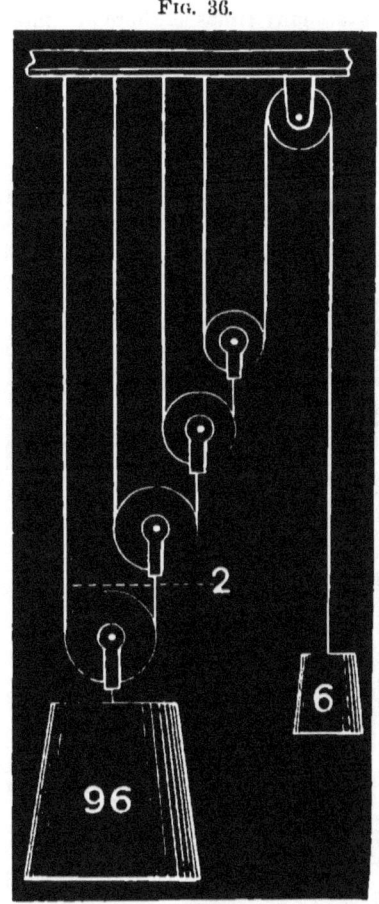

fixed pulley affords no advantages in power, the conditions of equilibrium are the same as in the last case; that is,

P : W = 1 : 2, or $P = \dfrac{W}{2}$, and W = P × 2; or, in numbers, 6 : 12 = 1 : 2;

or $6 = \dfrac{12}{2}$; and 12 = 6 × 2.

78. **Figure 36.—A system of pulleys with more than one cord.**—In this arrangement each movable pulley holds the same relation to the one next below it, that the lowest one does to the weight, and the lowest one holds the same relation to the weight that the single movable pulley (Fig. 35) does to the weight; that is, the lowest pulley being sustained by *two* cords, if the weight be divided by 2 it will express the weight held by the next pulley above; and so on.

Hence, equilibrium obtains when the power equals the weight *divided* by 2 as many times as there are movable pulleys; and, conversely, the weight equals the power *multiplied* by 2 as many times as there are movable pulleys. Or,

$$P = \frac{W}{2 \times 2 \times 2 \times 2}, \text{ and } W = P \times (2 \times 2 \times 2 \times 2).$$

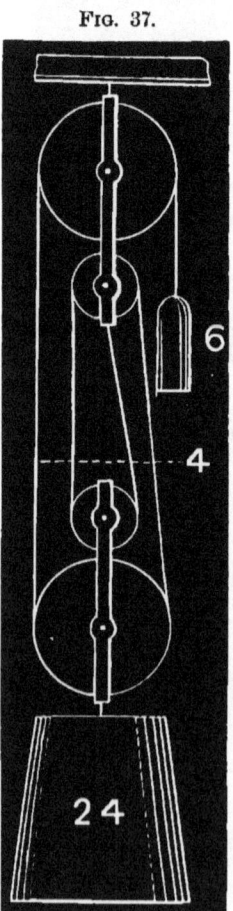

Fig. 37.

79. **Figure 37.—Compound pulleys with two or more movable pulleys.**—Pulleys of this kind are arranged in two blocks, one block being movable, and the other immovable, and the weight is divided equally among the cords passing around the pulleys of the movable block; and as the power required to sustain a given weight is diminished one-half by a single movable pulley, it follows that, in this arrangement, equilibrium will obtain when the power is equal to the weight divided by twice the number of movable pulleys. Hence,

P : W = 1 : twice the number of movable pulleys; or

P : W = 1 : number of cords; and

P : W = velocity of W : velocity of P; or 6 : 24 = 1 : 4.

$$P = \frac{W}{\text{num. pulleys} \times 2}, \text{ or } 6 = \frac{24}{2 \times 2}; \text{ and}$$

$$P = \frac{W}{\text{num. cords}}, \text{ or } 6 = \frac{24}{4}; \text{ and}$$

W = P × twice number pulleys; or, 24 = 6 × (2 × 2); and W = P × number cords; or, 24 = 6 × 4; and number cords = $\frac{W}{P}$; or,

$$4 = \frac{24}{6}.$$

Or, as the weight is sustained by four cords,

MECHANICAL POWERS. 69

and all being parts of the same cord, it is evident that each cord must bear one-fourth of the weight.

80. **Figure 38.—Compound pulleys with one movable pulley.**—It is evident, in this combination, that as the weight is sus-

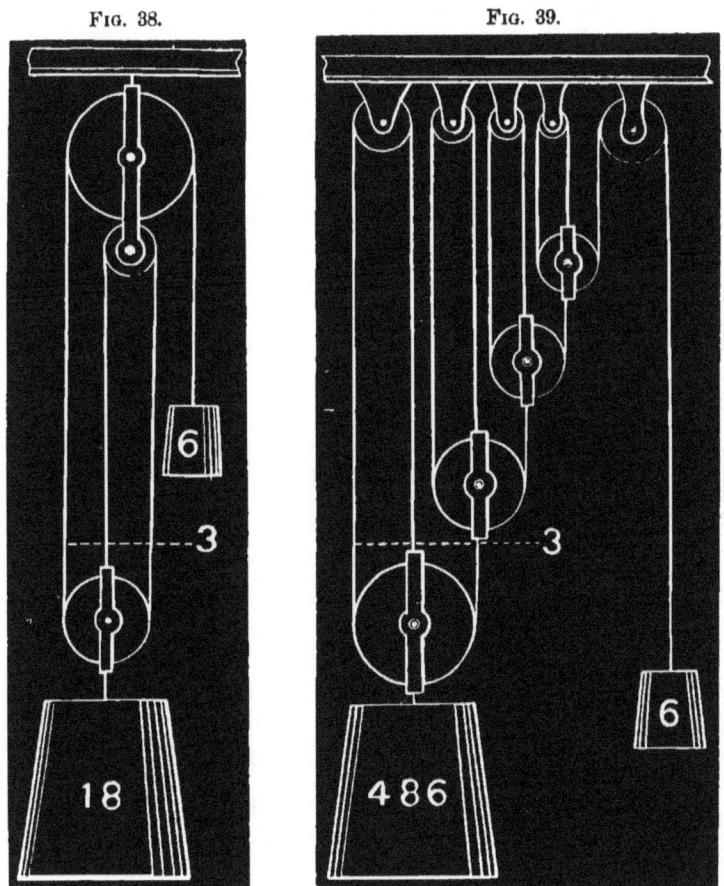

Fig. 38.   Fig. 39.

pended by three cords, all being parts of the same cord, the $W = P \times$ number of cords; or, $18 = 6 \times 3$; and
$P = W \div$ number of cords; or, $6 = 18 \div 3$; and the number of cords
$= W \div P$; or $3 = 18 \div 6$; and
$P : W =$ velocity of W : velocity of P; or $6 : 18 = 3 : 1$.

81. **Figure 39.—A system of pulleys with more than**

one rope and three cords to each pulley.—As the first pulley next to the weight is sustained by three cords, all of which are parts of the same cord, it is evident that each cord will bear one-third of the weight; but as only *one* of these three cords attaches to the second pulley, of course each one of its cords will sustain only *one-third of one-third* of the weight; and so on. Hence, the

W = P *multiplied* by 3 as many times as there are movable pulleys; and

P = W *divided* by 3 as many times as there are movable pulleys.

W = (6 × 3 = 18), (18 × 3 = 54), (54 × 3 = 162), (162 × 3) = 486.
P = (486 ÷ 3 = 162), (162 ÷ 3 = 54), (54 ÷ 3 = 18). (18 ÷ 3) = 6.

W : P = velocity P : velocity W, or
6 : 486 = 1 : 81.

Fig. 40.

Such a system is not practical, as the motion of the weight is so slow. It will be noticed that it would require 81 feet of rope at the power to raise the weight 1 foot.

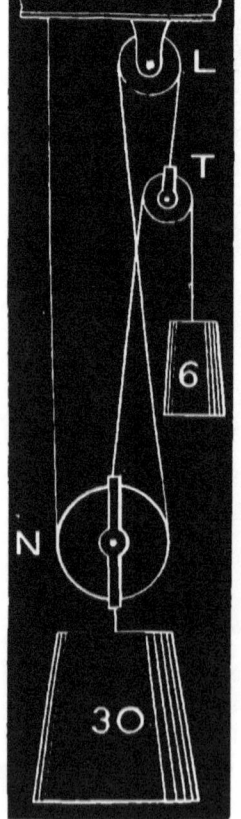

82. **Figure 40.—A system of pulleys with two ropes, having one fixed and two movable pulleys.**—This system, by sailors, is called the *burton*, by means of which 6 pounds of power overcomes 30 of resistance. For, suppose the weight to be 30 and the power 6, the cord which passes around T being attached to the power and weight, the power will balance 6 pounds of the weight, which leaves 24 pounds to be held by the two cords passing around the pulley N, half of which, 12 pounds, will be held by the cord passing over the fixed pulley L. But these 12 pounds being again divided by the pulley T, will be held by the 6 pounds of power; and, the power having already taken up 6 pounds of the weight, therefore 6 pounds sustain 30; and we have the

P : W = 6 : 30, or 1 : 5, or

$P = \dfrac{W}{5}$, and $W = P \times 5$.

P : W = velocity W : velocity P.

This system is considered quite indispensable on shipboard.

Inclined Plane.

83. **Figure 41.—Inclined plane.**—An inclined plane is one inclined to a horizontal plane. In every such plane three parts are to be considered, *height, length,* and *base,* for upon the relative proportions of these depends its power. The advantage gained by its use is due to the fact that it *supports a part of the weight.* If a body be placed on a horizontal plane it will support its entire weight, but if the plane be gradually elevated at one end it will support less and less of it, until the plane reaches the perpendicular position, when it will cease to sup-

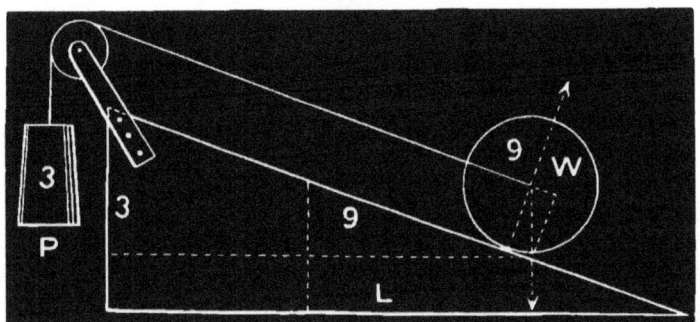

Fig. 41.

port any part of the weight. The power may be applied in a direction parallel to the length or parallel to the base, or in other directions. In any case, by resolution of forces, it can be found what amount of power is required to retain a body upon the inclined plane. Suppose, in the figure, the force to be applied in a direction parallel to the plane; draw, from the centre of the weight, the vertical dotted arrow, which represents the force of gravity, then draw the other dotted arrow perpendicular to the plane at its point of contact with the weight; then construct the dotted parallelogram, and the short side of the parallelogram will represent the direction and relative amount of force necessary to keep the weight in equilibrium on the plane.

Suppose the weight to be 9 pounds, length of plane 9 feet, power 3 pounds, and height of plane 3 feet, and the height and length divided off into equal spaces of a foot.

In moving the weight over one-third of the plane it will be elevated one foot, as shown by drawing the horizontal dotted line from the W to the perpendicular; hence, as one is a third of three, a force of one-third of the weight must be applied. Or, *equilibrium will obtain when the power is to the weight as the height is to the length of the plane.* Hence,

P : W = height : length, or 3 lbs. : 9 lbs. = 3 ft. : 9 ft.

$$W = \frac{P \times \text{length}}{\text{height}}, \quad \text{or, } 9 \text{ lbs.} = \frac{3 \text{ lbs.} \times 9}{3}; \text{ and}$$

$$P = \frac{W \times \text{height}}{\text{length}}, \quad \text{or, } 3 \text{ lbs.} = \frac{9 \text{ lbs.} \times 3}{9}; \text{ and}$$

$$\text{height} = \frac{P \times \text{length}}{W}, \quad \text{or, } 3 = \frac{3 \text{ lbs.} \times 9}{9 \text{ lbs.}}; \text{ and}$$

$$\text{length} = \frac{W \times \text{height}}{P}, \quad \text{or, } 9 = \frac{9 \text{ lbs.} \times 3}{3 \text{ lbs.}}.$$

84. **Figure 42.—The screw a modification of the inclined plane.**—The screw is an inclined plane wound spirally around

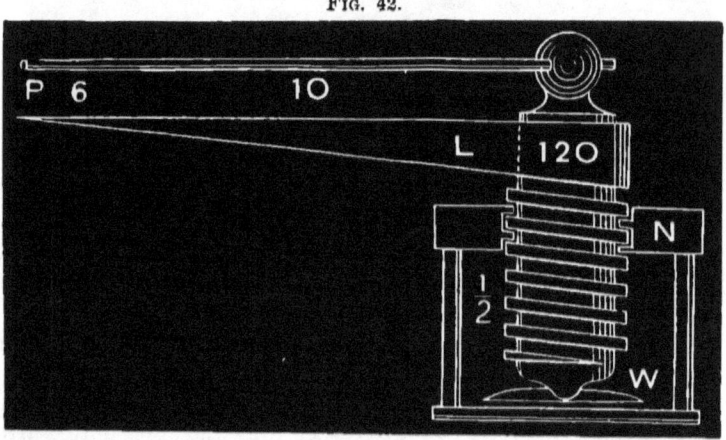

Fig. 42.

a spindle, and holds the same relation to the ordinary inclined plane that a spiral staircase does to a straight one. In the figure a part of the inclined plane L, forming the screw, is extended off to the left at the top of the spindle, instead of off to the right at the bottom, which inverts it.

The thread projects from the surface of the spindle, and fits into corresponding depressions in the nut, N. The point of the screw bears upon an iron plate, W, between which and the lower beam of the frame is placed the resistance to be overcome. In the head of the spindle is a lever which combines its power with that of the screw.

The distance between the threads of the screw depends upon the inclination of the inclined plane. Suppose a small insect to travel down the inclined plane L and around the screw, and it will, at last, arrive at W; and every time it goes around the screw it will make the same vertical descent as it did in travelling the same distance on the straight portion of the inclined plane L.

The resistance bears upon the inclined face of the thread, and the power on the lever parallel to the base of the screw. Equilibrium, therefore (without a lever), will take place when the

Power is to the weight as the distance between the threads is to the circumference of the screw; and (with a lever) when the

Power is to the weight as the distance between the threads is to the circumference of the circle described by the end of the lever. Or

$$P : W = \text{dis. between threads} : \text{sweep of lever.}$$

Supposing the distance between the threads is $\frac{1}{2}$ an inch; length of lever, 10 inches; and power 6 pounds; and we have,

$$W = \frac{P \times \text{sweep of lever}}{\text{dis. bet. threads}}; \text{ or, } W = \frac{6 \times 60}{\frac{1}{2}} = 720; \text{ and}$$

$$P = \frac{W \times \text{dis. bet. threads}}{\text{sweep of lever}}; \text{ or, } P = \frac{720 \times \frac{1}{2}}{60} = 6; \text{ and}$$

$$\text{dis. bet. threads} = \frac{P \times \text{sweep of lever}}{W}; \text{ or, } \frac{6 \times 60}{720} = \frac{1}{2}; \text{ and}$$

$$\text{sweep of lever} = \frac{W \times \text{dis. bet. threads}}{P}; \text{ or, } \frac{720 \times \frac{1}{2}}{6} = 60$$

$$W : P = \text{velocity of P} : \text{velocity of W}.$$

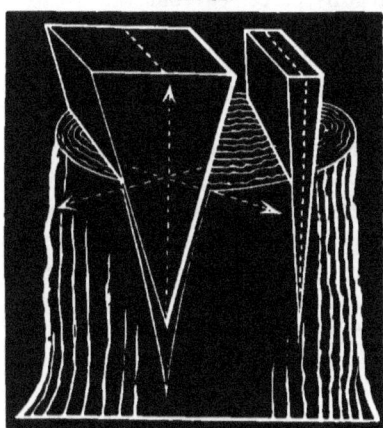
Fig. 43.

If 720 be divided by 6, we have 120 lbs. as the weight which 1 pound will raise, but this weight is elevated only *half an inch* while the power describes 120 half inches. Hence, in this, as in all mechanical devices, what is gained in power is lost in time and space.

85. **Figure 43. — The wedge a modification of the inclined plane.**—Instead of lifting a load by moving it over an inclined plane, the same result may be obtained by moving the plane under the load. When used in this way it is termed a *wedge*, and usually consists of two inclined planes joined base to base, as shown by the dotted lines in the figure.

The *back* of the wedge is that face to which the power is applied; the inclined faces, the *sides;* and the distance from point to back, its *length*.

The resistance may act at right angles to the *sides*, as shown by the two transverse arrows; or it may act at right angles to the *length*.

In the first case, therefore, equilibrium obtains when the power is to the resistance as the back of the wedge is to its *side ;* and, in the second case, when the power is to the resistance as the back of the wedge is to its *length*. Or,

P : W = back : side; and P : W = back : length.

Hence, in the first case,

$$P = \frac{W \times \text{back}}{\text{side}}; \text{ and } W = \frac{P \times \text{side}}{\text{back}}; \text{ and}$$

$$\text{back} = \frac{P \times \text{side}}{W}; \text{ and side} = \frac{W \times \text{back}}{P}.$$

And, in the second case,

$$P = \frac{W \times \text{back}}{\text{length}}; \text{ and } W = \frac{P \times \text{length}}{\text{back}}; \text{ and}$$

$$\text{back} = \frac{P \times \text{length}}{W}; \text{ and length} = \frac{W \times \text{back}}{P}.$$

The great amount of friction, and the method of applying the force in the use of the wedge, render it difficult to definitely calculate the power exerted by it; but it will be readily perceived that the greater the difference between the length and back, the greater will be the force from a given power. Including the swinging of the hammer or maul, much time and space are exchanged for power.

86. **Figure 44.—Endless screw—and combination of the five mechanical powers.**—The large cog-wheel, in this figure, works into a screw on the shaft A, and this shaft is worked by a crank, which acts as a lever. Every time the crank is turned the screw will turn the wheel the distance of the width of one tooth. Hence, equilibrium between the power and resistance offered by the teeth of the wheel, will obtain when the *power is to the resistance as the distance between the threads is to the sweep of the crank.*

Combination of the five mechanical powers.—By such a combination, could materials of sufficient strength be had, there could be exerted almost an unlimited force, but only through a correspondingly limited space.

It is only by means of combined action of the mechanical powers, that sufficient force can be exerted to haul vessels out of the water for repairs.

Fig. 44.

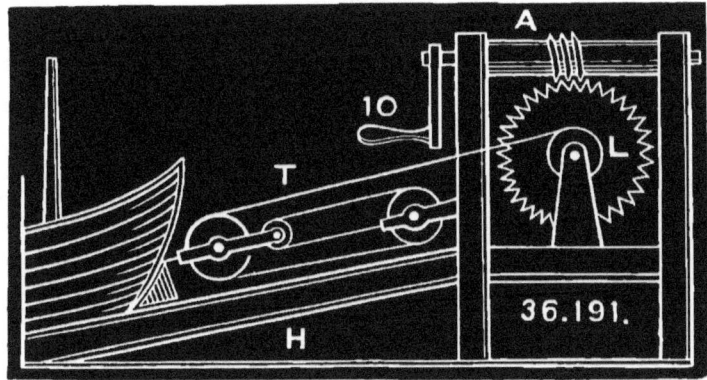

In estimating the force of this engine, suppose the dimensions of its several parts to be as follows:

Length of the lever or crank....................18 inches,
Distance between threads of screw..................1 inch,
Diameter of the toothed wheel......................4 feet,
Diameter of the axle, L, of the wheel................1 foot,
Compound pulley, T.............................4 ropes,
Height of inclined plane, H, (half its length).........2 feet,
Power applied to handle of the crank............10 pounds.

The sweep of the crank is twice its length multiplied by 3.1416, which equals 113.0976.

Then we shall have, first,

$$\frac{P \times \text{sweep of crank}}{\text{dis. bet. threads}} = \frac{10 \times 113.0976}{1} = 1130.976 \text{; and}$$

$$\frac{P \times \text{wheel radius}}{\text{axle radius}} = \frac{1130.976 \times 2}{\frac{1}{2}} = 4523.904 \text{; and}$$

$$P \times \text{num. ropes} = 4523.904 \times 4 = 18095.616 \text{; and}$$

$$\frac{P \times \text{length of plane}}{\text{height of plane}} = \frac{18095.616 \times 2}{2} = 36191 \text{ pounds.}$$

Thus (allowing nothing for the fraction), 10 pounds would exert a force of 36.191 pounds; or a power of 100 pounds, which is less than the power of a man, would exert a force of 361.910 pounds.

CHAPTER VI.

(CHART NO. 2.)

HYDROSTATICS.

Distinguishing Properties of Solids, Fluids, and Gases.

87. **Attraction and repulsion.**—As previously stated (22), it may be supposed that within all bodies there are two forces, *attraction* and *repulsion*. In rigid bodies, as iron, stone, wood, etc., the attractive force (cohesion) preponderates, holding the molecules firmly together, which causes the *rigidity*. In fluid bodies, these two forces, being in equilibrium, allow the molecules perfect freedom to move in all directions among themselves, which causes the *fluidity*. In gaseous bodies, the repulsive force preponderates, driving the particles from each other, which causes the greater *elasticity* and *compressibility* of these fluids.

Definition.—Hydrodynamics treats of the peculiarities, as weight, pressure, equilibrium, and motion, of fluid bodies, both liquids and gases. It is subdivided into *hydrostatics*, which treats of non-elastic fluids at *rest;* and *hydraulics*, which treats of non-elastic fluids in *motion;* and *pneumatics*, which treats of the properties of *elastic fluids*.

88. **Mobility of liquids.**—Owing to the equilibrium between these two forces (cohesion and repulsion), the particles or molecules of liquids are so free and mobile, that liquid bodies possess no definite form, but adapt themselves to the shape of the vessels that contain them. Liquids, however, vary in fluidity, and consequent mobility; as between water or alcohol and thick *viscous* bodies, like oils and tars.

In viscous fluids the imperfect fluidity is owing to a greater or less preponderance of the cohesive over the repulsive force, causing their molecules to slightly adhere or stick together. Heat increases the repulsive force, and converts viscous into thin fluids.

With greater or less intensity of heat the repulsive force can be so far increased (or the cohesion so far diminished) as to bring all bodies not only to a fluid, but to a gaseous condition; different substances being changed from one to another of these states by adding or abstracting heat (23); as in the case of water, which, when kept at a temperature between 32° and 212° F., is a liquid, but if the heat be less than 32°, this liquid becomes a solid (ice), and if it be more than 212°, then it becomes gas, or an elastic fluid (steam).

It is supposed that the molecules or ultimate atoms of an elastic fluid, like the air, are as hard and impenetrable as those of any solid, like iron and stone. Even though the air offers so little resistance to other bodies passing through it, yet it *can* be so far condensed that, bulk for bulk, it will weigh as much as the metals.

89. **Compressibility of liquids.**—Though liquids and gases are spoken of as *non-elastic* and *elastic* fluids, yet the distinction is not absolute, since *all* liquids possess some elasticity. It has been shown that water, by being submitted to a pressure of fifteen thousand pounds to the square inch, will be compressed about *one* part in 24; or about 33 ten-millionths of its bulk for each atmosphere of its pressure.

90. **Cohesion in liquids.**—Although cohesion and repulsion are spoken of as being in equilibrium in liquids, yet there is a slight preponderance of cohesion; as shown by their gathering and adhering in small masses or drops (37). This is illustrated by the method of making shot.

91. **Repulsion in gases.**—Gases or elastic fluids have so much preponderance of the repulsive force existing between their particles, that they continually dilate in volume, unless confined to a certain bulk by pressure (23).

Water may be taken as the type or representative of fluids, and common air as the type of gases.

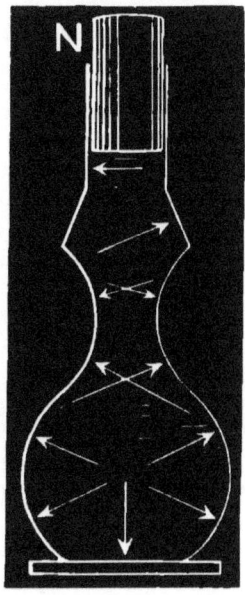

Fig. 1.

Pressure of Liquids.

92. **Figure 1. — Liquids transmit pressure equally in all directions.**— If the vessel be filled with water, and the cork, N, tightly fitted to the bottle, and pressed down upon the water, the pressure will be transmitted to the molecules in contact with it; these molecules will press upon those next in position, and so on, from molecule to molecule, in every direction, until the pressure is finally transmitted to every point of the interior surface of the bottle.

By experiment it is shown that the pressure thus transmitted is equal to that applied to the cork, surface for surface; that is, the pressure upon each square inch of the interior surface of the vessel is equal to that upon a square inch of the cork.

The direction of the pressure is at every point *perpendicular to the surface* of the vessel, as shown by the arrows. This law of transmission of pressure holds good irrespective of the shape and size of the vessel.

The whole theory of Hydrostatics depends upon this principle of transmission of pressure.

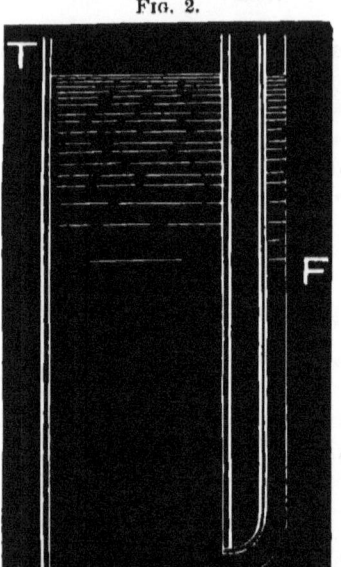

Fig. 2.

93. **Figure 2.—Pressure of liquid not in proportion to its quantity, but to its height.—** In this vessel, as shown, the water in the small division or pipe, F, stands on a level with that in the large division, T; thus showing that the large column of water presses against the small column with no greater force than the small column presses against the large one. Hence, columns or bodies of liquids of different magnitudes, when connected together, will be in equilibrium when they have the same depth or height.

94. **Figure 3.—Equilibrium of liquids in communicating vessels.—**A solid body is in equilibrium when its centre of gravity is supported, because the particles of the body are held together by cohesion. In liquids the particles do not cohere, and unless restrained they would flow away and spread out indefinitely. A liquid, therefore, can be in equilibrium only when restrained by a vessel or its equivalent.

This figure represents several vessels, differing in both size and shape, and all connected together by the pipe N. If either of these be filled with water to a given height, the liquid will rise to the same height in them all, as shown. Or, communicating liquids in different vessels will take a common level, whatever be the size, shape, or position of the vessels, or however small the communicating passage; because the pressure of liquids, at equal depths, is equal in all directions.

This figure is referred to in connection with the explanation of Figs. 9 and 10 (101 and 103).

HYDROSTATICS. 79

Fig. 3.

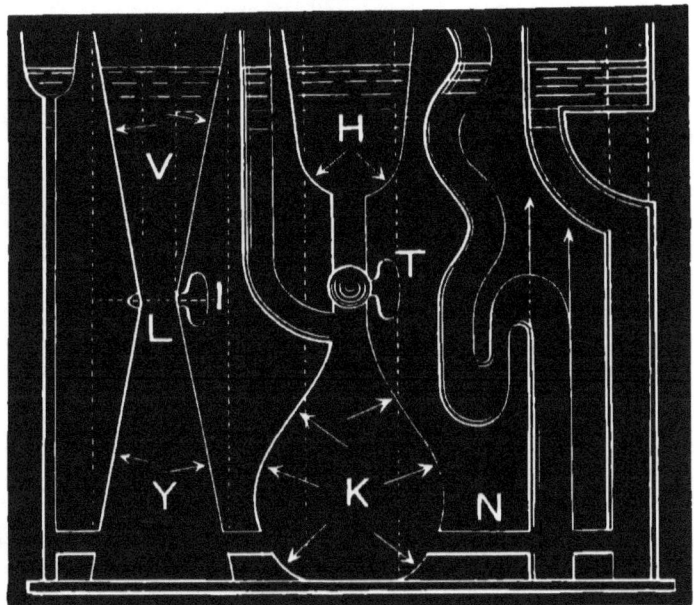

95. **Artesian wells.**—All springs and fountains illustrate the law of equilibrium of liquids in communicating vessels, artesian wells being the most remarkable examples. The water accumulates between two impervious strata of the earth's crust, which curve up to the surface of the ground like a basin. Suppose a common bowl, half full of dirt, to be placed in another a little larger than itself, and the space between the two filled with water. If now a tube be driven down through the dirt and the bottom of the inner bowl, the water will spirt out of the tube above the dirt, as high as the level of the water between the bowls. This is a miniature Artesian well.

96. **Figure 4.—The water-level.**—The surface of still water at any place corresponds to a limited horizontal plane. If, however, the water extends far, as in case of a lake or sea, the surface will be oval, and conform to the shape of the earth, as shown in Fig. 23 (122). But practically, for limited distances, the surface may be considered a horizontal plane, or a plane at right angles to the direction of gravity or the plumb-line.

Now, as water in communicating vessels (94) also seeks a level, it is easy to construct an apparatus for finding horizontal lines and directions with a small and portable quantity of water, as shown in the instrument known as the *water-level;* which consists of two upright tubes, connected at right angles with a horizontal tube, as shown in the figure. These tubes are partly filled with water or mercury, and upon the surface of the liquid are placed floats, II, carrying upright

FIG. 4.

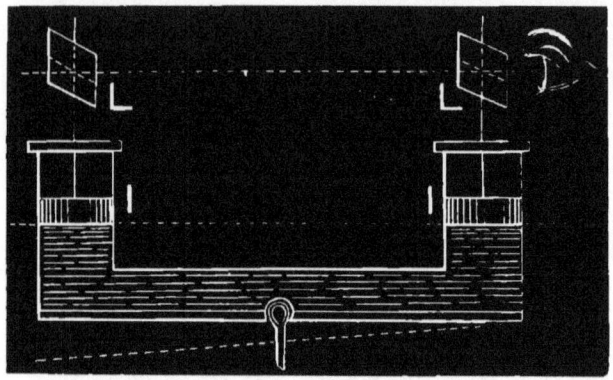

wires, to the ends of which are attached sights, LL, which consist of two fine hairs or threads, stretched at right angles across a square frame. The instrument is mounted on a stanchion, provided with a ball and socket joint. Suppose the instrument to be placed in a horizontal position (as in the diagram), and the dotted line, drawn through the *sights* to the eye, will be horizontal. If now the instrument be lowered at the left end, to correspond, for instance, with the dotted line below, the liquid, seeking a common level, will rise in one tube and fall in the other; thus sustaining the sights on a horizontal line. The accuracy will depend upon the length of the horizontal tube.

97. **Figure 5.—The spirit-level.**—This consists of a glass tube, FF, nearly filled with alcohol, and imbedded in a piece of wood. The bubble of air, N, will be equally distant from either end when the tube is horizontal. If one end be raised, as up to the dotted line,

FIG. 5.

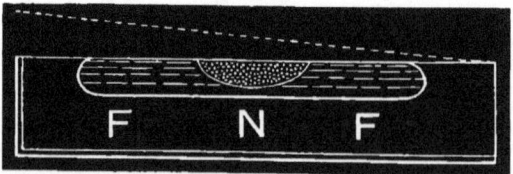

the fluid will run to the lower end, and the bubble to the higher end. This instrument is chiefly employed by builders, to level their work.

98. **Figure 6.—Tendency of liquids to seek a level shown by aqueducts.**—Let the dotted line represent a pipe conveying water over inequalities of the earth in the direction shown by the arrows. Whatever be the head or height of the supply, and the number of inequalities over which the pipe extends, the water will rise and be discharged at any outlet not vertically higher than its source.

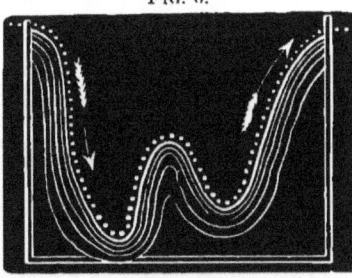

Fig. 6.

It is upon this principle that public water-works are constructed.

99. **Figure 7.—Intermitting springs.**—See Siphons (189).

Fig. 7.

100. **Figure 8.—Upward pressure of liquids equal to downward pressure at the same depth.**—Let E be a vessel partly filled with water. Take a tube, F, with a movable disk or false bottom, N, fitted water-tight, and held to the bottom of the tube F by means of a cord; then thrust the tube down into the liquid, as shown, and let go the string, and on the lower surface of the false bottom N the upward pressure will be equal to the downward pressure on an equal surface at the same depth. This is proved by the fact, that if water now be poured into the vessel, F, the false bottom will fall off when the liquid rises to the same level as that in the outer vessel.

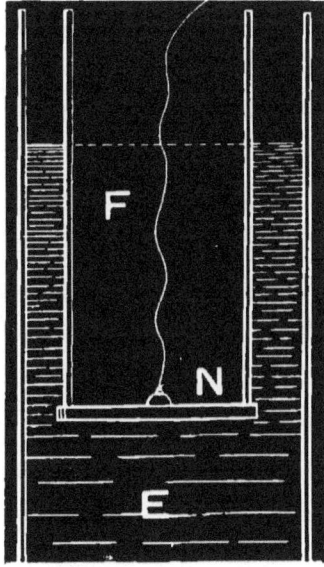

Fig. 8.

The upward pressure of fluids is called their *buoyant effort*.

HYDROSTATICS.

101. Figure 9.—Downward pressure of liquids independent of shape and capacity of containing vessels.— The pressure on the horizontal base of vessels depends only on the size of the surface pressed, and its vertical distance below the upper surface of the liquid. Or, the pressure is equal to the weight of a column of the liquid, whose base is that of the vessel, and whose height is equal to the depth of the liquid.

FIG. 9.

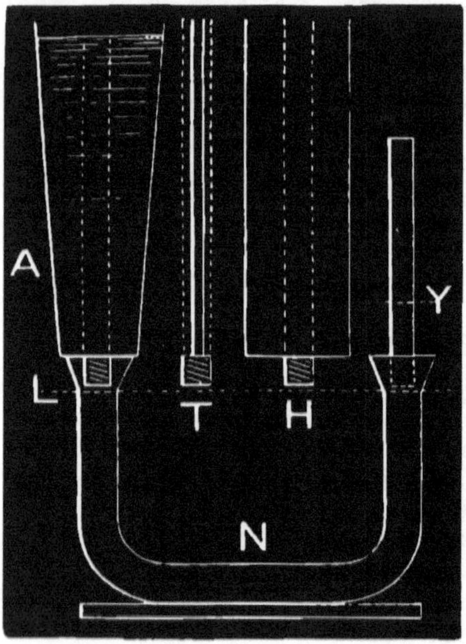

Let N be a bent tube, filled up to the horizontal dotted line, L, with mercury, and let the three vessels, A, T, H, of the same length and base, but otherwise differently shaped, be fitted to screw into the left arm of the bent tube; and Y, a glass tube fitted to the right arm.

Now, screw the vessel A to the left arm, and fill it up with water, and the mercury will rise in the right arm or tube Y, until the two liquids are in equilibrium. Mark the rise of the mercury with the dotted line Y. Detach the vessel A, and, in turn, put on the vessels T and H, and fill them with water, and it will be found that the mercury rises to the same height in every case. The perpendicular dotted lines in the three vessels represent columns of water of equal base and height, which, also, indicate equal pressure.

In Fig. 3 (94), the vertical dotted lines in the several vessels represent, respectively, the columns of water whose downward pressure would equal the pressure on the base of the several vessels; and the arrows indicate the direction of the pressure in different parts of the vessels.

102. Equilibrium of liquids of different densities.— When liquids of different densities are contained in communicating vessels, they will be in equilibrium when the heights of the columns are inversely as their densities; or (in Fig. 9), the height of the mercury in Y will be to the height of the water in A as the density of water is to the density of mercury.

HYDROSTATICS.

103. **Figure 10.—Pressure of a liquid is in proportion to its height and the area of its base.**—Let F and E be vessels of equal base and height, but, in form and capacity, quite unlike, each having for a base a disk held up by a cord attached to one arm of a balance, and sustained with weights on the opposite arm. By pouring water into the vessel E, to a given height, and adjusting the weights, the disk will fall off by the downward pressure of the liquid, and the weights will indicate the amount of pressure on the base at the moment of separation. If the string in F be attached to the arm of the balance, and water poured into the vessel, up to the *same* height, the pressure on the base, at the moment of its separation, will be the same, though much less liquid is employed.

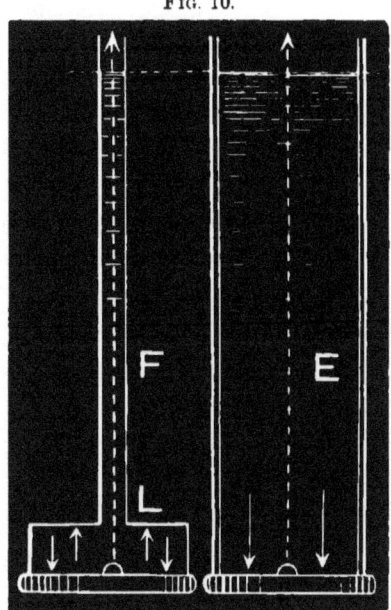

FIG. 10.

The reason of this is that the upward pressure on the surface L (shown, by Fig. 8, to be equal to the downward pressure), reacts on the base, as shown by the short arrows, while in the other vessel there is no upward pressure.

This principle is further illustrated by Fig. 3 (94). If the second vessel on the left were cut off from the other vessels and filled up to the faucet L, the pressure on the base would equal a column shown by the outside dotted lines up to the faucet. If the faucet be closed and the upper part of the vessel be filled, the pressure on the faucet will equal the small dotted column V. But if the faucet now be opened, the pressure on the lower base will equal the large dotted column the full height; which is *greater than the sum* of the two short columns, though no water has been added.

This is owing to the fact that in the upper part of the vessel some of the *downward* pressure is supported by the slanting sides, as shown by the arrows; while in the lower part, the pressure on the base is increased by the *upward* pressure on the slanting sides, as shown by the arrows.

Again, suppose the faucet T, in the central vessel, to be closed, and all the vessels filled, except H, above the faucet T; then the pressure on the base of this central figure will equal the dotted column extending the whole height of the vessel. If now the upper part of this vessel be filled, there will be a certain amount of pressure on the faucet, but if the faucet be opened it will add no pressure to the base of the vessel. This is because the *upward* pressure on the faucet, before it was opened, was just equal to the *downward* pressure from the water in H.

104. **Figure 11.—Pressure of liquids on the sides of a vessel.**—As liquids transmit pressure in all directions alike, it follows that the pressure of a liquid on any portion of a lateral wall is equal to the weight of a column of the liquid, which has for its *base* this portion of the wall, and for its *height* the vertical distance from its centre to the surface of the liquid. Hence, lateral pressure increases with the depth of the liquid.

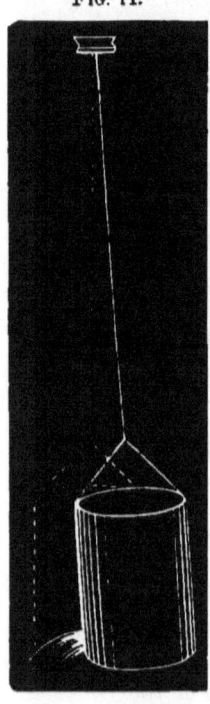

FIG. 11.

To sensibly show side pressure of liquids, suspend a pail of water by a cord, as in the figure, and remove a portion of one side of the vessel, which will destroy the equilibrium, and cause the pail to swing to the side opposite the opening, as shown by the dotted lines. Were it not for the resistance of the atmosphere on the stream, the force with which the pail would be moved would equal the weight of a column of the fluid, whose base equals the opening; and height, the distance from the centre of the opening to the surface of the liquid.

105. **The total pressure upon the walls of a vessel.**—This is equal to the weight of a column of the liquid, whose base is equal to the *area* of the sides, and whose height is equal to *one-half* the depth of the liquid.

106. **The total pressure on the bottom and sides of a vessel.**—This is equal to the weight of the liquid added to the side pressure; and as the lateral pressure on one side of a cubical vessel would be *one*-half of the weight of the liquid, on the *four* sides it would be four times one-half, or twice the whole weight, making the total pressure, on bottom and sides, three times the weight of the liquid contained in the vessel.

HYDROSTATICS.

107. Figure 12.—Hydrostatic paradox.—This paradox is another experimental proof that liquids press according to their height and not their quantity.

Fill a glass jar, T, with water, and balance it on a scale-beam with a

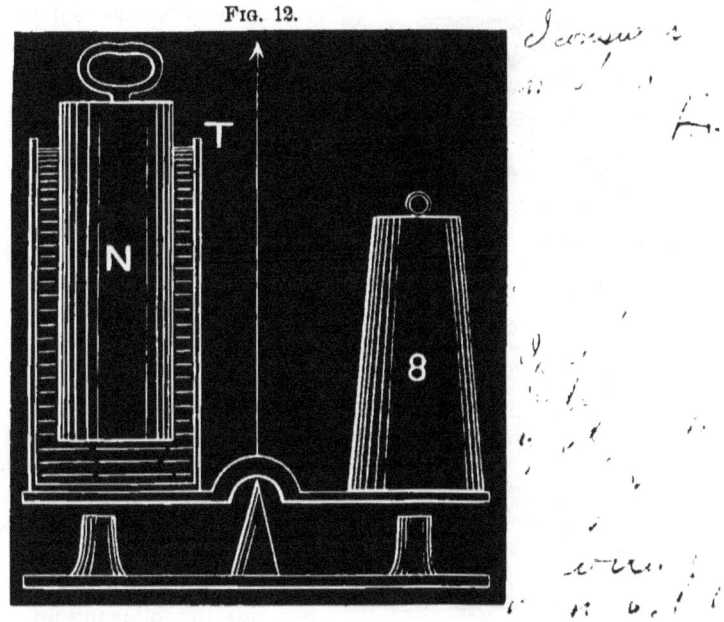

FIG. 12.

weight, 8; then pour out most of the water, letting the balance-weight remain, and replace the jar, which, of course, will not balance the weight. If now there be introduced into the jar a cylindrical piece of wood, or other solid substance, a trifle smaller than the jar, crowding it down until the water rises to its former level, the weight will again be balanced; though the cylinder is not in contact with the jar, and there remains but a small fraction of the water. Showing that, if the base of the vessel and height of the liquid remain the same, the *pressure* upon the base will be the same, irrespective of the quantity of liquid employed.

The result will be the same, whether a light substance, as cork, or a heavy material, as lead, be placed in the jar; the only condition being, that, in each case, the water shall rise to the same height.

The cylinder merely taking the place of the water, it will have the same effect upon the scale that its equal bulk of water did, which it has displaced. Hence, the cylinder may be any body which will displace water, be it solid or hollow.

108. **Figure 13.—Practical use of the principle that liquids transmit pressure in all directions alike.**—Suppose T and L to be pistons of equal diameter, fitted water-tight in cylinders which are partly submerged in confined water. If now there be placed upon the piston heads (T and L) equal weights—say 5 pounds—they will be in equilibrium. But, if *more* weight be placed on one of the pistons it will be depressed while the other will be raised, and the equilibrium will again be restored, when the weight of the water in the pistons, standing between their respective levels, equals the extra weight.

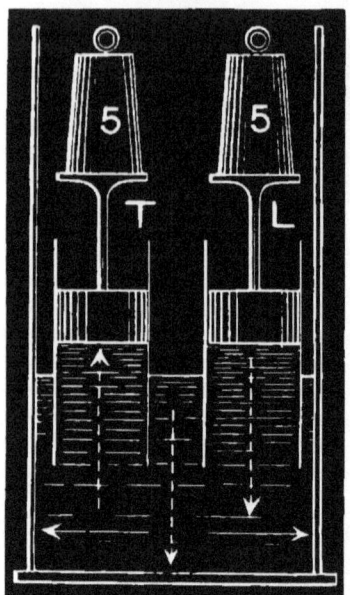

Fig. 13.

Again, if the weights are equal and the area of the pistons unequal, the equilibrium will be destroyed; for the reason, heretofore shown (103), that the pressure of liquids is as the base and height. Hence, leaving out weight of fluid and friction of parts, we have as conditions of equilibrium between force and resistance, acting upon pistons through the intervention or medium of confined liquids or fluids, the following formula:

The force is to the resistance as the area of the piston receiving the force is to the area of the piston acting upon the resistance.

Or, substituting *power* or P, for force; and *weight* or W, for resistance; and *power piston* for the area of the piston on which the force acts; and *weight piston* for the area of the piston acting upon the resistance, and we have:

P is to W as *power piston* is to *weight piston.*

This is the principle employed in the hydrostatic press (109).

109. **Figure 14.—The hydrostatic press.**—This press is extensively employed for exerting immense force through short distances.

Instead of using a high column of water to obtain pressure on the *power piston,* for convenience a lever force-pump is employed.

N Y L is a strong frame of wood or iron, and I is the bed-plate of the press, upon which is placed the object to be pressed, or the resistance to be overcome.

The bed-plate is rigidly connected with the *weight piston*, T, by a large shaft of iron; and the piston works in a heavy iron cylinder, E; into which, and below the piston, the water is forced by the *power piston* F, with the lever A—this lever and piston constituting the force-pump. The water is drawn by the pump from the cistern or well, and forced into the press and kept from returning, while the pump is reversed, by means of the ball valve, 2 —the pump valve being shown at 1.

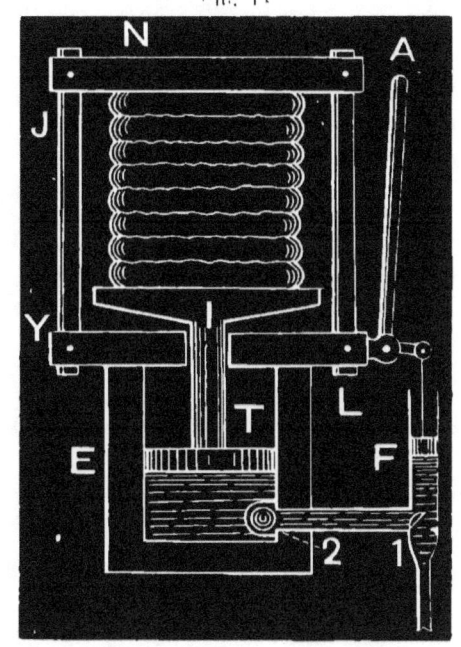

Fig. 14

The force of the press will depend upon the power of the pump lever, A, and the relative areas of the two pistons. According to the formula previously stated (108), we have (omitting the advantage of the lever)

W is to P as *weight piston* is to *power piston*.

For clearness, substitute *press piston* for weight piston, and *pump piston* for power piston; then we have

W is to P as press piston is to pump piston.

Or, including the advantage of the lever,

$$W = \frac{P \times \text{press piston}}{\text{pump piston}} \times \text{leverage}.$$

Suppose the pistons to be as 2 to 200 inches, the power 100 pounds, and the leverage as 10 to 1; and we shall have, as the W, or force of the press,

$$W = \frac{100 \times 200}{2} \times 10 = \frac{20000}{2} \times 10 = 100{,}000 \text{ pounds.}$$

Or, 100 pounds on the lever gives 1000 pounds on the pump piston; and this multiplied by 100, the number of *pump pistons* required to equal the *press piston*, gives 100,000 pounds.

The above formula, of course, will serve to find the P, leverage, or either piston, when the other dimensions are given.

The cylinder should be furnished with a discharge cock (not shown in the diagram), to take off the pressure after the completion of its work.

The hydraulic press is the most powerful and convenient mechanical engine in use. Its power is limited only by the strength of the machinery and materials used in its construction. It is extensively employed for pressing cotton, hay, and other substances into bales, raising ships for repairs, testing the strength of cables, pipes, steam-boilers, etc.

110. **Figure 15.—Bursting a cask with hydrostatic pressure.**—To further illustrate that the pressure of a liquid does not depend upon its bulk, but upon its height and base, take a cask holding 50 or 60 gallons, fill it with water, and into its head insert a tube, T, 40 or 50 feet long. If this tube be filled with water, which in quantity need not be more than a pint, it will burst the cask, exerting as much pressure on its interior surface as if the sides of the cask were extended up in the direction of the arrows to the full height of the tube, and then filled with water.

This serves to show also the upward pressure of liquids; for if a stop-cock be inserted in the upper head of the cask, and opened when the tube is kept full, the water will spirt up nearly as high as the tube.

111. **Figure 16.—Hydrostatic bellows.**—This is still another instrument to illustrate the great pressure of a small vertical column of liquid.

The bellows is made of leather nailed to two circular disks of wood, having a vertical pipe, P, opening into the interior. If it be filled with water to the top of the tube, the upward and downward pressure on the disks will equal the weight of a column of water whose base is equal to the face of the disks, and whose height equals that of the tube.

A pint of water, in this instrument, may be made to elevate thousands of pounds. The arrows, if extended as high as the tube, would show the size of the column of water, whose weight would equal the pressure on the disks; or, the pressure on one of these disks will be to the weight of the water in the tube as the area of one of the disks is to the area of the tube.

Striking effects of the pressure of water, by its own weight, are exhibited in the ocean. A strong square glass bottle, empty and firmly corked, will have its sides crushed in by being sunk in water, at a depth less than sixty feet. Divers cannot descend far below the surface, and even fish cannot descend beyond a given limit, in consequence of the increased pressure of the water.

HYDROSTATICS.

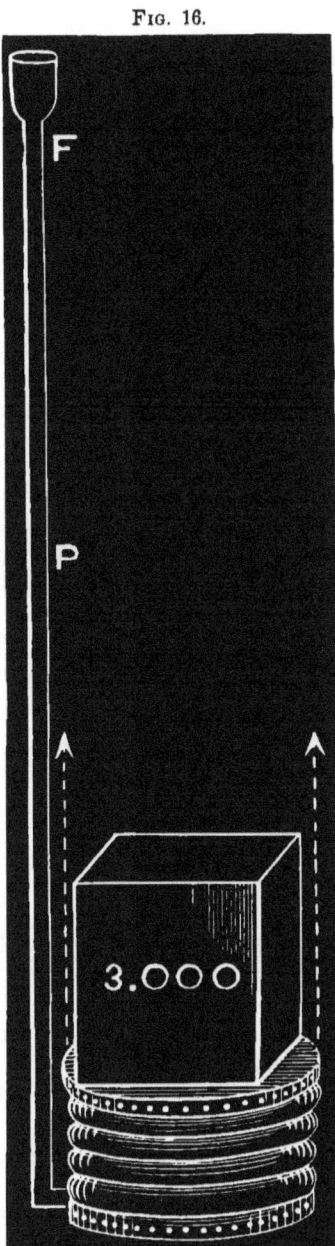

Fig. 15.   Fig. 16.

Fig. 17.

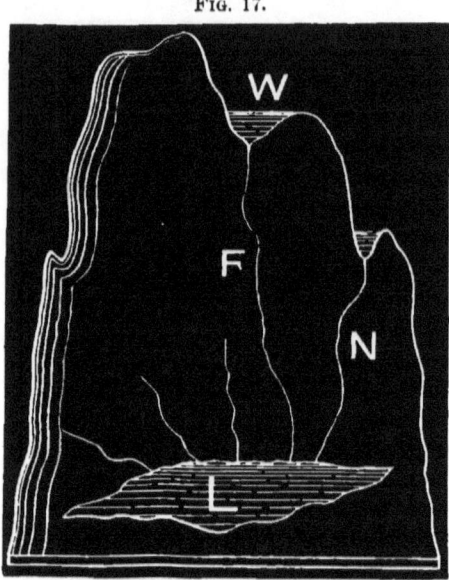

112. Figure 17.—Hydrostatic pressure in mountains.—Suppose L to represent a small pool of water, of only a few yards in extent, but several hundred feet below the surface water, at W; and F a small passage leading from W to L; then the pressure on the pool of water would be equal to the weight of a column of water whose base is equal to the surface of the pool, and whose height is equal to the distance from L to W. Of course, it matters not how shallow be the water in the pool, or how small the stream, F, that supplies it. It is not improbable that mountains have thus been ruptured.

Fig. 18.

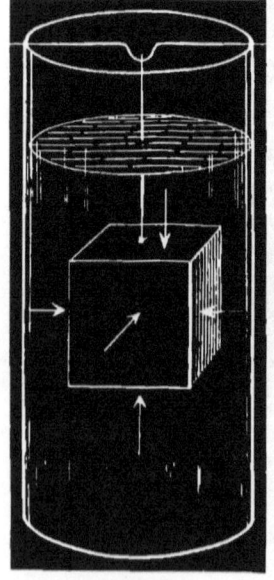

113. Figure 18.—Submerged bodies not pressed in all directions equally.—Suppose a cube to be immersed in water, as shown. The opposite lateral faces will be equally pressed, and in opposite directions, as indicated by the arrows.

The lower side will be pressed upward by a force equal to the weight of a column of the liquid whose base is that of the cube, and whose height is the distance from its lower face to the surface of the fluid. The pressure on the upper face will be downward, and equal to the weight of a column of the liquid laterally as large as the cube, and whose height equals the distance from the top side of the cube to the surface of the liquid; and the resultant of these two pressures is an *upward* force, equal to the weight of a volume of the liquid equivalent to that of the cube.

This upward pressure is the *buoyant effort*

HYDROSTATICS. 91

of the fluid. Hence, *a submerged body displaces a quantity of fluid equal to its own bulk, and loses a portion of its weight equal to that of the fluid displaced by it.*

Specific Gravity.

114. **Specific gravity.**—By specific gravity of a body is meant its weight, compared with that of another body of the same magnitude, assumed as a standard, or its relative weight. Distilled water, at 60° F., is taken as the standard for solids and liquids. If a cubic inch of gold, for example, weighs 19 ounces, and a cubic inch of water 1 ounce, it shows that the relative weight of water and gold is as 1 to 19; or, that the specific gravity of gold is 19, being 19 times heavier than water.

115. **Figure 19.—Method of finding specific gravity of solids.**—The body (if not lighter than water) is suspended by a hair

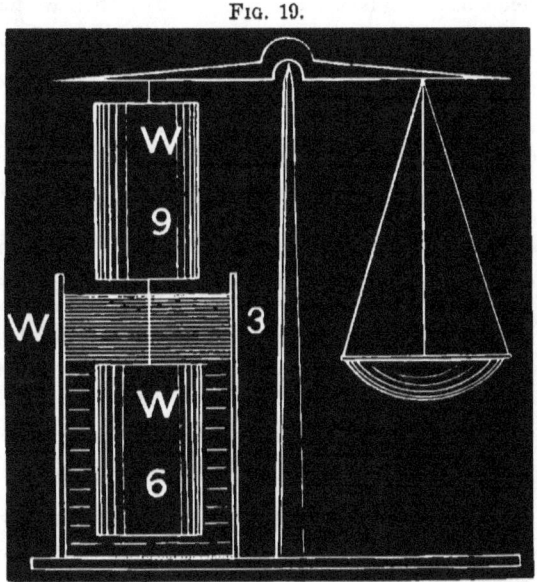

FIG. 19.

or a fibre of silk to the scale-beam, and weighed *out* of water, in the air, as shown in the figure, where its weight is 9 pounds. It is then weighed in water (by lengthening the string), where its weight is 6 pounds, showing that the loss is 3 pounds. The bulk of the water displaced (shown between W and 3) is equal to the bulk of the body, and weighs 3 pounds (shown by the loss of weight in the object); therefore, the body is as many times heavier than water as 3 is contained in 9.

RULE.—Divide the weight of the body *out* of water by the *loss* of weight *in* water. Or,

$$\text{Sp. gr.} = \frac{\text{weight out of water}}{\text{loss of weight in water}}; \text{ or, } \frac{9}{3} = 3.$$

For solids lighter than water.—When the body is lighter than water, it must be attached to some solid (whose weight in air and water is known) sufficiently dense to sink it in water. The compound mass being weighed in air and water, and the loss determined, subtract the loss of the heavy body from the loss of the compound body, and divide the weight of the light body in air by the difference of these losses.

EXAMPLE.—A substance weighed in air 200 grains. Attached to a piece of copper, it weighed in air 2247 grs., in water 1620 grs., suffering a loss of 627 grs. The copper itself, when weighed in water, lost 230 grs. Difference of losses is 627 less 230 = 397; then we have,

$$\text{Sp. gr.} = \frac{200}{627 - 230} = .504.$$

For liquids.—Select some heavy body, as a cubic inch of lead, and weigh it in air, then in water, and finally in the liquid in question. Subtract the second and third weights from the first separately; and the results obtained will be respectively the weights of a volume of *water* and of the liquid, equal to that of the cube. Divide the latter by the former, and the quotient will be the specific gravity required.

FIG. 20.

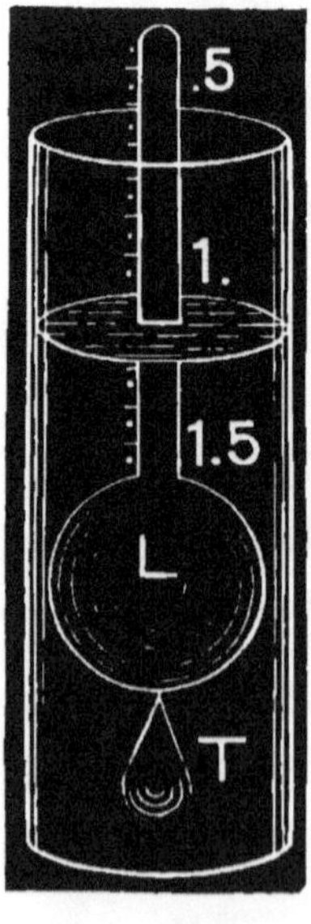

Suppose the cube, weighed in water, loses 253 grs., and in alcohol only 204 grs.; then the weight of alcohol and water will be to each other as these losses, or as 253 to 204; or, the sp. gr. of alcohol is 204 divided by 253 = .809 +.

116. **Figure 20.—Specific gravity of liquids, continued—Hydrometer.**—The hydrometer is an instrument by which the specific gravities of liquids are ascertained from the depth to which the instrument sinks below the surface. It consists of a light glass tube with a hollow ball or float, L, attached to one end, and on the ball, opposite the tube, is fastened a small piece of metal, T, to keep the instrument upright in the liquid.

Within the tube is a printed graduated scale. The scale is made thus: the instrument is adjusted to sink *in water,* up to the point, say, midway from the ball to the top of the tube. This point is marked 1 on the tube (water being the standard), and above and below this mark others are made, which indicate, *in weight, grains.* For convenience, therefore, the 1 is marked 1,000, standing for 1,000 grains, as the weight of water. Above this the numbers *decrease,* and below, *increase.*

Now if the instrument be placed in alcohol, which is lighter than water, it will sink down to .809, which indicates the specific gravity.

In a liquid heavier than water, it would stand higher than 1, or 1.000.

The specific gravity of liquids of commerce, as alcohol, acids, solutions, milk, etc., being well established, this instrument becomes a convenient means to determine whether or not they have been diluted with water, or, in many cases, otherwise adulterated.

117. **Figure 21.—Liquids of unequal density seek different levels in the same vessel.**—If two or more liquids, which do not chemically or mechanically unite, are poured into the same vessel, they will adjust themselves one above another, in the order of their respective specific gravities; the heaviest falling to the bottom, and the lightest rising to the top.

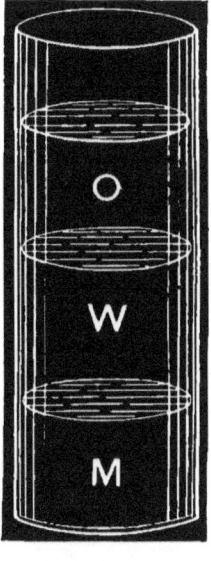

FIG. 21.

The figure represents a glass jar containing three liquids of unequal specific gravities; viz.: mercury, water, and oil.

It is in accordance with this principle that cream rises on milk, oil on water, etc.

118. **Figure 22.—Principles of flotation.**—When a body is plunged into a liquid, it is urged downward by its weight, and upward by the buoyant effort of the liquid. Three cases may arise, depending on the relative intensities of these forces: 1st, when the density of the body is *greater* than that of the liquid; 2d, when the density of the body is *less* than that of the liquid; and, 3d, when the density of the body and liquid are *equal.*

When a floating body comes to rest, the plane of the upper surface of the liquid is called the *plane of flotation.*

When a body is so shaped as to displace more than its bulk of liquid,

FIG. 22.

as in the case of a hollow dish, it may float, though the density of the material be many times greater than that of the liquid. This is the case with iron ships. The "Great Eastern," though it is the heaviest movable object in the world, and made of iron, is as buoyant and light on the water as a bamboo stick.

The figure is a toy to illustrate the principles of flotation. The hollow ball, when partly filled with water, and fastened to the metallic fish, is adjusted to float just below or at the surface of the water; that is, so that the specific gravity of the apparatus will just equal that of the water; and the jar covered air-tight, with a rubber or some other elastic cup.

If now the cap be pressed down with the fingers, the air above the liquid will be compressed, and the pressure communicated to the water (as indicated by the arrows), thence to the air in the ball, which will be compressed by the water being driven into the small opening on the lower side of the ball, which, of course, increases the weight, or rather diminishes the buoyant effort of the toy, and thus causes it to sink to the bottom. If the pressure on the cap be removed, the elasticity of the air in the ball will drive the water out of the opening, and so increase the buoyancy, when the toy will again rise to the surface.

This is similar to the process in fish, their "air-bladder" taking the place of the ball.

CHAPTER VII

(CHART NO. 2.)

PNEUMATICS.

119. **Definitions.**—Pneumatics treats of the properties of *elastic fluids;* which may be divided into two classes, *gases* and *vapors.*

In *gases*, the molecular force of repulsion (22, 23, 88, 91) prevails over the force of attraction; and in permanent gases this force has never been overcome.

Vapors differ from gases chiefly in that they are produced by the action of heat upon liquids (as steam from water), and by their returning again to the liquid state by loss of heat.

Tension is an expression for the tendency of a gas to expand.

120. **Gases, simple or compound.**—Of the thirty-four known gases, four only are simple or elementary, viz.: oxygen, nitrogen, hydrogen, and chlorine. The first three of these, together with the compound gases, oxyd of carbon and bynoxide of nitrogen, are the only aeriform bodies which have not, by cold and pressure, been reduced to the liquid or solid state. Hence they are termed *permanent or incoercible* gases.

Expansion is the most characteristic property of gases; and, for all that appears, this molecular force would dilate them indefinitely through all space, were there no counteracting causes.

121. **Mechanical condition of gases.**—Perfect freedom of motion among their particles, and being also elastic, ponderable, and impenetrable, it follows that all the characteristic properties of liquids apply also to gases. Hence, they transmit pressure in all directions alike, have buoyancy, inertia, specific gravity, etc.

Atmospheric air is the type of permanent gases, and is employed as the standard of weight for gases.

Atmospheric Air.

122. **Figure 23.—The atmospheric air an aerial ocean enveloping the earth.**—This diagram shows the globular form of the earth, its uneven surface, and the relation of its surface to the water and atmosphere. The land-surface of the earth, instead of being even, as might be shown by the true interior circle of the figure, is rough and jagged, as illustrated by the line drawn above and below the water. The inequalities shown by the figure, however, are immensely exaggerated. About three-quarters of the earth's surface is covered with water, filling up its inequalities. Yet there are mountains extending five miles above the water; and when the earth is viewed within the narrow limits of vision it seems to be exceedingly rough and uneven. Yet, relatively to its size, it is smoother than an orange; and, considering its elastic or atmospheric envelope, its surface is relatively softer than velvet, and smoother than polished steel.

If vision could extend from the eye, in the diagram, to F, it would take in mountain-tops thousands of miles apart; but when it is considered that the distance between the two radii, drawn from E to N, is over a thousand miles, it is plain that within the reach of vision (say, twenty-five to thirty miles), the surface of the water would appear to be a horizontal plane, instead of a portion of a sphere.

The outer circle in the figure represents the limit of the atmosphere, but its distance from the land and water surface of the earth, relatively to the size of the drawing, is far too great.

Fig. 23.

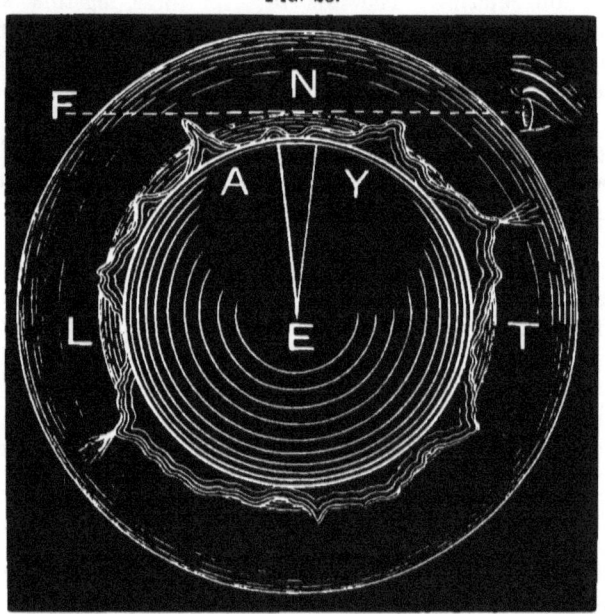

123. **Height of the atmosphere.**—The atmosphere does not extend more than fifty miles from the land and water; therefore, relatively, it is a mere film on the face of the earth. On a twelve-inch globe it would be less than an eighth of an inch in depth. It is the most dense at the surface of the earth, and becomes exceedingly rarefied at its greatest altitude. Yet it is held to the earth and kept in equilibrium, against its elastic or repulsive force, by gravity. And though the earth is moving around the sun at the rate of 68,000 miles an hour, the atmosphere is not disturbed, showing that the planets meet with no resistance in space.

124. **Composition of the atmosphere.**—Air is chiefly composed of the two incoercible gases, nitrogen and oxygen, in the proportion of 79 parts of the former and 21 parts of the latter.

Though oxygen, when thus mixed with nitrogen, supports animal life and combustion, it would, of itself alone, so intensify combustion and the animal functions, as to destroy life, and burn up the world; while nitrogen, of itself, would not support life and combustion at all. Hence, the purpose of nitrogen seems to be to dilute the oxygen.

Respiration of animals and combustion consume oxygen and supply carbonic acid, while the growth of vegetables consumes carbonic acid and throws off oxygen. The air, therefore, contains, besides oxygen and nitrogen, small quantities of carbonic acid (from 1 to 2 parts in 2,000), and also variable quantities of vapor of water (without which we could not breathe it), and traces of ammonia.

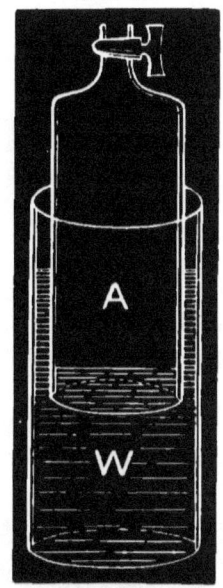

Fig. 24.

125. **Figure 24.—Impenetrability of gases.**—Let W be a glass jar partly filled with water, and A, a glass cylinder with a faucet at the top, as shown. If the faucet be closed, and the cylinder pushed to the bottom of the containing vessel, the water will rise higher outside than inside the cylinder, owing to the impenetrability of the air within; and equilibrium will be established between the elasticity of the air and the upward pressure of the water. If the faucet now be opened, the air will escape, and the water will rise within the cylinder until it finds a common level in the containing vessel; showing that it was the resistance of the air that kept the water from rising before the faucet was opened.

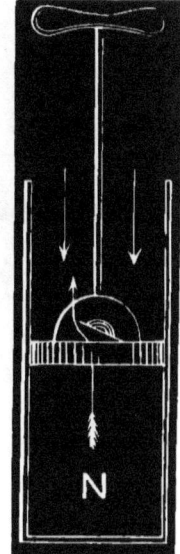

Fig. 25.

126. **Figure 25.—Pressure or weight of the atmosphere.**—Fit into a strong glass cylinder a piston, provided with a valve opening outward, and crowd it down to the bottom of the cylinder. As it is pushed down, the air in the cylinder will open and pass through the valve, as shown by the arrow. When the piston has reached the bottom of the cylinder, the valve will close by its own weight. If now the piston be drawn up, no air can find its way into the cylinder below it, consequently there can be no upward pressure of air acting upon it; and as the pressure on the upper surface can be accounted for only by the downward pressure of the air (shown by the small arrows), it is taken for its weight; which, it has been found by experiment, is 15 *pounds to the square inch*, at the level of the sea. Hence, as fluids press in all directions alike, *the pressure of the atmosphere upon every object in every direction is equal to 15 pounds per square inch.*

The surface of the human body, being about 2,000 square inches, is submitted to an atmospheric pressure of 30,000 pounds, or about 15 tons; which, of course, could not be sustained, only that it presses internally, externally, upward, downward, and laterally alike.

Every physical pore of all organic structures, animal and vegetable, all the pores of the ground, every nook, hole, and crevice in the rocks and hills, are thus filled with and pressed by the atmosphere.

127. **Figure 26.—Compression and expansion of the atmosphere.**—Provide a strong cylinder, N, having a faucet, T, at the bottom, and a tightly-fitted piston; enter the piston at the top, and, by pressing it down with sufficient force, the air within can be compressed into a hundred times less than its usual bulk. Air is found to be compressible in proportion to the force employed; that is, the bulk of a given weight of air is reduced to *one-half* by doubling the original pressure, to one-*third* by trebling it, and so on.

FIG. 26.

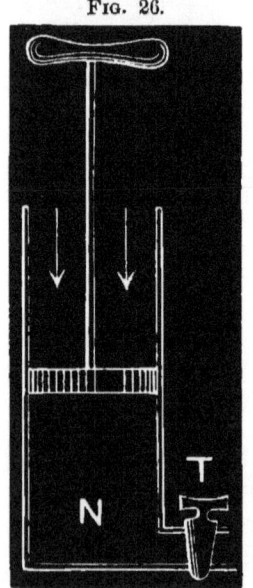

Expansion.—Open the faucet, T, and drive out most of the air by crowding the piston down to within an inch or so of the bottom of the cylinder, then close the faucet and draw the piston up, and the small quantity of air will expand and fill the entire cylinder.

It is found that the air, when its usual pressure is diminished, expands in the same ratio that it condenses; that is, if *half* the pressure is removed from a given weight of air, it will occupy twice the space it did before; if subjected to one-*third* the first pressure, *three* times the space; and so on. Air has been condensed 27 times, and expanded 112 times. See 147.

128. **Figure 27.—Air-pump, receiver, and vacuum.**— The air-pump is an apparatus to draw the air out of vessels. The vessel so exhausted is called a *receiver;* and the space within, thus deprived of air, is termed a *vacuum.*

In the figure, the inverted glass vessel, W, is the receiver, fitting airtight on a smooth surface, called *the plate.* In this plate is an aperture into which is fastened a pipe, I, that communicates with the pump N.

OPERATION.—As the piston is drawn up to L, the upper valve (situated in the centre of the piston) closes by its own weight and downward pressure of the air, and the downward pressure on the lower valve, T, being thus removed, the air in the receiver will, by expansion,

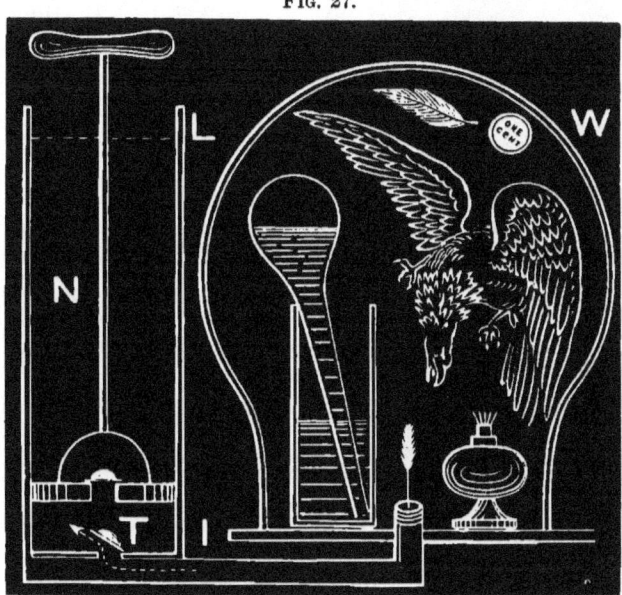

FIG. 27.

open and pass through it; as shown by the arrow passing into the pipe and through the valve. Now, if the piston be pushed down, the lower valve will close, and the dilated air in the pump will be compressed and pass through the upper valve. By again raising the piston, the air in the receiver will be further expanded; and so on ; until the air is so intensely rarefied, that it will no longer open the valves, when the process must cease. The pump does not, therefore, produce a perfect vacuum.

129. **Various phenomena in vacuo.**—The unlighted lamp under the receiver, indicates that, without air, there can be *no combus-*

100 PNEUMATICS.

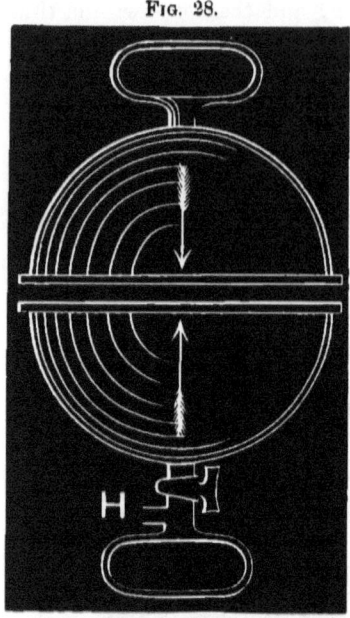

Fig. 28.

tion; the dead bird, that without air there can be no *flight* or *animal life;* the coin and feather, that in a vacuum, *light and heavy bodies will fall, by force of gravity, with equal rapidity;* the inverted flask of water, that without the downward pressure of the air on liquids, *the "suction-" pump will not operate.*

130. Figure 28.—Pressure of air equal in all directions shown by hollow hemispheres. —This apparatus consists of two brass hemispheres, fitted to each other air-tight, and provided with handles. In the shank of the handle of one of them is a faucet, and a pipe, H, to connect them with the air-pump. Having placed them together and attached them to the pump, exhaust the air. It will then require, to separate them, a force equal to 15 pounds to the square inch of the surface between them. This is the case, whichever side up they are placed, which proves that the pressure of the atmosphere, which holds them together, is the same in all directions. These hemispheres have been made so large as to require fifteen horses on each side to draw them asunder; yet by opening the faucet they would fall apart.

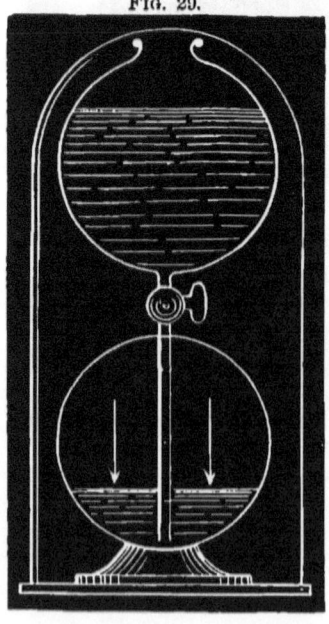

Fig. 29.

131. Figure 29.—Expansion fountain.—This consists of two glass globes, the upper one being open at the top, and furnished with a faucet and tube, the tube being open at the bottom, and reaching nearly to the bottom of the lower globe. The lower one being nearly filled with colored liquid, the upper one, with the pipe, is fastened to it, and (with faucet open) placed under the receiver of the air-pump, as seen in the figure.

If, now, the air be exhausted from the receiver, the air above the water in the lower globe will expand and press upon the water (as shown by the arrows), and drive it up through the pipe into the upper globe. By allowing the receiver to be filled with air, the water will, by its gravity, return again to the lower globe. This process can be repeated any number of times.

132. **Figure 30.—Atmospheric pressure.— It varies with variations of altitude.**—Suppose the figure to represent a tube not less than thirty-five feet long, having a tightly fitted piston, with a rod or handle as long as the tube. Set the lower end of the tube into water, so that the water will be in contact with the lower side of the piston. If, now, the piston be drawn up by the handle, it will remove the downward pressure on the water *within* the tube, and the downward pressure on the water *outside* the tube will force it up under the piston, as shown in the figure, until the weight of the column of water will equal the atmospheric pressure, which, as heretofore shown, is 15 pounds to the square inch.

The height to which the water will thus rise is about 33 feet 9 inches. Hence, the pressure or weight of a column of water 33 ft. 9 in. high is equal to the pressure or weight of an equal column of air as high as the atmosphere extends, be the height more or less.

If the piston be drawn up higher than 33 ft. 9 in. the water will cease to follow it, and the space between it and the water will be a vacuum.

The column will be 33 ft. 9 in. if the experiment is performed at the level of the sea, but less if at an elevation.

This is what is erroneously called "suction."

133. **Atmospheric pressure sustains different liquids at different heights.**—If the above experiment be tried with liquids of different densities, the heights to which the columns will rise are inversely as their specific gravities. Mercury, for example, is $13\frac{1}{2}$ times heavier than water; hence, 33

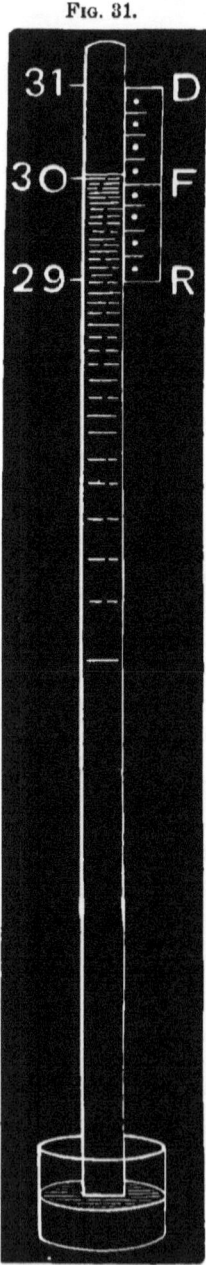

Fig. 31.

height of mercury as sp. gr. mercury (13½) is to sp. gr. water (1). Or, reducing 33 ft. 9 in. to inches, we have,

405 inches is to height of mercury as 13½ is to 1;

or, $(405 \times 1) \div 13\frac{1}{2} = 30$ (inches),

as the height to which mercury would rise in the experiment. Many practical tests have proved that this is the average height.

Atmospheric pressure varies at the same place.—It is found, however, that columns of water or mercury do not always stand at the same height at the same place, showing that the pressure of the atmosphere varies at the same place. (See next figure.)

The Barometer.

134. **Figure 31.—The barometer and its uses.**—The construction and operation of this instrument depend upon the principles of atmospheric pressure, Fig. 30 (132). Take a glass tube, about 34 inches long, open at one end and closed at the other; fill it with pure mercury, place the finger over the open end, invert the tube, place the open end in a cup of mercury, remove the finger, and the barometer, essentially, is made, as shown in the figure. The mercury will, at first, vibrate up and down, and come to rest (if the weather be fair) at an elevation of 30 inches, when at the level of the sea.

As the mercury is sustained in the tube only by the pressure of the atmosphere, whatever affects this pressure will vary the height of the mercurial column. As the pressure of the air depends upon its depth, the mercury, of course, will fall as it is elevated above the level of the sea. Many experiments having proved the amount of its fall for different elevations, it has become a convenient instrument for taking altitude, as of mountains, balloon ascensions, etc., and also for testing the pressure of the atmosphere at different times and places, and for indicating approaching changes of weather, etc.

135. Height of the mercury at different elevations.—
At the level of the sea it stands   at 30   inches.
5,000 ft. above the sea it stands   " 24.773   "
10,000 "   "   " [height of Mt. Ætna]   " 20.459   "
15,000 "   "   " [height of Mt. Blanc] " 16.896   "
3 miles "   "   " 16.36   "
6 "   [above the loftiest mountains]   " 8.923   "
9 "   " 4.866   "
15 "   " 1.448   "

136. Barometer as a weather-glass.—When the air is moist or filled with vapors, it is lighter than usual, which causes the mercury to stand low; but when the air is dry and free from vapor, it is heavier, and supports a longer column of mercury. The barometer, therefore, generally stands *high* in fair, and *low* in foul weather.

Rules for reading the changes of the barometer.—1. Sudden falling of the mercury is followed by high winds and storms, the mercury sinking lowest when the wind approaches from the south.

2. Sudden rising of the mercury indicates coming fair weather.

3. A fluctuating and unsettled condition of the mercurial column indicates changeable weather.

4. If the mercury falls slowly, a long continuation of foul weather may be looked for. If it rises slowly, continued fair weather may be expected.

5. In sultry weather the falling of the mercury indicates coming thunder. In winter the rising of the column indicates frost. In frosty weather its fall indicates thaw, and its rise indicates snow.

For convenience of noting the variations in the barometer, a graduated scale is attached to the upper part of the tube, as shown in the diagram (31); D indicating dry weather; F, fair; and R, rain. Opposite the letters are figures, showing the height of the mercury.

137. Diurnal variations of the barometer.—The mercury also rises and falls, slightly, daily. At the equator the maximum height corresponds to 9 o'clock in the morning, and the minimum height to 4 o'clock in the afternoon; and it is highest again at 9 o'clock, P.M., and lowest at 4 o'clock, A.M.

Capillarity and changes of temperature must be taken into consideration in making close observations with the barometer.

138. **Figure 32.—The wheel barometer.**—In the common barometer, the rise and fall of the mercury is indicated by a scale of inches and tenths of inches, fixed behind the tube (Fig. 31); but it has been found that slight variations in the density of the atmosphere are not readily perceived by this method; yet it is desirable, many times, to note these minute changes. The object, therefore, of the wheel barometer is to make the rise and fall of the mercury more sensible.

The tube is bent at the bottom, as shown in the figure, and in its short arm, on the mercury, is placed a float, L, to which is attached a cord, passing over a pulley, having a weight, T, fastened at the other end. As the mercury rises and falls in the long arm of the tube, the float also rises and falls; which communicates motion to the pulley. To the pulley is attached an arrow-pointer that rotates in front of a graduated circular disk, as shown.

Of course, the motion of this pointer will be as much greater than that of the mercury in the tube, as the circular disk is greater than the pulley.

On the outer portion of the disk are printed (not shown) the different conditions of weather, to correspond with the movements of the pointer.

Changes in the weight of the atmosphere, hardly perceptible by the ordinary barometer, will become quite apparent by this instrument.

139. **Figure 33.—Density of the atmosphere at different altitudes.**—Suppose the whole height of the atmosphere to be forty-five miles, as indicated by the figures and graduated scale on the left of the diagram, then its relative density, at different altitudes, will correspond to the relative distances between the horizontal parallel lines. The relative pressure or weight at different altitudes is shown by the numbers on the right of the figure. If it be 30 half pounds at the level of the sea, then, at the tops of the highest mountains (or about five miles) it will be between 20 and 10 half pounds (say about 12), and at 20 miles elevation it will be but about 1 half pound.

The whole amount of air, therefore, above the altitude of nineteen miles, equals only the amount contained between the earth and the lowest horizontal line.

Thus it is seen that the difference in the density of the atmosphere, at different altitudes, is very great, rapidly diminishing as the altitude increases, which is due to the *weight* and extreme *compressibility* of the air.

The weight, and consequent pressure of the atmosphere upon bodies near the surface of the earth and upon the earth itself, was not generally known, until Torricelli first announced it in 1643, notwithstanding

PNEUMATICS.

FIG. 32.   FIG. 33.

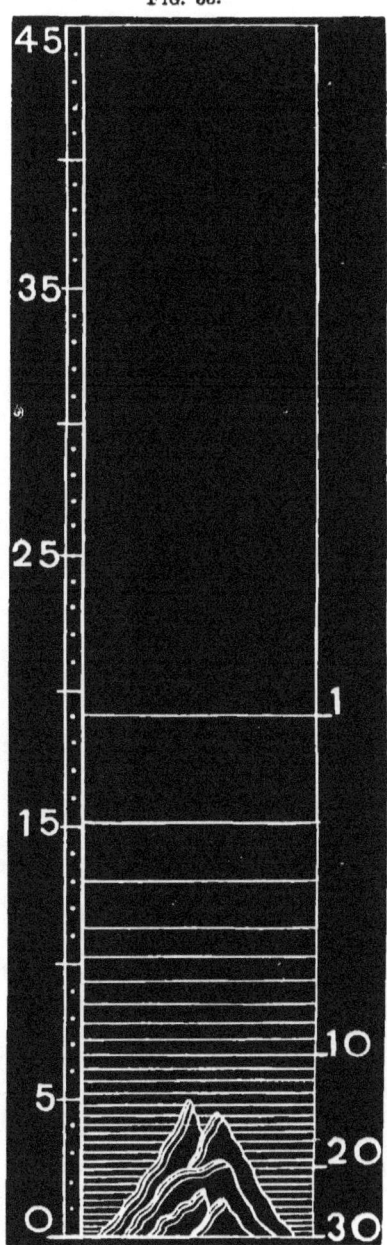

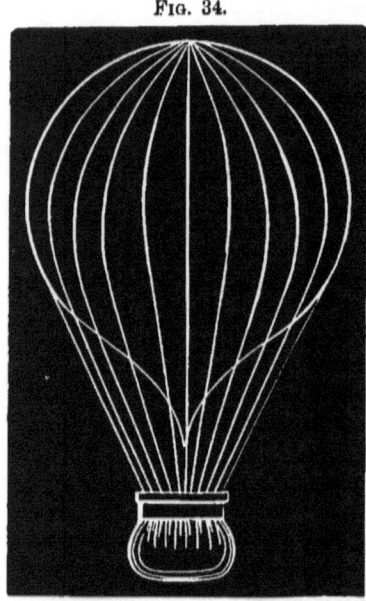

Fig. 34.

valuable use had been made of atmospheric pressure for many centuries, as in pumps, siphons, etc.

140. **Figure 34.—Balloons.**—Bodies in air (like solids plunged in liquids) lose as much of their weight as equals the weight of the air displaced. Hence, if a body weighs less than an equal volume of air, it will rise in the atmosphere until it meets with air of its own density. This is the principle upon which heated air, smoke, etc., rise.

The buoyant effort of a balloon of a given size, will depend upon the lightness, or specific gravity, of the gas employed to fill it. Hydrogen gas is usually employed. For convenience, common burning gas is used, though it is several times heavier.

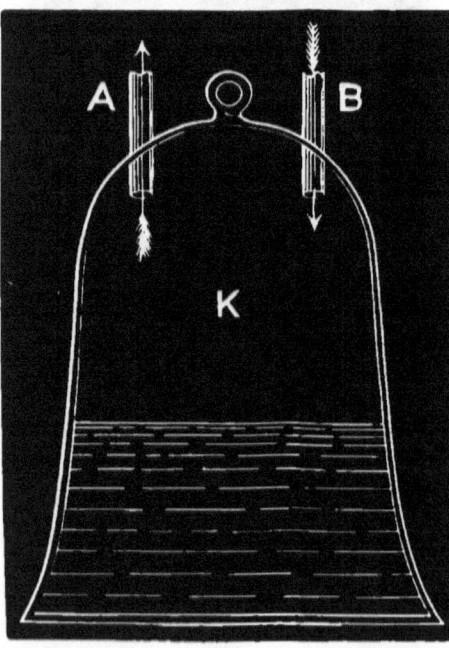

Fig. 35.

The balloon must not be completely filled, otherwise the expansion of the gas is liable to burst it, as the pressure of the atmosphere diminishes.

When the aeronaut wishes to *descend*, he opens a valve by means of a cord, in the upper part of the balloon, to allow the gas to escape; to *ascend*, he throws out ballast.

141. **Figure 35. — Diving-bell.**—As the balloon is the means of ascending into the air, so the diving-bell is the means of descending into the water. It consists of a heavy inverted vessel of suitable size and shape—usually bell-shape.

Within are seats upon which the diver sits while the bell is being lowered into the water, by means of a rope fastened into the eye at the top.

The atmosphere in the upper portion, K, though compressed by the upward pressure of the water, furnishes air for the diver to breathe; though only for a short time. By means of the two pipes, A and B, extended up to the surface of the water, the foul air is removed and fresh air supplied; as indicated by the arrows.

The diving-bell affords another illustration of the impenetrability and compressibility of the air.

142. **Figure 36.—Atmospheric pressure shown by inverted tumbler of water.**—If a tumbler be filled with water and covered with paper, and then inverted, the water will not fall out, owing to the upward pressure of the air on the paper.

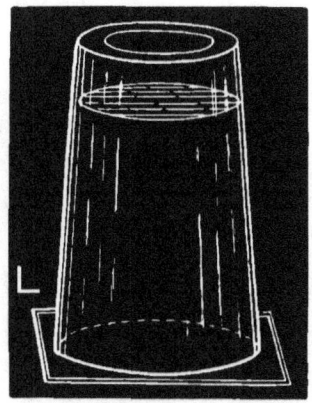

Fig. 36.

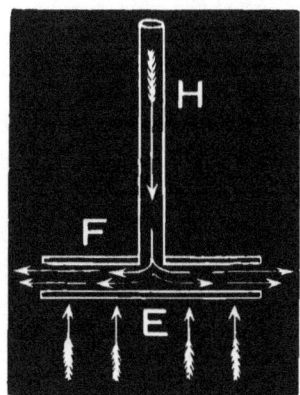

Fig. 37.

143. **Figure 37.—Atmospheric pressure shown by currents of air.**—Let E and F be two circular disks of card-paper, about the size of the diagram, having a quill or other small tube, H, passing through the centre of the upper disk, as shown. Place the upper disk parallel to, and about a quarter of an inch above, the lower disk. By blowing through the tube, the lower disk will leap up and adhere to the upper one; and the harder the blowing, the firmer it will stick. If the apparatus be inverted, the card cannot be blown off. The reason of this is, that the blowing more or less drives the air out from between the disks, which diminishes the pressure of the air on their *inner* surfaces; thus allowing them to be forced together by the balance of atmospheric pressure *without*, as indicated by the system of arrows.

108　　　　　PNEUMATICS.

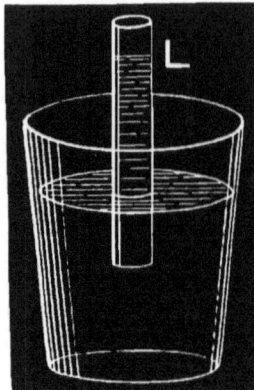

FIG. 38.

144. **Figure 38.—Atmospheric pressure shown by tubes and water.**—If a tube, L, open at both ends, be vertically sunk in water, and then the thumb placed over the upper end, it can be lifted full of the liquid; owing to the downward pressure of the air within the tube being excluded, and thus allowing its pressure on the outside to drive the water into the tube.

145. **Figure 39.—Vacuum fountain, showing atmospheric pressure.**—Let A be any shaped glass vessel, provided with a short pipe and faucet, and means for connecting it with the air-pump. Exhaust the air, close the faucet, remove it from the pump, insert the pipe in a dish of water, open the faucet, and the down-

FIG. 39.　　　　　　　　　FIG. 40.

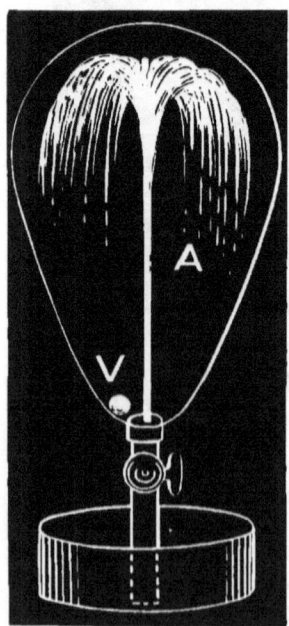
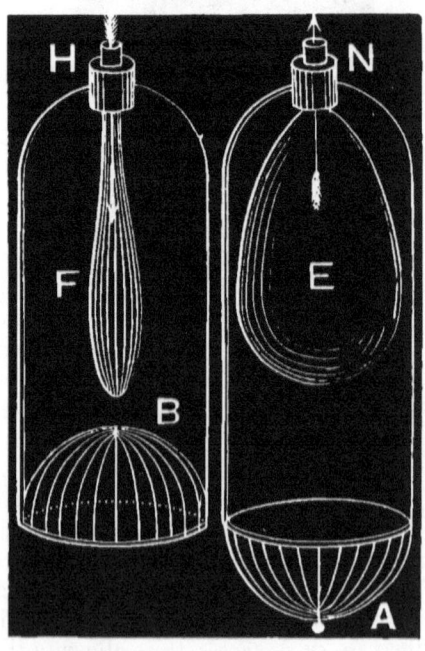

ward pressure of the air on the water in the dish will drive it into the vacuum with great force, as shown in the figure. The vacuum simply removes the downward pressure of the air from the water in the jet-opening of the pipe. The ball, V, will be alluded to hereafter (149).

146. Figure 40.—Animal respiration dependent upon atmospheric pressure.—Water is not raised in pumps by "suction," nor do we breathe by drawing or "sucking air" into our lungs.

Let E and F be two air-tight sacks or bladders, situated in glass jars, and communicating with the external air; A and B, leather caps, tightly fastened to the jars.

Now, if the cap, B, be drawn down (as shown at A), a partial vacuum will be formed within the jar, and external air will rush in at H, and distend the bladder, F (as shown at E). This is equivalent to *inspiration*. If, now, the cap, A, be forced up into the jar (as seen at B), the air in the bladder, E, will be forced out at N, leaving the bladder collapsed (as seen at F). This is equivalent to *expiration*.

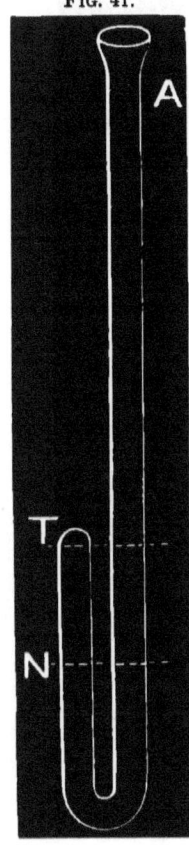

FIG. 41.

The jars take the place of the chest; the caps, A and B, the diaphragm; the bladders, E and F, the lungs; the apertures, H and N, the mouth. The upward and downward motions of the ribs aid the process.

147. Figure 41.—Mariotte's law, relating to the elastic force of gases.—The elastic force of any given amount of gas, whose temperature remains the same, *varies inversely as its volume*. Hence it follows that (if the temperature remains constant), *the elastic force varies as the density*.

Pour mercury into the bent tube, A, just sufficient to fill the bend at the bottom; then the air in both arms will be alike compressed; that is, by its own weight (15 pounds to the square inch). If, now, the long arm be filled with mercury until it comes to stand 30 inches higher than in the short arm, the air in the short arm will be submitted to the pressure of *two* atmospheres (30 pounds to the square inch), or double as much as before; which compresses it into half the space it before occupied, indicated by the dotted line N. That is, with *twice* the pressure we have *half* the volume; with *three* times the pressure, one-*third* the volume; and so on. Or, if half the pressure be removed, the volume

110   PNEUMATICS.

will be doubled, and so on. By this law, at a pressure of 814 atmospheres, air would become as dense as water.

148. **Figure 42.—Condenser, and condensed air.**—Let W be the vessel in which the air is to be condensed, provided with a faucet. The balance of the figure represents the condenser, which is a cylinder, with an opening, L, at the top, and an outward working valve, T, at the bottom, having a tightly-fitted piston.

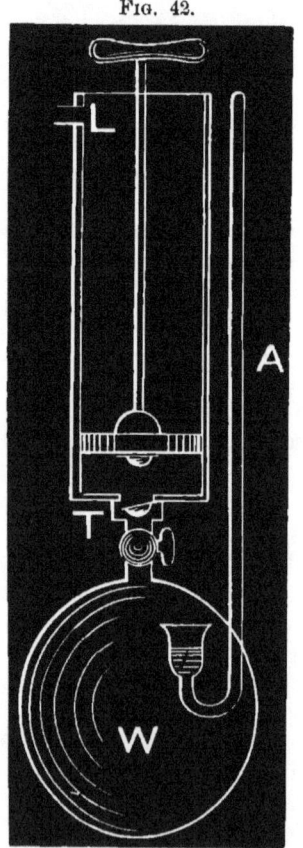

Fig. 42.

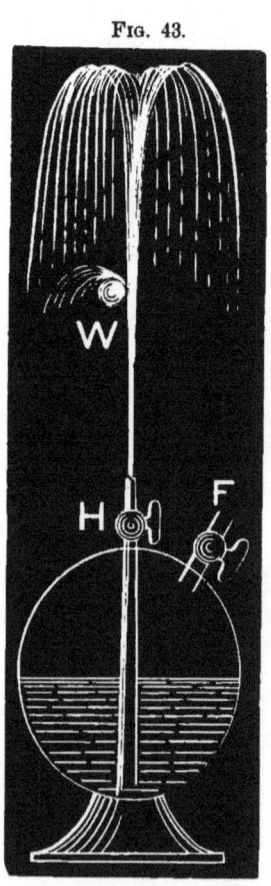

Fig. 43.

If the piston be drawn up, the expansion of the air in the vessel, W, will close the valve, T, and the air in the cylinder will pass through the valve in the piston. If the motion of the piston be reversed, the air below it will be compressed and driven through the valve, T, into the condenser, while the cylinder will be refilled through the open-

PNEUMATICS. 111

ing, L. By this means the air can be condensed to any desired extent. The mercurial tube shows the degree to which the condensation is carried, and operates upon the principle explained in the last paragraph.

149. **Figure 43.—Condensed-air fountain.**—Fill the vessel here shown about three-quarters full of water, and then, by means of the condenser just described, condense the air above the water (through the pipe and faucet F), then open the faucet, H, and the expansive force of the compressed air will act upon the water, and drive it up through the tube, as shown.

The ball or ring, W, on the side of the stream, is held up against gravity by the upward force of the jet, and at that point where the velocity of the stream equals the force of gravity. The ball is crowded against the stream by the unequal lateral pressure of the air; which on the side of the jet is less than on the opposite side; owing to the motion of the water driving the air away from this side, and so somewhat diminishing the pressure; which is proved by the fact that the same ball or ring will not rise on the same stream in a vacuum, as seen in figure 39 (145).

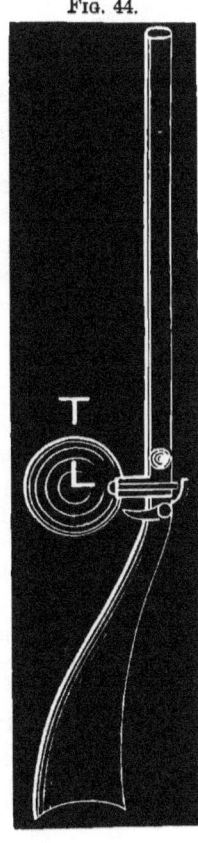

Fig. 44.

150. **Figure 44.—Air-gun.**—Air is condensed in the hollow globe, T, and this is so attached to the gun, that by means of the lock of the gun, the valve, L, is opened, and the air is thus instantaneously allowed to escape behind the ball, which throws it out with great force.

The velocity of the ball will depend on its size, and on the density of the air in the magazine, T. When the bore of the gun is no more than half an inch, or so, in diameter, it is estimated the ball will have a force not much less than that of a musket-shot.

As these guns, in their discharge, make no report, they become dangerous secret weapons in the hands of the assassin, and therefore their use is generally prohibited by law.

For practical use, the breech of the gun is made of strong copper plate, and constitutes the magazine, which is far more convenient than the copper globe, T ; while the barrel may serve as the tube of the condenser.

CHAPTER VIII.

(CHART NO. 3.)

HYDRAULICS.

General Principles.

151. **Definition.**—Hydraulics is that part of hydro-dynamics which treats of liquids in motion, or their flow and elevation—especially of water—and the construction of all kinds of instruments for moving them, and to be moved by them.

152. **Shape of orifices.**—All other conditions being the same, the greatest amount of water will flow through an orifice when its *length is twice its diameter.*

153. **Friction between liquids and solids.**—The central part of a stream in a pipe flows faster than that next to the pipe, thus showing there is friction between liquids and solids. Hence, pipes for conveying water should be smooth as practicable. Sudden turns in pipes are partial obstructions to the rapid flow of water, and should be avoided when possible (190). When a given quantity of water is required, considerable allowance must be made for friction. Though the capacities of an inch and a two-inch pipe are as 1 to 4, yet it is found, in practice, that they are as 1 to 5, if their lengths be 100 feet.

154. **Figure 1.—Velocity and gravity.**—If a vessel be filled with water, and three openings, A, E, F, made at different heights, the water will be driven out by the lateral pressure of the liquid; and as the pressure depends upon the height of the liquid in the vessel, of course the lower the orifice the greater the velocity of the stream and the amount of the discharge. These streams, being acted upon by gravity, take the curves resulting from the two forces (62).

The projectile force varying with the height of the liquid, the curves will not be alike. The fluid, therefore, obeys the same laws that solids do when projected, and falls in curved lines depending on the velocity (62).

The jet E, flowing from half the height of the fluid, has the greatest possible horizontal range, and all jets made equally distant above and below this orifice, as A and F, will have equal horizontal range with each other.

Fig. 1.

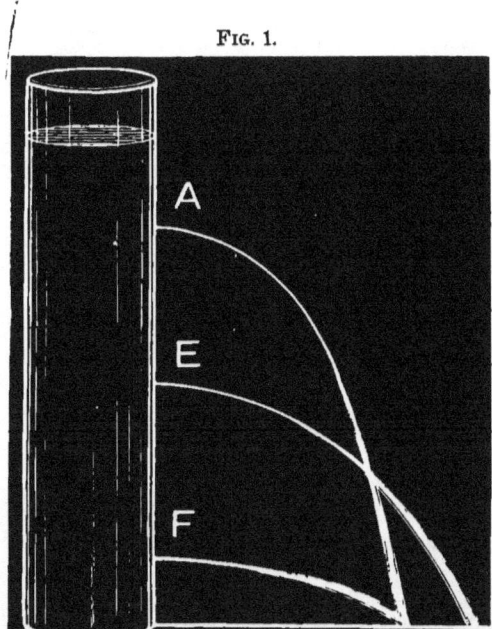

155. Figure 2.—Velocity of discharge.—The velocity of flow of liquids from an orifice is as the square root of the head. Let the vessel be graduated into 25 equal spaces (say inches) on the left side, as shown.

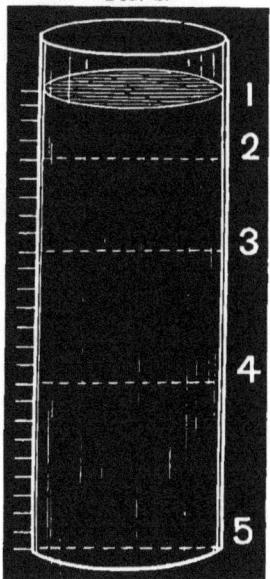

Fig. 2.

Opposite the 1st division set 1, the square root of 1.
Opposite the 4th division set 2, the square root of 4.
Opposite the 9th division set 3, the square root of 9.
Opposite the 16th division set 4, the square root of 16.
Opposite the 25th division set 5, the square root of 25.

Streams flowing from this vessel, where their velocities would be to each other as 1, 2, 3, 4, and 5, would start opposite the divisions indicating the depth of the fluid 1, 4, 9, 16, and 25. Or, in tabular form:

114   HYDRAULICS.

Velocity	1	2	3	4	5	6	7	8	9	10	11	12
Depth	1	4	9	16	25	36	49	64	81	100	121	144

This is the same as the law of falling bodies (55). Hence, the velocity of discharge, at any orifice, is the same as the velocity of a body falling freely through a height equal to the depth of the centre of the orifice below the surface of the fluid.

156. **Figure 3.—Flowing of rivers.**—Owing to the friction between fluids and solids, the sides and bottom of a river flow less rapidly than the central and upper parts of the stream. This is shown in the figure by a weighted stick, floating in a river, with the top, H, leaning in the direction of the current, whereas in still water it would stand upright. The arrow-heads show the direction of the current.

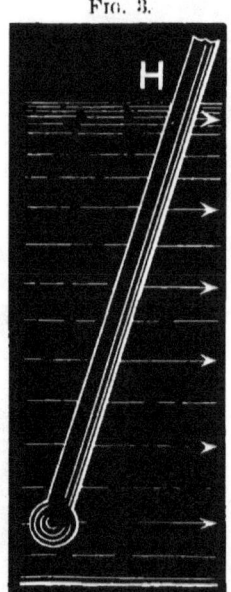

FIG. 3.

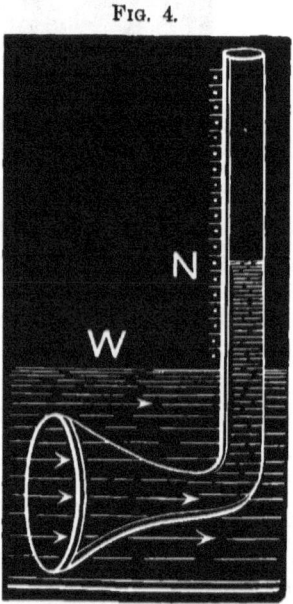

FIG. 4.

157. **Figure 4.—Finding the velocity of rivers.**—This is done by stationary revolving wheels, and floating bodies, and also by means of a tunnel-shaped tube, open at both ends and bent at right angles, as shown in the figure. The current, W, and its direction, are indicated by the horizontal lines.

The tube is placed in the water with its mouth toward the current, and the rapidity of the stream is estimated by the height to which the water is forced into the tube, N, above the surface of the river.

HYDRAULICS.

Water as Motive Power.

158. **Many devices** have been invented for utilizing the fall or gravity of water as a motive power. The principles involved in those most extensively employed are illustrated and briefly described.

Though various reciprocating and rotary *water-engines*, similar to steam-engines, have been used, the most simple and common way of applying the fall of water is by means of various kinds of wheels, called *water-wheels;* which may be divided into four classes, as represented by the following illustrations.

159. **Figure 5.—Overshot water-wheel.—**The water falls from the canal, W, upon the top of the wheel, and fills the buckets,

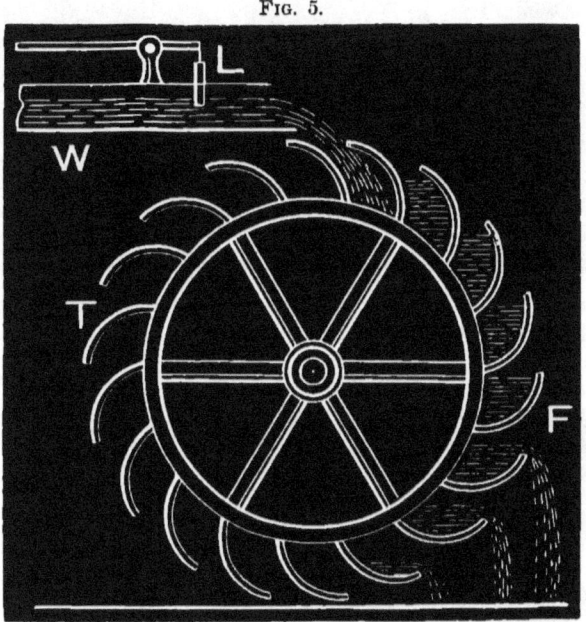

Fig. 5.

TF, which are pitched toward the stream, and hold the water until they reach the position F, where they begin to discharge. This is the most powerful of all the water-wheels of similar construction, and is moved principally by the gravity, and slightly by the momentum, of the water. L is a gate for shutting off the stream. The operation of this wheel is too evident to need further description. Water has the greatest effect on this wheel when its buckets move about three feet per second.

160. **Figure 6.—Breast water-wheel.**—This wheel receives the water at about half its own height, and is moved both by the weight

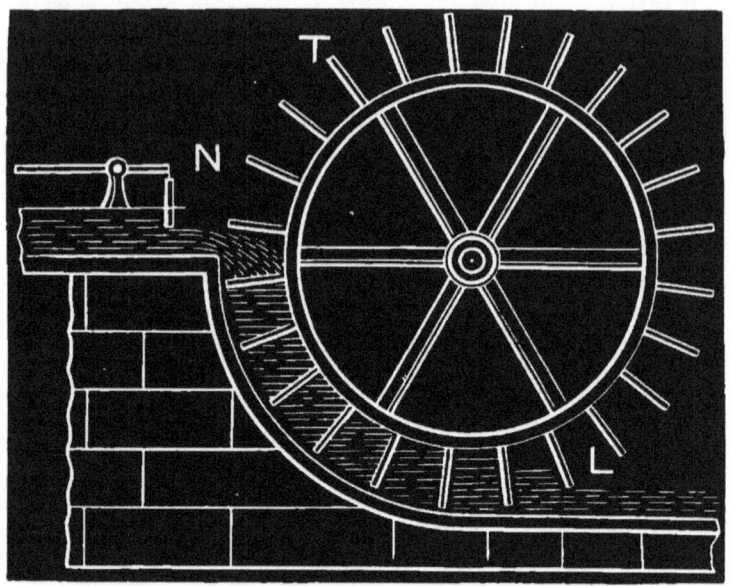

FIG. 6.

and momentum of the water. It is furnished either with buckets or float-boards, TL, fitting the water-course. N is the gate for shutting off the water.

FIG. 7.

161. **Figure 7.— Undershot water-wheel.**—This is provided with vanes, or float-boards, projecting from its periphery into the stream, as shown, and is moved principally by the momentum of the water; requiring no fall, but a rapid flow of the stream. To yield the greatest effect, the floats in this wheel should move about five-twelfths as fast as the water. This wheel is extensively employed for elevating (166).

162. **Figure 8.—Turbine water-wheel.**—The turbine, of which there are many modifications, is a horizontal wheel. It works submerged, and is the most energetic and economical of all the water-wheels; some of them having utilized eighty-eight per cent. of the entire power of the water. They are applicable to large and small streams, and great and small falls of water. W is the wheel, N the guides, to change the direction of the water so it shall strike the flanges of the wheel at the most advantageous angle. T is the shaft which carries the wheel and the driving pulley, F. The water falls vertically upon these stationary guides, which change its direction (as shown by the long arrows) so it shall fall upon the flanges of the wheel nearly at right angles to their faces (as indicated by the points of the arrows); when, by reaction on the blades of the wheel, its course is again changed, and it passes out below the wheel, as shown by the short arrows.

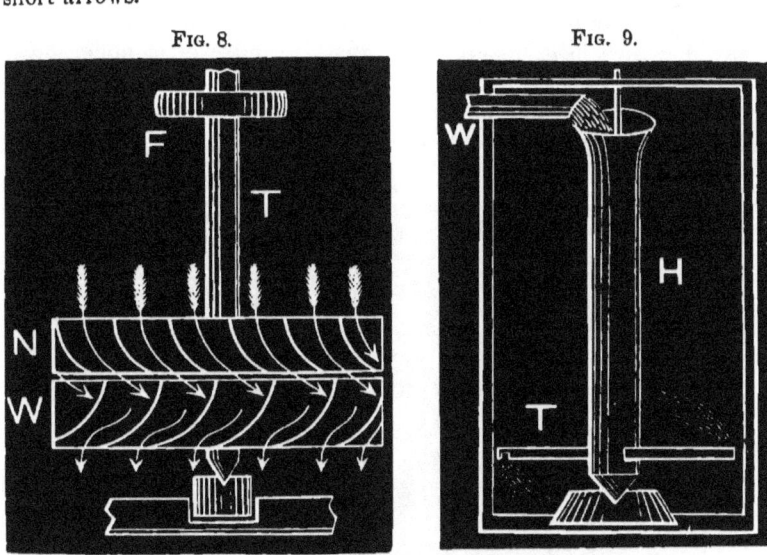

FIG. 8.   FIG. 9.

163. **Figure 9.—Reaction and centrifugal machine, or Barker's Mill.**—H is an upright cylinder, funnel-shaped at the top, to receive the stream of water from the pipe, W—standing on a point and held in position by a projecting spindle at the top; the arms, T, are tubes communicating with the cylinder. In the tubes are openings from which the water issues. These openings, removing a portion of the internal surface of the tubes, destroy the equilibrium of the lateral pressure of the fluid within, and set the cylinder to moving, with great velocity, in the direction of the resultant force of pressure; that is, in the opposite direction to the flow of the jets. The cylinder must be kept full of water.

The remarkable feature about the operation of this machine is its great velocity; which is caused in part by the centrifugal force of the water in the tubes, which, of course, greatly increases the reactionary force, and this again increases the speed, which again further increases the centrifugal force, and so on; each force increasing the other.

Machines for Elevating Water.

164. **Variety of water-elevators.**—In the earliest ages there were devices for elevating water, and every subsequent age has added new ones, until machines for this purpose are almost without number —volumes would be required to describe them. Yet, in this country, as well as others, some of the earliest and crudest of these are still employed, as the well-sweep, windlass, and rope and pulley. In fact, few, if any, machines have undergone a greater number of metamorphoses than that class of these devices termed *pumps*.

Only a few of the ancient and some of the best of the modern contrivances for elevating water are here described.

FIG. 10.

165. **Figure 10.—Lifting-wheel.**—This is a wheel consisting of a series of hollow or tubular spokes, bent at right angles at the extremities, to form cups or buckets, TL. The wheel is set so that when it is revolved by hand or other power, these cups will be filled with the water to be elevated. As each cup rises to the level of the axis, the water will run through its spoke to the centre, F, of the wheel, where it is discharged, as shown in the diagram.

If floats or disks were fastened to the extremities of the spokes, the current of a stream would revolve the wheel.

166. Figure 11.—Wheel and buckets, or Persian Wheel.—This consists of a series of swinging buckets, fastened to the rim of an undershot water-wheel (161), as seen in the diagram. As the wheel is revolved by the stream, the buckets are filled as they pass into the

Fig. 11.

water; carried up, and overturned by coming in contact with a pin in the trough. Arrows in the water-lines show the direction of the current and the motion of the wheel.

This is an ancient Persian invention. The greatest work in France, for artificial irrigation, was a series of these wheels, in Languedoc, raising water thirty feet. They are still used in various parts of Europe and Asia for supplying cities with water, irrigating land, etc. In Hamath, an ancient city of Syria, celebrated for its water-works, these wheels are employed; some of them being *seventy feet* in diameter.

The construction of the water-works of Hamath have remained unaltered, in their general design, from very remote times. The peculiar locality of the river (named El Ausi, *the swift*), and its consequent adaptation to *undershot* wheels, render it probable that the present mode of raising water is much the same as when this city flourished under Solomon.

120   HYDRAULICS.

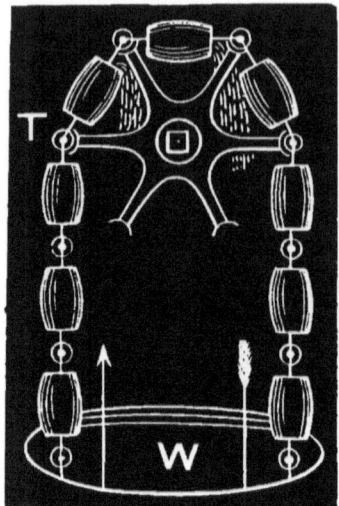

FIG. 12.

167. Figure 12. — Endless chain of pots.—The chain of pots is an ancient invention, and is used as an overshot water-wheel, where the fall of water is great, and the stream small; though it is chiefly employed for elevating water, cleaning docks, deepening harbors, etc.

The chain is hung on arms, T, of a wheel, as seen in the diagram. As the wheel is revolved, the pots rise *filled* on one side, and descend *empty* on the other; their contents being discharged into a cistern as they pass over the wheel. The direction of the movement is indicated by the arrows seen at the mouth of the well, W.

168. Figure 13.—Chain pump.—This consists of a cylinder, E, with its lower end standing in the water of the reservoir or well, N,

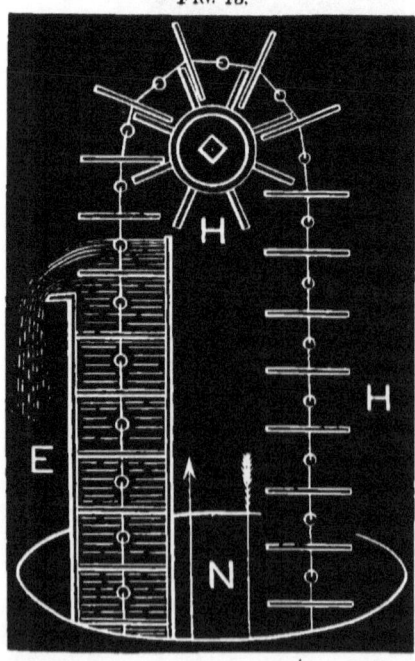

FIG. 13.

and its upper end terminating in a trough. An endless chain is carried around a wheel, H, above and below, and is furnished, at equal distances, with circular disks which fit closely in the cylinder.

As the wheel is revolved (usually by a crank) the disks successively enter the cylinder and carry the water up before them, into the trough, from which it is discharged. The arrows indicate the direction of the movement.

The chain pump is made in various forms. In China the cylinder or trough is usually made square, and often inclined to the horizon. Instead of the circular disks and an iron chain, stuffed globular cushions made of leather, and attached at regular intervals to a rope, have been substituted. It has been used in all countries, and is extensively employed at the present day. It had its origin, probably, in China, many centuries ago.

This pump seems to be the connecting link between the chain of pots and the ordinary lifting and suction pump; hence, in connection with the history of hydraulic devices, the place and date of its origin are matters of considerable interest.

In their various forms, the *Persian wheel*, the *chain of pots*, and the *chain pump*, are now, as they ever have been in all Eastern countries, among the principal devices for elevating water.

169. **Figure 14.—First invented centrifugal pump.—** This pump was invented in 1732. It is merely a straight tube, N,

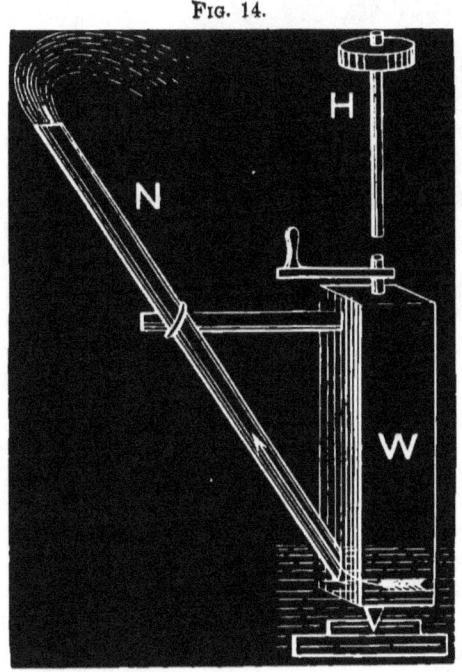

Fig. 14.

attached, in an inclined position, to a vertical axis, W, and whirled around by the crank, or by a pulley, H.

As the motion begins, the water, by centrifugal force, is thrown into the tube (as indicated by the arrow), and out of its mouth, as shown. In the figure the vertical axis is a box, open at the bottom; but a simple shaft of wood may be substituted for it.

170. **Figure 15.—The T-centrifugal pump.**—This pump consists of two communicating tubes, united in the form of the letter T. The main tube, F, has openings at the bottom, and stands on a point, being held upright by a stem and brace at the top, and has a valve, H, in the bottom. On the top is a cross-tube, LL, underneath which is a circular trough, TT, to receive the discharged water; and above is a grooved pulley to connect with the power.

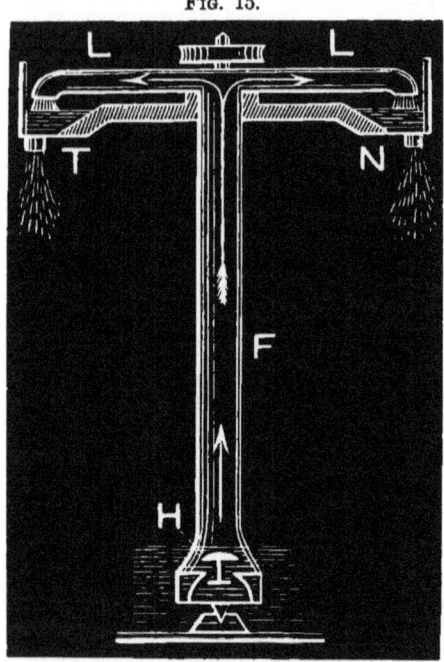

FIG. 15.

OPERATION.—Having first filled the tubes with water, if the pump be started by rotating the arms, LL, the water contained in these will be thrown out by centrifugal force, and the atmospheric pressure on the surface of the water below will force the liquid up through the valve to keep the arms supplied, as shown by the arrows. The water is delivered from the trough through the apertures T and N.

171. **Figure 16.—Archimedes' screw.**—Wind a pipe spirally around an inclined cylinder, provided with bearings and a crank, H; the lower end being immersed in a reservoir, so the end of the pipe will dip into the water. In the figure there are two pipes, but the principle is the same.

OPERATION.—Suppose the machine to be at rest, and a metallic ball dropped into the pipe at T; it is plain that it will roll down to the position of 1, and remain at rest. Suppose, as shown, there is a ball in each bend. Now, by revolving the cylinder, the pipe will fall in *front* and rise *behind* each ball, which gives each of them a forward motion (that is, toward the handle); but if the cylinder be revolved the other way, they will have a backward motion. Hence, by one revolution the ball 1 would move forward to the position of ball 3; and ball 2 to that of ball 4; and so on; until they would drop out of the upper end of the pipes. If water be poured (or scooped) in with the balls, it will go along, and be discharged with them, as indicated in the diagram.

FIG. 16.

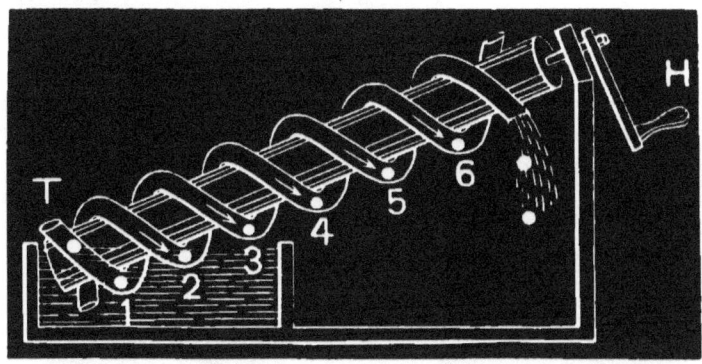

Such screws are employed to elevate, besides water, ores, grain, etc., and are commonly set at an inclination of about 45°.

172. Figure 17.—Hydraulic ram.—In this machine the *momentum* of a part of the fluid in motion is effective in raising another

FIG. 17.

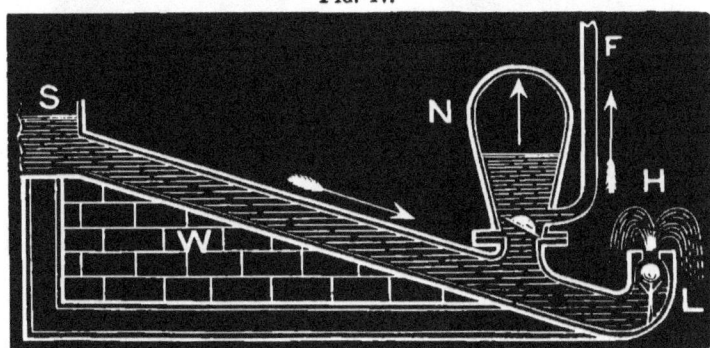

portion; and, by means of which, a large stream, with small fall, will elevate a small stream to a great height.

OPERATION.—The water from the cistern or stream, S, runs down through the pipe, W, and out at the aperture, H, until the velocity of the current is sufficient to lift and close the ball-valve, L. This aperture being closed, the *momentum* of the water is suddenly checked, which drives a portion of the liquid through the valve of the air-chamber, N, where it compresses the air, as indicated by the small arrow. The elasticity of the air reacts on the fluid, closes the chamber-valve, and drives the water up through the discharge pipe, F. The water in the pipe, W, having now come to a state of rest, the ball-valve, L, by its weight, will drop down and again open the aperture, H, when the same operation will be repeated, and so on.

Suction Pumps.

173. **Figure 18.—The principle of suction pumps.**—The operation of suction-pumps, so far as regards the *suction*, consists in producing, by means of a cylinder and piston, or other device, a vacuum, which becomes filled with water, by the downward pressure of the atmosphere. As fast as the piston lifts the air *out* of the cylinder, F,

Fig. 18.   Fig. 19.

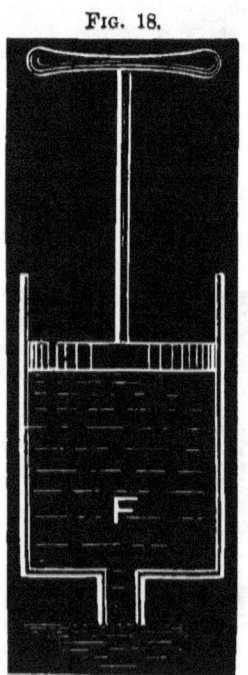

the pressure of the air drives the water *in*. Or, in other words, a suction pump consists of a tube not more than 34 feet long, with any sort of contrivance, at the top, that will remove the downward pressure of the air *within*, so that its pressure on the water *without* will force the liquid up the tube. *A piece of straw and the mouth*, therefore, are a suction pump—being, probably, the first pump known, and that which led to the invention of others.

HYDRAULICS.   125

The figure represents a simple cylinder and piston. If the piston be raised, the vacuum formed below it will be filled with water. If the piston is not held up, the downward pressure of air will bear it down, and the water in F will return to the cistern.

Water will rise, by suction or atmospheric pressure, 34 feet, theoretically; practically, it should be rated about 2 feet less.

For conditions of the atmosphere, and other circumstances affecting the operation of this principle, see 131 and 132.

174. **Figure 19.—Proof of atmospheric pressure in pumps.**—To prove that water rises in suction pumps only by pressure of air on the fluid outside of the pump, let the reservoir, E, which supplies the pump, be a closed vessel, provided with a faucet, as shown. If the faucet be closed, which shuts off the air, and the piston, L, drawn up, the water will not follow it; and a vacuum will exist at N. If, now, the faucet be opened, the air will rush into the reservoir, and press the water up the pipe into the vacuum at N.

Rotary Pumps.

175. **Figure 20.—Double-cylinder rotary pump.**—There are many kinds of rotary pumps; of which three are here represented. All rotary pumps are both sucking and forcing machines.

FIG. 20.

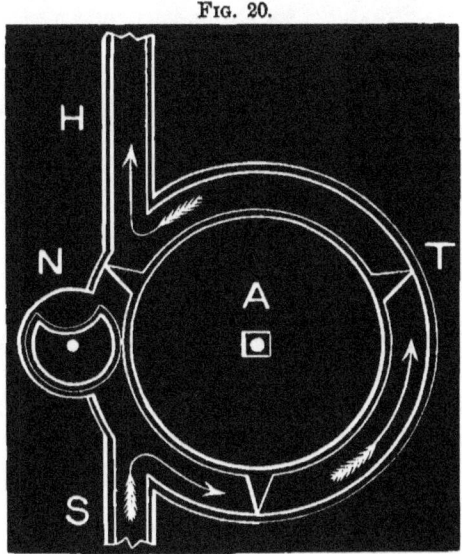

T is a cylindrical case (with head removed); A, a cylinder considerably smaller than the case, provided with three teeth or blades, which, acting as pistons, work water-tight against the interior surface of the case; N, a small cylinder (termed the butment), revolving against the large one, and provided with a curved indentation on one side to allow the blades to pass; S, the supply-pipe; H, the discharge-pipe; and at the centre of the cylinder is a shaft to which is applied the power. The arrows indicate the direction in which the water and the large cylinder move.

OPERATION.—The lower blade, for instance, drives the water before itself, and leaves a vacuum behind, which is filled with water from the supply-pipe. The blade, T, also drives the water in front of itself; and, as the liquid cannot pass around between the cylinders, it is driven up through the discharge-pipe; while the indentation in the small cylinder allows the blades to pass by itself without causing an opening for the escape of the water.

176. **Figure 21.—Single-cylinder rotary pump.**—In this pump is a solid wheel, T, formed into three spiral wings, L, acting as pistons, and turned round within a cylindrical case (the head in the figure being removed).

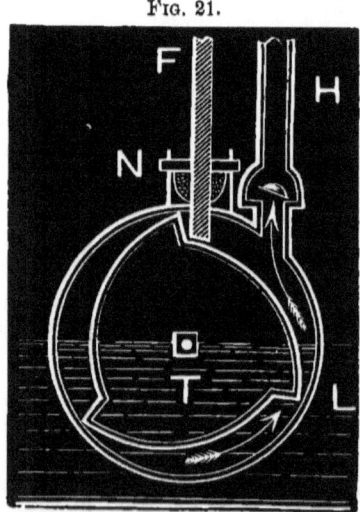

FIG. 21.

The butment, F, is a heavy piece of metal, working water-tight through a stuffing-box, N, and as wide as the wings; and, by its *weight*, bears water-tight on the face of the wings; being kept upright by passing between rollers (not shown). The arrows indicate the motion of the wheel and water. A stuffing-box is a contrivance for making a tight-working fit. See Fig. 42, Chart 4 (353).

OPERATION. — As the wheel is turned, the wings, working water-tight in the case, drive the water before them through the valve into the discharge-pipe, H; and the butment, F, rising and falling on the face of the wings, prevents the water from passing around with the wheel. The water is admitted into the case through openings (not shown) in the bottom. The valve in the discharge-pipe is to prevent the water from returning while the pump is at rest.

177. **Figure 22. — Double cog-wheel rotary pump.**— This is one of the oldest rotary steam-engines, but now principally employed as a suction and force pump, for which purpose it is a powerful machine.

It consists of two cog-wheels, the teeth working water-tight into each other, and against the interior surface of a cylindrical case—the front head in the figure being removed. It is worked by power applied

Fig. 22.

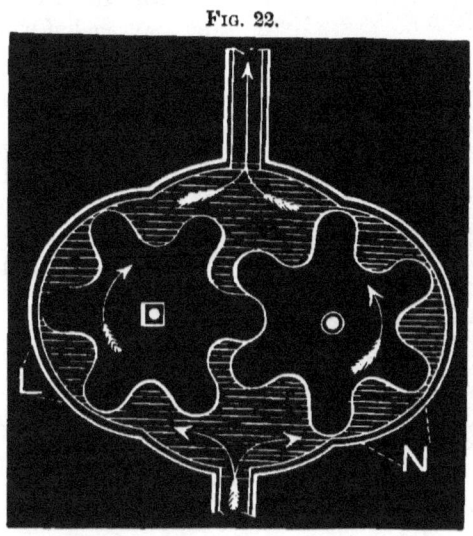

to the shaft of one of the wheels. As one wheel turns the other, they revolve in opposite directions.

OPERATION.—As the wheels revolve (in the direction of the arrows), a portion of the water below is carried between their teeth and the case, as at N and L, around to the upper side, and as it cannot pass down between the wheels, is forced into the discharge-pipe above, as shown by the double arrow; while the vacuum thus formed below is filled from the supply-pipe, as indicated by the other double arrow.

Many volumes would be required to describe the different kinds of rotary pumps which have been invented, yet they have never retained a permanent place among machines for raising water. Besides being more expensive than other pumps, they are too complex and too easily deranged to be adapted for common use. Theoretically considered they are perfect machines, but practical difficulties render them (like rotary steam-engines) inferior to others. In cases, however, where strong and rapid action, instead of durability and saving of expense, are the leading objects, as in the case of steam fire-engines, they are employed with great success.

178. **Figure 23.—The bellows suction pump.**—The bellows pump is the oldest of which history gives any account, and was probably suggested to some primitive inventor by sucking water through a straw.

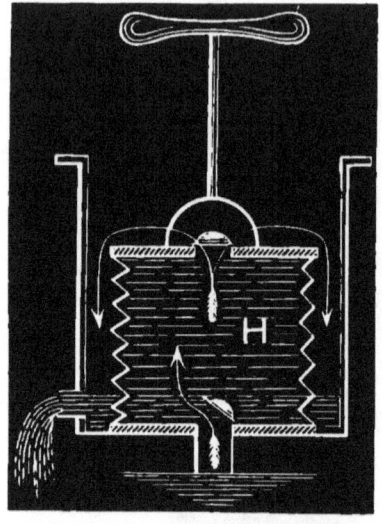

Fig. 23.

It consists of a leather bag, H, the lower end of which is fastened water-tight to the bottom of an open dish, and the upper end to a board or disk through which there is an aperture, the disk being provided with a suitable handle and an outward working valve, as shown.

OPERATION.—If the handle be drawn up, a vacuum will be formed within the bellows, which will be filled from the supply-pipe below, as indicated by the arrow. By reversing the motion, the valve over the supply-pipe will be closed, and the water, H, in the bellows will lift the upper valve and pass out into the open dish, and flow off, as indicated by the double arrow and spout.

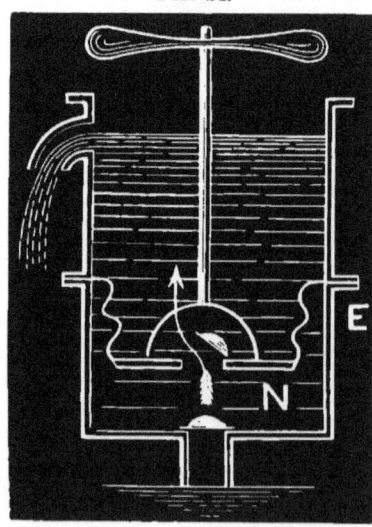

Fig. 24.

179. **Figure 24. — Diaphragm suction pump.**—This consists of a diaphragm, N, working in a cylinder or open dish. The outer edge of the diaphragm, E (made of leather), is fastened water-tight to the interior surface of the cylinder, in the manner shown, on the central portion of which is secured a disk, N, provided with an aperture, handle, and outward working valve.

OPERATION.—If the diaphragm be lifted by means of the handle, its valve will close, and the water above be raised and discharged at the spout, and the vacuum, formed below, filled with water from the cistern. By reversing the motion, the lower valve will close, and the water below the disk will open the upper valve and pass through the disk, as shown by the arrow.

180. Figure 25.—Plunger, force, and suction pump.—

This is chiefly employed for lifting or forcing small quantities of water against great resistance, as for feeding steam-boilers.

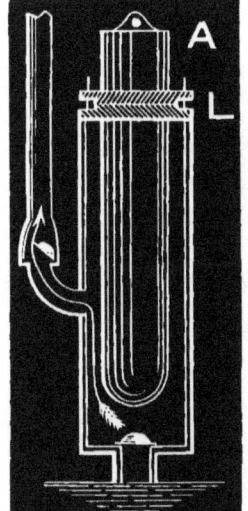

Fig. 25.

It consists of a cylinder, the usual valves, and a plunger, A, in place of a piston, which is a solid bar somewhat longer than the stroke of the pump. The plunger, instead of coming in contact with the interior surface of the cylinder, passes through a stuffing-box, L, at the top of the cylinder, as shown in the figure. The power is applied at the top of the plunger.

OPERATION.—As the plunger is drawn up, the valve in the discharge-pipe will be closed, and the vacuum, formed within the cylinder, filled with water rushing through the lower valve from the cistern. If the motion be reversed, the lower valve will be closed, and the water in the cylinder forced through the upper valve into the discharge-pipe, as indicated by the arrow.

181. Figure 26.—Single-cylinder suction pump.—

This is the most common of all pumps, being employed to draw water from house-cisterns, and consists of an open cylinder, piston, and the two usual valves. When the cylinder is extended much above the upper valve, the water above this valve being *lifted* instead of sucked, it is termed the *suction and lifting pump*, and in this form is used for wells, which are usually too deep for the simple suction pump. The upper valve is placed in the piston, and the lower valve at the bottom of the cylinder. In the ordinary wooden pump the bore of the log constitutes the cylinder, and extends the whole length of the pump.

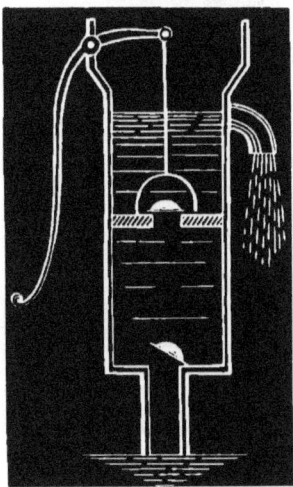

Fig. 26.

OPERATION.—As the cylinder descends

the lower valve closes, and the water above it passes through the upper valve. The motion being reversed, reverses the valves, and discharges the water above the piston, while the vacuum, thus formed below it, is filled from the cistern or well.

182. **Figure 27.—Suction and force pump.**—This is the pump usually employed for conveying water from cisterns to upper

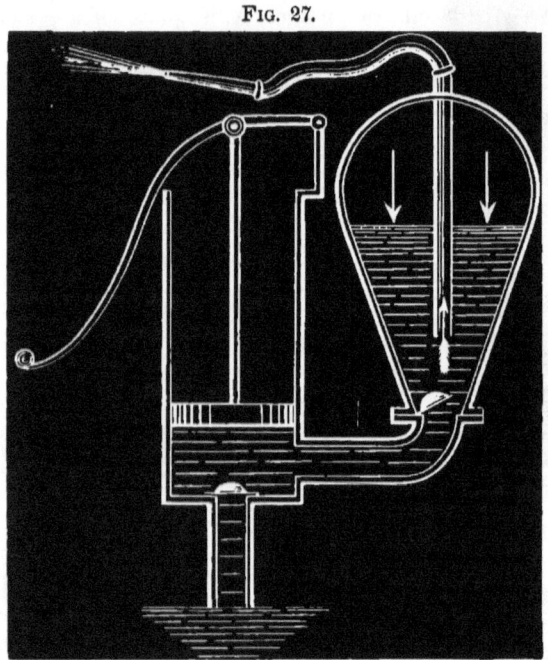

Fig. 27.

rooms, sprinkling door-yards, etc. The upper valve is placed in the mouth of an air-chamber, instead of the cylinder. The object of the air-chamber is to soften the action of the pump and render the discharge continuous.

OPERATION.—By raising the piston the upper valve will be closed, and the vacuum, formed under the piston, filled with water from the cistern passing through the lower valve. If the motion is reversed, the lower valve closes, and the piston forces the water below it through the upper valve into the air-chamber faster than it can escape through the discharge-pipe; and the air above, being thus compressed, will, by its elasticity, press upon the water (as indicated by the arrows) and keep up a discharge, while the piston is refilling the cylinder.

183. **Figure 28.—Double-acting suction and force pump.**
—This consists of a cylinder, piston, and four valves, with supply and discharge apertures at both ends of the cylinder.

OPERATION.—The cylinder and all the pipes being full of water, if the piston be drawn up, the valve N will close and prevent the return of water from the discharge-pipe, and the valve H will also close and prevent the water above the piston from returning to the cistern through the supply-pipe, thus causing the water above the piston to be forced through the valve F into the discharge-pipe; and the valve E will be opened by the water rushing up from the cistern to fill the vacuum formed below the piston, as indicated by the position of the valves and the two double arrows. If the movement of the piston be reversed, it will reverse all the valves, and the cylinder will be filled through the valve H, and emptied through the valve N; the valve F will close to prevent the return of water from above, and the valve E will close to prevent the water, W, below the piston from returning to the cistern.

FIG. 28. FIG. 29.

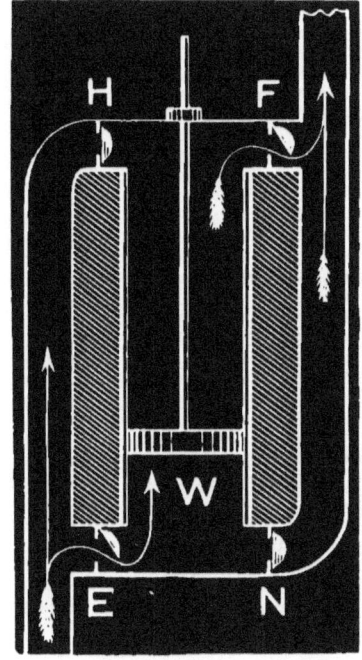

184. **Figure 29.—Single-acting suction and force pump.**
—This is a strong, powerful force pump, usually employed where force

pumps of large capacity are required, as in large low-pressure steam-engines.

Its operation is the same as the one illustrated by Fig. 25 (180), only, instead of a plunger, a heavy piston is employed.

The object of the valve in the discharge-pipe, H, is to relieve the lower valve from strain, while the piston is descending.

185. **Figure 30.—Double-acting suction and force pump with two valves.**—This pump, though it throws a steady stream without an air-chamber, has but two valves; but it has two cylinders and two pistons; and is constructed as shown in the figure.

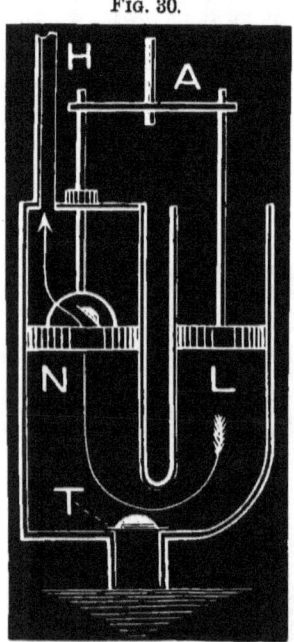

Fig. 30.

OPERATION.—By means of the cross-bar, A, both pistons are simultaneously moved in the same direction. As they are raised up, the upper valve in piston N closes, and the water in *it* is discharged through the pipe, H, and the vacuum produced under both pistons is filled through the lower valve, T. By reversing the motion, not only will the water in the left-hand cylinder pass through the upper valve, but the water below the piston, L. will also be forced through it; and thus a quantity of the liquid, equal to the capacity of the right-hand cylinder, will be forced into the discharge-pipe, as shown by the long arrow, while the piston is descending, which, of course, keeps up a constant discharge.

186. **Figure 31.—Fire-engine.**—This important machine is a four-valve, two-cylinder, double-acting suction and force pump, provided with a strong air-chamber. Connected with the piston-rods is a powerful lever, in the extremities of which, VY, are provided long bars or rods of wood (not shown), by means of which many men can work the engine at the same time.

OPERATION.—As one piston descends the other ascends. Supposing the piston, F, to be forced down, the valve, E, will close, and the water in this cylinder will be driven through the valve, H, into the air-chamber; the valve, L, will be closed to prevent the water from escaping into the cistern, and the valve, A, will be opened by the water from the supply-pipe, as indicated by the long arrows. Reversing the motion will reverse the valves. From the air-chamber the water, W, is

FIG. 31.

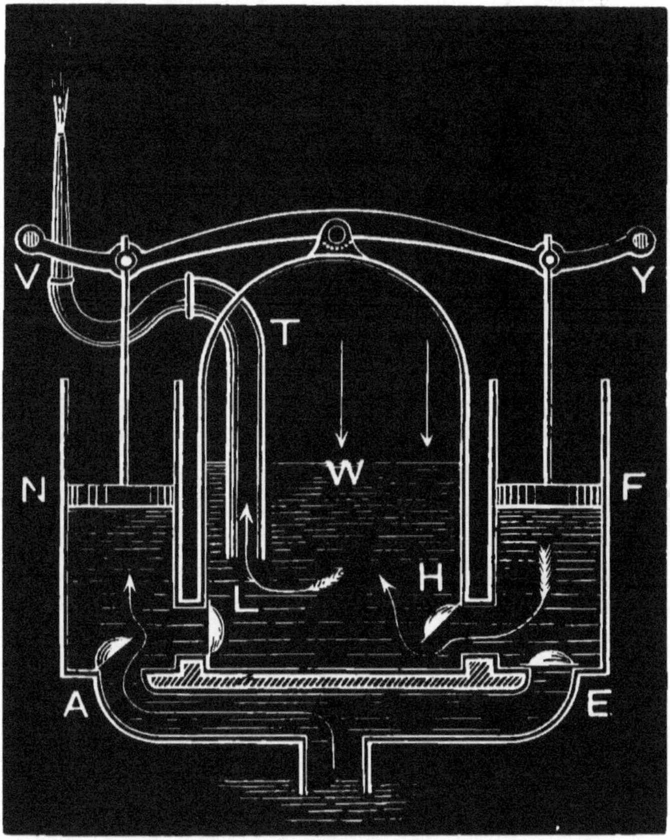

forced through the pipe, T. The object of the air-chamber is to produce, by means of the elasticity of the compressed air, a steady and continuous jet from the nozzle of the hose-pipe.

Fire-engines were first employed in Egypt. Not only were such engines used in early times, but the construction of those of remote antiquity was similar to that of the ordinary machines now employed; including even the air-chamber, notwithstanding it is supposed the ancients were wholly unacquainted with atmospheric pressure.

Rotary pumps, worked by steam, are rapidly taking the place of these hand-engines, one of which is more effective than a dozen of the ordinary machines.

187. **Figure 32.—Stomach pump.**—The object of this useful instrument is to throw fluid into the stomach, and then withdraw it, without changing the apparatus, only by altering its *position*. It consists of a syringe, A, provided with two ball-valves. T and H, and two flexible pipes, D and S, to be the required length.

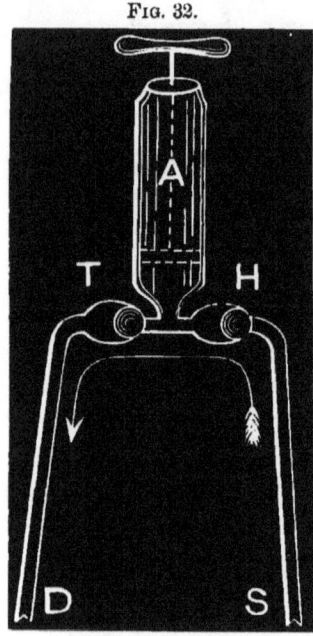

FIG. 32.

OPERATION. — The syringe must be held horizontally, and the pipe that is to bring the fluid *to* the syringe must have its valve lowermost. For instance, if the pipe, S, comes from the stomach, then, by drawing out the handle of the syringe, the fluid coming from the stomach would lift the ball, H; by reversing the motion of the piston, this ball would fall, and the other ball, T, be raised by the contents of the syringe, as indicated by the arrow. Then, to reverse the flow of the fluid, to pump liquids *into* the stomach, without withdrawing the pipe, it is only necessary to place the pipe, D, in the fluid, and turn the valve, T, lowermost.

Siphons, Fountains, etc.

188. **Figure 33.—The siphon dependent on atmospheric pressure.**—The siphon is used principally for decanting liquids, and consists of a bent tube, having one of its arms longer than the other; and depends, for its operation, upon atmospheric pressure. To put it in operation, fill it with fluid and put the mouth of the short arm into the liquid.

OPERATION.—Suppose the long dotted arrow in the siphon, III, (Fig. 34), to be a chain passing over a pulley at L, and it is evident that the greater weight of the longer end would cause it to fall out of the pipe. So, if the siphon were filled with water, the fluid in the longer arm being the heavier, it would commence to fall, and if the mouth of the short arm were in water, it would, by atmospheric pressure, supply the long arm; and so it would continue to flow.

The velocity of the flow will be the same as if the liquid fell freely from a height equal to the distance between the level of the liquid in the vessel and the end of the long arm; or, from L to H in Fig. 33.

HYDRAULICS.

To prove that this instrument operates by pressure of air, place the short arm in an air-tight vessel, N (Fig. 33), provided with a faucet. When the siphon is operating, *close* the faucet and the flow will *cease ;* *open* the faucet and the flow will again commence.

As siphons operate by pressure of the air, the short arm cannot be over 34 feet long; that is, its vertical height must not exceed this distance; though the short arm may be many times this length, and the long arm but a small part of 34 feet; it being required, only, that the discharging arm have a vertical height greater than that of the receiving arm, irrespective, too, of their relative size.

Very *short* siphons will work in a vacuum, by the tenacity of the liquid, caused by the force of cohesion among its particles (36).

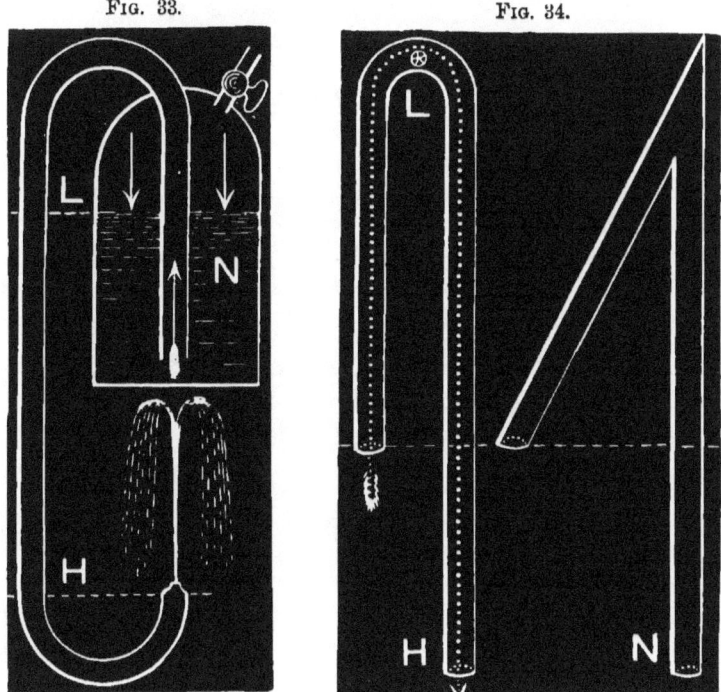

FIG. 33.   FIG. 34.

189. Intermittent springs.—There are in nature intermittent springs, the water flowing regularly for a time, and then suddenly ceasing. One of these is illustrated by Fig. 7, Chart 2 (99), in which T is a subterranean cavity, having an outlet, L, shaped like a siphon. As the water now stands, the opening of the short arm is under water, but when the water falls, so air can enter it, the spring will instantly cease, and not flow again until the water from the hills, HH, above, fills the cavity up to the level of the highest point of the siphon, L (shown by the dotted line), which may require a long time.

190. **Figure 34.—Sharp angles obstruct the flow of liquids, shown by siphons.**—Let the two siphons in this figure be every way alike, except one has an oval bend, and the other a sharp turn; and it is found that the one with a rounded turn will discharge much more rapidly than the other.

FIG. 35.

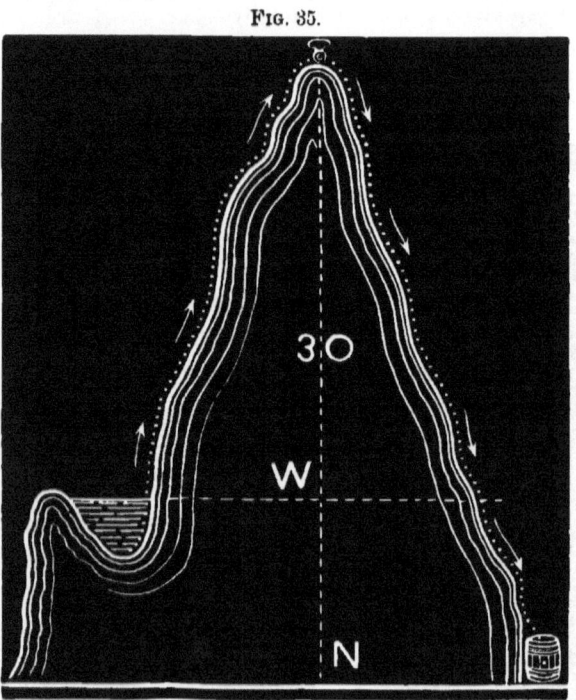

191. **Figure 35.—Conveying water over hills with siphons.**—The ancients made extensive use of the siphon for conveying water over elevations. Let the diagram represent a hill, which may extend many miles *over ;* and if its vertical height be not more than about 33 feet from the level of the supply-water—and the supply-water not far above the level of the sea—the liquid can be conveyed over it with a pipe, as shown by the dotted line. To put such a siphon as this in operation, first plug up both ends of the pipe, and then fill it by means of an opening at its highest point, then close the opening and draw the plugs. The diagram will be otherwise understood without further description.

HYDRAULICS.

192. Figure 36.—Siphon for the chemical laboratory.
—As it is often necessary to employ the siphon in acids and other liquids which are unpleasant to handle, they are so constructed that they can be charged by sucking. Such an one is illustrated in the figure. The mouth is placed at N, and the finger at the bottom of the open tube below. When the liquid reaches the bulb, N, withdraw the mouth, then remove the finger, and the siphon will operate. S shows the sediments in the jar, which, by means of this instrument, are left undisturbed, while the clear fluid is being drawn off.

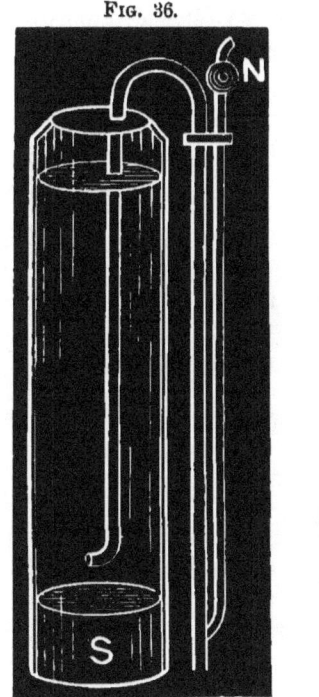

FIG. 36.

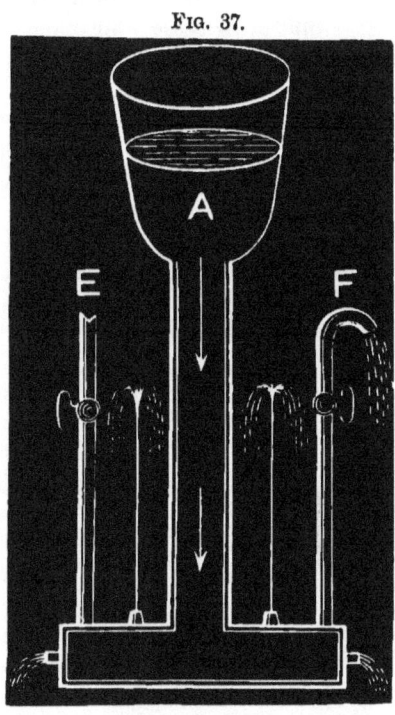

FIG. 37.

193. Figure 37.—Loss of effective head in public waterworks.—Though the head in the reservoir of public water-works may remain the same at all times, yet, at remote points, the water, especially during business hours, will not rise to the same, or even to an approximate, level. This is because the pressure, at any given place, is more or less diminished by every other opening intervening between this place and the reservoir; which is in accordance with the law relating to pressure of confined fluids—that *pressure increased or diminished at one point, is increased or diminished at every other point.*

Suppose A, in the figure, to represent the reservoir, communicating with the horizontal section at the bottom, in which there are six openings, as shown, two of them being small jets. These jets do not rise to only about half the height of the level of the water; but if one of the other apertures be closed, they will rise higher; and if they were all closed, the jets would rise nearly to the level of the reservoir.

194. Lateral pressure of liquids diminished by motion. —The lateral pressure of water in pipes is also diminished by the velocity of the fluid within them; that is, if a jet issue from the side of a large pipe of *running* water, under a given head, it will not rise so high as when there is no current within the main pipe.

Fountains, etc.

195. Fountains and vertical jets of water.—According to the laws of falling and rising bodies (55) and pressure of liquids, vertical jets should rise to the level of the water in the reservoir, but this never quite takes place, because of, 1st, the friction in the tubes diminishing the velocity; 2d, the resistance of the air; 3d, the returning water falling upon that which is rising.

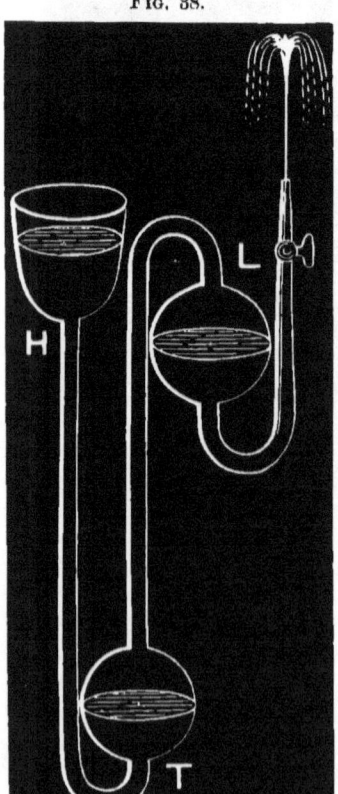

Fig. 38.

196. Figure 38. — Hiero's fountain.—In this curious fountain the water seems to rise higher than its source, by one body of water acting upon another through an intervening column of air. There are many modifications in its form, the one represented illustrating the principle rather than the deception.

This fountain may be considered the oldest pressure-engine known, a volume of air acting as the piston.

OPERATION.—Construct the apparatus as shown. Through the nozzle, fill the bulb, L, nearly full of water, and close the faucet. Then pour water into the vessel, H, until it is nearly filled, as shown. The water in H is prevented from passing through the bulb, T, and so up into the bulb L, by the compressed air intervening between the water in T and in L. The water in L, through the medium of the compressed air, is now pressed with a force equal to a column of water extending from its surface in T, to its surface in H. Hence, if the faucet be opened, the water from the bulb, L, will rise to a distance above its surface equal to the height of the column from H to T. It will be observed that none of the liquid from H to T passes out of the nozzle; this water serving only to supply the force which drives the water out of the bulb, L.

By ingeniously combining the two long pipes and two upper vessels, H and L, so that one pipe and vessel will contain and conceal the other, a person unacquainted with the apparatus could easily believe that water, after all, *will* rise higher than its source.

197. **Figure 39.—Intermittent fountains.**—An intermittent fountain is one in which the flow takes place at regular intervals. These exist in nature. An artificial one is represented in the figure.

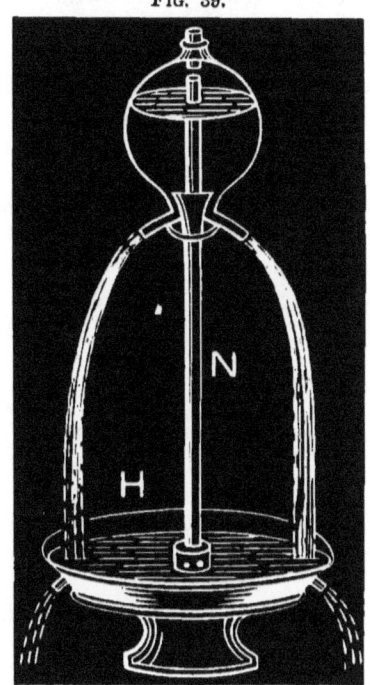

FIG. 39.

Fasten a glass globe, closed with a stopper, on the upright tube, N, so that the tube will extend quite to the top of the vessel; provide two small pipes at the bottom of the globe for jets, and secure the lower end of the tube to the bottom of the basin, H. Around the bottom of the tube provide small holes through which air can enter it, and thus reach the upper part of the globe. The two side apertures in the basin must be smaller than the jets.

OPERATION.—The globe and basin are first nearly filled with water. The small holes at the foot of the tube, N, being above the water, will allow the air to pass above the surface of the liquid in the globe, and the water will flow from the jets into the basin until it is filled so as to cover these small holes, which shut off the air from the globe, thereby causing the flow of the fountain to cease. But when the water has been drawn from the basin, by its apertures, so as to again expose the small holes to the air, the fountain will again begin to flow, and so on.

Importance of water.—Water, in many respects, is the most important substance known. Every comfort of civilized or savage life is more or less dependent upon it. Without it, vegetation would cease, and every animated being would perish. It enters into nearly every combination of matter. Even the atmosphere we breathe, deprived of moisture, would destroy life. The mechanical effects produced by it render it of equal importance in the arts. It was the earliest source of inanimate motive-power, and without it, man could not bring to his aid that mighty machine, the *steam-engine*.

Importance of hydraulic and hydro-pneumatic machines.—The universal importance of water, and its scarcity in many countries, and the fact that, in its liquid form, it always seeks the lowest levels and places of the earth, while it is ever needed at more elevated situations, and often in vast quantities, as for irrigating lands and supplying large cities, render water-elevators of the utmost importance. Hence, from the earliest times, the ingenuity of man has been at work to produce machines for this purpose; which finally led to the invention of the *steam-engine*, which now not only excels all other means for this purpose, but, more than all other mechanical devices, is subserving the general wants of civilization.

CHAPTER IX.

(CHART NO. 4.)

HEAT AND STEAM-ENGINE.

Preliminary General Principles relating to Heat.

198. **Definitions.**—The term *caloric* is the agent which excites in our bodies the sensation of *heat*. For convenience, however, in this work these terms are used synonymously.

199. **Heat and cold relative terms.**—*Heat* and *cold* are only relative terms, cold being the absence of heat. That is, any body, whatever its temperature, is said to be *hot* when compared with bodies *colder* than itself, and *cold* when compared with bodies *hotter* than itself. Hence, we say, ordinarily, that bodies are warm or hot and cool or cold when they seem so to the touch, whatever be the temperature of the hand at the time.

200. **Temperature.**—The term *temperature* does not imply the *quantity* of heat in a body, but merely its relative heat, at a given time, as compared to an arbitrary standard—like the common thermometer.

201. **Nature of heat.**—The real nature of heat is unknown. Scientific opinion is divided between two views respecting it. These are the *corpuscular or emission theory* and the *undulatory theory*.

According to the *emission* theory, heat is a subtile fluid, destitute of weight, existing in all bodies, is capable of flowing from one body to another, and, though attracted by particles of other bodies, its own particles mutually repel each other.

According to the *undulatory* theory, heat is attributed to the vibratory movements of the molecules of a hot body communicated to those of other bodies by means of a highly elastic fluid called *ether*, in the same manner that sound is transmitted through air.

This ether pervades all space, and, by other kinds of motions, is supposed to produce *light* and *electricity*.

By the former theory, bodies cool by losing a portion of this subtile fluid; by the latter, they simply lose a part of their vibratory motion.

Herein the emission theory, for convenience of explanation, is assumed, though at present the undulatory theory is generally received.

202. **General effects of heat.**—1st. Heat, by penetration, unites with the ultimate molecules (4 and 5) of all bodies, and, with its repellent forces, counteracts those of cohesion (22 and 23), and thus *expands* all bodies. Particles of bodies, with sufficient heat, are so far repelled as to move freely among themselves, and so become *liquids;* and with still greater heat, the liquids pass into a state of vapor. Vapors, if deprived of heat, return to the liquid state; and the liquids, by further abstraction of heat, become solids (88); and, if the process be continued, the solids go on contracting. Hence, heat dilates, and cold contracts, bodies, but in different degrees. The most dilatable are gases, then vapors, then liquids, and finally solids. Hence, heat determines the *size* and *state* of bodies.

2d. Heat, by its powerful repellent force, so readily and extensively expands other bodies, that it has come to be the most available and universally-employed inanimate power known. In its application to the expansion of water to steam, it is already exerting more mechanical energy in subjugating the earth, and otherwise subserving the wants of man, than all the inanimate forces of the globe combined.

3d. The distribution of heat on the earth's surface determines, principally, the distribution of animals and plants.

4th. This agent or fluid has very great control over all chemical transformations of substances. In some, heat is evolved; in others, cold is produced.

5th. The power of heat is not limited to the inorganic world. Life, on this planet, cannot take place only within certain limits of temperature, that is, between the freezing and boiling points of water; while variations of its intensity, within these limits, are indispensable to the laws of vitality and physiological changes.

203. **Equilibrium of heat.**—A heated body (whatever its temperature) surrounded by cooler bodies, gives off its heat, and the surrounding bodies attract and take it up. This process will go on until *it* and all the adjacent bodies have a common temperature; or if a *cold* body be surrounded by hotter ones, then it will *attract* heat from all the rest, which give it off, until the intensity is uniform in all. This removal is termed *transference;* and when the temperature has declined or increased to that of the adjacent bodies, an *equilibrium* is said to have been attained.

HEAT. 143

There are two methods by which this transference takes place: 1st, by *radiation*—both general and interstitial; 2d, by *convection*.

204. **Luminous and obscure heat.**—Heat radiated from non-luminous bodies, as a ball heated below redness, is called *obscure* heat; that radiated from luminous bodies, as the sun, or a ball heated to redness, is called *luminous* heat.

SOURCES OF HEAT.

There are four principal sources of heat: *physical, chemical, mechanical,* and *physiological.*

Physical Sources of Heat.

Physical sources of heat are solar radiation, stellar radiation, terrestrial radiation, and electricity.

205. **Solar radiation** is the principal source of heat to our globe; though the distance of the sun from us is 95,000,000 of miles. Its size or volume is 1,400,000 times greater than the earth. Opinions are divided as to the cause of the sun's heat.

206. **Quantity of heat emitted by the sun.**—The quantity of heat annually received by the earth from the sun, is sufficient to melt a crust of ice surrounding the earth 101 feet thick. The atmosphere absorbs nearly 40 per cent. of this heat. It is also estimated that the *whole* amount of heat emitted by the sun is 2,381,000,000 times greater than that received by the earth; which is sufficient to melt a cylinder of ice 45 miles thick, at the rate of 190,000 miles a second.

207. **Extremes of natural temperature,** on the earth, vary from 70° F., below, to 146° above, zero. In this latitude (New York), from the coldest to the hottest seasons, the variations are often 110°, F.

208. **Terrestrial radiation.**—There are many theories regarding terrestrial heat, but it may be partly accounted for by local chemical action.

The heat of the sun does not penetrate the earth more than from 50 to 100 feet. Descending into the earth, after passing the point of constant temperature, the heat regularly increases about 1°.8 for every 100 feet. At the depth of 2 miles, water would boil; at 23 miles, cast iron would melt. Hence, it is estimated that the crust of the earth is not more than 100 miles thick; or one-fortieth of its radius; which, relatively, is thinner than an egg-shell.

209. **Atmospheric electricity** is a source of heat which is but little understood. Its intense calorific powers are shown by flashes of lightning not unfrequently fusing metals and earthy matter, and cutting chains and bars of iron in two, as with a blade of fire, *instantaneously.*

Chemical Sources of Heat.

210. **Chemical sources of heat.**—When chemical combination of two substances takes place, it is usually attended with an elevation of temperature, but sometimes with a depression.

211. **Combustion.**—When the heat developed by the chemical combination of two bodies produces luminosity, the bodies are said to *burn,* and the phenomenon is termed *combustion.* If one of the bodies be a solid, it is called *fire;* if gaseous, *flame.* Oxygen combining with other substances, constitutes all ordinary combustion. It is supposed that the *cause* of heat in combustion is the vibratory motions of the constituent atoms of the bodies, as they combine together. The amount of heat evolved by chemical combination varies with different substances.

212. **Mechanical sources of heat.**—The principal of these are *friction, compression,* and *percussion.*

When two bodies are rubbed together, heat is generated by the *friction* of their surfaces; which must be attributed to a molecular movement of the bodies, excited by the friction.

The quantity of heat developed by friction depends, 1st, on the nature and state of the surfaces; 2d, on the pressure; 3d, on the velocity.

Compression.—When any substance is diminished in volume, there is, generally, a development of heat; strikingly seen in gases, when they are suddenly compressed (236).

Percussion is a combination of friction and compression, produced by hammering; and the heat evolved is principally due to the diminution of bulk of the body hammered.

213. **Physiological source of heat.**—Animal heat is the result of a series of chemical actions taking place within the living body, the principal of which is combustion in the lungs; oxygen of the air combining with the carbon and hydrogen of the blood, forming carbonic acid and vapor of water. The heat thus developed is equal to, and so compensates for, that lost from the exterior, which keeps the body at a uniform temperature in all climates and seasons.

Vegetable life is also attended with chemical changes and consequent evolution of heat. The temperature of plants is, in general, from 0°.9 to 1°.1 higher than that of the surrounding air.

214. **Difference between quantity and intensity of heat.**—No amount of heat of low temperature can be so applied to another object as to raise it to a higher temperature than that of the source from which the heat emanated. For instance, with a lens the heat of the sun will ignite combustible substances, but the *same quantity* of solar heat, after being absorbed by a blackened wall and then radiated, cannot be brought to that degree of intensity necessary to ignite the same substances. For the same reason solar heat, reflected from the moon, loses its intensity.

EXPANSION.

Linear Expansion.

215. **Figure 1.—Linear expansion of solids.—Pyrometers.**—Place any kind of metallic rod in the two supports, L and H,

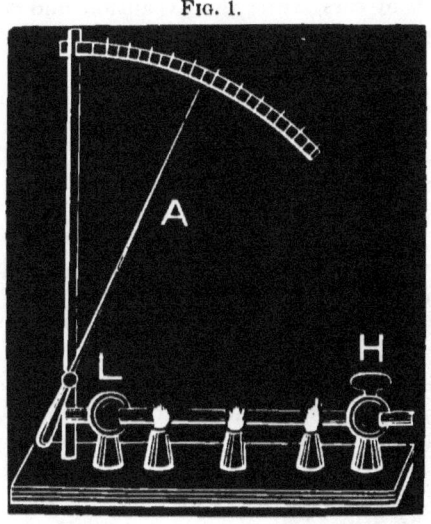

Fig. 1.

so that one extremity will abut against the short arm of the lever, A, when it stands in a vertical position; then secure the other extremity by the clamp-screw H. When the rod is heated, by lighting the lamps, it will expand; and the extent of expansion will be indicated by the movement of the long arm of the lever on the graduated index. If the lamps be extinguished, the bar, on cooling, will contract to its original length; shown by the lever again returning to the vertical position.

This instrument is called the *pyrometer* (there are other and better ones), and by its use it is found that the laws of expansion are:

1. *The extent of the expansion and contraction of the same metal varies with variations of temperature.*
2. *The extent of the expansion and contraction of different metals varies with the same temperature.*

Iron rail-tracks are laid with reference to the first law, by leaving a space between the ends of the rails, to prevent the track from *"lifting,"* as it is called.

The second law is practically applied in the construction of compensating pendulums (60).

The contraction and expansion of metals by heat and cold are also employed to exert powerful force through short distances; as setting tires on wheels, drawing walls of buildings together, etc.

The immense Croton water-pipe at High-Bridge, New York, rests on rollers to facilitate its movement, caused by expansion and contraction.

The Niagara Suspension Bridge is deflected only about six inches by the heaviest trains of cars, while the expansion and contraction of its cables, by change of temperature, cause the bridge to rise and fall about *two feet.*

The cables of the suspension bridge being constructed between New York and Brooklyn, will expand and contract about *seven feet;* to provide for which, the towers over which the cables will pass are to be 160 feet higher than the floor of the bridge.

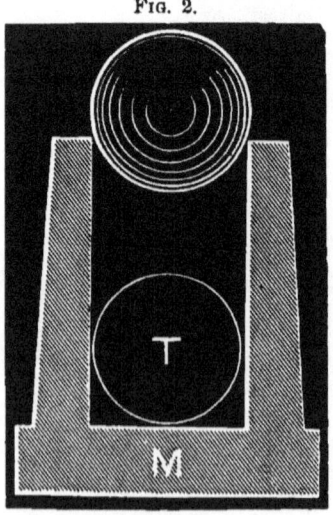

FIG. 2.

216. **Co-efficient of expansion.** —*The co-efficient of lineal expansion* is the small amount gained in the length of a rod, a foot long, when heated from 32° to 33° F.

The co-efficient of cubic expansion is the small fraction of its volume, by which a solid, liquid, or gas is increased when heated from 32° to 33° F.

Cubic Expansion.

217. **Figure 2.—Cubic Expansion of solids.**—By this is meant expansion in three directions, or expansion of *volume.* T is a metallic ball of just sufficient magnitude, at ordinary temperature, to fit between the upright arms of the bed-piece, M, as shown. If the ball be taken out and heated in a furnace, it cannot be placed between the arms, in whatever position it be turned; showing it has been expanded in all directions. If it be left on the points of the arms, as shown, it will, on cooling, drop into its original position.

If the experiment be performed with a cube, instead of a sphere, the result will be the same.

Different solids expand unequally with the same heat; and the same solids unequally with different degrees of heat.

218. **Relation between linear and cubical expansion.—** If the linear expansion is *one*-thousandth of the original length, then the cubical expansion will be *three* one-thousandths of the original bulk.

219. **Amount of expansion of solids, absolute and relative.—**The most expansible metal, zinc, increases only one three hundred and fortieth ($\frac{1}{340}$) of its length, with change of temperature from the freezing to the boiling point; while glass expands only one-third as much as zinc. The relative expansibility of metals and glass is as follows, commencing with the most and ending with the least expansible: zinc, lead, tin, silver, brass, gold, copper, bismuth, iron, steel, antimony, platinum, glass.

The compressibility of these substances is about in the same order. The most expansible are, in general, the most fusible.

The ratio of expansion increases with the temperature.

EXPANSION OF SOLIDS.

By increasing the temperature from 32° to 212° F.

SUBSTANCES.	EXPANSION.	
	IN LENGTH.	IN BULK.
English Flint-glass.......	1 in 1248	1 in 316
Platinum	1 " 1131	1 " 377
Tempered Steel	1 " 926	1 " 309
Iron....................	1 " 847	1 " 282
Gold	1 " 682	1 " 227
Copper	1 " 582	1 " 194
Brass...................	1 " 536	1 " 179
Silver	1 " 524	1 " 175
Tin	1 " 516	1 " 172
Lead	1 " 351	1 " 117
Zinc....................	1 " 340	1 " 113

Expansion of Liquids.

220. **Figure 3.—Expansion of liquids.**—All liquids expand by heat more than solids; for, mercury, the *least* expansible of all liquids, expands more than the *most* expansible metal, which is zinc. Their expansibility, however, is more variable than that of liquids.

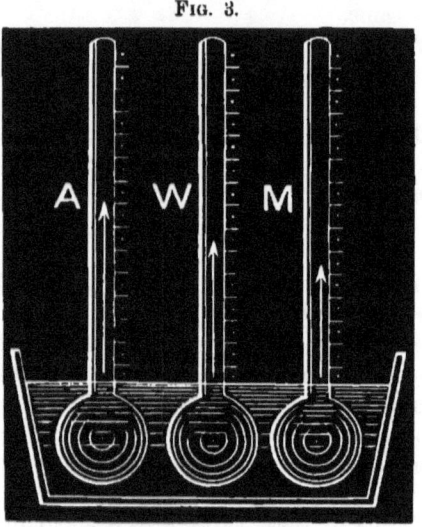

Fig. 3.

Fill the bulb of the glass vessel, A, in the figure, up to the tube, with any fluid, then place the bulb over a spirit-lamp, and as the liquid becomes heated, its expansion will be shown by its rising in the tube; and, on being allowed to cool, it will return to its original bulk.

221. **The amount of expansion of liquids.**—*Liquids expand unequally for equal increments of heat.*

The same liquid expands more the more it is heated; and the higher the temperature rises the greater will be the expansion for a given increase of heat. This is owing to the fact that the higher the temperature becomes, the further the particles are removed from each other, and, therefore, the cohesive or antagonistic power (23) diminishes in a greater ratio than the repulsive force of heat increases.

222. **Different liquids expand differently for the same increase of temperature.**—In the diagram (Fig. 3) let A, W, and M be three glass bulbs of equal dimensions, with narrow graduated tubes, filled, each to the same level, with different liquids; say, alcohol, water, and mercury. On pouring hot water into the trough, the fluids will expand and rise in the tubes; but, not expanding equally, they do not rise to the same height, as indicated by the arrows. The alcohol in A will rise the highest, and the mercury in M the least; while the water in W will rise to a point intermediate between the other two.

EXPANSION OF LIQUIDS,

By increasing the temperature from 32° to 212° F.

Mercury .... 1 part in 55.
Pure Water .... 1 " " 21.3
Sulphuric Acid .... 1 " " 17.
Oil of Turpentine .... 1 " " 14.
Fixed Oils .... 1 " " 12.5
Alcohol .... 1 " " 9.

The most expansible liquids, generally, are those whose boiling points are the lowest.

223. **Water, at certain temperatures, an exception to the laws of contraction and expansion.**—Water, in cooling, ceases to contract at about 42° F.; and at about 39°, just before it reaches the freezing point (32°), it begins to expand again, and more and more rapidly as the freezing point is reached. This expansion is about *one-eleventh* of its bulk, and accounts for the bursting of pipes, vessels, etc., when water is freezing within them.

224. **Beneficial effects of unequal expansion of water.** —By this exception to the law of expansion, *ice* is rendered specifically lighter than water, which causes it to float, and so form a cover to lakes, rivers, etc.; and, being a good non-conductor of heat, it prevents radiation from the water below it; and thus keeping the water warm, preserves animal life below, and prevents the accumulation of vast quantities of ice. If it were not for this grand exception to the otherwise general law, ice would sink and fill the beds of rivers, causing them to overflow, and be exposed in large surfaces to the air; and so, besides inundating the country, produce fields and masses of ice that, in higher latitudes, would not melt from one cold season to another; and thus render even our own climate uninhabitable.

225. **Freezing of water in small tubes.**—Water freezes at a much lower temperature than 32° in small tubes, like sensible pores; which, doubtless, is one of the many universal means of the All-Wise for protecting organic nature from harmful effects of extreme cold.

Expansion of Gases.

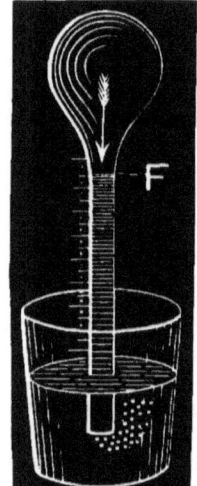

Fig. 4.

226. Figure 4.—Expansion of gases.—Gases and vapors, being under the influence of repulsion (23), and having little cohesion, expand, for equal increments of heat, much more than either solids or ordinary liquids.

Invert the bulbed tube, F, and insert its mouth into a tumbler of water; then, by heating the bulb, if only with the hand, the air will expand and escape, as indicated by the bubbles in the water. If the heat be removed, the air, cooling, will contract, and water will rise to take the place before occupied by the air that has escaped. Hence, the height to which the liquid rises in the graduated tube will indicate the amount of expansion of the air.

227. The general laws of expansion of gases by heat:

1. *All gases have the same co-efficient of expansion as common air.*
2. *The co-efficient of expansion remains the same, whatever may be the pressure to which the gas is subjected.*
3. *Under the pressure of the atmosphere, the co-efficient of expansion for all gases may be considered as 0.3666, between the freezing and boiling points of water;* or $\frac{1}{481}$ of the volume at 32° for each degree of Fahrenheit's scale.

228. Relation between compressibility and expansibility.—The expansibility and compressibility of a substance increases with the temperature.

Solids expand less than liquids, and are less compressible; while liquids are less expansible and compressible than gases.

The most expansible solids are generally the most easily compressed.

229. Density of gases.—Density of gases and vapors is compared, for a standard, with common air, when the barometer stands at 30 inches, and thermometer at 32° F., air being called 1, or 1.000.

The method of determining the density of a gas is, in principle, the same as for the density of liquids.

The density of air being 1.0000, that of hydrogen is 0.0692; nitrogen, 0.9714; oxygen, 1.1056; carbonic acid, 1.5290.

Hydrogen is the lightest known body.

SPECIFIC HEAT.

230. **Figure 5.**—**Calorimetry,** *or the measurement of the quantity of heat which different bodies absorb or emit during a known change of temperature.* Let AA be a large vessel made of ice, having a heavy slab of ice, M, for a cover. Suppose it were required to determine the relative capacity of water and mercury for heat. In a glass flask, T, put one ounce of water, and raise its temperature, say, to 200° F.; then place the flask in the ice vessel, and cover it over. Let the water cool down, as it will, to 32°. Now, pour off the water that is in the *ice-vessel* (which has come from the warm water melting the ice), and measure it. Do the same with an ounce of mercury; and it will be found that the mercury melts only one *thirty-third* as much ice as the water. And as the relative amount of water obtained from the ice-vessel shows the relative amount of heat that is necessary to raise an ounce of water and an ounce of mercury from 32° to 200° of temperature, it follows that water has 33 times the capacity of mercury to absorb heat in undergoing a given change of temperature.

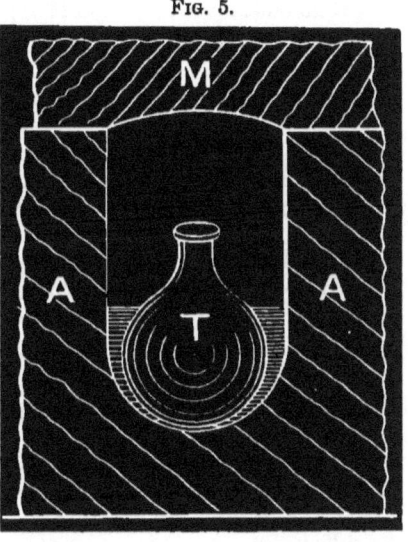

FIG. 5.

231. **Specific heat or caloric capacity.**—The amount of heat which a body is capable of absorbing, as above described, is called the *specific heat,* or *caloric capacity* of the body.

232. **The unit of heat, or thermal unit,** is the quantity of heat required to raise a pound of water from 32° to 33° F.

233. **Standard of specific heat.**—From such, and other experiments, as above shown, tables have been formed expressing the specific capacity of different bodies for absorbing heat; *water* being taken as the standard, and marked 1.000.

152   HEAT AND STEAM-ENGINE.

TABLE SHOWING SPECIFIC HEAT OF DIFFERENT SUBSTANCES.

Water	1.000	Cobalt	106.96
Ice	513	Zinc	95.55
Charcoal	414	Copper	95.15
Sulphur	241	Arsenic	81.40
Glass	203	Silver	57.01
Diamond	147	Gold	32.44
Iron	114	Platinum	32.43
Nickel	109	Mercury	33.32

234. **Effect of specific heat of water on climate.**—The universality of water and its high specific heat, or its great capacity to absorb and emit heat, greatly modifies the rapidity of natural transitions, or sudden changes from hot to cold and cold to hot seasons.

235. **Specific heat of gases.**—If a unit of weight of any gas, allowed to expand without change of pressure, is heated from 32° to 33°, the amount of heat thus absorbed (measured in fractions of the unit), is called the *specific heat under a constant pressure;* but if the gas be *not allowed* to expand, then the amount of heat, so required, is called the *specific heat under a constant volume.*

236. **Figure 6.—Compression of air and other gases diminishes their capacity for heat.**—Let the figure represent a strong cylinder and piston; on the lower side of the piston let there be placed a piece of tinder, represented by the dots. If the air in the piston be suddenly compressed, by forcing down the piston, the tinder will be ignited, because the capacity of the air for heat is diminished with a diminution of its volume.

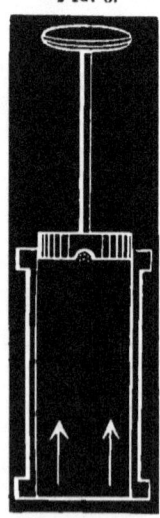
FIG. 6.

The variation of capacity of substances, under variations of volume, is clearly shown, and impressed on the mind with the *sponge and water* illustration. Thus: if a sponge, which has imbibed as much water as it can hold, be compressed, a portion of water exudes, just as the air in the cylinder allows a portion of the heat to escape when pressure is made. On relaxing the force on the sponge, and allowing it to dilate, it will take up an increased quantity of water; and air, when suddenly dilated, has its capacity for heat increased, and vice versa. Or: equal volumes of *all* gases (measured at the same temperature and pressure), set free or absorb the same quantity of heat

HEAT. 153

when they are compressed or expanded the same fractional part of their volume.

237. **Heat applied to warming apartments partly consumed in expanding the air.**—When air is heated, where it is free to expand, as in a room, only about *five-sevenths* of the heat applied is expended in producing elevation of temperature; the other *two-sevenths* being taken up by the expansion of the air, to be given out again as the air contracts by cooling.

238. **Specific heat affected by change of state.**—A body in the liquid state has a greater specific heat than in the solid form; owing to the fact that additional heat is required to convert the solid into a liquid; as, in the above table (233), it will be seen that the specific heat of water is nearly double that of ice.

On the other hand again, in the gaseous condition of a body, its specific heat is less than when it is in the liquid state.

The following table exhibits the dependence of the specific heat on the physical state of the substance:

SPECIFIC HEAT OF DIFFERENT STATES OF BODIES.

SUBSTANCES.	SPECIFIC HEAT.		
	SOLID.	LIQUID.	GASEOUS.
Water............	0.5040	1.0000	0.4805
Bromine	0.0833	0.1000	0.0555
Tin..............	0.0562	0.0637	....
Iodine	0.0541	0.1082	....
Lead.............	0.0314	0.0402	....
Alcohol	....	0.5475	0.4534
Ether............	....	0.5290	0.4797

See *latent heat* and *change of state*, 303.

COMMUNICATION OF HEAT.

239. **Heat is communicated in three ways:** 1st, By *conduction* (chiefly in solids); 2d, By *convection*, or circulation (in liquids and gases); 3d, By *radiation*.

Conductibility of Solids.

240. **Conduction of heat—conductors and non-conductors.**—If one part of a solid be heated, as one end of an iron bar, the heat will slowly travel along from particle to particle, until it reaches all parts of the body. This is called *conduction*. As the ultimate atoms or molecules of matter (4 and 5) are not supposed to be in actual contact (22 and 35), conduction is sometimes called interstitial radiation.

241. **Different solids conduct heat differently.** Hence some are called good conductors; others, bad conductors. Solids conduct heat better than liquids, and liquids better than gases.

242. **Figure 7.—Determination of the conductibility of solids.**—There are many ways of testing the relative conductibility of solids. Screw into a copper ball, T, three metallic rods, A, N, H, as copper, brass, and iron, of equal length and diameter; form their outer

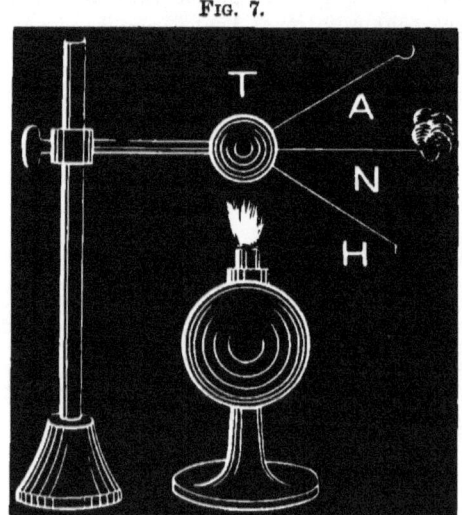

FIG. 7.

extremities into little cups; in each of these place a bit of phosphorus. If now the ball be heated with a spirit-lamp, the heat, conducted along the rods, will ignite the phosphorus, as shown at the extremity of the rod, N; the best conductor firing its phosphorus first, and the poorest last.

TABLE OF CONDUCTIBILITY OF SOLIDS (TYNDALL).

(Silver being rated 100.)

Silver	100	Iron	12
Copper	74	Lead	9
Gold	53	Platinum	8
Brass	24	German Silver	6
Tin	15	Bismuth	2

Good conductors of heat are also good conductors of electricity.

243. **Musical tones caused by conduction.**—Experiments have shown that conduction of heat produces vibratory motion of the conductor, accompanied by musical tones.

244. **Conductibility varies with molecular arrangement.**—In homogeneous solids, conductibility is equal in all directions. While in wood and crystals, it is greater in some directions than others.

In wood, it is found that there are three unequal axes of calorific conduction; the principal one being parallel to the fibres of the wood. The heat-conducting power of wood bears no definite relation to its density, some of the lightest being the best conductors. Green woods conduct heat better than dry.

The conductibility of a body is diminished by being pulverized, or otherwise minutely divided; as marble, powdered; or wood, worked into saw-dust.

245. **Figure 8.—Conduction the principle of the safety-lamp of Davy.**—The blaze of the lamp is surrounded or inclosed by a cylinder of metallic wire gauze, shown by the double-dotted lines. If the lamp or lantern be carried into a mine, or any place where there are inflammable gases, the blaze of the burning gas *within* the gauze cylinder will not communicate itself to the gas *without:* for the reason that, as the flame passes (or is passing) through the gauze, the wires conduct away a sufficient amount of its heat to reduce the temperature of the blaze below the combustible intensity, which, of course, extinguishes it.

FIG. 8.

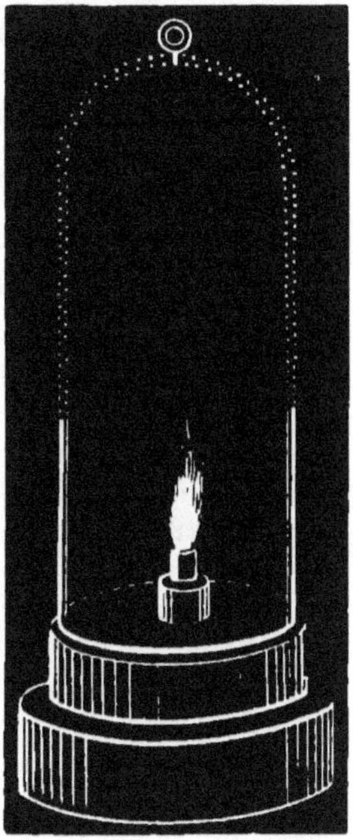

This lamp is of immense value in mines, and has been the means of preventing many explosions and much destruction of human life.

Conductibility of Liquids.

246. **Conductibility of Liquids.**—Formerly, from experiments, it was concluded that liquids were absolutely non-conductive, but later experiments prove that they do conduct heat, but only to a very limited degree—except mercury; which, being a metal, is a good conductor.

247. **Figure 9.—Heat in liquids not equalized by conduction.**—When water is to be heated in a vessel, it is indispensable that the heat be applied at the lower part of the containing dish; as will be presently explained.

(For explanation of this figure, see 253.)

FIG. 9.   FIG. 10.

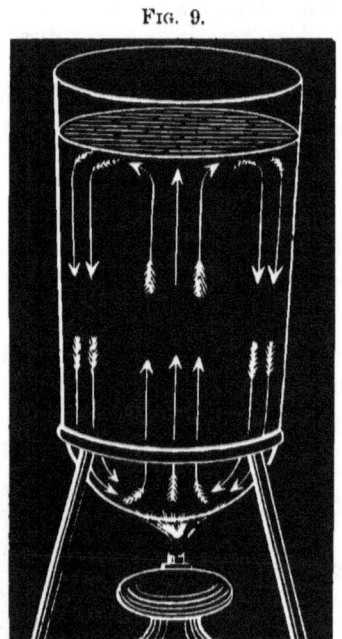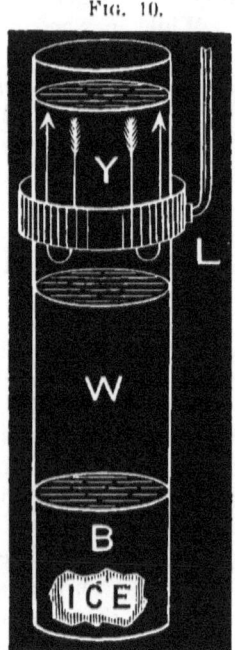

248. **Figure 10.—Non-conductibility of liquids shown by experiments with water.**—Place in the bottom of a wide tube a piece of ice; fill the lower portion, B, with *blue*, the intermediate portion, W, with *plain*, and the upper portion, Y, with *yellow water*, as shown. Take the heavy metallic ring, L, heat it red-hot, and place it as seen, just above the level of the plain water; and immediately the water on the outer portion of the column, as far down as the ring, will begin to ascend, and in the central portion to descend; as shown by the bent arrows; and soon it will boil without mingling with or raising the temperature of the plain water below. By placing the ring down just above the blue water, the plain water will boil and mix with the yellow. If the ring be placed still lower, a portion of the blue water can be made to boil and mix with the other colors; while yet the *ice* remains unmelted; thus proving that heat in water does not descend below the point of applied heat, either by *conduction* or *convection*.

HEAT. 157

Conductibility of Gases.

249. **Conductibility of gases.**—Gases are even more non-conductive of heat than liquids. Heat in these is so readily diffused by currents, it is difficult to make experiments. Substances which inclose large volumes of air within their pores, as down, feathers, wool, etc., are very poor conductors of heat; and, in the economy of Nature, are employed as non-conductors.

250. **Relative conductibility of moist and dry air.**—Air filled with moisture is rendered thereby a much better conductor than dry air, in the ratio of 230 to 80; hence, at the same temperature, a damp atmosphere seems colder to the senses than dry air, as it more rapidly conducts away animal heat.

251. **Relative conductibility of solids, liquids, and gases of the same temperature.**—We would be burned with a rod of metal heated to 120° F., but not scalded by water at 150°, while dry air has been endured without injury even as high as 300°.

252. **The philosophy of clothing,** as relates to heat, consists in wearing non-conducting materials when the heat of the air is greater than that of the body (98 F.), to shield the body from heat *without;* and when the air is colder than a comfortable temperature, to keep the heat from *escaping* from the body; and for all temperatures between these two limits, conductive materials should be worn, to allow the heat of the body to escape.

CONVECTION OF HEAT.

Convection of Liquids.

253. **Convection of liquids.**—Though liquids and gases do not readily conduct heat, yet, owing to their perfect mobility (88), and the fact that liquids and gases are made lighter by heat, they are readily heated by a process of circulation, called *convection;* illustrated by Figure 9 (247).

The heat being applied at the centre of the bottom of the containing vessel, an upward current of heated particles takes place through the centre of the water, and a corresponding downward current of colder particles supplies the place of the rising current. The downward current will take place where the body of the water is coldest, which, of course, in this case, is next to and near the sides of the vessel. The system of bent arrows will show the currents. In Fig. 10 (248) the descending currents were in the centre, because the heat was applied to the sides instead of the bottom or centre of the vessel.

Thick and viscid liquids do not circulate so freely, and need to be stirred when heated.

254. **Ocean currents.—The Gulf-Stream.**—Different parts of the ocean being subjected to unequal heat, causes regular and constant currents of great magnitude and extent, which are modified, in their direction, by the form and distribution of land and water, and the earth's rotation around its axis.

The water becomes heated under the tropics and flows off to the north and south, conveying heat to and evaporating it in the colder regions; while colder currents flow from higher latitudes toward the equator. These streams exert a great effect in equalizing and modifying the temperature of the regions through which they pass.

The *Gulf-Stream* is one of the most remarkable of these currents. It is called the Gulf-Stream because, in its circuit, it sweeps around into and out of the Gulf of Mexico.

255. **Figure 11.—Heating buildings by convection of fluids in pipes.**—If the boiler, W, and system of pipes are filled with water, and heat be applied to the boiler, by a suitable furnace, the heated water will rise from the boiler and pass up into the turns, N, of the pipe, and, by radiation, becoming cooled, will flow down in the descending pipe into the boiler again, as indicated by the system of arrows. The furnace is placed in the cellar, F representing the floor of the room above. The pipes are filled and replenished through the opening, L. This is different, somewhat, from heating by steam, as will be hereafter shown.

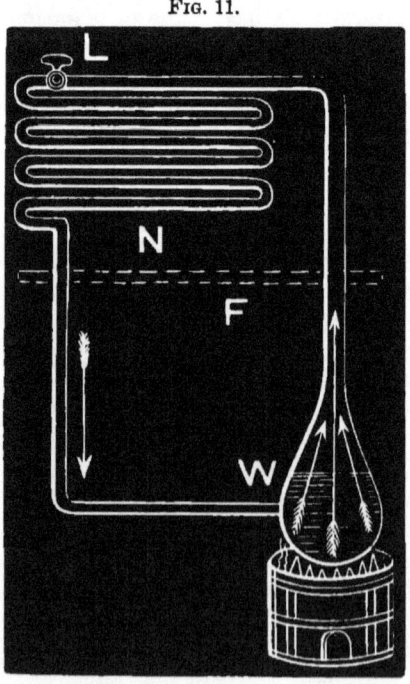

Fig. 11.

Convection of Gases.

256. **Convection of gases.**—Heat is distributed in gases by circulation in the same manner as in liquids. A current of heated air rises above a lighted candle, and currents of colder air rush in below to take its place, as shown by the arrows about the flame in Fig. 37 (344).

A room is heated principally by convection. Furnaces in the lower parts of houses heat the upper apartments by the circulation of air, which conveys the heat to and imparts it at the desired locality.

257. **Heating buildings by steam.**—The apparatus for this purpose is not unlike that employed for heating with hot water, Fig. 11 (255); the pipes not being filled with water but with steam, and water in the boiler carried to a greater temperature.

OPERATION.—The steam is condensed in the pipes above, and runs back to the boiler in the form of liquid. Every pound of water converted to steam in the boiler takes up (from the fire) over 900 units of heat (232), and renders it latent (303), and every pound of steam condensed in the pipes gives out this heat into the rooms above. The water is thus made to convey the heat from the furnace below to the apartments above.

258. **The atmosphere an immense steam heating apparatus.**—The intense heat of the tropical regions evaporates an immense quantity of water and passes it into the air, freighted with a relative amount of latent heat. This vapor is carried, by atmospheric currents (also caused by heat, 262), northward and southward to colder regions, where, by the cold, it is condensed, and compelled to liberate its latent heat. The condensed vapor falls as rain—thus *watering* as well as warming the colder parts of the earth—and, through rivers, lakes, and oceans, finds its way back to the equatorial regions.

Thus the atmosphere acts as a universal steam apparatus, in which the atmospheric currents and the rivers are the pipes; and the sun, the furnace. This apparatus excels the device of man; for it not only warms the cold regions, but, by conveying away the heat, it cools the hot regions, and universally supplies one of the most indispensable elements, which is water.

259. **Relation of air to the earth same as glass to a hot-house.**—A hot-house catches and entraps the heat of sunbeams. The *luminous* heat (204) from the sun passes readily through glass, but, after being reduced to *obscure* heat, by absorption, radiation, and reflection, it cannot pass back through the glass; as glass (besides being a poor conductor) will not transmit obscure heat.

The watery vapor in the atmosphere, while it quite readily allows the passage of luminous rays, is almost opaque to obscure heat. Hence, the atmosphere may be considered an immense hot-house to catch and entrap the luminous heat of the sun.

WIND.

260. Definition.—Wind is air in motion. The winds are an illustration of convection on a large scale.

261. Kinds of wind.—1. *Regular* winds are those which blow constantly in nearly the same direction, as the trade-winds (262).

2. *Variable* winds are those which blow sometimes in one and sometimes in another direction.

3. *Periodical* winds are those which blow regularly in the same direction at the same seasons of the year or hours of the day, as the land and sea breezes (264).

4. *Hurricanes* or cyclones.

5. *Tornadoes* or whirlwinds.

262. Figure 12.—Cause of winds.—Trade-winds.—The air in the region of the equator, being rarefied by tropical heat, rapidly

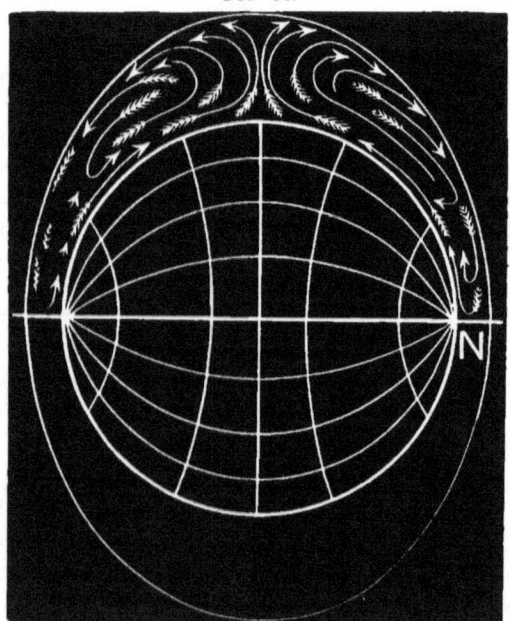

FIG. 12.

ascends and passes, in the upper atmospheric regions, over toward the poles, and a current of cold air sets in, in the lower atmospheric regions, from the north and south, to take the place of the rising current; as illustrated by the arrows.

These currents, toward the poles above and toward the equator below, would be due north and south were it not for the rotation of the earth from west to east. The surface of the earth moves faster at the equator than in high latitudes. Hence air, coming down from the poles, is continually coming to places where the earth is moving faster and faster, and it therefore lags behind. This effect, near the equator, is so great that the currents seem to blow from the *northeast* and *southeast;* while it is, really, only the earth sweeping under the currents in the opposite direction. These are called the *trade-winds*.

263. **Variable winds.**—The direction of the upper currents is just the opposite of the lower ones (above described). In intermediate latitudes, as our own, the upper currents, becoming cooled, begin to settle down, which commingle the upper and lower currents; and, flowing in opposite directions, cause the extreme variableness of the winds of our climate.

Variableness of winds is also produced by more local causes, as hills, valleys, mountains, relation of land and water, etc.

264. **Land and sea breezes.**—Owing to the greater specific heat of water (234), the sea becomes less heated, during the day, than the land. Hence, toward evening, the air over the land rises, and a surface current, called the *sea-breeze*, sets in *from the water.* At night the land cools faster than the water, and, consequently, toward morning a current, called the *land-breeze*, sets in *from the land.* These breezes are most marked on islands, especially in tropical regions. The change of seasons modifies winds.

265. **Hurricanes or cyclones.**—These are distinguished from other tempests by their extent, power, and sudden change in direction. They revolve around an axis, upright or inclined, while they move over the surface of the earth. Their progressive velocity is from 10 to 40 miles per hour; their rotary velocity is sometimes 100 miles per hour. In diameter they vary from 100 to 500 miles. They rotate in a direction contrary to that of the course of the sun.

266. **Tornadoes or whirlwinds** differ from hurricanes chiefly in extent and continuance; being rarely more than a few hundred rods in breadth, with a track usually not more than twenty-five miles in length. They continue but a few seconds; many times acting with fearful energy; overturning buildings, uprooting trees, etc.

Water-spouts are whirlwinds filled with water or vapor, instead of leaves, sticks, dust, etc.

267. **Physical properties of winds.**—Winds are *hot, cold, dry,* or *moist.* From sandy deserts, they are hot; from the sea, in lower latitudes, they are warm and moist; and from the north they are cold and dry. Our northeast winds are *cold* and *moist,* because they come over the Atlantic ocean. The Simoon is a hot wind that blows from the deserts of Africa. Its temperature is often 120° F.

268. **General direction or frequency of different winds.** —In the Table the relative frequency of different winds is given, the total number of winds in each country being 1,000.

FREQUENCY OF DIFFERENT WINDS.

COUNTRIES.	N.	N. E.	E.	S. E.	S.	S. W.	W.	N. W.
England	82	111	99	81	111	225	171	120
France	126	140	84	76	117	192	155	110
Germany	84	98	119	87	97	185	198	132
Denmark......	65	98	100	129	92	198	161	156
Sweden	102	104	80	110	128	210	159	106
Russia	99	191	81	130	98	143	166	192
North America.	96	116	49	108	123	197	101	210

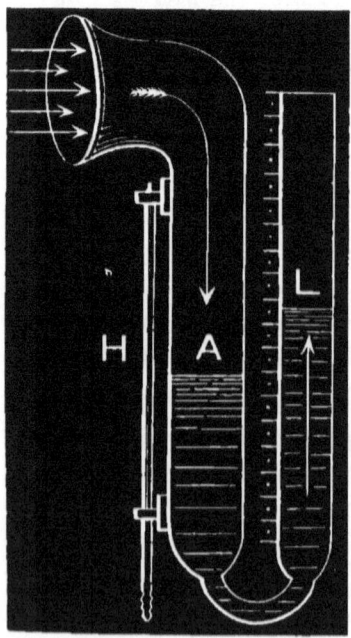

FIG. 13.

269. **Figure 13.—Anemometers. — Pressure of winds.** — Anemometers, of which there are many kinds, are instruments for measuring the pressure and velocity of winds.

The anemometer here shown consists of a tube, open at both ends, bent in the form of the letter U; the end of one arm being bent to the horizontal direction, and the mouth widened to receive the wind; the whole being nicely adjusted, as a vane, on the rod, H (which is screwed into a block of wood or other support), so the mouth will turn to the wind. Fill the instrument about half full of water and it is ready for use.

OPERATION.—The wind will press upon the fluid, depressing it in one tube, as at A, and elevating it in the other, as at L, as indicated by the

HEAT.   163

several arrows. The weight of the water standing between the level of A and L, equals the *pressure or force* of the wind, but *not its velocity*.

270. Velocity of winds.—The velocity of winds is indicated by the force or pressure which they exert.

The effect of moving the instrument through still air being the same as if it were at rest and the air in motion, to prepare the instrument for testing the velocity of different winds, let the above anemometer be moved through still air, on a calm day, by any means, as on a carriage or an open rail-car, at various rates of speed, and mark the rise of the fluid for the different velocities on the tube, as shown by the graduated scale.

The tube is diminished at the bottom to check the undulations of the water.

The force of the wind is as the square of the velocity; and, hence, the velocity is as the square root of the force.

The velocity of winds varies from that which scarcely moves a leaf to that which overthrows a forest.

The following table shows the corresponding height of water, velocity of wind, and force exerted, upon a square foot of surface.

VELOCITY AND FORCE OF WIND.

HEIGHT OF WATER IN INCHES.	FORCE OF WIND IN POUNDS.	VELOCITY PER HOUR IN MILES.	COMMON APPELLATIONS OF SUCH WINDS.
		1	Hardly perceptible.
		4	Gentle breeze.
		6	Pleasant wind.
		10	Brisk wind.
		15	} Very brisk wind.
¼	1.3	18	
½	2.6	25.5	High wind.
1	5.2	36	Very high wind.
2	10.4	50	Storm.
3	15.6	62	Great storm.
4	20.8	76	} Hurricane.
5	26.	80	
6	31.25	88	
7	36.5	95.2	} Violent hurricane.
8	41.7	101.6	
9	46.9	108.	
10	52.1	113.6	
11	57.3	119.2	
12	62.5	124.	

MEASUREMENT OF TEMPERATURES.

Thermometers.

Before explaining the principles of *radiation*, the use, construction, and method of making thermometers will be explained.

271. **Thermometers.**—A thermometer (heat-measurer) is an instrument for measuring temperature (200); and depends upon the principle that bodies expand when heated, and contract when cooled. Thermometers have been made of many different substances, each being selected as a standard. For special purposes they are made either of solids, liquids, or gases. For common purposes, however, mercury is preferred, because of its great range of temperature between its freezing and boiling points; and because it affords nearly uniform increments of expansion for uniform increments of heat; and because it does not vaporize in the vacuum, and is not too bulky.

272. **Figure 14.—Mercurial thermometer.**—This consists of a bulb of glass, at the upper extremity of which is a narrow tube of uniform bore, hermetically sealed at its upper end, as shown by F, C, and R.

FIG. 14.

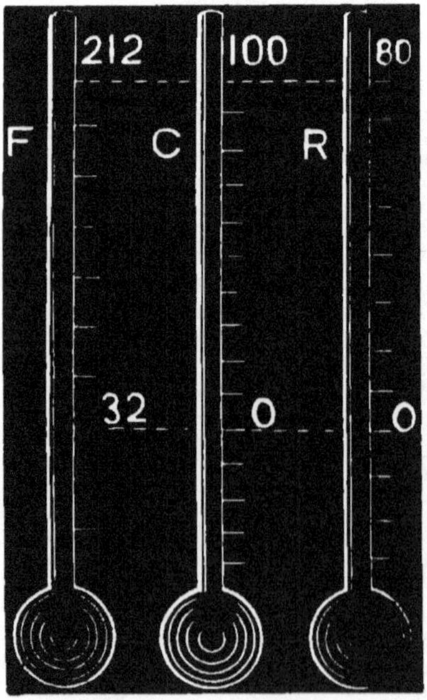

The bulb and part of the tube are filled with pure mercury, and the whole is attached to a frame, on which is a graduated scale for measuring the rise and fall of the mercury in the tube.

Of the ordinary mercurial thermometers there are three kinds, *Fahrenheit, Centigrade,* and *Réaumur;* respectively represented in the diagram by F, C, and R. The F. is mostly employed in the United States and England; the C., in France; and the R., in Germany. The principle of operation is the same in all; the difference between them consisting in the graduation, as shown in the figure.

In the *Fahrenheit*, the intermediate space between the freezing and boiling points (of water) is divided into 180; the freezing point being marked 32°, and the boiling point, 212°. The zero in this is 32° below the freezing point.

In the *Centigrade*, the freezing point (zero) is marked 0, and the boiling point, 100°.

In the *Réaumur*, the freezing point (zero) is also marked 0, but the boiling point 80°.

All degrees below zero are designated by prefixing the sign minus (—).

273. **Conversion of thermometric scales.**—In reading foreign books, it is often necessary to convert one of these scales into another; hence the following rules:

The *Centigrade* is reduced to the *Fahrenheit* by multiplying the given number of degrees by 9, dividing the product by 5, and adding 32 to the quotient: and,

The *Réaumur* to the *Fahrenheit* by multiplying by 9 and dividing by 4, and adding 32: or,

The Fahrenheit to the others by reversing these processes. Examples:

Cent. 100 × 9 = 900 ÷ 5 = 180 + 32 = 212° Fah:
Réau. 80 × 9 = 720 ÷ 4 = 180 + 32 = 212° Fah.
Fah. 212 — 32 = 180 × 5 = 900 ÷ 9 = 100° Cent.
Fah. 212 — 32 = 180 × 4 = 720 ÷ 9 = 80° Réau.

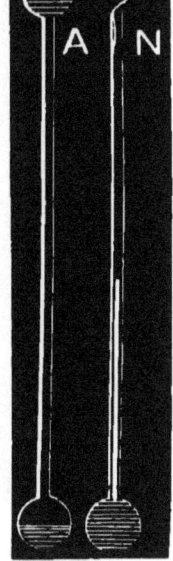

FIG. 15.

274. **Figure 15.—Method of making a thermometer.**—The glass bulb and tube being provided with a funnel at the top, as shown at A, is nearly filled with mercury, as seen at N. The whole is then heated till the mercury boils, thus filling the tube; when the funnel is melted off, and the tube hermetically sealed. On cooling, the mercury descends to some point of the tube, as shown in N, leaving a vacuum at the upper end. It only remains to graduate it, and attach a suitable scale.

275. **Standard points in the thermometer.**—If there existed a natural or absolute limit to temperature, either of heat or cold, it could be taken as the natural zero, from which the thermometric scale might be numbered, either upward or downward, from it. But, as there is no such natural limit or zero, the thermometric scale must be arbitrary. As the melting point of ice and the boiling point of water, under certain given conditions, are always the same (respectively called the *freezing* and *boiling points*), they have been adopted in all countries as the two temperatures with reference to which thermometric scales are constructed.

276. **Figure 16.—Method of graduating thermometers. —Fixing the freezing point.**—To fix the freezing point of a thermometer, thrust the bulb and part of the stem into a vessel of powdered ice, as exhibited in the drawing, which will contract the mercury down to the temperature of the melting ice. With a diamond mark the position of the mercury on the tube, or by other means, on paper previously attached to the tube.

If it is to be a Fahrenheit thermometer, mark this point 32, as shown; if a Centigrade or Réaumur, mark it 0. This will constitute the *freezing point;* and in the Centigrade and Réaumur, the zero.

FIG. 16.　　　　　FIG. 17.

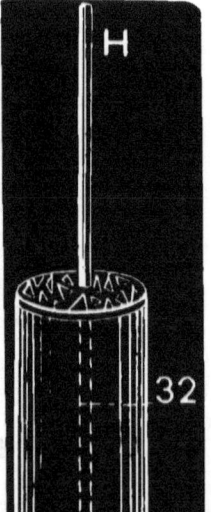
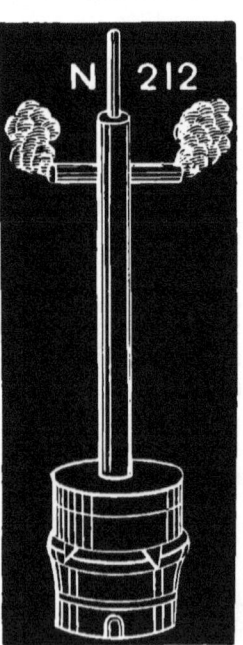

277. **Figure 17.—To fix the boiling point of thermometers.**—To fix the boiling point, plunge the instrument into boiling water, or, what is more accurate, a steam-bath, by means of a vessel, as seen in the figure, leaving the top of the stem or tube in view, as shown

HEAT. 167

at N. After the mercury ceases to rise in the tube, **mark its position**, as in the last case.

If it is to be a *Fahrenheit*, mark it 212, as shown; if a Centigrade, 100; if a Réaumur, 80; and this will constitute the *boiling point*.

To complete the graduation, divide the space between the freezing and boiling points into as many equal parts as there are designed to be degrees in the scale. The divisions are continued both above and below the fixed points. The figures expressing the number of degrees, increase upward and downward from zero (0). Prefix the sign minus (—) to all degrees below zero (276).

278. **Tests of thermometers.**—For ordinary uses thermometers may be tested by thrusting them into melting ice and boiling water, to determine if the freezing and boiling points are correctly fixed or marked. When inverted, the mercury should fall with a sudden click, and fill the tube, thus showing the perfect exclusion of air.

279. **Sensibility of a thermometer** is of two kinds. It may indicate very small differences, or it may be very sensitive to *sudden changes* of temperature. The former obtains when the *bulb is large* and the *bore of the stem is small;* the latter, when the *bulb is small* and the *glass thin*.

280. **Limits of the mercurial thermometer.**—Though mercury is by far the most available thermometric fluid, yet it has its limits; that is, it boils at 662° above zero, and freezes at 39°, F., below zero. Hence, for testing temperatures above and below these points, other substances must be employed. For degrees above the boiling point of mercury, *pyrometers* are used; for degrees below the freezing point of mercury, alcohol is employed.

Pyrometers are made in various ways—the principle employed in most of them being the expansion of solid metals by heat.

281. **Spirit thermometers.**—Alcohol has never been frozen, and is, therefore, generally employed for the estimation of *low* temperatures. For this purpose it is usually colored red, to render it more visible.

For *higher* temperatures, however, alcohol cannot be employed, as its limit, in this direction, is soon reached; its boiling point being 174° F.

Air thermometers are the best, because most accurate, for very high temperatures.

282. Figure 18.—Self-registering thermometers.—It is desirable, sometimes, to ascertain the highest or lowest temperature, or both, in places and at times where or when it is impossible or inconvenient to make observations of the instrument; as in deep water, or in the night, or at some inaccessible distance.

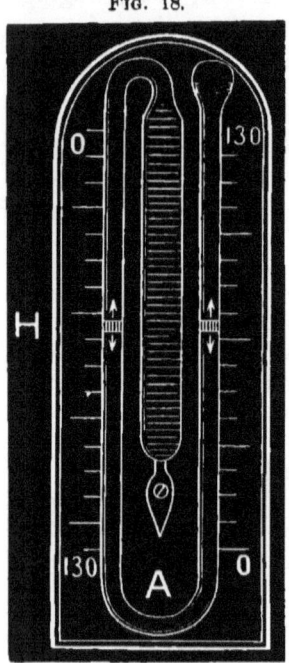

Fig. 18.

For this purpose, self-registering thermometers of various kinds are constructed. The one here represented consists of a single tube twice bent, having a long cylindrical bulb, filled with alcohol, which reaches down the small tube to H, where it rests on mercury; the mercury extending down the small tube around to opposite H; above this, the tube is filled with alcohol and air; so that the lower part of the tube, A, is filled with a heavy, and the upper part with a light, fluid. Opposite H are little iron disks or floats, made to work in the tube with a little friction, by means of hair springs, which keep them in any given place, unless moved by the mercury; and past which the alcohol can freely pass. These disks are put in contact with the mercury (on which they float), by means of a magnet carried along outside of the glass.

OPERATION.—When the alcohol in the large bulb expands by heat, it drives the mercury and floats around before it; when it contracts by cold, the float on the *right* hand is held in its highest position by the friction spring, while the mercury is driven back by the alcohol and expansion of air above it. When the alcohol in the large bulb has contracted by cold, and then again expanded by heat, the float on the left hand will be left at *its* highest point.

So, after the instrument has been submitted to different temperatures, as, for instance, at some place in a distant forest, or on a mountain, unobserved for a whole year, it can then be inspected, and the position of these floats will show the *lowest* and *highest* temperature that has obtained during the year.

283. Figure 19.—Differential thermometers.—The object of these instruments is to determine the difference of temperature of two different points or substances. The one here represented consists of a two-bulbed tube, bent twice at right angles; the tube being partly filled with alcohol or sulphuric acid, and air occupying the balance of the space. If both bulbs are equally heated, the liquid will stand at the same height in both branches of the tube; but if one, as

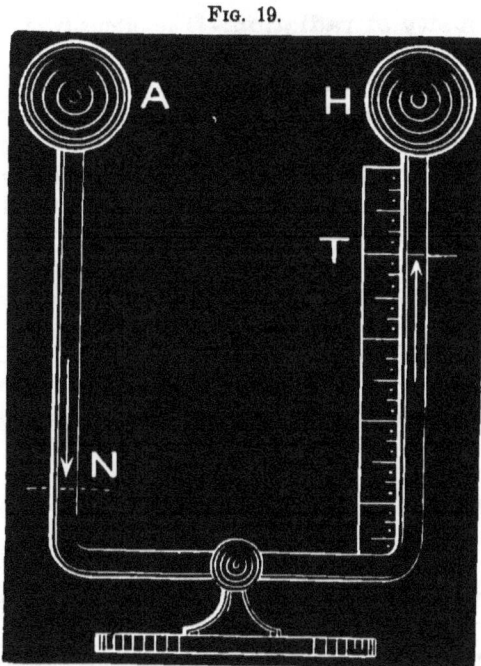

Fig. 19.

A, is heated more than the other, the liquid will be depressed in its branch, as at N, and rise, as at T, in the other branch, as indicated by the arrows, until the tensions in the two bulbs balance each other; and the graduated scale attached to one of the arms will show the difference of temperature of the two bulbs.

RADIATION OF HEAT.

284. **Radiation of heat.**—1st. Hot bodies radiate heat *equally in all directions.*

2d. Radiated heat proceeds in *straight lines*, diverging in every direction from the points where it emanates, same as rays of light from a luminous body. These lines are called *thermal rays* or *heat rays*.

It is the radiant heat of the sun, a common fire, a burning lamp, etc., that warms us.

285. **Cooling by radiation.**—Thermal rays continue to issue, until the heat of the body sinks to the actual temperature of the air, or surrounding medium (203).

Conduction of heat may be internal radiation from particle to particle, termed *interstitial radiation* (240).

286. **Intensity of radiation.**—The intensity of radiant heat is according to the following laws:
1st. *It is proportional to the temperature of the source.*
2d. *It is greater in proportion as the rays are emitted in a direction more nearly perpendicular to the radiating surface.*
3d. *It is inversely as the square of the distance from the source.*
This law is the same as that of the force of gravity and the intensity of light, and is illustrated and explained by paragraph 47.

287. **Radiant heat is partially absorbed by the medium through which it passes,** but is not sensibly affected by the *motion* of the media, as of winds in air.

The sun's rays lose about one-third of their heat in passing through the atmosphere, the remainder being absorbed or reflected at the surface of the earth.

288. **Radiation in vacuo.**—Radiation takes place more freely in a vacuum than in the air.

289. **Universal radiation and constant mutual exchange of heat between bodies.**—*Heat is radiated from all bodies at all times*, whether their temperatures be the same as, or different from, that of surrounding bodies; for it is the tendency of heat to place itself in equilibrium (203). Of several bodies of different temperatures, the hotter ones give off more than they receive, and the colder ones absorb more than they give off; and when thus equilibrium is restored, each body *continues* to give off and absorb, but in equal quantities.

ACTION OF DIFFERENT BODIES UPON HEAT.

Surface Action.

290. **Incident heat absorbed and reflected.**—A ray of heat falling upon the surface of a body, is divided into two parts, one of which enters the body and is absorbed, and the other is deflected or bent from its course. This bending is called *reflection*. The laws of reflection, as relate to the angles of incidence and reflection, are the same as for light, sound, and motion (57). The point where the bending occurs is called the *point* of incidence; before incidence the ray is called the *incident ray*; after incidence, the *reflected ray*. A perpendicular to the reflecting surface at the point of incidence is termed the *normal*. The angles formed by the incident and reflected rays with the normal, are called, respectively, *angles of incidence and reflection*. The plane of the incident ray and the normal at the point of incidence is called the *plane of incidence*. The plane of the normal and the reflected ray is called the *plane of reflection*.

291. Figure 20.—Laws which govern the reflection of heat.
1st. *The planes of incidence and reflection coincide.*
2d. *The angles of incidence and reflection are equal.*

Let W be a tin box, with blackened faces, and filled with hot water; T, an intercepting screen, provided with a small opening; A, a reflecting surface; and F, a differential thermometer. NL is a normal to the

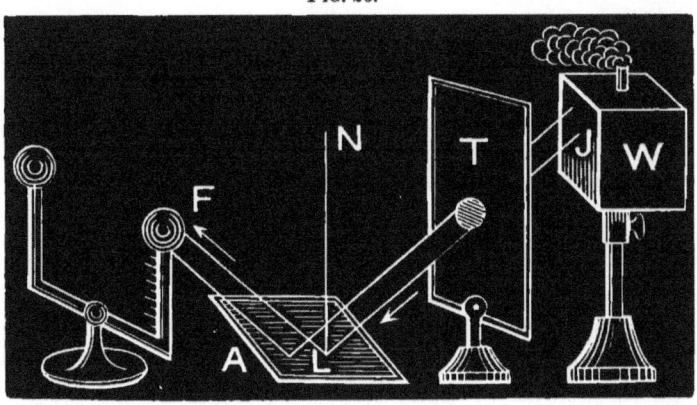

FIG. 20.

reflecting surface. The surface, J, radiates heat in all directions, but, by means of the screen, T, as shown, only a single ray is permitted to fall on the reflector. By this apparatus it is demonstrated that, whatever be the value of the angle of incidence, the planes JLN and NLF coincide with each other, and the angles JLN and NLF are equal to each other.

292. Figure 21.—Reflection of heat from concave mirrors.—This figure represents two concave mirrors, which are parabolical in shape (392), turned face to face, called *conjugate mirrors*. The axis of such mirrors is a normal to the surface at the middle point.

In accordance with the laws just explained, rays of heat, as well as rays of light, parallel to the axis of such mirrors, will be reflected to a single point, called the focus of the mirror; and, conversely, rays radiating from the focus will be reflected in lines parallel to the axis. This is demonstrated by placing a piece of inflammable substance, as phosphorus, in the cup, A, at the focus of the mirror on the right, and a heated

FIG. 21.

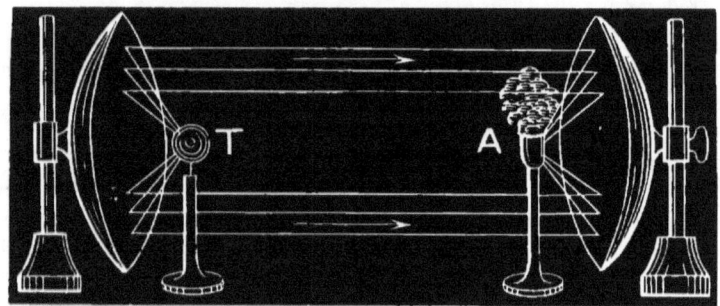

cannon-ball in the focus, T, of the other mirror. As indicated by the lines, arrows, and smoke, the heat from the ball, T, will be reflected from the left-hand mirror to the right-hand mirror in parallel lines, and again reflected to the cup, igniting the phosphorus. The mirrors may be several yards from each other. Single parabolic mirrors, called *burning mirrors*, are employed to collect the rays of the sun.

The reflection of heat in vacuo takes place according to the same laws as in air.

293. **Reflective power of different substances.**—Different bodies possess different powers of reflection. Some substances *reflect* more and absorb less; others *absorb* more and reflect less than others; hence, there are *good and bad absorbers*. Good reflectors are *bad absorbers;* and bad reflectors are *good absorbers*.

294. **Determination of reflective power.**—The source of heat is a tin canister, F (Fig. 22), filled with boiling water. The thermal rays are converged by the concave mirror, E, and thrown upon a small plate of the substance to be tested, by placing it between the mirror and focus, so that the rays reflected from the substance shall fall upon the bulb of the differential thermometer. The substance is not shown in the figure.

Polished brass possesses the highest reflecting power; silver reflects nine-tenths, tin eight-tenths, glass one-tenth as much as brass. Plates blackened by smoke do not reflect heat at all.

295. **Figure 22.—Absorptive power.**—As previously stated, different substances possess very different powers of absorbing heat. The absorptive power of a substance is in the reverse ratio of its reflective power; the best reflectors being the worst absorbents; and vice versa.

FIG. 22.

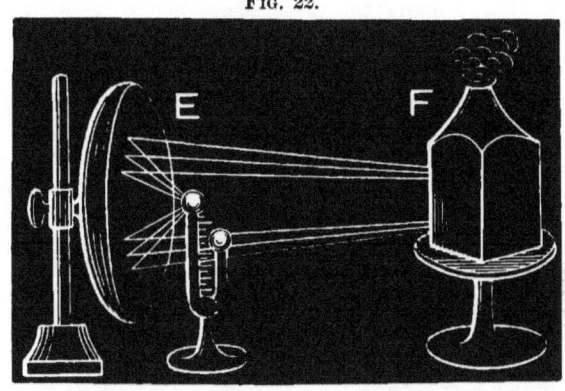

Let the source of heat be a canister, F, of boiling water; bring the thermal rays to a focus by means of the parabolic mirror, E, as represented. In the focus place the bulb of the differential thermometer, successively covered with the different substances to be tested.

Substances blackened with smoke, or covered with carbonate of lead, absorb nearly all the radiated heat thrown upon them; glass, $\frac{90}{100}$; polished cast-iron, $\frac{25}{100}$; tin, $\frac{14}{100}$; silver, $\frac{3}{100}$.

Absorptive power of colors.—The same cloth differently colored has different absorptive powers. According to their absorbent power, the colors stand in the following order; black (warmest), violet, indigo, blue, green, red, yellow, and white (coldest). Hence, summer clothing is made of *light-colored* and winter clothing of *dark-colored* fabrics.

296. **Emission or radiating power.**—The emission power of a body is its capacity to emit or radiate the heat it contains. To determine the emission power of different substances, the apparatus (Fig. 22) above described is employed,—The different sides of the canister being made of the different substances to be tested, as tin, brass, blackened surfaces, glass, paper, etc. On turning these different faces toward the mirror, the thermometer indicates different degrees of temperature. Experiments show that radiating powers of bodies are the same as their absorbing powers; that is, a good radiator is a good absorber, but a bad reflector; and vice versa.

297. **Causes which modify the reflective, absorbent, and emission powers of bodies.**—These causes are *polish, density, direction of the incident rays, nature of the source of heat,* and *color.*

1st. Other things being equal, polished bodies are better reflectors and worse absorbers than unpolished ones.

2d. Other things being the same, dense bodies are better reflectors and worse absorbers than rare ones.

3d. Other things being equal, the nearer the incident rays approach the direction of the normal, the less will be the portion *reflected* and the greater the portion absorbed.

4th. The nature of the source of heat sometimes modifies the reflective and absorbent powers. For example, a body painted with white lead absorbs more heat from a canister of boiling water, than though the same heat were emitted by a lamp. But if a body be painted with lamp-black, the amount is the same, whatever be its source.

5th. Other things being the same, light-colored bodies absorb less and reflect more heat than dark-colored ones (295).

DIATHERMANCY—REFRACTION—POLARIZATION.

298. **Transmission of radiant heat.**—Light passes through all transparent bodies, from whatever source it may come. The rays of *heat* from the *sun* also pass through transparent substances. Radiant heat, however, from terrestrial sources, is in a great degree arrested by many transparent substances, as well as by opaque bodies. For example, window-glass remains cold while the heat of the sun passes through it, but the same glass held before a common fire arrests a large part of the heat, and none of the light. Rock-salt, however, will transmit the heat of the fire.

Bodies which transmit heat are termed *diathermanous,* or diathermic (signifying, *through* and *to heat*).

Many substances are eminently diathermic, which are nearly opaque to light; smoky quartz, for example. Hence, solids that are transparent to light do not necessarily allow the passage of heat, and vice versa.

Rock-salt is the only substance that transmits an equal amount of heat from all sources. *This substance, therefore, is to heat what glass is to light;* and, hence, Melloni called it *the glass of heat.*

299. **Causes which modify the diathermanic power of bodies,** are, the nature of the source of heat, the degree of polish, the thickness and number of the screens through which the heat has been previously transmitted.

300. **Diathermancy of the air.**—The atmosphere is very diathermanic. If it were not, the upper layers would be much heated by the solar rays passing through them; and the earth would receive correspondingly less heat from the sun.

301. **Figure 23.—Refraction of heat.**—Heat, like light, is refracted or bent out of its course in passing obliquely through diathermanic substances, as shown by the figure, illustrating the *burning*

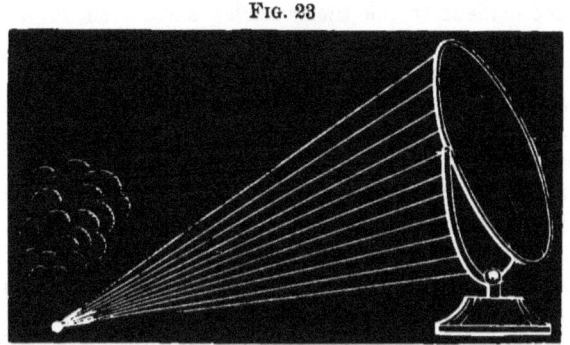

FIG. 23

glass; which consists of a double convex lens. By such a lens the rays of heat, not only of the sun but other heated bodies, are concentrated and brought to a focus, same as rays of light. Glass lenses are used for condensing the heat of the sun, but they will not condense the heat from *other* sources; besides, they would themselves become heated. It is only with a lens of *rock-salt* that heat from other sources than the sun can be condensed by refraction.

Gunpowder, paper, and other combustibles have been inflamed with a lens of *ice.*

Lenses of thin, pure glass, from one to three feet in diameter, have volatilized the most fixed metals at the focal point, and fired ships and houses at a considerable distance.

302. **Polarization of heat.**—Heat is polarized in the same manner as light (513). It undergoes double refraction by Iceland spar, and the two beams are polarized in planes at right angles to each other. A pencil of heat polarized by a plate of tourmaline is transmitted or intercepted by another tourmaline plate, under the same circumstances that a pencil of polarized light would be transmitted or intercepted.

Polarization of heat is also effected by reflection from plates of glass, and by repeated refraction.

CHANGE OF STATE OF BODIES BY THE ACTION OF HEAT.
Latent Heat.—Liquefaction and Solidification.

303. **Latent heat of fusion.**—During the conversion of a solid into a liquid, or a liquid into a gas or vapor, a certain quantity of heat is absorbed and disappears, so that the thermometer and the senses give no evidence of its existence. But when the same vapor or gas is again converted to a liquid, or the liquid to a solid, there will be given off and rendered evident to the thermometer and senses, or set free from the substance, the same amount of free heat as before was absorbed.

This heat, thus absorbed or rendered insensible by changing matter from a *dense to a more rarefied form*, and again set free and rendered sensible by changing matter from *a rarefied to a denser form*, is called *latent heat*.

EXAMPLE.—If a pound of pulverized ice, at 32° F., be mixed with a pound of water at 174°, the heat of the water will be just sufficient to melt the ice; and there will result two pounds of water at the temperature of 32°. Hence, 142° of heat of the water have been absorbed and rendered latent in converting the ice to water. But if a pound of the water be reconverted to ice, then the 142° would be again set free. Hence, we say the latent heat of water, at 32°, is 142°.

304. **Liquefaction and solidification, or melting and freezing.**—When a body passes from a solid to a liquid state, it is said to *melt* or *fuse;* and the act of conversion is called *fusion*, or *liquefaction*. The act of passing from the liquid to the solid state is termed *freezing, congelation*, or *solidification*.

Expansion, the first effect of heat, has a limit, at which solids become liquids. The force of cohesion is then subordinate to the power of repulsion, and fusion results.

The laws of liquefaction and solidification are:

1. All solids enter into fusion at a certain temperature, invariable for the same substance.

2. Whatever may be the intensity of the source of heat when the fusion commences, the temperature remains the same until the whole mass is fused.

3. If a liquid body be allowed to cool, it solidifies at the same temperature at which it fuses.

4. The temperature of a body remains the same from the commencement to the end of its solidification.

5. The temperature at which fusion takes place is different for different bodies: for some it is very low; for others, very high, as shown by the following table.

MELTING POINTS OF DIFFERENT SUBSTANCES.

SUBSTANCE.	TEMPERATURE.	SUBSTANCE.	TEMPERATURE.
Mercury	−39° F.	Bismuth	507° F.
Ice	32°	Lead	635°
Tallow	91°	Antimony	842°
White Wax	140°	Zinc	933°
Sulphur	232°	Silver	1832°
Tin	442°	Gold	2192°

Some bodies do not melt, but are decomposed by heat, as paper, wood, bone, marble, etc. Bodies composed of a simple element, or but one kind of matter, always melt; though carbon has resisted all attempts, as yet, to fuse it.

Substances difficult of fusion are called *refractory* bodies.

305. **Peculiarities in the fusion of certain solids.**—Certain solids soften before they melt; as tallow, butter, wax, etc. This is because they are composed of several substances, which melt at different temperatures.

Metals that are capable of being welded, as iron and platinum, soften before they fuse.

Glass and certain metals never attain perfect fluidity.

306. **Melting and freezing always gradual,** *owing to the absorption or evolution of heat during these processes.*

As solids cannot pass into the liquid state without absorbing and rendering latent a great amount of heat (303), the very act of melting deprives the immediately surrounding air of so much of its heat as to partially arrest the melting process. And as the act of freezing liberates latent heat, the freezing body becomes surrounded with a layer of warm air, and thus the process of freezing is partially arrested by the very freezing itself. Hence the seeming paradoxes, that *melting is a cooling process,* and *freezing, a warming* process. Yet it is true, that all processes of freezing are processes of warming, and all processes of melting are processes of cooling.

Were this not the case, melting and freezing would be instantaneous, and so, dangerous. Water, at 32°, would immediately become ice; and ice and snow would, by a slight increase of temperature, instantaneously return to water, causing destructive freshets, etc.

307. **Why ice does not acquire great thickness.**—It is owing to this law of absorption and liberation of heat, by melting and freezing of water, together with the law of its *irregular expansion* (223) and its high specific heat (234), that ice never acquires any very great thickness.

308. **Latent heat of water graduates the changes of temperature.**—It is also owing to the law of absorption and liberation of heat, by melting and freezing of water, together with the law of its irregular expansion (223) and its high specific heat (234), that we have such a gradual and healthful approach of hot and cold seasons. In autumn the water has 142° of heat to give out before it solidifies; in the spring it must receive the same amount before it will melt; serving as a check upon the sudden changes of temperature.

309. **Freezing mixtures.**—These are made in accordance with the above law of absorption of heat. Salt and pounded ice, for instance, mixed together, and acting upon each other to mutually hasten their liquefaction, will so rapidly absorb heat from surrounding bodies (cream for example) as to freeze them.

In a mixture of salt and snow, the thermometer may be reduced to 0, F.

310. **Crystallization.**—When bodies pass slowly from the liquid to the solid state, their particles, instead of arranging themselves in a confused manner, tend to group themselves into regular forms, called crystals, by a process termed crystallization (25).

Sugar-candy, alum, common salt, and snow-flakes, are examples of crystallized bodies.

VAPORIZATION.

311. **Definitions.—Vaporization.**—A liquid sufficiently heated is converted into the gaseous form, and is called a *vapor*. This change of state is called *vaporization*.

Conversely, if heat be abstracted from a vapor it will return to the liquid form. This change of a vapor to a liquid is called *condensation*.

Thus water, at 212° F., is rapidly converted into steam, an invisible vapor.

Vapors are generally colorless, and endowed with an *expansive force* or *tension;* which, when heated, may become very great.

Boiling or *ebullition* is the rapid formation of vapor throughout the whole mass, producing agitation.

Evaporation occurs gently and invisibly, only at the surface of liquids, as on the surface of water in an open dish.

Sublimation is the change of *solids* to vapors without the intermediate *liquid* condition; such as camphor, iodine, musk, and odorous bodies generally.

312. **Volatile liquids and fixed liquids.**— *Volatile liquids* are those which have a natural tendency to pass into a state of vapor at ordinary temperatures; such as alcohol, ether, essences, essential oils, turpentine, and the like.

Fixed liquids are those which do not pass into a vapor at *any* temperature; as, for example, fish-oils, olive-oils, and the like; which, at high heat, are decomposed into various gases, but to no true vapors that can be again condensed into the original liquid.

313. **Latent heat of evaporation.**—A large amount of heat disappears, or is rendered latent, during evaporation; and is again liberated, or set free, by condensation. See latent heat of fusion (303).

314. **Latent heat of steam.**—The amount of heat absorbed or rendered latent in converting ice to water is 142° F. (303); and in converting water to steam there is absorbed or rendered latent 967°.5 F.

315. **Latent and sensible heat of steam at different temperatures.**—The whole amount of heat in steam is the *latent heat* plus the *sensible heat*. Thus the heat of steam at the temperature of ebullition is 967°.5 + 212° = 1179°.5 F. The heat absorbed in evaporation is less as the temperature of the vaporizing liquid is higher.

FIG. 24.

Experiments show that *the sum of the latent and sensible heat of steam* increases with the temperature, by a *constant* difference of $\frac{305}{1000}$ of a degree for each degree F.

Ebullition or Boiling.

316. **Figure 24.—Ebullition.**— Ebullition or boiling is a rapid evaporation in which the vapor escapes in the form of bubbles. The bubbles are formed in the interior of the liquid (represented by the specks between the bottom of the liquid and its surface), and, rising to the surface, they collapse, permitting the vapor to pass into the air. The cloudy vapor seen above the vessel, commonly called steam, is *not* steam, but minute globules of water; *steam itself being invisible.*

317. Laws that govern the phenomena of ebullition.

1. *Under the same pressure, each liquid boils at a fixed temperature.*

The temperature at which a liquid boils is called its *boiling point.* The boiling point is very different for different liquids; that of pure water is 212° F., when the pressure on its surface is equal to 30 inches of mercury; in other words, when the barometer stands at 30 inches. The boiling point of ether is 96°; alcohol, 174°; and mercury, 662° F.

2. *The pressure remaining the same, a liquid cannot be heated higher than the boiling point.*

The additional heat does not raise the temperature, either of water or steam, above 212°, for the reason that it becomes latent in the steam (314).

Causes Modifying the Boiling Point.

318. Figure 25.—Variation of pressure on the surface of the liquid varies the boiling point. — This is because ebullition consists of the formation of a vapor of the same elasticity of the superincumbent atmosphere or pressure. To prove that this is the case, fill a glass flask half full of water, and, having caused the water to boil, remove the flask from the fire or lamp, and, in a moment or two, cork it tight, and then plunge it into a vessel of cold water, as represented in the figure, when the water will again begin to boil, and will continue to do so until the temperature is reduced quite low.

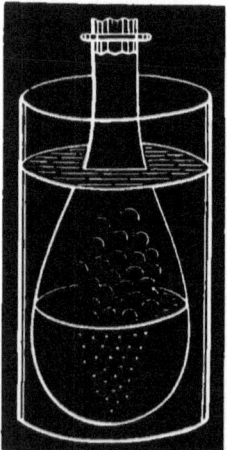

FIG. 25.

The reason why water boils by the application of cold is, that the steam which filled the space in the flask above the water is (by the cold water) condensed; thereby producing a partial vacuum, which diminishes the pressure on the surface of the water; thus proving that *liquids under less pressure boil with less heat.*

This is shown, also, by placing water, heated to less than 212°, under the receiver of an air-pump; where it will begin to boil when the pressure of the air is partially removed by the pump.

If the pressure be increased the temperature of the boiling point will be raised (334).

319. **Useful applications of boiling water under diminished pressure** are made in concentrating vegetable extracts, cane-juice (sugar), etc., and consequently at a temperature below that which would injure the substances treated.

Boiling point affected by altitude.—On ascending mountains, the boiling point of liquids *falls*, because the atmospheric pressure is less; and, conversely, on descending into mines, etc., it *rises* (134). Experiments prove that a difference of about 543 feet in elevation produces a variation of 1° F. in the boiling point of water.
It is impossible to cook meat, by *boiling*, on high mountains.

Figure 26.—Franklin's pulse glass is a further illustration of the law, that liquids under less pressure boil with less heat. This consists of a glass tube terminating with bulbs, as shown, and partly

FIG. 26.

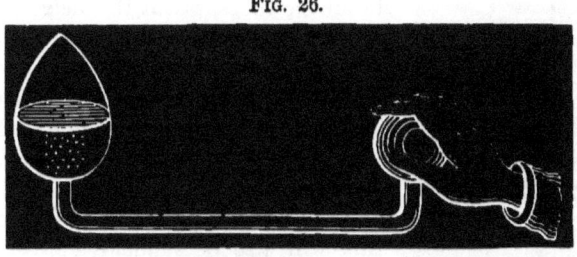

filled with ether, or water, and sealed while the liquid is boiling. When the liquid is cooled, the space above the fluid will be a vacuum; then, if only the heat of the hand be applied to one bulb, the liquid will be set to boiling in the other, as indicated in the drawing.

320. **Solids in solution in liquids raise their boiling points** in proportion to the quantity dissolved. For example, water which holds in solution as much common salt as it is capable of dissolving, requires 227° F. to raise it to the boiling point.
If, however, the body dissolved is more volatile than water, then the boiling point is lowered.

321. **The nature of the vessel varies the boiling point.**—When the interior of the vessel is rough, the projecting points form centres for developing vapor, and the boiling point is lower than when the surface is smooth. Water boils at a lower temperature in iron than in glass vessels.

Evaporation.

322. **Evaporation** takes place slowly in the open air, owing chiefly to atmospheric pressure. If the pressure be partially removed, evaporation will take place more rapidly; if wholly removed, it will occur instantaneously, like the flash of gunpowder; especially if the liquid is very volatile.

323. **Figure 27.—Evaporation in a vacuum** takes place in obedience to the following laws:
1st. *All volatile liquids volatilize instantly.*
2d. *At the same temperature the vapors of different liquids possess unequal elastic force or tension.*

The figure represents four barometer tubes, filled with mercury, and inverted in a cistern of mercury, with a graduated scale in the centre.

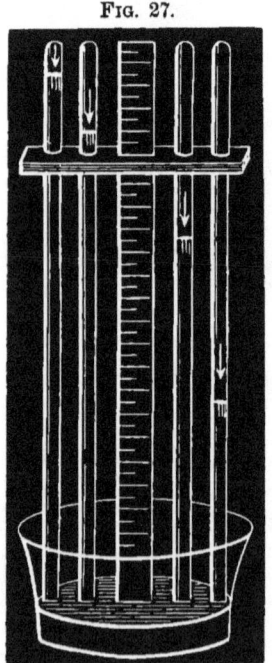

FIG. 27.

The mercury will stand at the same height in all the tubes, say at the height of that in the one on the left, as shown by the arrow.

If now a drop of ether passes up the right-hand tube to the top of the mercury, it instantly flashes into vapor and depresses the mercury half its height or more, as shown by the arrow; which illustrates the *first law.*

A drop of alcohol introduced into the next tube will also be suddenly converted to vapor, and depress the mercury; and so with a drop of water in the next tube. The different heights of the columns will show that the three several fluids possess different degrees of volatility and elasticity; thus proving the *second law.*

If more ether be introduced until it remains on the mercury and ceases to further evaporate, it is said to have reached its point of *saturation,* or *maximum tension,* or *limit of tension.* In this case, the tension of the vapor balances the tendency of the liquid to pass into a state of vapor. Yet the quantity of watery vapor necessary to saturate a given space is always the same, whether that space is a vacuum, or whether it contains air or any other gas.

Heat will increase and cold diminish the tension, as illustrated by the next figure: hence,

The limit of tension of a given vapor varies with the temperature.

The amount of vapor required to saturate a given space also varies with the temperature.

Rain is caused by the vapors (which are less dense than the air in low regions) rising to regions where they are condensed by the colder air.

The tension of different vapors varies. Ether, for example, being 25 times as great as water, and 6 times that of alcohol.

324. **Figure 28.—Evaporation under pressure.**—Let the end of the short arm of the bent tube be closed, and leave the other end open, and fill the tube two-thirds full of mercury, which, of course, will completely fill the short arm. If, now, a drop of ether be introduced into the top of the short arm, A, the pressure of the air on the mercury in the long arm will prevent its evaporation at any ordinary temperature. If, however, the tube is plunged into a vessel of water heated to 112° F., the ether will be converted into vapor and occupy a certain portion, as AT, of the tube, holding in equilibrium the pressure of the atmosphere, together with the weight of the mercurial column whose height is TN.

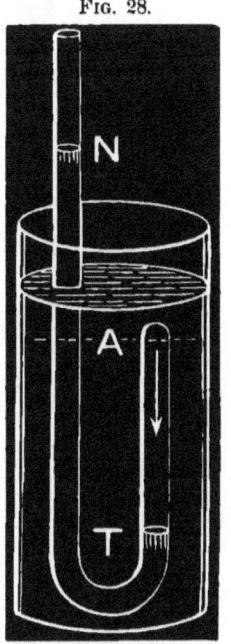

FIG. 28.

If the tube be withdrawn and cooled, the vapor will return to the liquid form again.

325. **Heat increases and cold decreases the tension of vapors.**—The illustration and proof of this principle have just been given (324).

The evaporation of liquids, however, takes place at temperatures much below their boiling points. Even at ordinary temperatures, water, many liquids, and some solids, vaporize. Mercury, whose boiling point is as high as 662° F., evaporates at all temperatures above 60°.

326. **Causes that accelerate evaporation.**—The principal causes which influence the amount and rapidity of evaporation are:

1. *Pressure.*—Increased pressure diminishes evaporation. The rapidity of evaporation is inversely as the pressure upon the surface of the liquid. Were the pressure of the air entirely removed, many liquids would assume a permanently aerial form.

2. *Increased surface* facilitates evaporation.
3. *Increased temperature* increases evaporation.
4. *Diminished quantity of vapor in the air,* or dry air, facilitates evaporation.
5. *Renewal or circulation of the air over the fluid* accelerates evaporation by constantly carrying away the saturated air, and allowing drier air to take its place.

327. **Causes of condensation.**—Condensation of vapor is its change from a vaporous to a liquid state. There are three causes of condensation: *chemical action, pressure,* and *diminution of temperature.*

1. *Chemical action.*—The affinity (2) of some substances for the vapor of water is so strong that they absorb it from the air, even when the latter is not saturated; such are quick-lime, potash, sulphuric acid, and others.

2. *Pressure.*—That pressure will condense vapor is shown by compressing a volume of saturated air.

3. *That a diminution of temperature* causes condensation is shown by the escape of steam, or breath, into cool air, which condenses the vapor into minute globules of water. This principle is shown, too, by Fig. 28 (324); also by the accumulation of water in warm weather, on the outside of a pitcher filled with ice-water.

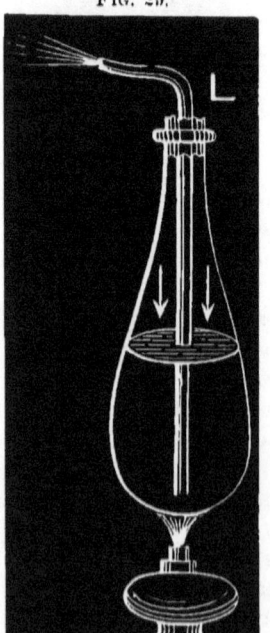

Fig. 29.

328. **Dew-point.**—If air, saturated with moisture, is cooled, a portion of the moisture will be precipitated as dew. The *dew-point* is the temperature at which this deposition takes place. The more fully the air is saturated with moisture, the nearer the dew-point is to the temperature of the atmosphere.

329. **Figure 29.—Pressure exerted by steam or heated vapor.**—This figure illustrates the pressure of heated vapor by confining the vapor over the surface of the evaporating liquid.

Fill the flask about two-thirds full of water, and pass a tube, L, through the stopper, so it will extend nearly to the bottom of the vessel. Let the steam or vapor be generated faster than it can escape at the nozzle of the pipe; then, as the generation of steam goes on, the increased pressure will be shown by the increased force with which the water will rush out of the nozzle, by the elastic force of the steam exerted on the surface of the liquid; indicated by the arrows. It is this elastic force of steam that constitutes the power of *high-pressure* steam-engines.

330. **Figure 30.—Candle-bombs, illustrating the explosion of steam-boilers.**—These are globules of glass, about the size of a pea, with a neck an inch, or so, long, in which *a drop* of water is confined by hermetically sealing the neck. When one of these is stuck into the wick of a lamp, as shown, the heat vaporizing the water, and there being no passage for the escape of the steam, the bulb is burst to pieces with a loud explosion. The mechanical force is wonderful, when it is considered how little water is employed. This is a miniature of what takes place in the bursting of high-pressure steam-boilers.

Fig. 30.

331. **Spheroidal state of liquids.**—If a few drops of water be poured upon a red-hot metal plate, as a common fire-shovel, they gather into a globule which rolls about without boiling, or coming into contact with the plate. In this condition the water is said to be in the *spheroidal state.*

The temperature of the plate is *higher* and that of the spheroid *lower* than the boiling point of the liquid. The temperature of the vapor from the spheroid is nearly the same as that of the plate. When the temperature of the plate falls to a certain point, the liquid will come into contact with it, and burst into ebullition, and quickly evaporate.

Causes of the spheroidal state of liquids.—1. *The repulsive force of heat* exerted between the plate and liquid. 2. *The hot plate converts a portion of the liquid into vapor,* upon which the spheroid rests. 3. *The vapor, being a poor conductor,* prevents the conduction of heat from the plate to the spheroid. 4. *Evaporation carries off the heat* as it is absorbed by the liquid, which assists in preventing it from entering into ebullition.

It is in accordance with these principle, that the hand may be bathed without harm in molten metals. The moisture of the hand, assuming the spheroidal state, prevents immediate contact between the hand and metal.

332. **Figure 31.—Condensation of steam.**—As a vapor will bear no *increase of pressure*, so neither will it suffer any *reduction of temperature*, without instantaneously condensing.

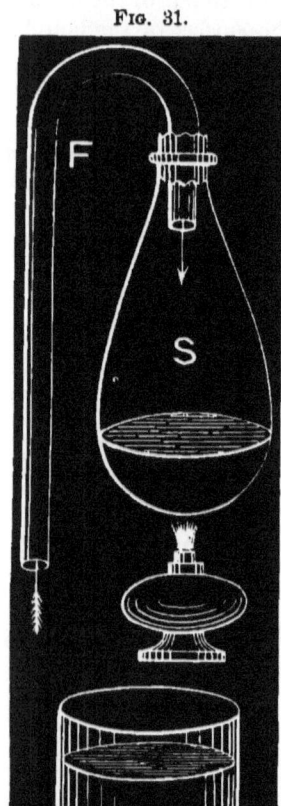

Fig. 31.

Pour some water in the vessel, S, provided with an open tube, F, and stopper, as shown; set the water to boiling by means of a spirit-lamp; and when the air has been expelled by the steam, remove the flask from the lamp, and insert the lower end of the tube into cold water, in the vessel, W. The vapor or steam in the tube will be condensed by the cold water, causing a vacuum, and the atmospheric pressure will force the water from W into the pipe, to fill it. In this way the entire flask and pipe will be filled. This operation will take place so rapidly and with such force as to dash the vessel to pieces or throw it from the grasp of the experimenter. The violence with which the water rushes into the flask, is due to the suddenness with which the condensation of the steam takes place throughout the entire vessel.

The low-pressure steam-engine depends upon this principle of rapid condensibility of vapor or steam for its superiority over the high-pressure engine.

333. **Figure 32.—Illustration of the principle of the low-pressure engine.**—This apparatus consists of a glass cylinder, blown into a bulb at its lower extremity, into which is placed some water. Into the cylinder is fitted a piston, with its rod or handle projecting through the cap or cover of the cylinder. In the cover are two openings to admit the egress and ingress of the air.

OPERATION.—If heat be applied to the bulb, and steam generated, the piston will be driven *upward* by the steam with a force equal to its elasticity, as indicated by the arrows at W. If now the cylinder be suddenly cooled, by dipping it in cold water or dashing cold water upon it, the steam will be condensed, and the *downward* pressure of the air will drive the piston down to fill the vacuum, with a force equal to 15 lbs. to the square inch, indicated by the arrows passing through the cover. This operation can be repeated at pleasure.

This apparatus, simple as it is, affords a practical illustration of the expansion and condensation of steam, and the atmospheric pressure, which constitute the motive power of the low-pressure steam-engine.

FIG. 32.   FIG. 33.

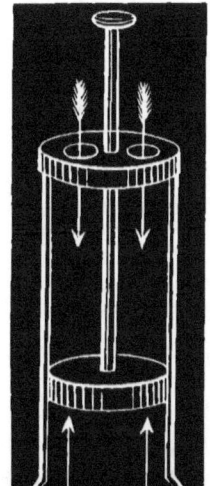
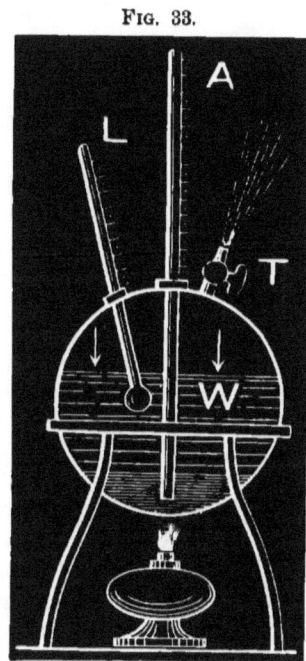

334. **Figure 33.—High-pressure steam.**—Under an increase of pressure the boiling point rises, and the elastic force of the steam evolved becomes correspondingly greater.

To demonstrate this, a spherical boiler is provided, having an inverted mercurial tube, A, with its mouth near the bottom of the boiler; a thermometer, L, with its bulb near the centre; and a stopcock, T. Sufficient mercury is poured into the boiler to supply the tube, A (shown by the fine lines); and sufficient water, W, to cover the thermometer bulb.

OPERATION.—With a spirit-lamp, set the water to boiling with the faucet open; and the thermometer will stand at 212°, which is the boiling point under the pressure of the air, or *one atmosphere* (15 lbs. to the square inch). If now the faucet be closed, the steam, exerting its elastic force on the surface of the boiling liquid, presses the mercury up the tube, A. The height of the mercury indicates the amount of

188 HEAT AND STEAM-ENGINE.

this pressure; and the thermometer, the corresponding change in the temperature of the boiling point. When the pressure equals *two atmospheres*, the thermometer will show that the boiling point has risen to 249°.5 F.

BOILING POINT OF WATER AT DIFFERENT ATMOSPHERIC PRESSURES.

NUMBER OF ATMOSPHERES.	BOILING POINT OF WATER.	NUMBER OF ATMOSPHERES.	BOILING POINT OF WATER.
1	212° F.	11	364°.2 F.
2	249.5	12	371.1
3	273.3	13	377.8
4	291.2	14	384.
5	306.	15	390.
6	318.2	16	395.
7	329.6	17	400.8
8	339.5	18	405.9
9	344.8	19	410.8
10	356.6	20	415.4

FROST-BEARER.—RAIN, SNOW, ETC.

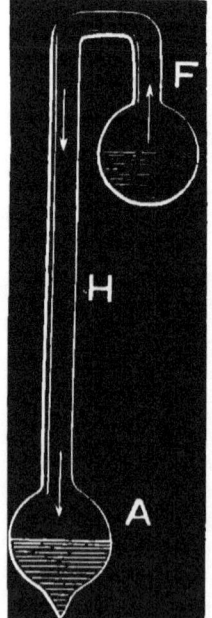

Fig. 34.

335. **Figure 34.—Freezing by evaporation—the cryophorus, or frost-bearer.** —In this simple instrument water may be frozen by cold *produced by its own evaporation*. It consists of a bent tube, half an inch or more in diameter, with a bulb, A and F, at each end, as represented. The bulb, F, is filled about a third full of water, and the rest of the space in the instrument is full of air, and only filled with vapor of the water.

If now the bulb, A, be immersed in a freezing mixture (309) of nitric acid and snow, the water in the distant bulb, F, will soon be frozen. The explanation is simple. The vapor in A is rapidly condensed, and the rapid evaporation of the *water* in F, to supply the place of the vapor condensed below, absorbs or renders latent (303) so much of its own heat as to reduce it to the freezing point. The movement of the vapor is indicated by the arrows.

336. **Rain** is the vapor of the clouds, or of

the air, condensed and precipitated to the earth in drops. Rain is generally occasioned by the union of two or more volumes of humid air, differing considerably in temperature; the several portions, when mingled, being incapable of absorbing the same amount of moisture that each would retain if they had not united. Hence the production of rain is the result of the law, that the capacity of air for moisture decreases in a *greater ratio* than the temperature.

If the excess of moisture or vapor is great, it falls as drops or rain; if it is of slight amount, it appears as clouds.

337. **Snow** is the *frozen* moisture that descends from the atmosphere. The largest flakes occur when the atmosphere is loaded with moisture, and the temperature is about 32° F.; as the cold increases, the flakes become smaller.

338. **Hail** is the moisture of the air frozen into globules of ice. Hail-stones are generally pear-shaped; and formed of alternate layers of ice and snow, around a white, snowy nucleus.

339. **Figure 35.—Rain gauge.**—This is an instrument designed to measure the quantity of rain which falls at any given time and place. It may be made of copper or zinc, and in the form represented.

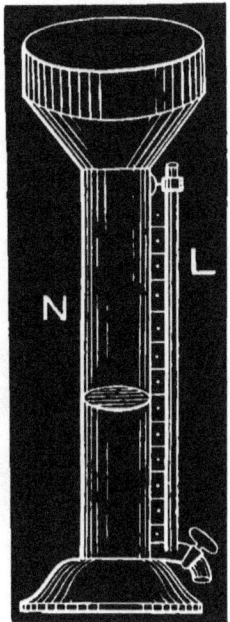

Fig. 35.

For convenience, a communicating glass tube, L, is arranged outside of the receiving vessel, and provided with a graduated scale, as shown. The faucet is provided for drawing off the water. If the funnel at the top is twice the size of the cylinder, N, then *an inch* on the scale would indicate *half an inch* in the gauge.

340. **Distribution of rain.**—As a general rule, it may be stated that the higher the average temperature of a country, the greater will be the amount of rain that falls. Local causes, however, produce remarkable departures from this rule.

In Egypt it scarcely ever rains. Along the coast of Peru, for a long distance, it *never* rains. No rain ever falls on some portions of the coast of Africa, while in Guiana it rains during a great part of the year, as also at the Straits of Magellan, and in the Islands of Chiloe (S. lat. 43°).

341. **Days of rain.**—The *rainy days* are more numerous in high than in low latitudes, as is seen in the following table, although the *annual amount* of rain which falls is smaller.

North Latitude.	Mean Annual Number of Rainy Days.
From 12° to 43°	78.
" 43° " 46°	103.
" 46° " 50°	134.
" 50° " 60°	161.

342. **Annual depth of rain.**—The greatest annual depth of rain occurs at San Luis, Maranham, 280 inches; the next in order are Vera Cruz, 278; Grenada, 126; Cape François, 120; Calcutta, 81; Rome, 39; London, 25; Uttenburg, 12.5; Hanover, N. H., 38; New York State, 36; Ohio, 42; Missouri, 38.

343. **Figure 36.—Hygrometer, or moisture measurer.**—The use of this instrument is to show the state of moisture in the atmosphere. It consists of two glass bulbs, connected by a glass tube twice bent, as shown. The bulb, A, contains a small quantity of ether, by the boiling of which the air has been expelled from the instrument. It contains a small thermometer with its bulb in the ether. The bulb, T, is covered with muslin. Upon the supporting column is attached another thermometer.

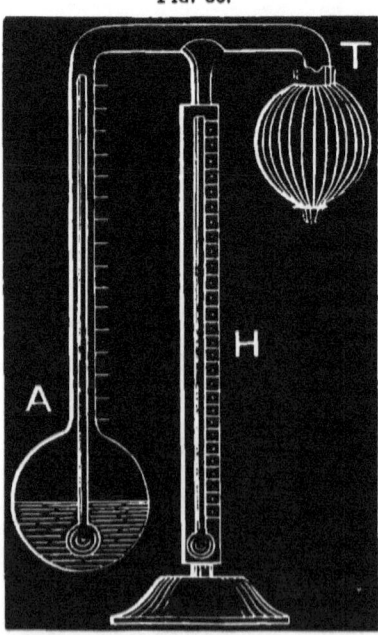

FIG. 36.

OPERATION.—Let fall a few drops of ether upon the bulb, T, and its evaporation will reduce the temperature of the bulb, A, by causing the ether within to evaporate to supply vapor to take the place of the condensed vapor in T (see Fig. 34). When the temperature of the bulb, A, is thus sufficiently reduced, the moisture of the air will begin to accumulate upon the outside. This is called the *dew-point*, the temperature of which is shown by the thermometer within. The temperature of the dew-point varies with the amount of moisture in the air (328). The greater the amount of moisture, the nearer the dew-point is to the temperature of the air; hence the difference between the two thermometers will indicate the relative humidity of the atmosphere. The drier the air the greater is this difference.

344. **Figure 37.—Combustion and structure of flame.—** The diagram illustrates some of the principles involved in the burning of a jet of illuminating (hydro-carbon) gas.

There are four simple elements or kinds of matter, which, combined in various proportions, make up the great bulk of all organic bodies, both animal and vegetable. These are *oxygen, hydrogen, carbon,* and *nitrogen,* and may be called *the four organic elements.*

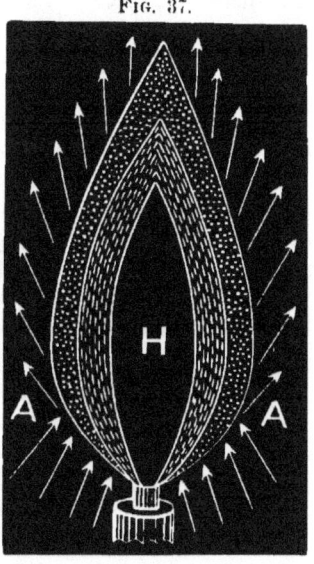

Fig. 37.

Of these four elements, *carbon* and *hydrogen* are those which impart to organic compounds the property of *combustibility;* the oxygen and nitrogen in them only regulating the intensity with which they burn. The compounds employed as sources of heat and light, contain organized hydrogen and carbon. Carbon and hydrogen burned separately, give rise each to a large amount of heat; but they exist in different forms, and burn in different ways. Carbon is a solid, and remains so during combustion. Hydrogen is a gas, and burns as a gas; and if set free, it diffuses into the air, and thus burns while in motion, giving rise to flame, and heating the particles of carbon to a white heat, which is the principal source of the luminosity of flame.

The best illuminators, therefore, are pure hydro-carbons, composed of an equal number of atoms, or equivalents, of each.

The diagram represents a section of a gas-jet flame. The burning of other substances, as tallow, liquid oils, etc., involve the same principles; for these must be, and are, *converted into gas before they are burned.*

The gas-jet or candle-flame is not a solid mass of fire, but a hollow shell of light, and is dark within, as shown by the diagram; H being the dark space. The dark chamber within is filled with the combustible gas.

Illuminating gases being composed, in part, of hydrogen, they are lighter than the air, and tend to rise, which, with the heat of combustion, produce an upward current, causing the flame to ascend, and giving it a conical or pointed form.

The air being composed of 1 part of oxygen to 4 of nitrogen (124), affords just enough free oxygen to support safe combustion (211). The free oxygen of the air chemically combining with the hydrogen and carbon, constitutes the combustion; which results in water and carbonic acid gas.

The hydrogen is oxidized first, producing intense heat, which sets free the minute particles of carbon, and heats them to whiteness, giving rise to a vivid white light. But if the particles of carbon are sufficiently heated, they become oxidized and lose their luminosity or whiteness.

Now, by observing an actual gas-jet, it will be noticed that at the lower part of the flame, where the arrows (in the diagram) point *toward* the jet (up as far as AA), the flame is dark, or nearly so. This is because the abundant supply of air (represented by the same arrows) affords sufficient oxygen to cause complete combustion at this point of the flame; and the outer portion of the flame (shown by the dots) is also *bluish* instead of *white*, for the reason that, coming in contact with the air, it receives sufficient oxygen to render the combustion more complete than it is a little deeper in the flame, but not so complete as at the bottom; hence the surface is not *as* dark as the bottom. That part of the flame between the dark chamber, II, within, and the bluish portion without, is the principal illuminating part of the blaze. In this part of the flame the amount of oxygen of the air is only sufficient to burn the hydrogen, the heat of which only whitens, but does not *burn* the carbon; while the dark chamber within is nothing but the hydro-carbon gas itself; no oxygen of the air coming in contact with it to set up combustion.

The arrows above AA show the upward currents of the air and gases after combustion.

STEAM-ENGINES.

345. **Origin of the steam-engine.**—A steam-engine is any contrivance for converting heat into mechanical energy through the medium of water.

The first rudiments of knowledge of steam as a motor date back of modern times. As early as 130 years before the Christian era, Heiro describes, among other curious contrivances, the *eolipile.*

346. **Figure 38.—The eolipile.**—A form of this apparatus is shown by the figure. It consists of a metallic globular boiler, A, provided with two hollow arms, holding a hollow cross-bar, T, from which project two other arms, at the ends of which, on opposite sides, are openings for steam to escape. In the boiler is water, which is converted to steam by heat. The steam passes into the cross-bar, where it comes in contact with the side-arms of the boiler, and escapes at the openings, as shown. The escaping steam recoils on the atmosphere, and revolves the cross-bar with great rapidity. The mechanical principle involved is the same as that of Barker's Mill (163), the pressure of steam taking the place of the pressure of water.

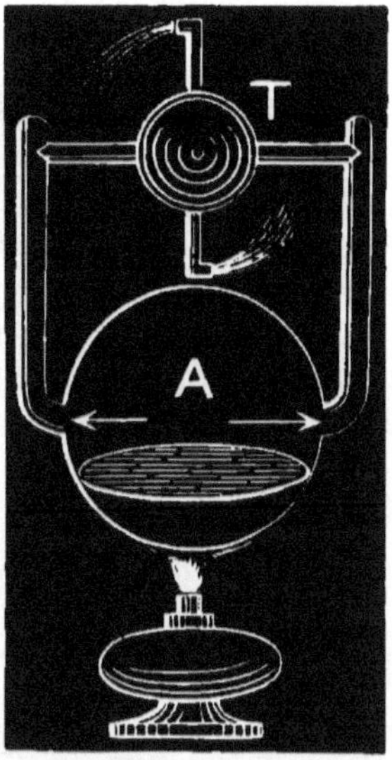

FIG. 38.

347. **Improvements in steam-engines.**—It cannot be expected that in a work like this an explanation and history can be given of the many improvements which, from time to time, have been made in the construction of the steam-engine. The essential principles, however, involved in the application of steam as a motor, and the principal parts of high-pressure and low-pressure engines, will be understood by reference to what has already been said, and to the following five illustrations and their explanations.

Whatever may have been the construction of the first contrivance that merited the name of *steam-engine,* or when, or where, or by whom invented, there was nothing that could compare with the improvements made by James Watt, in 1769. What was done before was important chiefly in leading the way to his improvements. Of course, many minor and some important improvements have been made in the construction of engines since Watt's time; but no general principles of importance have since been discovered.

348. **Reciprocating and rotary motion of engines.**—There are rotary steam-engines, but these are not commonly employed. All steam-engines in general use are reciprocating; that is, they are provided with a cylinder and piston. The steam works the piston back and forth in the cylinder (as will be seen); and this is called *reciprocating motion;* which is converted, by means of a crank, into *rotary motion.* There are many objections to reciprocating engines which would be wholly obviated by rotary engines, were it possible to simplify the construction of the latter, and render them as durable as the former.

349. **Figure 39.—The high-pressure engine.**—The high-pressure engine is employed for railroad locomotives and small steamboats, especially harbor tugboats, and all, or nearly all, stationary engines.

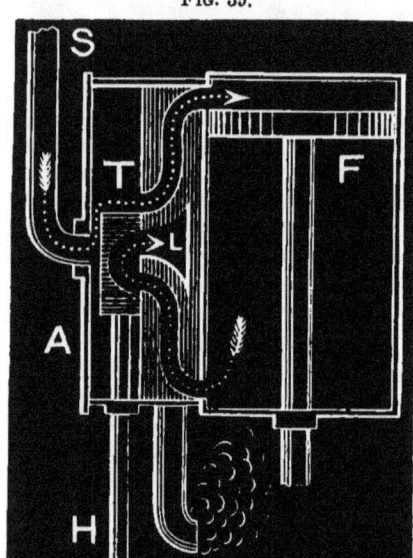

FIG. 39.

In this machine, the escape steam is driven out against the pressure of the atmosphere; and instead of advantage being taken of the condensibility (332 and 333) of the steam and atmospheric pressure, the steam must exert a force of 15 lbs. to the square inch, to overcome the atmospheric pressure, *before* it becomes effective for use; yet the lightness, simplicity, compactness, and low cost of the high-pressure engine render it available, notwithstanding its uneconomical use of steam, in many places where the low-pressure or condensing engine could not be employed.

In the figure, F is the piston, fitted steam-tight to the cylinder which surrounds it; S, the steam-pipe that conveys the steam from the boiler into the steam-chest, A, which communicates with the interior of the cylinder at the top and bottom. N is the discharge or ejection pipe, which communicates with the opening, L, in the bottom of the steam-chest; T, the cut-off or slide-valve, which is fastened to and operated by the rod, H, passing through the end of the steam-chest.

OPERATION.—As the piston stands (in the figure), the steam from the steam-pipe passes into the steam-chest and through it into the cylinder above the piston, as shown by the arrow, which presses it down to the bottom of the cylinder, while the steam below the piston is driven out through the lower passage into the opening, L, as shown by the other arrow, which communicates with the ejection-pipe.

If now the sliding-valve, T, be moved up, by means of its rod, H, until its upper bearing (now between the arrows) passes the upper passage, it will connect the upper passage with the discharge-pipe, as now the lower passage is, while it will open a communication between the steam-chest and the lower end of the cylinder, as now there is between it and the upper end.

The sliding-valve being thus moved, the steam will now force the piston back. By alternately shifting the valve, the steam is alternately admitted and discharged at the opposite ends of the cylinder, above and below the piston.

The supply of steam, and the connection of the piston-rod to the resistance to be overcome, and the means of working the valves, will be shown hereafter.

350. **Figure 40.—The eccentric.—Its importance.**—As at every stroke of the piston the valves must be shifted or reversed, it is important that the engine itself be made to perform this operation; as it is only by this means that the steam-engine can be made automatic in its operations, and without which it would possess but a limited usefulness.

To accomplish this indispensable part of the operation is the object of the eccentric, which consists of a wheel, keyed on the main shaft of the engine; the hole, through which the shaft passes, being made, instead of at the centre, at one side of the centre, as at S. Around the periphery of this wheel, in a groove, is clasped an iron band, bolted together, as at LL. E is simply an opening in the wheel, made to lighten it and save metal. From this band extends a rod, A, called the eccentric-rod, which is welded to, and is a part of, the valve-rod, as H in the last diagram.

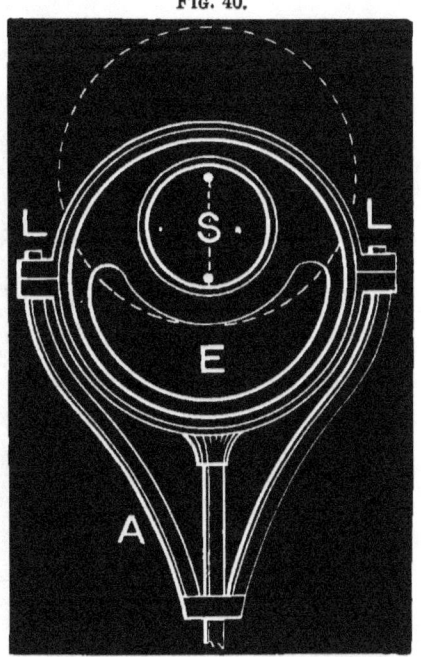

Fig. 40.

OPERATION.—As the shaft, S, revolves, the wheel turns in the band. Suppose the shaft to be revolved half a turn, which is accomplished by a single stroke of the piston of the engine; then the wheel will take the position of the dotted circle, which will lift the eccentric-rod, A, a distance equal to the distance from the upper point of the circumference of the wheel, in its former position, to the upper point of the dotted circle; which is sufficient to shift or reverse the valves. Thus, at every stroke of the piston and every half revolution of the shaft, the valves are reversed by the eccentric.

351. **Figure 41.—Steam-boiler and operation of steam-valves.**—Boilers are made of heavy plate-iron, firmly riveted together, provided with suitable means for heating them, to produce steam. They are partly filled with water, the balance of the space being filled with steam, which supplies the engine.

The object of the three faucets, 1, 2, 3, is to enable the engineer to ascertain, at any moment, the amount of water there may be in the

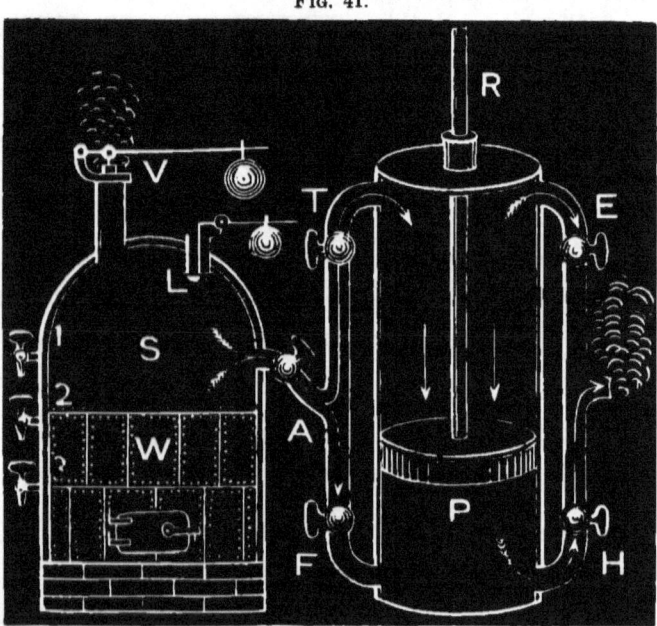

Fig. 41.

boiler. As the water, W, should be kept about on a level with the middle faucet, if the *upper* faucet be opened there should escape from it only *steam;* but if *water* should escape, it shows there is too much water in the boiler. If mingled water and steam escape from the *middle* faucet it shows the boiler is properly filled; but if only steam escapes, it shows the water is low; and if steam issues from the lower faucet it indicates the water is *dangerously low.* The level of the water in the boiler is also shown by communicating glass tubes arranged on the outside of the boiler.

V is an outward-acting safety-valve, to allow the steam to escape when its pressure has reached the point beyond which it is unsafe. The ball and lever, and the size of the valve, enable the engineer to determine and fix the limit of pressure at different times.

The inward-working safety-valve, L, is to prevent the boiler from being collapsed by the atmospheric pressure without, in the event of the steam becoming condensed within.

A is the *throttle-valve*, which governs the supply or flow of steam to the cylinder; P, the piston; R, the piston-rod, passing through a stuffing-box at the head of the cylinder. The action of the steam on the piston is controlled by the four valves, T, E, F, and H. By tracing the arrows (which represent steam) out of the boiler, it will be seen that T is open and F closed, so that the piston is being driven down by the pressure of the steam on its upper surface, as indicated by the two short arrows; while the steam below the piston is being driven through the valve H, and kept from escaping above the piston by the closed valve E, as the arrows indicate.

By reversing the valves, the piston will be forced in the opposite direction; and so on.

There are many ways of arranging the valves in different engines; but, however constructed and arranged, the principle of reversing them is the same.

352. **Condensation in steam-engines.**—Referring to the above diagram (Fig. 41), if by any means the valve, H, could be closed, and the steam, below the piston, suddenly condensed, the upward pressure or resistance of the atmosphere (15 lbs. to the square inch) would be removed; which would be equivalent to increasing the elastic force of the steam 15 lbs. to the square inch. This, however, is accomplished by the condensing or low-pressure engine (Fig. 43).

The advantage of the atmospheric pressure on a piston of *two feet diameter is nearly three and a half tons.*

353. **Figure 42.—Stuffing-boxes.**—The object of these is to furnish a working steam-tight joint or fitting between the piston-rod and cylinder-head; as also to provide such a joint or packing in all cases where gases, vapors, or fluids are to be confined against pressure.

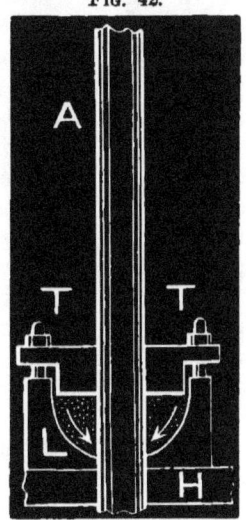

Fig. 42.

Let H be a section of the piston-head, with a hollow, dish-like projection, L, on its upper surface, filled with cotton, hemp, or other fibrous substance, shown by the small dots; over which is placed a downward projecting disk or collar, which crowds upon the fibrous substance, and drives or presses it against the rod, A, as represented by the direction of the arrows. The force with which the hemp or other material is pressed against the piston-rod is regulated by the two bolts and nuts, TT.

354. Figure 43.—The low-pressure or condensing engine (see frontispiece).—The low-pressure engine is employed on all large steamboats, and in situations where economy of fuel and the greatest mechanical effects from it are the principal considerations.

Owing to the nearly perfect vacuum obtained by the condenser and air-pump, about 14 lbs. to the square inch of the atmospheric pressure is removed, which adds so much to the mechanical energy of the steam (352). Hence, with a pressure of only 10 lbs. of steam to the inch, a mechanical force of 24 lbs. to the inch is obtained; which shows the propriety of the term *low-pressure* engine.

S is the steam-pipe, which conveys the steam from the boiler to the engine; just at the opening of which is seen the throttle-valve, which controls the flow of steam. B is a double-acting cylinder; N, the valve-rod, provided with adjustable arms, and connected to the valves in the steam-chests; Y, a right-angular bar or lever, which works the valve-rod; F, the eccentric-rod, that operates the valve-lever; U, the fly-wheel, on the shaft of which is the eccentric; D, the pitman, which connects the working-beam above with the crank of the shaft; Z, a beam on which rests the bearing of the working-beam; HIJK, the parallelogram which produces parallel motion and vertical action of the piston-rod; JR, the radius-rod. The beam, on which the working-beam rests, is supported by an iron column in the centre; O, a triangular bar to communicate the action of the governor to the throttle-valve, S, in the steam-pipe. EE is the cold-water cistern, in which is contained and immersed the condenser, L, and air-pump, T; V, the rod which opens the passage for cold water to pass from the cistern into the condenser; P, the pump which draws the hot water from the hot-water chamber (above A) in the cistern, and sends it to the boiler; W, the pump which supplies the cistern with cold water from the well or other source.

Operation.—By means of the eccentric on the shaft, the eccentric-rod, F, and right-angle lever, Y, and arms on the valve-rod, N, the valves in the steam-chests (at the upper and lower ends of the cylinder) are alternately reversed, as the piston is moved up and down. The exhaust-steam is met in the condenser, L, by a jet of cold water from the cistern, EE, which condenses the residuum steam and produces a vacuum (332) in the cylinder, on the side of the piston opposite to the pressure of the steam. The condenser, L, is kept exhausted of water and air by means of the air-pump, T. The outward-working valve at the bottom of the condenser, and the upward-working valve in the plunger of the air-pump, will be readily understood.

As the piston of the air-pump, T, descends, the valve in the hot-water chamber closes to prevent the hot water from returning to the air-pump; and the valve between the air-pump and condenser closes to prevent the contents of the air-pump from returning to the condenser.

The air-pump discharges its water into the hot-water cistern above A, from which it is drawn by the pump P, and, to economize heat, is sent through the dotted pipe in the brick-work to contribute toward feeding the boiler.

The cistern, EE, is kept supplied with cold water by the pump, W.

The governor.—The throttle-valve, S, which admits steam to the piston, is controlled by the governor; which consists of two heavy iron balls, suspended on arms, as shown. These arms are pivoted on a central spindle, which is made to revolve by means of a cord or belt (shown by the dotted lines passing over the two friction rollers) connecting the main shaft with a pulley at the bottom of the spindle. The balls are swung out from the spindle by centrifugal force. If the engine is running too fast, the balls, by rising higher, will draw the sliding collar or sleeve, M, down on the spindle, which throws the perpendicular arm of the right-angle bar to the right; which, being connected to the arm of the throttle-valve by an iron rod, partially closes the valve, and thus diminishes the supply of steam. When, by this means, the speed of the engine is sufficiently reduced, the balls, being depressed by gravity, reverse the motion of the throttle-valve and again let on more steam.

The arm of the throttle-valve is provided with a series of holes to regulate its opening, to adjust the supply of steam to the amount of work to be performed by the engine at different times.

The fly-wheel.—As the crank revolves, there are two points or positions where it is said to be on "*the dead-centre.*" When the pitman, D, works vertically, the dead-centres are at the highest and lowest points reached by the crank-pin. If the engine is at rest and the crank is in either of these two positions, the fly-wheel must be revolved a little, by hand, before the steam can move it, as all its force would act in a straight line running through the centre of the shaft, which would have no tendency to revolve the wheel.

There are also two points, in the revolution of the crank where the power of the steam is the most *effective* in revolving the wheel; and these are at right angles—or 90°—from the dead-centre points. From 2 (one of the dead-centres) the power obtains a stronger and stronger hold on the crank until it reaches the position of 1 (the piston being at "half stroke"); then its hold grows less and less until it reaches the opposite dead-centre point, where, again, the power becomes wholly ineffective to revolve the crank; and so on.

This will explain one of the reasons why a heavy fly-wheel is indispensable with a single-crank engine. As there are but two points in each revolution of the crank where the power of the steam can exert its entire force, it becomes necessary to employ the fly-wheel, to equalize the power in its application to the resistance, and give the engine a steady and uniform motion.

In steamboats, however, the weight of the crank and wheels, together with the motion of the boat, act as a substitute for a fly-wheel. The wheels of railroad locomotives and the momentum of the entire machines act as fly-wheels.

The unequal resistance offered to the engine from one moment to another, as in rolling-mills, etc., also makes it necessary to employ the fly-wheel, as otherwise the engine at one moment would be resisted beyond its power, while at another it would have no resistance.

Parallel motion.—The object of the parallelogram, HIJK, is to produce an upright or vertical motion to the piston-rod without slides; though slides are now usually employed. The radius, JR, being fixed at R to the beam, determines the arc of the circle through which the point, J, moves, which causes the point, K, or head of the piston-rod, to travel in a straight perpendicular line.

CHAPTER X.

(CHART NO. 5.)

OPTICS.

General Properties of Light.

355. **Definitions.—Optics.**—Optics is that branch of Physics which treats of the nature and properties of light.

Light is that mysterious agent which, acting upon the organs of vision, produces the sensation of sight. Light unfolds to us the beauties of nature, and brings us into convenient and pleasing relation with surrounding objects.

356. **Nature of light.—Theories.**—Two theories have been advanced to account for the phenomena of light; the *Corpuscular* or *Emission Theory,* and the *Wave* or *Undulatory Theory.*

According to the *corpuscular* or *emission theory,* light consists of infinitely small particles of matter shot forth from burning or luminous bodies, with immense velocity, which, falling upon the retina of the eye, produce the sensation of sight.

According to the *wave* or *undulatory theory,* light consists of waves or undulations in the ethereal medium, caused by luminous bodies acting upon it; and that these waves dash upon the retina of the eye, producing sight; same as waves of air fall upon the ear, and produce the sensation of sound. By this theory no matter whatever is thrown off from the luminous body. The ethereal medium which the luminous body acts upon or sets in motion, is supposed to be universally existent, impalpable or imponderable, and extremely elastic.

Though there has been a great diversity of opinion respecting the nature of light, the *undulatory* theory is now most generally received, as it more satisfactorily accounts for the various phenomena; though it is difficult to explain all the phenomena of light even on this theory. No theory of light is entirely satisfactory.

357. **Sources of light.**—Bodies which give out or emit light are called *luminous bodies.* The sources of light are the *sun, stars, heat, chemical combinations, phosphorescence,* and *electricity.*

Nothing is known of the cause of the light emitted by the sun and stars. It is known, however, that bodies become luminous at a high temperature, and the greater the intensity of the heat, the more vividly they shine.

Artificial light, as of candles, lamps, gas, etc., is due to combustion of substances containing carbon and hydrogen. See structure of flame, 344. The chemical action in such cases disengages more or less intense heat, as the burning body becomes luminous.

Phosphorescence is a pale light emitted in the dark by certain substances which do not appear to emit any sensible heat, a beautiful specimen of which may be seen by looking at cold boiled lobster in the dark. It has been observed in animals, vegetables, and minerals; the glow-worm and fire-fly emit it. Under certain conditions of the air and water, magnificent displays of it may be seen in the track of a steamboat in salt-water. The cause of phosphorescence is not known, but in some cases it appears to depend upon electricity.

Electricity is a source of light so intense that its brightness is equal, in some cases, from one-fifth to one-fourth that of the sun.

358. **Similarity of light and heat.**—There are several reasons for supposing that the *thermal, luminous,* and *chemical* rays (420) of sunbeams are one and the same; among which are:

1. Light and radiant heat are reflected, refracted, dispersed, and polarized in the same way.

2. The dark lines in the solar spectrum are devoid of heat.

3. Similar dark and cold lines exist in the obscure part of the spectrum beyond the red end where the heat is most intense.

4. There is an absence of both heat and chemical action in the dark lines found in the luminous part of the spectrum.

359. **Relation of different bodies to light.**—Bodies, as related to light, are either luminous, non-luminous, transparent, translucent, or opaque.

Luminous bodies are those in which light originates, as the sun and burning bodies.

Non-luminous bodies are those which are seen by reflected light, as the earth, the moon, a rock, a house, etc.

Transparent bodies, also said to be diaphanous (meaning to shine through), permit light to pass through them freely, as glass, water, and air.

Translucent bodies are such as imperfectly transmit light, but not sufficiently to show the outlines of objects, as ground glass, oiled paper, thin porcelain, etc.

Opaque bodies are those which do not ordinarily allow any light to pass through them, as wood, iron, etc.; though thin leaves of some metals partially transmit some colors; thin leaves of gold, for instance, transmit a beautiful violet-green light.

360. **A medium.—Propagation of light in a homogeneous medium.**—A medium is *luminiferous* when it transmits light, and it is *homogeneous* when its composition and density are the same in all its parts. All space is supposed to be pervaded by such a medium, called *luminiferous ether*. In a homogeneous medium light always moves in straight lines, as may be shown by admitting light into a dark chamber by a very small opening, which renders the course of the light visible, by its illumination of the fine particles of dust always floating in the air. Media, such as water, air, and glass, are pervaded among their particles by the luminiferous ether, but not always in such a state as to permit the transmission of light.

361. **Absorption of light.**—No body is perfectly transparent; all intercept or absorb a portion of light. Some media, which in thin layers are transparent, intercept or absorb most of the light, if they be very thick. Opaque bodies absorb all of the light falling upon them which is not reflected (see Opaque Bodies, 359). The cause of absorption is some peculiarity of molecular constitution, which breaks up and neutralizes the waves of light that enter them.

Though the air appears perfectly transparent, much of the light of the sun is absorbed by it in reaching the earth, shown by the greater brilliancy of the stars when viewed from high mountain-tops. In fact, so great is the clearness of vision in the higher regions of the atmosphere, that it becomes exceedingly difficult to judge of distances.

FIG. 1.

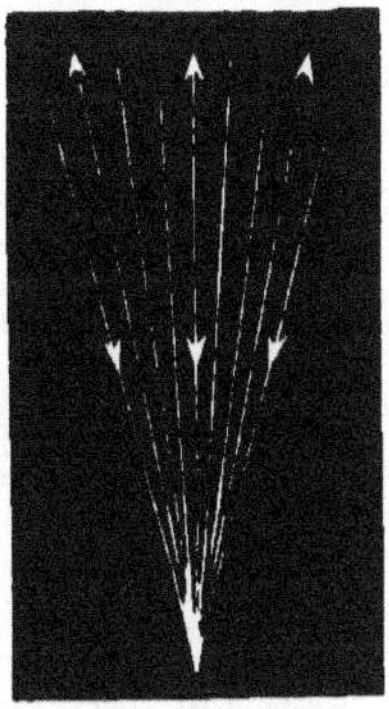

362. **Figure 1.—Rays, pencils, and beams of light.**—A single line of light is called a *ray*.

A *pencil* of light is a collection of rays diverging from or converging to a common point, as shown in the diagram. Hence there are *converging* and *diverging* rays.

A *beam* of light is a small collection of parallel rays, such as would pass through a hole in a shutter, from a distant body, as the sun.

363. **Figure 2.—Visible bodies emit light from every point, and in every direction,** the rays diverging from each point in straight lines. The two eyes, in the figure, receive rays of light from the same three points of the arrow, but not the same rays. So each and every point of the object emits light in every direction, but the eye in any one position only takes in the rays that come in its direction. There are no vacant spaces among the rays, as at B, in the diagram, but the entire space is filled with rays crossing each other at every point.

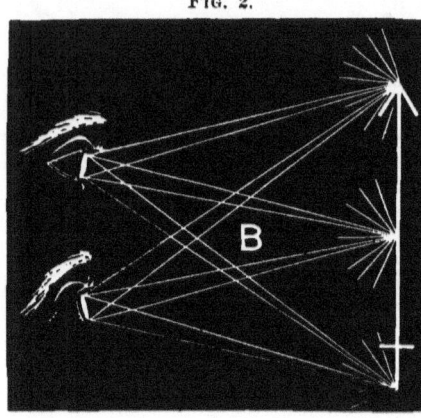

Fig. 2.

364. **Properties of light.**—Light falling upon any substance is either absorbed, dispersed, reflected, or refracted.

Absorption.—Light falling upon a black substance partly disappears, and is said to be *absorbed*. No substances absorb all the light.

Dispersion.—Light falling upon opaque bodies causes them to emit light in all directions, and thus become visible. Such bodies are said to *disperse* light, because they scatter it. Light is thus dispersed by the innumerable little *facets* of the particles composing the rough surfaces.

Reflection.—Light falling upon polished surfaces is thrown off in a regular manner, as a ball rebounds from a floor.

Refraction is the bending of a ray of light, caused by passing obliquely from one transparent medium to another.

CATOPTRICS, OR REFLECTION OF LIGHT.

Reflectors—Mirrors—Specula.

365. **Reflectors** are solid bodies bounded by regular surfaces, highly polished, and capable of reflecting a large portion of the light which falls upon them.

366. **Mirrors and specula.**—*Mirrors* are reflectors made of glass and coated with an amalgam of tin and quicksilver.

Specula are reflectors made of metal, highly polished. Thirty-two parts of copper to fifteen of tin make the best metallic reflectors.

367. Forms of reflectors.—Reflectors are either *plane* or *curved*. Curved mirrors or specula may be *spherical, elliptical,* or *paraboloid*. A *concave* spherical mirror is a portion of the interior surface of a sphere. A *convex* spherical mirror is a portion of the exterior surface of a sphere.

A line passing through the centre of and perpendicular to a spherical reflector, is called the *axis* or *principal axis*. The centre of the sphere, of which the mirror forms a part, is called the *centre* or *optical centre*. The middle point of the mirror is called the *vertex*. For *paraboloid* reflectors, see 392.

In the use of glass mirrors, a portion of light reflected from the first surface interferes with the perfection of the image (398); hence, where the most perfect instruments are required, metallic reflectors are employed.

368. The laws of reflection of light are the same as those of reflection of heat, illustrated by Fig. 20, Chart 4 (291), and are thus stated:

1st. *The incident ray, the perpendicular at the point of incidence, and the reflected ray, are all situated in the same plane.*

2d. *The angles of incidence and reflection are equal.*

369. Direction in which objects are seen.—Whenever the light passes in a straight line from the object to the eye, the object will be seen exactly where it is; but when, by reflection or refraction, the rays are turned from their first direction, *the object will be seen, and so appear to be, in the direction in which the rays are passing at the point where they enter the eye.*

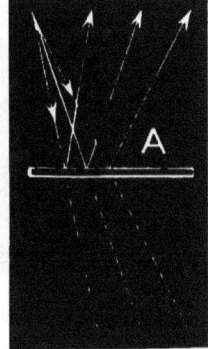

FIG. 3.

Reflection at Plane Surfaces.

370. Figure 3.—Reflection of diverging rays.—In accordance with the second law of reflection (368), diverging rays before reflection will be equally divergent after reflection, as shown by the diagram, in which A is the plane mirror.

Reflection from a plane mirror, therefore, changes the direction of the rays, and removes the point of *apparent* convergence or divergence to the opposite side of the reflector. The dotted lines show the course which the rays would take if the mirror were removed.

***371*. Figure 4.—Reflection of converging rays.**—In accordance with the same law, converging rays before reflection will converge after reflection. The degree of convergence before and after reflection will be the same; and the reflected rays will meet at a point as far in *front* of the mirror, E, as the point at which they would meet (shown by the dotted lines) is *behind* it, if the mirror were removed.

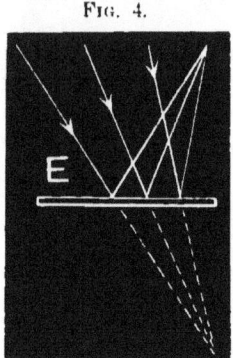

Fig. 4.

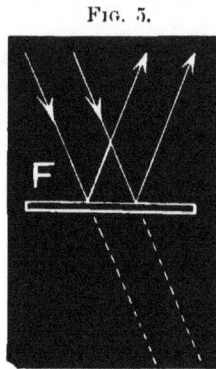

Fig. 5.

***372*. Figure 5.—Reflection of parallel rays.**—In accordance with the same law, parallel rays before reflection will be parallel after reflection, as illustrated by the diagram.

***373*. Figure 6.—Convex, plane, and concave mirrors.**—A ray of light from the lamp, T, falling upon the point, H, of the plane mirror, KP, will be reflected to the eye at L. The line, HN,

Fig. 6.

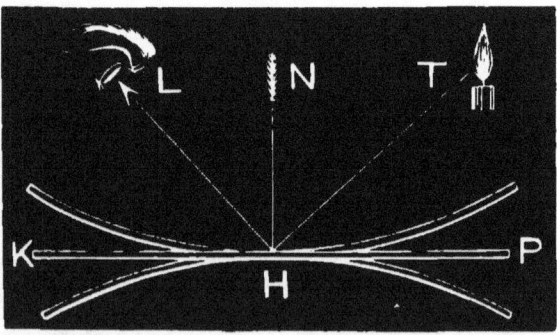

being perpendicular to all three of the mirrors at the point, H, the same ray, TH, in accordance with the second law of reflection, would be reflected to the same point, L, by each of the three mirrors.

374. **Figure 7.—The intensity of reflected light** increases with the magnitude of the angle of incidence. If the light of the candle be reflected by a piece of paper to the eyes, E and F, it will be more intense at E than at F, because the angle of incidence (THN, Fig. 6) is greater at B than at A.

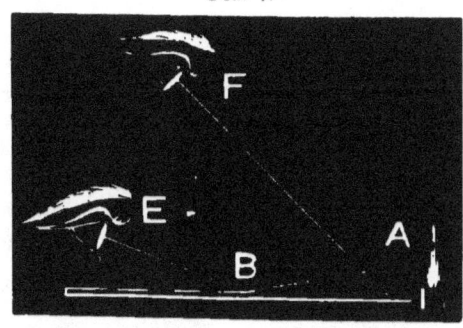

FIG. 7.

This is illustrated by the fact, that near sunset the reflected rays of the sun are so brilliant, the eyes can hardly bear to look at them, while at mid-day we observe them without difficulty.

Highly-polished metallic surfaces, however, reflect more light as the angle of incidence diminishes, the greatest amount being reflected when the incident rays are perpendicular to the surface.

The intensity of the reflected light will also depend upon the nature and degree of polish of the reflector.

The most perfect reflector does not reflect all the light, but diffuses a part of it.

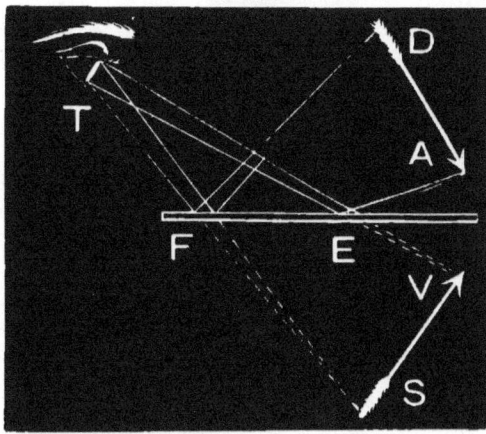

375. **Figure 8.—Images formed by plane reflectors.— Virtual image.**—Let AD be an object placed in front of a plane horizontal mirror. The light from the points, A and D, will be reflected to the eye at T. The rays from A will *appear* to come from a

point, V, as far behind the mirror as A is in front of it. The same is true of the point, D, and every other point of the object. Hence, *the object will appear to be situated as far behind as it actually is in front of the reflector.*

If we stand with our right arm toward the mirror, the image will *appear* to have the *left* arm toward the mirror; or the image is reversed laterally. This is because the image of *each point* is as far behind the mirror as the point of the object is in front. The image will also be erect and full size. Hence, *the object and image are symmetrically situated with respect to the mirror.*

The *virtual image*, therefore, is an image which *appears* to exist.

If a person approaches a mirror, his image seems to come forward to meet him.

376. **Figure 9.—Multiplicity of images** of a single object seen by means of inclined reflectors. When an object is placed between two mirrors, which make with each other an angle of 90°, or less, several images are produced, varying in number according to the inclination of the mirrors. If they are perpendicular to each other, *three* images will be seen, as represented by the diagram. Let L be the object, and the heavy lines the two mirrors. Place the dividers at N, and draw the dotted circle, and an image of the object will be seen by the eye at each of the points, 1, 2, and 3. The plain arrow-lines represent the incident and reflected rays by which the object is seen. The straight dotted lines show where the object *seems* to be, and hence the three images. It will be noticed that the image 3 is the result of double reflection.

FIG. 9.

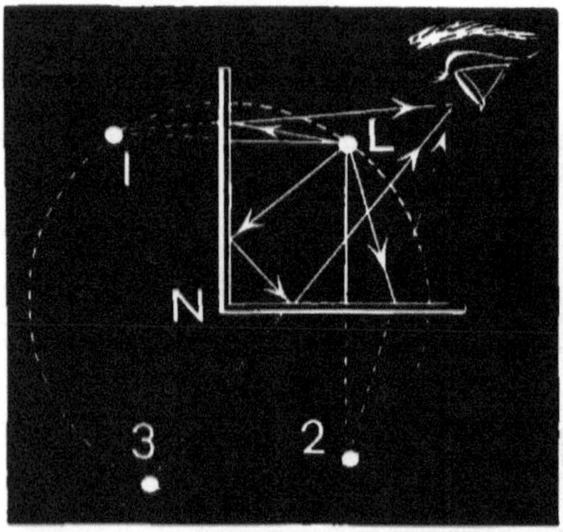

377. **Kaleidoscope.**—This toy depends upon the multiplication of images by inclined mirrors, as just explained; the mirrors being placed at angles varying from 30° to 60°, and inclosed within a suitable case or tube. In the end of the tube, behind ground glass, is a narrow cell, containing several small objects, as bits of colored glass, tinsel, etc., which are free to tumble about.

378. **Figure 10.—Deceptions practised by use of mirrors: seeing through a brick.**—This is done by means of four mirrors, and five short tubes joined together at right angles, as represented. The mirrors, 1, 2, 3, and 4, are placed successively at an angle of 45° to the incident ray coming from the object. The rays of the candle are reflected by the mirror 1, vertically to the mirror 2; and from the mirror 2, horizontally to 3; and from 3, vertically to 4; and from 4, horizontally to the eye. Thus the candle will be seen, apparently, in a direct line passing through the brick, or other opaque body, A.

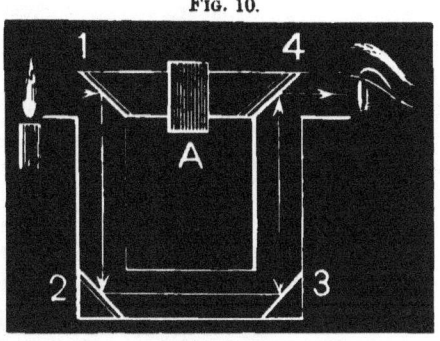

FIG. 10.

379. **Figure 11.—Plane mirrors may reflect objects double their own length.**—Let D be the mirror, of half the length of the object, ET. The *point* of the arrow is reflected from the top of the mirror back to the eye, the reflected ray taking the track of the incident ray. The opposite extremity of the object is reflected by

FIG. 11.

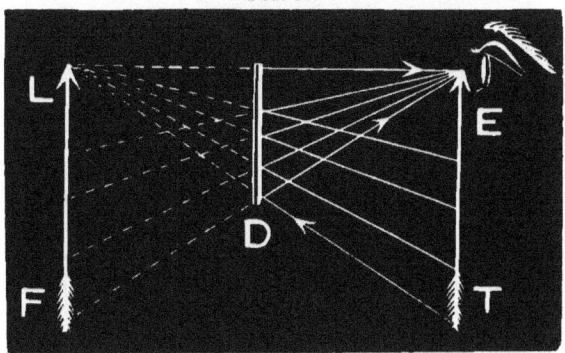

the lower end of the mirror, the incident and reflected rays forming equal angles with the surface of the mirror. In the same manner all points of the object will be reflected to the eye; and the object will *appear* to be at LF, a distance as far *behind* as it is in *front* of the mirror, as shown by the dotted lines, which are imaginary continuations of the incident and reflected rays.

OPTICS.

gure 12.—**The mariner's sextant.**—This is an in-
 measuring the altitudes and angular distances of the
 ودies, and depends on reflection from two mirrors.

The mirrors, A and L, are so mounted that their angle of inclination can be varied. The mirror, A, is attached to the movable arm AF, by which its inclination is changed by moving the arm along the graduated arc. The mirror, L, is firmly attached to the frame of the instrument, a little of the silvering of its outer portion being removed, so that the eye can have a direct view of the horizon or other objects.

FIG. 12.

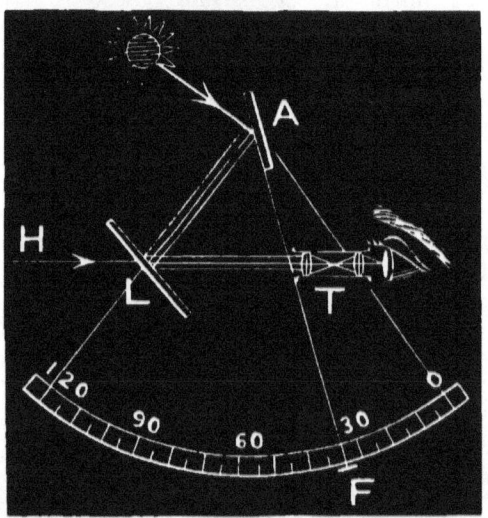

The mirror, A, is turned, by the arm AF, until the rays of any object, as the sun, moon, or a star, are twice reflected, and so directed to the eye; when they will coincide with the rays of the horizon or other object, H, seen by direct vision, and from which the angular distance of the star is to be measured. The angular distance of the object is shown by the position of the index-arm on the graduated arc. The telescope, T, is to facilitate accurate observation.

Reflection at Curved Surfaces.

381. **Figure 13.—Convex spherical mirrors illustrated by plane mirrors.**—A convex mirror may be considered as made up of an indefinite number of infinitely small plane mirrors. If E be two of these small plane mirrors, which, taken together, represent a portion of a convex mirror, the effects of convex mirrors, in changing the direction of the rays of light which fall upon them, will be easily understood.

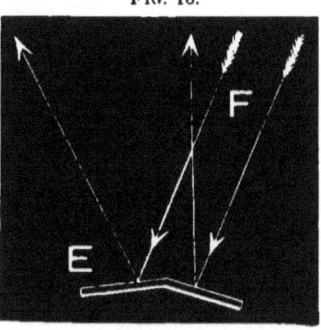

FIG. 13.

Let the two arrows, F, be parallel rays; the one on the right falling upon the mirror on the right, while the other ray falls upon the mirror on the left. Now, as the angles of incidence and reflection are equal in both cases, the rays after reflection cannot be parallel, but divergent. The degree of divergence will depend upon the angle formed by the two mirrors, or upon the amount of curvature of the mirror. Hence, *parallel rays, falling on a convex mirror, are reflected divergent; converging rays are reflected less convergent or parallel; and diverging rays are rendered more divergent.*

382. **Figure 14.—Convex spherical mirrors.**—Let A be the optical *centre* of the mirror. The ray 2 is perpendicular to the surface of the mirror, and, if continued, would pass through the centre, A. This line is called the *principal axis* of the mirror. The two rays, 1 and 3, being parallel to this, the three rays would fall on a plane mirror in a perpendicular direction, and be reflected in the direction of their incidence. But, owing to the obliquity of the convex surface, the parallel rays 1 and 3 will be reflected divergent

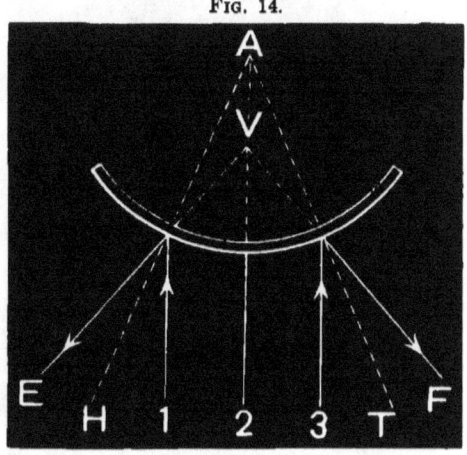

FIG. 14.

(as shown by the last diagram). Draw the dotted lines. H and T, perpendicular to the reflecting surface, and they will, if continued, pass through the centre A. The ray 1 will be reflected to E, in such a direction that the angle of reflection, between E and H, will equal the angle of incidence, between 1 and H; and so with the ray 3. If E and F be continued, as shown by the dotted lines, they will meet behind the mirror at V. Hence, since the image is always seen in the direction of the reflected ray, an object placed at 1 and 3 would be seen at V, or respectively in the directions of E and F.

212   OPTICS.

The point, V, is the *principal focus* of the mirror, and, for parallel rays, is situated equally distant from the mirror and its geometrical centre, A; and, being behind the mirror, is called the *principal virtual focus*.

Converging rays would seem to meet at a point between the principal focus and the mirror; and *diverging* rays, at a point between the principal focus and the geometrical centre, A.

383. **The apparent size of an object**, seen by direct vision, depends upon the magnitude of the angle formed at the eye by the rays of light coming from the extreme borders of the object; therefore, any cause, as reflection or refraction, which changes the direction of the rays by which an object is seen, so as to enlarge or diminish this angle, at the point where it meets the eye, will render the apparent size of the object larger or smaller than the object appears by direct vision.

384. **Figure 15.—Formation of images by convex reflectors.**—*Images formed by convex reflectors are always erect and virtual, and smaller than the object.*

Fig. 15.

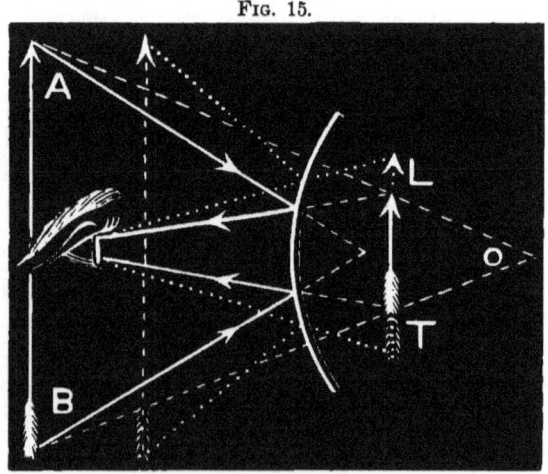

Let AB be the object, and LT will be the image, which, as represented, is erect, virtual, and smaller than the object. The converging rays from the extremities of the object fall upon the mirror, and are reflected, *less convergent*, back to the eye; and, as the object is seen by these reflected rays, it will appear to be smaller than it would if seen by the same rays before reflection (383); which is shown by continuing the reflected lines behind the mirror, until they meet the two long broken lines, drawn from the extremities of the object to the centre, O, and perpendicular to the surface of the mirror.

385. **Images formed by convex mirrors are larger the nearer the object approaches the mirror, and vice versa** (Fig. 15).—Let the object, AB, be removed toward the mirror to the position of the dotted arrow, and the reflected rays, represented by the dotted lines, will form a larger angle at the eye than when the object was in the former position, which, of course, renders the image correspondingly larger, as shown by the dotted prolongation of the first image, LT.

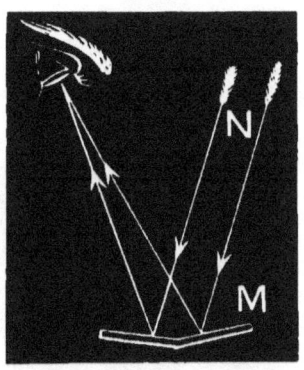

Fig. 16.

386. **Figure 16.—Concave reflectors the reverse of convex reflectors.**—The surface of the concave mirror, like that of the convex, Fig. 13 (381), may be considered as made up of small plane mirrors. Concave mirrors render parallel rays convergent, instead of divergent; and convergent rays *more* convergent, instead of less; and divergent rays *less*, instead of more divergent; as illustrated by the parallel rays, N, being reflected convergent, by means of the two small plane mirrors, M, set at an angle with each other, to represent a portion of a concave mirror.

Fig. 17.

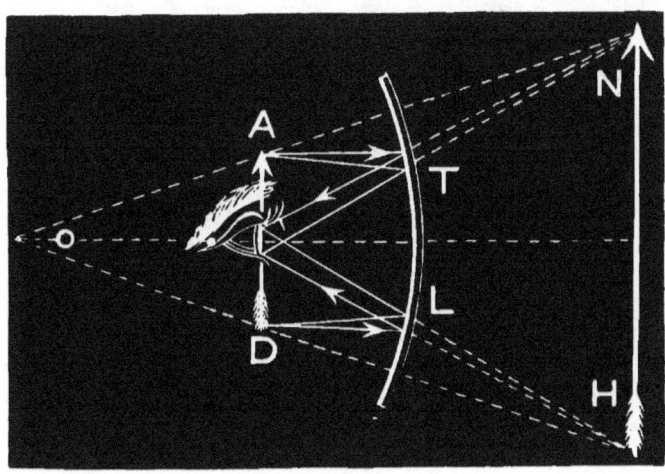

387. **Figure 17.—Formation of images by concave reflectors.**—In this diagram the object is placed between the mirror and principal focus. The centre of the mirror is at O, and the principal focus is shown by a dot between the eye and eyebrow.

Let AD be the object; and the converging rays AT and DL will be reflected back to the eye more convergent; thus enlarging the angle under which the virtual image is seen at NH, in the direction of the reflected rays; thus showing that, when the object is between the mirror and principal focus, *the image is erect, virtual, and larger than the object.*

388. Figure 18.—Foci of concave mirrors for parallel and convergent rays.—Parallel rays falling near the axis of a concave mirror converge, after reflection, to a point equidistant between the mirror and the centre of the sphere, of which the mirror forms a part.

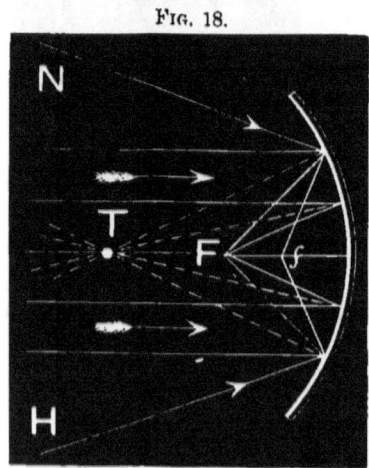

Fig. 18.

In the diagram, T represents the *centre* and F the *principal focus.* The central line passing through the centre and focus is the *axis.* The dotted lines from the centre to the mirror are perpendicular to the mirror.

Rays emanating from the principal focus, F, will be reflected parallel to the axis and to each other; and, conversely, rays parallel to the axis, after reflection, will meet at the principal focus, F.

Converging rays and virtual focus (Fig. 18).—If the radiant point passes from the principal focus, F, toward the mirror, as to f, the reflected rays, N and H, will diverge, as though emanating from a point behind the mirror called the *virtual focus;* and converging rays, as H and N, falling upon the mirror, will be reflected to some point between the mirror and the principal focus, as at f.

The lines N and f form equal angles with the dotted or perpendicular line between them, being, respectively, the angles of incidence and reflection, according to which way the ray proceeds. In the same way the parallel rays and their reflected rays, to F, form equal angles with the dotted perpendiculars.

389. Figure 19.—Foci of concave mirrors for divergent rays.—If the rays of light emanate from some point of the axis, as A, not infinitely distant from the mirror, they will be brought to a focus, after reflection, at some point of the axis between the principal focus and the centre of the mirror. The candle on the right is at the principal focus, the one in the middle, at the centre of the mirror.

Fig. 19.

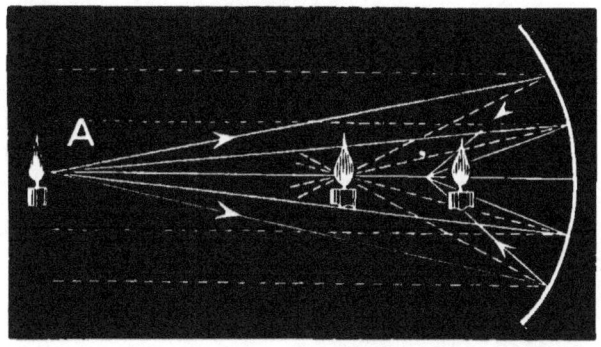

The point, A, and the point where its reflected rays meet the axis, are called the *conjugate foci*. Conjugate foci, therefore, are any two points so related that a pencil of light, emanating from either one, is brought to a focus at the other. The one from which the light emanates, as A, is called the *radiant*.

As the dotted lines, crossing at the centre of curvature, are perpendicular to the mirror, if the radiant, A, be moved toward the centre of curvature, its conjugate focus or reflected rays will also approach the centre; otherwise the angles of incidence and reflection would not be equal; and when the radiant reaches the centre, the conjugate foci will meet, and the incident rays will be perpendicular to the mirror and be reflected back to the centre from whence they came.

Some of the properties of conjugate foci are as follows:

1. If the radiant approaches the mirror, the focus recedes from it.
2. If the radiant is beyond the centre, the focus is between the centre and principal focus.
3. If the radiant is at the centre, the focus is also at the centre.
4. If the radiant is between the centre and principal focus, the focus is beyond the centre.
5. If the radiant is at the principal focus, the focus is at an infinite distance; that is, the reflected rays are parallel.
6. If the radiant is between the principal focus and the mirror, as at *f*, Fig. 18 (388), the rays are reflected so as to diverge, and on being produced backward meet at a point behind the mirror, which will be the focus, and which is called the *virtual focus*.

390. **Secondary axes.—Oblique pencils.**—If the radiant, A (Fig. 19), is not situated in the principal axis, but at any point near it, a line drawn from the radiant through the centre of curvature will constitute a *secondary axis*, and the focus of the *oblique pencil* of rays diverging from the radiant will be found *in* this secondary axis; and the radiant and focus will possess properties entirely analogous to those above explained (389).

391. **Figure 20.—Spherical aberration of reflectors.— Caustics.**—It would appear, from what has been said, that concave and convex spherical mirrors reflect rays to single points called foci, but this is not strictly the case, only for rays falling near the vertex or centre of the mirror.

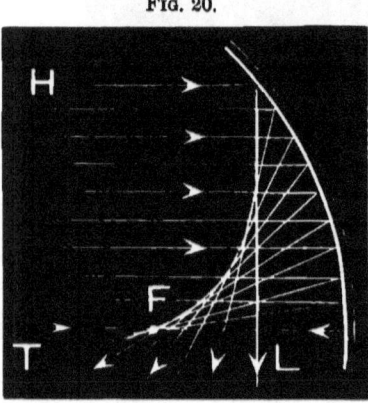

FIG. 20.

Let TL be the axis; F, the principal focus; and the several parallel lines, rays of light. It will be seen that the axial ray is reflected back upon itself, the angle of incidence and reflection being nothing; while the ray next above is reflected back, sensibly, to the principal focus, forming a slight angle of incidence and reflection; but, as the distance from the vertex increases, the angles of incidence and reflection increase in size, and the reflected rays sensibly depart from the principal focus; so that the outer ray, H, will be reflected to L. This scattering of the reflected rays along the axis, from the principal focus toward the mirror, is called *spherical aberration by reflection;* and the brilliant surface formed in space by the crossing of the reflected rays, two by two, is called *a caustic.*

The want of clearness or distinctness in the image, caused by this aberration, makes it necessary to construct concave and convex mirrors in the form of paraboloid surfaces (392).

392. **Figure 21.—Paraboloid reflectors.**—The nature of a parabolic curve is such that rays parallel to its axis will be reflected to a single point, called the *focus.* Let F be the focus, and the lines FN and HN will form equal angles with the mirror, and the line, NH, will be parallel to the axis; and this is true of each of the other rays drawn from the focus. And, conversely, all rays parallel to the axis, LF, will be reflected exactly to the focus, F. Or, if a line be drawn perpendicular to any point of the reflector, as LN, the angle of incidence, HNL, will equal the angle of reflection, FNL.

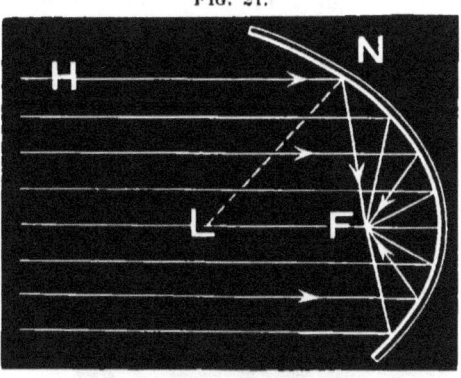

Fig. 21.

If the lines parallel to the axis be intersected by a line perpendicular to the axis, then each of the parallel lines plus its reflected line, as HN plus NF, will equal each of the other parallel lines plus its reflected line.

Parabolic reflectors are employed in reflecting telescopes, and on railroad locomotives, for illuminating the track at night, etc.

393. **Figure 22.—Formation of images by concave mirrors when the object is beyond the centre of curvature.—** Let 1 be the centre of curvature and F the principal focus. The lines A1 and H1, drawn from the extremities of the object through the

Fig. 22.

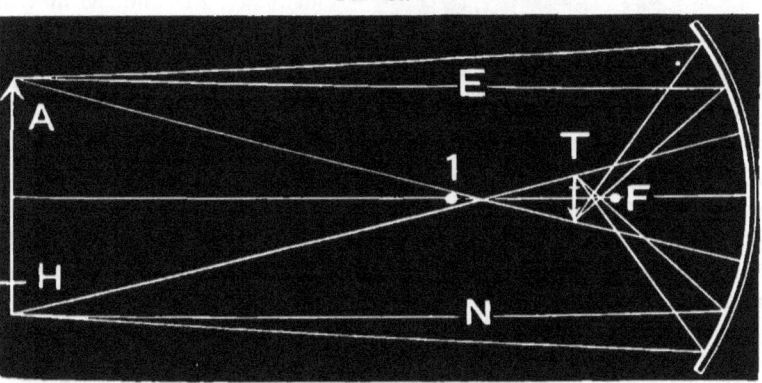

centre of the mirror, are the secondary axes (390), in which the extremities of the image, T, will be formed, at a distance from the mirror equal to the conjugate foci (389) for the extreme points of the object.

This image is *real, inverted, smaller than the object, and placed between the centre of curvature and the principal focus.*

The image will be very bright, as all the light incident upon the mirror will be gathered into a small space.

As the object approaches the mirror, the image recedes from it and approaches the centre, 1, in the same manner as do the conjugate foci. Therefore, when the object is at 1, or the centre, the image will be as large as the object. When it is at any point between the centre and the principal focus, F, it will be reflected, enlarged, and more distant from the mirror than itself (387); and when it arrives at F, the image becomes infinite, the rays being reflected parallel (see Conjugate Foci, 389).

DIOPTRICS, OR REFRACTION OF LIGHT.

394. **Figure 23.—Definitions.**—The diagram represents a dish filled with water. Refraction is the deviation or bending which a ray of light undergoes in passing obliquely from one medium into another, as FLT.

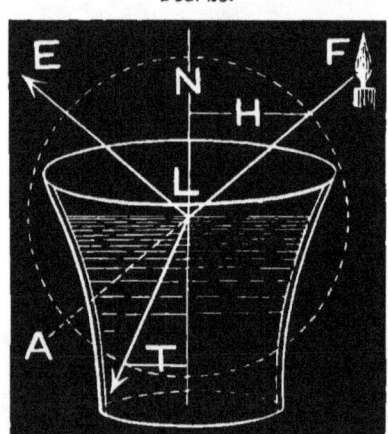

FIG. 23.

The ray, FL, before refraction, is called the *incident ray.*

The point L, at which the ray is deviated or bent, is called the *point of incidence.*

The ray, LT, after deviation, is called *the refracted ray.*

The angle formed by the incident ray, FL, and the normal, LN, at the point of incidence, L, is *the angle of incidence ;* and the plane FLN of the angle, *the plane of incidence.*

The angle formed by the refracted ray, LT, and the normal, at the point of incidence, L, is *the angle of refraction ;* and the plane of this angle, *the plane of refraction.*

As a portion of the incident ray, FL, is reflected by the surface of the water, let LE be the *reflected ray ;* then the angle NLE is *the angle of reflection.*

Describe the dotted circle, of any convenient size, from the point of incidence, L, and draw the line H, from the intersection of the circle and incident ray, so it will fall perpendicular to the normal NL; and also the line T, perpendicular to the normal.

The line, H, is *the sine of the angle of incidence ;* and the line T, *the sine of the angle of refraction ;* and H divided by T is invariably the same for any given medium, whether the angle of incidence is increased or diminished.

The quotient obtained by dividing H by T is called *the index of refraction.*

The index of refraction varies with different media. For light passing from air into water, it is about $\frac{4}{3}$; from air into glass, $\frac{3}{2}$; from air into diamond, $\frac{5}{2}$. These fractions inverted will, of course, express the index of refraction for light passing *out* of water, glass, and diamond, into air.

395. **Laws of refraction.**—1. *When light passes from a rare to a denser medium, it is refracted toward the perpendicular or normal; and, conversely, when it passes from a dense to a rarer medium, it is refracted from the perpendicular or normal.*

2. *The planes of incidence and refraction coincide, both being normal to the surface separating the media at the point of incidence.*

3. *The sine of the angle of incidence bears a constant ratio, in the same medium, to the sine of the angle of refraction.*

396. **The cause of refraction** is a change in the elasticity of the ether in passing from one medium into the other, which causes a change in the velocity of the ray. The density and elasticity of ether in water are different from what they are in the atmosphere, so that light travels faster in the latter medium than in the former, which causes the ray, on passing from air into water, to bend toward the normal at the point of incidence.

397. **Figure 24.—Refraction by parallel strata of different media.**—If a ray of light passes through one, two, or several plates of dense media, all the refracting surfaces being parallel planes, the emergent ray is parallel to the incident ray.

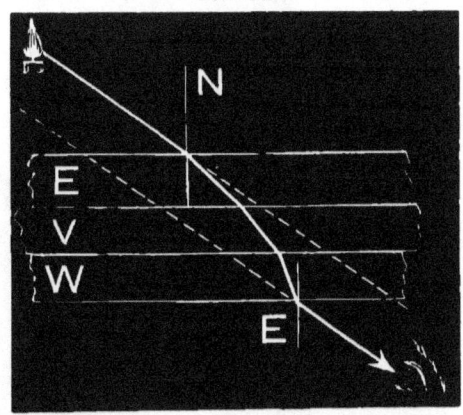

Fig. 24.

Let EVW be three media of greater density than air, and the second more dense than the first, and the third more dense than the second. A ray of light from the candle, incident at the foot of the perpendicular, N, will be refracted at the upper surface of E; and at the upper surface of V it will be again refracted, and at the upper surface of W it will be still further refracted; but on emerging into the air at E, it will be parallel to the incident ray, and, to the eye, the candle will appear to be situated at the extremity of the dotted line below the object.

398. **Figure 25.—Refraction and internal reflection.— Double reflection of mirrors.**—When light falls obliquely upon a transparent medium, as a plate of glass, it will be divided in various ways. Let the light from the candle fall upon the plate of glass, F, at the foot of the normal, N. At this point a portion will be *absorbed* and another portion *dispersed* (364), and still another portion will be *reflected* in the direction of 1, and the balance will be *refracted* to E, on the opposite surface of the glass. At this point it is further divided.

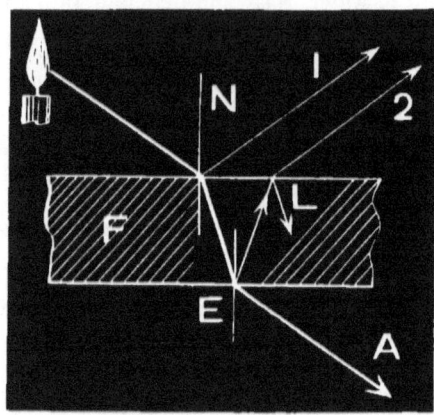

FIG. 25.

A part emerges into the air and is again refracted, parallel to the incident ray; and the balance is reflected back to L, which is again divided, a portion emerging into the air and passing to 2, parallel to the first reflected ray, 1, and the balance is reflected back parallel to the first refracted ray, and so on; until, by absorption and emergence, the light is lost.

In general, only the rays 1, EA, and 2, have sufficient intensity to be visible to the naked eye. If the lower face of the glass plate were silvered, that is, if the plate were a mirror, most of the light would be reflected by the silvered side, and pass in the direction of the line 2, which would give the principal image of the object; and a faint image of the object would be formed by the first reflection, and be seen in the direction of the line 1.

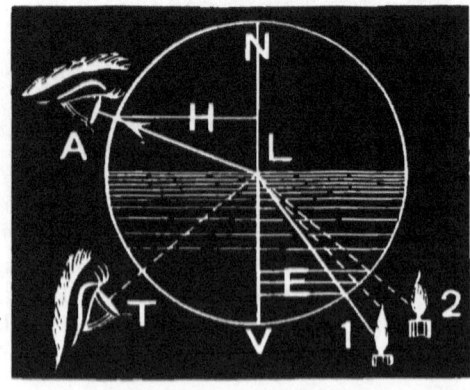

FIG 26.

399. **Figure 26.—Refraction and total reflection.**—When light passes from a dense to a rarer medium, the angle of refraction is greater than the angle of incidence (395), and when the angle of refraction is 90°, the angle of incidence is much less. For water, it is 48° 35', for ordinary glass it is 41° 49'; consequently, when the angle of incidence, in the case of water, exceeds 48° 35', refraction cannot occur, and the light will be totally reflected.

Let the diagram represent a glass globe half-full of water. A ray of light passing from 1 to L, being normal to the surface of the globe, suffers no refraction there, but coming to the surface of the water at L, it is refracted away from the normal, NV, to the eye at A (395). The angle of incidence, 1LV, being less than 48° 35', the angle of reflection, NLA, will be greater than 48° 35', but less than 90°, as shown by the sine II, being less than the radius LA. But a ray from the candle, 2, forming a *greater* angle of incidence than 48° 35', would not emerge from the water, otherwise the sine of its angle of refraction would be greater than the radius, LA, which is *impossible;* therefore the ray from 2 will be wholly reflected by the surface of the water, and pass to the eye T, forming an angle of reflection, TLV, equal to the angle of incidence, 2LV.

Suppose the ray, between the rays 1 and 2, to form an angle of incidence of just 48° 35', then the angle of refraction would be 90°, and the refracted ray would fall on the surface of the water, and the sine of the angle of refraction would equal the radius of the globe.

This kind of reflection, at the surface which separates two media, is called *internal reflection*, or *total reflection*.

This is the only way in which total reflection occurs, however smooth reflecting surfaces may be made.

It is impossible to see the bottom of a pond of water when looked at obliquely, because the rays return, by total reflection, to the water, instead of emerging into the air.

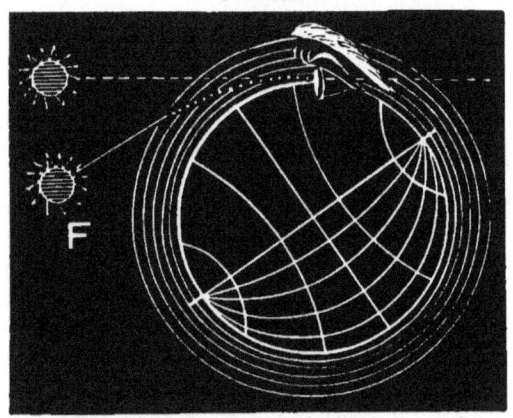

FIG. 27.

400. **Figure 27.
—Effects of refraction on the rising and setting of the heavenly bodies.**
—Suppose the dotted line, in the diagram, to represent the horizon; the several circles, the atmosphere; and F, the sun in its *actual* position. The rays of the sun entering the atmosphere in straight lines, become more and more refracted, until they reach the

eye in the horizon. Now, as the *apparent* position of an object lies in the direction in which the light from it passes at the point where it enters the eye, the sun will be seen on the dotted line of the horizon when it is *actually* at F, below it. Hence, heavenly bodies, by the amount of this refraction, rise earlier and set later than they would were there no atmosphere surrounding the earth.

The crimson appearance of the horizon, at sunset and sunrise, is owing to the fact that the red rays of the sun, being the least refrangible, are the first to appear in the morning and the last to disappear at night.

401. Figure 28.—Refraction by dense media spreads out the light.—When a ray of ordinary daylight or sunlight is refracted by a dense transparent medium, the refracted light is not confined to a single line, but it is spread out into a fan-like form, as represented in the figure.

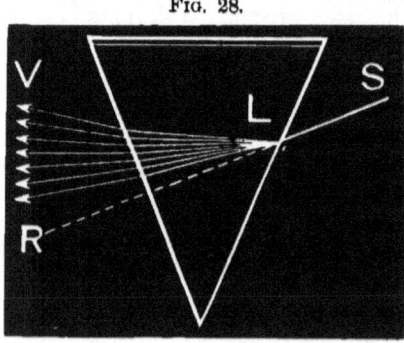

FIG. 28.

Let S be the incident ray, and, after refraction by the prism L, it will have the form shown by the several lines between V and R. The different parts of the refracted pencil show different colors; the most refracted part, V, being violet, and the least refracted, R, being red. The index of refraction for any one color is uniform for any given medium, but the index in the same medium varies for the different colored light.

402. Figure 29.—Mirage.—Mirage is an atmospheric phenomenon, caused by refraction and total reflection; and depends upon the different strata of the atmosphere being unequally heated, which causes rays coming from distant objects to become curved in their passage to the eye; and sometimes a layer of atmo-

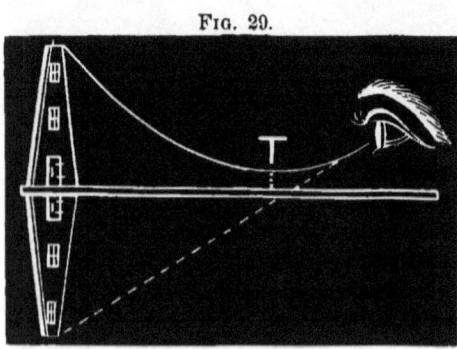

FIG. 29.

sphere next the earth becomes a reflector, causing total reflection (399) of the oblique rays falling upon it; which will cause objects to appear inverted, as if reflected from water. In this way portions of the earth, especially on deserts, appear to the traveller as lakes and ponds. To heighten the illusion, trees are often seen reflected from these *apparent sheets of water.*

In the diagram, the ray of light passing from the top of the tower toward T, is gradually curved by the unequal refractive power of the different layers of unequally heated atmosphere, the lower stratum being most heated; and when the ray reaches the point T, its obliquity, or angle of incidence on the stratum of air, is such that total reflection takes place; causing the ray to be turned in its course toward the eye; and the ray seeming to come from the direction in which it is passing at the point where it enters the eye, will give the object the appearance of being inverted, as if reflected by water. In this case both the tower and its image are seen.

403. **Figure 30.—Looming** is an atmospheric phenomenon caused by extraordinary refraction, by which objects, on the shores of lakes and seas, appear to be thrown up higher than their real positions. It is most common in very hot and very cold countries, and where the sea and land are more equally divided. It is due to different strata of the atmosphere being unequally heated. The lower layers, in this case,

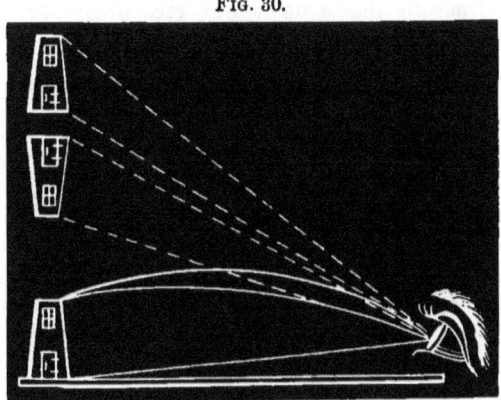

Fig. 30.

being the coldest, cause the rays, coming from a distant object, to become curved *upward* instead of downward in the passage. When some stratum of the air acts as a reflector, as previously explained (402), the object will not only be elevated but inverted, as shown in the diagram.

By *looming*, ships have been seen at so great a distance that the curvature of the earth would render it impossible for them to be but partially seen by direct vision. By this means the French coast, for several leagues in length, has been seen at Hastings, in England, fifty miles distant.

404. **Figure 31. The depth of water rendered apparently less by refraction.**—This is shown by a dish of water and a piece of coin. Let L be the piece of coin, placed in the bottom of the empty dish; then let the observer take such a position, that the side of the vessel will cut off his view of the coin. By filling the dish with water the coin will be brought to his view, and have the appearance of being situated at T, in the direction of the refracted rays.

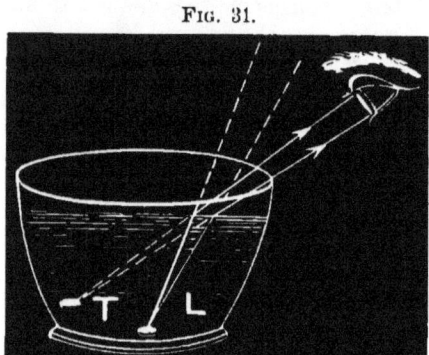

Fig. 31.

In this way the bottoms of rivers, ponds, etc., seem to be nearer the surface of the water than they really are; sometimes causing people to venture into water too deep for their safety.

It is by refraction that oars, spiles, etc., when partly plunged in water, seem to be bent at the surface of the water.

Prisms and Lenses.

405. **Figure 32.—Prisms and Lenses.**—These are usually made of glass, and are of various forms.

A *prism* is a refracting medium, bounded by three or more (usually three) plane faces, variously inclined to each other. In the diagram, 1 represents a section, or end-view, of a *triangular prism*. The angle formed by the two adjacent faces, through which a ray of light passes, is called *the refracting angle of the prism.*

A *lens* is a refracting medium, usually glass or crystal, bounded by curved surfaces, or by one plane and one curved surface.

Lenses are bounded by spherical surfaces, or by one spherical and one plane surface.

When the surfaces of lenses are of different kinds, they are named in reference to the side on which the light first falls.

OPTICS.

A *plane glass*, section 3, is a plate of glass having two plane surfaces, parallel to each other.

If the several sections, 2, 4, 5, 6, 7, 8, 9, were revolved around the straight line passing through them, they would severally describe the solid lenses they are intended to represent.

A sphere, shown in section 2, has all parts of its surface equally distant from a certain point within, called the centre.

A double convex lens, 4, is bounded by two convex surfaces.

A double concave lens, 5, has two concave surfaces opposite to each other.

A plano-convex lens, 6, has its first surface plane and the other convex.

A plano-concave lens, 7, has its first surface plane and the other concave.

A meniscus, 8, has one surface convex and the other concave, the concave surface being the least curved.

A concave-convex lens, 9, has its first surface concave and the other convex, the concave surface being the most curved.

An achromatic combination consists of two or more lenses of different kinds of glass, so constructed as to neutralize the effect of dispersion (438). This combination is of great importance in the construction of optical instruments.

Lenses either *converge* or *diverge* rays of light.

Convergent lenses have greater *convexity* than concavity, and, therefore, are thicker in the middle than at their edges. These are 2, 4, 6, and 8.

Divergent lenses have greater *concavity* than convexity, and, therefore, are thinner in the middle than at their edges. These are 5, 7, and 9.

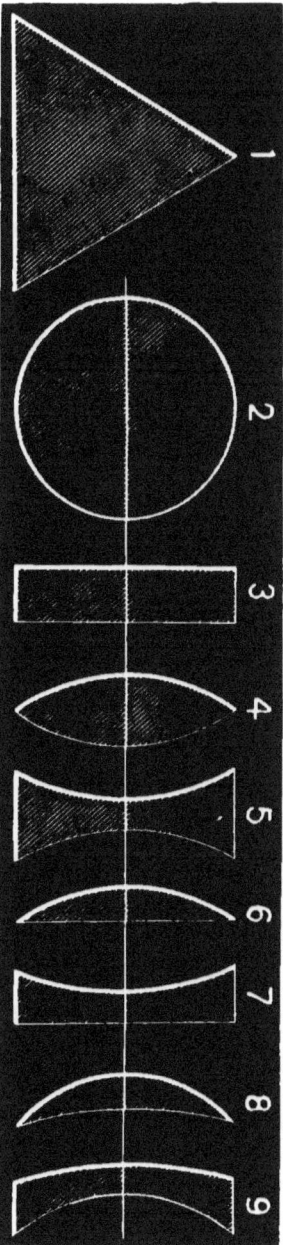

FIG. 32.

226 OPTICS.

406. **Figure 33.—Refraction by prisms.**—*Finding the direction of the refracted and emergent rays.*—Let the triangle represent a section of a crown-glass prism whose index of refraction (394) is 1.5; and AL, a ray of light, from the candle, falling obliquely upon the prism at L.

FIG. 33.

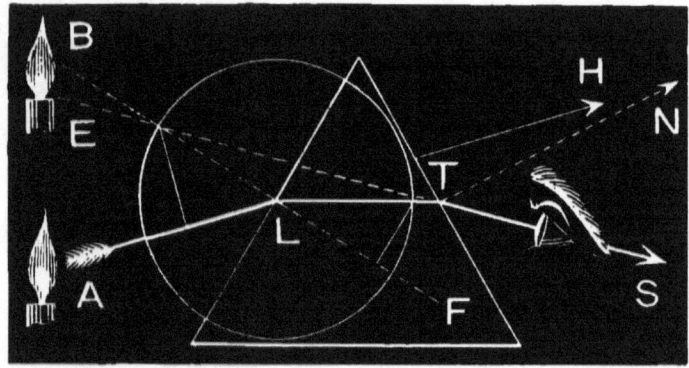

To find the point at which the ray will emerge from the prism on its opposite face, first draw the dotted line, BF, through the point of incidence, perpendicular to the face of the prism, and ALB will be the angle of incidence, which will be to the angle of refraction as 1.5 is to 1. Now erect a line, which (by some scale, say inches) is 1.5, perpendicular to AL at a point where it will meet BL; then describe a circle from L, passing through the point where these lines meet. On LF erect a perpendicular line equal to 1, at a point where it will meet the circle, and through this point the refracted ray, LT, must pass; for the perpendicular to AL is the sine of the angle of incidence and the perpendicular to LF is the sine of the angle of refraction, and these are to each other as 1.5 is to 1.

If it were not for this refraction, which has turned the ray toward the perpendicular BF, it would have passed on in the direction of TH.

By a like process, TS will be found to be the direction of the ray after emergence. In this case, as the ray passes from a dense to a rarer medium, it will be turned *from* the perpendicular TN (394) toward the face of the prism.

As the eye views the object by the emergent ray it will seem to be at E, in the direction of ST.

By slowly turning the prism backward and forward about its axis, one position will be found where there is the least distance between the *real* position of the object, as at A, and its *apparent* position, as at E. This position of the prism is when the emergent ray, TS, deviates the *least* possible from the incident ray AL, which will be the case when the refracted ray, LT, is parallel to the base of the prism. In this position the angles, at which the ray enters and leaves the prism, will be equal.

Effects of a plane-glass.—For the effects of a plane-glass upon an oblique ray of light, see Figs. 24 and 25 (397-8).

407. **Figure 34.—The course of light through a sphere of glass or spherical lens.**—Let AB represent three parallel rays of light incident upon the crown-glass spherical lens, represented by the circle, the middle ray passing through its centre, L; and let HTL be a perpendicular to the surface at T. The ray AT, on entering the

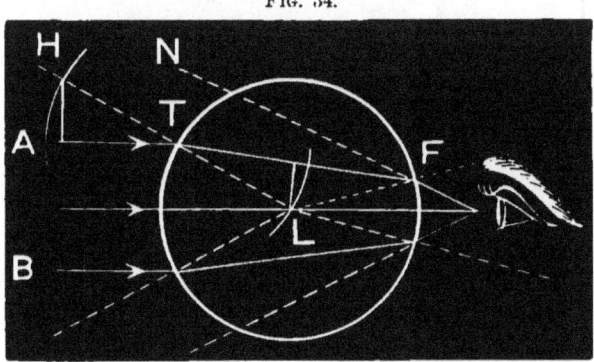

FIG. 34.

lens, will be refracted toward the perpendicular. From the point T describe the arcs, as shown, one of which passes through the centre of the circle; then draw TF, in such a direction that the sine of the angle of incidence, ATH, will be to the sine of the angle of refraction, FTL, as 1.5 is to 1; or, as the index of refraction of crown-glass is to that of air.

By the same process, and the perpendicular, LF, the direction of the emergent ray may be found; which, coming from a dense to a rarer medium, will be turned *from* the perpendicular LF, and pass to the eye, where it will meet the ray, B, and with it form the angle under which the eye would view an object, whose *real* position and magnitude is AB, but whose apparent magnitude, of course, would be much larger. The central ray, being normal to the sphere, passes through it without deviation.

The point where A and B meet is the *focus* for parallel rays.

To find the distance of the focus from the centre of the lens, divide the index of refraction, of the material of which the lens is made, by twice its excess above 1—the radius of the lens being 1.

Action of Convex Lenses.

408. **Figure 35.—Definitions.**—The centres of the bounding surfaces of a lens are called *centres of curvature;* thus, the centres of

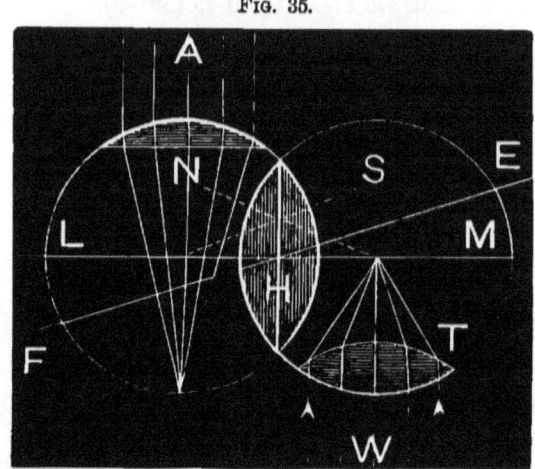

FIG. 35.

curvature of the several lenses in the diagram, are the centres of the two circles.

The *axis* of the lens is the straight line drawn through the centres of curvature, as LM, for the lens H.

In higher optics, it is demonstrated that there is always one point on the axis of a lens, such, that rays of light, passing through it, are not deviated by the lens. This point is called the *optical centre,* and is of much use in the construction of images.

If the surfaces of double convex and double concave lenses are equally curved, the *optical centre* is on the axis, midway between the two surfaces, as H; and any ray, as EF, passing through it, is not deviated by the lens.

To find a normal at any point of the surface of a lens, draw a line through that point to the corresponding centre of curvature; thus, the dotted lines, S and N, are normals to the points where they enter the lens.

Action of convex lenses on light (Fig. 35).—A ray of light falling upon one surface of a double convex lens is refracted *to-*

ward the normal; and, passing through the lens, is again incident upon the other surface, and is, therefore, refracted *from* the normal; the deviation, in both cases, being toward the thicker portion of the lens, which is analogous to the action of the prism; see Fig. 38 (411). Therefore, rays of light, as W and A, parallel to the axis, will be collected, by refraction, to a single point, called the *principal focus;* and its distance from the lens is called the *principal focal distance*.

If the lens be made of glass, whose index of refraction is 1.5, then the principal focus, for *double convex lenses*, as T (Fig. 35), is the centre of curvature. Hence, the principal focal distance is equal to *the radius of the curvature*.

The principal focus for *plano-convex lenses*, as N, is on the axis at a point in the circle of which the convex surface of the lens forms a part. Hence, the principal focal distance is equal to *twice the radius of the curvature*, as represented in the diagram.

409. **Figure 36.—Conjugate Foci.**—These are any two points on the axis of a lens, so situated that a pencil of light from one is brought to a focus at the other. The *radiant* is the one from which the light proceeds.

Let the two white dots be the principal foci of the lens, that is, for

FIG. 36

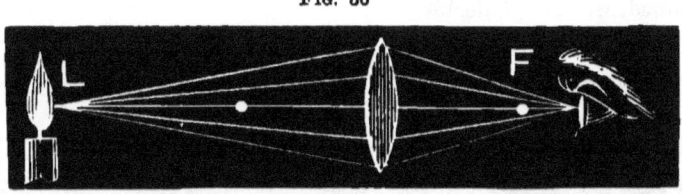

parallel rays. If the radiant, L, be situated beyond the principal focus, as it is, the diverging rays will be brought to a point at the eye, somewhere beyond the principal focus on the right. These two points, L and the eye, are conjugate foci; and it matters not upon which side of the lens the radiant is placed.

If the radiant be placed at *twice the distance* of the principal focus from the lens, the corresponding focus will be equally distant from the lens; or, the points at which the conjugate foci will be equally distant from the lens is when either of them is double the distance of the principal focus.

If the radiant is at an infinite distance the rays are parallel; in which case the corresponding focus will coincide with the principal focus.

410. **Figure 37.—Conjugate foci, continued.**—As the radiant *approaches* the principal focus on its side of the lens, the corresponding focus will *recede* from the principal focus on the opposite

Fig. 37.

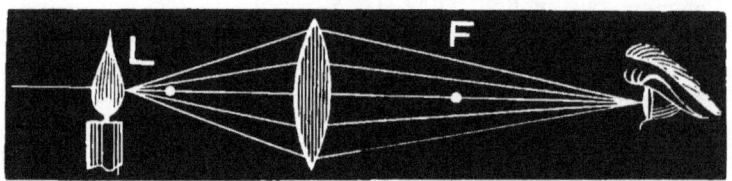

side, as shown; and when the radiant, L, reaches, or coincides with the principal focus, the corresponding focus, (the eye) will be at an infinite distance, as, in this case, the refracted rays will be parallel.

If the radiant is nearer to the lens than the principal focus, the rays will diverge, as shown by the lines A and B (Fig. 38), and will meet only by being produced backward, as at E; in which case the focus is *virtual*, the radiant being at the intersection of the lines A and B.

If the radiant be placed, instead of on the axis, on *any* line (not much inclined to the axis) passing through the optical centre (408), called a *secondary axis*, the corresponding focus will be on that line, and the laws which regulate the positions of conjugate foci, already explained, will be applicable.

411. **Figure 38.—Analogous effects of prisms and double convex lenses,** shown by their action on *diverging, parallel*, and *converging rays*.

Fig. 38.

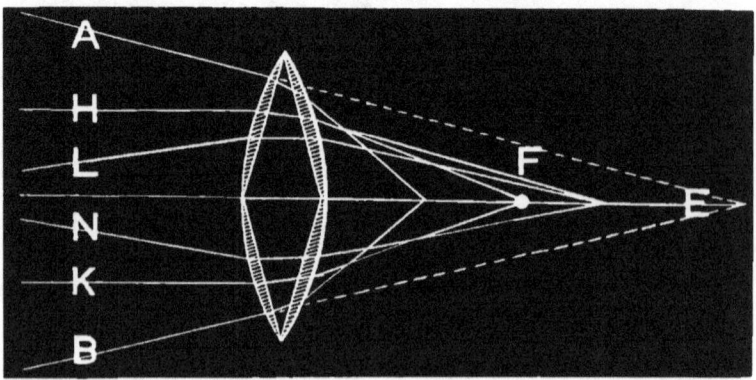

Within the double convex lens draw sections of two prisms so that their angles of refraction shall coincide with the edges of the lens, and their opposite sides with the axis of the lens, as represented.

Let the rays, H and K, be *parallel* to the axis, and, by the lens, they will be refracted to its principal focus, F; the *diverging* rays, L and N (coming from beyond the principal focus on the left), will be refracted to some point beyond the principal focus on the right; and the *converging* rays, A and B, will be refracted to some point between the principal focus, F, and the lens.

If, now, the lens be removed, and the inscribed prisms substituted, they will have the same effect as the lens upon the several rays of light.

412. **Figure 39.—Longitudinal spherical aberration of lenses,** and the principles determining the foci of lenses. A double convex lens may be regarded as composed of a number of segments of

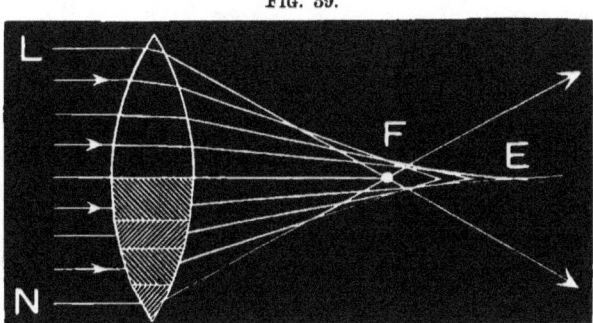

FIG. 39.

prisms, as illustrated by the lower half of the lens in the diagram. The further the segment is from the centre of the lens, the greater is the inclination of its faces, and, therefore, the greater will be the refraction of the rays passing through it. The central segments may be regarded as a *plane glass*, with nearly parallel faces, while the outer segments approximate the form of prisms.

Now, since the deviation of a ray, passing through a prism, increases as the inclination of the faces of the prism increases, the rays L and N will be refracted more than the two rays passing through the central segments; therefore the rays, as L and N, passing through the edges of the lens, will meet nearer to the lens, as at F, than those passing through the central portion of the lens, which will meet at a greater distance from the lens, as at E; while all intermediate rays will meet at various points along the axis between F and E.

This scattering of focal points of different rays along the axis, from F to E, is called *longitudinal spherical aberration*, and is provided against by giving the faces of lenses a peculiar curve; but owing to the difficulty of grinding them in this form, the aberration is practically obviated by making the lenses relatively thin, which diminishes the inclination of their faces.

A **plano-convex lens** has, in general, the same effect as the double convex lens, only its foci are at double the distance; the principal focus being at a distance equal to twice the radius of the curved surface (408).

Formation of Images by Convex Lenses.

413. **Figure 40.—Formation of images by convex lenses, when the object is twice the focal distance.**—If an object, as AE, be placed before a lens, all points of it, on either side of the principal axis, may be regarded as *radiants*, situated on secondary axes, sending out pencils of rays. For instance, let A and E be two such

FIG. 40.

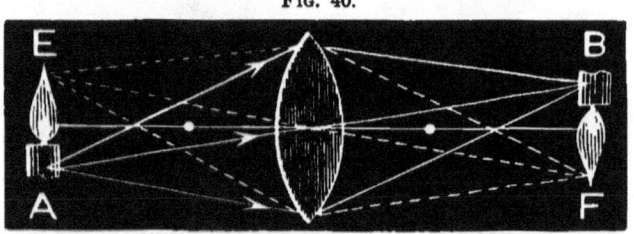

radiant points. Draw the secondary axes AB and EF, and let the two dots on the principal axis be the principal foci of the lens. The point A being beyond the principal focus, its rays will meet on its secondary axis, at B, beyond the principal focus on the right; and, in the same way, the rays from E will meet on its secondary axis at F; and so on, for all points of the radiant EA.

As all the secondary axes cross the principal axis, the image, BF, will be inverted.

The size and position of the image will depend upon the distance of the object from the lens.

In this case, the object, EA, is at twice the distance of the principal focus, and, consequently, according to the law regulating the positions of conjugate foci (409 and 410), the image, BF, must be at an equal distance from, and on the opposite side of, the lens, *real* and *virtual*.

414. **Figure 41.—Images formed by convex lenses when the object is at more and less than twice the focal distance.**—1. Let the two dots on the principal axis be the principal foci; and AB, the object, situated *more* than twice the focal distance from the lens, in which case the image, HN, will be *smaller than the object, real, inverted,* and *situated between the principal focus and the point at twice the focal distance.*

Fig. 41.

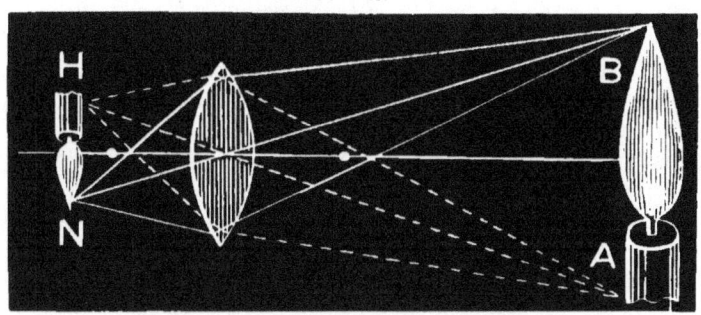

2. If HN be the object, situated between the principal focus and twice the focal distance, then the image, AB, will be *larger than the object, real, inverted,* and *situated at more than twice the focal distance.*

If AB, as an object, be moved toward the lens, the image, HN, will grow larger and *recede from* the lens. If AB be moved *from* the lens, the image, HN, will move *toward* the lens and become smaller.

The image, however, can never approach nearer to the lens than the principal focus, as this is the focus for parallel rays, in which case the object would be at an infinite distance.

The linear magnitude of the image, as compared with the object, will be proportional to their respective distances from the lens.

415. **Figure 42.—Images formed by convex lenses when the object is at less than the focal distance.**—If the object,

Fig. 42.

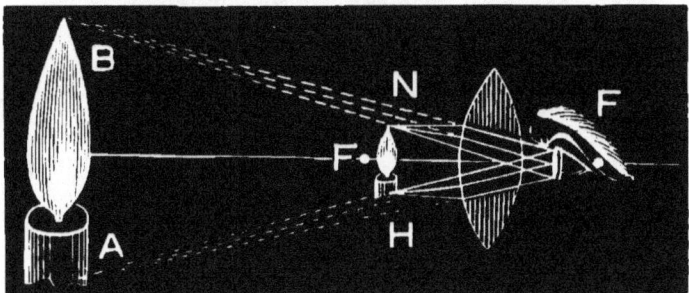

NH, and the eye, be placed nearer to the lens than the principal foci, FF, the image, AB, will *increase,* will be *erect* and *virtual.*

The image being virtual can only be seen by looking through the lens; while, in the former cases, the images, being *real*, would be seen on an intercepted screen.

In this case, the lens becomes what is called a *single microscope*.

The rays from the object are refracted to the eye by the lens, and the eye will see the image, AB, in the direction of the dotted lines.

416. **Figure 43.—Light-houses.—**These are towers erected along the coast, upon the tops of which are large lanterns, lighted, at night, as guides to mariners.

In early times light-houses were illuminated by fires, made of wood, coal, or other substances; subsequently by means of oil-lamps, placed in foci of concave reflectors. But the metal reflectors, becoming tarnished by sea-air, soon lost much of their reflective power, which led to the invention of a new system of illumination, which is being adopted in all civilized countries.

FIG. 43.

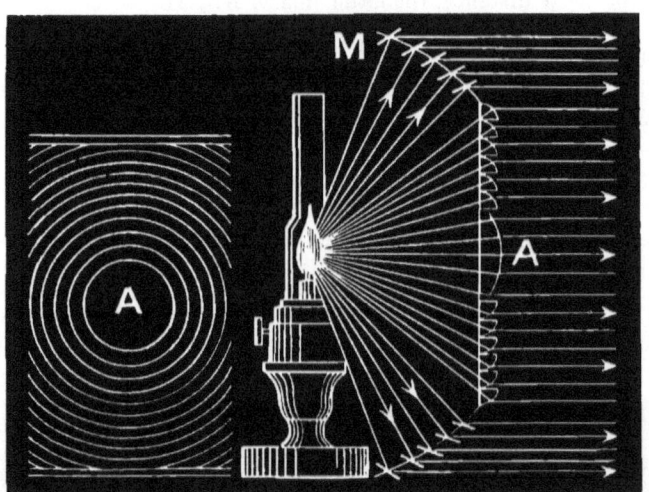

This consists of substituting, for the reflectors, plano-convex lenses, in the principal foci of which are placed powerful lamps, with several concentric wicks. The difficulty of making large plano-convex lenses, together with their great absorption of light, led to the adoption of a *system* of lenses, known as *échelon lenses*.

A lens of this kind is represented by the diagram; A (on the left) being a front view, and (in the main figure) a side view. It consists of a plano-convex lens in the centre, a foot or so in diameter, around

OPTICS. 235

which is disposed a series of plano-convex annular lenses, with such a curvature that each shall have the same principal focus as the central lens, A. Around about this compound lens are several ranges of small reflectors, M, so arranged as to reflect such light as would otherwise be lost.

This double combination sends forth, in a single direction, an immense beam of light, as shown in the diagram, which is visible for fifty or sixty miles.

To make the light visible in more than one direction, eight such systems are arranged on different sides of the lamp; which, for lighthouses of the first order, present an appearance of a pyramid of glass, nine or ten feet high.

To make the light visible in all points of the horizon, the whole is set upon a vertical shaft or spindle; which, by the employment of machinery, like clock-work, is made to revolve. By this means an observer at any point will see eight flashes of light during one revolution, which are followed by as many intervals of darkness, called *eclipses*.

One light-house is distinguished from another by varying the revolutions of the lights.

Concave Lenses.

417. **Figure 44.—Effects of concave lenses on rays of light.**—Lenses of greater *concavity* than *convexity* (405) render parallel rays divergent; converging rays, less convergent; and diverging

FIG. 44.

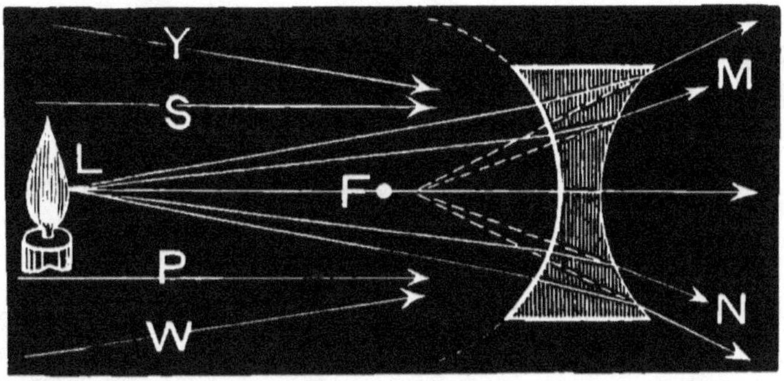

rays, more divergent. The divergent rays from the radiant L, by passing through the double concave lens, are rendered more divergent, and take the directions of M and N, as though proceeding from a point behind the lens, as shown by the dotted lines. This point is called the *virtual focus*.

The parallel rays, S and P, would become *divergent*, and the converging rays, Y and W, would become *less convergent*, on passing through the lens. The *principal focus*, F, is the centre of curvature.

418. **Figure 45.—Formation of images by concave lenses.**—Let F be the centre of curvature, and AB the object. A pencil of light coming from A, is deviated, and *appears* to come from the *top* of the image, H, situated on the secondary axis or line drawn

FIG. 45.

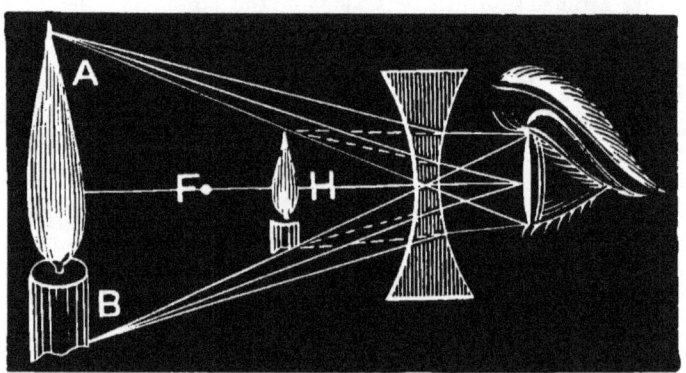

from A to the optical centre of the lens. A pencil of rays coming from B, is deviated, so as to appear to come from the *bottom* of the object, H, situated on the secondary axis or line drawn from B to the optical centre of the lens. Therefore, H is the image of the object, AB. Hence, images formed by concave lenses are *erect, virtual*, and, being nearer the optical centre, *smaller than the object.*

CHROMATICS, AND DECOMPOSITION OF LIGHT.

The Solar Spectrum.

419. **Figure 46.—Solar spectrum.—Primary colors.**—A beam of sunlight let into a dark room, through a small hole in the shutter, and passing through a triangular prism, P, will be twice refracted out of its course, instead of passing on, as to T; and instead of being refracted to a single round point, on an intercepting screen, it will be diffused or spread out over a considerable space, from V to R, called *the solar spectrum*, in which will be seen all the colors of the rainbow. This dispersion is owing to the unequal refrangibility of the different colors. Beginning with the color least refracted, they are *red, orange, yellow, green, blue, indigo,* and *violet,* as shown in the drawing.

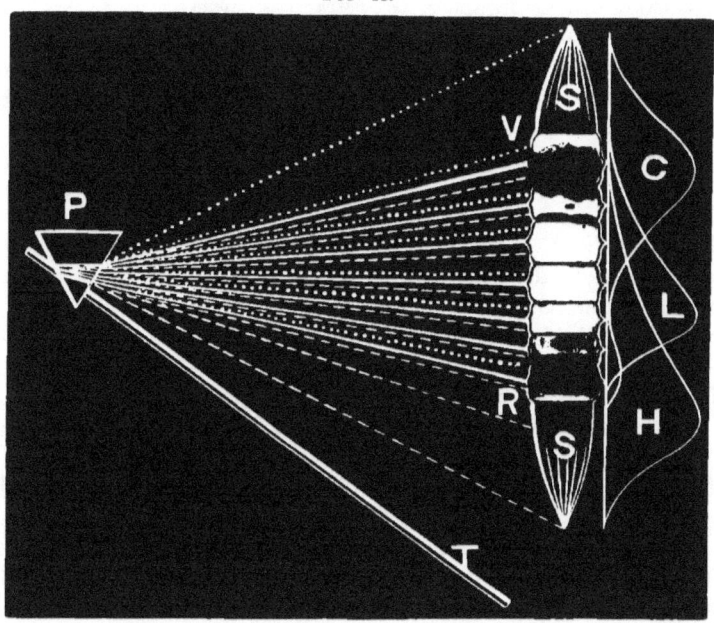

Fig. 46.

The property which a refractive medium possesses of decomposing and scattering solar light, is called its *dispersive power.* The dispersive power of different substances varies. For example, the spectrum formed by *flint* glass is nearly twice as long as that formed by *crown* glass.

Primary colors.—If a hole be cut through the screen opposite any one of these colors, and the light allowed to pass through and fall upon another prism, it is found that it can be further refracted, but it cannot be further decomposed or separated into other colors by refraction. Hence, the colors of the solar spectrum are generally called *primary colors.*

420. **Properties of the solar spectrum** (Fig. 46).—Whether or not light and heat are one and the same, or whether their difference consists only in the rate or velocity of the vibrations of the ethereal medium, yet it is evident that there are *three* classes of effects produced by the solar radiations, which are widely different, namely: *luminous effects,* which act upon the eye; *thermal* or *calorific effects,* which expand all bodies; and *chemical effects*, which play between different elementary substances, causing chemical changes.

These three kinds of force, being unequally refrangible, are separated, and so examined, by means of the refractive power of the prism, in the manner previously shown for separating the colors of light (419).

By referring to the diagram (Fig. 46) it will be noticed that from the prism, P, to the spectrum, SS, there are three kinds of lines, which represent these three *forces, agents,* or *properties* of the solar rays. Of course, they are not distinctly separated from each other, as the lines are, but they blend together like the colors in the spectrum or rainbow.

The *plain lines* represent the luminous rays; the *dotted lines*, the chemical rays; and the *broken lines*, the calorific rays. The beam of sunlight, therefore, instead of being separated into only seven rays, is decomposed into twenty-one rays; seven luminous, lighting or coloring; seven calorific or heating; and seven chemical rays.

These three forces or agents are not equally powerful in all parts of the spectrum. There are points where each has a maximum and minimum intensity.

Below the red ray, quite out of the color, is the most powerful *calorific ray* (represented by the first broken line below R), each calorific ray diminishing in intensity of heat as we pass up, and lying just below its respective lighting ray. On the contrary, the most powerful *chemical ray* is at the top, above the violet, and quite out of the color, each chemical ray diminishing in intensity of effect as we pass down, until we reach the strongest lighting ray (which, as will be seen, is the yellow), where the chemical effect diminishes to *nothing;* then increasing again, and, finally, diminishing to nothing at the lower extremity of the spectrum; thus showing *two maxima* of chemical influence.

The most powerful *coloring* or *lighting ray* is the yellow, the lighting effect diminishing from this color to nothing at either end of the spectrum.

The chemical effect extends as high as the dotted line at the extreme upper end of the spectrum, S, and the heating effect as low as the broken line at the extreme point of the spectrum, S, below.

By experiment it has been found that the change wrought within the vegetable leaf, namely, the de-oxidization of carbon and hydrogen, or the decomposition of carbonic acid and water, by which oxygen is liberated, takes place with far the greatest activity in the yellow ray, where the light is most intense and the chemical effect is least. Now, notwithstanding the point of greatest intensity of this de-oxidizing force, agent, or property of the solar rays corresponds with that of the lighting or coloring rays; yet its effect on vegetation is so different from that of light upon the eye, it is not improbable that this is a distinct property of solar radiation.

The intensity of heat, in different parts of the spectrum, may be tested by a delicate thermometer; the intensity of chemical effect by paper, previously prepared with nitrate of silver; and the intensity of light by the distance at which fine print, placed in different parts of the spectrum, can be read.

The position of the maximum intensity, for the calorific rays, varies with the nature of the material of the prism.

On the right of the spectrum are three curved lines, C, L, and H, which are called, respectively, the *curve of chemical intensity*, the *curve of luminous intensity*, and the *curve of thermal intensity*. The most prominent point of each curve stands opposite to that part of the spectrum in which is found the maximum effect of the property which the curve represents. From these points the intensity diminishes in proportion as the curves approach the straight base-line, until the curves and base-line meet, opposite to which points the effects cease.

421. **Complementary colors.**—Any two colors are said to be complementary to each other, which, by their union, would produce white light. If all the colors of the solar spectrum, *except any one of them*, be reunited by means of a double convex lens (Fig. 54), or by a second prism, the resulting color will be complementary to the color left out, as it only lacks this color, mixed with it, to produce white light. If the red, for example, be left out, the recomposition of the other colors will give a bluish-green; hence *red* and *green* are complementary. In this manner it is found that

Red is complementary to		....	Green.
Violet red	"	"	Yellow green.
Violet	"	"	Yellow.
Violet blue	"	"	Orange Yellow.
Blue	"	"	Orange.
Greenish blue	"	"	Reddish Orange.
Black	"	"	White.

422. **Analysis of colors by absorption.**—Although the colors of the prismatic spectrum cannot be further divided by refraction, yet any of these colors may be still further decomposed by transmission through various colored glass; by which means it has been found that *red, yellow*, and *blue*, are in all parts of the spectrum; and that any color whatever may be formed by suitably combining these three. Hence it is inferred, that there are really only *three*, instead of *seven*, primary colors, *red, yellow,* and *blue;* the other four being considered as *secondary colors* of the spectrum.

423. **Figure 47.—Union of two primary colors of the spectrum, to produce a secondary color.**—Let a solar ray of light be dispersed by the prism P, and intercepted by a screen, A, so perforated as to allow the primary colors *yellow* and *blue* to pass through it, and fall upon the two prisms, H and N, by which the rays

FIG. 47.

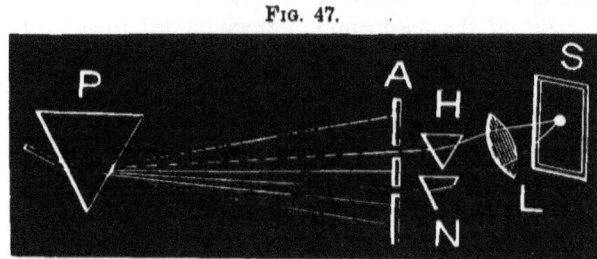

will be still further refracted, but not dispersed. If, by means of the double convex lens, L, they be converged so as to meet on the screen S, they will form *green.*

By the same process it is found that yellow and red form *orange;* red and blue form *violet* and *indigo.* Still, no two colors alone make a third color in the solar spectrum, as more or less of all the primary colors are necessary to form either of the four secondary colors.

424. **Figure 48.—Composition of the several colors of the solar spectrum.**—The colored spaces represent the relative

FIG. 48.

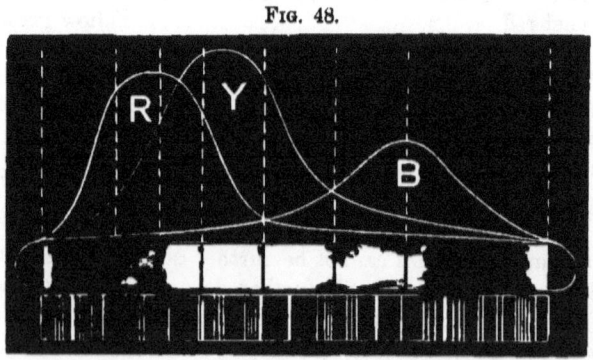

lengths of the several colors of the spectrum. The three curves, R, Y, and B, represent, respectively, the distribution, along the spectrum, of the three primary colors, red, yellow, and blue, and the relative amount of each of these necessary to produce the secondary colors of the spectrum, *orange, green, indigo,* and *violet.*

The curved line, B, shows that very little blue is found at the red end of the spectrum; and the curved line R, that there is hardly any red at the blue end; while the curved line Y, shows that but a small portion of yellow is found at either end.

The spaces between any two of the vertical dotted lines, lying between the curved lines and spectrum, represent the relative amount of each of the primary colors necessary to form the secondary color that lies directly below.

425. **Refraction and dispersion of the solar spectrum.**—If a glass tube or a plain drinking-glass, or any glass instrument of similar form, be held in the path of the colored rays of the spectrum, in a dark room, a beautiful system of colored rings will be produced, which vary in form, position, and color, with every change in the position or form of the interposed glass. The great variety and exquisite beauty of the tints and hues exhibit the infinite resources of color in the sunbeam.

Dark Lines in Light.

426. **Dark lines in the solar spectrum** (Fig. 48).—If the spectrum be formed from a narrow line of light, and by a fine flint-glass prism, and viewed through a telescope, there will be seen crossing the spectrum a large number of dark lines, of different sizes; varying in number from 600 to 2,000, according to the power of the telescope. None of the dark lines coincide with the boundaries of the colored spaces.

The position of some of the largest of these lines is shown by the diagram, the lines being drawn in their relative positions *below* instead of across the spectrum.

427. **Lines in light vary with different sources of light.** —The position of the dark lines of the spectrum is *invariable* when the light comes from the sun, whether the spectrum be formed from direct rays or from rays reflected by the moon, planets, or terrestrial objects. When the spectrum is formed from light of a star, the position and number of the lines are not the same as when it is formed from the light of the sun. Their position and number are not the same when the spectrum is formed from light of different stars. Electrical light and light of flames, from whatever burning body, give bright lines instead of the dark lines.

16

428. **Fixed lines in the spectra of different colored flames.**—Salts of various metals impart characteristic colors to the flame of alcohol, and spectra from flames thus colored possess characteristic fixed lines. For instance, the spectrum of a soda-flame is characterized by two bright lines in the position of two dark lines in the solar spectrum. Flames of potash-salts give other bright lines in the place of certain other dark lines.

Experiments with such and various other flames have led some philosophers to infer, that the atmosphere of the sun contains compounds of sodium and potassium.

Colors of Bodies.

429. **Color of opaque bodies.**—The color of a body may be temporary or permanent. *Temporary colors* arise from some modification of light, of a transient character. The colors of a rainbow, for instance, are caused by refraction, and are temporary.

Respecting *permanent colors* there are various opinions. Newton held that bodies absorbed some of the rays of the spectrum and reflected the remainder. According to this theory, the color of a body would be that resulting from a mixture of the reflected rays. For instance, vermilion was supposed to reflect only the red rays, while it absorbed all the other rays. All bodies placed in red light appear red, in blue light, blue, and so on for other colors.

Arago was of the opinion that the color of bodies arose from light admitted into the body and then emitted again, undergoing thereby certain modifications. According to this theory, the color would depend upon the *molecular condition* of the body.

430. **Color of transparent bodies.**—All transparent bodies absorb more or less of the light which enters them, and if sufficiently thick, must appear colored. Their color, therefore, is due to that part of the light which is transmitted. If, for example, all the solar rays, except the red ones, are absorbed by a medium, it will appear red by transmitted light. Hence water, in large masses, appears greenish, by absorbing more rays of the other colors and transmitting more of this hue. In the same way air appears blue, and hence the color of the sky.

431. **Recomposition of light.**—The seven colors of the spectrum may be reunited so as to produce white light. This can be done in several ways.

1. If a circular disk of card-board be painted in sectors with the seven colors of the spectrum, in the proportion of 56° red, 27° orange, 27° yellow, 46° green, 48° blue, 47° indigo, 109° violet, and then rapidly

revolved, it will appear to be painted *white;* illustrated by Fig. 52 (p. 245). In this case, the colors are mixed in the eye.

2. If the spectrum be received upon a concave mirror, it will be reflected to a focus, producing white light.

3. If the rays of the solar spectrum be passed through a double convex lens, shown by Fig. 54 (p. 247), they will be reunited; and if a screen, S, be held at the focus of the lens, an image will be formed entirely free from color.

4. If light be decomposed by a prism, and then received upon a second prism, of the same form and material, having its refracting angle reversed, it will be recomposed and emerge as white light; as shown by Fig. 4, Chart 6 (p. 251). The incident ray, L, will emerge from the second prism in the direction of H; the incident and emergent rays being parallel, as represented by the dotted lines.

Rainbows.

432. **Figures 49 and 50.—Rainbows—primary and secondary.**—The rainbow is a semi-circular band or arch, composed of

FIGS. 49 AND 50.

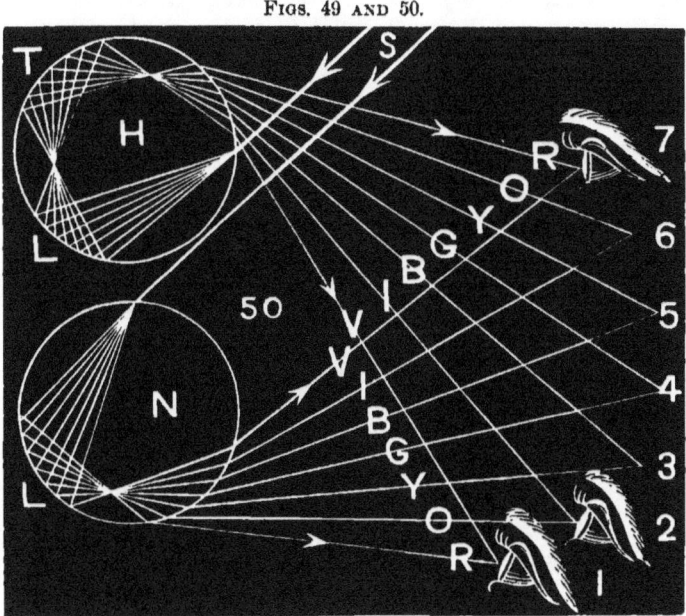

the seven different colors, seen in the air opposite to the direction of the sun, during the occurrence of rain in sunshine, when the sun is less than 42° above the horizon.

This beautiful phenomenon in nature is caused by *reflection, refraction, dispersion,* and *interference* of sunbeams by drops of rain.

Sometimes there are two rainbows, one within the other; the inner one being called the *primary bow,* and the outer one the *secondary bow.*

Let H and N be two drops of rain falling through air, and S two rays of light, one of which falls upon N, and the other upon H. N belongs to the primary and H to the secondary bow.

The ray falling upon N will first be refracted and dispersed, then internally reflected at L, and, finally, on emerging from the drop, be again refracted. The red ray, R, falling the lowest, will pass to the eye, 1, while the other rays are thrown *above* the eye.

The ray falling upon H, will first be refracted and dispersed, then *twice* internally reflected, at L and T, and, finally, on emerging from the drop, be again refracted. The violet, in this case, owing to the double reflection, falling the lowest, will also pass to the eye 1, while all the others will be thrown above the eye. A person, therefore, standing in this position, will observe a *red* ray from the *primary* and a *violet* ray from the *secondary bow;* while the eye 2 will observe the *orange* ray of the primary bow, and the *indigo* ray of the secondary bow; and so on, until the eye 7 will take in the *violet* ray of the *primary* bow and the *red* ray of the *secondary bow.* Hence it will be seen, that by placing the eye in seven different positions, it will observe all the colors of the rainbow in *one drop,* and in *two drops* all the colors coming from both bows.

FIG. 51.

433. **Figure 51.—How we see all the colors of the rainbow from one position.**—It has just been shown how, from different positions, all the colors of the rainbow may be seen in *one drop*. It will be seen by this diagram, how, by a series of drops, all the colors can be seen from *one position*.

Let SS be rays of the sun incident upon the series, or constant succession of drops on the left, and it will be seen that the uppermost drop will send the *red* ray to the eye; and the next drop, the *orange* ray; and so on, to the lowermost drop, which will furnish the *violet* ray.

Hence, as two persons cannot occupy the same place of observation, it is evident that, although different persons observe this phenomenon at the same *time*, no two persons behold exactly the *same* rainbow.

The unequal brilliancy of the two bows is due to a greater loss of light in the secondary than in the primary bow, caused by the light being twice, instead of once, reflected.

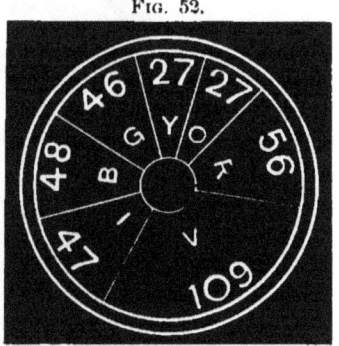

Fig. 52.

Figure 52.—For an explanation of this diagram, see 431.

434. **Figure 53.—The arch of the rainbow.**—It is not so difficult to understand the refraction, reflection, and dispersion of a ray of light by a drop of water, as it is to comprehend the construction of the arch of the bow.

Width of the bow.—By referring to Fig. 51 (433), it will be seen that the angle formed by the incident ray and the reflected or *red* ray (passing to the eye) of the uppermost drop, is *larger* than the angle formed by the incident ray and the reflected or *violet* ray (passing to the eye) of the lowermost drop.

Now, as the eye, in both cases, is in the same position, and the sun's rays are parallel to each other, the difference in the size of the two angles is owing to the fact that the reflected ray of the lowermost drop, being the violet, is more refracted than the reflected ray of the uppermost drop, which is the red ray.

The angle formed by the sunbeam and *red* ray being 42° 4', and that formed by the sunbeam and *violet* ray being 40° 17', their difference will be 1° 47', which is the width of the *primary* bow.

The width of the *secondary* bow (the light being twice reflected) is greater, by 3° 10'. In this bow the angle formed by the sunbeam and *red* ray is 50° 57'. As the red ray is on the outside of the primary bow and on the inside of the secondary bow, the distance *between the bows* will be the difference between the two angles formed by the sunbeams and the two red rays, that is, 50° 57′ minus 42° 4′ equals 8° 53′.

The arch of the bow (Fig. 53). Let the uppermost drop of the primary

FIG. 53.

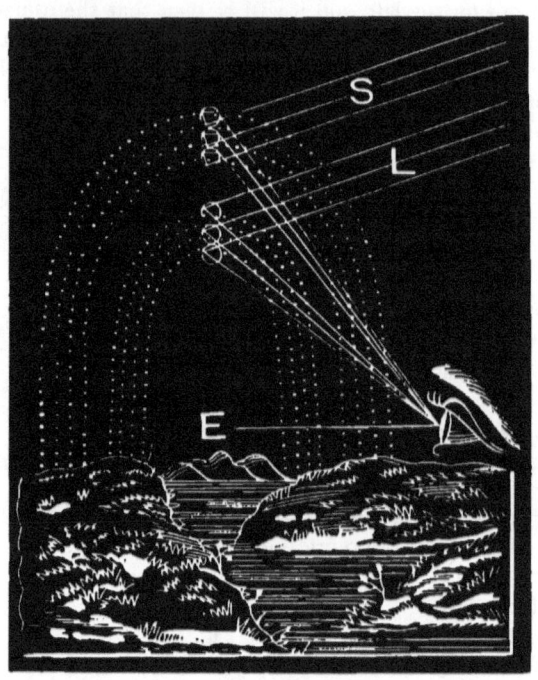

bow, and the lowermost drop of the secondary bow, represent drops reflecting the red rays. The angles formed by the sunbeams, S and L, and these red rays, as above shown, are respectively 42° 4′ and 50° 57′, and constant or invariable, whatever be the position of the drops. Therefore, although the air on the one side is filled with drops of rain, and on the other side with sunbeams, and every drop refracts, reflects, and disperses the light, yet the observer, in any *one* position, can view only those rays which are embraced within the several angles as above explained. That is, if a spectator stand with his back to the sun, and a straight line be drawn from the sun, through the eye to the shower of rain, it will also pass through the centre of the bow; and the observer will perceive the violet of the *primary* everywhere 40° 17′ from this line; and the red of the primary 42° 4′; and the red of the secondary

OPTICS. 247

50° 57'; and the violet of the secondary 54° 7'. Hence, if the angle of the sun's elevation above the horizon exceeds these angles, no rainbow can be seen; and the nearer the sun is to the horizon, the higher will be the rainbow.

The purity of the several colors in the rainbow is the result of interference, which produces dark bands for each particular color, giving a clear space for the delineation of the other colors of the rainbow before the first color is repeated. The colors are most clearly defined when the drops of rain are uniform in size.

For a further explanation of the rainbow, or the effects of a drop of water on a ray of light, see Fig. 1, Chart 6 (435).

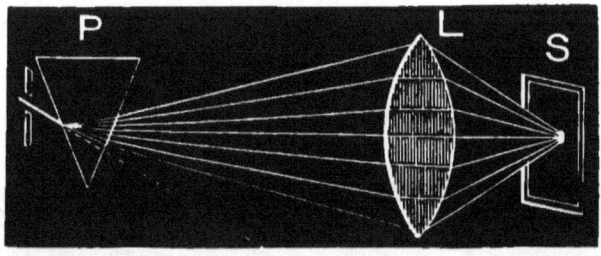

Figure 54.—Recomposition of Light by means of a double convex lens. For an explanation of this diagram, see 431.

CHAPTER XI.

(CHART NO. 6.)

OPTICS, CONTINUED,—OPTICAL INSTRUMENTS.

435. **Figure 1.—Effects of a drop of water upon parallel rays of light, further explained.**—Let the circle represent a drop of water, and S, T, H, F, parallel rays falling upon it. The ray F, being perpendicular to the drop, will pass straight through it, as shown; though a little of its light will be externally reflected back upon itself at the first surface, and internally at the second. The ray H will be refracted to A, where it will be reflected to the opposite sur-

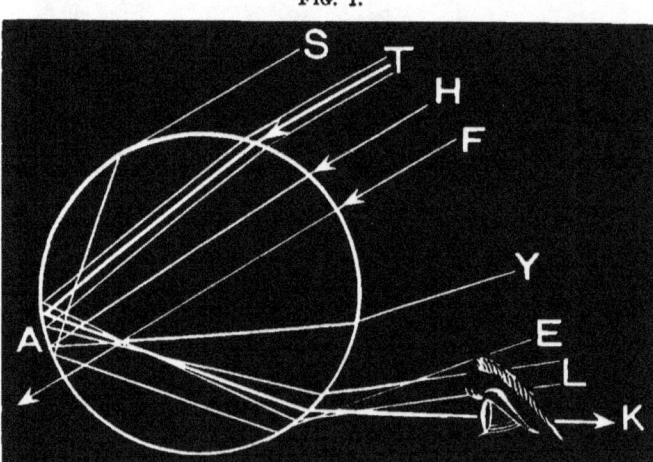

FIG. 1.

face and then refracted in the direction of Y, making a certain angle with its original direction H. As the distance of the incident ray from the centre increases, the emergent ray will make a greater angle with the incident ray, until a distance is reached where the angle formed by the incident and emergent rays will be the *largest possible*, as shown by the heavy incident line T, and its emergent ray K ; for, the more distant ray S will emerge at E, nearer parallel to itself than the heavy line T. Hence, any incident ray on either side of T, will emerge parallel to some other emergent ray, whose incident ray is on the opposite side of T; as shown by the two finer lines drawn close to the heavy line T, which emerge in the direction of L, parallel to each other.

Now, as the emergent ray K makes the *greatest possible angle* with the incident rays, it follows that all the parallel rays which enter the drop will emerge and spread over and be limited to the space between the rays K and F, having the greatest intensity near the direction K, and rapidly diminishing toward Y, until they fade to nothing.

The angle of greatest deviation, TAK, for red rays, is 42° 4', and for violet rays, 40° 17', as previously stated (434).

Since there are, at every angle between K and F, parallel rays, which have traversed different paths, and so unequal distances, through the drop, there will be exhibited all the phenomena of bright and dark bands, produced by *interference*, to be hereafter explained.

The intersection of the emergent rays will form a *caustic curve* (391).

436. **Fogbows. — Halos. — Coronas.** — *Fogbows* differ from rainbows by the minuteness of the globules of water from which the reflection takes place.

Halos are prismatic rings seen around the sun or moon, varying from 2° to 46° in diameter, caused by reflection from minute crystals of ice floating in the air.

Coronas are formed about the moon by reflection from the external surface of aqueous vapor, the light thus reflected *interfering* with direct light from the same source.

437. **Figure 2.—Chromatic aberration.**—From the analogous action of prisms and lenses, previously shown (411–12), it is evi-

FIG. 2.

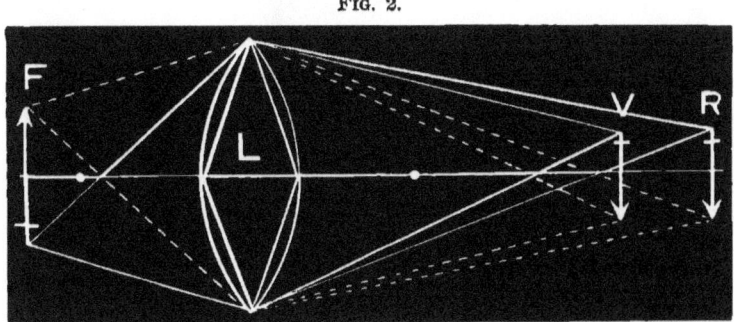

dent that white light will be dispersed by convex lenses, in the same manner as by prisms, producing all the colors of the spectrum.

Let F be an object situated beyond the principal focus of the lens L; which, having the same effect as the two inscribed prisms, will refract the most refrangible rays, which are the violet, to a focus nearer the lens, than the least refrangible, which are the red rays. Hence there will be formed, as at V, a violet image of the object, F; and a red image, beyond, as at R; while images of the other colors of the spectrum will be formed between the violet and red. Though the image of a point or line formed at V is violet, yet it will be surrounded by fringes composed of all the colors of the spectrum, the outer border of the fringe being red. If the lens be 28 inches focus, the distance between the images, V and R, will be 1 inch; if 28 feet, it will be 1 foot.

This scattering of the different colored foci, which occurs with the use of all single lenses, formed of whatever substance, is called *chromatic aberration*.

Hence, for many nice optical purposes, as for the telescope and microscope, a lens or any combination of lenses, formed out of the same glass, is almost entirely useless.

438. **Figure 3.—Achromatic combination of lenses.**—To overcome the chromatic aberration of lenses, and render them suitable for such optical instruments as the telescope, microscope, etc., has led to a combination of lenses, which has the effect of neutralizing their *dispersive*, by partly destroying their *refractive*, power.

Such lenses consist of a combination of two or more lenses of different shapes, and made of materials of unequal dispersive power; by which images can be produced unattended with prismatic phenomena.

The *double convex* crown-glass lens L (acting as two prisms, base to

FIG. 3.

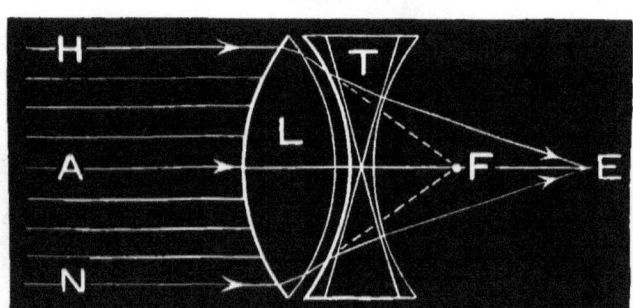

base) will refract the parallel lines, HN, to its principal focus, F, attended with the prismatic colors. If, however, the *double concave* crown-glass lens T, having its concavity equal to the convexity of L, be placed in the position as shown, it will act as two prisms, apex to apex, and render the converging rays parallel. In this case one lens just neutralizes the other in every respect. To retain a part of the refractive effect, and, at the same time, neutralize the prismatic or dispersive effect, the concave lens, T, is made of *flint* glass, which material having double the dispersive power of crown-glass (419), may be made plano-concave, instead of double concave, and so *still* neutralize the dispersive effect of the double convex crown-glass lens, L, while it will neutralize only *half its refractive effect;* therefore, in such a combination, the refractive power is equal to a single plano-convex lens of crown-glass, of the same curvature as L. Hence, the focus of the combination will be at the point E, double the distance from the lens of the focus F, and free of prismatic colors.

In forming an *achromatic combination* the following conditions must obtain:

1st. It must be composed of two or more lenses, formed of media having different dispersive powers.

2d. One of the lenses must be concave and the other convex.

3d. The two lenses must have focal lengths directly proportional to the dispersive powers of the media of which they are respectively composed.

If the combination is made of crown and flint glass, the focus of the *crown* should be to that of the *flint* as 2 to 3, or rather, in ordinary cases as to 3 to 4; since most specimens of flint-glass, when formed into an equal prism with one of crown, make a spectrum whose length compared with that of the crown is as 4 to 3, instead of 3 to 2, as heretofore stated.

FIG. 4.

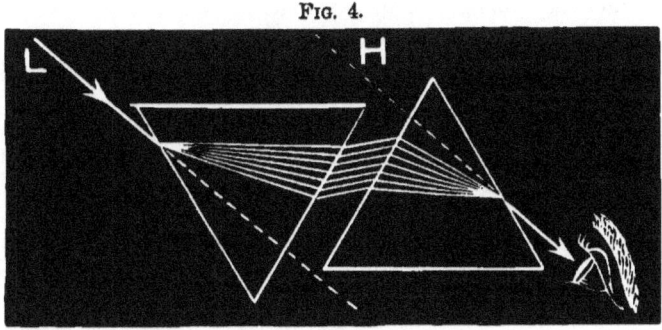

Figure 4.—Recomposition of light by means of reversed prisms. For an explanation of this diagram, see 431.

VISION.

439.—**Figure 5.—The camera obscura.**—The camera obscura as the name implies, is a dark chamber, and, in a portable form,

FIG. 5.

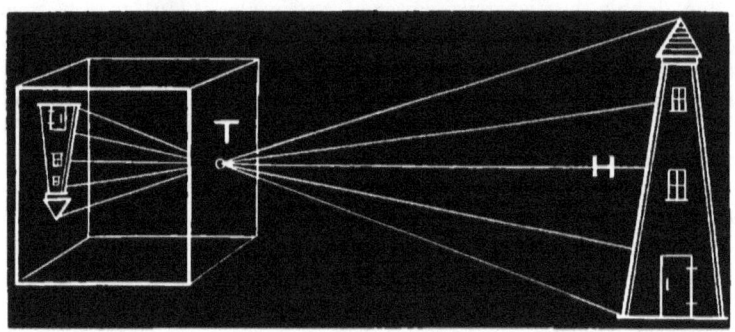

is employed to take pictures of objects. In its simplest construction, it consists of a dark room, provided with a small opening, as a hole in a shutter, on one side of the room, the wall on the opposite side serving as a screen, to receive the image.

The principle of its operation is, that the rays which form the image, coming from any object, as the tower H, must converge in order to pass through the opening T; hence, all rays, except the axial, necessarily *cross* each other as they enter the box or chamber; and, as all other rays are excluded, an inverted image will be formed, as represented.

To render the camera obscura portable, there is substituted, in place of the room with an aperture in the shutter, a wooden box, with a small hole in óne side, with a ground-glass or paper screen on the other, upon which to receive and trace the image.

If the box be moved toward the object, the image increases in size, and diminishes if it be moved from it. If it be held at a given distance, and the opening moved up or down, or to the right or left, as if the box were held by a central point within, the image will remain the same size, but be shifted about on the screen. The image is rendered more distinct with a small hole than with a large one, since, in the first case, rays from any particular part of the object fall on the corresponding part of the image.

The images are the same whatever be the shape of the aperture, provided it be quite small.

The images thus formed are not sufficiently distinct, but if the aperture be made larger and provided with a double convex lens, the picture will be formed, on a screen placed at the focal distance, which will represent, with great beauty and distinctness, whatever is in front of the lens, all the objects having their proper relations of position, light, shadow, and color.

This instrument affords aid in sketching outlines of landscapes, buildings, etc.; but its principal importance at present consists in its application to the various branches of Photography (487).

The camera obscura will be alluded to again, and it is thus far explained in this connection, to assist in explaining the construction of the eye and the phenomena of vision.

440. **The eye a camera obscura.**—The eye is a self-adjusting camera obscura; the eyeball being the dark chamber or box; the pupil, the aperture; the retina, the screen; the contents of the ball, the lens. Its portability is evident, as we always have two of them with us. Its position is adjustable by the motion of the head in every direction on the neck, and by the partial rotation of the ball within its socket. The size of the pupil or aperture adjusts itself to the intensity of the light: the humors and lens adjust themselves to vary the focal distance to the retina or screen, according to the distance of the object, and they have neither the fault of spherical or chromatic aberration.

By these various and wonderful contrivances, we can stand in one position, and, without moving the body below the neck, so set and adjust this natural camera obscura, as to photograph upon the retina a perfect image of every object, from a simple speck to a complicated landscape, in whatever direction, and for a vast distance. Hence the eye may be considered an optical instrument embracing every perfection.

441. **Figure 6.—Method of adjusting the pupil or aperture of the eye.**—The circular portion of the figure represents the *iris,* or that part of the eye which determines its color, as black, hazel, blue, gray, etc.; the dark part being the aperture or pupil, which admits the light.

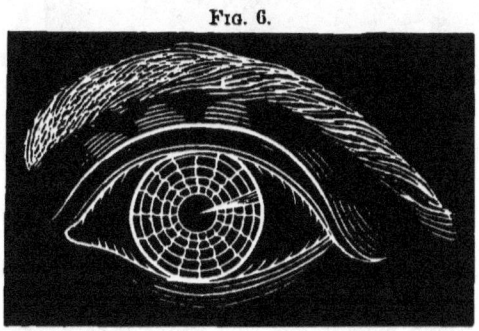

Fig. 6.

The iris is provided with two sets of muscles, *radiating* and *circular.* The radiating muscles, represented by the wavy

254   OPTICS.

radiating lines, will contract and the circular ones expand, when the intensity of the light is *insufficient*, and so enlarge the pupil, that more rays may enter. The circular muscles, represented by the circles, on the contrary, contract, and the radiating ones expand, when the intensity of the light is *too great*, and thus exclude a portion of the light.

The variation of the size of the pupil may be noticed by observing the eye at different distances from a bright light, at night. Its sudden contraction gives pain, as when going immediately from a dark to a brilliantly lighted room, or on suddenly opening the eyes in the morning light. The pain on such occasions is partly due to the effect of too much light on the retina, before the pupil can sufficiently contract to exclude it.

The owl is unable to see by daylight because he cannot contract the pupil sufficiently to prevent the blinding effect of the rays, while it admits sufficient light to enable him to see in the night.

The pupil in man is round; in the feline tribe it is vertically elongated; in ruminating animals its elongation is horizontal.

442. **Figure 7.—The means of adjusting and holding the eye in the direction of the object.**—The diagram represents the exterior of the eyeball, P being the pupil, and FME, muscles.

These and other muscles are attached, at one end, to the eyeball, and at the other end to the back part of the bony socket. By their alternate contraction and expansion the eye can be turned in any direction, necessary to direct the pupil toward the object to be viewed; as if the ball were turned about a central point within; while they serve also to firmly hold the eye in any given position.

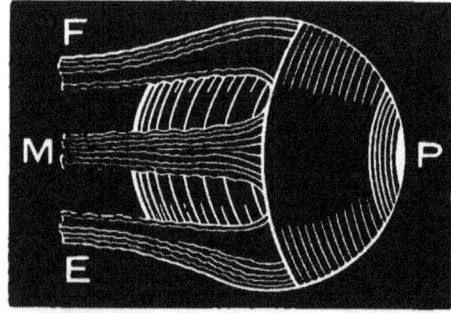
FIG. 7.

443. **Figure 8.—Structure of the interior of the eye.**—The figure shows a horizontal section of the eye, the upper part representing the side toward the nose.

The principal parts of the eye, not already described, are the *sclerotic coat, cornea, choroid coat, retina, optic nerve, crystalline lens, aqueous humor,* and *vitreous humor.*

1. *The sclerotic coat* is the outer covering, being a strong, thick, opaque membrane; that which is called the *white* of the eye being a

part of it. This membrane has a posterior, sieve-like opening, T, for the transmission of the fibres of the optic nerve.

2. *The cornea* is a transparent membrane which is joined to the

FIG. 8.

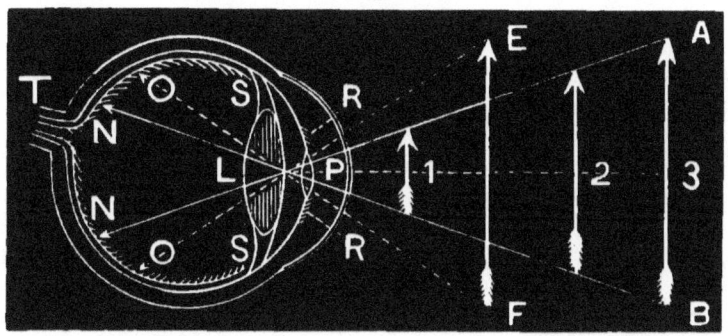

edges of an opening in the anterior part of the sclerotic coat, through which the light passes to the eye; and holds the same relation to the sclerotic covering that the crystal of a watch does to the case. The cornea is more oval than other parts of the ball, as represented in the diagram.

3. *The choroid coat* is a vascular membrane lining the sclerotic coat, and is covered internally with the pigmentum nigrum, a dark pigment which darkens the chamber and prevents internal reflection of light.

To the edges of an opening in the front part of this membrane is joined the outer edge of the iris, RR.

4. *The retina and optic nerve*. The retina is the third or inner membrane of the eye, and consists of an expansion or spreading out of the optic nerve, into millions of fine fibres, forming a whitish, delicate, lining membrane of nerve-substance, upon which the images of external objects are formed.

5. *The crystalline lens*, L. is a transparent body, of the consistence of gristle, placed just behind the iris. and is enveloped in a transparent membrane or capsule. which adheres by its borders to the ciliary process, SS. The posterior surface of the crystalline lens is more convex than the anterior, as shown. This lens is made up of serrated fibres, arranged in layers, which increase in density from the circumference to the centre of the lens.

6. *The aqueous humor* is a transparent liquid which fills the space between the cornea in front and the crystalline lens, L. In this liquid freely floats the annular curtain or iris. RR; which divides this space into the anterior chamber (between the cornea and the iris) and the

posterior chamber (between the iris and crystalline lens). These two chambers communicate freely with each other through the pupil, P.

7. *The vitreous humor* is a transparent, gelatinous fluid, nearly filling all the posterior compartment of the eye, which includes all the space behind the crystalline lens. This humor is enclosed in delicate cellular tissue.

444. **The lachrymal or tear gland, and eyelid.**—The eye being necessarily sensitive, in order to be susceptible to the delicate impressions of light, requires to be kept moist, clean, and free from dust, and protected from the air and light while we sleep.

These requirements are admirably provided for by the lachrymal gland and eyelid. These, taken together, may be called a delicate washing apparatus, ever at work, during our waking hours, moistening and cleansing the eye every time we wink. The gland may be likened to a sponge, concealed and situated just above the eye, which gathers tear-fluid from the blood-vessels and passes it down to the eye; where the lid, acting as a soft, suitable cloth, wipes or washes the natural glass of the eye, and coats it with an essential film of moisture. Without winking, vision soon becomes indistinct.

445. **Figure 9.—Adjustability of the eye to different distances.**—That the crystalline lens must adjust itself, in order to vary its focal distance, and so produce on the retina distinct images of objects situated at different distances, is evident from the laws previously explained, relating to lenses.

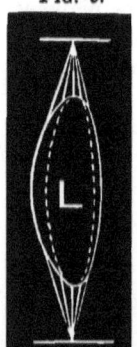
FIG. 9.

This variation in the convexity of the crystalline lens is accomplished by means of its elasticity, and the attachment of its membrane or capsule to the ciliary process, SS, Fig. 8.

Let L represent the lens within its capsule or bag. If the case or bag be fastened to the short parallel lines, and these lines be separated, the lens will be compressed and flattened (shown by the dotted lines), as if it were made of some soft elastic substance, like rubber. If then these points of attachment be brought nearer together, the lens will restore itself to its former convexity. The distance of the lens from the retina, also, may be changed.

446. **Optical axis.**—The principal axis of the eye, called the *optical axis*, is a straight line passing through the eye in such a direction that the organ is symmetrical on all sides of it; which is a right line passing through the centre of the cornea, pupil, and crystalline lens. Lines drawn near the optic axis, which are sensibly right lines, are secondary axes. Objects are seen most distinctly in the principal optic axis.

447. **Optic angle.**—The angle formed by drawing straight lines from the two eyes to the object, is called the *optic angle*, or the *binocular parallax*.

This angle, and difference of direction, will be appreciated by looking at an object first with one eye and then with the other, without moving the head, which will cause the object to apparently change its position.

448. **Angle of vision** (Figure 8).—The angle formed at the eye, by lines drawn from the extremities of an object to where they cross in the eye, is called the *visual angle* or *angle of vision*.

This angle bears a proportion *directly* to the linear magnitude, and *inversely* to the distance of the object.

1. Let AB be an object, and the lines AN and BN will intersect at the eye, forming a certain angle; and an image, NN, of the object, of a certain size, will be formed on the retina. If the object, AB, were made double its length, the visual angle and the image would be twice as large.

2. If the object, AB, be placed at EF, half as far from the eye, the visual angle and image will be twice as large, as shown by the dotted lines.

The reason of this is, that the diverging lines depart from each other in proportion as they are extended from the point of their intersection, as shown by the objects 1, 2, and 3.

As the superficial magnitude of an object is as the square of the lineal magnitude, the *apparent* superficial magnitude of an object will be *inversely as the square of the distance*.

The smallest visual angle under which an object can be seen, with the naked eye, is about *twelve seconds*.

449. **Inversion of images formed in the eye.**—The camera obscura (439) and the structure of the eye are sufficient proof of the inversion of images on the retina; but, for ocular proof, take the eye of an ox, cut away the posterior part of the sclerotic and choroid coats; fix the eye in an opening in the shutter of a dark room, look at it with a magnifying glass, and external objects will be seen beautifully delineated in an inverted position on the retina.

450.—**Why we see objects erect, their images being inverted,** is explained in different ways by different philosophers; but probably it is because, the image *always* being inverted, the mind, by unconscious training, is habituated to it; learning from the beginning to refer the impression it receives to the upright position of the object.

451.—**The brightness of the ocular image.**—The intensity of light diminishes as the square of the distance it travels increases; see Fig. 50 (529). Hence, the brightness of an object, by this law, would be inversely as the square of the distance. The apparent superficial magnitude of an object also diminishes as the square of the distance increases (447). Hence, as the intensity of the light (or brightness of the object) will be *increased* by the apparent diminution of surface over which it is spread, in the same ratio that its intensity will *diminish* by the increase of distance, it follows that

The apparent brightness of an object, and consequently of its image, will remain constant, whatever may be the distance of the object.

452. **Figure 10.—Indistinct vision.**—If an object, F, be brought too near the eye, say within an inch or two, its image becomes

FIG. 10.

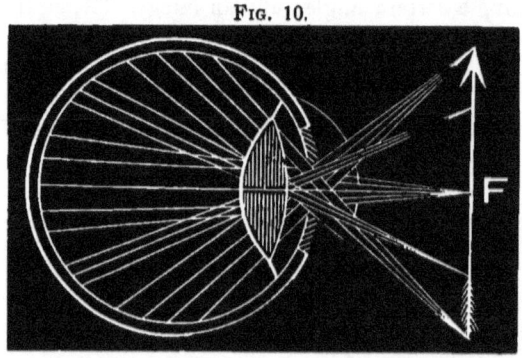

confused and indistinct, because the rays, flowing from it, fall too divergent on the crystalline lens to be refracted to a focus on the retina.

If we could see objects distinctly when placed quite near the eye, we should be able to examine things that are now invisible at the limit of distinct vision (455), since the visual angle (448) would then be increased, and consequently, the image on the retina enlarged, in proportion as objects were brought near the eye.

Sufficiency of illumination.—In order to have distinct vision, the image must not only be well defined on the retina, but it must not be so faint as to produce no sensation, nor so intensely brilliant as to dazzle the eye, which produces pain, and consequently destroys distinctness of vision.

453. Figure 11.—How to see objects close to the eye.—
The images of objects held close to the eye may be rendered distinct by intercepting the more divergent rays, and thus preventing them from entering the eye.

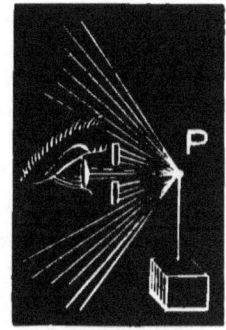

Fig. 11.

Let the object, P, be a pin-head, brought close to the eye. Interpose a piece of paper, sufficiently large to shut off all the light that would fall upon the eye, and admit only such rays as will pass through a pin-hole in the paper, as represented. These few rays, being sensibly parallel, will be converged, and form, on the retina, not only a distinct but an *enlarged* image. The brightness of the image will be *diminished*, owing to the pin-hole being smaller than the pupil.

454. Figure 12.—Brilliancy of vision is dependent on the number of rays that enter the eye, that can be brought to a focus on the retina.

If the object, F, be a pin-head, and L, a small double convex lens, the eye will receive all the rays that would diverge between the two

Fig. 12.

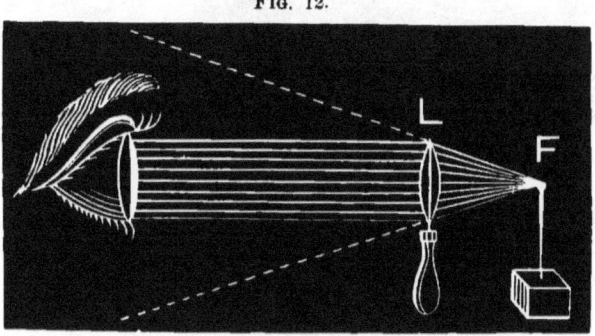

dotted lines; rendering the vision more distinct than if only those rays were received which would diverge to the eye without the lens.

This is the whole theory of the single *microscope*, the word meaning, to view small things.

455. Limit of distinct vision.—Although we see objects at both great and small distances, most persons, when they wish to see the minute structure of an object clearly, place it from six to ten inches from the eye. This point is called the *limit of distinct vision*.

456. **Figure 13.—Visual rays must be nearly parallel.—** When the eye is adjusted to view near objects, the diameter of the pupil being only about one-tenth of an inch, and the limit of vision from six to ten inches, it will be found that the cone of divergent rays from a single point will be included within an angle of from *one* to a little more than *one-half* a degree. Therefore, the rays of vision differ but slightly from parallel rays. While, for all objects more remote, the rays may be considered as parallel.

Hence, *distinct vision is obtained only by rays that are sensibly parallel or very slightly divergent.*

This is illustrated by the diagram. From the extremities, as well as from all other points of the object, L, rays diverge in every direction;

Fig. 13.

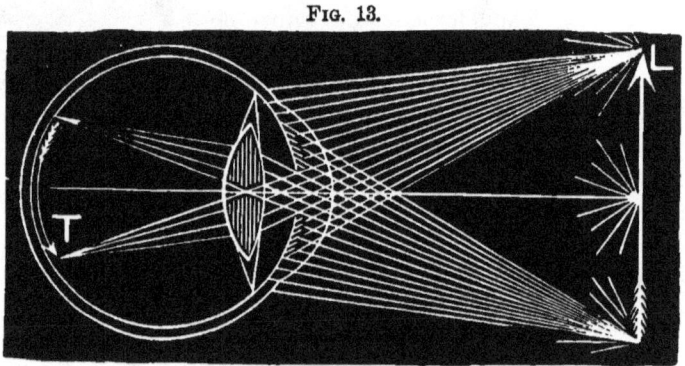

but the image, T, of the point, L, on the retina, is formed by the few nearly parallel rays that pass close to the secondary axis, LT; and what is true of the point L is true of all other points of the object.

457. **Size of the image on the retina.—**The actual size of the image on the retina, capable of exciting sensation and producing vision, may be exceedingly small. For example, a human hair can be seen, with the naked eye, at a distance of twenty or thirty feet, yet the image is many times smaller than the object.

It has been estimated that the image on the retina, of a man seen at the distance of a mile, is not more than one five-thousandth part of an inch in length.

458. **Figure 14.—Near-sightedness and long-sightedness.—**Persons who see objects at very short distances, say less than about six inches, are called *near-sighted;* while those who see objects distinctly only at a greater distance than about twelve inches, are said to be *long-sighted.*

OPTICS.

Near-sightedness is caused, in some cases, by *too much curvature* of the cornea and crystalline lens, by which the rays of light, that form the image, are brought to a focus before they reach the retina, as shown by the image T, of the object A, which falls short of the retina. The object will be seen, but not *distinctly*. To obtain distinct vision, therefore, the object must be brought nearer to the eye, or concave spectacles employed, either of which means will cause the rays to enter the eye with a greater degree of divergence, and so, by increasing the focal distance, throw the image back upon the retina.

FIG. 14.

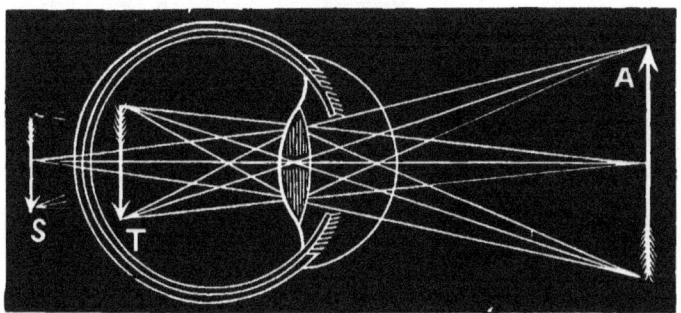

Long-sightedness, on the contrary, is caused by *too little curvature* of the cornea and crystalline lens, which throws the image S, of the object A, beyond the retina. This defect, therefore, is corrected by holding the object at a greater distance from the eye, or by employing convex spectacles, either of which means will render the rays less divergent, and, thus shortening the focal distance, will bring the image within the eye and throw it upon the retina.

FIG. 15.

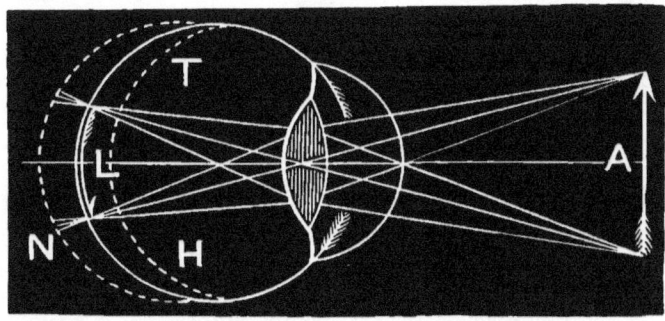

459. **Figure 15.—Short-sightedness and long-sightedness caused by defective forms of the eyeball.**—Although the cornea and crystalline lens have the proper curvature, and all parts of the eye possess their usual powers of adjustment, yet *short-sightedness* may result from an elongation of the eyeball, which would locate the retina beyond the focal distance, and thus out of the reach of the image.

Long-sightedness may be caused by the shortening of the diameter of the eyeball in the direction of the optical axis; which would bring the retina between the crystalline lens and its focal distance, as shown in the diagram.

In case of elongation, as shown by the exterior dotted line N, the image, L, would fall short of the retina; and in case of shortening, as shown by the interior dotted line, TH, the image, L, would fall beyond the retina.

460. **Long-sightedness of old people** is due principally to the loss of convexity and elasticity of the crystalline lens, and to more or less diminution of curvature of the cornea, and a partial absorption of the humors of the eye.

461. **Conditions of distinct vision** are, 1st. That *an object be situated at such a distance as to form an image on the retina.*

2d. *That the image be of some appreciable magnitude.*

3d. *That the object be sufficiently illuminated to produce a distinct impression upon the retina.*

An image may be so faint as to produce no sensation, or it may be so intensely brilliant as to dazzle the eye, destroy the distinctness of vision, and produce pain.

462. **Sensibility of the retina** is diminished by long exposure of the eye to intense light, and increased by remaining a long time in feeble light or in the dark (441).

That that part of the retina, receiving a very bright image, will be temporarily insensible, is shown by turning the eye directly from a bright to a dim object, when a dark spot will be seen. If the bright object be of one color, the part of the retina on which the image falls becomes insensible to rays of that color, but not to rays of other colors.

This explains the appearance of *complementary* colors (421). For example, a bright red image will blind the retina to red light, but leave it sensitive to the remaining colors which make up white light; and when red is taken from white light, the combination of the other colors gives a greenish hue. Hence, on turning the eye from a bright red object, other objects, for a moment, will appear *greenish*: conversely, if the bright object be green, other objects will appear *red*.

463. **Color-blindness.**—Some persons are unable to distinguish colors at all; and others but indifferently; while some can detect the slightest difference in shades of the same color. Some confound red and green, and can distinguish other colors. Persons who cannot see the difference in the colors of the spectrum, or cannot distinguish between any two of the simple colors, are said to be *color-blind.*

464. **Effect of different colors on vision.**—The distance at which an object can be seen varies with its color and the amount of illumination. A white object, illuminated by the sun, can be seen at a distance equal to 17,250 times its own diameter; a red object, about half as far; and a blue object at a distance somewhat less than a red. Objects can be seen about twice as far when illuminated by direct rays of the sun, as when illuminated by ordinary daylight.

465. **Effects of background.—Irradiation.**—When a white object is seen against a black ground, it appears larger than it really is; while a black object on a white ground, appears smaller than it really is. This effect is called *irradiation.*

This is caused by the impression, produced by the light-colored object on the retina, extending beyond the outline of the image. It bears the same relation to the space occupied by the image, as the duration cf the impression does to the duration of the image.

466. **Estimation of distance and magnitude of objects.**—The appreciation of the distance and magnitude of objects depends upon the visual angle, optic angle, comparison with familiar objects, and distinctness or dimness of the image, caused by intervening air or vapor.

The visual angle of an object, as previously shown (448), varying with the distance, can afford no evidence of the *size* of an object, unless we appreciate its distance. We must, therefore, know the *distance* of a body in order to estimate its size. By knowing its distance we instinctively appreciate its size. A chair, for example, at the opposite side of the room, has a visual angle only half as large as when at half the distance, yet we cannot make it seem any smaller in one part of the room than another, if we try. But if we are, in any way, deceived as to the distance of an object, we are also deceived as to its size.

One of the means by which we judge of the distance of an object, is by knowing its *size.* Being familiar with the size of many bodies, as men, animals, trees, etc., the visual angles under which they are seen enable us to estimate their distance; and, knowing their distance, we instinctively estimate the magnitude of adjacent objects, with whose magnitude we are not familiar.

This is the reason why the moon appears larger near the horizon than overhead. When near the horizon it seems further off, because it is beyond all other objects, and so we judge it is larger than when it is in the zenith, where there are no intervening objects to make it appear equally distant.

We also judge of the distance of an object by the *distinctness* with which we see it. The brighter it is the nearer it seems. It is for this reason that objects seem larger in a fog. Their indistinctness impresses us that they are far off, and hence, we judge they are larger than they are. It is for this reason, too, that distant objects seem less distant in very clear atmosphere.

Infants reach out to grasp the blaze of a candle which is many feet from them; showing that, without experience of touch, they have no notion of distance.

The *optic angle*, or binocular parallax (447), is an essential means in appreciating distance. This angle increases or diminishes inversely as the distance. The effort we make to turn the eyes inward, to vary the optic angle, or converge the optic axes of the two eyes upon the object, gives us an idea of its distance.

467. Why, with two eyes, we see objects single.— Though an image of an object is formed in both eyes, yet we see but the one object. This is accounted for by the bifurcation of the optic nerves. That is, the optic nerve from the right lobe of the brain sends a portion of its fibres to each eye, and also sends some branches across and backward to the left lobe of the brain; and a portion of the optic nerve from the right *eye*, instead of proceeding to the brain, curves around to the optic nerve and retina of the left eye. The optic nerve of the left side is related to that of the right side in the same manner.

In this way a perfect sympathy is established between the two eyes, the inner side of one corresponding to the outer side of the other. As the images are always formed with their centres at the centres of the eyes, the right and left parts of the images will be on corresponding parts of the eyes, and, therefore, they will appear as one.

By pressing the finger upon the eyeball, the images will not fall upon corresponding parts of the two retinæ, and the object is seen double.

468. Double vision.—Both eyes being fixed steadily upon one object, any other object seen at the same time will be seen double.

Fix both eyes upon any near object, and a pencil, held between the eyes and the object, will appear double.

Any cause, as drunkenness, disease of the nerves, etc., which prevents the eyes from being steadily fixed upon the same object, will cause double vision.

469. **Binocular vision.**—Though a picture of an object is formed on the retina of each eye, yet the two pictures, notwithstanding they are formed from the same object, are not precisely alike. This is because the object is not observed from the same point of view by both eyes.

If a thin book, for example, be held up edgeways to the centre of and a few inches from the face, one eye will see one side of the book and the other eye the other side.

If an oval object, like a bottle, be held before the face, both eyes will see some portion of it, while each eye will see some parts of it that the other cannot see; so that we partially see *around* the bottle.

While the mind is impressed with the idea that there is but one object, yet the judgment naturally determines the object to be a projecting body (see 495).

470. **Duration of impression upon the retina.**—The impression made by light on the retina does not cease instantly, on removing the light, but lasts for an *eighth of a second* or more.

A lighted stick, as every one has observed, whirled rapidly around a circle, appears like a ring of fire. The rapidity of revolution required to produce this impression is one-third of a second in a dark room, and one-sixth of a second in the daylight. It is owing to the continuation of the impression on the retina that the seven simple colors, revolved on a disk (431), produce white light; and that the spokes of a rapidly revolving wheel cannot be distinguished.

Winking does not interfere with distinct vision, because the act of winking requires less time than is needed to remove the impression from the retina.

471. **Optic toys.**—It is upon the principle that impressions remain on the retina for a sensible length of time, after the object has changed its place, that optical toys are constructed, and pyrotechnic exhibitions owe their effect.

472. **Time required to produce visual impressions.**—If an object moves across our vision with great velocity, as a projected cannon-ball or rifle-ball, its image does not remain on the retina long enough to produce any impression.

Motions describing less than one minute of arc in a second of time are not appreciable to us. Hence, we cannot perceive the movement of the hour-hand of a clock, or the motions of the heavenly bodies.

473. **Sensations of light may be excited by other causes.**—The sensation of light may be excited by anything which can excite the optic nerve. An electric shock sent through the eye produces an apparent flash of light. If a piece of zinc be placed in the mouth and one end of a silver pencil held in the corner of the eye, a flash will be experienced when the silver and zinc are brought in contact. Pressing the eyeballs with the fingers produces a luminous image; and so will a blow on the head enable us to "see stars."

OPTICAL INSTRUMENTS.

474. Variety and principal uses of optical instruments.—There are many kinds of optical instruments, varying in construction and magnitude, from simple eye-glasses or spectacles to telescopes weighing many tons, and costing hundreds of thousands of dollars.

Though the unaided eye extends its limits far and wide, beyond the reach of our other senses, picturing on the brain an infinite variety of objects, yet our unassisted power of vision is limited, in its observations of the vast field of nature, to a mere speck, compared with the scope of our senses aided by various optical instruments.

The *microscope* (the word meaning to view small things) has made us acquainted with a world, which, though too minute to be seen with ordinary eyes, is filled with greater curiosities and wonders, and with more important operations, than all we can see by direct observation.

The *telescope* (the word signifying to see far off) has made it possible for us to bring to view countless worlds, which, though of immense magnitude, were beyond the reach of our vision.

With the aid of the *camera*, instead of *painting* pictures we *print* them with rays of light.

With *simple lenses*, or eye-glasses, the skill of the artist is increased, and the dim sight of old age is repaired.

475. Spectacles.—The most common and simple of all optical instruments are spectacles. These are employed to remedy the defects of eyes. The principles involved in their application were explained under the head of short-sightedness, etc. (459).

Microscopes, Opera-glasses, Etc.

476. The simple microscope is a simple double convex lens, of short focal distance. These are called magnifying glasses, and are used to magnify, to an ordinary extent, small objects. They are employed by various artisans, as watch-makers, engravers, etc., whose labors are performed on minute structures.

Such lenses may be used single or double. They are usually set in a rim provided with a handle, or fixed in a short cylinder of ivory or horn. Such a magnifying glass is seen at L, Fig. 12 (454). These instruments occupy a place between spectacles and regular microscopes, composed of several parts.

Magnifying power of a lens is found, for ordinary purposes, by dividing ten inches (the limit of distinct vision) by the distance of the principal focal distance of the lens.

In using the simple microscope the object is placed a little nearer the lens than the focal distance, in which case the divergent rays from the object will be made to pass to the eye as parallel rays, and the object will appear as large as if the eye were placed at the optical centre of the lens, as shown by Fig. 12 (454).

If the focal distance be half an inch, the magnifying power will be $10 \div \tfrac{1}{2} = 20$.

477. **Figure 16.—The compound microscope** consists essentially of a double convex lens, L, called the *object-glass*, and a second double convex lens, F, of larger size, called the *eye-piece*.

Fig. 16.

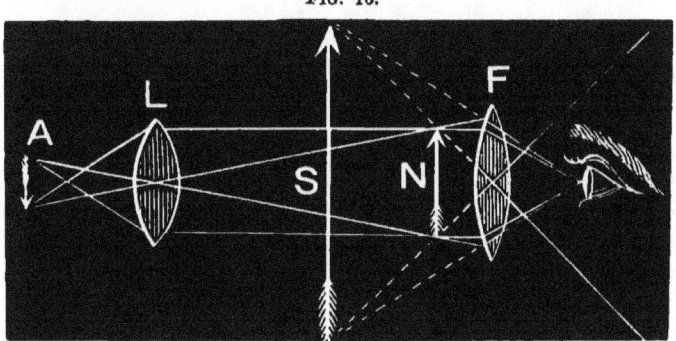

The object, A, is placed a little beyond the principal focus of the object-glass L. This lens produces a real image, N, which is inverted. The eye-piece or lens, F, is so placed that its principal focus is a little beyond the image N. This then acts as a simple microscope and magnifies the image; causing it to appear as a virtual image, in the situation of, and as large as, S.

The lenses, of course, are made achromatic, to avoid prismatic colors (438).

A good magnifying power, of length and breadth, is 600, which, being squared, gives in surface 360,000. If the power be greater than this, distinctness is lost.

The object, when transparent, is illuminated with a concave mirror;

when opaque, it is illuminated by concentrating light upon it with a lens.

The microscope is employed in the study of botany, entomology, anatomy, physiology, and for many purposes.

To find the power of a compound microscope, *multiply the power of the object-lens by the power of the eye-glass.*

478. **Figure 17.—The magic lantern.**—This is an apparatus for projecting upon a screen enlarged images of objects painted on glass.

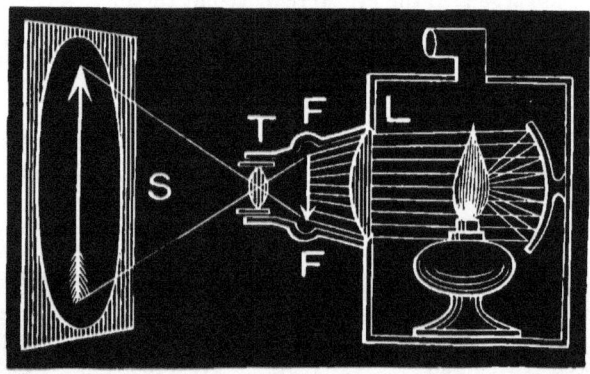

FIG. 17.

It consists of a dark box, in which a lamp is placed before a parabolic reflector; the light being concentrated and reflected upon a plano-convex lens L; by which it is further concentrated, and directed upon the object painted upon the glass slide, inserted at FF. The magnifying lens, T, is placed so as to throw its focus a little beyond the object, which forms an image of the illuminated picture upon the screen S, placed at its conjugate focus.

The magnifying power is equal to the distance of the screen from the lens T, divided by the distance of the lens from the object. Therefore the power of the instrument depends upon the lens T.

To provide for the adjustment of magnifying lenses, of different powers, to the painted objects, they are held in a slide, T.

The picture-object should be inverted, in order that its image may appear erect.

479. **Figure 18.—The solar microscope** differs in principle from the magic lantern, only in the method of illuminating the object.

It is usually employed for producing on a screen images of natural objects, highly magnified.

It is mounted in a dark room, before an opening in a shutter. A plane mirror, M, being arranged outside the shutter in such a position as to receive the direct rays of the sun, and reflect them through the condensing lens H, which highly illuminates the object A, the object is adjusted to the focus of the magnifying lens L, and a greatly enlarged image, formed at the conjugate focus, will be received upon a suitable white screen, S.

FIG. 18.

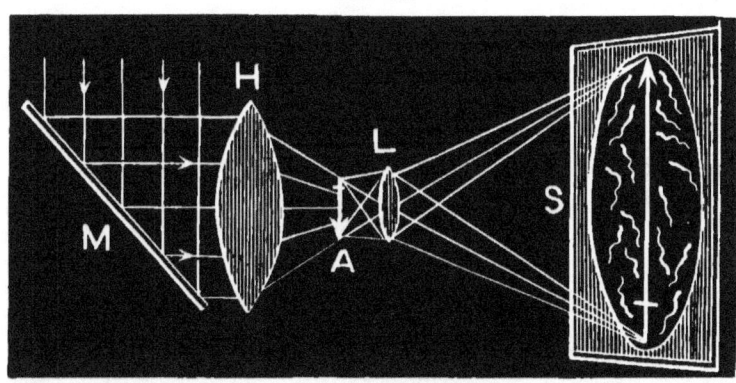

The magnifying lens may be a small globule of glass, or a compound achromatic object-glass of short focus. The power of the instrument depends upon this lens.

Instead of illuminating the object with light of the sun, electric light, or the oxyhydrogen light may be, and often is, employed, and with great effect. For some purposes, this is superior: being free from the heat that attends a concentration of the solar rays, animalcules are not so soon destroyed, and the instrument may be used in any place and at any time.

Upon the screen, S, is represented a magnified drop of vinegar; the live, snake-like insects being sometimes magnified to the length of two or three feet, which are seen swimming in every direction.

Not only are small objects brought to view, but minute *operations* are distinctly exhibited, as the manœuvres and habits of insects, the circulation of the blood, the phenomena of crystallization, and a great variety of Nature's processes, which, to the unaided eye, would forever remain unobserved.

The objects are held in position by suitable contrivances. Live insects, and painted ones, and drops of liquid filled with animalculæ, different kinds of vegetable substances, animal tissues, etc., constitute interesting objects.

480. **Polyrama and dissolving views.**—The polyrama consists of a double magic lantern. The dissolving views are obtained by using both lanterns.

If a scene, painted by moonlight, be put upon one side in the lantern, and a painting of the same scene by daylight be put upon the other side, of course, first one scene and then the other can be thrown upon the screen, by alternately covering and uncovering the two tubes of the lanterns. But by gradually cutting off the light from one picture, and, at the same time, gradually admitting it to the other, the first will insensibly fade away, whilst the other as insensibly grows brighter. In this manner all the effects, intermediate between full daylight and full moonlight, may be obtained in succession.

481. **Figure 19.—Opera-glasses.**—The opera-glass consists essentially of a convex object-lens, which collects the rays, and a concave lens as an eye-piece, by means of which the rays from each point of the object are rendered parallel, and thus capable of producing distinct vision.

FIG. 19.

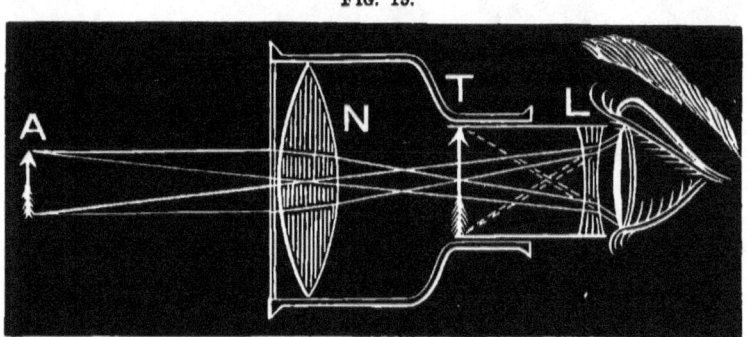

The object-glass, N, converges the rays coming from the object A, upon the concave eye-glass, L, by which the converging rays are rendered slightly divergent before entering the eye, as though emanating from the position T, at a distance of distinct vision; the image being virtual and erect.

The large object-glass, of long focal distance, and the eye-piece, of short focal distance, are placed at a distance apart equal to the difference of their principal foci, which collects a large number of rays from the object and brings them to such a state of divergence as to produce distinct vision in the eye.

As the eye-piece is concave, the magnifying power of such an instrument is found by dividing the principal focal distance of the convex lens by the principal focal distance of the concave lens.

This instrument was first constructed by Galileo and employed as a telescope; hence it is called the Galilean telescope.

When employed as an opera-glass it is made double to provide for both eyes.

482. **Night-glasses,** employed by seamen, have the same construction as opera-glasses, except they are larger and have less magnifying power; the object being to concentrate a large amount of light in such a condition as to allow of distinct vision, to enable the observer to see objects distinctly at night.

The Camera Obscura.

483. **Figure 20.—The camera obscura,** as employed by artists for tracing landscapes, etc.

Having explained the general principles of the camera obscura in connection with the description of the eye (439), it only remains to show the manner in which it is adapted to the use of the artist.

FIG. 20.

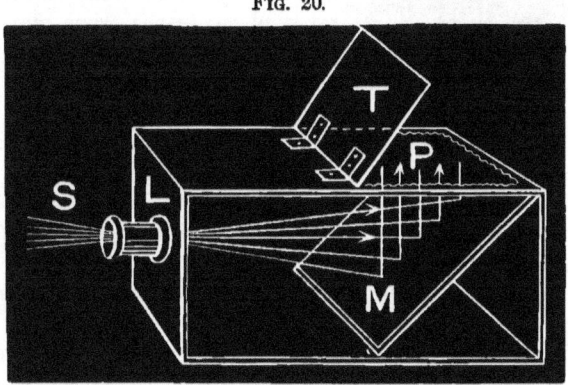

In the dark box is provided a plane mirror, M, inclined at an angle of 45°, upon which the rays S, coming from the object or scenery, are received, and by which they are reflected upward to a glass plate or transparent screen, upon which is laid the paper P, and on which the tracing is made. The lens, in L, gives the proper convergence to the rays. The box is placed on a stand or any convenient support. The cover, T, serves to protect the glass screen when the instrument is not in use.

484. **Figure 21.—Another form of the camera obscura.**
—Upon the frame, FF, is mounted a horizontal head-piece, in which is fitted a plane mirror, M. To exclude the light, a black cloth is thrown over the frame. The rays of the object, A, or scenery, are received upon the mirror and reflected through the lens, and received upon the paper laid on the table, H, below, as shown. The lens is held in a sliding tube, TT, to render its focus adjustable. Different lenses are employed. The artist seats himself under the cloth (not shown) thrown over the frame-work, FF.

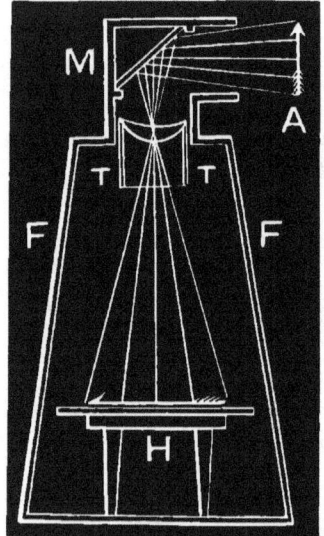

FIG. 21.

485. **The camera lucida** is another instrument employed for sketching from nature. It consists of a prism having one right angle and two angles of 135°, by which total reflection (399) takes place; or the prism may have one right angle, and, opposite to this, an angle of 135°, and two other angles of $67\frac{1}{2}°$ each. In this case the light will be twice totally reflected, entering the eye in the direction in which the object will be seen. Hence, the instrument may be so placed that the object will be seen on the paper where it is to be traced. The dimensions of the image will be as much smaller than those of the object, as the distance of the prism from the paper is less than its distance from the object; therefore, by varying the position of the prism, the size of the image can be varied to suit the occasion.

486. **Daguerreotyping** is the art of producing pictures by the actinic or *chemical* action of light; involving, besides the chemical action, all the principles of the camera obscura.

Instead of receiving the image on a screen of paper, to be traced with pen or pencil, it falls on a metallic or glass plate, previously made sensitive to the action of light, by iodine, bromine, or other chemical preparation. The action of the light upon the chemicals is such, that, by certain chemical treatment of the plate by the artist in the dark laboratory, the image is further *developed* and *fixed*.

The daguerreotype, ambrotype, crystallotype, etc., are thus produced. Of course, there are minor details connected with the art, which it is not necessary to describe.

The achromatic compound lens is employed in the camera.

487. **Photography** is the art of fixing upon paper the picture produced by the camera. If the picture be taken by the camera upon glass, it has the lights and shades reversed, and is called a *negative*. By laying the negative upon chemically prepared paper, the action of the sunlight reverses the position of the lights and shadows of the picture on the paper, which, being fixed by further chemical treatment, may be pasted on card-board for use.

Any number of copies may be made or *printed* from the same negative.

Telescopes.

488. **The different kinds of telescopes.**—A telescope is an optical instrument for viewing objects at more than ordinary distances; and, in effect, to bring them apparently nearer to the eye, by increasing the apparent angles under which such objects are seen.

Telescopes are first divided into two classes, *refracting telescopes* and *reflecting telescopes.*

In the first class, an *object-lens* is used to form an image; in the second class, a speculum or mirror is employed for this purpose. In both classes the image thus formed is viewed by a lens, or combination of lenses, termed the eye-piece.

The manner in which the component parts are arranged, together with the nature of the auxiliary pieces, determines the particular kind of telescope.

489. **Figure 22.—The refracting astronomical telescope.**—This instrument consists essentially of two convex lenses, the one, L, being the object-glass, and the other, N, the eye-piece.

The pencils of rays coming from the object, A, are converged by L to a focus, forming the real inverted image, T. The eye-piece, N, is

FIG. 22.

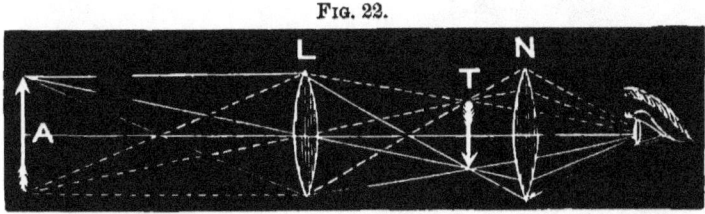

placed at a distance from the image, T, equal to its principal focal distance. The pencils of light from this image are refracted and converged to the eye, so as to form a visual angle many times larger than it would be if the object were viewed with the naked eye; and, consequently, the object appears to be magnified.

274   OPTICS.

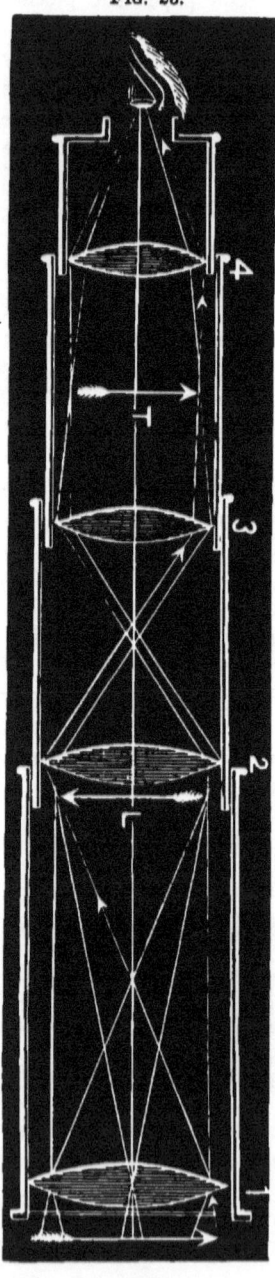

Fig. 23.

All telescopes are rendered adjustable, to view objects at different distances, by altering the position of the eye-piece, which, for this purpose, is set in a sliding tube.

The object-lens should be achromatic, to prevent prismatic colors; but slightly convex, to increase the distance between the lenses; and as large as possible, to illuminate the image.

The magnifying power is found by dividing the principal focal length of the object-glass by that of the eye-glass.

Of course, the image, and, therefore, the object, will be seen inverted, but this is not objectionable in viewing heavenly bodies.

One of the finest telescopes of this class in the world, is in the Observatory at Chicago, Illinois. Its object-glass is 18 inches diameter. This instrument takes in about 6,000 times as much light as the eye.

490. **Figure 23.—The terrestrial telescope or spy-glass.**—The principles involved in the construction of this instrument are the same as in the one just described; but as it is desirable to see terrestrial objects erect, it becomes necessary to *invert* the inverted image. This is accomplished by the introduction of two other lenses, besides the usual object-glass and eye-piece.

The diagram shows the course of the rays in a terrestrial telescope. The arrow in front, or object, is supposed to be remote from the instrument.

The object-lens, 1, forms the inverted image, L; the lens 2 converges the rays of the image to a focus between the inverting lenses 2 and 3, where, after crossing, they pass on and diverge to the second inverting lens, 3, and are brought to a focus between the lenses 3 and 4, forming the erect image, T; which is magnified by the eye-piece, 4.

The several tubes, which slide one within another, allow the instrument to be reduced to a convenient length when not in use.

491. **Figure 24.—Herschel's reflecting telescope.**—There is a great variety of reflecting telescopes, in all of which a parabolic metallic speculum or mirror (392) is employed, instead of the object-lens, to form an image of the object, and an eye-piece is used to magnify the image.

The figure represents Sir William Herschel's telescope. AA is a sheet-iron tube, in one end of which is a parabolic speculum, M, some-

FIG. 24.

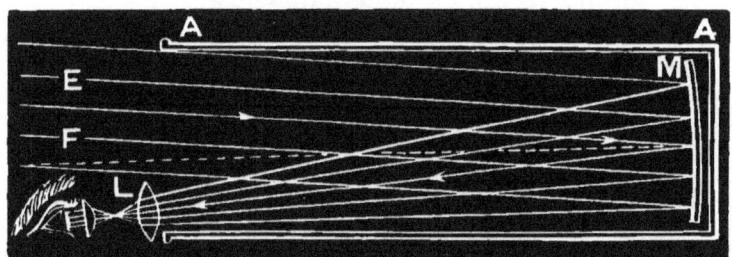

what less in diameter than the tube, with its axis directed to one side of the tube, shown by the dotted line. The parallel rays, EF, from some very distant object, are received upon the mirror and reflected, converging, to the eye-piece, L. The size of the tube and the inclination of the axis of the speculum are so adjusted, that the observer does not intercept any light which can fall upon the reflector.

This is called the *front-view telescope*. The speculum of Herschel's great telescope was 4 feet in diameter, 3½ inches thick, weighing 2,118 pounds, with a focal distance of 40 feet, and magnifying power of 6,450 diameters.

This telescope is a modification of the Newtonian telescope.

FIG. 25.

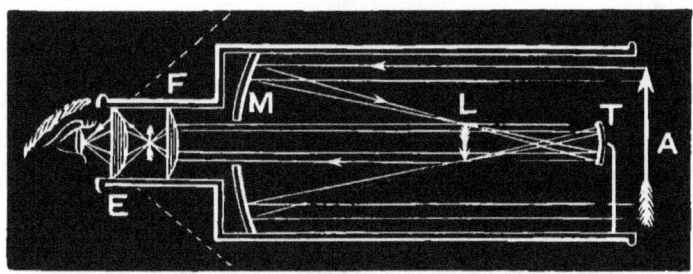

492. **Figure 25.—The Gregorian reflecting telescope.**— M is a concave metallic speculum, having a hole in its centre. This reflector will form, at its focal distance, an inverted image, L. At T is placed a small concave mirror, about one-fourth the focus and diameter of the speculum, M, and facing toward it, and at a little greater distance from L than its own focal distance. Rays diverging from L are rendered less divergent after reflection by T, and are thrown back, in nearly parallel lines, to the plano-convex eye-piece, F, by which they are brought to a focus, forming an erect image. The rays then passing the second eye-piece, E, are converged at the eye, where the object seems to appear under a much enlarged visual angle, shown by the two dotted lines.

493. **Figure 26.—The Newtonian reflecting telescope,** as improved and constructed by M. Froment, of Paris.

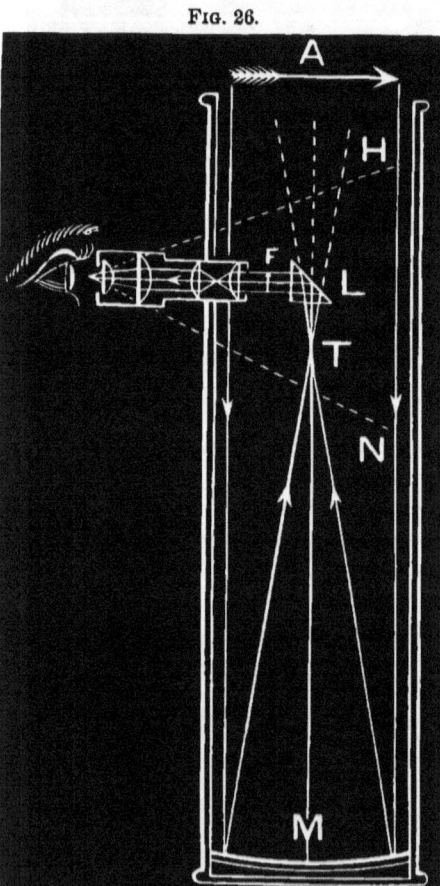

FIG. 26.

M is a concave reflector, placed at the bottom of a long tube. The reflector tends to form a small image of the object, A, at the other end of the tube; but before the rays reach the image they are intercepted by the glass prism, L, so arranged that the rays, entering its first face, will be totally reflected, and form an image of the object at F. This image is viewed by an eye-piece through the side of the telescope, as represented. The eye-piece is made of two plano-convex lenses, the combined effect of which is to cause the image to appear under the much enlarged visual angle indicated by the two dotted lines H and N.

494. **Lord Rosse's reflecting telescope** has a tube 56 feet long by 7 feet diameter, with a speculum of 6 feet diameter, weighing 4 tons; and the entire instrument weighs more than 18 tons, and cost $60,000.

OPTICS. 277

495. **Figure 27.—The telestereoscope.**—Owing to the fact that the two eyes do not view an object from the same point (447), the image formed on the two retinæ are not exactly alike (469), and by the difference in the images we are aided in judging of the distance and figure of the object (466). The nearer the object the greater is this difference. If the object is very distant the images will be sensibly identical, and we lose the aid just mentioned, in estimating the distance and bodily figure.

The object of the telestereoscope is to increase the optic angle or binocular parallax (447) of *distant* objects, by presenting to each eye such a view

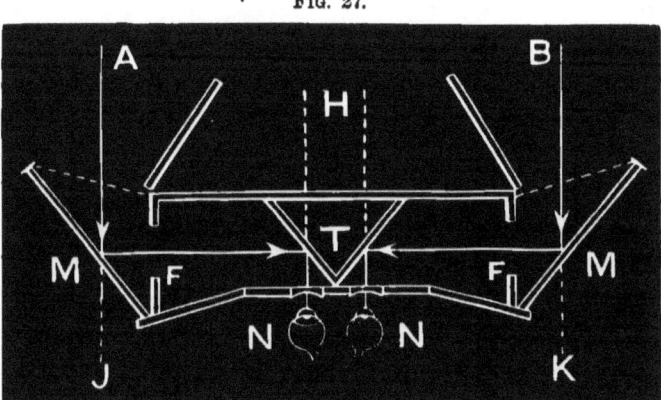

FIG. 27.

as would be obtained if the distance between the eyes were greatly increased, which increases the difference in the images on the two retinæ, and gives the same appearance of relief to the object as if it were brought near to the observer.

Let AB, rays of light coming from some distant object, fall upon the two mirrors, MM, and be reflected to the two mirrors, T, and, being again reflected from these mirrors to the eyes, NN. of the observer, the two views seen will evidently be the same as if the eyes were separated to the positions of J and K.

The relief with which objects are seen by this instrument is increased as much as the distance between J and K exceeds that between the eyes, NN.

Though the perspective difference of the images seen by the two eyes is increased, the visual angle under which each object is seen remains unchanged, and hence, as the apparent *distance* of the object is diminished, their dimensions appear diminished in the same proportion.

278   OPTICS.

If lenses (such as are used in opera-glasses) are inserted, the object-glasses being placed at FF, between the large and small mirrors, and the concave eye-pieces between the small mirrors (T) and the eyes, the effect will be to increase the visual angle of every object in the field of view.

If the glasses magnify as many diameters as the distance between J and K exceed the distance between the eyes, every object will appear in its due proportions, and the appearance will be as though the observer had been transported to the immediate vicinity of the objects themselves.

The distance between the large mirrors should not exceed the breadth of an ordinary window, unless the instrument is to be used in the open air.

496. **Figure 28.—The stereoscope** (from words signifying *solid* and *to see*) is an instrument by which two flat pictures are made to appear like a single solid or projecting body.

Fig. 28.

This figure represents the exterior appearance of the instrument. The pictures are inserted at the opening seen on the right; the lid at the top admits and regulates the light on the pictures. The pictures are seen through the tubes.

497. **Figure 29.—The principles of the stereoscope.—** This instrument is constructed upon the principles explained in connection with Fig. 27 (495). The two pictures to be viewed by the stereoscope are not taken from the same point of view. In taking stereoscopic photographs of near objects, one picture is taken by placing the camera in the position of the left eye, and the other by placing it in the position of the right eye. If the scene or object to be photographed be *distant*, the two points from which they are taken must be wide apart. Pictures thus taken, when viewed by the stereoscope, will stand out in relief as the scene or object itself would if viewed by direct vision.

Let a corresponding point of each picture be represented by FF, and rays from these points, falling upon the semi-double convex lenses, HII, will be refracted to the eyes, EE, and the mind will refer both points, FF, to the central position L. What is true of these two points, FF, is true of all other points of the two pictures.

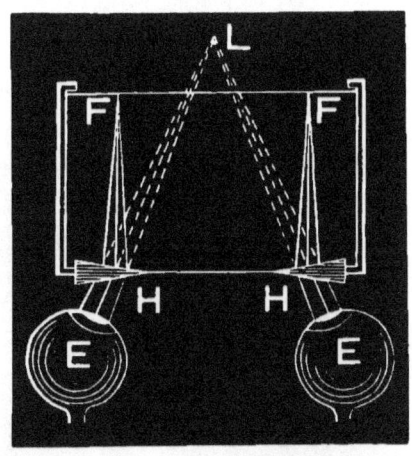

FIG. 29.

As one picture represents the real or projecting object, as observed by the right eye, and the other as seen by the left eye (though appearing, when viewed through the lenses IIII, to proceed from the same object), the impression made on the mind will be the same as if both images were derived from *one solid or projecting body*, instead of from two somewhat unlike flat pictures.

The distance between the two positions in which the camera is placed to take stereoscopic pictures, varies from a few inches to any distance necessary to produce the desired effect.

498. **Figures 30 and 31.—The stereomonoscope.**—This is an instrument by which a single image is made to present the ap-

FIG. 30.

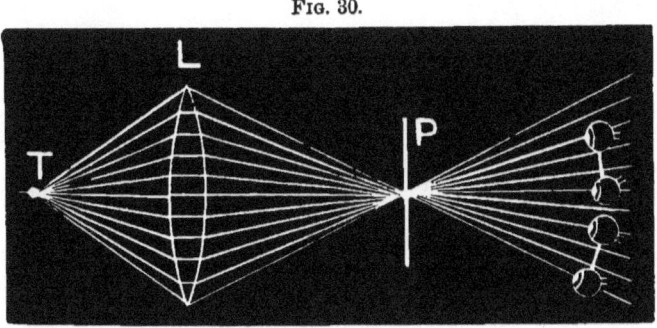

pearance of relief, as seen in the stereoscope, and by means of which several persons can view these effects at the same time.

If an object, T, be placed before a large double convex lens, L, an image of the object will be formed at the conjugate focus, which may be received on a plate of ground glass, P. From the image, rays of light will diverge, as from a real object, which will be seen wherever the eyes may be placed, within the cone of diverging rays, as shown by the figured eyes on the right.

The stereomonoscope (Fig. 31) consists of *two* such lenses, L and N, so placed as to form images of stereoscopic pictures, A and B, on a

FIG. 31.

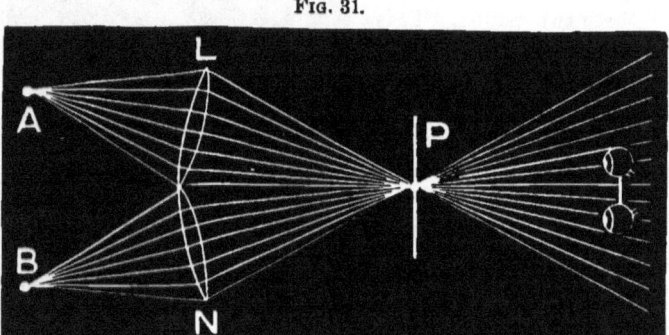

screen of ground glass, P. Though the two pictures have their images superimposed on the same part of the screen, P, yet each picture can be seen only by the rays emanating from the photograph by which it was formed.

If the eyes be placed, as figured, so that rays coming from one lens will enter the right eye, and those from the other lens the left eye, the object (from which the pictures were taken) will appear in relief, as in the stereoscope. Several persons can witness the effect at the same time.

WAVE THEORY OF LIGHT.
Interference, Diffraction, etc.

499. **Figure 32.—Waves of light.**—As previously stated (356), the undulatory or wave theory is most generally received. According to this theory, the cause of light is an undulatory movement in the ethereal medium. In this elastic medium undulatory movements can be propagated in the same manner as waves of sound in air. The ether and light are not the same. The latter is the effect of movements in the former; as air is one thing, and the sound which traverses it another. These waves advance at the rate of 192,000 miles per second. The particles of ether do not advance at this rate, but only the waves. This may be illustrated thus:

Having fastened one end of a cord to a fixed obstacle, F, commence agitating the end A, up and down, and the cord will be thrown into wave-like motions, passing rapidly from one end to the other.

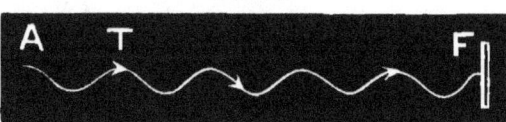

FIG. 32.

The particles composing the cord do not advance or retreat, however rapidly the undulations may pass. So, too, floating objects on water only rise and fall with waves, when the waves pass on; thus showing that the water itself does not advance forward with its undulations.

The *vibration* is the cause of *undulation*. In case of the cord, the vibration is represented by the movement exerted by the hand; the undulation is the wave-like motion.

As a vibrating string agitates the surrounding air, and makes waves of sound pass through it, so does an incandescent or shining particle, vibrating with surprising rapidity, impress a wave-like movement on the ether, and this movement, finally impinging on the eye, is what we term *sight*.

500. **Figure 33.—Directions of vibrations and waves of light.**—If the free end of the cord be vibrated horizontally, vertically, or diagonally up and down, as indicated by the arrow-heads, or in any intermediate directions, these directions will all be transverse, or at

FIG. 33.

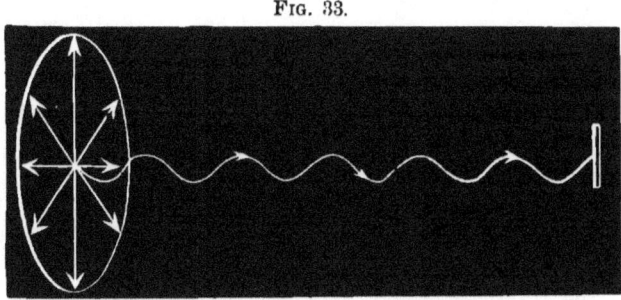

right angles to the length of the cord, or the direction of the waves. This is the peculiarity of the movement of light; that is, its *vibrations are transverse to the course of the ray*. With sound, the vibrations are executed in the direction of the resulting wave, and not at right angles to it. Hence, the undulatory theory of light, by some writers, is designated the *Theory of Transverse Vibrations*.

282 OPTICS.

501. Brilliancy dependent on amplitude of waves.—
Lights differ from each other in *brilliancy* and *color*, which depend on
qualities in the waves. As waves of water may vary in height, by
which is meant *amplitude*, so waves of light vary in amplitude. A
wave of great amplitude impresses us with a sense of intensity or brilliancy, while a wave of small amplitude is less brilliant. Therefore,
the brilliancy of light depends on the *magnitude of the excursions of
the vibrating particles*, as the amplitude of the waves in the cord
(Fig. 33) depends upon the distance which the hand is moved, which
causes the waves.

502. Color dependent on length of waves.—By length
of wave is meant the distance from the crest of one wave to that of the
next, as from A to T, Fig. 32 (499), or from depression to depression.
The length of the waves determines the color of light. The longer
waves give rise to red light; the shorter ones, to violet, and those of
intermediate lengths, the other colors, in the order of their refrangibility.

503. Figure 34.—Interference of light.—If two waves of
water encounter in such a manner that the concavity of the one corresponds with the convexity of the other, they mutually destroy each
other's effect. So it is with waves of *sound*. If waves thus encounter
they destroy each other's effect. Hence, two sounds, at the point of
their encounter, produce silence. In like manner, if two waves of *light*
similarly encounter they destroy each other's effect. Therefore, two
rays of light, however brilliant they may be separately, will produce
darkness at these points of encounter. This is called *interference of
light.*

FIG. 34.

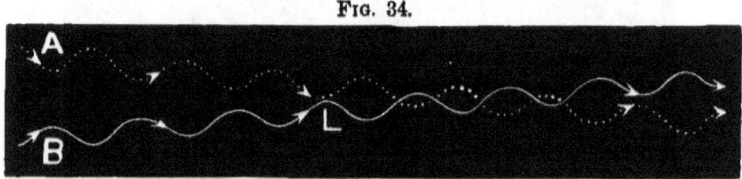

Let A and B represent two encountering rays of light, in which the
two systems of waves or undulations are in opposite phases, the convexity of the one corresponding with the concavity of the other,
and interference will take place, as at L, producing darkness at this
point.

504. Figure 35.—Non-interference of light.—If two rays
of light, as A and B, encounter each other in such a manner that the

OPTICS. 283

concavities and convexities of their undulations respectively correspond, there is no interference; and where they encounter, as at L,

FIG. 35.

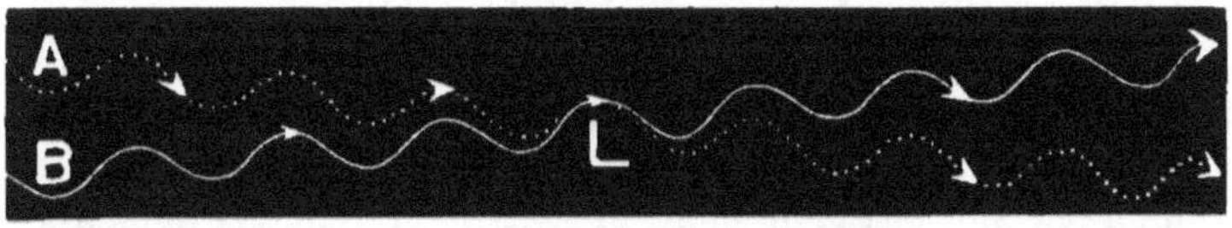

instead of *darkness* being the result, an *intenser light* is produced at this point.

505. Figure 36.—Demonstration of interference of light.
—Produce a lucid point at S, by bringing rays of the sun to a focus by a double convex lens, or by passing a sunbeam through a pin-hole. In the diverging rays from this lucid point place a cylindrical body, as a piece of wire, F (seen endwise in the figure); at some distance beyond, place a screen of white paper. The object, F, will throw a shadow on the screen, reaching from H to W. This shadow, instead of being uniformly dark, is found to consist of light and dark stripes, as represented by the figure A, caused by interference. The cause of the interference is thus explained:

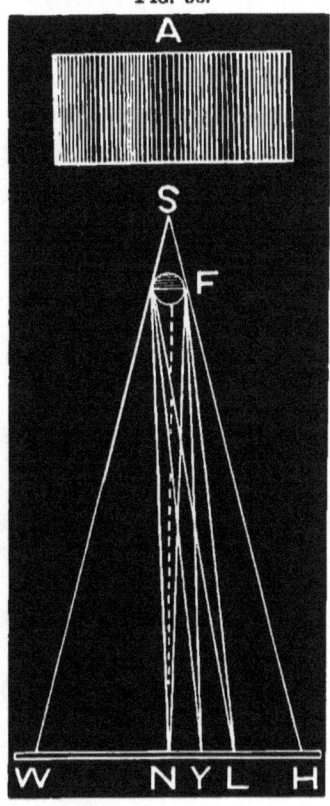

FIG. 36.

Waves of water pass round to the back of an object on which they impinge, and the undulations of light, in the same manner, flow round at the back of the piece of wire, F. The two series of waves which have passed from the opposite sides of the obstacle to the middle point, N, of its shadow, having passed through paths of equal length, will encounter in such a manner as *not to interfere;* and, therefore, they will exalt each other's effect, and produce a *light* line at this point.

The systems of waves which have passed from the sides of the obstacle to the point, Y, having come through distances which differ in length by *half* a wave, will encounter at Y in such a manner as to *interfere* and destroy each other's effect, and so produce a dark stripe at this point.

At the point, L, the waves from each side of the obstacle again have come through unequal paths which differ in length by a *whole* wave, and, therefore, they will again encounter in such a manner as not to interfere, and another white stripe is produced.

The correctness of this explanation is shown by placing an opaque screen on one side of the obstacle, F, so as to prevent the light passing, when the fringes will disappear.

506. **Laws of interference and non-interference of light.**—1. *If two systems of waves, of the same length, encounter after having come through paths of equal length, they will not interfere.*

2. *Nor will they interfere though there be a difference in the length of these paths, provided that difference be equal to one whole wave, or two, or three, etc.*

3. *But if the paths be of unequal length, they will interfere, and the interference will be complete when the difference of the length of the paths is half a wave,* 1½, 2½, 3½, *etc.*

507. **Figure 37.—Interference colors** are seen in thin films of varnish, cracks in glass, and other thin transparent substances, as in soap-bubbles.

Let FH represent a section of a thin transparent bulb of glass or of a soap-bubble. If a ray of light, S, is incident at V, a portion of the light, after refraction and transmission, will pass on in the direction of

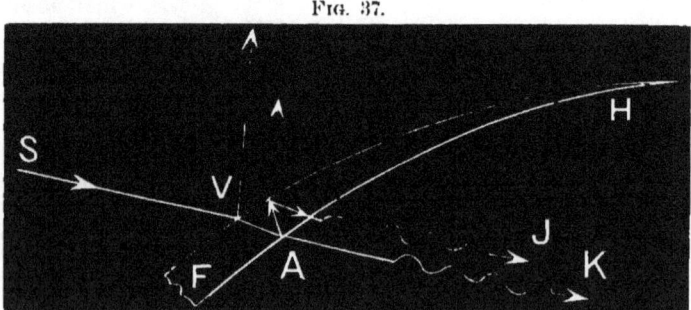

Fig. 37.

K, and another portion will be reflected at V, as shown by the first vertical arrow. At the point, A, a portion of the light is internally reflected from the second surface, and is divided by transmission and a second internal reflection at the first surface, the reflected portion being transmitted in the direction of J.

The curves, in the rays J and K, represent waves. The second ray at the first surface, reflected from the second surface, will be retarded behind the first a distance equal to twice the thickness of the bubble, shown by the difference in the length of the two vertical arrows. The ray J, having traversed the thickness of the film twice, will fall behind the ray K a distance equal to twice the thickness of the bubble. If these retardations equal the interval of an odd number of half waves they will interfere, and produce dark lines.

The difference in the intensity of the rays J and K being greater than that of the two rays proceeding from the first surface, the dark lines in the former are less distinct than in the latter.

The difference in the dark and bright bands thus produced is different for different colors of the spectrum, being least for violet and greatest for red. The dark bands and peculiar tints of the soap-bubble are thus due to interference.

508. Figures 38 and 39.—Determining the length of waves of light.—The thickness of soap-bubbles cannot be accurately measured; but dark rings can be produced by other means, which facilitate the measurement of the distances between the reflecting surfaces.

Place upon a flat, smooth plate of glass another slightly curved piece, whose curvature is that of a portion of a sphere whose radius is 40 or 50 feet, as represented by Fig. 38.

FIG. 38.

When this curved glass is pressed down upon the plate, the centre appears black, and is surrounded by colored rings (Fig. 39), as in the soap-bubble. If homogeneous light, as red, be allowed to fall vertically upon the upper glass, rings will be formed at 1, 2, 3, and 4; and the diameter of these rings, shown by the dotted lines, can be easily measured. They are always found to be in the proportion of $1 - 1.414 - 1.723 - 2.000$, and so on. These numbers are the square roots of 1, 2, 3, 4, and so on; and it is known, from the form of the sphere, that the distances 1R, 2N, 3S, 4H, etc., are to one another as the squares of the cords or dotted diameters. Hence the distance between the reflecting surfaces of the second bright ring is twice that of the first, and so on. The diameters of the bright rings being as the square roots of 1, 2, 3, 4, and so on, the diameters of the dark rings will be as the square roots of $1\frac{1}{2}$, $2\frac{1}{2}$, $3\frac{1}{2}$, $4\frac{1}{2}$, etc.

The distance between successive rings of violet will be much less than that between successive rings of red.

509. **Length of waves or undulations of light** (Fig. 39).
—The light reflected from R must travel half a wave-length (see 3d law of interference, 506) further than that reflected from 1, in order that the waves reflected from these points may meet in the same phase, and so give a bright ring. But the wave reflected from R travels over the space 1R *twice;* therefore 1R must be only ¼ the length of a luminous wave. But 1R, as previously shown, is ¼ of 4H. The length of 4H is easily found. Thus: 4F is half the diameter of the fourth

FIG. 39.

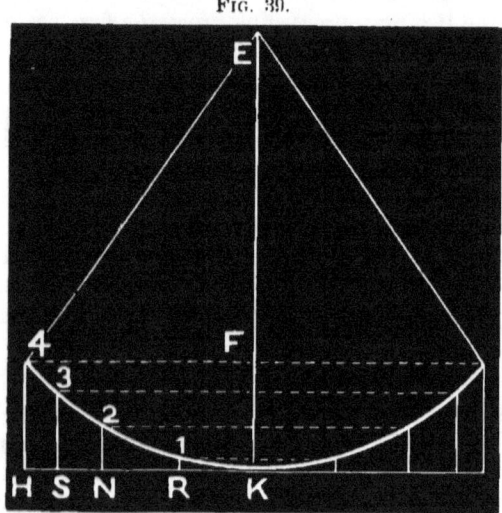

ring, and can be found by actual measurement; and the length of the radius, 4E, is known, and 4FE is a right angled triangle. The hypothenuse, 4E, and the side, 4F, being known, the length of EF is found. Having found EF, and knowing EK, 4H is found by subtracting EF from EK, or EK − EF = 4H.

By this and other methods, the length of waves, or undulations, required to produce different colors, has been estimated, and the number of waves that enter the eye per second.

The length of the vibrations in the extreme red ray is just double the length of the vibrations of the invisible rays beyond the violet, which, concentrated, produce the lavender light of Herschel. The entire range of rays, therefore, extends only over what is equivalent to a single octave of music.

The following table exhibits the numerical results which have been deduced for the length and velocity of luminous waves of different colors.

OPTICS. 287

COLORS.	LENGTH OF UNDULATIONS IN PARTS OF AN INCH.	NUMBER OF UNDULATIONS IN AN INCH.	NUMBER OF UNDULATIONS PER SECOND.
Extreme red....	0.0000266	37640	458,000000,000000
Red............	0.0000256	39180	477,000000,000000
Orange.........	0.0000240	41610	506,000000,000000
Yellow..........	0.0000227	44000	535,000000,000000
Green...........	0.0000211	47460	577,000000,000000
Blue............	0.0000196	51110	622,000000,000000
Indigo	0.0000185	54070	658,000000,000000
Violet...........	0.0000174	57490	699,000000,000000
Extreme violet..	0.0000167	59750	727,000000,000000

510. **The cause of the waves of light** is supposed to be the vibrations of the particles of a luminous body.

In ordinary combustion, one of the sources of light, the atoms of oxygen in the air are rushing into combination with the atoms (hydrogen and carbon) of the burning body (344); and the collision of these atoms is likely to set them vibrating. These vibrations will be communicated to the atoms of the surrounding ether, and by these transmitted to the eye.

FIG. 40.

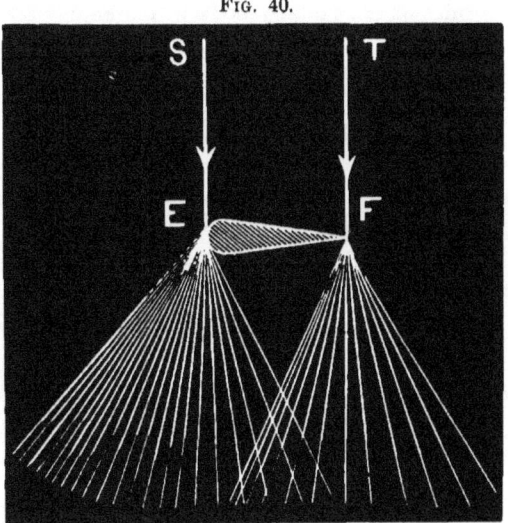

511. **Figure 40.—Diffraction fringes caused by interference.**—A convenient method of showing diffraction fringes consists of allowing the rays of the sun to fall on the flat side of a razor.

The rays, S and T, passing in close proximity to the back and edge of the instrument, will be deflected as represented. A portion of the rays are deflected outward as if *reflected*, the back of the razor, E, deflecting more of the rays outward, and the edge, F, more of them inward. If the body be narrow, like a needle or hair, Fig. 36 (505), the rays deflected inward cross each other and produce interference, in accordance with the wave-theory. The rays deflected outward produce interference with rays not deflected. All the bright and dark lines are bordered with colored fringes, as in ordinary cases of interference.

If a beam of sunlight pass through a lens in a dark room, and fall upon a white screen, and any small opaque body placed in the light so its shadow will also fall on the screen, the shadow, instead of being sharply defined, is surrounded by three colored fringes, the outer one being very faint. If homogeneous light be employed, instead of the fringes, there will be seen bright rings, separated by dark spaces—the breadth of the rings varying with the color of light. When white light is used, these different sets of colored rings blend, producing the fringes.

Polarization of Light.

512. **Poles in physics.**—The name *poles* is given, in physics, in general, to the sides or ends of any body which enjoy or have acquired any contrary properties.

513. **Figure 41.—Transmission of luminous waves.**—The subject of polarized light constitutes the most interesting branch

Fig. 41.

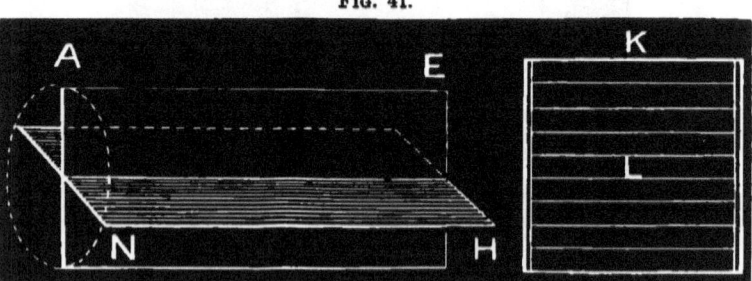

of optics. The scope of this compendium, however, will admit of only a brief explanation of a few of its leading phenomena.

In connection with Fig. 33 (500), it was shown that vibrations take place in every possible direction transverse to the ray; but for convenience of explanation, we will *suppose* they take place only in two directions, as in the directions of the horizontal and vertical arrows

(Fig. 33), and that every ray consists of two sets of colorless undulations.

Let AE (Fig. 41) represent the plane in which one set of these undulations takes place; and NH, the plane in which the other set of waves occurs—the planes intersecting each other at right angles.

Let K represent a frame, provided with fixed cross-bars, L; and suppose the planes AE and HN to be intersecting pieces of card-board. If now an effort be made to thrust these card-boards through the frame, K, it is evident that while *one* slip of paper will pass, the *other* will be checked; but if the frame, K, be turned one-fourth round, the slip of paper which was before checked will now pass through the bars, L, but the one which passed in the first case will be stopped.

If, instead of the frame, K, we take a thin plate of a certain gem, called the tourmaline, and, instead of the slips of paper, the ray of light composed of the two sets of undulations, which, as we have supposed, vibrate in planes at right angles to each other, it will be found that one set of these undulations will be transmitted, and the other set intercepted, when the tourmaline is held in one position; but, if the tourmaline be turned one-fourth round, the rays that before passed are now stopped, and those that in the first case were intercepted now pass.

When light has been thus treated, or when, by any means, but one set of undulations is obtained, the light is said to be *polarized*.

Opaque bodies allow no luminous vibrations to pass through them. Some bodies transmit nearly all the luminous vibrations which fall upon them; while other bodies are capable of transmitting only those vibrations of light which move in a single plane, or those undulations which can be resolved into that plane. Other bodies, which are themselves capable of vibrating in two directions, reduce all the vibrations which they transmit to vibrations in the two planes in which they themselves vibrate. Other bodies alter the direction of vibrations of light, which fall upon them at certain angles of incidence, so as to transmit vibrations which lie in a single plane.

FIG. 42.

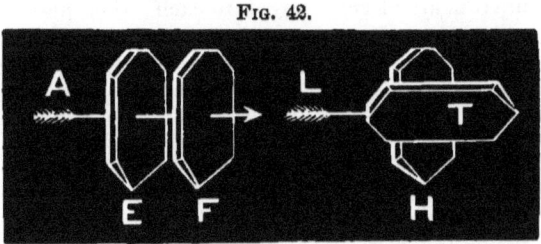

514. **Figure 42.—Action of tourmaline on ordinary light.**—Let EF be two tourmaline plates symmetrically held, and the arrow, A, a ray of light; and, as shown, the ray will pass through both plates. If now one of the plates, as T, be turned a quarter round, as shown, a ray of light, L, will pass through the first plate, H, as before, but not through the second plate, T.

If the light which has been transmitted through the first plate be received upon a plate of glass at an angle of incidence of 56° 45', it will be wholly reflected, in a certain position of the glass, and wholly transmitted if the glass be turned round through 90°.

A plate of tourmaline affords a convenient means of determining whether a ray of light has been polarized by other means.

515. **Figure 43.—Polariscope.—Polarization by reflection.**—An instrument employed for polarization of light by reflection is called a *polariscope*. If the light of the candle falls upon the mir-

FIG. 43.

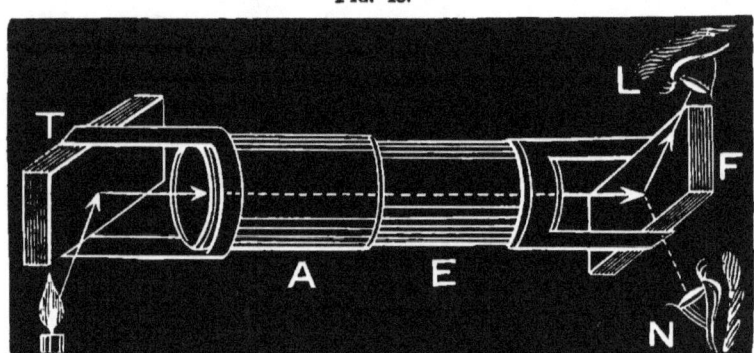

ror, T, making the angle of incidence 56° 45', from this mirror it is reflected, through the tube AE, to the mirror F, falling upon it at the same angle of incidence, 56° 45', and is thence reflected to the eye, at L. The mirrors are at right angles to each other, and the candle is hardly perceptible to the eye at L. If now the mirror, F, be gradually turned, by revolving the tube, E, in the tube, A. the image of the candle grows brighter and brighter, and is the brightest possible when the planes of the mirrors are parallel to each other. Hence, from the position of the eye, N, the image is perfect, though it can scarcely be discerned at L.

Light is polarized, more or less, by reflection from many different substances, such as glass, water, air, ebony, mother-of-pearl, surfaces of crystals, etc., provided the light falls at a certain angle peculiar to each surface, called the *polarizing angle*.

516. **Plane polarization.**—When light has been polarized so that all its undulations move in a single plane, it is said to be *plane polarized*.

If a bundle of stretched cords of different sizes were vibrating in the same direction, it would represent plane polarized light; and the difference in size or tension of these cords would cause a difference in the length of their waves; hence the different cords may represent the different colors, which also differ in the length of their undulation.

517. **Waves in any number of planes resolved to two planes.**—If, instead of two, Fig. 41 (513), there are an infinite number of planes intersecting each other in the manner of AE and NH, and undulations of a beam of light are passing in all these planes, these undulations can all be resolved to two planes, which shall intersect each other at any required angle. When resolved to two planes, intersecting each other at right angles, the sum of resulting intensities in the one plane will equal the sum of intensities in the other. A ray of ordinary light, therefore, may be considered as consisting of undulations moving in two planes at right angles to each other.

Any medium that will, either by its position or molecular constitution, separate light into two parts, undulating in planes at right angles to each other, will produce the change denominated *polarization of light*.

518. **Partial polarization of light.**—Light reflected or refracted at any oblique angle, is, in general, partially polarized; and by repeated reflections and refractions the degree of polarization is increased, until, at last, it is apparently completely polarized.

519. **Double refraction** is a property which certain transparent crystals possess, of causing a ray of light, in passing through them, to undergo two refractions; that is, the single ray of light is divided into two separate rays, causing objects, seen through such a crystal, to appear double.

A common mineral, called Iceland spar, which is a crystallized form of carbonate of lime, possesses, to a remarkable degree, these refracting properties. The form of this crystal is that of a rhomb, or rhomboid.

In all such crystals there are one or more directions along which objects, when viewed through them, appear *single*: these directions are termed the axes of double refraction, or major axes. In the case of Iceland spar, there is one such axis which joins the two obtuse three-sided angles. If the summits of these angles be ground down and polished, no double refraction will be seen through the crystal in this direction.

One of the refracted rays will conform to the law of ordinary refraction, and is, therefore, called the *ordinary* ray. The other ray does not lie in the same plane as the incident and ordinary rays, and does not conform to the law of sines (394); and, therefore, it is called the *extraordinary* ray.

In the case of Iceland spar, the index of refraction for the ordinary ray is constantly 1.6543; that of the extraordinary ray varies, being 1.4833, when it makes an angle of 90° with the major axis.

The phenomenon of double refraction is due to the molecular structure of the medium through which the light passes.

520. **Polarization by double refraction.**—When light is transmitted through a double refracting substance, both the ordinary and extraordinary rays are thereby completely polarized, whatever be the color of the light employed. The tourmaline plate, or other analyzer, will transmit the ordinary image, and wholly intercept the other; but if the tourmaline be rotated 90°, it will then transmit the extraordinary and intercept the ordinary ray.

521. **Useful applications of polarized light.**—Since the discovery of polarized light, its principles have been applied to many practical results.

Thus, it has been found that all *reflected* light, come from whence it may, acquires certain properties by which it can be distinguished from direct light.

It has been found that light from incandescent bodies, as red-hot iron, glass, etc., is polarized light; but that light from an inflamed gaseous substance, as illuminating gas, is always in a natural state, or unpolarized. Applying these principles to the sun, it has been discovered that the light-giving substance of the sun is of the nature of a gas, and not a red-hot solid or liquid body.

By means of polarized light, the chemist can detect one-thirteen millionth of a gramme of soda, and distinguish it from potassa or any other alkali.

Polarized light is found to be of great value in various microscopic investigations.

Especially important is such light in physiological chemistry, as in the examination of crystals found in various cavities and fluids of both plants and animals.

Polarized light is of great importance in many departments of natural science.

Shadows.

522. Figure 44.—Shadows of bodies larger than the illuminating body.—When rays of light radiate from a luminous point through the surrounding space, on account of moving in straight lines they will be excluded from the space behind the body. The comparative darkness thus produced is called a *shadow*.

When the luminous body is smaller than the opaque body, the shadow of the opaque body will gradually increase in size with the distance, without limit. Thus, the ball, L, being larger than the luminous point of the candle (supposing the light of the candle to emanate from a point), will cast a shadow upon the screen, in the three positions,

FIG. 44.

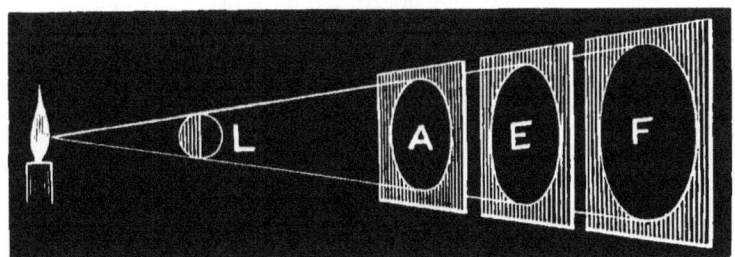

A, E, F, of different sizes, depending upon the distance, as shown. The shadows on the screens will be larger the nearer the ball is placed to the light.

If the luminous body is a mere point, the body will cast a well-defined shadow upon the screen. If either of the straight diverging lines be carried around the sphere, L, touching it all the way, it will mark the exact limits of the shadow cast by the sphere, which, being round, shows that light moves through air in straight lines.

If the luminous and opaque bodies be of the same size, the shadow will not increase or diminish; and its shape will be cylindrical.

FIG. 45.

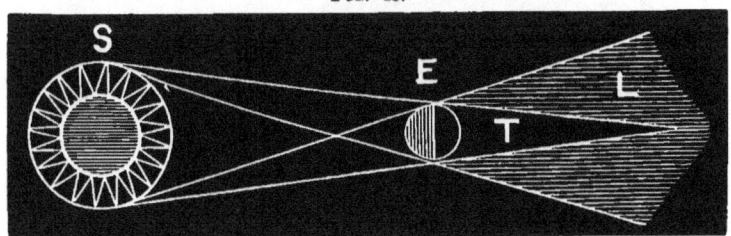

523. Figure 45.—Shadows of bodies smaller than the illuminating body.—When the luminous body, S, is larger than the opaque body, E, the shadow will gradually diminish in size until it terminates in a point. The shape of the shadow of a spherical body will be that of a cone, T. The length of the cone will be increased by increasing the distance between the luminous and opaque body.

524. **Umbra and penumbra** (Fig. 45).—If the illuminating body is not a mere point, the shadow cast will have an indistinct outline, called the *penumbra;* from *pene*, almost, and *umbra*, a shadow.

S represents the sun; E, the earth; T, the shadow or umbra of the earth; L, the penumbra of the earth. If the line, SE (to the end of the shadow), be carried around the earth and the sun, it will describe the circumference of the umbra, T. If either of the cross-lines be carried around the earth and sun, it will describe the circumference of the penumbra, L, as far as the extent of the shadow.

The breadth of the penumbra increases with the diameter of the luminating body, and with the distance which the shadow extends behind the opaque body. The darkness of the penumbra gradually increases from the borders toward the umbra.

525. **Figure 46.—Density of shadows.**—Shadows are of different degrees of darkness, because the light from other luminous

FIG. 46.

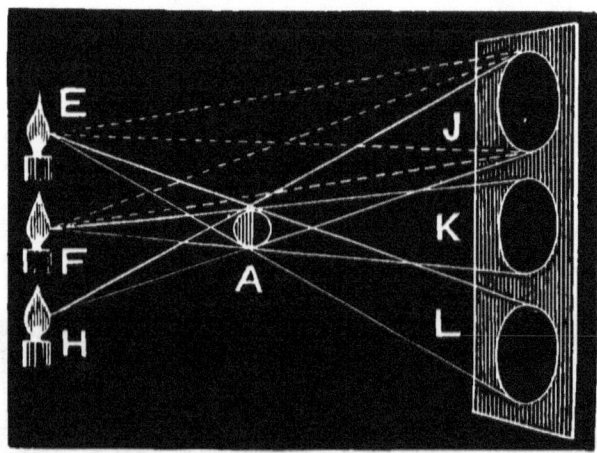

bodies (or from bodies reflecting light) reaches the place where the shadow is formed. This is shown by light from two or more luminous points falling on the same opaque body.

Let A be an opaque body illuminated by three candles. The light E will produce the shadow L; the light F, the shadow K; the light H, the shadow J. But, as the light from each of the candles shines upon all the shadows except its own, the shadows will all be faint.

For instance, the shadow J is illuminated by the candles E and F, as shown by the dotted lines. If the candle E be extinguished, the shadow L will disappear, and the shadows J and K will be darker. If the candle F be extinguished, the shadow K will disappear, and the shadow J will be still darker and well defined.

The darkness of a shadow, when it is produced by the interruption of the rays from a single luminous body, is proportioned to the intensity of the light.

The forms of shadows prove that light moves through the air in straight lines.

526. **Figure 47.—Velocity of light.**—Light moves with such rapidity that its movement through any distance, limited by the surface of the earth, cannot be appreciated by our unaided senses. Its velocity was first determined about two hundred years ago, by the astronomer, Roemer; who observed that the occurrence of the eclipses of Jupiter's first satellite were subject to certain uniform changes.

Let A and E represent the earth in different parts of its orbit; J, Jupiter; F and L, Jupiter's first moon. The direction in which the

FIG. 47.

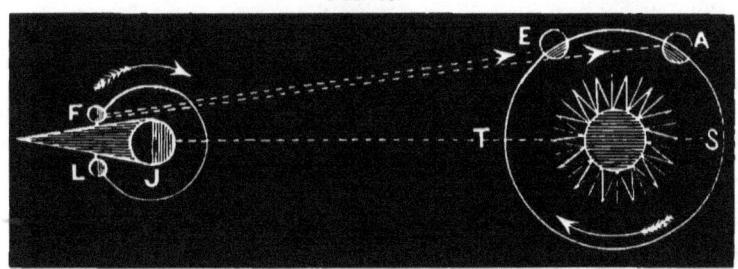

earth rotates around the sun is indicated by an arrow, as also the motion of the satellite around the planet.

As the earth moves from T, its nearest position to Jupiter, to S, its most remote position, the intervals between the consecutive eclipses of the satellite gradually grow longer; whilst in moving from S back to T, these intervals grow shorter. The total retardation in passing from T to S is nearly $16\frac{1}{2}$ minutes, and just equal to the acceleration in passing from S back to T. As the distance from T to S is 190,000,000 miles, of course, the velocity of light (reducing $16\frac{1}{2}$ minutes to seconds) equals 190,000,000 divided by 990, or about 192,000 miles per second.

At F the satellite is just emerging from the shadow of the planet, and will be seen from the earth in its position at E; now, while the satellite passes around to L and again emerges at F, the earth will have moved on, say to some point, as A; hence the light from the emerging satellite will be retarded from E to A as long as it will take for light to pass from E to A, and so on. As the satellite revolves around the planet every 48 hours, this process will be repeated 104 times while the earth passes from T to S; and 104 times, with reverse effect, while it moves from S to T.

Velocity of light is ascertained by other means (see 509).

The mind cannot conceive a velocity of 192,000 miles per second. Yet it takes more than four hours for the light of Neptune to reach the earth. It is susceptible of proof, that light is three years in coming from the nearest fixed star to the earth; while many stars have been seen, by the aid of instruments, which astronomers infer are more than a thousand times as far from us as the nearest one; requiring more than *three thousand years* for their light to reach the earth, notwithstanding its inconceivable velocity of 192,000 miles per second. How vast, therefore, must be *our* universe. Yet all this system, called our cluster of stars, is but a small part of the Grand Whole—the Boundless.

527. **Figure 48.—Intensity of light.**—The intensity of light is the amount of disturbance which it imparts to the ether.

The illuminating power of a light depends upon several conditions:

1. As the *distance* increases it becomes less, as will be explained presently.

2. The *absolute intensity* of the light also determines the result; thus, there are flames that are very brilliant and others that are paler.

3. The *absorbent effect* exerted on the passing rays by the air, or other medium traversed.

4. The *direct or oblique* manner in which the rays are received on the illuminated surface.

This last condition is illustrated by the figure. The parallel lines representing a given number of rays of light, falling upon the oblique and vertical mirrors, M and N, will not illuminate them equally; for, all the rays that fall on M will fall on N, by removing M; but M has a larger surface than N. Hence, the greatest illuminating effect, other things being equal, will be realized when the rays fall upon the illuminated body perpendicular to its surface.

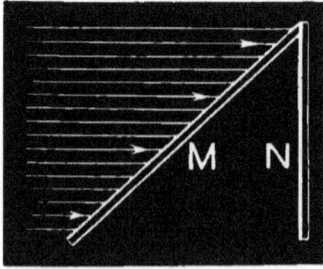

Fig. 48.

Photometers.

528. Figure 49.—Photometers are instruments used to measure the comparative intensity of different lights. There are several kinds of these instruments, but none of them are as satisfactory for measuring the intensity of lights as thermometers are for measuring the comparative heat of bodies.

Ritchie's photometer depends on the equal illumination of surfaces. It consists of a box, AA, six or eight inches long, by one inch

FIG. 49.

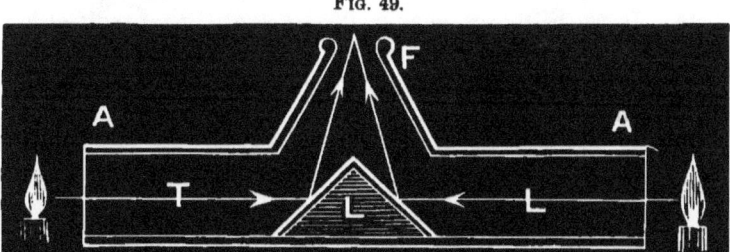

square, in the middle of which is a double inclined plane, L, which is covered with white paper, neatly doubled to a sharp edge at the top or angle. In the top of the box is a conical tube, F, at the upper end of which the eye is placed. Place the two lights, the comparative intensities of which are to be determined, at opposite ends of the box, and the reflected light of each will be seen at the top of the tube, F, as represented by the arrows. Now place the brighter light of the two at such a distance that its reflected light will equal that of the other. Then, measuring their distances from the paper on the inclined planes, L, their illuminating powers are as the squares of those distances.

Rumford's photometer depends on the principle, that of two lights, the more brilliant one will cast the deepest shadow,—the brighter light being removed from the ground-glass screen until the shadows are of equal density. Then, as before, their relative intensities are as the squares of the distances of the lights from the shadows. A partition may be placed between the lights.

Silliman's photometer is the reverse of Rumford's, comparing two disks of light thrown up by two equal triangular prisms, upon a disk of ground glass in the body of a dark chamber.

Bunsen's photometer is convenient, and consists of a disk of paper, four or five inches in diameter, rendered translucent by washing it with paraffine dissolved in oil of turpentine, except a small part of it in the centre. Place this disk between the two lights, and if their intensities are unequal the translucent part can be distinguished from the central part of the paper; but when the disk is placed so that the two parts of the paper appear the same, the disk is equally illuminated by the two lights, for which reason no light shines through. Of course, the relative intensities of the two lights, as before, will be as the squares of their distances from the disk.

529. **Figure 50.—Intensity of light at different distances.**—It can be shown, mathematically, that the intensity of light, coming from the same source, *varies inversely as the square of the distance from its source.*

If a board, one foot square, be placed one foot from the luminous point, it will cast a shadow that will cover a space two feet square at

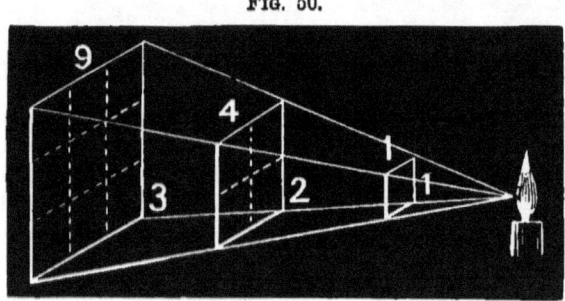

FIG. 50.

double the distance, and three feet square at three times the distance, and so on (448). The *areas* of these shadows will be as the square of their distances from the luminous point, or as $1^2, 2^2, 3^2$, etc., or as 1, 4, 9, as shown in the diagram, by the dotted lines. But as no more light would occupy the space at 3 feet than at 2 feet or at 1 foot from the luminous point, the intensity of light at 1, 2, 3, etc., feet, is as 1, $\frac{1}{4}, \frac{1}{9}$, etc., or as 9, 4, 1.

Hence it is seen that light follows the same law, with regard to its intensity at different distances, that is observed for gravity, heat, and sound.

CHAPTER XII.

(CHART NO. 7.)

ACOUSTICS.

PRODUCTION AND PROPAGATION OF SOUND.

530. **Definition.**—Acoustics (signifying to hear) is that branch of Physics which treats of the nature, phenomena, and laws of sound.

531. **Sonorous or sounding bodies.**—If an elastic body, for example, a glass bell-jar, held by the knob, be struck with the knuckle, its particles execute a series of tremulous movements, and gradually return to a position of rest. Bodies thus capable of vibrating are said to be *sonorous bodies.*

532. **Mediums.**—A medium is that substance which intervenes between the sonorous body and the organ of hearing, or the auditory nerve. The ordinary medium is the atmospheric air.

A medium, therefore, transmits the vibrations of the sonorous body to the organ of hearing. The air adjacent to the sonorous or vibrating body is thrown into a wave-like motion, and this movement of the air is communicated to the air next beyond, and so on, until the *sound-wave* dashes against the drum of the ear; whence it is transmitted, by a complex mechanism, to the auditory nerve, and so to the sensorium, or seat of sensation. In rapid successions, these condensations and rarefactions, or sound-waves, flow from the sonorous body until its vibrations cease.

Other substances, besides air, act as media, such as wood, water, iron, etc.

533. **Sound a sensation.**—Sound is the sensation produced on the organ of hearing, by the vibrations of sonorous bodies, communicated by undulations or sound-waves of intervening media. The particles of the medium do not pass from the sonorous body to the ear, but only the undulations. The sonorous body may exist and the waves pass, but these do not constitute sound; the *sensation* which they produce on the sensorium is what is called sound.

534. **Different sounds.**—The quality of sound, or the character of impression on the auditory nerve, depends upon the peculiarity of the waves or undulations which fall upon the ear; and these will depend upon the nature of the sonorous body, and the character of the medium or media through which the vibrations of the sonorous body are transmitted to the ear.

535. **Sonorous difference of bodies.**—The quality of sonorousness of a body depends upon its nature and molecular structure, its shape, its size, etc. For example, every bell will differ in its vibrations from every other bell, from which it differs either in composition, size, or shape. Every kind of wood has its own quality of sonorousness; and a piece of any particular kind of wood will vary with its shape, size, dryness, etc. The same is true of different metals and other solids.

If strings be stretched between two fixed points, and made to vibrate, the quality of the vibrations will vary with their composition, tension, length, diameter, etc.

It is upon this difference of sonorousness, depending on exact conditions, that we are enabled to construct language, speech, music, and, in many ways, to extend scientific investigation. It is made valuable use of in the investigation of certain diseases of the human body. If the forefinger be placed upon the body, over any particular organ, as the liver, lungs, heart, etc., and rapped with the ends of the fingers of the other hand, a certain sonorousness will be perceived, varying in different positions on the body. The physician, having become familiar with these different sounds for the *healthy* and for the *unhealthy* states or conditions of these different organs, is enabled, in any given case, to determine almost the precise condition of an internal organ by this means, known as *percussion* (to strike) and *auscultation* (to listen).

536. **Time is required for the transmission of sound.**—The blows of a hammer at a distance are *heard* a sensible interval of time after the hammer is seen to fall. The flash of a cannon is seen an appreciable time before the report is heard, though the gun be but a little distance from the observer. Thunder is heard after the flash of lightning is seen, etc.

537. **Calculation of distance by sound.**—Knowing the velocity of sound, and considering that of light to be instantaneous, the distance between the observer and the sonorous body may be calculated by observing, as in the case of the cannon, the length of time intervening between the flash and report.

Velocity of Sound.

538. **The velocity of all sounds is the same.**—The velocity of sound is the space that it traverses in a second. The velocity of the vibrations of sonorous bodies, in the same medium, is the same for all sounds, grave or sharp, strong or feeble, and whatever may be their pitch. For example, there is no confusion in the effects of music, at whatever distance it may be heard.

539. **Velocity of sound in air.**—By numerous experiments, it has been found—

1. That velocity of sound decreases with the temperature. At 50° F., it is 1106 feet per second. The velocity diminishes about one foot and a tenth for every degree of fall of temperature.

2. That, at the same temperature, the velocity remains the same, whether the sky is bright or cloudy, the air clear or foggy, the barometric pressure great or small, provided the air is tranquil. The *intensity* of the sound, however, as it falls upon the ear, is more or less affected by all these conditions (556).

3. That the velocity varies with the direction and velocity of the wind (556).

540. **Velocity of sound in different gases and vapors.**—The velocity of sound in the different gases, is in the inverse ratio of the square root of their densities.

At the temperature of 32° F., the velocity of sound in carbonic acid is 860 feet per second; in oxygen, 1040 feet; in air, 1092.54 feet; in hydrogen, 4163 feet.

541. **Velocity of sound in liquids.**—Sound is transmitted through liquids as well as through gases. Experiments prove that the velocity of sound in water is 4708 feet per second, being greater than in hydrogen gas, and four and a half times greater than in air.

Agitation of the liquids does not affect either the velocity or intensity of the sound. But the interposition of solid bodies, as walls, etc., almost destroys the sound in water—an effect which does not take place to the same degree in air.

542. **Velocity of sound in solids.**—Solid bodies transmit sound with much greater rapidity than gases or liquids; but the velocity is not equal in all solids, varying with their elasticity, density, homogeneity, and structure.

Want of homogeneity interferes with the propagation of sonorous vibrations. The velocity of sound in iron is 11,609 feet per second.

It would require nearly three years for sound to be transmitted by an iron rod extending from the sun to the earth, the distance that light travels in eight and a half minutes. In wood the velocity is from ten to fifteen times greater than in air.

543. Time required to distinguish sounds.—The ear cannot distinguish one sound from another, if they succeed each other at an interval of less than *one-ninth* of a second.

REFLECTION OF SOUND.

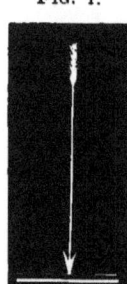

Fig. 1.

544. Figure 1.—Reflection of sound at right angles.—When waves of sound, or rather waves of air on which sound is borne, impinge on a solid surface, they are reflected from it. The laws regulating reflection of sound are the same as those which govern the reflection of motion (57), and heat (291), and light (368).

The waves have the same velocity and curvature after as before reflection. If the undulations fall upon a body in the direction perpendicular to the reflecting surface, they are reflected in the direction of the incident wave, as indicated by the arrow.

545. Figure 2.—Sounds reflected at oblique angles.—If HL be the direction of incident waves, upon the plane surface EF, the reflected waves will take the direction LT, making the angle of reflection, NLT, equal to the angle of incidence NLH.

Fig. 2.

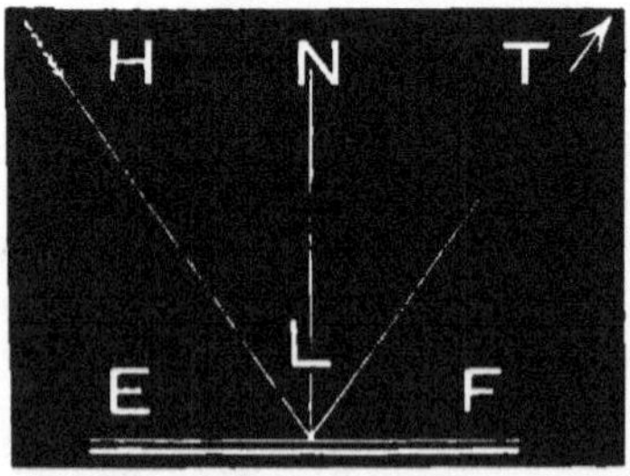

546. Circular waves reflected from a plane.—If a circular wave fall upon a plane surface at right angles to it, after reflection it has the same curvature, with the curve reversed; the same as it would have been had the wave originated from a point on the opposite side of the plane, and as far back as the point of origin itself is in front of the plane.

547. Echoes.—An echo is a repetition of sound, caused by reflection of the sound-waves from an obstacle, as a rock or building, more or less remote. Thus, a sound, emanating at a distance from a hearer, is heard first by the direct or original undulations, and afterward by the reflected waves.

In order to produce an echo, therefore, the reflecting body must be sufficiently distant from the source of sound, to make the time between the arrival of the original and reflected waves equal to or greater than *one-ninth* of a second (543); otherwise the original and reflected sounds will blend together, and produce what is called a *resonance*, and not an echo. Hence, in small rooms, less than about 63 feet across, there can be no echo; for, as sound-waves move at the rate, say, of 1,125 feet per second (539), they would cross the room and return to the hearer in less time than one-ninth of a second, if the walls were nearer to each other than about 63 feet; thus producing a resonance (549), instead of an echo.

At this distance, only the echo of the last syllable of a sentence will be heard. If the distance be twice, thrice, etc., as far, then there will be echoes of two, three, etc., of the last syllables. The direct sound and reflected sound of the other syllables will be confounded with each other.

548. **Figure 3.—Multiple echoes.**—The same sound may be reflected from several objects situated in different directions and at different distances, producing what are called *multiple echoes.*

If AH and BF represent two parallel walls, and a sound emanate at

FIG. 3.

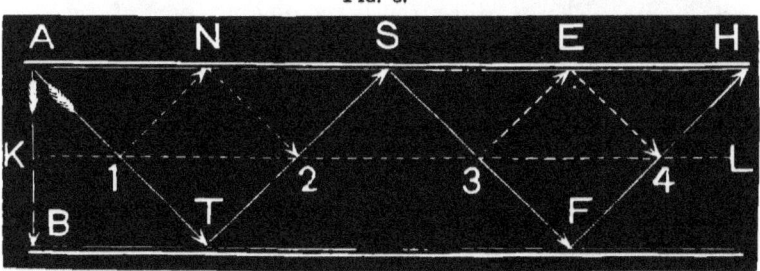

A, it will radiate in all directions toward the opposite wall. In passing to B, it will be reflected back to A; in passing to T, back to S, whence it will be again reflected to F and back again to H, and so on. If the wall BF be nearer to the wall AH, as in the position of the line KL, the number of reflections will be increased. One track of the waves, in this case, would be A1, 1N, N2, 2S, S3, and so on.

If the sound emanate, for instance, from S, it would be reflected from T to A and from F to H; or, in case of the wall being at KL, then from 2 to N, N to 1, etc.; and from 3 to E, E to 4, etc.

There are parallel walls which are said to repeat sound from twenty to thirty times.

Echoes modify the tones of sound; some rendering them with a softened, others with a roughened tone, others with a plaintive accent, etc.

Reflecting surfaces do not necessarily require to be hard and smooth, for sounds are reflected from the clouds; and a feeble echo occurs even when sound passes from one mass of air to another of different density.

549. **Resonance.**—When sounds are reflected from obstacles at a less distance than about 63 feet, or echo-distance (547), the reflected sound is superimposed upon the direct one, thus giving rise to a strengthened sound, which is called *resonance.*

It is easier to speak in a closed apartment than in the open air, in consequence of the resonance from the walls.

The resonance is more perceptible when the walls are plain and elastic. Hence, it is more clearly perceived in rooms devoid of furniture, draperies, and carpets.

FIG. 4.

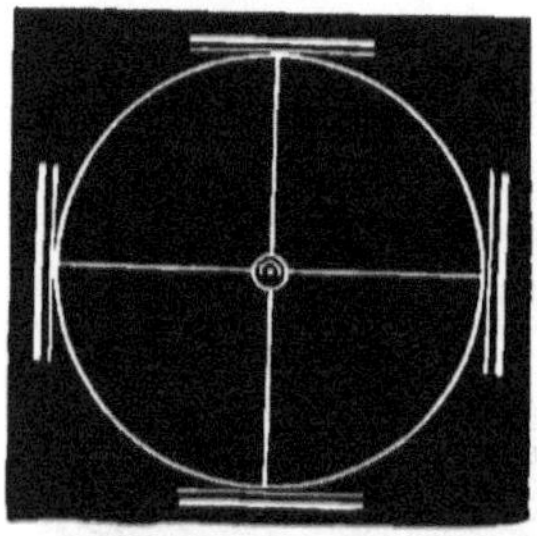

550. **Figure 4.—Sound reflected in a sphere.**—If sound were to emanate at the centre of a hollow sphere, the undulations would reach the interior surface at all points at the same time; and, falling on the surface at right angles, would all be reflected back to the centre at the same time, causing a concentration of echo or resonance, depending upon the size of the sphere.

551. **Figure 5.—Sound propagated from the foci of an ellipse.**—If the figure be an ellipse and a wave emanate from F,

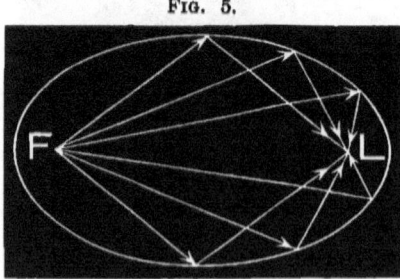

FIG. 5.

one of the foci, all the rays will converge, so as to fall simultaneously, after reflection, at the other focus L, as shown by the lines. This is because the angles of incidence are equal to those of reflection, from focus to focus.

552. **Whispering galleries** are so called because a low whisper uttered in one point in them may be heard distinctly at another and distant point, while it is inaudible in all other positions.

Such galleries are of ellipsoidal shape; and the whispering takes place at one focus and is heard at the other. The reason the whispering cannot be heard at other points, is because there is no other point where the rays converge. For this reason, too, the whispering cannot be heard unless it takes place in one of the foci.

553. **Audience rooms.**—In the construction of public rooms for the purpose of speaking, such forms should be avoided as produce echoes and reverberation, which impair the distinctness with which the speaker is heard.

By an elaborate series of experiments and observations, it is found that the best form for an audience room is one shaped like a fan, the breadth in front of the speaker being sixty-four feet, and the length one hundred feet. The height of the room should not exceed thirty or thirty-five feet.

554. **Figure 6.—Reflection of waves by parabolic curves.** —The nature of a parabolic curve, as previously shown (392), is such that heat, light, and sound proceeding from its focus will be reflected, by the curve, in parallel lines; or, conversely, parallel rays, falling upon the curve, will be reflected to the focus.

This is proved by the fact, that if two such curves be placed opposite to, and several yards from, each other, as represented, and a watch

FIG. 6.

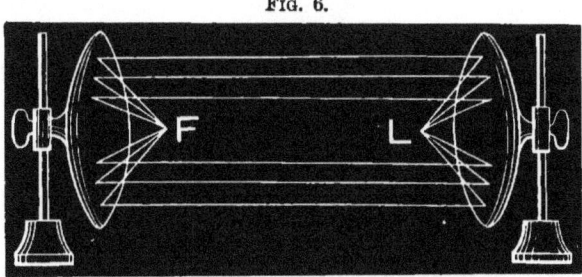

be made to tick in the focus, F, of one, it will be heard in the focus, L, of the other, although it tick so faintly that it cannot be heard at any other point between them, even if the ear be placed quite near the watch.

This proves, again, that the angles of incidence and reflection are equal.

Intensity of Sound.

555. **The Intensity of sound** is its loudness; which depends upon the amplitude of the waves; which, in turn, depends upon the force or amplitude of the vibrations of the sounding or sonorous body.

556. Causes which modify the intensity of sound.—The following are some of the causes which modify the intensity of sound:

1. It is shown by theory and experiment that the intensity of sound at different distances is subject to the same law which governs heat and light and gravity. That is, *the intensity of sound varies inversely as the square of the distance from the sonorous body.*

2. The intensity of sound diminishes with the *amplitude* of the vibration of the aerial particles. This will be appreciated by looking at the vibrations of a musical cord or a tuning-fork, and observing that the sound grows fainter as the amplitude of the vibrations diminishes.

3. Sound is modified by the *density of the air.* If the air is rarefied, the intensity is diminished, as shown by ringing a bell in the exhausted receiver, Fig. 23 (575). Hence, as a diminution of heat increases the density of air, sounds are louder in cold than warm weather.

4. *Watery vapor* being a good conductor of sound, its presence in the air increases the intensity of sounds.

5. *The wind modifies sound.* The effect of wind is to move the whole mass of air, carrying along the sound-waves unaltered. Hence the velocity of sound is increased or diminished by the velocity of the wind, according as the direction of the wind corresponds with or is opposed to the direction of the sound.

6. The intensity of sound is increased if the sonorous body is in contact with or not far from another body, capable of vibrating in unison with it.

It is upon this principle that sounding-boards are employed in musical instruments, as the piano, etc. In the case of the violin, the air in the body of the instrument vibrates in unison with the cords or strings.

557. Intensity of sounds in tubes.—If the sound-waves are prevented from spreading in all directions, the particles of air lose but little of their motion, and the sound but little of its intensity. Hence the employment of speaking tubes, through which conversation can be conducted in a low tone of voice by persons situated a mile from each other.

This will be understood by referring to Fig. 3 (548). The wave or sound, AT, is more intense at 1 than at T, and more intense at T than it would be further on in its direct course. Hence the intensity at S is greater when the wave takes the track, A1, 1N, N2, 2S, than when it takes the track AT, TS.

558. Figure 7.—The ear-trumpet.—This is an instrument employed to intensify sound, to assist persons who are hard of hearing.

The mouth, M, of the instrument is turned in any convenient direction, and the small end, N, is placed in the ear.

It was formerly supposed that the advantage of the instrument was due to reflection of the sound within the trumpet, in such a manner as to converge the undulations and direct them to a focus at the point of contact between the instrument and the ear, as illustrated by the

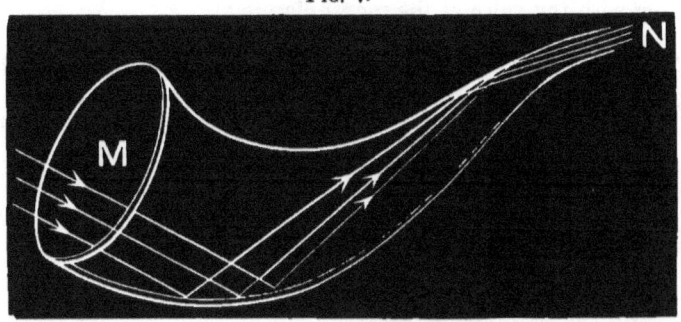

lines; but it has been found that the instrument does not operate upon this principle. Its advantage is due, 1st, to the principle explained in the previous article, and 2d, to its wide mouth and conical shape, irrespective of its otherwise exact form, by which the portions of compressed or dilated air, which arrive at the exterior opening, transmit their compressions or dilatations to portions of air smaller and smaller, and consequently transmit them with increased intensity.

The form of the external ear of animals favors the collection of sound in the same manner.

559. **Figure 8.—Speaking-trumpet.**—This is an instrument employed to intensify the voice, that it may be heard in the midst of other sounds, and also for conveying the voice to a great distance.

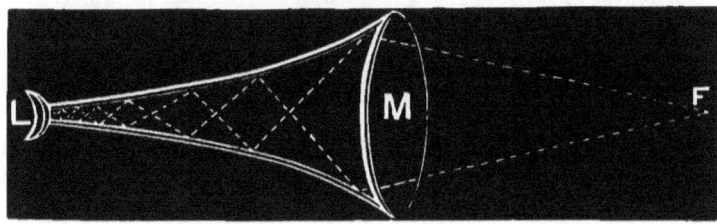

The instrument is conical, terminated by a bell-shaped extremity, M, and provided with a suitable mouth-piece, L.

308　　　　　　　　　　ACOUSTICS.

As in the case of the ear-trumpet, it was formerly supposed the advantage of the speaking-trumpet was due to the reflection of the undulations, in such a manner that they issued in the direction of the axis of the instrument, as represented by the dotted lines. It has been shown, however, that the efficiency of the instrument is not due to reflection of sound from its walls, but simply to the greater intensity of the pulsations produced in the column of confined air, which vibrate in unison with the voice at the mouthpiece.

560. **Figure 9.—Vibrations of sonorous bodies illustrated by the Jews-harp.**—This little instrument, familiar to every one, affords a convenient illustration of the vibrations of sonorous bodies. If its tongue be struck with the finger, its vibrations can be distinctly *seen*.

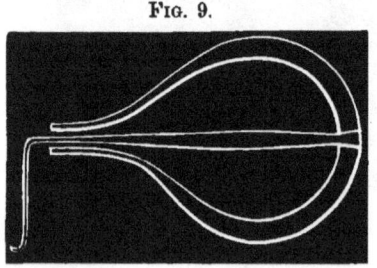
Fig. 9.

The different sounds given out by this instrument, when in use, depend upon the variation of the currents of air blown across its tongue by the player, and upon varying the relative position of the lips and instrument (585).

561. **Figure 10.—Sound-waves caused by striking a bell.**—The vibrating bell causes the air to be thrown into waves of

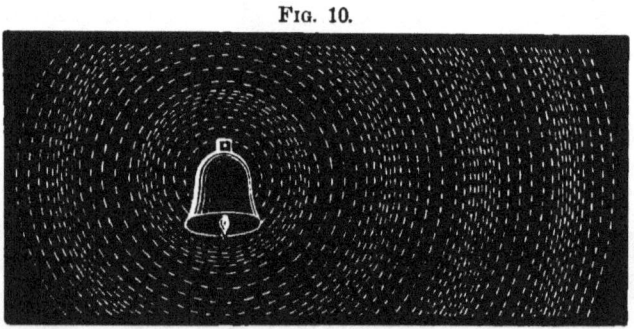
Fig. 10.

condensation and *rarefaction*. The rarefactions are shown by the darker portions of the figure, and the condensations by the lighter portions (567).

562. **Figure 11.—The cause of vibrations in sonorous bodies illustrated by a bell.**—Let the dotted circle represent

ACOUSTICS.

the rim of a bell at rest. If the rim of the bell be struck with a hammer, it is thrown out of the circular shape into the form of an ellipse, shown by either of the elliptical curves. Now, as the bell is an elastic body, it will spring back, not only to its circular form, but to the form of an ellipse situated at right angles to the first ellipse, and so on; alternately approaching and receding from the position of equilibrium, each vibration diminishing in amplitude, until all parts of the bell come again to a state of rest.

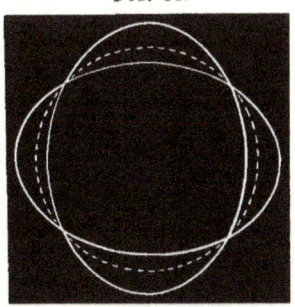

FIG. 11.

It is the springing of the bell forward and backward, in this manner, that propagates the undulations shown in the previous figure.

As the bell springs forward, striking the air, a wave of *condensation* is produced, and as it recedes *from* the air, a wave of rarefaction is produced (567).

563. **Figure 12.—Harmonicon.**—This is a musical instrument, consisting of a number of glass goblets of different sizes, fastened

FIG. 12.

to the bottom of a box which acts as a sounding-board, and so attuned to each other as to form the harmonical scale. The glasses are made to vibrate by touching the edges with the wet finger, and their tones may be prolonged, and made to swell or diminish, like those of the violin. This simple contrivance, first invented by Franklin, affords music, which for sweetness, delicacy, and smoothness, is hardly surpassed by that of any other instrument.

Interference of Sound.

564. Figure 13.—Interference of sound.—If two series of sonorous undulations encounter each other in opposite phases of vibration, the phenomena of interference will be produced.

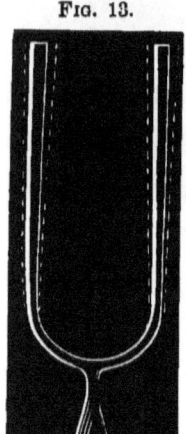

FIG. 13.

If both arms of the tuning-fork are vibrating, they will recede from and approach each other, as indicated by the dotted lines. If the instrument be placed about a foot from the ear, with the branches equidistant, both sounds will be heard, for the waves combine their effects. But, if the fork be slowly turned around, the sound will grow more and more faint, until a position will be reached in which, owing to interference, total silence will result. If, however, one of the arms ceases to vibrate the other will be heard. See interference of light (503).

565. Combination of waves of liquids.—Combination and interference of waves are of universal occurrence in all media in which force of any kind is propagated by undulation.

Two systems of waves encountering each other, several effects may follow.

1st. If the elevations of two waves coincide, and, consequently, their depressions also, then a new wave will be formed, whose elevation and depression will be the *sum* of those of the originals. In case of an elastic fluid and sound-waves, the sound at this point would be *louder*.

2d. If the two waves are of equal amplitude, and so superimposed that the elevation of one falls into the depression of the other, then both waves disappear, and the surface remains horizontal. This constitutes *interference*. In case of an elastic fluid and sound-waves. *silence* would occur at this point.

3d. When one wave has greater amplitude than the other, if they meet in the same phase, the resulting wave will have a height equal to the difference between them. In case of an elastic fluid and sound-waves, *partial silence* would occur at this point.

566. Figure 14.—Interference in an ellipse.—If the figure represent an elliptical dish of water, and a system of waves be formed about each of the foci, the two sets of waves will encounter each other, as represented by the several circles, and exhibit the phenomena of interference.

If the heavy lines are the elevations and the lighter lines are the depressions, then the points where the heavy and light lines intersect are

Fig. 14.

points where an elevation coincides with a depression, which, therefore, are points of interference.

At these points, in case of an elastic fluid, there would be silence, if the waves were those of sound.

567. **Waves of condensation and rarefaction.**—The undulations of liquids, described in the last two articles, are *surface* waves, and undulations of the same kind may be produced in elastic fluids. But *waves of condensation* and *waves of rarefaction* are of a different character, and peculiar to elastic fluids.

Such waves are produced, in air and gases, by any disturbance of density. If the elastic fluid be compressed, and again suddenly relieved from compression, it will expand, and in its expansion exceed its former volume to a certain extent; after which it will contract and expand, and thus oscillate alternately on either side of the position of repose (561–2).

568. **Interference of sound-waves** (Figs. 20 and 21).— Two sets of undulations, represented by the two curved lines, TS and LN, Fig. 20 (p. 315), would interfere and produce silence, as at *i*, because their phases are so related to each other that the depressions of one set correspond with the elevations of the other.

If a vibrating tuning-fork, Fig. 21 (p. 315), be held over the mouth of a cylindrical glass vessel, E, the air within the vessel will assume sonorous vibrations, and a *tone* will be produced. If now a second glass cylinder, A, be held in the position shown, the musical tone previously heard will cease; but if either cylinder be removed, the sound will be renewed again. The silence is caused by interference of the two sets of *sonorous waves*.

Co-existence of sonorous waves.—Many sounds may be transmitted through the air simultaneously. In listening to a concert of instruments, a practiced ear can detect the particular sound of each instrument; which shows that the sound-waves cross each other without modification, notwithstanding the effects of interference, as previously explained.

569. **Undulation of solids.**—Solid bodies exhibit the phenomena of vibration in various forms and degrees, according to the form of the body and the manner of applying the force.

Linear bodies, as tense wires, strings, etc., are susceptible of three kinds of vibrations, called transverse, longitudinal, and torsional.

Vibration of Cords.

570. **Figure 15.—The elasticity of cords and wires is developed by tension.**—If a cord, TL, be stretched, and secured at each end, and then drawn out in the middle from its position of

FIG. 15.

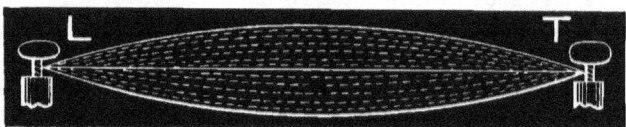

equilibrium, as shown, upon being let go, its elasticity causes it to return to its former position with accelerated velocity, which carries it past the position of equilibrium, to some position from which it returns; and again passes the central position, and so on; until, after a great number of oscillations, it at length comes to rest.

These oscillations, at first, will be manifest to the eye, if the string be of considerable length.

One complete movement from side to side, is termed *an oscillation* or vibration; and the time occupied in performing it, is called the *time of oscillation*.

L and T are thumb-screws for tightening the cord.

571. **Figure 16.—Nodal points of vibrating cords.**—If the vibrating cord (Fig. 15) be touched in the middle, its vibrations will assume the form shown by the dotted line in this figure. FE will

FIG. 16.

equal AE; the elevation, f, will equal the depression, l; and that point of the cord, E, where the phases of elevation and depression intersect, will be at rest. A piece of paper placed on this point will rest undisturbed, while it would be thrown off of any other part of the cord. This is called a *nodal point* (from the Latin, *nodus*, a knot).

Figures 17 and 18.—Two or more nodal points in one string.—If the cord be touched at two points, dividing the string into

FIG. 17.

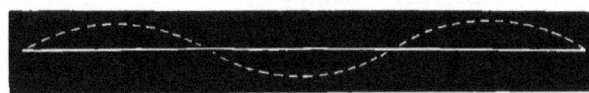

three equal parts, the vibrations will assume the form shown by the dotted line in Fig. 17.

If the cord, HN, Fig. 18, be touched at its centre, L, and at S, midway from N to L, the vibrations will assume the form represented by the dotted lines.

FIG. 18.

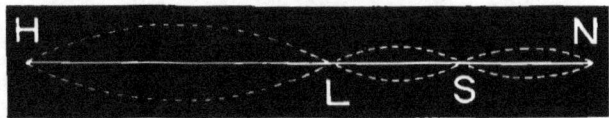

Any number of nodal points may exist in the same string, but rarely more than four, when they spontaneously occur.

572. **Laws of the vibration of cords.**—The number of vibrations of a stretched cord, in any given time, as in one second, depends upon its *length, thickness, tension,* and *density.*

Calculation and experiment have demonstrated that cords vibrate in accordance with the following laws.

1. *The tension being the same, the number of vibrations varies inversely as its length.*

This property is utilized in the violin. By applying the finger, the length of the vibrating portion of the cord is reduced at pleasure.

2. *The tension and length being the same, the number of vibrations varies inversely as its size or thickness.*

A cord, therefore, of any given size, makes twice as many vibrations as one of double the size. Other things being equal, the notes rendered differ by an octave.

3. *The length and size being the same, the number of vibrations varies as the square root of the tension.*

Hence, a cord, which renders a given note, will, if its tension be quadrupled, render a note an octave higher, and so on.

4. *Other things being equal, the number of vibrations varies inversely as the square root of the density.*

Hence, dense cords render graver notes than those of less density. Large, dense, and long cords, not tensely stretched, give grave notes; while small, light, and short cords, tensely stretched, yield acute notes.

573. **Figure 19.—Verification of the laws of vibration.—The sonometer.**—The laws just enunciated are verified by means of an instrument called a *sonometer*, or sound-measurer. This instrument consists of a wooden box about four feet long, upon which

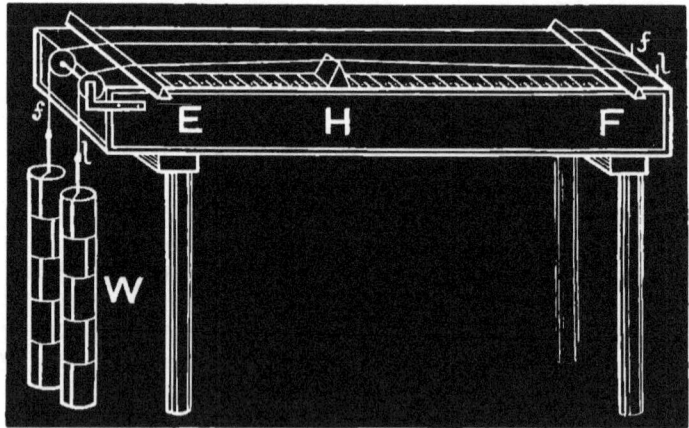

FIG. 19.

are mounted two fixed bridges, F and E, and one movable bridge H. Passing over the fixed bridges are two cords, ff and ll. One end of each cord is fastened to the box, and the other ends, after passing over pulleys, are drawn down with equal force, by means of equal weights, W, as shown. On the edge of the box is a graduated scale. The

ACOUSTICS. 315

length of the vibrating part of the cords will depend upon the position of the bridges.

If the movable bridge, II, is placed so that the distance, FH, is equal to half the distance, FE, the notes of the two cords will differ by an octave; that is, ll will vibrate twice as fast as ff. If, by moving the bridge II, FH be made equal to one-third of FE, then ll will vibrate three times as fast as ff. This verifies the *first* law.

Remove the bridge, II, and substitute two other cords (of the same material), one of which is twice as large as the other; and it will be found that the notes differ by an octave. If one cord be three times as large as the other, the smaller cord will vibrate three times as fast as the other; which verifies the *second* law.

If the cords are every way alike, and one is stretched by a weight four times as great as that used to stretch the other, the notes will differ one octave. If the weights are as 1 to 9, the rapidity of the vibrations will be as 1 to 3. This verifies the *third* law.

If the cords are of different densities, but every other way alike and equally stretched, it will be found that the *fourth* law is verified in each case.

FIG. 20.

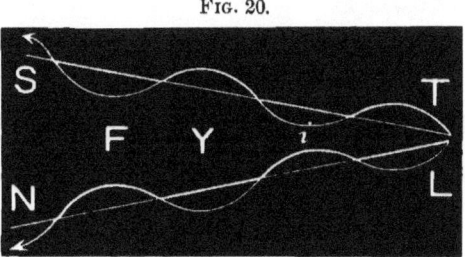

Figure 20.—Interference of sound illustrated by two vibrating cords. — For explanation of this figure, see 568.

Figure 21.—Interference of sound further illustrated, by means of a common tuning-fork and two cylindrical glass vessels. For the explanation, see 568.

FIG. 21.

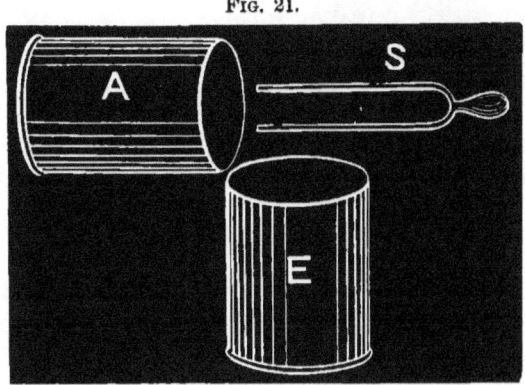

FIG. 22.

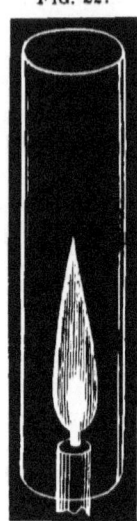

574. **Figure 22.—Sounds caused by burning hydrogen.**—When a small jet of hydrogen is burned within a glass tube of about an inch in diameter, as shown, pleasant musical tones are heard, which are varied by raising the tube up and down.

The vibrations and sounds are due to the successive explosions of small portions of free gas, mingled with common air. The ascending current of air, caused by the heat, momentarily extinguishes the flame, permitting the mixture of the air with the inflammable gas. The expiring flame kindles this explosive mixture and relights the jet. These successive phenomena occur with great rapidity and at regular intervals, producing the musical note.

The hydrogen may be generated by the action of dilute sulphuric acid on zinc, placed in a common bottle. It is better, however, to regulate the flow of the gas to the tube by means of a faucet.

575. **Figure 23.—Sound is not propagated in a vacuum.**—That some medium is necessary for the transmission of sound may be shown by experiments with the exhausted receiver.

FIG. 23.

In the top of the receiver is a rubber plug, L, fitted air-tight. Extending through the plug is a rod, upon the end of which, within the receiver, is a bell. The rod is bent at right angles above, to form a handle, T, with which to ring the bell.

The sound of the bell can be distinctly heard when the receiver is filled with air. If the air be exhausted, the bell cannot be heard. By exhausting the air and ringing the bell at the same time, the sound of the bell grows fainter and fainter, until it ceases. Hence, sounds at high altitudes, as on high mountains, are not so loud as at the level of the sea.

Vibrations of Rods and Plates.

576. **Vibrations of rods.**—Rods, like cords, vibrate. If they are fixed firmly by one of their extremities, as in a vice, they will, when set in motion, be divided by stationary undulations into several vibrating parts. The nodal points may be ascertained by placing upon the rods light rings of paper; which will be thrown off all along the rod, except at the nodal points, where they will remain unmoved.

The space between the free extremity and the first nodal point is equal to half the length contained between two nodal points.

577. **Means of vibrating plates.**—Vibrations are readily excited in elastic plates by friction or blows, and sounds are evolved. The plate is confined either at its centre or one corner, in a vice (Fig. 26), resting on a cone of cork and pressed by a screw, also tipped with cork, as represented.

578. **Nodal lines of plates.**—In the vibration of plates nodal lines will be formed, which do not participate in the movements of the plane, but remain in a state of rest.

579. **Determination of nodal lines of plates.**—The position of the nodal lines may be determined by scattering sand or other fine material over the plate, and causing the plate to vibrate, as by means of a violin-bow drawn across the edge. The grains of sand will be thrown from the vibrating portions of the plate, and come to a state of rest on the nodal lines and points.

580. **Nodal figures.**—These always have symmetry of form. A great variety of these have been determined. The same plate may furnish an infinite number of them, which pass from one to another in a continuous manner, and not by sudden changes.

A few of these figures are represented, in order to give a general idea respecting their formation.

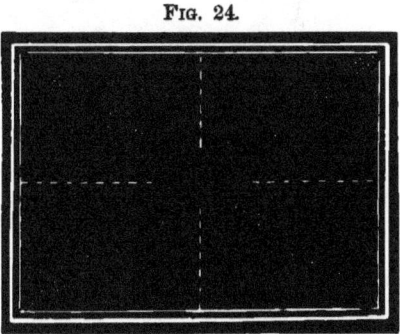

FIG. 24.

Figure 24.—If a square plate of glass be grasped in the centre by the hand-vice, and sand scattered over its surface, and the violin-bow drawn rapidly across it, close to one of its angles, the sand will be thrown into the position shown by the dots.

Powdered litmus, previously mixed with gum-water, dried and pulverized to a uniform size, may be used instead of sand. Figures thus made can be transferred to paper, simply by moistening the paper with gum-water, and pressing it upon the plate.

Figure 25.—If the plate be confined near one of its angles, and the bow applied to the middle of one of its sides, the sand will be arranged as shown by the dots in the figure.

FIG. 25.

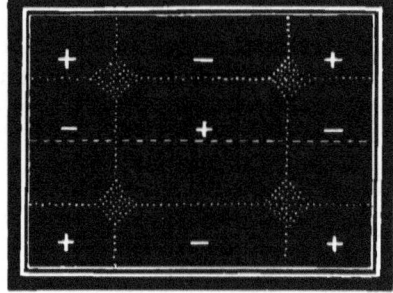

The space between the nodal lines is just double the distance between the nodal lines and the edges of the plate. The signs plus and minus represent opposite phases of vibration.

FIG. 26.

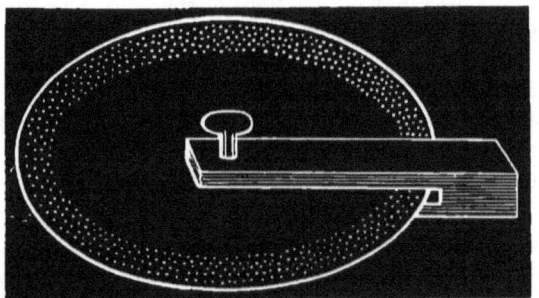

Figure 26.—If a circular plate of glass be confined at the centre and the violin-bow drawn across the edge, the sand will take the position represented by the dots.

FIG. 27.

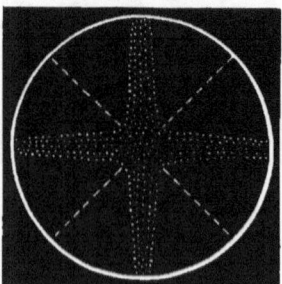

Figure 27 represents another nodal figure of a circular plate.

Many hundred forms of nodal figures have been determined. Triangular and polygonal plates all give symmetrical figures, analogous to those obtained with square plates, as represented by the following two illustrations.

Figure 28 represents a nodal figure of a polygonal plate.

FIG. 28.

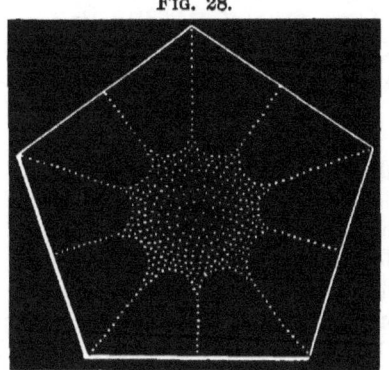

Figure 29 represents nodal figures of a triangular plate.

FIG. 29.

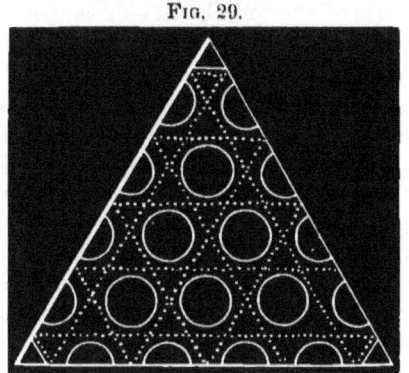

Refraction of Sound.

581. **Figure 30.—Refraction of sound.**—Although sound is reflected by any surface of different density from that in which it

FIG. 30.

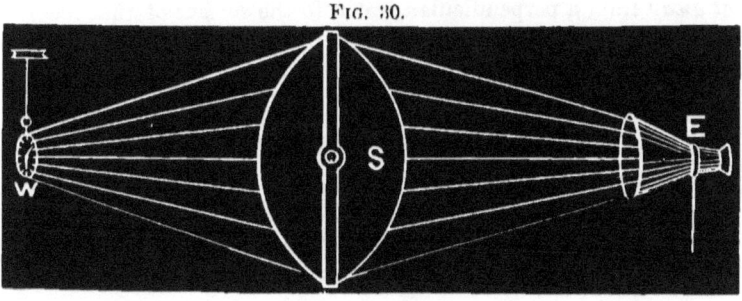

originates, the sound also enters the second medium by means of new vibrations, originating at the interposed surface.

A cell, S, made of two films of collodion, united at the edges, and having the form of a double convex lens, as shown, will serve to demonstrate refraction of sound. The cell is held at the edges by a frame, and provided with an opening, by which it can be filled with different gases.

If the cell be filled with carbonic acid gas, which transmits sound-waves with less velocity than air (540), the waves will be converged by passing through the cell.

A watch, W, held on the axis of the lens-shaped cell will be heard on the opposite side of the cell, at some point, as at the small end of the funnel E, on the axis. If the watch be held nearer to the cell, the ticking will be heard at a greater distance from it; but if the watch be held at a greater distance from the cell, then the ticking will be heard at a nearer point. If the watch, the lens, or the ear is placed out of the line of the axis of the cell, the ticking cannot be heard. Hence, the refraction takes place in accordance with the principles of refraction of light.

Let the sound-waves be represented not by the lines, but by the *spaces* between the lines. Then, as the outer space, or wave, from the watch, comes in contact with the cell, that portion of the wave falling on the cell first will be retarded more than that portion meeting the cell later, which, of course, will bend the wave toward the axis, or principal perpendicular line. But, in accordance with this, if the cell were filled with some medium, as hydrogen gas, which transmits sound with greater velocity than air, then the waves would be refracted *away* from the axis or perpendicular line.

582. **The laws of the refraction of sound** are—

1. Sound-waves passing obliquely into a medium of different density, will be *refracted*.

2. If they travel more rapidly in the new medium, they will be *bent away* from a perpendicular drawn to the surface of that medium.

3. If they travel less rapidly in the new medium, they will be *bent toward* the perpendicular drawn to the surface of that medium.

Sounds from Pipes.

583. **Sound from pipes.**—Air put into vibration in a *pipe*, or hollow tube, yields a sound. The air is the sonorous body; the character of the sound depending upon the form of the pipe, and the manner in which the vibrations of the air are produced.

The contained air is thrown into successive condensations and rarefactions by introducing a current of air through a suitable *mouthpiece*. Two principal forms are given to the mouthpiece. In one of these the parts are fixed, and in the other there is a moveable tongue, called a *reed*.

The difference in the *quality* of the tones produced by pipes of different materials, may be owing to a feeble vibration of the pipes themselves.

584. **Figure 31.—Pipes with fixed mouthpieces.**—These are made of wood or metal, are rectangular or cylindrical, and are of considerable length compared with their cross-section. The flute, the organ-pipe, the whistle, or flageolet, etc., are examples of this class of pipes.

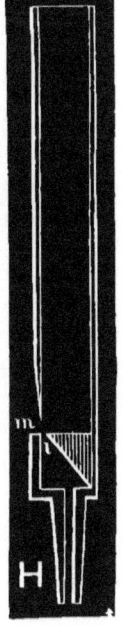

Fig. 31.

One of the forms given to this class is represented by the figure. H represents the tube through which air is forced into it by the bellows. The air passes through a narrow opening, i, called the *vent*. Opposite the vent is an opening, m, in the side of the pipe, called the *mouth*. The upper border of the mouth is beveled, and is called the *upper lip*, the lower border (not beveled) is called the *lower lip*.

When the air is forced through the vent, i, it encounters the edge of the upper lip, by which it is partially obstructed, causing a shock, so that the air passes through the mouth, m, in an intermitted manner. These pulsations are transmitted to the air in the tube, making it vibrate, and thus producing a sound.

In order to have a pure sound, there must exist a certain relation between the dimensions of the lips and the opening of the mouth; and the length of the tube must bear a certain ratio to its diameter. Holes or openings in the side of a wind-instrument, as the flute, flageolet, etc., have the effect of virtually varying the length of the tube.

585. **Reed-pipes.**—In reed-pipes the mouthpiece is provided with a vibrating tongue, called a *reed*. The reed is made of elastic metal, or wood, and attached to an opening in such a manner that a current of air, passing into the opening, causes the reed to vibrate. This vibration is propagated to the surrounding air.

Some of the reed instruments are the clarionet, the trumpet, the bassoon, the accordion, the Jews-harp (560), etc.; the last being the most simple of this species of instruments.

586. **Figure 32.—Arrangement of reeds.**—The reeds may be so arranged as to beat against the sides of the opening, or they may play freely through the opening.

The figure shows the arrangement of a reed of the first kind. A piece of metal, *f*, shaped somewhat like a spoon, is fitted to an elastic tongue, *l*, which can completely close the opening shown between them. A piece of metal, *i*, which can be elevated or depressed by a rod, L, serves to shorten or lengthen the vibrating part of the reed; which, of course, increases or diminishes the rapidity of vibration.

FIG. 32.

When a current of air is forced into the tube, TN (the front of which is cut away to show the parts just described), the reed, *l*, rapidly vibrates, producing a succession of rarefactions and condensations in the air of the pipe, S, thus causing it to emit sound. The air entering TN, first closes the opening by pressing the reed against it; the reed then recoils by the force of its elasticity, permitting a portion of condensed air to enter the pipe, when the reed is again pressed against the opening, and so on.

587. **The organs of the voice a reed instrument.**—At the top of the trachea, or windpipe, is a pair of elastic bands, called the *vocal cords*, stretched across the opening of the trachea, so as nearly to close it, and forming a kind of double reed. When the air is forced from the lungs through the slit between these cords, they are made to vibrate. Their rate of vibration, within certain limits, is varied at will by changing their tension, upon which depends the pitch of the voice. The cavities of the mouth and nose act as resonant tubes.

The various organs which constitute the entire vocal apparatus of man, are the *lungs*, the *trachea*, the *larynx*, the *pharynx*, the *mouth*, and the *nose*, with their appendages.

A minute description of the construction of these, and an explanation of the part that each performs in the utterance of sound and speech, belong to the department of Anatomy and Physiology

Musical Sounds.

It cannot be expected that more than a few leading principles relating to musical sounds, would be explained in an elementary compendium for schools. Music and musical instruments are the subjects of a special treatise.

588. **Difference between musical sounds and noises.**— A musical sound results from a succession of atmospheric vibrations of equal duration. Noise is the sensation produced by unequal vibrations. If a stone be thrown into the middle of a still sheet of water, a single wave circles off to the shore, which may illustrate the effect upon the air when a *tone* is produced. If several stones be thrown into the water together, each stone produces its own circle, and the several circles intersect each other and become confused to the eye. This may be compared to the effect upon the air when a *noise* is produced.

589. **Qualities of sound.**—The ear distinguishes three qualities of sound: 1. *Pitch*, or *tone*, which depends upon the frequency of the vibrations. Rapid vibrations yield *acute* or *high* sounds, and slow vibrations give *low* or *grave* sounds.

2. The *intensity*, by virtue of which sounds are loud or soft. Loudness depends upon the amplitude of the oscillations.

3. *Quality*, in virtue of which sounds of the same intensity and pitch are relatively distinguishable.

590. **Limits of perceptible sounds.**—The gravest perceptible sound is produced by 16 vibrations per second, and the most acute, by 48,000 vibrations per second. Supposing the velocity of sound to be 1,090 feet per second, the length of the waves of the gravest sound would be 68 feet, and those of the most acute, a little more than a quarter of an inch.

The limits in music are much narrower, especially in singing. The lowest sound of the male voice being 190 vibrations per second; for the female voice, 572; for the highest sound of the male voice, 678 vibrations; for the female voice, 1,606.

591. **Unison.**—Sounds produced by the same number of vibrations per second are said to be *in unison*.

592. **Melody.—Chord.—Harmony.**—When the vibrations of a progressive series of single musical sounds bear to each other such simple relations as are *readily perceived*, an agreeable impression is produced, called *melody*.

When two or more sounds, having to each other such simple relations, are produced simultaneously, it is called *a chord*.

A succession of chords, succeeding each other in melodious order, constitutes *harmony*.

It is invariably found that the sounds caused by vibrations which are to each other in some simple numerical proportion, are pleasing; such as 1 to 2, 2 to 3, 3 to 4, etc. The science of music does not admit of any proportions except those which arise from the limited combination of these very simple numbers.

593. **The principal harmonies.**—The principal harmonies are represented in the following diagrams, the upper line in each representing the acute and the lower the grave notes. Those vibrations which occur simultaneously, and, therefore, increase each other's power, are connected by vertical lines.

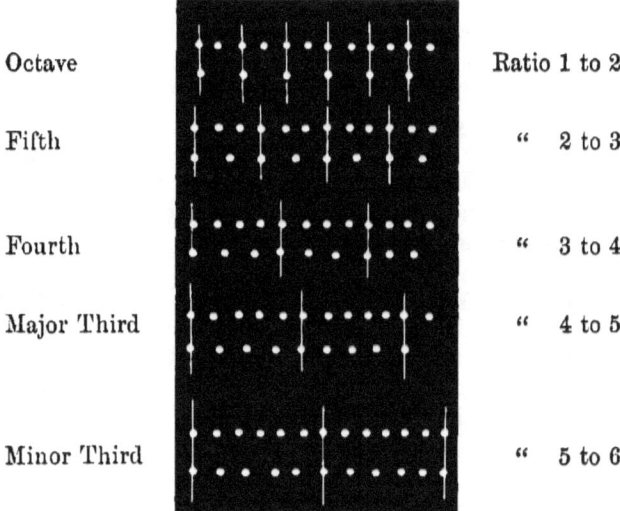

Octave		Ratio 1 to 2
Fifth		" 2 to 3
Fourth		" 3 to 4
Major Third		" 4 to 5
Minor Third		" 5 to 6

The concord 1 to 2 is most pleasing, every second vibration of the acuter chord coinciding perfectly with each vibration of the graver; it is called the *octave*, as it comprehends an interval of eight notes in the musical scale. The concord 2 to 3 is the next most pleasing, each third vibration of the acuter corresponding with the second of the graver; it is called the *fifth*, as it comprehends an interval of five notes from the fundamental in the musical scale. The concord 3 to 4 is quite pleasing; it is called a *fourth*, as it comprehends an interval of four notes in the scale; each fourth vibration of the acuter chord corresponds with the third of the graver. The concord 4 to 5 is pleasing: it is called the *major third*, because it not only comprehends an interval of three notes, but its ratio 4 to 5 is greater than the ratio 5 to 6, which also comprehends an interval of three notes, and is called a *minor third ;* in the first case, five pulsations of the acuter chord correspond to four of the graver, and in the latter, six of the acuter to five of the graver.

594. **The most pleasing harmonies.**—The combination of two notes is the more pleasing to the ear, the smaller the two numbers which express the ratio of their vibrations.

595. **The limit of harmonies.**—The limit beyond which a musical ear, and the mind generally, will not tolerate the combination of two sounds, is that expressed by 5 to 6, or that of minor third.

596. **Musical scale.—Gamut.**—The tones forming a melodious series between any two adjacent sounds which are as 1 to 2, are called the *musical scale* or *gamut*.

The sounds which compose the musical scale or gamut, are the alphabet of music. To find the relation which exists between the fundamental note (C) and the other notes, the *sonometer* is employed (573).

The names of the sounds composing the scale are, in English, C, D, E, F, G, A, B. In French and Italian, do, re, mi, fa, sol, la, si.

By means of the sonometer, it is found that the length of the cord corresponding to each note is represented by the following fractions:

Notes........................ C D E F G A B C'
Relative length of cord........ 1 $\frac{8}{9}$ $\frac{4}{5}$ $\frac{3}{4}$ $\frac{2}{3}$ $\frac{3}{5}$ $\frac{8}{15}$ $\frac{1}{2}$

597. **Formation of the musical scale.**—It has been shown that the number of vibrations is in the inverse ratio of the length of the string (572). Hence, the relative number of vibrations, corresponding to each note in the same time, will be expressed by inverting the fractions of the preceding table.

Representing, therefore, the number of vibrations corresponding to the fundamental note C, by 1, we have:

Notes........................ C D E F G A B C'
Relative number of vibrations.... 1 $\frac{9}{8}$ $\frac{5}{4}$ $\frac{4}{3}$ $\frac{3}{2}$ $\frac{5}{3}$ $\frac{15}{8}$ 2

To avoid fractions, whole numbers bearing the same ratio may be substituted, thus:

        C   D   E   F   G   A   B   C'
       24 27 30 32 36 40 45 48

Absolute number of vibrations corresponding to each note.—The notes of the scale whose gamut corresponds to the gravest sound of the bass are indicated by 1. To notes of gamuts, more elevated, are affixed the indices 2, 3, etc.; to graver notes are affixed the indices —1, —2, etc. The number of simple vibrations corresponding to the note C, is 128 per second. Hence, by multiplying this number by the several fractions (597), we have:

Notes	C	D	E	F	G	A	B
Absolute number of simple vibrations	128	144	160	170⅔	192	213⅓	240

The absolute number of vibrations for superior gamut is obtained by multiplying the numbers in this table successively by 2, by 3, etc.

The following table indicates the length of the waves corresponding to the C of successive scales:

	LENGTH OF WAVES IN FEET.	NUMBER OF VIBRATIONS IN A SECOND.
C—3	70	16
C—2	35	32
C—1	17.5	64
C1	8.73	128
C2	4.375	256
C3	2.187	512
C4	1.093	1024

It will be noticed (597) that the interval C—C', as indicated by the figures, bears the ratio of 1 to 2, and is called an *octave*.

The interval C—G is called a *fifth*, comprehending five notes, the ratio being 2 to 3.

The interval C—F, and also E—A, is called a *fourth*, comprehending four notes, the ratio in each case being 3 to 4.

The interval C—E and F—A is called the *major third*, the ratio being 4 to 5, and the interval three notes.

The interval E—G and A—C' is called the *minor third*, the interval being three, and the ratio 5 to 6, which is less than the ratio 4 to 5; hence the name, *minor third*.

CHAPTER XIII.

(CHART NO. 7.)

MAGNETISM.

GENERAL PROPERTIES OF MAGNETS.

598. **Definitions.**—Magnetism, as a science, is that branch of Physics which treats of the properties of magnets, and of their action upon each other, and upon other bodies.

The real nature of the magnetic force is unknown; but the analogies offered by electro-magnetism and magneto-electricity indicate, that it is one mode of electrical excitement.

599. **Lodestone, or natural magnets.**—Lodestone (*to lead* and *stone*) is an ore of iron, found in a natural state in many parts of the earth, possessing the power of attracting iron and a few other substances. This power is called *magnetism*, from the name of the ancient city Magnesia, near which this ore was first found. It is a compound of one equivalent of peroxyd of iron with one of protoxyd.

600. **Figure 33.—Magnetic manifestations of lodestone.**
—If a piece of this ore be dipped in iron filings they will collect and cling together at two opposite extremities, as represented in the figure. The magnetic property, whatever it may be, seems, therefore, to be collected, and to act with the greatest energy, at two opposite extremities. These are termed *poles* (512).

FIG. 33.

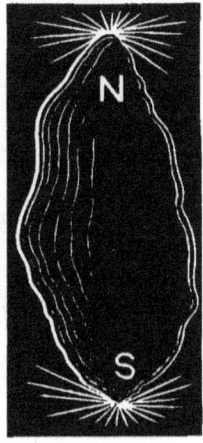

If a piece of the ore, as shown, be laid down on a piece of board, and the board floated on water, the lodestone will invariably arrange itself so that the same pole will be directed to the *north* and the other to the *south*. Hence the pole which turns to the north is called the *North* pole and the other the *South* pole, as indicated by the letters in the figure. Pieces of this ore are called *natural magnets*.

601. **Figure 34.—The armature.**—The effective power of the lodestone is improved by means of what is termed an *armature;* which

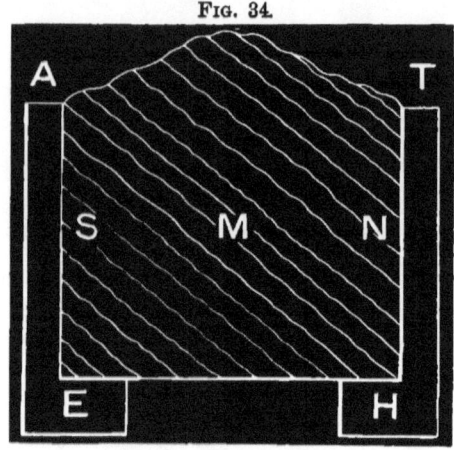

FIG. 34.

consists of pieces of soft iron, AE and TH, applied to the opposite polar surfaces, S and N, of the lodestone, M. The attractive force is thus transmitted to the artificial poles of iron, E and H.

602. **Figure 35.—A fully-mounted lodestone magnet.**—This consists of the armatures secured to the lodestone, M, by brass binders, A and E; a ring, H, for suspending the apparatus; a keeper, K, which is a soft piece of iron, connecting the poles, S and N, as shown.

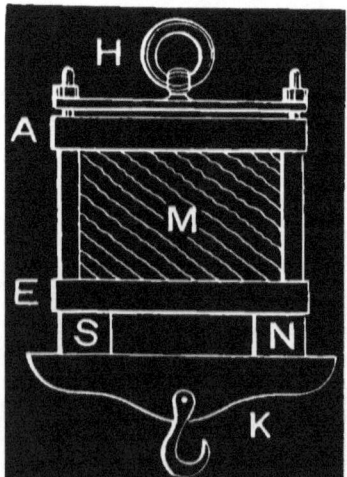

FIG. 35.

This keeper is found to preserve and increase the attractive force of the poles, especially if the whole be suspended by the ring, and weights be attached to the hook of the keeper.

603. **Artificial magnets** are bars of iron, steel, or tempered steel, to which the property of the natural magnet has been imparted.

Artificial magnets are either *permanent* or *temporary.* Permanent magnets are made of tempered or hardened steel; temporary magnets are made of untempered steel and of soft iron.

MAGNETISM.

Artificial magnets are more powerful and useful than the lodestone or natural magnet, and possess properties identical with it. Temporary magnets do not retain their magnetism after the exciting cause is removed.

604. **Figure 36.—Method of making an artificial magnet with lodestone.**—ME represents a part of the mounted natural magnet (602), s and N being its poles.

FIG. 36.

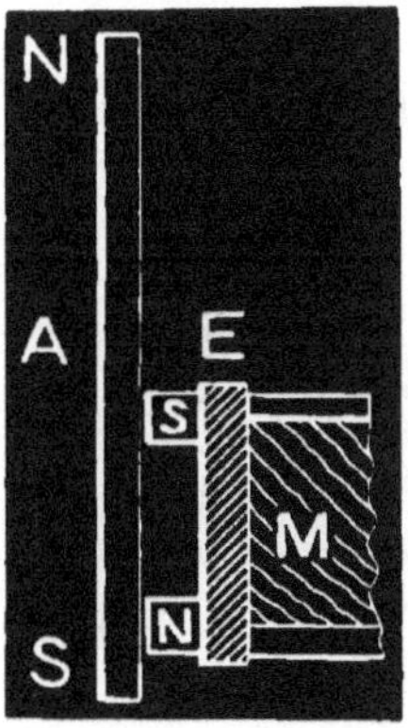

To impart the magnetism to the tempered bar of steel, A, and render it a permanent magnet, place it upon the poles, as shown in the figure, and slide it lengthwise back and forth a number of times, but not so far as to pass either extremity of the bar beyond either pole; finally bring the bar at rest, with its ends at an equal distance from the poles, and then lift it perpendicularly from the natural magnet. The bar will now manifest magnetic attraction and polarity.

The artificial magnet will have opposite polarity to the original magnet; that is, the south pole of the artificial magnet will have been developed by or at the north pole of the natural magnet, and vice versa.

605. **Figure 37.—Distribution of force in magnets.**—The magnetic force is not equally distributed in all parts of a magnet. The attraction is strongest at the ends, and diminishes toward the centre, where it is neutral. The ends, where the attraction is greatest, are called *poles;* the central part, where the attraction is nothing, is called the *equator*, or the *neutral line*.

FIG. 37.

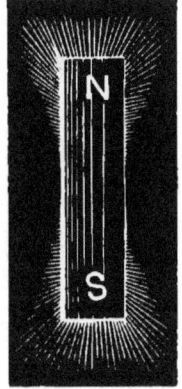

The positions of the poles and equator are shown by the figure, in which the radiating lines represent the attractive force. If the magnet be rolled in iron filings, the particles of iron will be attracted to, and held in the position of, these radiating lines.

Every magnet has at least two poles, and one neutral point.

The poles are distinguished by North and South (N and S), Austral or Boreal (A and B), or by the signs plus (+) and minus (−). These signs refer to the earth's attraction and antagonism between poles of unlike names.

330   MAGNETISM.

Sometimes, owing to inequality of temper in the steel, artificial magnets have minor poles, situated between the principal ones, called *secondary poles.*

606. The law of distribution of attraction. — The law regulating the distribution of magnetic force in a bar is, *that the force is nearly as the square of the distance of any given point from the magnetic equator.*

607. The force of magnetic attraction at different distances. — Magnets attract at all distances, but *their power decreases as the square of the distance from their poles increases*, being in accordance with the common law, that regulates all forces which act from a centre, as that of heat, light, gravitation, etc.

The most powerful magnets sustain about thirty times their own weight.

608. Effect of heat on magnets. — The power of magnets is diminished by heat; but if they be heated only to *redness*, the power returns on cooling. *White-*heat wholly destroys their magnetic force. Their power is increased at low temperatures.

FIG. 38.

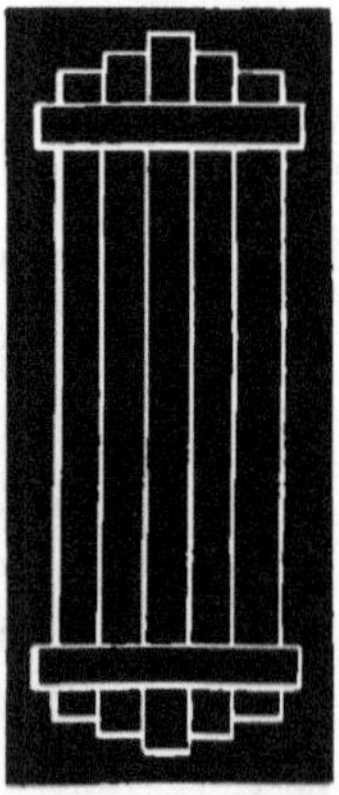

609. Figure 38.—Various forms of magnets.—The *bar magnet* is a simple straight bar of steel. The *horse-shoe* magnet is the bar magnet bent in the form of a horse-shoe.

The most powerful attraction takes place when both poles can be applied to the surface of a piece of iron at once; hence, to facilitate such an application, many magnets are made in the horse-shoe form.

A compound magnet consists of several magnets bound together. The figure represents a compound magnet made of several plain bar magnets.

The dimensions well adapted to magnetic bars, straight or curved, are such as to give the breadth about $\frac{1}{14}$ or $\frac{1}{15}$ of the length, and the thickness not more than half the breadth.

610. Figure 39.—Compound horse-shoe magnet.—This consists of several horse-shoe magnets bound together, with their similar poles in contact, by means of a clasp at the middle or neutral point, and with rivets or screws at the ends, as shown.

To preserve the magnetism, the poles are kept united, when the magnet

MAGNETISM.

is not in use, by means of a soft bar of iron, called the *keeper*. Such magnets are called *magnetic batteries*, and are often employed for charging other magnets.

Large magnets are not as powerful, in proportion to their weight, as small ones.

There is found a limit beyond which there is no advantage in extending these batteries.

Fig. 39.

Charging Magnets.

611. **Method of charging magnets.**—Artificial magnets are produced not only by *touch* or *friction* from other magnets; but by *induction;* and by *electrical currents*.

The method by touch is accomplished by various modes of manipulation, of which only two or three will be described.

612. **Figure 40.—Method of charging horse-shoe magnets.**—Let L be the bar to be charged or magnetised. Having secured it on a board, and united its extremities with a bar of soft iron, K, place the compound magnet, F, on one arm of the bar, as shown, and

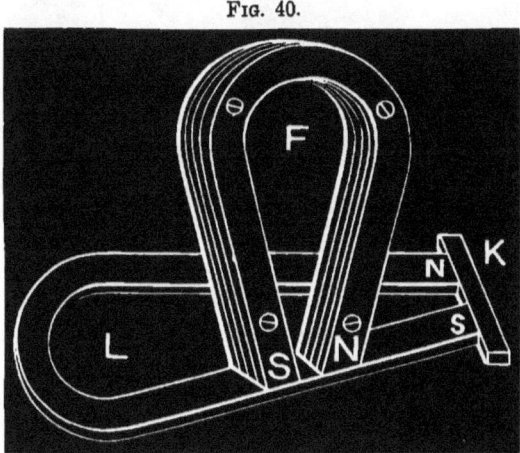

Fig. 40.

glide it around on the two arms several times; and having brought it to a state of rest at the neutral point, L, remove it. Then turn the bar over and repeat the operation on the other side, always observing to keep the unlike poles of the two magnets in contact with each other; that is, so that the N pole of the magnetizing magnet will be toward the S pole of the magnet which is being charged, as indicated by the several letters.

613. **Figure 41.—Method of magnetizing straight bars.**—Straight bars, and needles for compasses, are usually magnetized by rubbing them with other bar-magnets. There are three ways of doing this, known as the methods by *single touch*, by *separate touch*, and by *double touch*.

By *single touch*, the bar is magnetized by simply passing one end of a powerful bar-magnet several times over it.

By *separate touch*, the bar is magnetized by being rubbed in one direction with one pole of the magnet, and in the opposite direction with the opposite pole.

To magnetize by *double touch*, two or four magnets are employed,

FIG. 41.

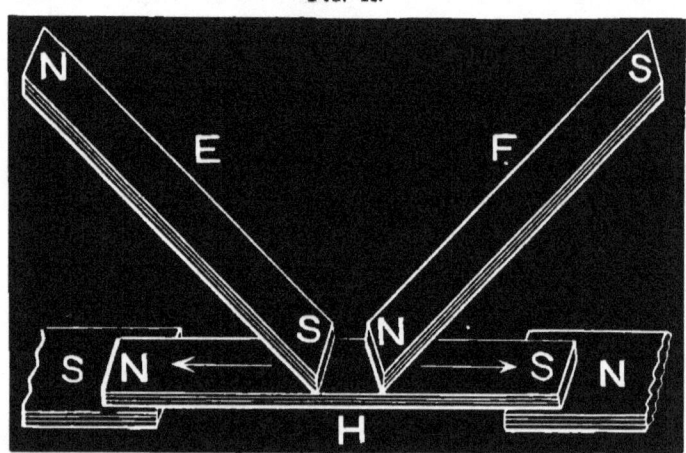

which may be simple or compound. In the drawing, four simple magnets, and the method of using them, are represented.

Let H represent the bar to be magnetized. First place it upon the opposite poles of two magnets (only one end of each of which is shown), then take two other magnets, E and F, and, having placed them as represented (that is, with their similar poles reversed), simultaneously draw them from the centre to the extremities of the bar, as indicated by the two arrows; then lift them up a foot or so, and again place them in the same position, repeating the process many times on both sides of the bar.

The N pole of the new magnet will be formed between the *south* poles of the magnets, and its S pole between the *north* poles, as indicated by the letters.

614. Figure 42.—Both poles must coexist in every magnet.—If a magnet be broken at the neutral point, as shown, each half will become a complete magnet of diminished force, having two opposite poles, like the original. The poles, formed at the broken ends, will be opposite in character to those of the corresponding extremities of the original magnet.

Fig. 42.

If these fragments be again and again broken, to the extreme degree of mechanical fineness, each particle, however small, will be a perfect magnet.

615. Magnetic and magnetized bodies.—A *magnetic body* is one which contains the two magnetic fluids or forces, but in a state of equilibrium; thus, iron, steel, nickel, and cobalt are such bodies.

Magnetized bodies contain the two fluids, but in a state of separation, each producing an opposite effect, whilst in the magnetic bodies the fluids are combined and produce no effect.

Induction.

616. Figure 43.—Induction.—Magnetism by contact.— Let M represent a bar-magnet, with its poles arranged as shown by the letters N and S. If a magnetic body, as an iron key, be placed in contact with one of the poles of the magnet, it will be magnetized, and adhere to the magnet.

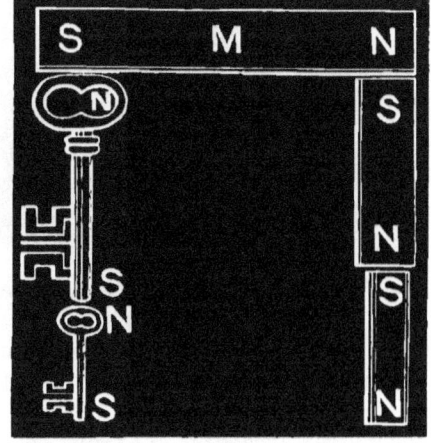

Fig. 43.

If a second key be brought in contact with the first, it also will be magnetized and adhere as shown, and so on. If iron keys, or other magnetic bodies, be brought in contact with the other pole of the magnet, they will be similarly magnetized; the only difference being, that their respective poles will be reversed.

In both cases the magnetized bodies in contact with the magnet have their poles reversed; or, generally, the adjacent extremities of all the bodies (including the magnet) have opposite polarity, as indicated by the letters.

If one of these magnetized bodies be reversed, or turned end for end, its polarity will also be reversed; that is, the end that was the N pole becomes the S pole, and vice versa.

This action of a magnet upon magnetic bodies is called *induction*.

Some substances besides the so-called magnetic metals, become *slightly* magnetic. Some minerals become magnetic by heating; and the alloy, brass, by hammering. The pure earths, and even silica, are found to have the same property. See Diamagnetism, 783.

617. **Figure 44.—Magnetic induction illustrated by a series of rings.**—If an iron ring be placed in contact with a magnet, it will, by induction, become itself a magnet. If a second ring be presented to the first, it will in like manner become a magnet, and so on, with a considerable number of them, as represented. If the bar be removed, the rings lose their magnetism, cease to adhere, and the chain falls to pieces.

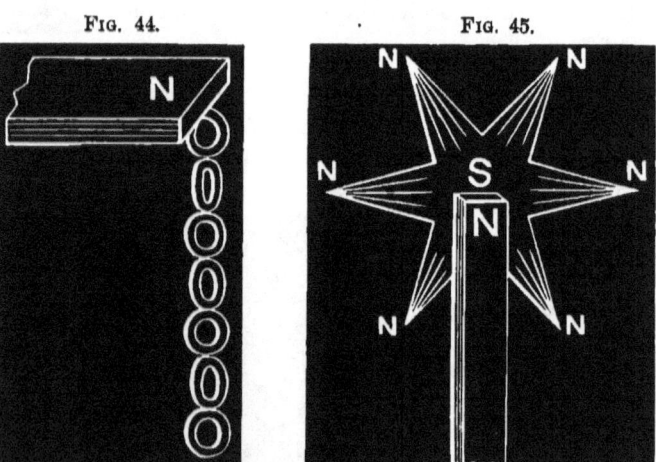

Fig. 44.   Fig. 45.

618. **Figure 45.—Arrangement of poles by induction in a star-shaped body.**—If a piece of sheet-iron be cut in the form of a star, and one end of a bar-magnet be placed on its centre, as represented in the figure, the central part will have the opposite polarity of the end of the magnet in contact with it, and the points will have the opposite polarity of the centre, as shown by the letters.

619. **Figure 46.—Production of two sets of poles in one bar by induction.**—If a bar-magnet, shown by the upright part of the figure, has one of its poles brought in contact with the middle portion of a bar of iron, there will be developed at the point of contact a polarity opposite to that of the contact end of the magnet, which will cause the extremities of the magnetized bar to have like poles with each other, but opposite to that of the centre, as shown by the letters.

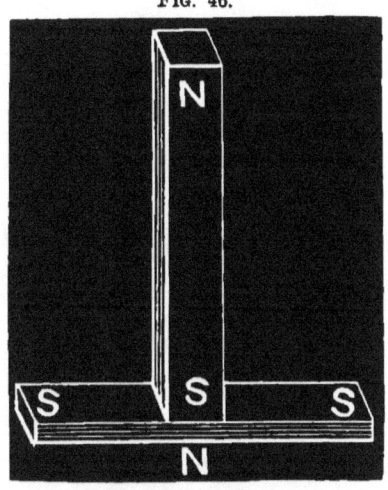

Fig. 46.

620. **Figure 47.—Induction without contact.**—Every magnet is surrounded by a *sphere of magnetic influence*, called its *magnetic atmosphere*. Magnetizable or magnetic bodies within this influence become, without contact, more or less magnetized; the parts contiguous to the magnet-pole having opposite, and those remote

Fig. 47.

from it a similar polarity, as shown by the letters in the figure; M representing the magnet, and the other parts of the drawing, small bars of iron.

621. **Figure 48.—Magnets do not part with their own power.**—Magnets do not part with or lose any of their own magnetic force by magnetizing other bodies. They simply act to develop or bring into action a power which already resides in the other bodies, but in a state of equilibrium. To prove this, let F be a bar-magnet, sustaining a small bar of iron, H, to which is attached a scale-pan. Place in the scale-pan just sufficient weight to cause the bar, H, to be severed from the magnet. Remove the weights from the pan, suspend it again to the magnet, and place the bar of iron, E, on the top of the magnet, which, of course, will be magnetized by the contact. While the bar, E, remains in this position, *more* weight than before is required to separate the small bar, H, from the magnet.

This not only shows that the magnet has lost *none* of its *own* force, but it has developed a force in the bar, E, which, acting in conjunction with its own, enables it to sustain a greater weight than it previously did.

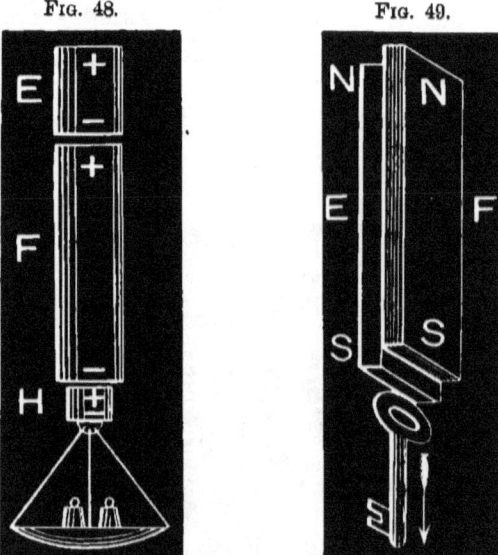

FIG. 48.   FIG. 49.

622. **Figure 49.—Unlike poles neutralize each other.**—A combination of two or more magnets, with their like poles in contact, exerts a greater force than one alone, or even greater than the sum of their forces, applied separately. But if two equal magnets be combined, with their unlike poles in contact, they mutually destroy each other.

If an iron key be suspended to the magnet, E, and another equal magnet, F, is brought in contact with E, and slid along, as represented in the figure, the key will not fall off if the like poles of the two magnets are in contact, as shown. But if the magnet, F, be reversed, end for end, the key will drop when the ends of the magnets are brought nearly even with each other.

FIG. 50.

623. **Figure 50. — Neutralization shown by the Y-magnet.**—Place on the arms, H and K, of the Y-shaped piece of soft iron, the two magnets, E and F, with their like poles turned in the same direction, and the lower end of the Y-shaped iron will attract and hold the key. If one of the magnets (say F) be removed, the key will still remain suspended; but if F be again applied, with its poles reversed, as shown in the drawing, the key will instantly fall; because of the mutual neutralizing effect of like poles at the bottom of the Y-shaped iron, as indicated by the several letters.

624. **Figure 51.—The inductive power of the earth's magnetism.**—Bars of iron and steel, by standing a long time in a vertical position, will acquire polarity (646); which is caused by the inductive power of the earth's magnetism. By testing such bars with a small needle, as shown in the figure, it is found that the end toward the earth is always *austral*, and the opposite end *boreal*, while the central portion is neutral.

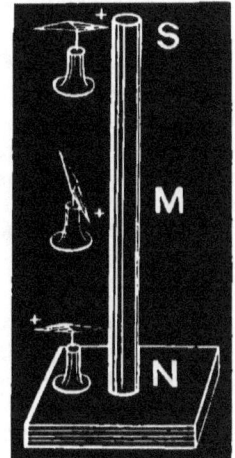

FIG. 51.

If the experiment were made south of the equator of the earth, the polarity of the bar would be reversed.

Ordinary crow-bars, which have been kept standing in one place for years (when not in use), are found more or less magnetized.

Globes of iron, like bomb-shells, a foot or more in diameter, become miniature copies of the earth, as regards magnetism, by virtue of the inductive force of the earth's magnetism.

Hypotheses and Laws of Magnetism.

625. **Figure 52.—Hypothesis of two magnetic fluids.—** The action of the two poles of a magnet upon a *piece of soft iron* is the same; but the action of the two poles is not the same upon another magnet. If a small magnet, like the needle shown in Fig. 57 (635), be balanced on a pivot, or suspended at the neutral point by a small string, and the N pole of a magnet be brought near to its S pole, it will be attracted by the magnet. But if the S pole of the magnet be brought near to the S pole of the needle, it will be not only *not* attracted, but it will be *repelled* by the magnet, and with a force equal to the attraction in the other case.

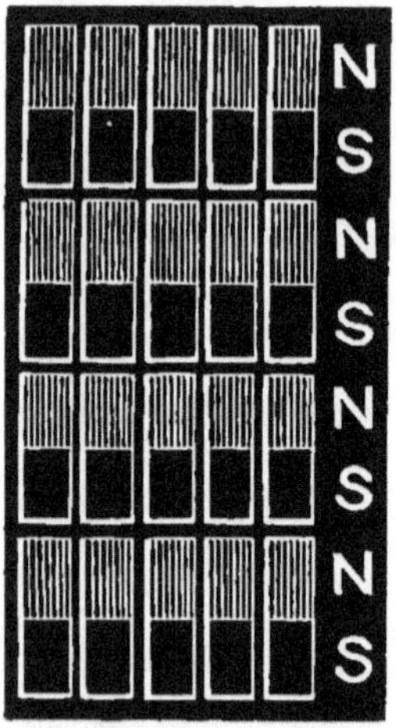

To explain these phenomena, it is supposed there are two *magnetic fluids*, or two kinds of subtle matter, surrounding the molecules of the magnet, each fluid repelling its own kind, and attracting the other.

Fig. 52.

According to this theory, a body is magnetized when these fluids are separated, and driven to its opposite extremities. Hence, the poles which contain the same kind of fluid *repel each other*, and those which contain opposite kinds *attract each other*. The attraction and repulsion are mutual.

Every magnet, in this view, must be regarded as an assemblage of numberless small magnets, every molecule of steel having its own poles antagonistic to those of the next contiguous particle.

In the figure, the small parallelograms represent the particles of the magnet, the N poles pointing in one direction, and the S poles in the opposite direction. These opposing forces, therefore, constantly increase from the central or neutral point, where they are in equilibrium, to the ends, where they are greatest.

626. **Laws of attraction and repulsion.**—The laws of magnetic attraction and repulsion are—

1. *Magnetic poles of contrary names attract, and those of the same name repel each other.*

2. *The forces of attraction and repulsion both vary inversely as the square of the distance between the attracting and repelling poles.*

627. **The coercitive force.**—The resistance which bodies show to the induction of magnetism is called the *coercitive force*.

The two fluids are more easily separated in some bodies than others. In soft iron they yield with less resistance than in any other substance; but in hardened steel a powerful magnetic force is required to induce any permanent magnetism. The harder the steel the more difficult it becomes to separate the two fluids.

Soft iron parts with its induced magnetism as readily as it receives it. The reverse is the case with hardened steel; it takes time and force to render it a magnet, but it retains its magnetism for a long time.

The force which resists the separation of the two fluids acts, after their separation, to prevent their reunion.

Magnetic Curves.

628. **Figure 53.—Magnetic curves rendered apparent to the eye.**—If a piece of paper be stretched on a frame, and placed over a powerful bar, SN, the magnetic attraction and repulsion will be exerted through the paper; which may be shown by projecting on the paper, through a lawn sieve, some fine iron-dust or filings. The particles will arrange themselves in a series of curved lines of magnetic force, proceeding from homologous or similar points on each

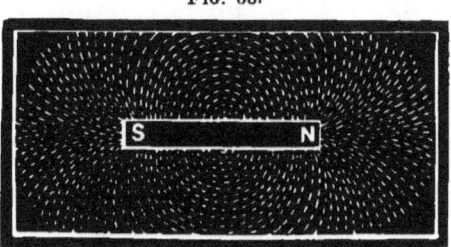

FIG. 53.

side of the middle of the bar, some uniting about the magnetic centre, others standing out at the extremities, as if repelled from the poles, N and S, and tending to turn at considerable distances into other curved lines of force, to unite their branches between the opposite poles.

629. **Figure 54.—Magnetic curves with two magnets and unlike poles.**—Place the stretched paper over dissimilar poles, SN, of two powerful bar-magnets, placed about two inches apart, and project over them the fine iron filings as before. Magnetic lines of force, both straight and curved, and proceeding from similar points of each bar, will be apparent, uniting the two poles by chains of reciprocal attraction.

FIG. 54.

630. **Figure 55.—Magnetic curves with two magnets and similar poles.**—Reverse the position of one of the magnets in the last experiment, so as to oppose two similar poles, NN, and the lines of force will then appear to be conflicting lines. The repulsive forces will cause a transverse straight line to appear upon the space between the poles. At this line, the opposed forces are struggling with each other, being exerted in repulsive directions from the opposed poles.

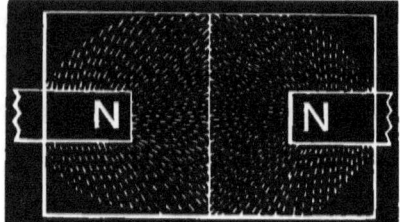

Fig. 55.

These phenomena afford satisfactory visual evidence of the existence of two distinct forces, of their reciprocal attractions and repulsions, and their mutual neutralization.

631. **Magnetic attraction not intercepted.**—Magnetic attraction acts through glass, paper, and solid and liquid substances generally, which are not capable of acquiring magnetic influence in the ordinary manner. Magnets manifest the same phenomena in water and in a vacuum as in air.

632. **Preservation of magnets.**—Magnets, if abandoned to themselves, would in time lose much of their power; hence it is that the armatures are employed. The armature is a piece of soft iron placed in contact with the poles of a magnet.

The poles acting by induction upon the armature, develop its polarity, and *its* two poles acting on the two poles of the magnet, prevent the recomposition of the two fluids, and thus preserve its magnetism. The armature is often called the *keeper*.

TERRESTRIAL MAGNETISM.

633. **The earth as a magnet.**—The earth may be considered a huge magnet, acting upon magnetic needles in the same way that magnetized bars do. Its magnetic poles are near the geographic poles, and its neutral line coincides nearly with the equator.

The fluid which is assumed to predominate at the north pole of the earth is called the *boreal fluid;* that which is supposed to predominate at the south pole is called the *austral fluid.*

As dissimilar poles attract and similar ones repel, the pole of a balanced magnetic needle which turns toward the north must contain the *austral fluid*, and the one which turns toward the south must contain the *boreal fluid*.

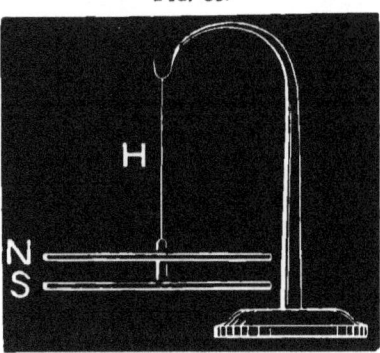

FIG. 56.

634. **Figure 56. The astatic needle** is an instrument in which the directive tendency of the earth's magnetism is neutralized, by placing two equal needles, NS, parallel one above the other, with their unlike poles opposed to each other. This system is suspended from a suitable support by a hair or fibre of raw silk, H, and is a sensitive test for feeble magnetic currents.

635. **Figure 57.—Magnetic needle.**—The drawing represents a simple magnetic needle, being nothing more than a piece of hardened steel, tapered from the middle to the extremities, thoroughly magnetized, and accurately balanced on a pivot, so it shall be free to turn in all horizontal directions, as indicated by the arrows.

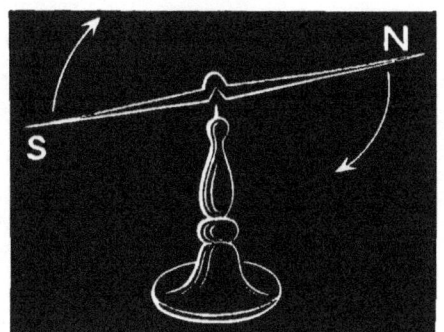

FIG. 57.

636. **Directive force of magnets.**—By the directive force of magnets, is meant, the tendency which they have to arrange themselves in such a manner that their like poles will be reverse to each other, which is in obedience to that fundamental law of magnetic attraction, which causes like poles to repel and unlike poles to attract each other.

The balanced magnetic needle assumes its position in obedience to the same law, and comes to rest with its austral or N pole toward the north pole of the earth, and its boreal or S pole toward the south pole of the earth. Hence, what we generally call the north pole of a needle is really its south pole, and its south pole is its north pole.

For simplicity, the mariner's compass and other needles are simply marked N on that point which turns to the north.

All bar-magnets, free to move in a horizontal plane, arrange themselves in this manner in all parts of the earth. Hence, the earth is regarded as an immense magnet, controlling the position of small magnets. The directive power of the earth is accounted for in another way, which will be explained hereafter.

The directive force simply rotates the magnet or needle.—If the needle be attached to a piece of cork, and placed in a dish of water, it will turn and come to rest in the same general direction as though it were balanced on a pivot. Though the needle is now free to move, it does not advance, either toward the north or south. Hence, it is inferred that the force exerted upon the needle is simply a *directive* force.

637. **Magnetic meridian.**—When a balanced magnetic needle comes to a state of rest, it lies in the direction of magnetic north and south. The imaginary plane passing through the needle and the centre of the earth, is called the *plane of the magnetic meridian,* or the *magnetic meridian.* A plane passing through the place and the axis of the earth, is called the *plane of the true meridian,* or the *true meridian.*

Variations of the Needle.

638. **Declination of the needle.**—The magnetic meridian and the true meridian, in general, do not coincide with each other. The angle which the magnetic meridian, at any place, makes with the true meridian, is called the *declination of the needle.* In other words, the declination of the needle is its deviation from true north and south. This is different at different places, and at the same place at different times.

If the north end of the needle rests on the east side of the true meridian, that is, points east of true north, the declination is said to be *to the east.* When it points to the west of true north, the declination is said to be *to the west.*

A line extending along the earth where the needle points to the true north, is called a line of *no declination.* Such a line extends from near Cleveland, Ohio, to Charleston, South Carolina.

This line of *no deviation* is moving to the westward at a rate that would carry it around the earth in about one thousand years. This is the most singular of all the phenomena of terrestrial magnetism.

For all parts of the United States east of this line, the declination of the needle is to the *west;* for all points to the west of it, the declination is to the *east.* The north end of the needle, at all places, is inclined toward the line of *no declination.*

There are two lines of *no declination,* eastern and western. In proceeding either west or east from either of these lines, the declination of the needle gradually increases, and becomes a maximum at a certain intermediate point between them. These two lines of *no declination*, in the present age, extend, one obliquely over North America and the Atlantic Ocean, and the other through the middle of China and across New Holland, and they are supposed to communicate near both poles of the earth.

The position of the northern magnetic pole is about 19° from the north geographical pole of the earth.

639. **Daily, annual, and other variations of the needle.** —It is found by observation, that there is a daily variation of the needle from east to west and from west to east, averaging a little less than one degree; caused, doubtless, by the action of the sun, and, therefore, this variation varies in different latitudes.

At London the north pole of the needle moves westward from eight A.M. until one P.M. Soon after one o'clock it begins to move eastward, and reaches its former position about ten P.M. During the night a small oscillation occurs, the north pole moving westward until three A.M., then returning as before.

Other variations of the needle.—There are annual variations of the needle, conforming to the movement of the sun in the solstices.

There are *irregular variations* of the needle, connected with the aurora borealis, or other cosmical phenomena, which have been called magnetic storms.

The magnetic needle also deviates more or less by the near approach of masses of iron.

640. **Inclination or dip of the magnetic needle.**—Besides the several kinds of variations already noticed, there is another, called *inclination* or *dip*. If a perfectly unmagnetized needle be suspended at its centre, by a fibre of raw silk, it will remain horizontal, and continue to point in any horizontal direction in which it may be placed. But if the same needle be magnetized and again suspended in the same manner, it will not only assume the magnetic north and south direction, but it will also assume an inclined direction; that is, its north pole will point more or less downward toward the north magnetic pole of the earth, and the south pole upward. This inclination is called the *dip*.

The *dip*, like the *declination*, is subject to continual and progressive changes. At London, in 1576, it was 71° 50'; in 1723 it was at its maximum, being 74° 42', while now it is only 68° 15'; showing it has decreased about 3' per annum for the last hundred and fifty years.

641. **Figure 58.—Action of the earth illustrated by the action of a magnet.**—The magnetic bar, SN, is placed horizontally on the diameter of a semicircle, representing an arc of the meridian.

FIG. 58.

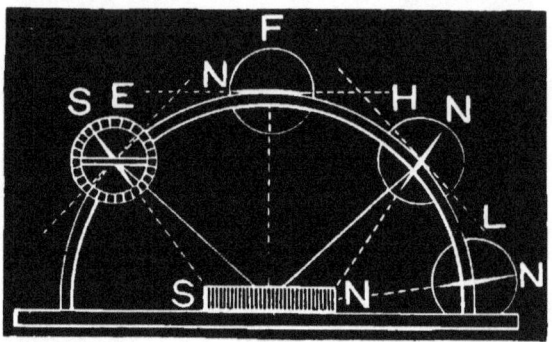

If a needle, free to move vertically, be placed at the magnetic equator, F, its two poles will be equally attracted by the magnet, and the needle will coincide with the horizon, shown by the dotted line; its *real* north pole standing in the direction of the south pole of the magnet.

If the needle be placed at E, its N pole will point toward the south pole of the magnet, as shown by the letters. If it be placed at H, its S pole will be turned toward the north pole of the magnet, as indicated by the letters.

FIG. 59.

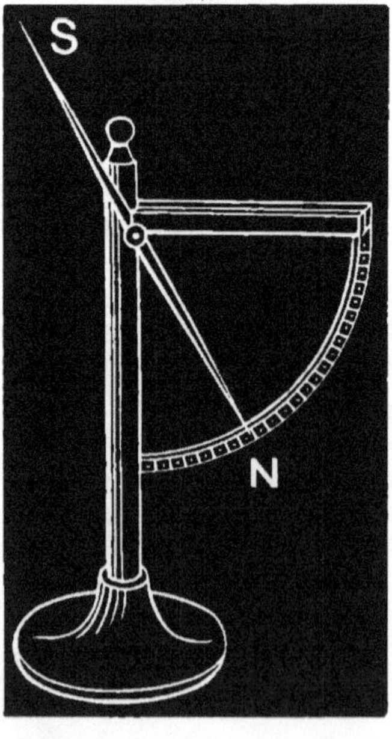

642. **Figure 59.—Dipping-needle.**—To show the dip, and to measure it at different places, a needle is so mounted as to be perfectly free to move or rotate in a vertical plane; the amount of dip being indicated by a graduated circle or quadrant, as represented in the figure. At any place, the dip will be greatest possible when the needle vibrates in the plane of the magnetic meridian (638).

The dip varies in passing from place to place, being greatest at the magnetic poles, and nothing at the magnetic equator, as clearly illustrated by the following diagram.

643. **Figure 60.—Position of the dipping-needle in different parts of the earth.**—SEN represents the magnetic meridian, and ME the magnetic equator of the earth. Let S, at one extremity of the line SEN, represent the north magnetic pole, and N, at the other end of this line, the south magnetic pole; and the several arrows, the dipping-needle, with the north pole at the point of the needle.

The angle which the needle makes with the horizon, at any place, is called the *dip* at that place.

At the equator (that is, at the magnetic equator), it will be seen

Fig. 60.

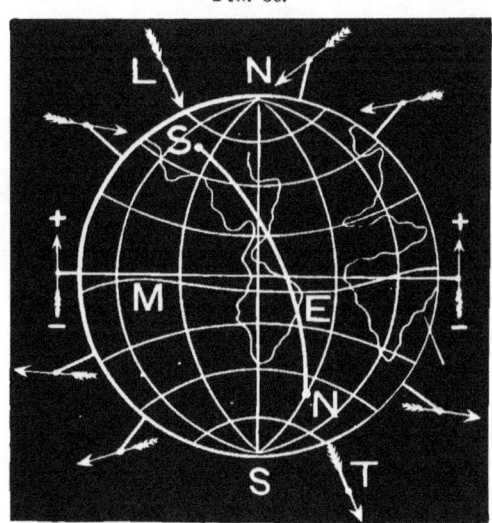

that the needle assumes the horizontal position, being equally attracted by the two magnetic poles of the earth.

At the magnetic poles the dip is 90°, the arrows being directed toward the magnetic poles. When nearer the north pole than the south, the *point*, or N pole, of the needle, points to the magnetic pole; but when nearer the south pole than the north, the feather end, or S pole, of the needle, points to the magnetic pole.

Hence, a needle, horizontally balanced at the equator, would dip toward the earth as it is carried toward the north pole, and vice versa if carried toward the south pole. Mariners' compasses, therefore, are provided with a sliding weight, with which to keep the needle balanced in different latitudes; and which can be shifted to the other side of the pivot, after crossing the equator.

644. **Figure 61.—The mariner's compass** is arranged in a box called a *binnacle.* The magnetic needle, delicately poised on a socket of agate, is attached to the lower side of a card, on which is

FIG. 61.

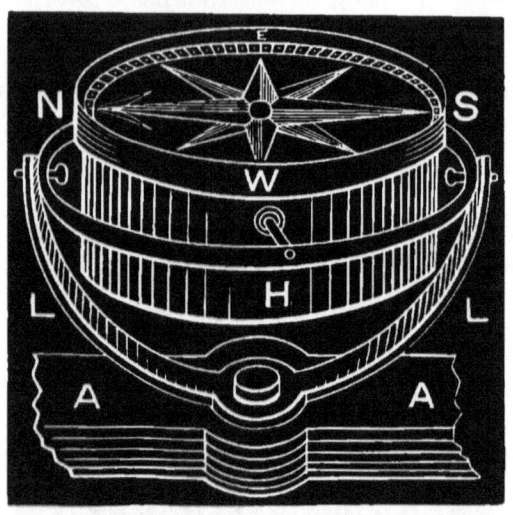

printed the star of thirty-two points; the cardinal points being N. S. E. W. The compass-box, H, is hung on points, called *gimbals,* one of which is seen at H, and two others at the tops of the arms LL; the whole being firmly secured to the support AA.

By this method of supporting the compass-box, it always remains horizontal, however the ship may roll.

Tables for correcting variations of the compass.—For most practical operations, as in navigation and surveying, the deviation of the needle from the true north and south is taken into account, and a rule of corrections applied. The amount of variation, east or west, for different localities, may be ascertained from *tables* accurately calculated and arranged for this purpose.

Discovery of the compass.—It is claimed that the directive tendency of the magnet was known to the Chinese some 2,000 years before the Christian era; but it was not known to the European nations until about 1,250 years after the Christian era. The compasses of that time were merely pieces of lodestone fixed to a cork, which floated on the surface of water; or a simple sewing-needle, rendered magnetic, thrust through a cork or reed, and placed on water.

645. **Magnetic intensity varies** in different parts of the earth. In general, it is greatest about the poles and the least intense about the equator. The relative intensity of different points is determined by the use of the *needle of oscillation.*

The greater the intensity the more rapidly will the needle oscillate; the relative intensity being as the *square of the numbers of oscillations.* This method of testing the relative intensity of terrestrial magnetism, is analogous to that of testing the force of gravity by the oscillations of the pendulum (61).

646. **The inductive power of the earth's magnetism** is manifested by the polarity of bars of iron and steel, which have been standing for a long time in a vertical position (624).

647. **Utilization of magnetism.**—Its directive power renders the compass invaluable to the explorer of the wilderness, to the navigator, to the surveyor, and the miner. The mineralogist and the general investigator find it indispensable in many researches. Different artisans make valuable use of the attractive force of magnets.

348   ELECTRICITY.

CHAPTER XIV.

(CHART NO. 8.)

ELECTRICITY.

STATICAL OR FRICTIONAL ELECTRICITY.

Fundamental Principles.

648. **Definitions.**—The name electricity is derived from the Greek *elektron*, which means *amber*.

Electricity is an imponderable agent, existing in all substances throughout nature, without affecting their volume or their temperature, or giving any indication of its presence when in a latent or quiet state. When, however, it is by some means liberated from this repose, it is capable of producing the most sudden and destructive effects, or of exerting powerful influences by a gentle and long-continued action.

Electricity, as a science, treats of the excitation, the manifestations, and the effects of this agent.

649. **Discovery of electricity.**—The ancients, six hundred years before the Christian era, knew that amber, when rubbed, would attract small pieces of straw, barbs of quills, and the like. Beyond this fact, which remained without value for more than two thousand years, nothing was known on the subject until the end of the sixteenth century. The success with which this subtle agent is handled and controlled at the present day, is shown by a large group of sciences to which it has given birth, and by the existence of the Atlantic Cable, and countless telegraphic wires stretching around the world, annihilating time and space, and enabling us to converse with our antipodes. Yet the exploration of this vast field of science is but just commenced.

650. **The sources of electricity.**—The chief sources of electrical excitement are—1st. *Friction* of dry substances; 2d. *Chemical action*, or chemical composition and chemical decomposition; 3d. *Magnetism*, producing magneto-electricity; 4th. *Heat*, or thermo-electricity; 5th. *Animal electricity*; 6th. *Electricity of Plants*.

651. **Figure 1.—Electrical effects.**—If a dry and warm glass rod or tube be briskly rubbed with cat's fur, or a piece of silk or woolen cloth, it attracts to itself bits of paper, shreds of cotton, gold leaf, feathers, pith, and other light substances, holding them for an instant, and then repelling them, as illustrated by the figure.

If the experiment be performed in the dark, a feeble bluish light is seen in the path of the rubber. If the glass is immediately presented

FIG. 1.

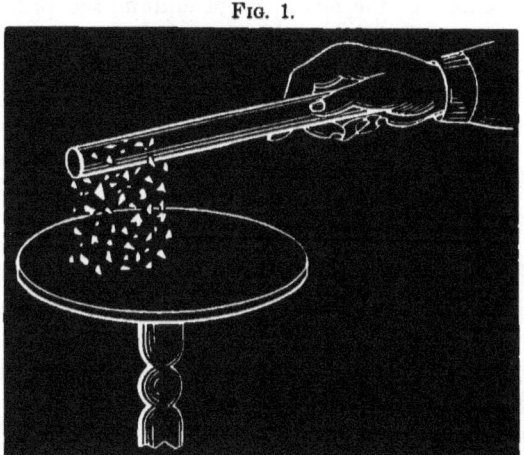

to a metallic body, or to the knuckle of the finger, a purple spark will dart off from the glass with crackling sound. If the glass be held near the face, a sensation is experienced similar to that produced by drawing a fine thread across the skin. The same effects are produced by the rubber. A peculiar odor accompanies electrical excitement, as also a peculiar taste, if the electricity be excited by voltaic action.

Bodies thus excited are said to be *electrified*, a condition which is only transient.

These simple experiments contain the germ of electrical science (671).

652. **Electroscope.—Electrical pendulum.**—An electroscope (of which there is a variety) is an apparatus to show whether or not a body is electrified. The most simple of these is the *electrical pendulum*, which consists simply of a small ball of elder-pith, or cork, suspended by a fine silk thread, which is fastened at the upper end to a stem of copper provided with a glass support.

If an electrified body be presented to the pendulum, the pith-ball will be attracted by it. If the body is not electrified, the ball will not move.

When very sensitive tests are required, more delicate instruments, called *electrometers*, are employed.

653. **Figure 2.—Vitreous and resinous, or positive and negative, electricities.**—There are two kinds of electricity, the difference between them depending upon the kind of material which is subjected to friction.

If a tube of glass, shown in the figure, be rubbed with a piece of silk, and then presented to the electrical pendulum, the pith-ball will be attracted and then repelled.

If, now, a stick of sealing-wax, as shown, be rubbed with flannel, and brought near the pith-ball (which is already charged with the electricity from the glass), it will be attracted to the sealing-wax, though it was repelled by the glass. If the wax be presented to the pith-ball first, the ball will be attracted to the wax, become charged with its electricity and then repelled. In this state the ball will be attracted by the glass.

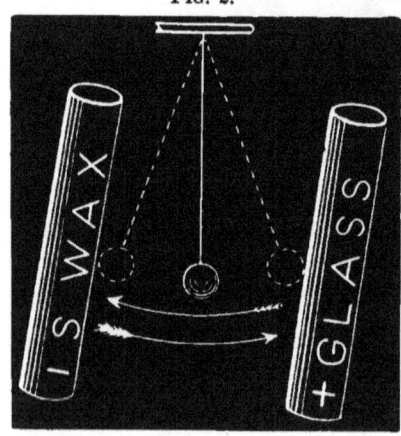

FIG. 2.

A pith-ball suspended between the glass and wax, as represented, will continue to swing back and forth from one to the other, as indicated by the arrows, as long as there is sufficient electrical excitement to charge it.

The ball being charged by the glass, is then repelled and attracted by the wax. The wax absorbs the electricity brought from the glass, and charges it with its own; when it will be repelled by the wax and attracted by the glass; and so on.

This shows that the action of electricity developed in glass and in resin is different; the one repelling when the other attracts.

The electricity developed by rubbing glass is called *vitreous or positive electricity;* that developed by rubbing resin or sealing-wax is called *resinous or negative electricity.*

Glass and resin are but types of two large classes of substances, which possess more or less perfectly this characteristic difference, as above explained.

654. **The theory of two fluids.**—This theory is based upon the supposition that two electrical fluids exist, in unexcited bodies, in a state of combination, forming what is called a *neutral fluid.* This neutral fluid has, of itself, no obvious properties. Hence, bodies which only contain it are said to be *neutral*. The earth is considered a great reservoir of this fluid.

If this neutral fluid is decomposed, and the two fluids separated, by whatever means, then various electrical phenomena are immediately manifested.

If glass is rubbed with silk, the positive fluid goes to the glass and the negative to the silk. But if sealing-wax is rubbed, the negative fluid goes to the sealing-wax and the positive to the silk.

All electrical phenomena are supposed to be due to the tendency of the two fluids to reunite and neutralize each other.

655. **The single fluid hypothesis** is simple, was for a long time adopted, and will account for most of the phenomena. It supposes the existence, throughout all space, of a subtle and exceedingly elastic fluid, called the *electric fluid;* that it is repulsive of its own particles, but attracted by particles of other matter; that all bodies contain a specific quantity of it; and that, when thus combined with other matter, it loses its self-repellent tendency. In its natural state every substance has exactly its own quantity of this fluid, and is consequently in a state of electrical indifference. If electrical excitement is developed in a body, by whatever means, this electrical equilibrium is disturbed; and the body becomes positively electrified when it is charged with *more* than its specific or natural quantity, and negatively electrified when it is *deprived* of a portion of its specific or natural quantity.

Hence, bodies positively electrified are restored to equilibrium by *parting* with the excess, and bodies negatively electrified, by *receiving* from surrounding bodies sufficient to satisfy the deficiency.

This hypothesis is strikingly similar to that commonly accepted in explanation of the equilibrium of heat.

On the principles of either of these hypotheses, it is impossible to produce one kind of electricity without the other simultaneously appearing. The positive and negative must be always co-ordinately generated.

The term fluid is calculated to convey an erroneous idea, for it is employed only as a convenient expression for an unknown cause. Instead of assuming the existence of a *separate* fluid or ether, as a medium for light, heat, or magnetic electricity, it is more in accordance with sound philosophy to suppose that these separate manifestations are only different functions of the one ethereal medium, which fills the entire universe, and from whose correlations to the particles of matter, all physical phenomena proceed.

656. **Figure 3.—Attraction and repulsion.**—If two pith-balls be suspended, as shown in the figure, and both charged alike, that is, with either positive or negative electricity, they will be mutually repelled, as represented by the dotted balls and the signs plus and minus. But if one ball be charged with positive and the other with negative fluid, as indicated, they will attract each other.

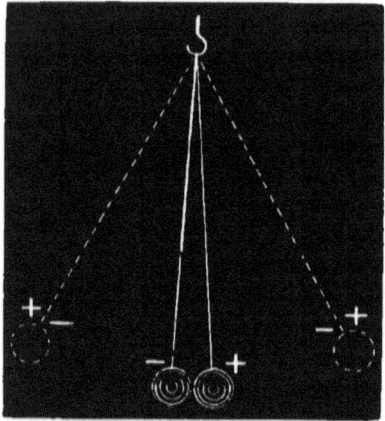

FIG. 3.

These simple experiments show a similarity between these actions and the law of *magnetic* attractions and repulsions (626).

657. **Laws of electrical attraction and repulsion.**—The following laws have been deduced from theory and confirmed by experiment:

1. *Fluids of the same name repel each other, and fluids of opposite names attract each other.*

2. *The intensities of the attractions and repulsions vary inversely as the square of the distances between them.*

3. *The distances remaining the same, the attractions and repulsions are directly as the quantities of electricities possessed by the two bodies.*

658. **Conductors of electricity.**—Conductors, or conducting substances, are those which permit electricity to pass through them.

Some bodies, electrically excited, part with their excitement instantly, others slowly, depending on the nature of the substance excited, and of those with which it is brought in contact. As bodies differ very much in their power to conduct electricity, they are divided into classes, called *good* and *bad conductors*, or conductors and non-conductors.

Good conductors propagate the excitement to all parts of their surfaces; and, when in contact with the earth, part with it as quickly as they receive it.

Among the good conductors are the following substances, placed in the order of their conducting power. The metals—silver and copper standing first, lead and quicksilver, last—charcoal, plumbago, coak, hard anthracite, acids, saline solutions, water, snow, living things, flame, smoke, vacuum, vapors of alcohol and ether, earth and moist rocks, etc.

Bad conductors receive and part with electricity very slowly; consequently they retain free electricity for a long time, and obstruct its passage from one body to another.

Among the best non-conductors are resins, gums, India-rubber, silk, glass, precious stones, spirits of turpentine, oils, air, and dry gases.

659. **Insulators.**—Insulators are non-conducting substances, placed between bodies to be electrified and the earth and other surrounding bodies, to prevent the passage of the electricity. A body, therefore, is said to be *insulated* when it is supported, and cut off from surrounding bodies, by good non-conductors. Insulators are usually made of glass. Gutta-percha and whalebone-rubber are among the best insulators known.

660. **The earth is the reservoir** into which all electrical excitements are returned. The air, unless saturated with moisture, is a poor conductor; hence it serves to insulate the earth, which is a good conductor.

Except for the non-conducting property of the air, all electrical phenomena would have remained invisible and unobserved.

It should be kept in mind that the earth is always negatively excited.

661. **Method of electrifying bodies.**—In order to electrify a conducting body, it must first be insulated from the earth and surrounding bodies, by placing it upon some sort of a glass or other non-conducting support. Thus supported, it must be rubbed by an insulated rubber. Conductors may be electrified also by contact and by induction.

If the body and rubber are not insulated, the excitement or fluid will pass to the earth through the support and body of the operator, as fast as generated.

Non-conducting bodies are only electrified by friction.

The method of electrifying by contact depends upon the conductibility of the body. If a conducting body be brought in contact with an electrified body, a portion of the electricity of the excited body flows into the unexcited body. If the two bodies are exactly alike, the electricity will be equally distributed over both. If they differ in size or shape, the electricity will not be equally distributed.

Electrifying bodies by induction is performed in a manner similar to that of magnetizing bodies by induction, as will be hereafter explained.

662. **Electrical tension** is a condition of constrained equilibrium, and when the fluids or electricities, to which it is due, reunite, an electrical current is produced from the reaction of the opposing fluids, analogous to mechanical motion from the recoil of a spring. The energy with which they reunite, when communication is made between them, shows the state of *tension* in which they existed.

All electrified bodies manifest electrical tension, and attract other bodies, decomposing their natural electricity, drawing from them a portion of the opposite fluid.

663. **Figure 4.—Electricity accumulates only on the outer surfaces of bodies.**—If a body be, however, thoroughly charged, the fluid does not penetrate the substance of the body; and if it be a hollow body, it does not even reside on the inner surface, but accumulates wholly on the outer surface.

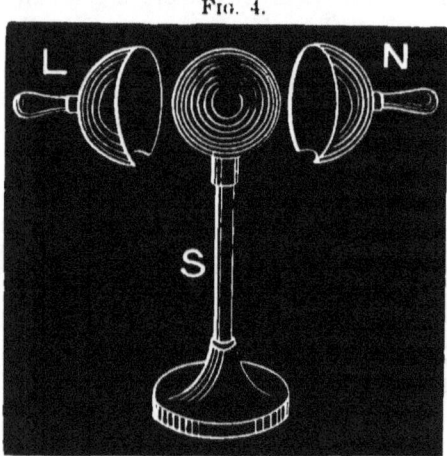

Fig. 4.

If a copper or other metal sphere, mounted on a glass or insulated support, S, be electrified, and then covered with the thin hemispheres, L and N, made of the same metal, and provided with insulating handles, it will be found, on removing the covers, that *they* are electrified, and the sphere is deprived of every trace of electrical excitement.

This is due to the repulsive power of the fluid within driving the excitement to the surface, where it meets the non-conducting air and is arrested; and also to the inductive influence of the electricity of surrounding bodies and of the walls of the room.

Figure 5.—That electricity accumulates only on the surface, shown in a different way.—This figure represents a ribbon, T, of metallic paper, wound around a metallic axis, insulated with silk threads; two sets of pith-balls are suspended by linen threads at the lower end of the ribbon. If the ribbon is wound up, by the insulating crank, and the whole apparatus is electrified, the pith-balls diverge powerfully. If the ribbon is now unwound, by drawing the insulating string at the bottom, the pith-balls gradually fall, and finally come almost in contact. But as the ribbon is again wound up, the balls diverge as before. This may be repeated several times.

As the surface increases the electricity is spread out; as the surface is diminished, it is concentrated and intensified; thus illustrating the relation of surface and intensity.

It is thus proved that all the electricity with which a conducting body is charged, is disposed on its surface.

Hence, a ball of wood or pith, covered with tin-foil or gold-leaf, can accumulate on its surface as much electricity as if it was of solid metal. A hollow and solid sphere, of the same size and material, will be charged with exactly the same quantity of electricity.

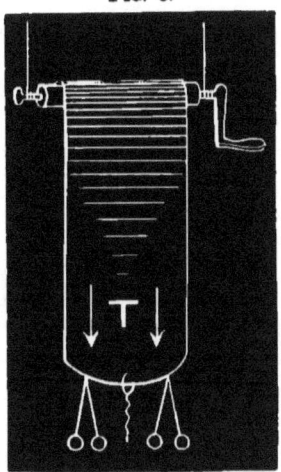

FIG. 5.

664. **Proof-plane.**—The proof-plane is an instrument for determining the relative quantities of electricity that are found on the different parts of an electrified conductor. It consists of a disk of gilt paper, attached to the end of an insulating rod, as gumlac, shown in the hand of Fig. 6. The rod is held in the hand, the disk applied to different parts of the electrified surface, and after each contact it is presented to the electrical pendulum.

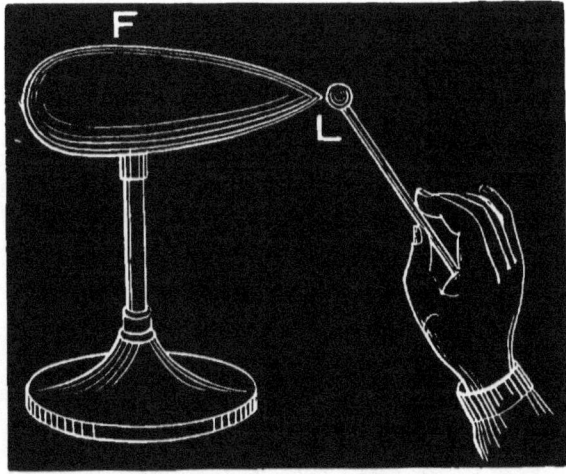

FIG. 6.

665. **Figure 6.—Distribution dependent on form.**—The distribution of electricity over the surface of bodies depends upon their form. If the body be a sphere, the distribution is uniform. If the proof-plane be applied at different parts of an excited ellipsoid, like the figure, it will be found that the electrical fluid is not equally distributed on all parts of the surface. The maximum is found at L, and the minimum at F; showing a tendency in electrical excitement to accumulate about the *extremities* of solids having unequal axes.

In cylinders, the concentration of force occurs not far from each end, and is feeble in the middle. In plates, the maximum is near the edges.

666. **The power of points.**—On the principle just explained, the power of points, in concentrating electricity, produces a tension sufficient to overcome the resistance of the air, causing it to pass off as rapidly as it accumulates, to the nearest bodies, or into the air, in an electrical brush or pencil, visible in the dark.

667. **The loss of electricity in excited bodies** is constant, chiefly from two causes: 1st, the moisture of the air; and, 2d, from the imperfection of the insulation, even when the best insulators are employed.

INDUCTION OF ELECTRICITY.

668. **Figure 7.—Bodies electrified by induction.**—E is a prime conductor of an electrical machine; NAP, a metallic cylinder, insulated by a rod or support of glass, having several pairs of pith-balls attached to its lower surface.

FIG. 7.

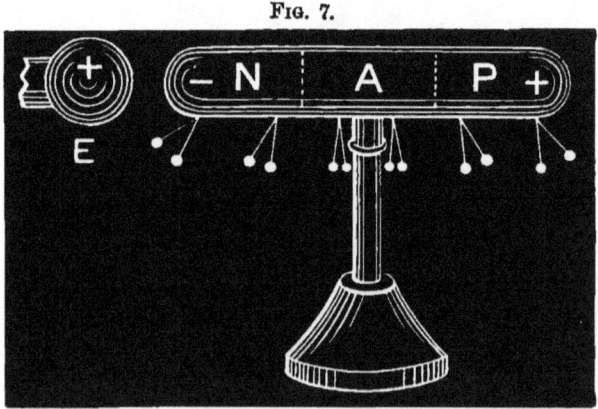

If the prime conductor be charged with positive electricity, and placed within a few inches of the cylinder, the pith-balls near the conductor, E, will be *attracted* and separated; those at the opposite end will be *repelled* and separated; while those in the central part will not be repelled, attracted, or separated. If the prime conductor be removed, the electroscopes, or balls, will cease to indicate any excitement.

The explanation of these facts is, that the neutral fluid of the cylinder has been decomposed by the influence of the prime conductor; the positive (+) fluid being repelled to P, and the negative (−) fluid attracted to N, while at the central part, A, a neutral point is found. When the prime conductor, the disturbing cause, is removed, the two electricities of NAP unite again, leaving the cylinder entirely passive; showing that none of the electric fluid is transferred from the prime conductor to the cylinder.

Bodies thus affected are said to be *electrified by induction.*

669. **Figure 8.—The two fluids separated and obtained by induction.**—Let three insulated cylinders be placed in a row, and in contact, as shown in the figure; approach the positively electrified prime conductor, E, toward the cylinder, N. By induction (668), the

FIG. 8.

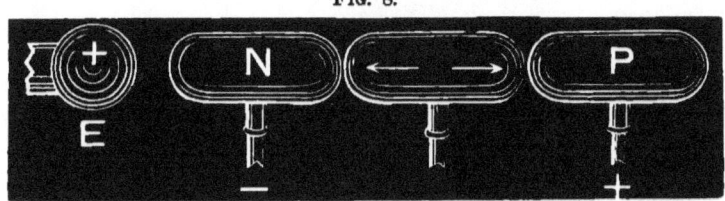

neutral electricity of the three cylinders will be decomposed; the negative (−) being attracted to and accumulated in N, and the positive (+) repelled to and accumulated in P. Whilst in this condition, remove the cylinders, P and N, at a distance from E, and from each other. The separated electricities will thus be kept from uniting; and, upon testing, N will be found *negatively*, and P *positively*, electrified, as indicated by the signs plus and minus.

By these principles of induction a great variety of electrical phenomena are easily explained.

The laws of electrical induction are thus stated:

1st. *A body electrized by induction, possesses no more electricity than before.*

2d. *If a conductor, electrized by induction, is touched, or made to communicate with the earth in any part of its surface, it parts with a portion of its electricity, always of the same name with the electrifying body, and it retains the fluid of the opposite name.*

670. **Figure 9.—Dielectrics.—Explanation of induction.**
—Induction takes place at a distance by polarizing the molecules of the intervening non-conductor. Because air, and other non-conductors, permit the passage of electrical influence in this manner, they are called *dielectrics*, in distinction from electrics.

Therefore, in the above experiments (668-9), the disturbance of the natural electric state of the cylinders is not produced by action at a distance. It takes place through the medium of the intervening air (a

FIG. 9.

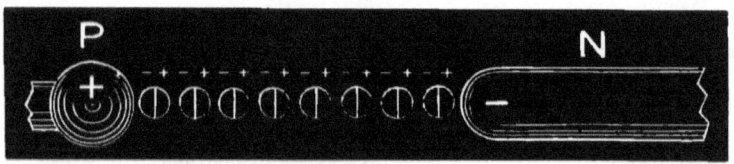

dielectric). Thus, if P (Fig. 9) be the prime conductor, and N the cylinder, let the small circles between them represent molecules of air (or any other intervening dielectric medium), and they will all be *polarized*, as it is termed, having their negative (−) parts or poles turned toward the positively excited body P, and their positive (+) parts or poles toward the cylinder N, which will attract the negative (−) fluid of the cylinder to the end nearest to the positive (+) prime conductor.

Dielectrics differ in their specific inductive capacity. If air (the lowest) be 1, the following will stand thus: air, 1; resin, 1.77; pitch, 1.80; wax, 1.86; glass, 1.90; sulphur, 1.93; shellac, 1.95.

671. **Attraction and repulsion of light bodies** (651) can be accounted for only by the laws of induction, as above explained (668, 669, 670). The excited glass or resin decomposes the neutral electricity of the bits of paper or pith-balls, repelling the electricity of the same name, which leaves them with an opposite excitement to the glass or resin, and, therefore, they become attracted to the electrified body.

Electrometers.

672. **Electrometers.**—The electroscope, previously described (652), serves only to indicate the presence and name of the electricity, but not the quantity. Electrometers are measures of electric force or intensity, and depend upon the principle, that like kinds of electricity repel and opposite kinds attract.

The two corks or pith-balls, suspended by linen threads (656) are one of the most simple of these contrivances. The distance to which they will diverge is a rough measure of the intensity of the electric force.

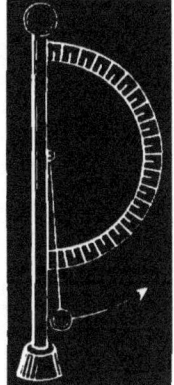

Fig. 10.

673. **Figure 10.—The quadrant electrometer** consists of a slender stem or support of baked wood, to which is affixed a semicircular piece of ivory, from the centre of which hangs a pith-ball, on a small arm of whalebone, as shown.

If this instrument is placed on the prime conductor (678), or other electrified body, the stem participating in the electricity, and repelling the pith-ball, as indicated by the arrow, the amount of repulsion may be read off on the graduated semicircle. The number of degrees do not express the true electrical intensity; and whatever may be the intensity, the ball cannot be repelled beyond 90°.

674.—**Figure 11.—The gold-leaf electrometer** consists of a bell-jar, provided with a copper rod, passing through a cork, terminated with a copper knob, T, at the top, and sustaining two strips of gold-leaf, E, placed face to face.

Fig. 11.

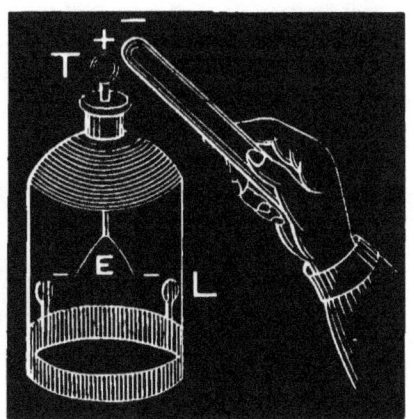

If the knob, T, be electrized, the gold-leaves diverge, and the extent of their divergence, measured on a graduated arc, serves to show the intensity of the electricity. Two strips of tin-foil, L, are pasted to the inside of the jar to discharge the diverging leaves, when they are repelled so as to reach the sides, to prevent the inside of the jar from becoming electrified by induction; otherwise the apparatus would be useless. To avoid dampness, the air within is dried by quick lime, and the top of the jar and cork are coated with an insulating varnish, made of sealing-wax dissolved in alcohol.

Instead of the gold-leaves, straws and pith-balls are sometimes employed.

When more exact *measurement* of electricity is required, the *torsion electrometer* is employed.

675. **Method of using the gold-leaf electrometer** (Fig. 11).—If the negatively electrized rod, in the hand, be brought near the knob, T, it will, by induction, attract the positive fluid, and repel the negative to the gold-leaves, and diverge them, as indicated by the signs plus and minus, and by the position of the leaves.

If, now, the finger be applied to the knob, T, the positive fluid passes off, through the body, to the earth; but, on withdrawing the finger, the leaves diverge under the influence of the negative fluid remaining in the apparatus.

If the rod were positively electrified the leaves would receive the positive fluid; yet, on applying the finger to the knob, the positive fluid passes off to the earth and the negative remains.

To ascertain the kind of electricity in a body, proceed, as just explained, to charge the leaves with negative fluid, then approach the body to be tested, to the knob. If the body is *negatively* electrified, the leaves will be still further separated; if *positively* electrified, the leaves will be drawn together.

ELECTRICAL MACHINES.

676. **Figures 12 and 13.—The electrophorus.**—An electrical machine is any apparatus by which electricity may be generated, and electrical phenomena obtained at pleasure.

The *electrophorus*, or carrier of electricity, is the simplest of all such devices. It consists of a cake of resin, or disk of whalebone India-rubber, W, eight or ten inches in diameter, and a wooden plate, S, covered with tin-foil, and provided with an insulating handle of glass.

Fig. 12.

To use this instrument, first excite the resinous cake by vigorously rubbing it with cat's fur or warm flannel, which developes negative electricity in the resin. Then apply the disk, S, to the resin, as shown in Fig. 12, holding it by the handle. The cake of resin acts upon the disk by induction, drawing its positive fluid to the tin-foil on the lower face, and repelling its negative fluid to the foil on its upper face. Now, touch the finger, as shown (Fig. 12), to the upper face, in order to allow the negative fluid to escape into the common reservoir (the earth, 660). If the disk now be raised by its handle from the resinous cake, and touched with the knuckle, as shown in Fig. 13, a spark will pass, which is due to the negative electricity passing from the body of the experimenter to the positively electrified plate.

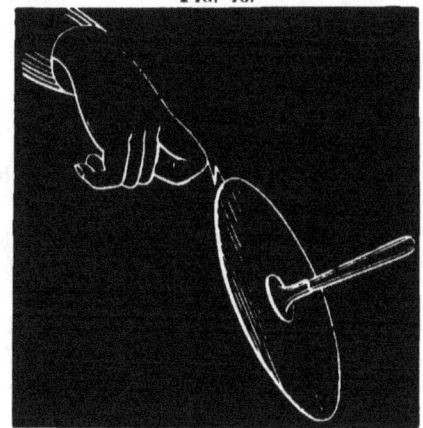

Fig. 13.

If the air is dry the disk can be applied to the resinous cake, and the spark evolved several times without further rubbing.

If the plate be left in repose on the resin, the apparatus will remain charged even for weeks. And the Leyden jar may be charged with the instrument at any time.

If the disk, S, were raised from the resinous cake, W, without applying the finger, as represented in Fig. 12, it would manifest no electrical excitement; the two fluids reuniting, as in the insulated conductor (668).

The phenomena involved in the electrophorus are in accordance with the *laws of induction* (669).

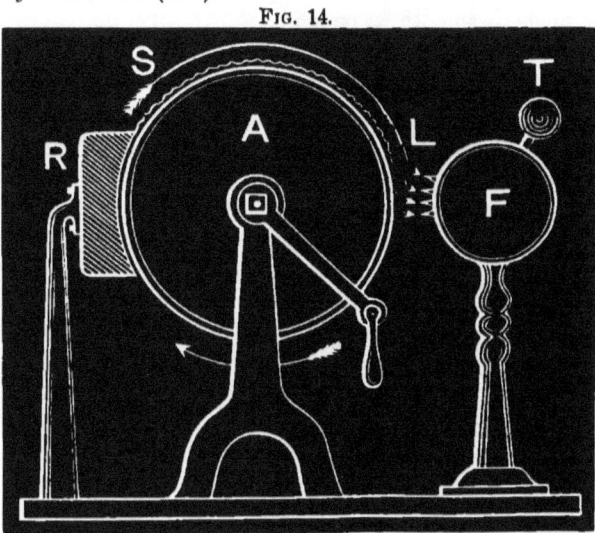

Fig. 14.

677. **Figure 14.—The cylinder electrical machine.**—To obtain larger quantities of electricity than can be supplied by means

362   ELECTRICITY.

already described, machines of various sizes and forms are made. However these may differ, there are at least three essential parts, viz.: 1st, a *non-conductor*, usually made of glass, and revolved on an axis, to produce friction; 2d, a *rubber* to press on the conductor, made of some soft, elastic, non-conducting body, as a cushion of leather, peculiarly prepared; 3d, conductors (one or two) insulated with glass supports, to receive the electricity as it is generated.

The figure represents an end view of the *cylinder* electrical machine. A is the *cylinder* of glass, which may be from six inches to two feet in diameter, and once and a half to twice its diameter in length, revolved, by means of a winch, between two upright supports of wood, dried and varnished. R is the *rubber*, somewhat shorter than the cylinder, made of wood and covered with leather, under which are several thicknesses of flannel, and covered, over all, with black silk. The face and lower side of the rubber are also coated with an *amalgam*, composed of 4 parts mercury, 8 zinc, and 2 tin, mixed with some unctuous substance. F is the *prime conductor*, placed opposite to the rubber, and consists of a hollow cylinder of brass or wood, covered with tin-foil, supported upon a glass rod. On the side next the glass it is furnished with points, L, nearly touching the cylinder, A, which draw off the electricity from the excited glass to the prime conductor (666).

To assist in preventing the escape of the fluid, an apron of black silk extends from the rubber over to the points, L. The prime conductor should be made as smooth as possible.

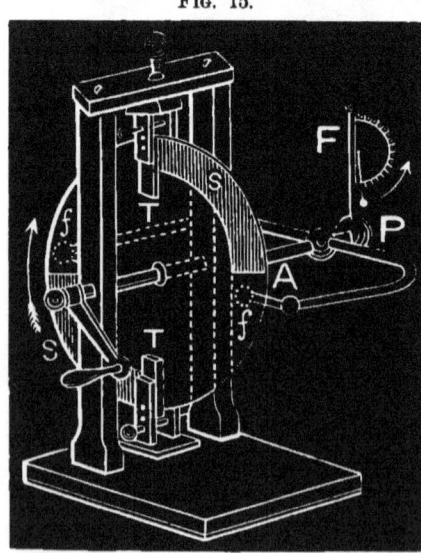

Fig. 15.

The rubber is sometimes mounted upon an insulated conductor, for the purpose of developing negative electricity.

The air inclosed in the cylinder should be free of moisture.

The arrow, S, represents the direction in which the cylinder is turned, and the flow of the fluid, which takes place, of course, under the silk apron. T is a small sphere attached to the prime conductor, from which the fluid is drawn in performing experiments.

678. **Figure 15.—The plate electrical machine.** —In this machine a large circular plate of glass is substituted for the cylinder, and is usually furnished with four rubbers, two of which, TT, are shown, held in suitable tightening clamps. The plate is revolved between these rubbers by turning the winch. Extending from the rubbers are silk aprons, SS; *ff* are points for collecting the fluid and conveying it to the prime conductor, P, which is supported by the glass rod, A. F is an electrometer. The arrow indicates the direction in which the plate is revolved.

These machines are variously modified, and some are made with two plates. One, at least, has been made with double plates *six feet* in diameter.

679. **Use of the electrical machines.**—When the plate is revolved, the friction develops a great quantity of positive electricity on the glass, whilst the negative fluid goes to the rubbers and is conveyed, through the frame, to the common reservoir, the earth, and so disappears. The neutral fluid on the conductors, or prime conductor, is decomposed; the negative fluid flows through the points to the glass plate, tending to neutralize the positive fluid on the plate. The conductors thus lose their negative electricity and become charged with *positive* fluid.

The prime conductor does not acquire positive electricity from the plate, but *gives to the plate its negative fluid*, thus becoming itself *positive.*

If a metallic point be held at some distance from a positively charged prime conductor, the electrometer, F (Fig. 15), begins to fall, showing a loss of electricity. But the point does not draw off the positive electricity from the conductor, but gives to the conductor negative electricity, which, uniting with the positive fluid, neutralizes it.

To produce *negative* electricity, the machine is insulated with glass supports, and the prime conductor connected with the earth by a metallic chain. The chain permits the positive fluid to escape from the prime conductor, whilst the negative electricity, being unable to escape, accumulates upon the cushions and frame of the machine.

680. **Measure of the quantity of electricity in the machine.**—The degree to which the machine is charged may be shown by placing a quadrant electrometer (673) upon the prime conductor, as seen at F, Fig. 15. When the machine is in operation, the ball rises along the quadrant, and, by its divergence from the vertical line, indicates the quantity of electricity developed.

Only a certain amount of the fluid can be retained on the prime conductor. After this quantity is accumulated, if the plate is turned, the tension becomes so great, it escapes through the air, and along the glass supports of the machine.

681. **Precautions in using the machines.**—A dry winter-air is best for working an electrical machine; and an apartment heated by dry furnace-air is very favorable.

In a damp day electrical experiments are seldom performed with success.

In carpeted rooms it is better to connect the rubbers with a gas-fixture, to secure a good communication with the common reservoir, the earth. The machine should not stand near the walls of the room, or any angular body. The glass columns should be coated with an insulating varnish (674), to prevent the deposition of moisture.

682. **Figure 16.—The hydro-electric machine.**—For furnishing electricity, the hydro-electric machine is superior to any above described. This is an apparatus for developing electricity from high steam. It consists of an insulated steam-boiler, about three feet long and twenty inches diameter, sufficiently strong to sustain a pressure of 200 lbs. to the inch, from which comes the steam-pipe, S, in the drawing. T is a box, containing a little water, through which the steam passes, in its passage from the steam-pipe, S, to the wooden jets, L. In these jets there is a sort of interrupted passage to produce friction. The vapor escapes against a number of metallic points in the frame above, which collect the electricity, and communicate with the insulated brass ball, H.

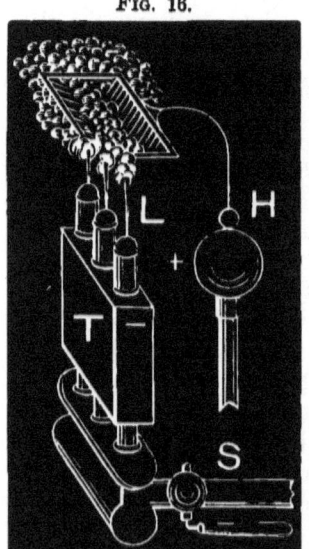

Fig. 16.

The evolution of electricity is due to *friction* between the particles of water (not steam) and the sides of the discharge apertures; the water being supplied by a small quantity in the box, T, through which the steam must pass, thereby becoming partially condensed. Steam is merely the vehicle and power by which the vesicles of water are expelled.

The boiler is negative, and positive electricity is collected at H, as indicated by the signs plus and minus.

Such an apparatus will develop, in a given time, as much electricity as four plate machines, forty inches in diameter, revolving sixty times a minute.

The discovery of electricity developed by steam was accidental. An engineer, endeavoring to cement a leak in a steam-boiler, observed electrical phenomena, which subsequently led to a scientific examination of the subject, and the production of the above described apparatus.

683. **Other sources of electrical excitement.**—1. Bands or belts of leather, India-rubber, or gutta-percha, used to drive machinery, often become powerful sources of resinous electrical excitement, giving sparks of negative electricity twenty or more inches in length.

2. Negative electrical excitement may be developed by briskly rubbing the feet, with shoes on, around on a woolen carpet, in rooms heated with hot-air furnaces; the person performing the operation being the electrical machine, prime conductor, and all. A person thus electrized, may light the gas by a spark from the finger, and give a shock to another person. This experiment is most successfully performed when the wind is northwest.

Experiments Illustrating Electrical Attractions and Repulsions.

684. **The insulating stool.—Electrical spark.—Electrical shock.**—Many instructive and amusing experiments may be made with an electrical machine, illustrating the laws of electrical attractions and repulsions. Limited space will admit of only a few.

The insulating or electrical stool is nothing more than a simple bench, provided with glass feet or legs, and sufficiently strong to sustain the weight of a person. A piece of board resting on four glass bottles or strong tumblers answers every purpose.

An electrical spark is a brilliant flash of light which passes when a conductor approaches a highly electrified body. For example, if the finger, which is a conductor, is held near to a charged prime conductor of an electrical machine, the positive fluid, acting at a distance by induction, drives the positive fluid of the hand to the earth, and the body of the experimenter becomes negatively electrified. When the tension of the positive fluid of the machine and the negative fluid of the body overcome the resistance of the air, they rush together with a sharp crack and a bright light, which constitutes the *spark*. If the electrical machine is sufficiently powerful, the sparks take a zig-zag course, like lightning, shown by Fig. 26 (700).

The electrical shock is the sensation experienced by the person who receives the electrical spark.

685. **Figure 17.—Electrical puppets** consist of little figures, made of cork, pith, or some similar substance, which are made to dance by means of electrical attraction and repulsion. These are placed between two metallic plates, as shown; the lower one being connected with the earth, and the upper one suspended to an arm of the prime conductor.

Fig. 17.

When the machine is turned, the upper plate, becoming electrified, attracts the images to it; these, becoming charged with positive fluid, are immediately repelled to the lower plate, where they lose this fluid, and are again attracted to the upper plate; and so on, dancing up and down as long as the machine is turned. This is but the same operation illustrated, in a simple way, by Fig. 1 (651).

686. **Figure 18.—The electrical chime** signifies the ringing of bells by means of electrical attractions and repulsions.

Attached to an arm of the prime conductor is a horizontal bar, from which is suspended three bells and two metallic balls, as shown in the figure. The outer bells, E and F, are suspended by metallic chains or wires, and the middle one, L, by a non-conducting substance, as a silk cord; the middle bell is also connected with the earth by a metallic chain.

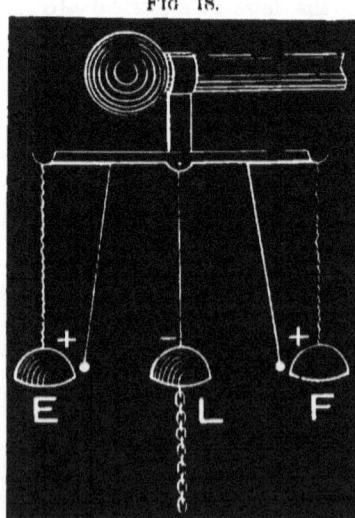

Fig. 18.

By turning the machine, the bells, E and F, becoming positively electrified by the prime conductor, attract the balls, which, becoming positively electrified, are immediately repelled; and, striking against the middle bell, L, they part with their charge, and are again attracted by the outer bells and again repelled. This alternate attraction and repulsion keeps the bells ringing as long as the plate is turned.

687. **Figure 19.—The electrical wheel** consists of four or more pointed arms, bent at right angles at the ends, and connected at the centre to a small cap, which is free to rotate on a pivot in a horizontal plane.

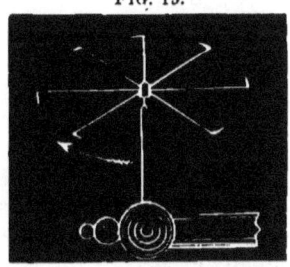

Fig. 19.

The wheel is sustained by a metallic support, set upon an arm of the prime conductor, as shown in the figure.

When the machine is in operation, the wheel becomes electrified, and revolves. The tension of the electricity at the points causes the fluid to escape, which causes the wheel to revolve by the reaction of the electricity on the air. The wheel will not revolve in a vacuum, though the fluid escapes the same; which shows that, out of the vacuum, its motion is due to the resistance of the air which causes the reaction.

688. **Figure 20.—The electrical blow-pipe.**—If a pointed metallic rod, with the point standing horizontal, be placed on the prime conductor, L, and the electrical machine put in operation, the escape of electricity from the point will create a current of air, which is rendered sensible to the eye by placing the flame of a burning candle before the point, as represented in the figure. The current from an active machine will even extinguish the flame.

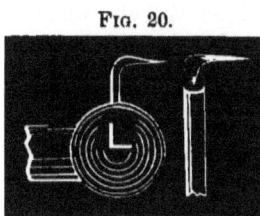

Fig. 20.

689. **Figure 21.—The electrical egg** is an egg-shaped light, produced by a flow of electricity through a vacuum.

The apparatus for exhibiting this light consists of a hollow globe or oval of glass, containing two small spheres of metal, F and H, at some distance apart. The upper one is connected with the prime conductor by the rod, T, and the lower one communicates with the earth. At the bottom of the glass is attached a pipe (provided with a stop-cock, N) by which the globe is attached to the air-pump.

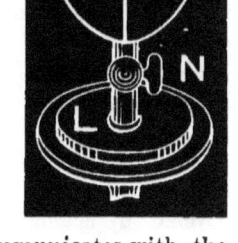

Fig. 21.

Having exhausted the air and closed the stop-cock, if the machine be turned, a flow of electricity will take place from the prime conductor to the earth. In passing from the ball F to the ball H, there is no obstruction. If the experiment is made in the dark, a beautiful violet-colored light, of an oval form, will be seen between the balls, as shown in the figure.

The rarer the air within the glass, the more globular will be the form of the light.

ACCUMULATION OF ELECTRICITY.

690. **Latent or disguised electricity.**—When two equal and insulated conductors, as metallic plates, are separated from each other by only a thin plate of glass, or other dielectric substance, and then equally excited by the two opposite electricities, no evidences whatever of any electrical excitement are communicated by either plate to an electroscope connected with them. The glass, or dielectric, prevents the union of the opposite fluids, but does not prevent their inductive action (670), whereby their presence is entirely masked to surrounding bodies.

By removing the plates to some distance from each other, the free electricity of each becomes manifest by its effect on the electroscope. If they be again brought together, with the dielectric still between them, this evidence of excitement again disappears; and so on, until, finally, the imperfect insulation of the air allows the free electricity to become neutralized.

The two fluids thus situated are said to be *latent* or *disguised,* or paralyzed by their mutual attraction.

691. **The electrical condenser.**—An electrical condenser is an apparatus employed for the accumulation of electricity.

Condensers are various in form, but in principle they are all essentially the same, being composed of two conductors separated by an insulator, and depend upon the principle above explained (690), of paralyzing the two fluids, or rendering them latent.

The Leyden jar is the most common of all the condensers.

692. **Figure 22.—The Leyden jar.**—This valuable piece of apparatus, named from the city where it was invented, was first discovered by accident, long before its principle of action was understood.

In its improved form it consists of a bottle or jar of thin glass, coated nearly to the top, on the inside and outside, with tin-foil; or, instead of coating it on the inside, it is better to fill it nearly full of loose tin-foil, or some other loose metallic substance, as shown in the figure. A metallic rod, passing through the cork, or non-conducting cover, reaches into the metallic filling; or, if the jar be coated inside, it terminates with a metallic chain, the lower end of which falls on the bottom of the jar. The rod terminates externally with a small sphere of metal, R, called the *button*.

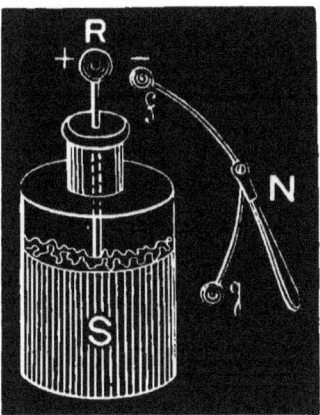

Fig. 22.

This is a condenser in which the glass of the jar serves as the insulator or dielectric medium, whilst the metallic substances, within and without, correspond to the two plates, previously mentioned (690).

The discharger, N, will be explained hereafter.

693. **Figure 23.—Charging the Leyden jar.**—The Leyden jar is charged by holding it in the hand (placing the hand on the tinned part) as shown, and bringing the button in contact with the prime conductor, F, of the electrical machine.

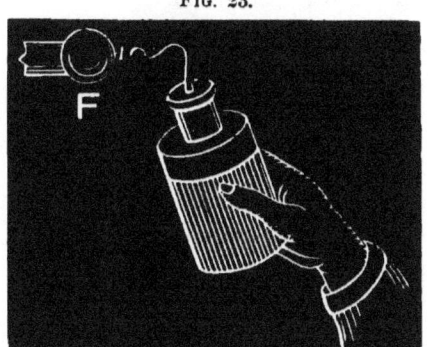

Fig. 23.

The positive electricity is accumulated in the interior, and acts by induction upon the outer coating, which becomes therefore negative, the positive fluid of the outer coating being conveyed by the hand through the body to the earth. The two fluids, reacting, accumulate a large quantity of positive electricity on the inside of the jar, and negative on the outside.

694. **Limit of the charge in a condenser.—Disruptive discharge.**—The amount of electricity that can be accumulated in a condenser is limited in two ways:

1st. By the limit of the tension of the fluid in the charging prime conductor; for, when the tension of the positive fluid on its plate or inner coating of the Leyden jar, becomes equal to that on the prime conductor, the fluid ceases to flow.

2d. By the cohesion of the insulating glass or dielectric medium between the two plates or coatings of the jar; for, if the electrical machine be sufficiently powerful, the tension of the opposing fluids goes on increasing until it overcomes the cohesion of the glass, shivering it in pieces, producing a loud explosion, and a brilliant spark.

Such a case as this is called a *disruptive discharge*.

695. The discharge of the condenser or Leyden jar may take place in four ways:

1st. *By disruptive discharge*, just explained (694).

2d. *Insensibly and gradually*, by imperfect insulation, especially if the air be damp.

3d. *By small successive discharges*. If the negative plate of a condenser or the outer coating of the Leyden jar is touched, no electricity is drawn off, because all that it contains is held in equilibrium by the positive fluid of the other plate or inner coating of the jar. But if the positive or inner coating of the jar is touched, all of its free electricity is drawn off, that is, all which is not neutralized by the other plate or coating of the jar. After this there will exist on the negative plate or coating of the jar a certain portion of unneutralized fluid, indicated by the pith-ball pendulum.

By continuing to touch the plates *alternately*, the whole charge may be drawn off in small quantities. By this process, whenever either plate or coating parts with its free electricity, an equal quantity of electricity is set free on the opposite plate or coating.

4th. *To obtain an instantaneous discharge*, it is only necessary to put the two plates, or the two coatings of the jar, in communication with each other, by means of a conductor. This can be done by touching one plate with the right hand and the other with the left; or, in case of the Leyden jar, by holding the jar in one hand and touching the button with the other; the arms and body being the conductor. The fluids flow through the body and neutralize each other. This produces a shock far more powerful than that produced by the simple spark from the prime conductor. To avoid the shock and produce the spark and explosion, without destroying the dielectric (694), an instrument is employed, called a *discharger*.

Dischargers.

696. The discharging-rod or hand discharger (Fig. 22) consists of a metallic rod, terminated at its two ends by small balls of metal, *f* and *g*, and having a hinge-joint at the middle, N, so it can be folded, to vary the distance between the balls. It is also provided with an insulating handle.

To discharge the Leyden jar with this instrument, it is only necessary to place one ball in contact with the outer coating, S, and the other with the button, R.

697. **Figure 24.—The universal discharger.**—Of the various contrivances for regulating the discharge of condensers and the electric battery, the *universal discharger,* represented by the figure, is considered the most useful.

FIG. 24.

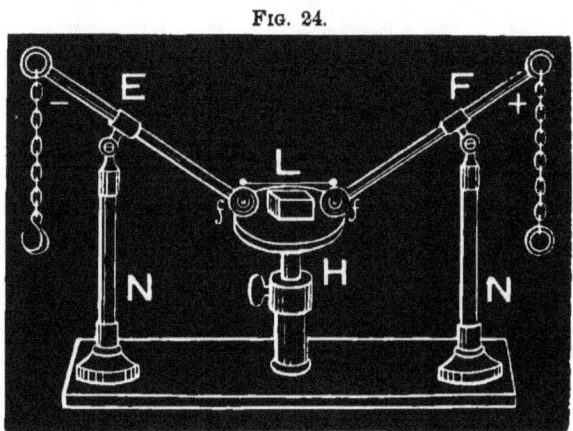

The two conducting-rods, sliding in the joints E and F, and provided with connecting chains, are mounted on insulating supports, N and N; by which the electrical fluid may be made to pass through any substance placed upon the table, H. The table may be elevated or lowered by means of the thumb-screw on the left. The substance experimented upon is insulated by a plate of glass, set into the top of the table.

The conducting-rods are pointed at the ends, and the points can be exposed by unscrewing the balls *ff.* The rod F connects with the positive side of the battery, while the rod E is brought into contact with the negative side, by means of the chains, or by applying one end of the discharging-rod (696) to the rod, E, and the other end to the negative side of the battery.

698. **Electricity in the Leyden jar resides on the glass.** —This is shown by an apparatus or jar consisting of three vessels (shaped like tapering tumblers), placed inside of one another. The outer and inner ones being thin metallic coatings, and the middle one, glass.

If this jar be charged, and placed on an insulating surface, and the vessels separated, the electrometer is not disturbed by either the outer or inner vessel, while the glass vessel remains strongly excited. If the parts be again put together, the jar is found to be charged as at first.

699. **Figure 25.—The electric battery.**—An electrical battery consists of several Leyden jars connected together in such a manner as to act as one jar. To establish a connection between their outer coatings, the jars are placed in a box which is lined, at the bottom, with thin metal. Their inside surfaces are brought into communication by connecting the several buttons with metallic rods, as represented in the figure.

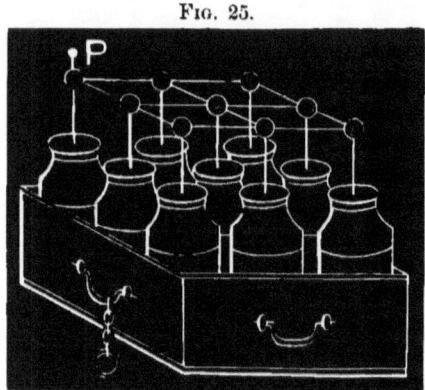

Fig. 25.

Though the power of jars, other things being equal, is directly as their surface, yet a limit of size is soon reached, which it is unprofitable to exceed, owing to the necessary thickness of glass, etc. Several batteries may be combined, by connecting their discharging-rods, which are preferable to more extended single series.

A battery is charged same as a single jar; that is, by connecting the interior with the prime conductor, and the exterior with the earth. The connection is made with the prime conductor by a rod passing from one of the buttons, as P; and with the earth by a chain attached to the ring in the handle of the box—the handle being in metallic contact with the lining of the box.

When handling powerful batteries, caution is requisite to avoid receiving their shocks, else serious consequences might follow.

A battery has been made embracing a hundred jars, each thirteen inches in diameter and two feet high. Such a battery magnetizes steel, deflagrates iron-wire, dissipates and vaporizes various metals, shivers blocks of wood several inches square, etc.

700. **Figure 26.—The electric spark.**—The explanation of this figure is contained in article 684. When a brass ball, at the end of a conducting-rod, is presented to a powerfully charged prime conductor, sparks are sometimes taken from it at a distance of thirty inches.

Fig. 26.

ELECTRICITY.   373

701. **The color of the electric spark.**—In air and oxygen gas it is white; though in heavy thunder-storms of this country it is sometimes purple, and at other times violet. In nitrogen it is blue; in hydrogen, crimson; in carbonic acid gas, green.

702. **Figure 27.—Difference between the positive and negative spark.**—The positive electricity gives an opening sheaf or brush of light; negative electricity gives only a star, as represented in the figure.

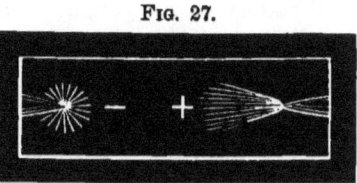

FIG. 27.

703. **Figure 28.—The electrical square.**—The electrical square consists of a square plate of glass, upon one surface of which is pasted a narrow strip of tin-foil, running backward and forward across the plate, as shown by the black line in the figure. The upper end of the strip is connected to the prime conductor by the rod P, and the lower end communicates with the earth by the chain T.

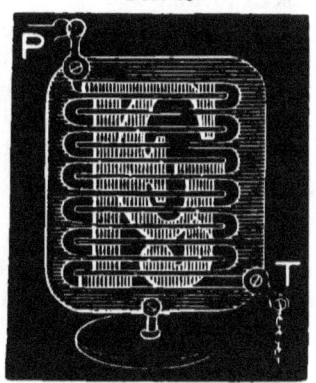

FIG. 28.

If the strip is unbroken, the fluid passes from the machine to the earth without emitting sparks; but if the strip be broken, the fluid, in passing over the break, produces a continuous light. And if several breaks be made, so as to mark out any design, as letters or other objects, the design will appear in light, as if traced on the glass with fire, whenever the machine is turned. The experiment is more striking in a dark room.

EFFECTS OF ACCUMULATED ELECTRICITY.

704. **The effects of the electric discharge.**—If the passage of electricity through bodies is impeded by their bad-conducting quality, or by want of proper dimensions, a powerful electric discharge, under such circumstances, will produce various effects, which may be classified as follows: 1st, *physiological;* 2d, *physical;* 3d, *mechanical;* 4th, *chemical.*

705. **Physiological effects of electricity** are the effects which it produces on men and animals. They consist of the shock, muscular contractions, more or less pain, and death, according to the power of the electrical apparatus.

Any number of persons, by joining hands, will be simultaneously and similarly affected by the same discharge. An electrical shock has been administered, in this manner, to five hundred persons at once.

A battery of six jars, of average size, would be dangerous. With more powerful batteries, cats, dogs, and larger animals may be killed outright. There are batteries of sufficient power to kill an ox instantly.

A person charged on an insulating stool (684), feels a prickly heat and glow, resulting in perspiration.

Many successful applications of electricity have been made in the treatment and cure of diseases.

706. **Heating power of electricity.**—This effect of electricity is shown in many ways. It is sufficiently intense not only to inflame ether, gunpowder, etc., but also to melt and volatilize the metals (699).

The heating effect is shown by stretching a fine wire, L, Fig. 24 (697), between the balls, *ff*, of the universal discharger, and discharging a powerful battery through it. The wire will undergo combustion, and be dispersed on all sides with vivid scintillations.

It is in this way that gunpowder is ignited under water, for blasting purposes, blowing up ships, etc.; the wire being protected from the water by suitable covering.

Though no heat is felt when the knuckle receives strong sparks from an active machine, yet a jet of burning gas can be inflamed by a spark from the finger (684); or, more strikingly, from an icicle held in the fingers of a person mounted on an insulated stool.

707. **The mechanical effects of electricity** are manifested when powerful charges of electricity are passed through imperfect conductors. The effects are expansion, with tearing, fracturing, and general shattering. These effects are exhibited by placing the body, as a billet of wood, a book, or a box, L, Fig. 24 (697), etc., on the table of the universal discharger, and passing through them a powerful charge from the battery. In this way blocks of wood may be torn to splinters, holes pierced in plates of glass, and through books of four or five hundred pages, etc.

708. **The chemical effects of statical electricity** are generally feeble. Small quantities of water have been decomposed with very small submerged points of gold. Various other chemical effects have been observed, but these belong rather to the subject of Chemistry than to this branch of Physics (see 752).

ATMOSPHERIC ELECTRICITY.

709. **Franklin's experiment with a kite proving the identity of lightning and the electrical spark.**—Franklin conceived the idea that the phenomena of a thunder-storm were due to electricity, and, to satisfy his inquiring mind, ingeniously tested the electrical condition of the clouds with a kite, and with such success that tears accompanied his joy.

Having prepared his silken kite, with a pointed wire on the top, and a hempen string, at the lower end of which he fastened an iron key, and to the key an insulating silken cord, he awaited the approach of a thunder-storm. The storm came, and up went the philosophic and famous kite, which soon gave the great philosopher hopes of success; and, finally, when the rain had increased the conducting power of the string, he enjoyed the unspeakable satisfaction of beholding long electrical sparks darting from the iron key—which unlocked the clouds to his searching mind.

Sparks ten feet long have been obtained from the clouds by means of kites.

Vivid sparks, often inconvenient and not without danger, flow from the receiving instruments in telegraph offices during a thunder-storm, the wires becoming charged with atmospheric electricity.

710. **Free electricity in the atmosphere.**—The existence of atmospheric electricity is not confined to clouds alone, for it often exists in the atmosphere when no trace of clouds is visible. An insulated conductor extended a few feet into the air, as by means of a long fishing-rod, will affect the electrometer. No evidence, however, is found of the existence of free electricity within three or four feet of the earth. But more and more is found the higher the conductor is raised, even at a height of two hundred and seventy-five feet.

From many experiments it is found that—

1st. The electricity of the atmosphere is always positive; is most abundant at night; increases after sunrise; diminishes toward noon; increases again toward sunset.

2d. The electrical state of the apparatus is disturbed by fogs, rains, hail, sleet, or snow; being negative when these approach; sometimes changing from positive to negative, and vice versa, every three or four minutes.

3d. The approach of clouds affects the instrument in a similar manner.

4th. Atmospheric electricity is more abundant in summer than in winter.

711. **The causes of atmospheric electricity** are: 1st. The inductive influence of the negatively excited earth; 2d. Evaporation; 3d, Condensation; 4th, Vegetation and animal life; 5th, Combustion; 6th, Friction.

The first of these causes is far more important than all the others. The denser air, near the surface of the earth, acts as a dielectric between the *negative* earth and *positive* higher layers of the atmosphere; the earth and air being an immense Leyden jar.

712. **Thunder-storms** are usually attended by an alteration in the direction of the wind. They generally prevail in the lower regions of the air, and are most frequent and violent in the equatorial regions, and in the summer than in the winter. They are attended with rapid condensation of atmospheric vapor, and an accumulation of electricity, in which they chiefly differ from other storms.

The origin of thunder-clouds is due to the rushing up of the lighter air to restore the normal equilibrium of the atmosphere, which had been disturbed by the gradual introduction, next to the ground, of warm and moist air. The upper end of such an ascending column of air is negatively electrified, as its lower end receives positive induction from the negative earth. The excess of watery vapor in such a cloud will be precipitated as it rises, and the ascending column becomes a conductor, through which a series of discharges will take place between the upper and lower parts of the cloud.

713. **Thunder** is the sound which follows a flash of lightning. The lightning passes through the air with such velocity, it violently displaces it, leaving void a space into which the air rushes with a loud report.

If the lightning proceeds from or toward the hearer, the sound will be somewhat prolonged, as, in this case, the sound from different parts of the vacuum has unequal distances to travel before it reaches the ear.

The loudness of thunder depends upon its nearness and the power of the electric discharge. Near by, it is sharp and rattling; at a greater distance it is dull and prolonged.

Lightning.

714. **Lightning.**—Air subjected to compression emits a spark; therefore it is, by some, contended that lightning is due to condensation of air in front of the electric fluid, in its rapid progress from point to point. At any rate, it is the result of electrical discharges. Clouds collect and retain electricity; and when different clouds are unequally or differently charged, and approach each other, the fluid rushes from one to another through the intervening air. In the same manner the fluid may pass from the clouds to the earth, when the discharge is called a *thunderbolt*. In such cases, elevated objects, as trees, church steeples, etc., often govern its direction, and suffer terrible consequences.

In low regions of the atmosphere lightning is white; in higher regions it is violet.

715. **Classes of lightning.**—Lightning has been divided into classes; namely, *zig-zag* or *chain lightning*, *sheet lightning*, *ball lightning*, *heat lightning*, and *volcanic lightning*.

Zig-zag or chain lightning.—The zig-zag form is due to the fact that the compressed air in front of the fluid resists its flow, causing it to be turned aside from a direct course. Sometimes the flash is thus divided into two or three branches; when it is termed *forked* lightning.

Sheet lightning is a diffused glow of light illuminating the borders of the clouds.

Ball lightning appears in the form of globular masses, sometimes remaining stationary, often moving slowly, and in a little time they explode with great violence.

Heat lightning occurs often in serene weather near the horizon, unattended with thunder. It is the reflection in the atmosphere of lightning at a remote distance.

Volcanic lightning is caused by rapid condensation of the vast volumes of heated vapor, thrown into the air from active volcanoes. This class of lightning is sometimes very terrific.

716. **The velocity of lightning** is estimated to be not less than 250,000 miles per second. The duration of a flash of lightning does not exceed a millionth part of a second.

717. **The return-shock** is a violent shock felt at a great distance from the place where the lightning strikes. It is due to the induction of an electrified cloud upon the ground and bodies beneath it, which are all strongly charged with electricity contrary to that of the cloud. When a discharge takes place, at whatever point of the cloud, the cloud returns to its neutral state, causing its inductive influence to cease instantly, whereupon all the bodies electrified by its induction instantly return to the neutral state. The violence of this return constitutes the *return*-shock, which sometimes causes death.

718. **Figure 29.—Lightning-rods** are rods of metal attached to buildings and ships, to protect them from injurious effects of lightning.

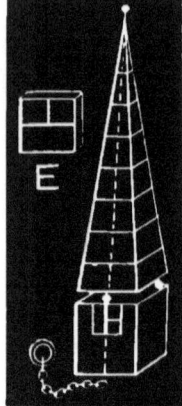

FIG. 29.

The protective influence of a rod extends to a distance from itself equal to four times its height above the building.

They receive the fluid on the point, and silently convey it from the clouds to the ground, even when no visible discharge takes place.

To render lightning-rods effective, they should be well insulated from the building by glass holders, pointed at the top and the point covered with non-corrosive metal, of ample size and good conducting material (copper is best), set deep enough in the ground to reach the permanently moist earth, connected with other metallic substances (if any) on the building, as gutters, gas pipes, etc.; and especially should they be *continuous*, otherwise they are a source of danger rather than safety, as will be seen by the following experiment.

The little tower (Fig. 29), constructed of separate wooden blocks, rests on three metallic balls or buttons, placed on a base block, as represented in the figure. The button in front stands upon a small square piece, shown separately at E. This piece has a metallic connection running through it in one direction, and half way through it in another; so that, by inserting this piece into its recess one side up, the lightning-rod (represented by the dotted line) is made continuous, from the top of the tower to the chain below. By turning the piece over, the metallic connection can be broken. If the charge of a Leyden jar is passed through the rod when the circuit is interrupted, the piece will be blown out, and the tower thrown down. By turning the block, and thus completing the metallic connection, the same charge is passed without disturbing the structure.

Means of safety.—Persons who suffer with fear of being struck by lightning, may feel a sense of security by putting on silk clothing, and sitting in an insulated chair placed in the middle of the room. The chair can be conveniently insulated with four glass tumblers, or pieces of thick glass. Or they may place themselves upon a feather bed. It is safer to avoid currents of air, and nearness to chimneys, and walls of the room, and metal conductors, as gilt frames, etc. If out of doors, it is prudent to avoid elevated objects, as trees, buildings, etc. For obvious reasons, it is safer to be in valleys than on hill-tops or hill-sides.

Liability of being struck by lightning.—The apprehension and solicitude respecting lightning are proportionate to the magnitude of the evils it produces, rather than the frequency of its occurrence. The chances of our being killed or injured by lightning are infinitely less than those which we encounter in travelling by boats and cars, or in our daily walks and occupations, or even in our sleep from the destruction of our dwellings by fire.

719. **Aurora borealis.**—By this term is meant the luminous phenomena which are often seen in the regions of the poles of the earth. In the northern hemisphere they appear in the north; in the southern hemisphere they appear in the south, and are then called *aurora australis.* There are different opinions concerning the cause of these phenomena. By some they are supposed to be due to the passage of electric currents through the higher regions of the atmosphere; the different colors being manifested by the passage of the fluid through air of different densities. Though philosophers cannot yet demonstrate the cause of these luminous appearances, still it is generally believed that the phenomena are intimately connected with terrestrial magnetic electricity.

That this light is not a local phenomenon is evident, for the reason that it is often seen simultaneously in places far apart, as Europe and America.

The height of the auroras has been estimated to be from one hundred to two hundred miles.

They appear to be more frequent about the period of the equinoxes than at other times.

During the prevalence of the auroras, all the magnetic elements show great disturbance, simultaneously, at the most distant stations.

That the auroras act upon telegraphic wires, is shown by the fact that several telegraphic lines in the United States were worked, in parts of August and September of 1859, for hours together, entirely by the magnetic current induced by the aurora, the batteries being detached.

Chemical decomposition, and heating and luminous effects, have been observed from the currents induced during auroral disturbances.

As everybody has observed, or may observe, the auroras, often called the Northern Lights, it is useless to describe their general appearance.

The phenomena of the auroras occur in the day-time as well as at night, but the superior light of the sun renders the auroral light invisible during the day.

720. Figure 30.—Slow discharge of a Leyden jar.—
Before leaving the topic of statical or frictional electricity, and taking up that branch of the general subject termed *dynamical electricity*, we will describe what may be considered a beautiful electrical toy, consisting essentially of a Leyden jar and two small bells.

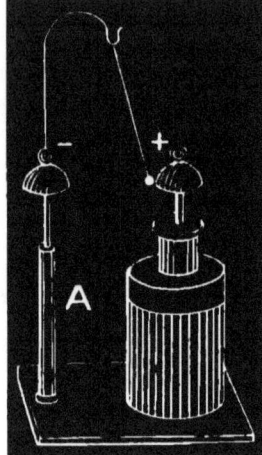

Fig. 30.

A charged jar, provided with a small bell in place of the button or knob, is set upon a board, near to a small brass ball fastened to a silken thread, which is held at the upper end by a metallic rod, A. This rod connects with the earth, and supports another small bell.

The positive electricity of the jar attracts the little ball, which, after striking the bell, is repelled, until it strikes the other bell, when its positive fluid is discharged, and itself is again attracted by the first bell, and so on, for many hours (653).

CHAPTER XV.

DYNAMICAL ELECTRICITY.

FUNDAMENTAL PRINCIPLES.

721. Galvanism.—Electricity excited or produced by chemical action is called *Galvanism*, in honor of Galvani, who first observed certain phenomena which led to the discovery of generating electricity in this way.

722. Figure 31.—Galvani's discovery and experiments.
—In the year 1786, Luigi Galvani, professor of anatomy in the University of Bologna, while making applications of atmospheric electricity to animal organisms, accidentally observed convulsive movements in the body of a frog, which he had prepared for some experiment, and hung on a copper hook near an iron frame of the window. By further observation and experiment, he found that the convulsions were strongest when he made connection, by means of *two metals*, between the lumbar nerves and the exterior muscles, denuded of the skin, as represented in the figure.

The instrument in the hand consists of two pieces of metal, zinc, Z, and copper, C, joined together at the contact with the handle. By simply placing the zinc in contact with the nerves, at N, no convulsion occurs, but as soon as the copper comes in contact with the limb below, the leg is convulsed and drawn up, as shown.

Galvani found also that these convulsions could be produced by bringing the interior surface of the nerves in contact with the exterior mucous surface, *without the use of metals.*

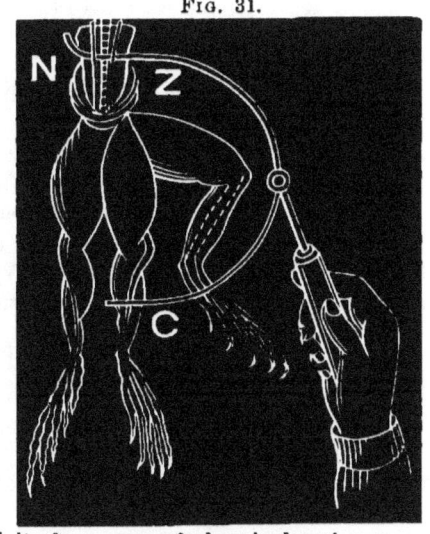

Fig. 31.

Thus began the discovery of the method of generating electricity by means of chemical action, now constituting one of the most important branches of science.

723. **Galvani's explanation.**—Galvani held that the convulsions of the frog were excited by a nervous or vital fluid, passing from the nerves to the muscles by way of the metallic communication, and that, falling on the muscles, it contracted them, like the electrical discharge from the machine. This view was soon shown to be incorrect, but was adhered to by Galvani until he died, in 1798, before the Voltaic Pile was given to the world.

724. **Volta's theory of contact.**—Volta at first accepted the views of Galvani, but after experiment and study, gave up this hypothesis and adopted one of his own. He attributed the electrical effects, manifested by the convulsions, to *the contact of dissimilar substances,* which, he claimed, caused a decomposition of the natural electricity of both bodies, the positive fluid going to one and the negative to the other; and that the frog's limbs were only the sensitive electroscope, indicating the current thus developed.

Though this theory held general sway for a long time, yet it was not the true explanation; hence it was gradually supplanted by the *electro-chemical theory,* which refers these phenomena to *chemical action.*

Volta discovered that *certain metals, particularly the oxydizable metals, disengage electricity and charge the condenser.*

This discovery soon led (1800) to Volta's second and great discovery, viz., the *Voltaic pile or battery.*

725. The electro-chemical theory.—The true cause of electrical excitement, occasioned by the contact of dissimilar metals, is now fully ascertained to be *chemical action.*

Electricity produced by chemical action is termed *Galvanic* or *Voltaic electricity.* Yet Galvani never even saw a galvanic battery; but, having been the first observer of the phenomena which set Volta to work, he shares the honor with Volta. Yet neither of them fully understood the discovery, which, through their instrumentality, is now so beneficial to mankind.

Fabroni first suggested the chemical theory, the truth of which was subsequently demonstrated by De le Rive and Becquerel, who also found that no chemical action takes place without developing electricity.

They also showed that whenever a metal is attacked by an acid, the former is positively and the latter negatively electrified.

726. Figure 32.—Simple voltaic couple. — Whenever two unlike substances, moistened by or immersed in an acid or saline fluid, are brought into contact, a voltaic current is established.

If a silver or copper coin and a piece of zinc be placed one above and the other below the tongue, so that their edges are in contact, a prickly sensation will be felt in the tongue, and, if the eyes be closed, a mild flash of light is also seen.

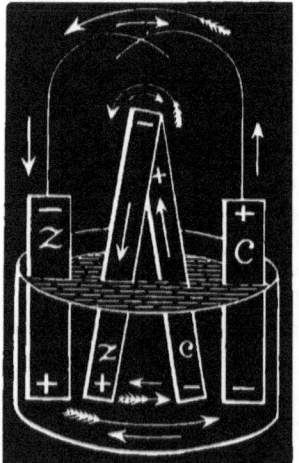

A mention of this simple experiment by Sulzer, a German author, is the first recorded phenomenon attributable to voltaic electricity. The saliva, in this case, is the saline fluid, exciting a voltaic current, due to its chemical effect on the zinc or copper, and the nerves of sense are the electroscope.

The figure represents the simplest form of a voltaic battery. It consists of a piece of copper (c) and a piece of zinc (z), partly immersed in a weak solution of sulphuric acid, resting in direct contact at the top, or united by means of copper wires, as shown in the figure. Thus, it is seen that a simple voltaic couple consists of three elements—*zinc, acid, copper.*

When the two metals are in contact (within or without the liquid), two electrical currents will be set up, flowing in opposite directions, as indicated by the two systems of arrows, in either of the two couples in the figure.

The positive fluid flows from the zinc to the copper in the liquid and from the copper to the zinc in the air, as indicated by the long arrows at the top and bottom; while the negative fluid passes from the copper to the zinc in the liquid and from the zinc to the copper in the air, as indicated by the short arrows at the top and bottom, and by the signs plus and minus.

Evidence of chemical action is seen by the constant flow of gas bubbles (hydrogen) from the zinc to the copper. This action ceases the instant the contact between the metals is broken.

727. **Figure 33.—The voltaic pile or battery.**—In the year 1800, Volta invented an apparatus by which the number of *contacts* could be multiplied, and the effect increased. This he did in accordance with his *contact theory*, previously mentioned (724).

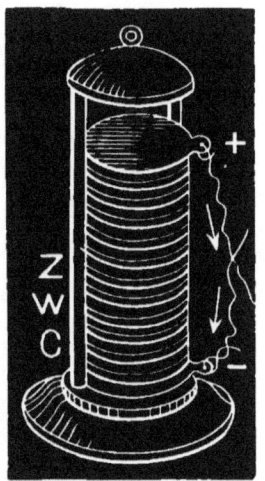

FIG. 33.

Such a pile consisted of alternate copper and zinc disks, laid up as shown in the figure, with disks of paper or cloth between them, moistened with brine or acidulated water; the couples being all disposed in the same order, that is, copper, cloth, zinc,—copper, cloth, zinc, and so on. W stands for the wet cloth in the drawing.

The terminal plates (copper at bottom and zinc at top) are provided with ears, for the convenient attachment of wires. The wires connecting the terminal plates are called *electrodes*.

Each couplet of copper and zinc may be soldered together, and then called a *couple, pair*, or *voltaic element*.

Other metals may be employed, but these are good, convenient, and cheap.

728. **Varieties of voltaic piles.**—As voltaic piles do not depend upon any particular form or substances, they have been made in various forms and of various materials. They have been made wholly of *animal* substances, and entirely of *vegetable* substances, as disks of beet-root and walnut-wood in contact; it being only required that the different substances act chemically upon each other.

A perfectly dry pile may be made of small disks of gilded paper and sheet-zinc, packed in a glass tube. They have been made in this way, consisting of 10,000 pairs, yielding sparks, charging Leyden jars, ringing bells, etc., for twenty years.

The voltaic or galvanic batteries, in use at the present day, are very different in form and efficiency from those formerly employed.

The *trough battery* was successful. It was with one of these that Davy made his invaluable and immortal discovery of the metallic bases of the alkalies.

729. **Polarity of the pile.**—The pile being insulated and tested, is found to possess electrical polarity,—one half of the pile being positive, the other half negative, and the middle neutral. In the zinc and copper pile, the end terminating with zinc is positive, the other end being negative, as indicated by the signs plus and minus, in Fig. 33.

The tension is greatest at the extremities; hence these are named poles. In any case, the end yielding positive fluid is the *positive pole;* the end yielding negative fluid is the *negative pole.*

The pile, therefore, may be regarded as a Leyden jar, or electrical battery, perpetually charged, if the necessary conditions are maintained.

730. **Electrical currents of the pile.**—The pile manifests no electrical action as long as the electrodes remain separated, but if these are brought near each other, a small spark will pass, which is caused by a re-combination of the two fluids. The passage of the spark does not discharge the pile, as in the case of the Leyden jar; but a succession of sparks will pass, showing that the process of decomposition of electricity in the pile is constantly going on, by which its poles are continually supplied with positive and negative fluids.

If the wires or electrodes are brought into actual contact, the sparks cease, but the flow of the fluid continues the same. This continuous flow of electricity is called *the electrical current.*

There are *two* currents of electricity, positive and negative (726), flowing in opposite directions. For convenience, only one of them will be considered, namely, that which flows from the positive to the negative pole.

731. **Electro-positive and electro-negative.**—The two metals, when placed in contact, are said to be *electro-polarized.* The one giving traces of free positive electricity is said to be *electro-positive,* and the other *electro-negative.* In case of zinc and copper, the zinc is electro-positive and the copper electro-negative.

These are only relative terms; as the same metal may be electro-positive when coupled with one metal, and electro-negative when coupled with another.

In any case, *the electro-positive metal is the one most easily corroded or oxydized.*

732. The difference between quantity and intensity.— The electricity evolved by a single voltaic couple is considerable in *quantity*, but weak in *intensity*. Electricity produced by the machine is *small in quantity*, but of *high tension;* that is, capable of passing through air, but producing slight chemical or heating effects. On the contrary, voltaic electricity is great in quantity and small in intensity; shown by the fact that the thinnest film of air is a perfect insulator,— and so are all dry woods,—but its chemical and heating effects are powerful.

733. Quantity increases with surface, intensity with number of pairs.—The quantity of electricity increases with the surface, but not with the number of the pairs; hence, to increase the quantity, large plates are employed.

The tension increases with the number of the pairs. *No greater quantity of electricity is obtained from a pile than a single pair of plates, its intensity alone being increased.*

734. Amalgamated zinc.—As all commercial zinc contains more or less of foreign substances, which stand in the electro-negative relation to the zinc, it is necessary to protect them from the action of the acid. Otherwise, each particle of the impurities forms, with the contiguous particle of zinc, a minute battery; which rapidly corrodes and roughens the surface, and correspondingly destroys the power of the whole couplet. This action of common zinc is called a *local action.*

To prevent this action, the freshly corroded zinc is rubbed with a little mercury, which covers it with a uniform coating of *zinc amalgam.* Thus prepared, zinc may be left in the acid water without injury, and when brought into contact with the other metal of the battery, it becomes far more energetic than before. This *zinc amalgam* is indispensable in practice.

Batteries.

735. Smee's battery consists of a plate of silver coated with platinum, suspended between two plates of amalgamated zinc. The three are attached to a wooden bar, which supports the whole in a tumbler partly filled with water, acidulated with one-seventh of its bulk of sulphuric acid (blue vitriol); or, for less activity, one-sixteenth. The electrodes are fastened to the zinc and silver plates by means of small screws. The *quantity*, but not the intensity, of this battery, is very great; and for many days it maintains a uniform action.

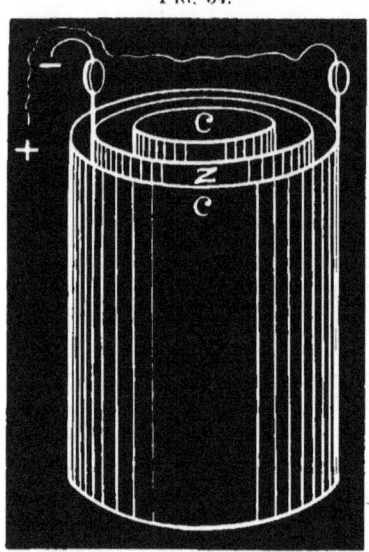

Fig. 34.

736. **Figure 34.—The sulphate of copper battery** consists of two concentric cylinders of copper, *cc*, tightly soldered to a copper bottom, and a zinc cylinder, *z*, fitting between them. The liquid employed is a solution of sulphate of copper (blue vitriol). The zinc cylinder is prevented from touching the copper by means of three pieces of wood or ivory (not shown) projecting from the top of the zinc cylinder, and resting on the top of the outer copper cylinder. The electrodes are connected, one with the outer copper cylinder, and the other with the zinc, as represented.

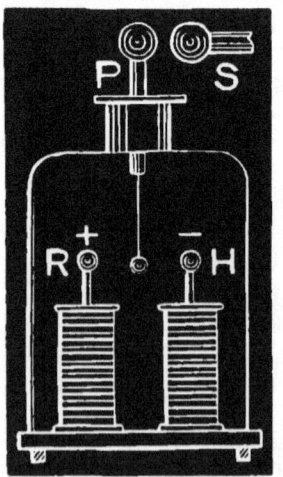

Fig. 35.

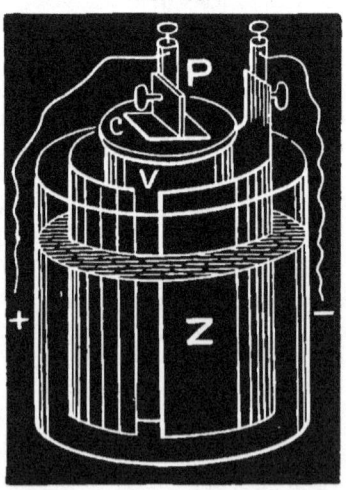

Fig. 36.

737. **Figure 35.—Bohnenberger's dry pile electroscope** consists of two dry voltaic piles (728), arranged under a glass jar,

ELECTRICITY. 387

having a strip of gold-leaf or a pith-ball suspended between their opposite poles, R and H, and connected with the rod and knob, P.

If a positively-electrified body, S, be brought near to the knob, P, the gold-leaf will be attracted to the negative pole, H, of the electroscope; but if a negatively-electrified body be brought near to the knob, the gold-leaf will be attracted to the positive pole, R. This is one of the most delicate electroscopes.

738. **Figure 36.—Grove's nitric acid battery.**—This is a powerful and intense sustaining battery. The outer vessel is glass, filled with from six to ten parts of water to one of sulphuric acid. In this fluid is placed an amalgamated zinc cylinder, Z, open on one side, as shown. The inner vessel, V, is a porous jar, filled with nitric acid, in which is immersed a piece of platinum, P. The porous vessel is covered to keep down the fumes of the acid. The connecting wires are held by binding screws, shown at the top.

In this battery there is a double chemical action, the hydrogen being engaged by the nitric acid, which it readily decomposes. There is therefore an increased flow of electricity.

739. **Figure 37.—Carbon battery.**—This battery is essentially like the one last described, with the exception that carbon is substituted for the platinum, to save expense.

FIG. 37.

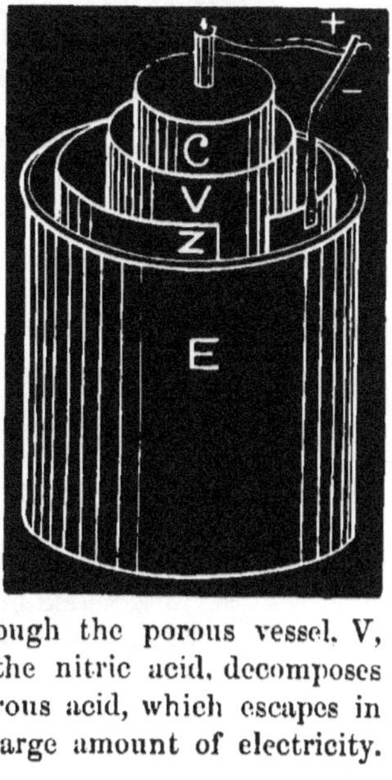

E is an earthen vessel, containing dilute sulphuric acid; Z, a zinc cylinder, open on one side, having a strip of copper soldered to its upper edge; V, a vessel of porous earthenware, containing nitric acid; c. a cylinder of well-calcined carbon or coke, which is a good conductor. In the top of this cylinder a stem of copper is inserted, to which is soldered a strip of the same metal, which, with the other strip of copper, constitutes the electrodes.

As in the Grove battery (738), there is a double chemical action. Water is decomposed in the outer vessel, giving its oxygen to the zinc, forming oxyde of zinc. The liberated hydrogen passes through the porous vessel, V, and, uniting with a part of the oxygen of the nitric acid, decomposes it, producing water, and also forming nitrous acid, which escapes in fumes. This double action developes a large amount of electricity.

The carbon is the positive and the zinc the negative pole of the couple. The positive fluid, therefore, passes from the carbon to the zinc.

740. **Figure 38.—Batteries of two or more couples.**— Any number of couples may be united by attaching the copper strip of the zinc cylinder in one couple to that of the carbon in the next couple, and so on throughout the combination. The remaining two strips, which will be one on the first and the other on the last couple, may be united by a conductor.

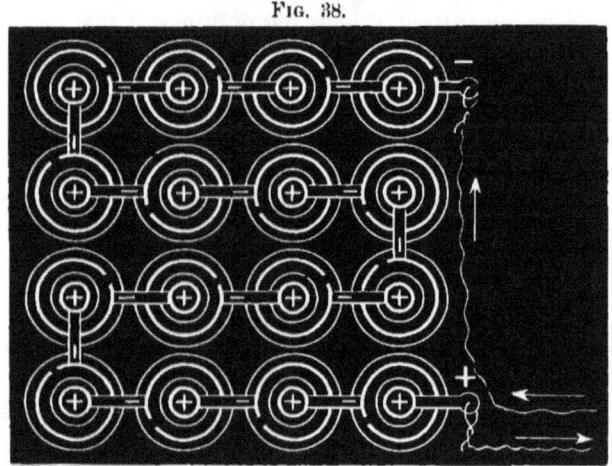

Fig. 38.

Such a combination is shown by the figure, consisting of sixteen carbon batteries, the view being from above, looking down upon the combination.

The outer circle of each couple represents the outer vessel; the next circle, the zinc; the next, the vessel containing the acid; and the central circle, the carbon.

It will be noticed that the carbon in all the couples is marked *plus* (+), showing that the positive fluid passes from the carbon to the zinc; and that the strips are marked *minus* (−), where they join the zinc, showing that the negative fluid passes from the zinc to the carbon.

741. **The electro-motive force.**—By the electro-motive force is meant the cause which gives rise to the electric current, which is the oxydation of the zinc; in other words, the chemical action.

742. **Resistance to the current.**—The electric current must proceed not only along the connecting wire, from pole to pole, but also through the couples; hence, there is a resistance to the flow of the current exterior to and within the apparatus.

743. **Laws determining the force of a voltaic current.**
1st. The *electro-motive force* varies with the number of the elements or pairs, the nature of the metals, and the nature of the liquids which constitute the elements; but it does not, in any manner, depend on the dimensions of their parts.

2d. The *resistance* of each element or pair is directly proportional to the distance between the plates within the liquid, the resistance of the liquid itself, and the length of the wire completing the circuit; and inversely proportional to the surface of the plates in contact with the liquid, and to the section or size of the connecting wire.

3d. The force of the current is equal to the electro-motive force, divided by the resistance.

744. **Difference between static and dynamic electricity.**—The nature of electricity is the same, whether it be produced by friction, chemical action, or other means.

The difference between frictional electricity and that evolved by chemical action, consists in the *low tension and great quantity* of the latter, as compared with that of the former. And to this difference is due the wide difference of effects caused by electricity produced in these two ways.

For example, it has been demonstrated that a miniature voltaic battery, consisting of two wires, the one of zinc, the other of platinum, five-eighths of an inch long and one-eighth of an inch diameter, excited by one drop of sulphuric acid mixed with four ounces of water, will liberate as much electricity in three seconds of time, as can be obtained by an electric battery, having 3,500 square inches coated surface, and charged by 30 revolutions of a plate-glass machine 50 inches in diameter. This quantity of electricity, in a state of tension given by the machine, would kill a small animal, and yet it is evolved by the solution of almost an inappreciable portion of the zinc-wire.

APPLICATIONS OF VOLTAIC OR GALVANIC ELECTRICITY.

Effects of the Voltaic Battery.

745. **The effects of the voltaic battery** may be divided into Physical, Chemical, Physiological, and Magnetic.

The effects of dynamical or voltaic electricity are all due to the re-combination of the two fluids, as in statical or frictional electricity; but they are more energetic, because of their continuous action.

Physical Effects.

746. Figure 39.—Illuminating effects.—If the electrodes of a powerful battery be terminated with points of well-burned charcoal, and brought insensibly near to each other, the points will immediately become incandescent, emitting a light of dazzling brightness. If the points are slightly separated, the current still continues to pass between them, and the light takes the form of a luminous arch, called the voltaic arch (747).

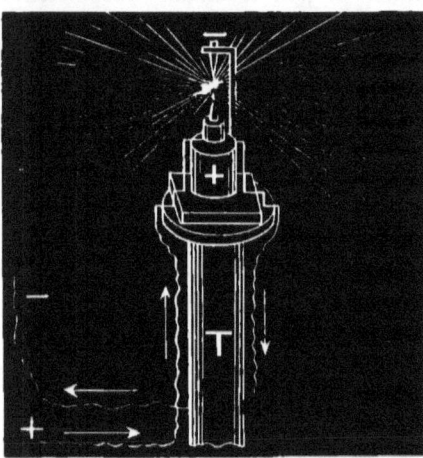

FIG. 39.

The figure, taken together with Fig. 38, will serve to illustrate the apparatus employed for illuminating streets, parks, etc., with electrical light. A suitable column, T, supports the electrodes of the battery; the wires being insulated with gutta-percha coverings. As one of the charcoal points slowly wastes away, while the other is somewhat elongated, provision is made, by means of clock-work (not shown), for keeping the points properly adjusted.

An electrical light, furnished by a battery of 48 carbon couples, equals that of 572 wax candles; the light produced by 100 couples dazzles the eyes; and that furnished by 600 couples is so intense, that it is as impossible to look at it as it is to look at the noonday sun.

747. Figure 40.—The voltaic arch.—The figure represents the charcoal points which are connected with the battery (746). The curved lines show the form of the arch of electrical flame, a white and

FIG. 40.

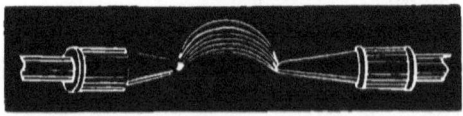

violet light of intolerable brightness, several inches in length, if the battery is very powerful.

As this flame is even more brilliant in a vacuum or in nitrogen or in carbonic acid, it follows that it cannot be produced by the combustion of the carbon electrodes. The action is accompanied by a hissing or rushing sound, caused, doubtless, by the removal and transportation of particles of carbon from the positive to the negative electrode.

748. **Figure 41.—The oval form of the arch.**—If the carbon electrodes are vertical, and the negative one uppermost, the arch will take an oval form, as shown. By inspecting this oval, through colored glasses, the particles of carbon can be seen moving from the positive to the negative electrode. When the image is projected on a screen, the growth of the negative and the decrease of the positive electrode can be easily observed. The negative carbon seems to glow first, but soon the positive becomes and remains the brightest part of the light. There is also seen in this form of the arch, a certain structure, in zones or bands of different brilliancy, as shown by the plain lines in the figure.

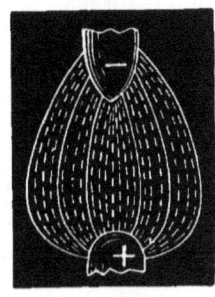

FIG. 41.

The arch is *magnetic*, that is, capable of influencing the magnet. If a magnet be brought near to the oval arch, the flame is deflected to one side, as shown in Fig. 43.

749. **Figure 42.—The shape of the electrodes.**—If the carbon electrodes be shaped, at first, both alike, as shown in Fig. 40, they will gradually take different shapes; the positive one taking the form of a cup, and the negative one remaining pointed, as shown in the figure.

FIG. 42.

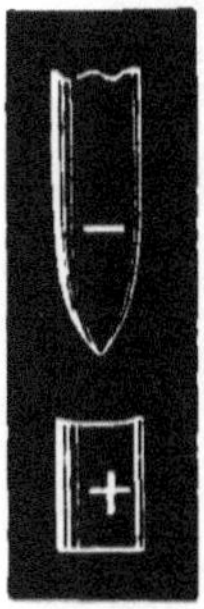

750. **Properties of the electrical light.**—The intensity of the electrical light depends more on the size of the individual couples or members of the pile than on their number. The light is unpolarized; it explodes a mixture of hydrogen and chlorine; acts on chloride of silver and other photographic preparations like the sun. Daguerreotypes are taken with it; and for taking microscopic photographs, it is preferable to solar light.

FIG. 43.

751. **Figure 43.—Heating effects.—Deflagration.**—The heat produced by a powerful battery, say of 600 couples, is so intense that even pure carbon has been softened by its power. When a current of voltaic electricity passes through a conductor, it heats it; and, according to the power of the bat-

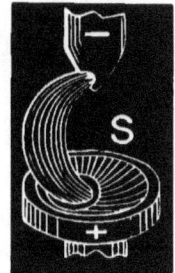

tery, it becomes fused or even vaporized. Small wires burn with splendid brilliancy.

When the positive electrode is formed into a small crucible of carbon, S, as shown in the figure, gold, silver, platinum, and other substances, are readily fused, deflagrated, or volatilized. Silver burns with a greenish, and gold with a bluish-white, light. Platinum, infusible in the hottest furnace, melts into spherical globules with a dazzling light.

Chemical Effects.

752. **Decomposition.**—The most important chemical effects of voltaic or galvanic electricity, are the decomposition of bodies traversed by it, and the transportation of their elements. Decomposition by means of electricity is one of the most valuable modern discoveries, yielding some of the richest gifts which abstract science ever bestowed upon the practical arts of life.

753. **Figure 44.—Method of electrotyping.**—This is a process of casting metals without heat; or the copying of medals, statues, type, and the like, in metal, by the aid of voltaic electricity.

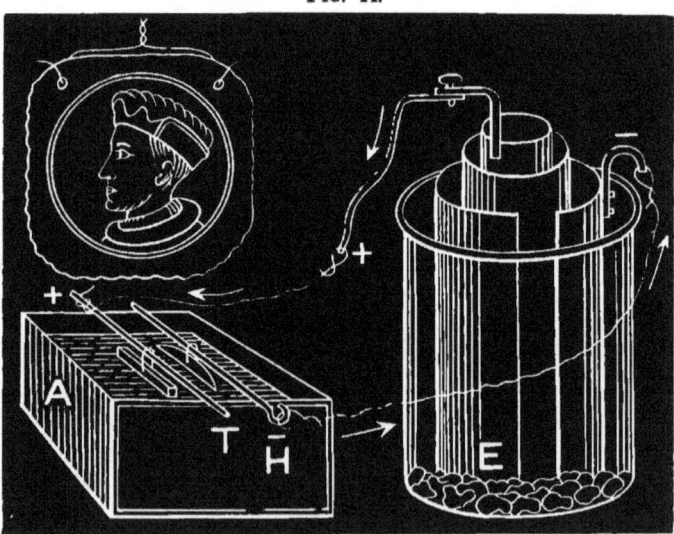

FIG. 44.

The battery shown in the figure differs from the carbon battery, Fig. 37 (739), by having a cylinder of zinc substituted for the carbon, and a cylinder of copper in place of the zinc. The outer vessel is of glass, and is filled with a solution of copper (blue vitriol), which is kept saturated by crystals of the sulphate, E, placed in the bottom of the vessel. The porous vessel (containing the zinc) is filled with dilute sulphuric acid (oil of vitriol).

The oxygen, resulting from the decomposition of the water, goes to the zinc, forming oxyde of zinc, which is dissolved by the sulphuric acid, giving sulphate of zinc. The hydrogen goes to the sulphate of copper and decomposes it. These chemical actions keep up the electric current, as shown by the arrows, which will continue as long as the outer vessel is supplied with saturated solution of sulphate of zinc.

Preparing the mould.—To produce a metallic duplicate of an object, as a medal, a wood-cut, or a form of type, it is first necessary to prepare an accurate mould of the object, made of some material, as plaster, wax, or gutta-percha, which will resist the action of the acids employed. Powdered black-lead is first rubbed on the wood-cut or other object, to prevent the warm wax, or other plastic substance, from sticking. The wax is then pressed upon the engraving, or object to be copied, until it touches every part. After hardening, the mould is removed, and, to render it a good conductor of electricity, it is coated with powdered black-lead. The mould, thus prepared to receive the metal, is made ready for the bath by attaching it to suspending wires, as shown in the upper part of the figure.

Method of depositing the metal upon the mould.—A is a vessel filled with a solution of sulphate of copper; T and H are metallic rods communicating with the two poles of the battery; the mould is suspended from the rod, H, and facing it is a plate of pure copper, suspended from the rod, T. The mould and the plate of copper constitute the two electrodes, the mould being the negative one.

The electric current of the battery passing through the solution, between the copper plate and mould, decomposes the sulphate into *sulphuric acid, oxygen,* and *pure copper.* The acid and oxygen go to the positive electrode, and, uniting with the copper plate, produce sulphate of copper; the copper goes to the negative electrode and is there deposited on the mould. In two days, or so, the coating of copper is sufficiently thick to be removed from the the wax mould. If the mould be perfect the casting will be a perfect fac-simile of the object.

If the object copied be a form of type, or a wood-cut, the metallic copy, being nailed to a wooden block, will serve to print from 100,000 to 200,000 impressions.

The positive electrode should be of the same metal as that in solution, and as large as the surface to be coated, and these should not be larger than the plates of the battery furnishing the current.

754. **Electro-gilding and electro-plating** consist in covering bodies, as spoons, watch-cases, etc., with gold, silver, etc., by a process similar to that of electrotyping. The object to be plated is first thoroughly cleansed and then suspended in a solution of the metal with which the object is to be plated.

755. **Figure 45.—Voltaic decomposition of water.—** Water is composed of oxygen and hydrogen gases, in the proportions of one measure of the former to two of the latter.

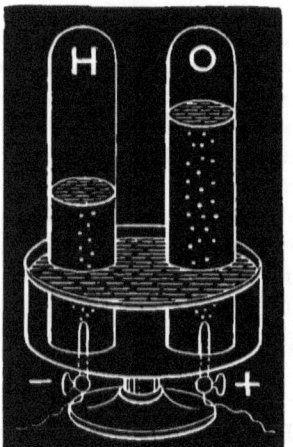

FIG. 45.

The process of decomposing water by a voltaic current is quite simple. Two glass tubes, filled with water, are inverted in a vessel of water. The vessel has a wooden bottom, through which the electrodes of the battery are passed, so as to enter the mouths of the tubes, as seen in the figure. To increase the conducting power of the water, a small quantity of sulphuric acid is added. The electrodes are platinum or gold, otherwise the oxygen would combine with one of them. When the current passes from one electrode to the other, through the water, the decomposition begins, as shown by the bubbles of gas rising in the two tubes. The oxygen rises in the tube O over the positive electrode, and the hydrogen in the tube H over the negative electrode.

The gases are pure, and their volumes are as 1 to 2, as indicated by the height of the water in the tubes.

The rapidity of the decomposition depends upon the intensity of the current.

756. **Figure 46.—Decomposition of salts.—**Fill a glass tube, as represented, with a solution of some neutral salt (as sulphate of soda), and color the solution with an infusion of litmus (blue cabbage), then pass a voltaic current through the saline solution, by dipping the platinum electrodes into the two arms. The dissolved salt will be decomposed, the acid constituent passing to the positive electrode in the arm R, and the alkaline to the negative electrode in the arm K, as will be shown by the infusion, which turns red by the acid, and green by the alkali.

The whole liquid will be turned to red and green. The arrows indicate the passage of the constituents. If the positive electrode be placed in the arm K, and the negative in the arm R, the constituents of the salt will be transposed in the tube, as shown by the red turning to green in the arm R, and the green turning to red in the arm K.

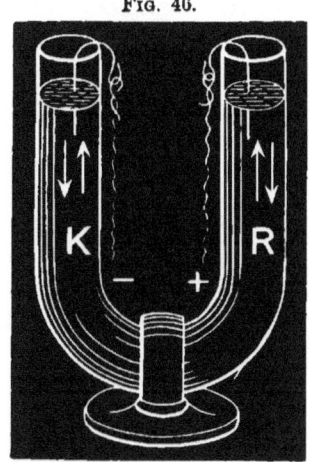

FIG. 46.

In all decomposition of substances containing acid and an alkali, the acid appears at the positive and the alkali at the negative electrode.

In all reduction of the metals from the solution of a metallic salt, the acid appears at the positive, and the metal at the negative electrode. That is, *oxygen and the acids appear at the positive, hydrogen and the metals at the negative electrode.*

Whenever a compound is decomposed by electricity, *electro-negative* elements appear at the *positive*, and the *elector-positive* at the *negative* electrode.

757. **The quantity of electricity required to produce chemical action is enormous.**—It has been demonstrated that it requires, to decompose *one grain* of water, an amount of frictional electricity equal to that furnished by the discharge of an electric pane having thirty-two acres of surface—" equal to a very powerful flash of lightning."

Physiological Effects.

758. **The physiological effects of the voltaic current** depend upon the number of the elements or pairs, rather than their size. No sensation is felt, with dry hands, from one or even a small number of pairs. From fifteen carbon couples a smart twinge is felt, reaching to the shoulders. The sensation is not like that produced by statical electricity, being continuous and less severe. It is only at the making and breaking of the contact that the *shock* is felt. The current from a very powerful battery becomes painful and dangerous, and even fatal.

The effect of the voltaic current on bodies of dead animals is peculiarly striking. It causes violent contractions of the muscles, similar to those of living beings. Experiments have been performed upon the dead bodies of criminals, which resulted in causing the lungs to act, the eyes to open, the lips to move, the body to writhe, and the face to contort, assuming expressions strange and horrifying beyond description.

Contact with but one of the poles of the battery produces no effect.

A gentle current hastens the germination of seeds and growth of plants.

CHAPTER XVI.

ELECTRO-DYNAMICS.

ELECTRO-MAGNETISM.

759. **Relation between magnetism and electricity.—** Magnetic and electric fluids have many analogous properties. In each case fluids of the same name repel, whilst those of an opposite name attract. A stroke of lightning often reverses the poles of magnets, and sometimes destroys magnetism. They have also points of dissimilarity. Magnetic fluids are not transmitted through conductors as electrical fluids are. Magnets do not return to a neutral state when brought into contact with the earth. Magnetism can only be developed in a few, whereas electricity may be developed in all bodies.

With such analogies on the one hand, and dissimilarities on the other, nothing conclusive could be affirmed respecting the identity of these two wonderful agents, until, in 1819, Ersted discovered that they are intimately allied, if not identical.

760. **Ersted's discovery.—** Though many philosophers had sought to evolve the phenomena of magnetism from the voltaic battery, they had experimented without connecting the poles. Ersted simply *closed the battery circuit by a conductor ; and discovered at once the important fact that wire (of whatever metal), connecting the poles, acts upon the magnetic needle as if the wire itself were a magnet.*

This constitutes the discovery of the fundamental principle of *electro-magnetism.*

761. **Figure 47.—Action of an electric current upon a magnet or needle.—**If positive electricity flows from south to north over a horizontal wire placed in the magnetic meridian, a needle would have its north end deflected to the *west,* if it is placed *below* the wire; and to the *east,* if placed *above* the wire. If the needle is placed on the *east side* of the wire, its north end is *depressed,* if on the *west side* of the wire, the north end of the needle is *raised*. If the current passes from the north to the south, the movements of the needle are all reversed.

By means of the rectangle surrounding the needle, in the figure, the current can be sent above, or below, or above and below, the needle, by changing the conjunctive wires in the connecting sockets at N and S.

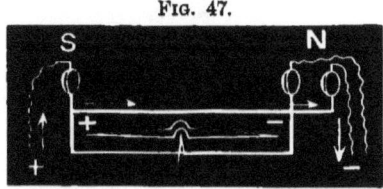

FIG. 47.

If the current passes around above and below the needle, in opposite directions, the opposite currents, instead of neutralizing, will assist each other, and the needle will move in accordance with the first direction of the current. Galvanometers are constructed upon this principle.

762. **Figure 48.—Galvanometers or multipliers.**—Galvanometers are instruments for measuring the force of electric currents. As just stated, the force exerted upon the needle is greater when the current is passed *once around*, instead of simply over or under it. It is also true that the force is multiplied in proportion to the number of times the conducting wire is passed around the needle.

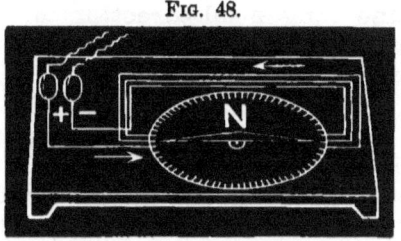

FIG. 48.

The figure represents a coil of copper wire, making thirty or forty convolutions around the needle, N, the wire being first covered with silk or cotton, like common bonnet-wire, for the purpose of insulating it. A graduated circle is fixed on the stand or bottom board, to measure the amount of the deflection. The coupling sockets serve to connect the ends of the coiled wire with the poles of the battery, the arrows indicating the direction of the current.

By this instrument a feeble current becomes quite sensible. For particular purposes, and when the current is very feeble, many thousand convolutions of fine wire are employed.

763. **The directive action of the earth.**—In all experiments the needle is more or less governed by the magnetic force of the earth, which must be neutralized in the experimental needle in order to accurately estimate the force of electrical currents; for, before the needle can be moved by the current, it must first exert a force equal to that exerted upon it by the earth's magnetism. This directive force of the earth is overcome by what is called the *astatic needle*.

764. **Figure 49.—The astatic needle** consists of two needles, placed and held one above the other, with their poles reversed, as indicated by the signs plus and minus.

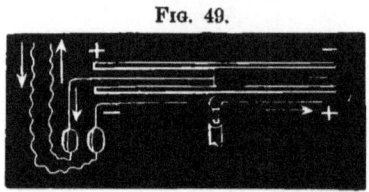

FIG. 49.

This needle, as shown in Fig. 56 (634), is suspended by a fine fibre of raw silk. The two needles are made so as not to quite neutralize each other, thus giving the system a slight directive force. While this needle is thus rendered nearly neutral as to the earth's magnetism, it is not thereby rendered less responsive to the electric current, as both needles tend to turn in the same direction, in consequence of one being *within* and the other *above* the coil or bend of the wire. Hence, the *astatic needle* is indifferent to the influence of the earth, and very sensitive to electric currents.

765. **The electro-magnetic force is exerted in a lateral and tangential direction** to the electric current. The electro-magnetic current or force moves at right angles to the course of the conjunctive wire.

A sewing needle or a bar of soft iron, held vertically on *one* side of the wire, instantly becomes a magnet, with its north pole toward the earth. If the bar or needle be held vertically on the *other* side of the wire, its polarity is instantly reversed. If the bar be revolved around the wire in a vertical plane, at right angles to the wire or current, it retains its polarity in every position. If it be a steel bar, it retains its magnetism after the current ceases.

The relation of the electro-magnetic and the electric currents, above explained, will be more easily remembered if thus stated: Suppose *the positive electric current or wire to enter the feet and pass out of the head of the observer, his face being turned toward the magnet, then the north pole of the magnet is invariably deflected to the left.*

When a magnetic pole is influenced by an electric current, it does not move either *directly toward* or *directly from* the conducting wire, but it tends to rotate around it, showing that the magnetic force of the electric current is exerted in a direction tangential to the conducting wire or current.

766. **Ampere's electro-magnetic theory** *supposes magnetism to be due to currents of electricity flowing around the ultimate molecules of a magnet, always in the same direction.* Or, differently stated, we may imagine each of the magnetic molecules to be replaced by a conjunctive wire bent on itself, in which a constant current of electricity is maintained, as from a battery. The interior currents neutralizing each other, the total effect is the same as that of a set of surface currents flowing around the magnet, in the direction of the hands of a watch, if the south end of the magnet is placed against the back of the watch, all acting at right angles to the axis of the magnet.

Hence, as the magnetic needle strives to place itself at right angles to the path of the current on the conjunctive wire, it follows that *currents of the magnet seek a parallelism to that in the conjunctive wire.*

767. **Figure 50.—Mutual action of electric currents.—** In accordance with the theory just stated, *parallel currents attract each other when they flow in the same direction; and repel each other when they flow in opposite directions.* These facts may be demonstrated by means of a *floating current,* which may be produced by fixing a piece of zinc and a piece of copper, Z and C, in a disk or float of cork, and connecting the metals with a wire; placing the whole in a dish of acidulated water, as shown. Along the conjunctive wire will flow an electric current from the copper to the zinc. If now a conjunctive wire of a battery be stretched between the two hands, and held parallel to the conjunctive wire of the floating couple, as shown by the long arrow, with the currents flowing in opposite directions, as indicated by the several arrows, the repulsion will be manifested by the movement of the floating couple. If either current be reversed, so that they will flow in the same direction, the conjunctive wire of the floating couple will assume a position parallel to the conjunctive wire of the battery.

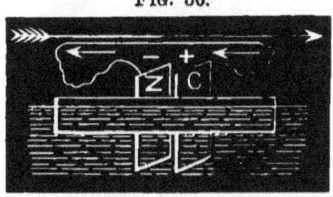

FIG. 50.

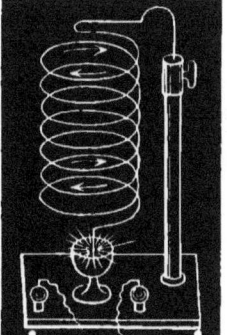

FIG. 51.

768. **Figure 51.—Attraction of currents shown by the oscillating spiral.—** The attraction of currents, flowing in the same direction, is neatly illustrated by the spiral wire, suspended as shown, and dipping into a glass of mercury. Below the platform the two poles of a battery are brought, one in contact with the mercury and the other with the metallic standard. As the current flows over the wire, as indicated by the arrows, each turn of the spiral attracts the next turn, shortening the spiral, and breaking the mercurial connection, which causes a *spark.* The attraction ceasing by the current being broken, the weight of the spiral again restores the connection, and so on, causing a continuous movement and emission of the spark.

769. Figure 52.—Action of magnets upon currents.—It has been shown that electric currents exercise a directive force not only upon magnets, but also upon each other. This figure will illustrate that magnets exert a directive force upon currents.

FIG. 52.

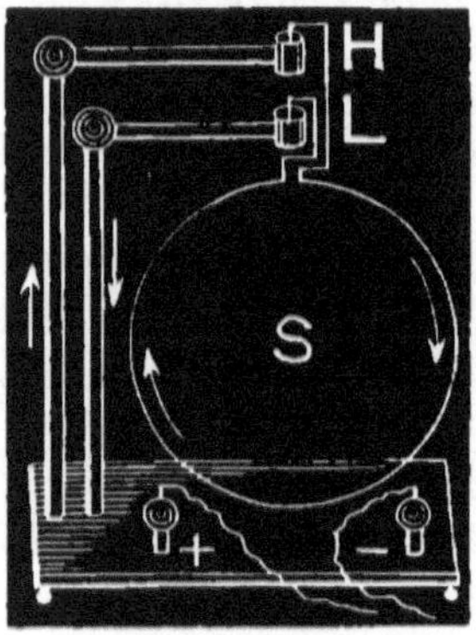

A copper wire, S, is bent into a circular form, and suspended to the two arms of the supports, as shown. The ends of the wire are tipped with steel, and rest in the cups of mercury, H and L, so that the wire hoop is free to revolve around the vertical line passing through the points. The wires of a battery, passing through the sockets, connect, under the platform, with the supports and mercurial cups, H and L. On completing the circuit, the current flowing as indicated by the arrows, the plane of the hoop, S, will assume the *east and west* direction, and come to rest at right angles to the magnetic meridian.

If a bar-magnet be held horizontally within the hoop, the axis of the magnet being in the plane of the circle, the hoop will turn around and come to rest at right angles to the axis of the magnet.

This experiment, made first by Ampere, is the reverse of Ersted's experiment and discovery (760).

770. Figure 53.—A single helix.—If the conjunctive wire be wound into a helix, as shown, and a current passed over it in the direction indicated by the arrow-points, the effects of the current, from R to L, will be neutralized by its return from L to Y, and there will

FIG. 53.

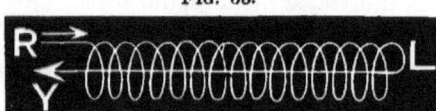

remain only the effect due to its spiral revolution about LY. The effect of the helix thus wound, is reduced solely to the influence of a series of equal and parallel circular currents. This form of the wire is called a *solenoid*.

771. **Figure 54.—A double helix.**—If a silk-covered wire be coiled into a double helix, as represented in this figure, and its ends tipped with steel points, P, and set into the cups of mercury (Fig. 52), the coil will be free to rotate in a horizontal plane. Thus placed, and the current passed over it, in the direction indicated by the arrows, it will assume the north and south direction, with the end O to the north.

It takes this direction because

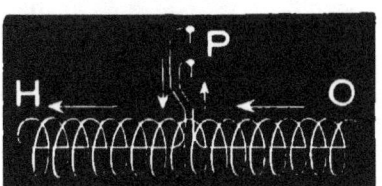

Fig. 54.

in no other position would the currents pass at right angles to the magnetic meridian of the earth (769).

The solenoid, therefore, simulates, in all respects, the character of a magnetic needle, although possessing not a particle of iron or steel in its composition.

If another solenoid, having a current passing over it, be presented to this one, they will manifest all the phenomena of attraction and repulsion, in the same manner as if the two helices or solenoids were magnets.

772. **Figure 55.—Magnetizing by the helix and electrical current.**—If a bar of iron or steel be placed within a helix of wire, as shown, and an electric current passed over the wire, the bar instantly becomes a magnet. If the bar is soft iron it loses its magnetism the instant the current is broken; if it be steel, it retains its magnetism.

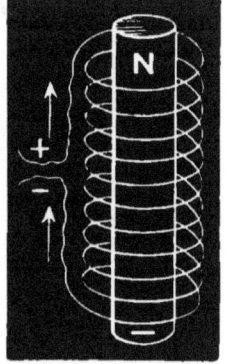

Fig. 55.

Insulated wire is employed for this purpose, and the coils repeated one over another, in order to multiply the convolutions.

Determining the poles.—If the bar stands on the floor or table and the current flows from plus (+) to minus (−), beginning at the top and moving around the bar in the direction that the hands of a watch move, the N pole will be uppermost, as shown in the figure. If the wire is wound in the opposite direction, the S pole will be uppermost. Magnets may be thus made with statical electricity.

The explanation of this is, that each volute of the helix, carrying an electric current, is itself an active magnet; hence, under the united influence of a great number of such circular and parallel currents or magnets, the *coercitive force* (627) of the bar is decomposed and active magnetism is induced.

773. **Figure 56.—Electro-magnets** are masses of soft iron wound with coils of insulated copper wire. They vary in form and size. The figure represents the form of those designed to sustain great weights. The spools, J and H, are virtually one: the direction of the whorl is only apparently reversed.

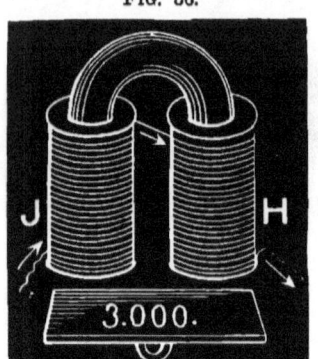

FIG. 56.

The surprising power of the horse-shoe electro-magnet is developed only when the armament is in contact with the poles. Their polarity is reversed, instantly, by reversing the poles of the battery.

Magnets of this kind are made that support 3,000 pounds or more; yet this enormous power can be alternately induced and paralyzed any number of times, and with inconceivable rapidity, by merely moving the end of a small wire through an almost inappreciable space.

774. **Bodies suspended without contact.**—If one end of a bar of iron be brought near to one extremity of a longitudinal helix, vertically placed, and connected with the battery, it will be attracted by and drawn into the helix, where it will remain suspended without visible contact or visible support, so long as the current is passing. Iron bars weighing nearly 100 pounds have been thus suspended in the air. Of course they fall the instant the current is broken.

775. **Utilization of electro-magnetic force.**—Many attempts have been made to utilize this very controllable force, by applying it as a motive-power; but the force (diminishing even more rapidly than the square of the distance from the magnet increases) acts through such a limited distance, that no important results have been achieved in its application, where much power is required. Jacobi expended $120,000, granted him by the Russian government, in experimenting for this purpose. The most valuable utilization of the electro-magnet is made in its application to the electric telegraph.

The Electric Telegraph.

776. **First experiments in electrical telegraphing.**—The observation of a simple phenomenon or the discovery of a single fact should not entitle the observer or discoverer to all the credit which mankind are ever ready to bestow for the achievement of great results;

for the discovery and practical application of all the general principles necessary to the accomplishment of any great good, are seldom, if ever, the result of single-handed efforts.

For example, in 1747, Watson employed frictional electricity, and transmitted messages over a single wire two miles or more in length, the wires being attached to chimney-tops. We now speak of Morse's electric telegraph worked by galvanic batteries; yet, Galvani never saw a galvanic battery, nor had he any knowledge of such a thing. All along from Watson's time to the date of Morse's improvements, extensive efforts were made, in several countries, to utilize the electric current by its application to telegraphy. Since Morse's improvements were made, many other useful and minor improvements have been invented.

The distinctive feature of Morse's invention, first employed in 1844, consists in permanently recording the message on paper, instead of indicating it by such signals as require to be observed at the instant they are made or not at all.

An electrical signal telegraph was employed in France, for ordinary purposes, until it was replaced by Morse's registering apparatus.

777. Figure 57.—Morse's recording telegraph.—The electro-telegraphic device embraces—

First, an apparatus for producing a force, by which mechanical results can be produced and controlled at a great distance. This apparatus consists of the *battery*, the *long wires*, and the *electro-magnet*.

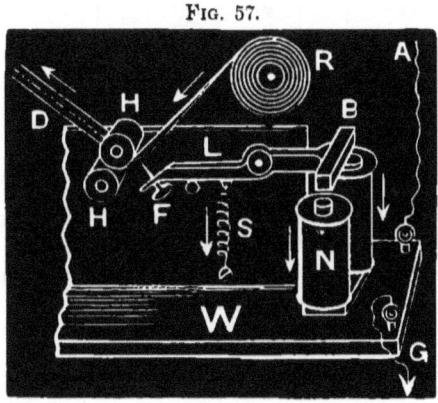

FIG. 57.

Second, two other instruments, one for dispatching the message, and the other for receiving or recording the message.

The receiving or recording instrument. This consists essentially of a simple lever, L, called the pen-lever, provided with a soft armature, B, arranged over the poles of an electro-magnet, N. This lever, L, can be worked on its centre or fulcrum by an operator situated in an office hundreds of miles away, by his completing and breaking the circuit. In the opposite end of the pen-lever, is fixed a point, F, called the *pen*. HH are a pair of rollers, which slowly revolve with uniform velocity, by means of clock-work. The rollers draw between them a fillet of paper, from the roll R. As the paper passes along, the pen, F, at the will of the distant operator, is made to puncture it, leaving the pin-hole mark. If the operator allows the current to flow for an instant, the pen will make an elongated impression or mark on the paper. So, by varying the length of time during which the current is interrupted, various marks, which represent the letters of the alphabet, are made. Some of these marks are seen on the fillet of paper at D. A feeble spring, S, serves to draw the pen from the paper, and lift the armature, B, from the magnet. The current is received by the wire A, and returned by the wire G, which passes into the earth, the earth serving as the return wire.

The various characters, which represent the letters of the alphabet, are shown in the following table:

MORSE'S ALPHABET.

a . —	j — . — .	s . . .
b — . . .	k — . —	t —
c . . .	l ——	u . . —
d — . .	m —— ——	v . . . —
e .	n — .	w . ——
f . — .	o . .	x . — . .
g —— —— .	p	y . . — . .
h	q . . — .	z . . . .
i . .	r . . .	

The instrument for transmitting the message is a simple apparatus, consisting of a light lever provided with a suitable knob, called the *finger-key*, for receiving the pressure of the fingers. It is so arranged that by gently pressing upon the knob, the circuit is *completed*, and, when the fingers are raised, the lever is lifted by a spring, which *interrupts* the current. By varying the length of time during which the current is interrupted and closed, all the above alphabetical characters can be made at the receiving station, many miles away.

House's telegraph, or the printing telegraph, differs from Morse's and others principally in an arrangement whereby the message, as transmitted, is printed in ordinary capital letters, on a narrow strip of paper, at the rate of two or three hundred letters per minute.

778. **The earth circuit.**—Watson and Franklin, in 1747-8, used the earth as the return circuit, but they employed statical or frictional electricity. Yet it was, for a long time, believed to be necessary, in using voltaic electricity, to employ two wires. Steinheil, in 1837, obviated the whole resistance of the return wire, by burying a large plate of copper at each station with which the circuit wire communicated.

This method, now universally adopted, of returning the current through the earth, and so obviating the resistance and expense of the return wire, must be considered one of the most important discoveries in connection with the telegraph.

Insulators.—Telegraphic wires are insulated from the poles, that support them from one station to another, by means of glass or some other non-conducting holders.

779. **Figure 58.—Electro-dynamic induction.**—*The revolving electro-magnet* operates by virtue of the attraction of dissimilar, and repulsion of similar, poles of magnets.

This instrument consists of a permanent U-magnet, between the poles of which an electro-magnet is horizontally supported on a vertical spindle passing through its axis, as shown. The wires of the electric battery pass through ivory collars, inserted in a frame, which sustains the upper end of the spindle. By a simple contrivance, called a break-piece, the continuity of the current is interrupted twice in every revolution, when the armature is in the position shown in the figure. The magnetic force being thus paralyzed, the momentum of the mass carries the armature by the poles of the fixed magnet, when the battery connection is again completed.

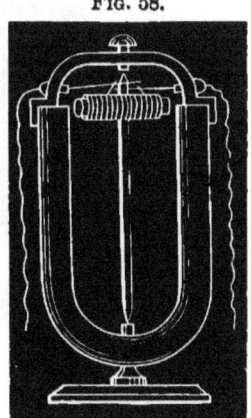

FIG. 58.

The revolution is caused by the mutual repulsion, and then the mutual attraction, between the two opposite poles of the two magnets, as the connection is broken and the poles of the electro-magnet are reversed.

The velocity with which the electro-magnet in this little machine revolves, is from 2,000 to 3,000 revolutions per minute, attended with from 4,000 to 6,000 reversals of polarity, and as many intervals of cessation of the magnetic force.

780. Figure 59.—Cause of the earth's magnetism.—If a metal ring be warmed at one point only, as with a spirit-lamp, no electrical effect is produced; but if the lamp be moved along the ring, an electric current is set up, which traverses the ring in the same direction the lamp has taken.

In this manner the sun continually heats successive portions of the earth, causing currents of electricity to flow around the globe from east to west, in a direction at right angles to the line joining the magnetic poles.

A magnetic needle, therefore (as also the double helix, Fig. 54), points north and south, because it is only when in this position that its electrical currents can be parallel to those of the earth (766–7).

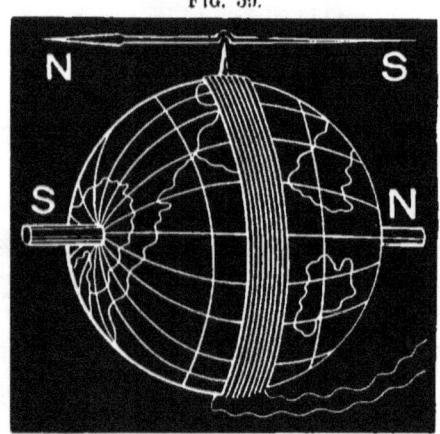

Fig. 59.

The figure represents a small artificial globe, surrounded by a coil of insulated wire, surmounted by a magnetic needle. When the current of the battery is transmitted through the wire, the needle points to the north pole of the globe.

The dip of the needle is accounted for in the same manner. At the polar regions it dips in order to place its currents parallel with those of the earth.

781. Figure 60.—Magneto-electricity.—Electricity generated by a magnetized bar is called *magneto-electricity*. If one of the poles of a powerful bar-magnet, A, be introduced within a helix of insulated wire, S, an electric current will be excited in the wire every time the magnet enters or leaves the coil. The current excited by one pole of the magnet will flow in the opposite direction to that induced by the opposite pole. An electro-magnet will produce the same results.

without alternately inserting and withdrawing it, provided its polarity be alternately reversed, by reversing the battery current.

The production of electric currents in this way is what might be expected, since magnetism is induced in a bar of iron by passing an electric current around it on a helix (772).

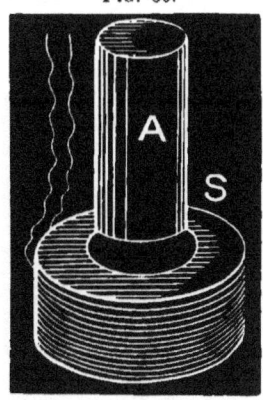

Fig. 60.

782. **Magneto-electric machines** are constructed in various ways, so as to reproduce all the phenomena of statical and voltaic electricity from permanent magnets.

Such machines are often employed in making application of electricity in the treatment of various diseases.

783. **Figures 61 and 62.—Diamagnetism.**—It has been demonstrated that all bodies, solids, liquids, and gases (which have been tested), are subject to magnetic influence.

If any substance be suspended between two opposite powerful poles of electro-magnets, as seen in the figures, it will assume either the axial position, as shown in Fig. 61, or the equatorial position, shown in Fig. 62.

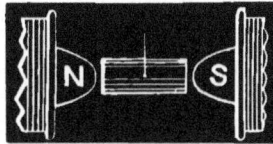
Fig. 61.

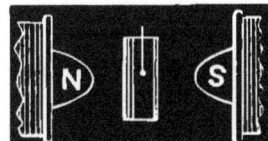
Fig. 62.

If the body assume the *axial* position, it shows it is attracted by the poles, and, therefore, it is said to be *magnetic* (615).

If the body assumes the *equatorial* position, it shows it is repelled by the poles, and, therefore, it is said to be *diamagnetic;* and the phenomena developed have received the general name of *diamagnetism.*

Fluids are tested by putting them in small homœopathic vials. Pieces of wood, meat, apples, leaves of trees, and every sort of substance, will assume either the axial or equatorial position.

The following list expresses the order of some of the most common *magnetic* substances, viz.: iron, nickel, cobalt, manganese, palladium, crown-glass, platinum, osmium. The zero is *vacuum.* The *diamagnetics* are arranged in the inverse order, commencing with the most neutral: arsenic, ether, alcohol, gold, water, mercury, flint-glass, tin, antimony, phosphorus, bismuth.

784. **Figure 63. Currents induced by other currents.—**
It has been shown that the electricity of the machine acts upon bodies by induction (668). And as it has been shown, also, that a wire carrying a voltaic current acts like a magnet, it ought, by induction to excite a current in another wire near it. By experiment this is found to be the case. The induced current, however, is excited only when the battery current begins to flow and when it ceases.

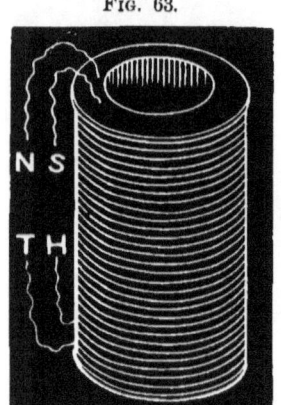

Fig. 63.

Two insulated wires are wound in the form of a helix, so that they run side by side through their whole course. Let NS represent the battery wire, and TH the other wire.

If a voltaic current be passed through NS, there is instantly a current produced by *induction* in TH, in the opposite direction. This current in TH ceases in a moment; but when the battery current is stopped or broken, then there is a secondary current produced in TH, in the opposite direction to that first produced. These are called induced currents, or secondary currents, but they are only momentary.

To facilitate the completion and interruption of the battery current with great rapidity, one end of the conjunctive wire may be attached to a coarse steel file or rasp, over which the other end of the wire is drawn, each notch on the rasp breaking the current.

785. **Figure 64.—Induced currents of different orders.**
—By using spirals of copper ribbon, alternating with helices of insulated wire, and arranging them in the order shown in the figure, it is demonstrated that secondary, or induced currents, produce other induced currents of the second, third, fourth, and even as high as the ninth order.

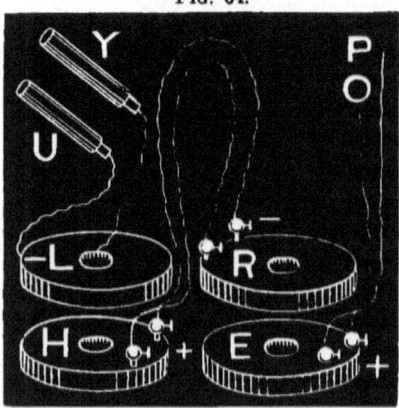

Fig. 64.

At every rupture of the primary, or battery current (from OP), the spiral ribbon, E, induces a *secondary* intense current, of opposite name, in the helix R, while the spiral of ribbon, H, receives from R a quantity current, inducing a *tertiary* intense current in the second helix, L, which will be realized by grasping the handles, U and Y.

786. **The properties of induced currents** are the same as those of other electrical currents. They produce violent shocks, give sparks, decompose water, salts, etc., and act upon magnets.

The longer the wires the more powerful the currents.

787. **Figure 65.—Thermo-electricity.**—If the junction of two metals, of unlike crystalline texture and conducting power, is heated, an electric current will flow from one to the other. Electricity thus produced is called *thermo-electricity.*

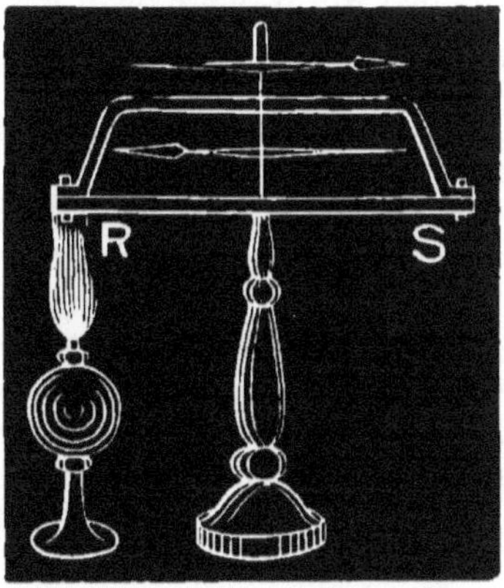

Let RS be a bar of bismuth, tin, lead, or zinc, over which place a strip of copper, binding the ends together with solder or rivets. Place between them an astatic needle (764). If the junction at R be heated, as by the spirit-lamp, the needle will be deflected in one direction; if the other junction, S, be heated, the needle will turn in the opposite direction.

FIG. 65.

Thermo-electric currents are developed by unequally heating different parts of the same metal (780).

Intense effects, analogous to those of the voltaic pile, are obtained from a compound thermo-electric series, if half of the solderings are heated and the other half cooled.

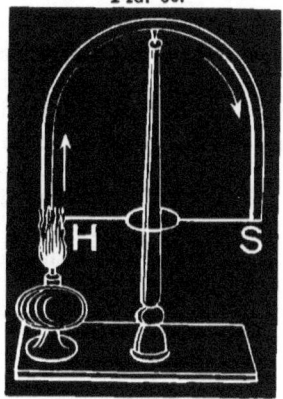

FIG. 66.

788. **Figure 66.— The thermoelectric revolving arch.**—A delicate reaction between the magnetism of the earth and the electric current may be had by this instrument. The arch is a piece of brass wire, nicely adjusted on a pivot at the top of the support, having its two ends connected to German silver wire, HS, encircling the support. If the stand be so placed that the wire, HS, points east and west, upon heating the junction at the east the arch will rotate. The thermo-electric current will be set in motion from the German silver, through the heated junction to the brass and through the arch to the German silver. The faces of the arch thus acquire polarity, the face turned to the north exhibiting south polarity. The arch, therefore, will move round to present its other face to this pole; but, in so doing, the other junction is brought into the flame, and the direction of the current reversed; this changes the polarity of the faces, and the arch again moves on; thus a slow but continuous revolution is produced.

If the arch be mounted upon one of the arms of a U-magnet, the rotation will be more rapid than in the above case.

ORGANIC ELECTRICITY.

789. **Animal electricity.**—It has been demonstrated that a current of positive electricity is always circulating from the interior to the exterior of a muscle. There is also an electrical current from the outer, or cutaneous, to the inner, or mucous, surfaces (722).

790. **Electrical animals.**—It has long been known that certain fishes possess the power of communicating an electric shock to persons handling them. The most remarkable of these are the *torpedo*, the *silurus electricus*, and the *gymnotus*. The electric organs of these animals bear a resemblance to the voltaic pile.

The most remarkable of these animals is the gymnotus, or electrical eel, found in abundance, by Humboldt, in South America. They are about five or six feet long. Electrical experiments are performed with them by means of two copper clasps, by which the animal is seized near the head and tail. It is found that the part nearest the head is positive, and that nearest the tail negative. The shocks received from this little animal are sufficient to throw a man upon the floor, magnetize needles, produce sparks, kill fish as if they were struck by lightning, deflect the galvanometer, produce chemical decomposition, heat small wires red-hot, and destroy the lives of large animals, even horses and mules, when attacked by them in their native waters.

791. **Electricity of plants.**—It is estimated that a surface of 100 square yards covered with vegetation, disengages, in a day, more negative electricity than is required to charge the most powerful Leyden battery.

SOLAR SYSTEM.

Fig. 1.

CHAPTER XVII.

(CHART NO. 9.)

ASTRONOMY.

Definitions, Introductory Observations, and Theories.

792. **Astronomy** (signifying the laws of the stars) is that branch of Physics or Natural Philosophy which treats of the heavenly bodies—the Sun, Planets, Satellites, Comets, and Fixed Stars.

793. **The general divisions of the subject** are—
1st. *Descriptive astronomy*, which treats of the magnitudes, distances, and densities of the heavenly bodies, and the phenomena dependent on their motions, such as day and night, the seasons, eclipses, etc.

2d. *Physical astronomy*, which treats of the causes of planetary motion, and the laws by which the movements of the heavenly bodies are regulated and maintained.

3d. *Practical astronomy*, which explains the construction and use of astronomical instruments, and the application of astronomical calculations.

794. **Different classes of heavenly bodies.**—The heavenly bodies are divided into three classes or systems, viz., the *solar system*, the *fixed stars*, and *comets*.

795. **Extent of space.**—There are no bounds to space. It is illimitable. If we imagine an indefinite number of objects, as arrows, to start from any point in space, and to fly, in straight lines, in different and opposite directions, with the speed of light or lightning, for billions of billions of years, they would then be no nearer to any bounds of space than before they started.

796. **Magnitude of heavenly bodies.**—Our vision being so limited, and the mind so familiar with objects of small magnitude, it is hardly possible to appreciate the real magnitude of even the earth on which we live. Yet the great green earth is, relatively, but an almost invisible speck within the boundless empire of Omnipotence.

Our own sun, which is but one of the minor countless stars, is a million and four hundred thousand times larger than the earth.

797. The number of the heavenly bodies.—It is estimated that one hundred millions of stars are visible through the telescope, which cannot be discovered with the naked eye. Yet all these, we may believe, are no more than a drop of water to the ocean, compared to the countless suns and systems of worlds that move in unmeasured orbits beyond the utmost reach of the telescope.

798. Distances between heavenly bodies.—Our notions of distance are so far influenced by the limited spaces over which we travel, it is no easy task of the mind to appreciate even 240,000 miles, the distance between the earth and the moon. The nearest fixed star, Sirius, is more than 20,000,000,000,000, or twenty millions of millions of miles from the earth. Yet it is believed, and partially proved, that other stars are five hundred times this distance from the earth. Light, travelling at the rate of 192,000 miles per second, would require 170 years to reach the earth from some of the stars of the sixth magnitude; while Herschel says that light would be *millions* of years in coming from some of the stars seen through his 40-feet telescope.

799. The orbital motions of heavenly bodies.—All the heavenly bodies embraced in the solar system are in motion. Not only do the satellites move around the planets, but the planets move around the sun, and the sun moves around some other body as its centre. And it is believed, and in some cases demonstrated, that all the so-called fixed stars revolve around other centres, each carrying with it a system of planets and satellites; and the central sun of these suns, around other orbs; and so on.

The extent of these orbital movements varies, of course, with different bodies. The distance of the sun's remotest planet, Neptune, is 2,862,000,000 of miles; while the distance of the sun from its own central orb is so great, that it requires 18,000,000 of years to complete one revolution, though it travels at the rate of 20,000 miles per hour.

800. The velocity of heavenly bodies.—The velocity of heavenly bodies is inconceivable. Mercury, the swiftest of our planets, flies in its orbit at the rate of about 100,000 miles per hour; and the earth about 68,000 miles per hour. The sun, carrying with itself thousands of comets, and all her planets and their satellites, travels around its central body, as above stated, at the rate of 20,000 miles per hour; while some of her comets, in some parts of their orbits, fly with the amazing swiftness of a *million miles an hour*.

Notwithstanding the vast magnitude and number of the heavenly bodies, and the immense extent of their orbits, and the inconceivable velocity of their movements, yet there is *room* for them all; and in their midst is the Great Unseen Hand that guides them.

801. **Early observations of astronomical phenomena.—** Observations of important astronomical facts and phenomena were made at an early date by the Egyptians, Chaldeans, Indians, and Chinese, who possessed many rules and methods of astronomical calculations.

The oldest recorded observations are those of the Chinese. Their annals contain an account of a conjunction of five planets at the same time, which occurred one hundred years before the flood. The truth of this account is confirmed by mathematical calculation.

The Greeks doubtless derived much of their knowledge of this science from Egypt.

The first of the Greek philosophers who taught astronomy was Thales, of Miletus, about 640 years before the Christian era. Then followed Anaximander, Anaximenes, Pythagoras, and Plato. Some of the views of these philosophers were correct, but they failed to produce a connected and complete system, and were unable to demonstrate their hypotheses.

802. **Ptolemy's Great System.—**Having collected the opinions of all antiquity, and those of the philosophers that preceded him, Ptolemy, an Egyptian philosopher, composed a work of thirteen books, called the Great System.

Though Pythagoras taught that the Sun was the centre of the universe, and that the earth had a diurnal motion on its axis, and an annual motion around the Sun, yet Ptolemy, who flourished 130 years after Christ, rejected these teachings of Pythagoras, as contrary to the evidence of the senses, and endeavored to explain the celestial phenomena by supposing the earth to be the centre of the universe, and all the heavenly bodies to revolve around it; that the earth was a plane, instead of a globe; and that it was inhabited only on one side; that the stars were supported in their places by being set or fastened into arches or hollow spheres, etc.

In explaining the celestial phenomena, however, upon his hypothesis, he met with a difficulty in the apparently stationary attitude and retrograde motions which he saw the planets sometimes have. To explain this, however, he supposed the planets to revolve in small circles, which he called epicycles, which were, at the same time, carried around the earth in larger circles, which he called deferents, or carrying circles.

803. **Copernicus' theory.**—About the middle of the 15th century, Copernicus, a native of Prussia, having an intense passion for the pursuit of astronomy, quitted the profession of medicine and turned his attention to this science. He conceived the idea that simplicity and harmony should characterize the arrangements of the planetary system. In the complication and disorder which he saw in the hypothesis of Ptolemy, he perceived insuperable objections to its being considered as a representation of nature.

In the opinions of the Egyptian sages, and those of Pythagoras and others, Copernicus recognized his own earliest convictions, that the earth was not the centre of the universe. By laboring more than thirty years, in clearing away various hypotheses, and gradually expelling the difficulties with which the subject was encumbered, he was permitted to see the true system of the universe.

The sun he considered as immovable, in the centre of the system, while the earth revolved around it, between the orbits of Venus and Mars, and produced, by its rotation about its axis, all the diurnal phenomena of the celestial sphere. The other planets he considered as revolving about the sun, in orbits exterior to that of the earth.

804. **Kepler's discoveries and laws.**—At the close of the 15th century, Kepler, a German, discovered and proved that the orbits of the planets, and those of their moons, were not circular, but elliptical. The supposition that they were circular had caused much error. He next determined the dimensions of the orbits of the planets, and found to what their velocities, and their motions through their orbits, and the times of their revolutions, were proportioned; which are truths of the greatest importance to the science.

The three great laws of Kepler are:

1st. *That all the planets revolve in elliptical orbits, having the sun in one of their foci.*

2d. *That the radius vector passes over equal areas in equal portions of time.*

3d. *That the square of the times of the revolutions of the planets around the sun, are proportional to the cubes of their mean distances from the sun.*

805. **Galileo's discoveries.**—While Kepler was discovering and demonstrating the above important laws, Galileo, an Italian, having improved the telescope, was discovering mountains and valleys upon the surface of the moon; satellites or secondaries were discovered revolving about Jupiter; and Venus, as had been predicted by Copernicus, was seen exhibiting all the different phases of the moon.

ASTRONOMY. 417

All these discoveries and many others served to confirm the Copernican theory, and to show the absurdity of the hypothesis of Ptolemy.

806. **Newton's discovery.**—Notwithstanding the important discoveries of Copernicus, Kepler, and Galileo, the force which causes the planets to revolve around in their orbits was yet unknown. To ascertain the cause of the planetary motions, and explain the laws by which these vast orbs, in their rapid flight, are directed, each in its own definite course, constituted the discovery of the illustrious Newton. He conceived the idea, that the same force which causes apples to fall from a tree might extend to the moon, and hold it in its orbit, and cause it to revolve around the earth. By a series of calculations he established the fact, that the same force which causes a pebble to fall from the hand to the ground, carries the moons in their orbits around the planets, and the planets and comets in their orbits around the sun. This force is the power of *attraction.*

THE SOLAR SYSTEM.

Classification.

807. **Figure 1.—The Solar System** (see frontispiece).—By the *Solar System* is meant the Sun and the heavenly bodies that revolve about it, including the satellites.

Planets (signifying *wanderers*) are primary or secondary. The *primary* planets are those which revolve around the sun as their proper centre; one of which is our earth. The *secondary* planets are those which revolve around the primaries, as they are carried around the sun; one of which is our moon.

The primaries are usually called *planets ;* the secondaries are called *moons,* or satellites.

The planets are dark opaque bodies, and shine only by reflecting the light of the sun. They may be distinguished from the stars by their *steady* light; while the stars appear to twinkle. They seem to change their relative places in the heavens, for which reason they are called planets; while those luminous bodies which are called fixed stars appear to preserve the same relative position.

Primary planets.—There are ninety-three primary planets; eighty-five of which revolve in orbits very near each other, situated between Mars and Jupiter; and, on account of their small size and star-like appearance, they are called *Asteroids.* Only five of these are represented in the illustration (Fig. 1).

27

The other eight of the primaries are, beginning with the one nearest to the Sun, Mercury, Venus, Earth, Mars (Asteroids), Jupiter, Saturn, Uranus, Neptune.

Satellites or moons.—There have been discovered twenty secondaries or satellites. Of these, the earth has *one*, Jupiter *four*, Saturn *eight* (and two rings), Uranus *six*, Neptune *one*.

The interior and exterior planets.—The *interior* planets are those whose orbits lie *within* the orbit of the earth. The *exterior* planets are those whose orbits lie *without* the orbit of the earth.

Comets are a singular class of bodies, belonging to the Solar System, revolving in greatly elongated orbits, and various in form; some being globular, and others having long trains of light. Two of these, S and R, are represented in the illustration (Fig. 1); only a part of the orbit of R being shown, while that of S is complete.

By *solar bodies* is meant those bodies which belong to the solar system.

808. **Figure 2.—Relative magnitudes of the planets.**— No. 1 represents one of the larger Asteroids; No. 2, the moon (drawn much too large); No. 3, Mercury; No. 4, Mars; No. 5, Venus; No. 6, the Earth; No. 7, Neptune; No. 8, Uranus; No. 9, Saturn; No. 10, Jupiter.

ASTRONOMY. 419

809. **Figure 3.—Approximate relative distances of the planets.**—Though it is impossible, as hereafter shown, to represent

FIG. 3.

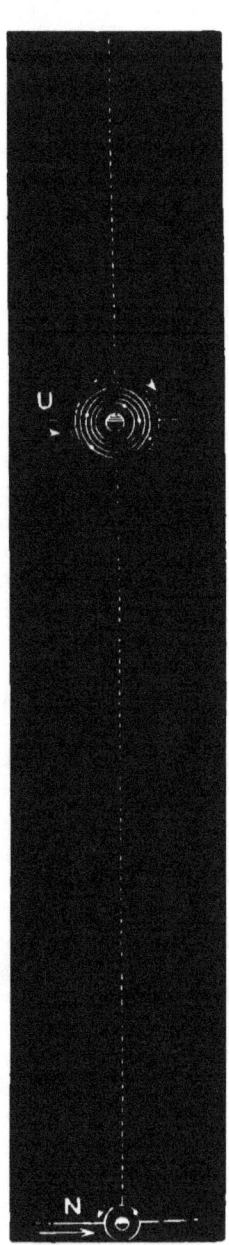

on paper the correct relative distances between heavenly bodies, yet this diagram will convey a less erroneous idea than Fig. 1. It is drawn *on the chart* to a scale of about 66,000,000 miles to the inch.

The first circle, which is drawn very near to the sun, represents the orbit of Mercury; the next beyond, the orbit of Venus; the circle, E, represents the orbit of the Earth; the line, M, a part of the orbit of Mars; the lines, A, a few of the orbits of the Asteroids; J, the orbit of Jupiter; S, the orbit of Saturn; U, the orbit of Uranus; and N, the orbit of Neptune.

The reader will imagine the cut on the right to be placed at the bottom of the one on the left, as it is drawn on the chart, where the figure is four feet long.

The arrows, in all cases, represent the direction of the motions of the various bodies. In these several orbits are represented the primaries, together with the satellites and their orbits.

810. **Impossibility of delineating the solar system.**—The magnitude of heavenly bodies and the distances between them are so great, and yet so unequal, that if the smallest and nearest are drawn on a scale large enough to be seen, then the largest become so great and the most distant ones so remote that they exceed all possible extent of drafting surfaces, as of paper, cloth, etc.

To illustrate (by referring to the diagram, Fig. 1), suppose the orbit of the earth (third from the centre) to be 95,000,000 of miles (its real distance) from the sun. Now, as the distance of Neptune, the most remote planet, is 2,862,000,000 of miles from the sun, it would require, in order to carry out the scale, that the outer circle of the diagram be about fourteen feet in diameter.

The fixed stars, as represented, appear to be situated just beyond the solar system, which conveys a very erroneous idea. The distance from the sun to Neptune is only 2,862,000,000 of miles, while the distance from the sun to the *nearest* star is 20,000,000,000,000 of miles. Therefore, to carry out the scale, the nearest of these stars, in the drawing, should be placed about a mile and a third beyond the orbit of Neptune.

Solar system represented by real objects.—To assist the student to obtain a more correct notion of the relative magnitudes and distances relating to the solar system, than can be gained from any possible delineation, let him imagine a globe of wood, representing the sun, a trifle less than five feet in diameter, to be placed upon an extensive plane, as a field of ice. Then, place about it other globes, of the sizes of those shown in Fig. 2, *on the chart*, which represent the relative magnitudes of the planets.

First take *Mercury*, No. 3, size of a small *pea*, and place it 194 feet from the sun; then *Venus*, No. 5, size of a *small cherry*, and place it 362 feet from the sun; next the *Earth*, No. 6, also the size of a *cherry*, and place it 500 feet from the sun; next *Mars*, No. 4, size of a *cranberry*, and place it 762 feet from the sun—omitting the *Asteroids*, some of which would be about the size of *pin-heads* and others the size of No. 1—then *Jupiter*, No. 10, size of a *small citron*, and place it 2,600 feet, or about half a mile from the sun; next *Saturn*, No. 9, also the size of a *citron*, and place it 4,768 feet from the sun; then *Uranus*, No. 8, size of a *peach*, and place it 9,591 feet, or about two miles from the sun; and last of all *Neptune*, No. 7, also the size of a *peach*, and place it 15,366 feet, or nearly three miles from the sun.

Now, at these several distances, describe circles around the globe of wood. These circles will represent the several orbits of the planets—the orbits themselves being, of course, only *imaginary circles*.

Hence it is seen that, although Mercury in this scale is only the size of a small pea, yet Neptune is nearly three miles from the sun, having an orbit of about *six miles* in diameter.

Representation of the motions of the planets.—To imitate the motions of the planets at the distances, as above described, suppose these small bodies to revolve around the globe of wood at such rates of velocity that each will describe its own diameter, as follows: Mercury in 41 seconds; Venus, in 4 minutes 14 seconds; the Earth, in 7 minutes; Mars, in 4 minutes 48 seconds; Jupiter, in 2 hours 56 minutes; Saturn, in 3 hours 13 minutes; Uranus, in 12 hours 16 minutes; and Neptune, in 23 hours 25 minutes.

The Sun.

811. **Influence of the sun.**—The sun is the centre of the solar system, around which all other solar bodies revolve, and by which they are all held in their orbits. It is a vast and fiery orb, the great source of light and heat to all the planets. All animal and vegetable life and growth are due to its influence.

812. **Magnitude of the sun.**—The sun is by far the largest of the heavenly bodies whose dimensions are known. Its diameter is 889,000 miles, and its volume 1,400,000 times larger than that of the earth, and 500 times larger than all the other bodies of the solar system put together. If it were placed where the earth is, it would extend 203,000 miles, on all sides, beyond the orbit of the moon. The weight of the sun is about 750 times the mass of all the rest of the solar system.

813. **The distance of the sun** from the earth is 95,000,000 of miles. It is useless, however, to attempt to impress the mind with any definite idea of such a vast distance. A ball fired from a cannon, and flying with undiminished velocity, would be 1,300 years in reaching the sun. Yet it requires great imagination to conceive the passage of a cannon-ball for 1,300 years, moving at the rate of 16 miles per minute, and its arrival at the sun.

814. **Telescopic view of the sun.—Dark spots.**—Viewed through the telescope, the sun presents the appearance of an enormous globe of fire, frequently in a state of violent agitation. *Dark spots*, of irregular form, frequently pass across its disk from east to west, in the period of nearly fourteen days. Some of these are 50,000 miles in breadth.

The sun was, for ages, and till lately, thought to be a globe of real fire; but it is now believed to be an opaque body, surrounded by a luminous atmosphere.

Motions of the sun.—The sun has three motions. 1st, It rotates on its axis once in 25 days, 9 hours, 36 minutes; its axis inclining 7¼ degrees to that of the ecliptic (847). 2d, It revolves around the centre of gravity of the solar system (845). 3d, It revolves around some other central body (893).

The Primary Planets.

815. **Periodic revolutions.**—The planets revolve around the sun from west to east. The passage of a planet from any point in its orbit, around to the same point again, is called its *periodic revolution*, and the time occupied in making such revolution is called its *periodic time.*

The periodic times of the planets are as follows:

Mercury	88 days.		Jupiter	11 years,	317 days.
Venus	225 "		Saturn	29 "	175 "
Earth	1 year.		Uranus	84 "	
Mars	1 " 322 "		Neptune	164 "	

Neptune travels in one periodic revolution as far as a train of cars, at 30 miles per hour, would travel in about 70,000 years.

The periodic time of a planet is called its *year;* hence, the year and seasons of Neptune are 164 times as long as those of the earth, and those of Mercury only about a quarter as long as ours.

816. **Velocity of the planets in their orbits.**—The following table shows the distance each planet moves in its orbit, per hour:

Mercury	95,000 miles.	Jupiter	30,000	miles.
Venus	75,000 "	Saturn	22,000	"
Earth	68,000 "	Uranus	15,000	"
Mars	55,000 "	Neptune	11,000	"

It will be noticed that the nearer the planet is to the sun, the greater its velocity, and the shorter its periodic time.

817. **Diurnal revolution of the planets.**—Besides the motion of the planets around the sun, they have a motion around their respective axes, producing the vicissitudes of day and night. The times of the revolutions, and, consequently, the length of days of the several planets, are as follows:

Mercury	24 hours.	Jupiter	10	hours.
Venus	$23\frac{1}{4}$ "	Saturn	$10\frac{1}{4}$	"
Earth	24 "	Uranus	unknown.	
Mars	$24\frac{1}{2}$ "	Neptune	unknown.	

It will be observed that the days and nights of Jupiter and Saturn are only about five hours long.

The fact that the planets revolve around their axes, is ascertained by observing spots on their surfaces, and noting the direction of the motions of these spots, and the times of their reappearance.

818. **Magnitude of the planets.**—As previously stated, Fig. 2 (808) represents the *relative* magnitudes of the planets. Their *absolute* magnitudes, expressed by the length of their diameters, are as follows:

Mercury	3,000 miles.	Jupiter	89,000	miles.
Venus	7,700 "	Saturn	79,000	"
Earth	8,000 "	Uranus	35,000	"
Mars	4,200 "	Neptune	35,000	"

819. **Relative magnitude of the planets,** the earth being taken as the unit (see Fig. 2).

Mercury	$\frac{1}{18}$.	Jupiter	1,400.
Venus	$\frac{9}{10}$.	Saturn	1,000.
Earth	1.	Uranus	90.
Mars	$\frac{1}{6}$.	Neptune	90.

The Sun.. ....1,400,000.

820. The distances of the planets from the sun, expressed in miles, are as follows:

Mercury	37,000,000	Jupiter	495,000,000
Venus	69,000,000	Saturn	900,000,000
Earth	95,000,000	Uranus	1,800,000,000
Mars	145,000,000	Neptune	2,800,000,000

Such are the vast distances over which the sun sends its genial rays to light and warm and develop its attendant worlds.

821. Density of the planets.—By density is meant compactness or closeness of parts. The weight of a body, of given bulk, depends upon its density.

The relative densities of the planets, and the substances with which they most nearly agree in weight, the earth being taken as the standard or unit of comparison, are as follows:

Mercury	3 — lead.	Jupiter	$\frac{1}{4}$ — water.
Venus	$\frac{8}{10}$ — earth.	Saturn	$\frac{1}{10}$ — cork.
Earth	1	Uranus	$\frac{1}{4}$ — water.
Mars	$\frac{8}{10}$ — earth.	Neptune	unknown.

The value of this table is seen in the following paragraph.

822. Attraction of the planets.—Attraction or gravitation is the force with which bodies are drawn toward each other. The essential law of this force is, that *its intensity is inversely as the square of the distance between the bodies* (47).

The attractive force of a planet, therefore, depends upon its *distance, density,* and *bulk.* Weight is the amount of attraction at the surface (39); hence, the weight of a given body, as a square foot of iron, upon the surface of any planet, will depend upon the density and bulk of the planet.

Assuming some object, as a piece of iron, to weigh on the earth 1 pound, then its weight on other planets will indicate their power of attraction, as compared with the earth. It would weigh on the several planets, respectively, as follows:

Mercury	1 lb. 1¼ ozs.	Jupiter	2 lbs. 8 ozs.
Venus	0 " 15 "	Saturn	1 " 5¼ "
Earth	1 "	Uranus	0 " 12¼ "
Mars	0 " 8 "	Neptune	unknown.

On the Sun the same object would weigh 28 lbs. 5½ ozs.

A person weighing 150 lbs. on the Earth, would weigh 375 lbs. on Jupiter, and only 75 lbs. on Mars.

823. **Light and heat of the planets.**—The intensity of solar light and heat diminishes as *the square of the distance from the sun increases;* hence, the amount of light and heat derived from the sun by the several planets is very unequal.

The relative intensity of these two elements or agents on the different planets (their intensity on the earth being taken as the unit of comparison), is as follows:

Mercury	6½	Jupiter	$\frac{1}{27}$
Venus	2	Saturn	$\frac{1}{90}$
Earth	1	Uranus	$\frac{1}{368}$
Mars	½	Neptune	$\frac{1}{1300}$

If the average temperature of the earth is 50° F., that of Mercury would be 325°, or 113° above that of boiling water, and that of Neptune 1,300 times lower than the average of the earth.

It does not necessarily follow that the heat is proportionate to the light received by the respective planets, as various local causes may modify the temperature. Mercury, for instance, may be surrounded by an atmosphere that arrests the light and screens the planet from the intense heat of the sun; while the atmospheres of the more distant planets, as Saturn, Uranus, etc., may act as a refracting medium, to gather and concentrate light and heat upon these planets.

The Asteroids.

824. **The Asteroids** (Figs. 1 and 3).—As previously stated (807), there are *eighty-five* small planets, whose orbits are situated between those of Mars and Jupiter, *five* of which are represented by the five lines drawn near each other (Fig. 1). Four of these, Ceres, Pallas, Juno, and Vesta, were discovered, respectively, in the years 1801, 1802, 1804, and 1807. In 1845, another, Astræa, was discovered; since when they have been discovered, one after another, until, up to 1865, they number in all *eighty-five*.

The asteroids all revolve at nearly the *same distance* from the sun, and perform their periodic revolutions in nearly the *same time*. Their orbits are *more* eccentric than those of the larger planets, and some of them *cross each other,* as shown in Fig. 1. From these and other circumstances, it is believed that these eighty-five small planets are the fragments of a large planet which once revolved between Mars and Jupiter, and which, by some convulsion or violence, was burst asunder.

Vesta appears like a star of the sixth magnitude, and is the only asteroid that can be seen with the naked eye.

The diameter of Ceres is 1,585 miles; that of Pallas 2,025 miles.

ASTRONOMY.

The following table comprises the names, distances, and periodic times of the Asteroids.

No.	Names.	Distance from the sun in Miles.	Periodic time in Days.	No.	Names.	Distance from the sun in Miles.	Periodic time in Days.
1.	Ceres............	262,764,110	1,680	44.	Nysa..........	230,886,670	1,384
2.	Pallas............	263,186,670	1,684	45.	Eugenia.......	260,568,660	1,659
3.	Juno............	253,524,410	1,592	46.	Hestia........	241,296,960	1,470
4.	Vesta............	224,327,205	1,325	47.	Aglaia........	273,641,325	1,786
5.	Astræa..........	244,767,500	1,511	48.	Doris.........	295,150,275	2,000
6.	Hebe............	230,414,710	1,380	49.	Pales.........	293,180,925	1,980
7.	Iris.............	226,683,965	1,346	50.	Virginia......	251,844,430	1,577
8.	Flora...........	209,131,670	1,193	51.	Nemausa......	225,901,640	1,339
9.	Metis...........	226,644,350	1,346	52.	Europa........	294,330,710	1,992
10.	Hygeia..........	299,190,435	2,041	53.	Calypso.......	248,224,930	1,543
11.	Parthenope.....	232,995,860	1,403	54.	Alexandra.....	258,811,540	1,642
12.	Clio.............	221,617,045	1,301	55.	Pandora.......	263,965,195	1,692
13.	Egeria..........	244,684,375	1,510	56.	Melete........	245,428,700	1,517
14.	Irene...........	245,989,960	1,522	57.	Mnemosyne....	299,942,265	2,049
15.	Eunomia.......	251,197,100	1,570	58.	Concordia.....	255,971,895	1,615
16.	Psyche..........	277,661,440	1,825	59.	Olympia.......	257,714,955	1,632
17.	Thetis..........	235,002,450	1,421	60.	Echo..........	227,203,995	1,351
18.	Melpomena....	218,125,700	1,271	61.	Danaë.........	285,377,815	1,902
19.	Fortuna.........	231,929,960	1,393	62.	Erato..........	297,430,750	2,024
20.	Massilia........	228,891,670	1,366	63.	Ansonia.......	227,654,200	1,355
21.	Lutetia.........	231,365,945	1,388	64.	Angelina......	254,437,170	1,601
22.	Calliope........	237,080,005	1,440	65.	Cybele........	325,996,965	2,322
23.	Thalia..........	249,738,280	1,557	66.	Maja..........	252,117,278	1,579
24.	Themis.........	299,244,965	2,043	67.	Aria..........	229,421,200	1,371
25.	Phocœa........	228,100,700	1,359	68.	Leto..........	258,652,510	1,641
26.	Proserpine.....	252,327,505	1,581	69.	Hesperia......	290,924,010	1,957
27.	Euterpe.........	222,993,975	1,314	70.	Panopæa......	253,662,065	1,594
28.	Bellona.........	263,641,815	1,689	71.	Feronia.......	203,783,740	1,148
29.	Amphitrite....	242,712,270	1,492	72.	Niobe.........	261,841,470	1,671
30.	Urania..........	224,598,905	1,328	73.	Clytie.........	254,435,102	1,589
31.	Euphrosyne....	299,835,010	2,048	74.	Galatea........	244,645,135	1,509
32.	Pomona.........	245,958,705	1,522	75.	Euridice.......	251,121,955	1,570
33.	Polymnia.......	272,372,125	1,773	76.	Freia..........	302,955,000	2,080
34.	Circe............	255,388,690	1,610	77.	Frigga.........	253,521,413	1,597
35.	Leucothea......	288,216,755	1,880	78.	Diana.........	262,418,500	1,677
36.	Atalanta........	261,126,975	1,665	79.	Eurynome.....	232,294,000	1,397
37.	Fides...........	255,981,165	1,568	80.	Sappho........	215,390,742	1,271
38.	Leda............	260,270,075	1,656	81.	Terpsichore...	263,981,794	1,693
39.	Lætitia.........	263,091,765	1,683	82.	Alemene.......	257,814,930	1,659
40.	Harmonia......	215,379,060	1,247	83.	Beatrix........	232,297,428	1,382
41.	Daphne.........	228,032,015	1,358	84.	Clio...........	225,900,271	1,324
42.	Isis..............	231,219,455	1,387	85.	Io.............	252,117,294	1,572
43.	Ariadne........	209,364,610	1,195				

The Secondary Planets or Satellites.

825. **Compound motion of the satellites.**—The relative magnitudes and distances of the satellites are not shown in Figs. 1 and 3, though their approximate relative *distances* are represented by Fig. 11 (853), which will be referred to again.

As the primaries revolve around the sun, so the satellites revolve around their primaries. Like the primaries, they all revolve from

ASTRONOMY. 427

west to east, except those of Uranus and Neptune, which revolve from east to west, as indicated by the arrow in Fig. 1.

Satellites not only revolve around the primaries, but accompany these in their journeys around the sun, besides revolving around their own axes; hence they have a compound motion. The actual track, therefore, which a satellite pursues through space is by no means a simple curve, as will be seen by observing the track of the Moon, as represented in Figs. 13, 14, and 15 (855, 859, and 860), to be explained hereafter.

Like the primaries, the satellites receive their light and heat from the sun. They serve, in the economy of nature, to reflect the light of the sun upon their primaries; thus diminishing the darkness of their shadows or nights.

The following tables show the *magnitudes, distances,* and *periodic times* of the several secondaries.

826. **The Earth's satellite or Moon.**—The diameter of the moon is 2,162 miles; its mean distance from the earth is 240,000 miles; its revolution on its axis, called *synodic revolution*, takes place once in 29 days 12 hours 44 minutes 3 seconds; its *periodic or sidereal* revolution is accomplished in 27 days 7 hours 43 minutes 11¼ seconds. The moon will be more particularly described hereafter. See paragraphs 855 to 864.

827. **Jupiter's satellites** (Figs. 1 and 3).—The following table exhibits the magnitudes, distances, and periodic times of Jupiter's satellites.

DIAMETERS IN MILES.	DISTANCES.	PERIODIC TIMES.
1st 2,500	280,000	1 day 19 hours.
2d 2,200	440,000	8 " 12 "
3d 3,500	700,000	7 " 14 "
4th 2,890	1,200,000	6 " 16 "

828. **Saturn's satellites** (Figs. 1, 3, and 9).—The distances and periodic times of Saturn's satellites are as follows:

Distances.	*Periodic Times.*	*Distances.*	*Periodic Times.*
1st ..118,000—	22½ hours.	5th.. 336,000—	4 days 12 hours.
2d ..152,000—1 day 9 "		6th.. 778,000—15 " 22 "
3d ..188,000—1 " 21 "		7th.. 940,000—22 " 0 "
4th..240,000—2 " 17 "		8th.. 2,268,000—76 " 7 "

829. **Uranus' satellites** (Figs. 1 and 3).—The distances and the periodic times of the satellites of Uranus are as follows:

Distances.	Periodic Times.	Distances.	Periodic Times.
1st ..120,000	—2 days 12 hours.	4th .. 380,000	— 13 days 11 hours.
2d ..171,000	—4 " 3 "	5th .. 777,000	— 38 " 2 "
3d ..288,000	—8 " 17 "	6th . 1,556,000	—107 " 16 "

These satellites move from east to west, as before stated; hence their motion is said to be *retrograde*.

830. **Neptune's satellites** (Figs. 1 and 3).—So far as known, Neptune is attended by only one satellite. It revolves around its primary in 5 days 21 hours, at a distance of 236,000 miles. Its motion is *retrograde*, that is, from east to west, same as the satellites of Uranus.

Comets—their Nature, Orbits, Motions, etc.

831. **Nature and appearance of comets** (Fig. 1).—Comets are bodies which revolve around the sun. They are distinguished from the planets and other heavenly bodies by a luminous tail, which is usually on the opposite side from the sun; though some are destitute of this appendage, while others have several, spreading out like a fan. It is generally believed that comets are nothing but a mass of vapor, more or less condensed at the centre. Some are transparent throughout their whole extent, and not sufficiently dense to obstruct the view of stars in their range, while others have an opaque and solid nucleus, called the *head*, as represented at R and S, Fig. 1. The head is sometimes surrounded by an *envelope*, which has a cloudy or *hairy* appearance. Others seem to be only globular masses of vapor. Comets assume a great variety of shapes. Probably most of them are only gaseous. In short, very little is known of the physical nature of comets.

There is so little density to comets, it is doubtful if one would do much harm were it to come in collision with the earth; while it has been mathematically demonstrated that the chances of such an event occurring is only as 1 to 281,000,000.

832. **Orbits of comets** (Fig. 1).—The orbits of comets are generally very eccentric, as shown by the diagram. Some comets fly many billions of miles beyond the orbit of Neptune, and then return. Drawn by the attraction of the sun, so nearly in a direct line toward the sun, through such vast distances, they acquire an amazing velocity.

The comet of 1680 had a tail 96,000,000 of miles in length. Coming from a distance of 13,000,000,000 of miles, this comet swept around

ASTRONOMY. 429

through its perihelion, within 130,000 miles of the sun, with the immense velocity of a *million miles per hour;* subject to a heat of the sun thousands of times more intense than that of red-hot iron.

833. **The periodic times of comets** are very various; some being limited to a few years, while others extend through centuries. Up to the beginning of the 17th century no correct notions had been entertained in respect to the paths of comets, while now the elements of about 137 have been calculated. Of these, 30 passed between the sun and the orbit of Mercury; 44, between the orbits of Mercury and Venus; 34, between the orbits of Venus and the Earth; 29, between the orbits of the Earth and Jupiter.

The periodic times of *three* well-known comets are as follows: Encke's, 1,212 days; Biela's, 2,461 days; and Halley's, 28,000 days.

834. **The number of comets** is not known. The number observed since the Christian era is 650. The best judges believe there are many thousands; while M. Arago, by a certain theory, estimates them by the billions.

835. **The direction of the motions of comets** is not uniform, like the planets. They observe no one direction, as from west to east. They move in every possible direction. Some move from west to east, others from east to west, while others seem to come up from the immeasurable depths below the ecliptic. Others appear to come down from the zenith of the universe; while others come and go in every possible direction, seeming to dash through space and whirl around the sun promiscuously. Yet, of the hundred or more whose elements have been calculated, 49 move from east to west, and 49 from west to east.

Telescopic Views of the Primaries.

836. **A few particulars relating to the telescopic views of the primaries.**—They all have the same general *figure,* that is, *spherical* or *spheroidal,* Fig. 7 (850). They all seem to be surrounded by an *atmosphere* of greater or less density. Spots and belts seen upon their surfaces seem to be permanent, and indicative of divisions of land and water, like the seas and continents of the earth.

Of *Mercury* but little can be seen, owing to its obscurity, caused by its nearness to the sun. It is claimed, however, that spots and mountains have been seen upon its surface. It has a faint bluish tint.

The surface of *Venus* is variegated with mountains; some of which are estimated to be twenty miles high. The spots vary in form and number. The atmosphere of this planet is supposed to be very dense, but only about three miles deep. Its color is silvery white.

If the *Earth* were viewed with a telescope, say from Mercury, the continents and islands would appear brighter than the rest of the surface, while the oceans, seas, and lakes, reflecting less light, would appear less bright. As the earth revolves on her axis, these different shades of light or spots would be seen crossing the earth's disk in twelve hours; while clouds and snows would cause changes in its appearance, and show that the earth is surrounded with an atmosphere.

The surface of *Mars* is variegated with oceans, seas, continents, mountains, and vales, which are discerned with perfect distinctness and outlines. The color of this planet is red, which is supposed to be the result of a dense atmosphere.

The *Asteroids* are so distant and small, that little is known regarding their appearance. Seen through a telescope, they have a pale ash color.

The axis of *Jupiter* has so little inclination to the plane of its orbit, there can be but little or no change of seasons at the same parallels of latitudes, nor any difference in the length of its days and nights. Hence, there is perpetual summer in the equatorial regions, and perpetual winter in the polar regions. Viewed through a telescope, Jupiter appears to be surrounded by a number of luminous zones, usually called *belts*. These are parallel to the equator and to each other, but subject to considerable variation, both in breadth and numbers.

The surface of *Saturn*, like that of Jupiter, is diversified with belts and dark spots. That which distinguishes this planet from every other, and which renders it, of all others, the most interesting solar body, is a magnificent zone or ring, surrounding the planet. This peculiarity, the only one within the reach of telescopic observation, will be referred to again.

Uranus, through a telescope, exhibits a small, round, uniformly-illuminated disk, without rings, belts, or spots.

Neptune is too far away from the earth to present any striking peculiarities.

Orbits, Eccentricity of Orbits, etc.

837. **Figure 4.—Orbits are elliptical.**—The orbits of heavenly bodies are not circular, but elliptical; and the central body around which another revolves, is always situated in one of the two foci of the ellipse. The revolving body, therefore, is sometimes nearer to the central body than at others. For example, the body, S, which may represent the earth, is nearer to the sun than when it is at T. The orbits of some bodies are more elliptical than others; those of comets being the most so of any.

838. **The eccentricity of a planet's orbit** is the distance of its centre from the centre of the sun. For example, the dotted line

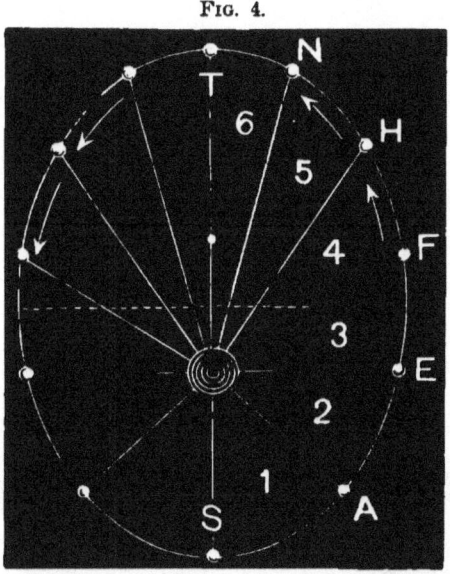

FIG. 4.

(Fig. 4) passes through the centre of the orbit, and the distance from the centre of this line to the centre of the sun below it, is the *eccentricity* of the orbit.

The eccentricity of the orbits of the several planets, expressed in miles, is as follows:

Mercury	7,000,000	Ceres	21,000,000
Venus	492,000	Pallas	64,250,000
Earth	1,618,000	Jupiter	24,000,000
Mars	13,500,000	Saturn	49,000,000
Vesta	21,000,000	Uranus	85,000,000
Juno	64,000,000	Neptune	unknown.

Although these distances seem very great, yet the orbits do not deviate so much from a circle as might be imagined at first thought. For instance, the mean distance of the earth from the sun is 95,000,000 of miles; hence, its eccentricity, being only 1,618,000 miles, would hardly be noticeable.

839. **Aphelion and perihelion.**—*Aphelion* is that point in the orbit of a planet which is at the greatest distance from the sun; and *perihelion* is that point in the orbit which is nearest the sun.

840. **The radius vector** is a line drawn from the sun to a planet in any part of the orbit, as the lines A, E, F, Fig. 4.

841. **The radius vector passes over equal areas in equal portions of time.**—That is, if the areas (Fig. 4) 1, 2, 3, 4, 5, and 6, are all equal to each other, then the planet, S, will pass from S to A in the same time that it would from A to E, and from E to F, and from F to H, and so on. If, then, the ellipse be divided into twelve equal areas, answering to the twelve months, the earth will pass through an equal area every month, but the space through which it passes in its orbit will be decreased during every month from the perihelion (at S) to the aphelion (at T), and increased during every month from the aphelion (at T) to the perihelion (at S).

842. **Figure 5.—Circular or curvilinear motion.**—It has been shown (58), that when a body is acted on by two forces perpen-

Fig. 5.

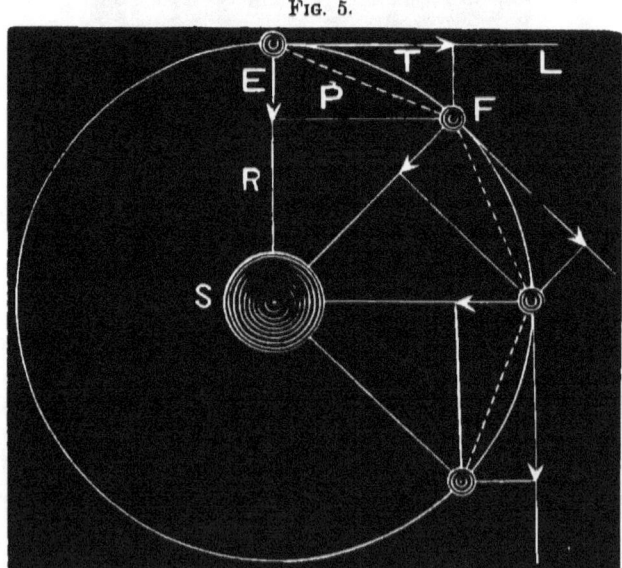

dicular to each other, its motion will be in a diagonal direction between the directions of the two forces.

Let S represent the sun, and E, the earth. Draw the line, R, and the line L, perpendicular to R. If the earth were moving in the direction of L, with a velocity that would carry it over the arrow, T, in the same time that the attraction of the sun would draw it over the arrow, E, then the resultant of the two forces would carry it over the dotted diagonal line to F. But the constant force of attraction of the sun causes the earth to move in the direction of the *curved* instead of the straight diagonal line. What is true in the passage of the earth from E to F, is also true for every other part of its passage around the sun, as will be understood by inspecting the diagram.

843. **Centripetal and centrifugal forces.**—If the sun should cease to attract the earth, the earth would instantly pass off in a straight line, tangent to its orbit. For instance, if the sun should cease its attraction when the earth is at the point E (Fig. 5), the earth would pass off in the direction of L. This tendency to pass off in a straight line is called the projectile or *centrifugal force*. Were this centrifugal force to cease, which it would do were the planet to cease moving in its orbit, then the sun would draw the planet to itself by the force of attraction. This force of attraction to the centre of motion is called the *centripetal* or *centre-seeking force*.

844. **Why the planets do not fall to the sun.**—From the explanation of the centrifugal and centripetal forces just given, it will be seen, that if these two forces were in exact and constant equilibrium the orbit of the planet would necessarily be a perfect circle. But as these two forces are not in constant equilibrium, the orbit is not a circle. Now, as these two forces are not in equilibrium, they must *alternately* preponderate, otherwise the planet would either pass off from the sun or be drawn to it. But within certain limits this is just what takes place.

The earth (Fig. 4) in moving from S to T, in the direction of the arrows, is passing further and further *from* the sun, and the sun's attraction is diminishing its velocity; and when the velocity is so far diminished that the centrifugal force is reduced to an equilibrium with the centripetal force, which takes place at the aphelion (or point T), the centripetal force begins to preponderate and increase the velocity; and when it has so far increased the velocity that the centrifugal force becomes greater than the centripetal, which takes place at the perihelion (or point S), then it begins again to sweep away from the sun; and thus the planet continues perpetually to revolve.

845. **Centre of gravity and motion of the solar system.**
—Not only do the planets revolve around the sun, and the satellites

around the planets, but between the sun and all the solar bodies that revolve around him there is mutual attraction. That is, each body attracts the sun just as much as the sun attracts it. In the same manner, each body of the solar system attracts every other body. Hence, in any given position of all the solar bodies, there is some one point which is the centre of gravity of the whole system. If, in this given position, all the bodies composing the solar system were rigidly fastened together, as by rods or bars, and the whole rigid system set to revolving, it would continue to revolve around this common imaginary centre of gravity. Now, as the quantity of matter in the sun is about 750 times greater than that of all the planets and other solar bodies, their whole united force of attraction is 750 times less than that of the sun. This common centre of gravity and motion, therefore, is not far *from* the sun. Were all the other solar bodies situated in their orbits on one side of the sun, even then he would not be more than his own diameter from this common centre of gravity and motion. Hence the sun is justly considered the centre of the system. As the planets are continually changing their relative positions around the sun, this common centre of gravity and motion is continually undergoing slight changes of position, as regards the solar system itself; yet it moves around some other central system at the rate of 20,000 miles per hour, completing its revolution in 18,000,000 of years.

846. **Planes of orbits.**—If a piece of wire be bent in the form of a circle, and paper stretched across and fastened to the wire, the wire may represent the *orbit*, and the paper the *plane of the orbit*. Of course, the orbit and plane are imaginary.

847. **Figure 6.—The ecliptic.**—Suppose the plane of the earth's orbit to pass through the centre of the sun, and to extend out on every side to the starry heavens. The great circle so made would mark the line of the *ecliptic*, or the sun's apparent path through the heavens. It is called the ecliptic, because eclipses happen when the moon is in or near this apparent path.

The *axis* of the ecliptic is an imaginary line passing through the centre of the sun, perpendicular to the plane of the earth's orbit, and the *poles* of the ecliptic are the extremities of this line.

In the figure the dotted line, OO, passes through the centre of the oval which represents the plane of the orbit of the earth, or the ecliptic; and the line E represents the axis of the ecliptic.

The other dotted line in the figure passes through the centre of the oval which represents the plane of the *equinoctial*. This plane passes through the centre of the earth, and coincides with the equator of the earth. The *axis* of the equinoctial is represented by the line A, which, of course, is parallel with the axis of the earth.

FIG. 6.

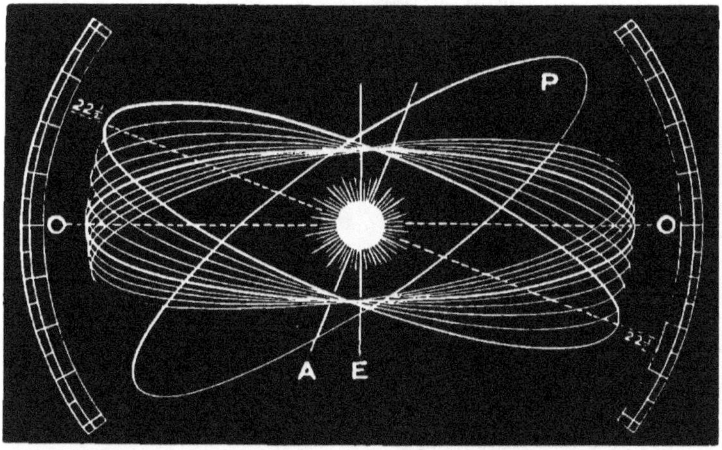

848. **Obliquity of the ecliptic** (Fig. 6).—The axis of the ecliptic. E. and the axis of the equinoctial, A, form an angle of $23\frac{1}{2}$ degrees: hence, the plane of the ecliptic forms the same angle with the plane of the earth's equator, or the equinoctial. This inclination of the ecliptic to the equator of the earth, is 23° 28', called the obliquity of the ecliptic. This will be more clearly shown hereafter.

849. **Inclination of the orbits of the planets to the plane of the ecliptic** (Fig. 6).—The planes of the orbits of the primary planets all pass through the centre of the sun, and form angles with the ecliptic or plane of the orbit of the earth. The inclination of the orbits to the plane of the ecliptic is shown in the following table, several of which are represented by the ovals in the figure.

Mercury	7	degrees.	Ceres	$10\frac{1}{2}$	degrees.
Venus	$3\frac{1}{2}$	"	Pallas	$34\frac{1}{2}$	"
Mars	2	"	Jupiter	$1\frac{1}{4}$	"
Vesta	7	"	Saturn	$2\frac{1}{2}$	"
Astræa	$7\frac{3}{4}$	"	Uranus	$\frac{3}{4}$	"
Juno	13	"	Neptune	$1\frac{3}{4}$	"

It will be observed that the orbit of Pallas, marked P. in the figure, forms a much larger angle with the ecliptic, OO, than any of the others.

850. **Figure 7.—The figure or form of the planets.**—The planets, and heavenly bodies generally, instead of being exactly round or spherical, as usually represented in the diagrams, are *oblate spheroids;* that is, their equatorial diameters are greater than their polar diameters.

It is supposed that the planets were once in a melted or liquid state.

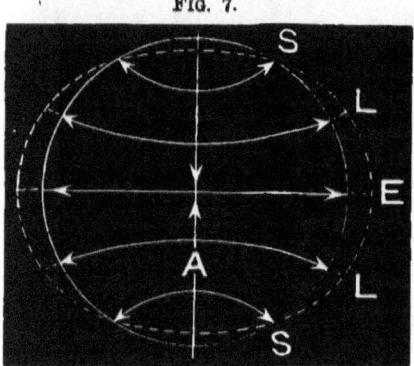

Fig. 7.

Suppose the figure to represent a planet in such a state, and perfectly round. If, now, it begins to revolve on its axis, A, it will take the form shown by the dotted line.

The reason of this is plain. At the equator, E, the centrifugal force is greater than at L and L; and greater at L and L than at S and S; while at the extremities of the axis A it is nothing. Hence, the relative intensity of this force, in different parts of the sphere, may be represented by the relative length of the several arrows; which show that the greatest elongation will be at the equator, and the greatest contraction at the poles.

The difference between the equatorial and polar diameters of some of the planets, is, respectively, as follows:

Earth.............. 26 miles. | Jupiter.......... 6,000 miles.
Mars.............. 25   " | Saturn.......... 7,500   "

Great magnitude and rapid rotation give Jupiter and Saturn a large difference between their equatorial and polar diameters.

851. **Figure 8.—Venus as morning and evening star.**
—Let the student suppose himself to stand with his face to the south, and the plane HH to represent the visible horizon; and the dotted line, the daily path of the sun; and S, the apparent position of the earth. The sun is shown as rising at E, and setting at W, and on the meridian at R, while Venus is seen revolving around the sun in the direction of the arrows, from west to east.

Now, it is obvious that when Venus is at T, or west of the sun, it passes below the horizon, or sets, as at N, before the sun; and rises before the sun, as at E. Hence, while Venus is in this part of her orbit, it will be *morning star.* When it is east of the sun, as at F. it will linger in the west after the sun sets, as at W, and is, consequently, *evening star.*

Fig. 8.

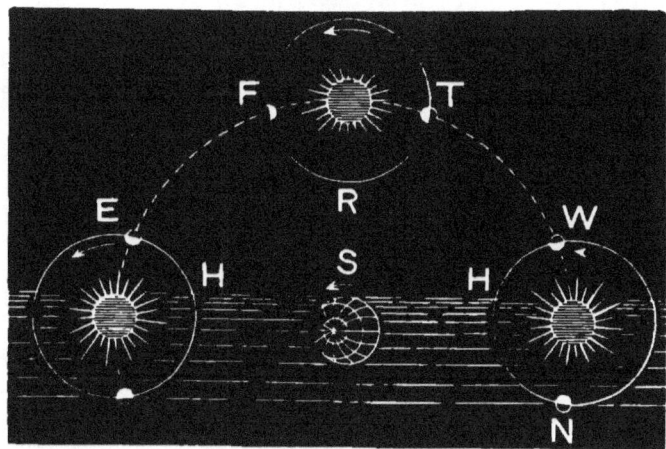

852. **Figures 9 and 10.—Saturn's rings.**—Fig. 9 represents Saturn as seen through the telescope. The light of the rings is more brilliant than that of the planet. The rings lie in the plane of

Fig. 9.

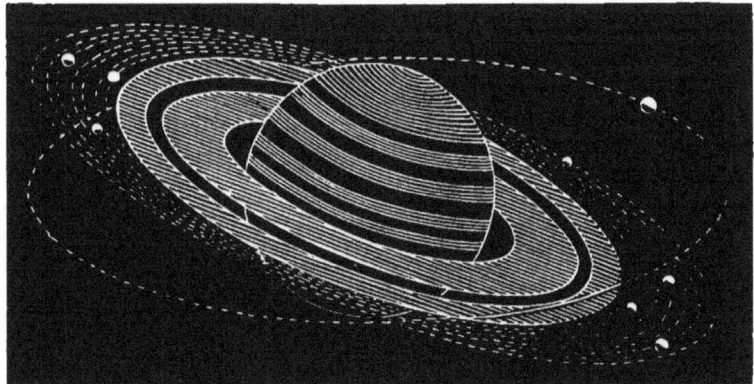

the planet's equator, and revolve around their centre of motion in the same time that the planet revolves on its axis.

As the axis of the planet, like that of all the other planets, *preserves its parallelism* in all parts of its orbit, the rings, as seen from the earth, will vary in appearance, as they are viewed in different parts of the planet's orbit. Sometimes they will be seen edgewise, when they will reflect no light to the earth, but appear like a dark line drawn across the planet. At other times they will be seen more or less obliquely, as

Fig. 10.

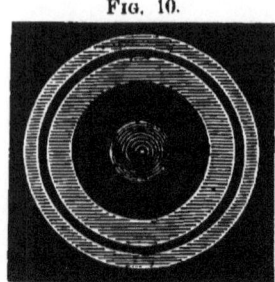

represented in Fig. 9; but they are never seen, from the earth, perpendicularly, as shown in Fig. 10. Were either pole of the planet exactly toward the earth, they would then present a perpendicular view.

As the planet revolves around the sun once in 30 years, of course, one side of the rings will be seen during part of this period, and the other side during the other part of its revolution.

As Saturn's moons (except one) revolve around the planet nearly in the plane of its equator, they are seldom eclipsed.

The diameters of the rings and their distances from the planet are as follows:

Diameter of the planet....................	79,000	miles.
Distance to the interior ring...............	20,000	"
Width of the interior ring..................	20,000	"
Space between the two rings...............	2,000	"
Width of the exterior ring	10,000	"
Thickness of the rings	100	"
The diameter of the outer ring.............	183,000	"

Hence, the thickness is but $\frac{1}{1830}$ part of the diameter, which, relatively, is thinner than a sheet of letter-paper. Yet these rings, according to Herschel, are composed of solid opaque matter, and probably are inhabited.

A third ring, interior to those above described, was discovered in 1850, by Mr. Bond, of Cambridge, Massachusetts.

To the inhabitants of Saturn these rings appear like vast arches, or semicircles of light, extending from the eastern to the western horizon. During the daytime, they appear dim, like a white cloud, but, as the sun goes down, their brightness increases.

Fig. 11.

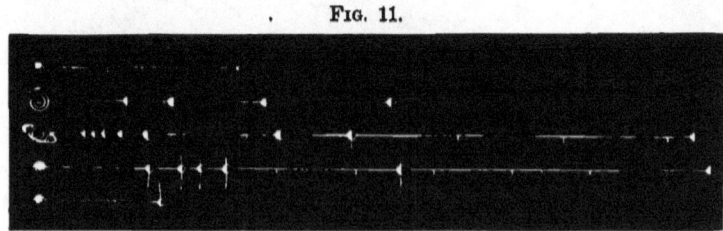

853. **Figure 11.—Distances of the satellites from their primaries.**—This figure represents the distances of the satellites from their primaries, measured in semi-diameters of the latter.

The line at the top represents the distance of the moon from the earth as being 60 times as far as the distance from the centre of the earth to its circumference. Each division of the line represents 10 semi-diameters of the earth. Taking the semi-diameter as 4,000 miles, we have 60 × 4,000 = 240,000 miles, as the distance of the moon from the earth. The short cross lines represent small parts of the orbits of the satellites.

The several planets, represented in the figure below the earth, are Jupiter, Saturn, Uranus, and Neptune. Compare 826, 827, 828, 829. and 830.

854. **Figure 12.—Solar and sidereal time.**—The rotation of the earth on its axis constitutes one of the most important elements in astronomical science; for the reason that it is taken as the standard of comparison for the revolution of all other celestial bodies.

The earth performs one complete revolution on its axis in 23 hours, 56 minutes, and 4.09 seconds. This is called *a sidereal day;* because, in that time, the stars *seem* to complete one revolution around the earth.

But, as the earth advances nearly one degree eastward, in its orbit, in the time it turns eastward around its axis, one rotation will not bring the same meridian around from the sun to the sun again; therefore, the earth must make somewhat more than one rotation to complete a *solar day.*

Suppose a man to be standing at a given point, at 12 o'clock, noon, on the earth, at E, under the line, SM; then, when the earth shall have turned on its axis so that he will again see the sun in the meridian, it will again be 12 o'clock, noon. The earth, in the meantime, will have

Fig. 12.

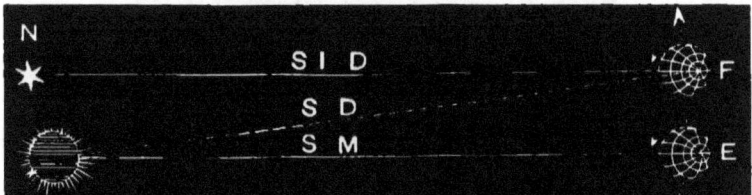

passed from E to F, and he will now see the sun in the direction of the dotted line, SD, instead of the direction of the line, SID, coming from the star, N.

The difference, then, between the *sidereal day* and the *solar day,* is the length of time it takes the earth to rotate from the line, SID, to the line, SD, which is *four minutes.*

440   ASTRONOMY.

If the earth were not revolving around the sun, the sidereal and solar days would be of the same length.

In 365 solar days the earth turns 366 times around its axis. This is true of all planets, whatever be the length of their days or years.

Sidereal days are always of the same length; but the solar days vary in length at different times of the year. This variation is due to two causes, namely, the inclination of the earth's axis to the plane of its orbit, and the inequality of its motion around the sun. Hence, the time shown by a well-regulated clock and that of a true sun-dial are scarcely ever the same. The difference between them, which, sometimes, is 16¼ minutes, is called the *Equation of Time*, or, the equation of solar days.

The Moon—its Path, Phases, etc.

855. **Figure 13.—The moon's path around the sun.—** Though the orbit of the moon is an ellipse, with respect to the earth, it is in reality an irregular curve, *always concave toward the sun*, as it will presently appear.

To obtain a correct idea of the path of the moon, it will be necessary to consider Figs. 14 and 15; but Fig. 13 will be first explained.

FIG. 13.

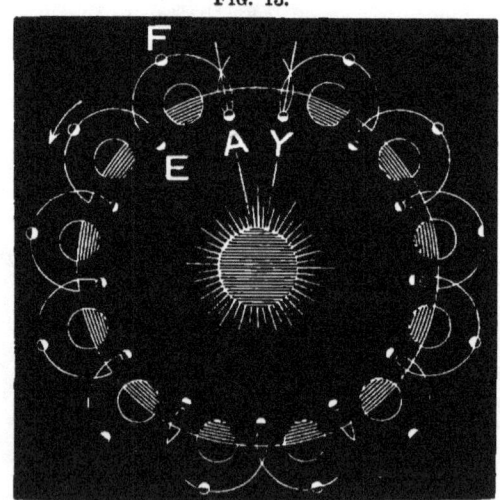

When the moon is at A, and the earth is in its orbit on the radius, A, it is *new moon*. In about 14 days the moon reaches F, and will be seen from the earth as *full moon*. In about 14 days more she reaches E, when it is new moon again; and so on, perpetually. When it is new moon, she is in *conjunction;* when it is full moon. she is in *opposition*.

It will be seen that the 12 revolutions of the moon, and the 1 revolution of the earth do not terminate at the same time. From the new moon, at A, around to the new moon, at Y, are just 12 lunar months or revolutions; but at this time the earth is 19° 20' short of her starting-point, or of completing her year. The lunar year, consisting of 12 synodical revolutions of the moon, or 346 days, is 19 days shorter than the civil year.

856. **Sidereal and synodic revolution of the moon.**—For the same reason that a sidereal day is shorter than a solar day (854), the sidereal revolution of the moon, which takes place in $27\frac{1}{3}$ days, is shorter than the synodic period, just explained, which takes place in $29\frac{1}{2}$ days.

857. **The rotation of the moon on her axis** takes place in the same time that she makes one synodic revolution. Hence, the same side of the moon is always turned toward the earth. Therefore, her day and night together cannot occur but once in $29\frac{1}{2}$ days. The moon, consequently, has but one night and one day in her year, containing, both together, 29 days, 12 hours, 44 minutes, and 3 seconds.

858. **The moon's libration in longitude and latitude.**— Owing to the ellipticity of the moon's orbit, and the consequent inequality of her angular velocity, she appears to *roll a little* on her axis from east to west, and west to east. This is called her *libration in longitude.*

The axis of the moon is inclined to the plane of her orbit only about one and a half degrees; but even this slight inclination enables us to see first one pole and then the other, in her revolution around the earth. These slight rolling motions are called her *librations in latitude.*

FIG. 14.

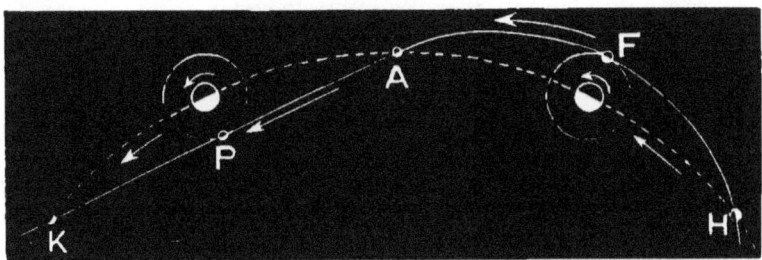

859. **Figure 14.—The actual path of the moon** is shown by the line, H, F, A, K. Suppose the dotted line to represent a part of the earth's orbit. At H the moon crosses the earth's track 240,000 miles behind the earth. Gaining on the earth, she passes it in 7 days at F, as a full moon. Continuing to gain on the earth, in 7 days more, she crosses its track at A, 240,000 miles ahead. From this point the earth gains on the moon for 7 days, when it overtakes her at P, where she is a new moon. The earth continues to gain for 7 days more, when the moon will again cross the track of the earth at K, 240,000 miles behind the earth; and so on perpetually.

The motion of the moon is never retrograde; that is, she never returns into her own path again; for the reason, that the earth moves much faster in its orbit than the moon in her orbit. In fact, the *forward motion* of the moon is never less than 67,500 miles per hour, for the reason that her hourly motion in her *own* orbit is only 2,300 miles per hour, while that of the earth is 68,000 miles per hour.

860. **Figure 15.—The moon's orbit always concave toward the sun.**—Let the long arrow represent the arc of the earth's orbit equal to that passed through by the earth during half a lunation.

Fig. 15.

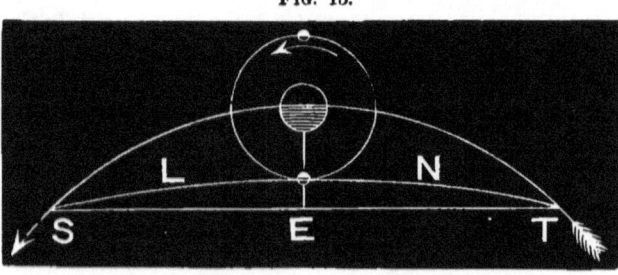

This arc and the cord, TS, being known, it is found that the cord, TS, must pass more than 240,000 miles within the earth's orbit; hence, the moon can never reach the cord, as at E; therefore the path of the moon, TNLS, must curve toward the sun.

861. **View of the earth from the moon.**—The appearance of the earth to the inhabitants of the moon is similar to the appearance of the moon to us. The earth, however, appears thirteen times larger than the moon. Hence it might be inferred that a fashionable trip, with those inhabitants of the moon who live on the side always turned *from* the earth, would be to journey around where they could view the sublime spectacle of a heavenly body, apparently *ten times* larger than any they had before seen.

862. **Figure 16.—The moon's phases.**—The parallel lines on the right represent rays of light from the sun; the circle around the earth, the orbit of the moon; A, B, C, D, F, G, H, the moon in different positions in her orbit. In all positions (except when she is eclipsed) the moon is illuminated by the sun. At A it is *new moon;*

FIG. 16.

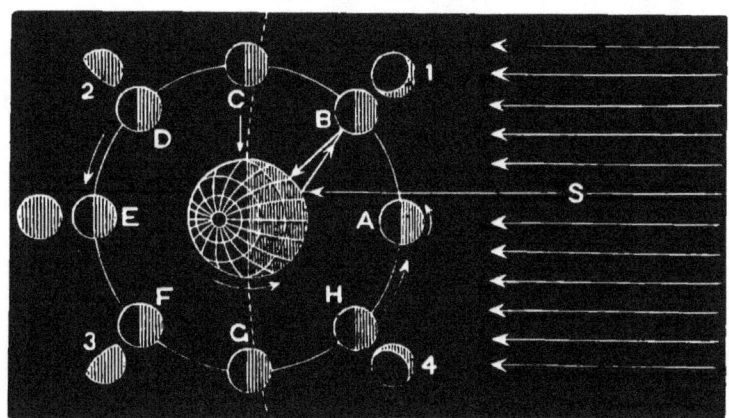

in which position she is not visible to us, as the unilluminated side is turned toward the earth. At B she appears like a crescent, as shown at 1. At C, more of her enlightened side is visible, when she appears to us like a half moon; which is the *first quarter.* At D, still more of the illuminated side is seen, where she appears as represented at 2. At E, the enlightened hemisphere is wholly in view, when she is said to be *full moon*, and in *opposition.* From E around to A again, the illuminated side becomes less and less visible. At F, she appears as seen at 3; at H, as seen at 4. When seen at D and F, the moon is said to be *gibbous.*

Importance of the phases and motions of the moon.—The phases and motions of the moon afford a great variety of interesting investigation. From them the astronomer ascertains the form of the earth, the vicissitudes of the tides, the causes of the eclipses, the distance of the sun, and, consequently, the magnitude of the solar system, etc. These phenomena, being perfectly obvious to the unassisted eye, served as a standard of measurement of time to all nations, until the advancement of science taught them the advantages of solar time.

These phenomena are of the greatest importance to the navigator, guiding him through the pathless ocean.

863. **Why the dark side of the moon is visible near conjunction.**—While near the position, A, the entire disk of the moon is faintly seen by the naked eye. This is because the dark side of the moon is so much illuminated by the reflected light of the earth, that the moon reflects the light of the earth back to the earth again, as represented by the ray of light S, which first is reflected from the earth to the moon, and then from the moon back to the earth.

864. **Other particulars relating to the moon.**—The size of the moon is one *forty-ninth* the size of the earth.

It is about $3\frac{1}{4}$ times the weight of water.

The light of the sun is 300,000 times greater than that of the moon.

The sun is 70,000,000 times larger than the moon; yet the moon appears as large as the sun, because it is 400 times nearer to us than the sun.

It rises about 50 minutes later every day, because it revolves around the earth from west to east; though the full moon, in Sept. and Oct., rises but a few minutes later for several successive evenings; owing to the moon's orbit being very oblique to the horizon. At these times it is called *harvest-moon*.

The moon has very little, if any, atmosphere. It appears covered with dark and light spots, caused by mountains, plains, and valleys. It seems to have no large bodies of water.

On the moon the stars would appear to revolve in $27\frac{1}{3}$ days, and the sun in $29\frac{1}{2}$ days. Though the moon reflects considerable light to the earth, it has been demonstrated that she reflects no heat. The eccentricity of her orbit is 13,333 miles.

CHAPTER XVIII.

(CHART NO. 10.)

ZODIAC, SEASONS, TRANSITS, PARALLAX, ETC.

865. **Figure 1.—The zodiac.**—The zodiac is an imaginary circular belt or zone in the heavens, 16 degrees wide; extending 8 degrees on each side of the *ecliptic*, within the limits of which lie the orbits of

FIG. 1.

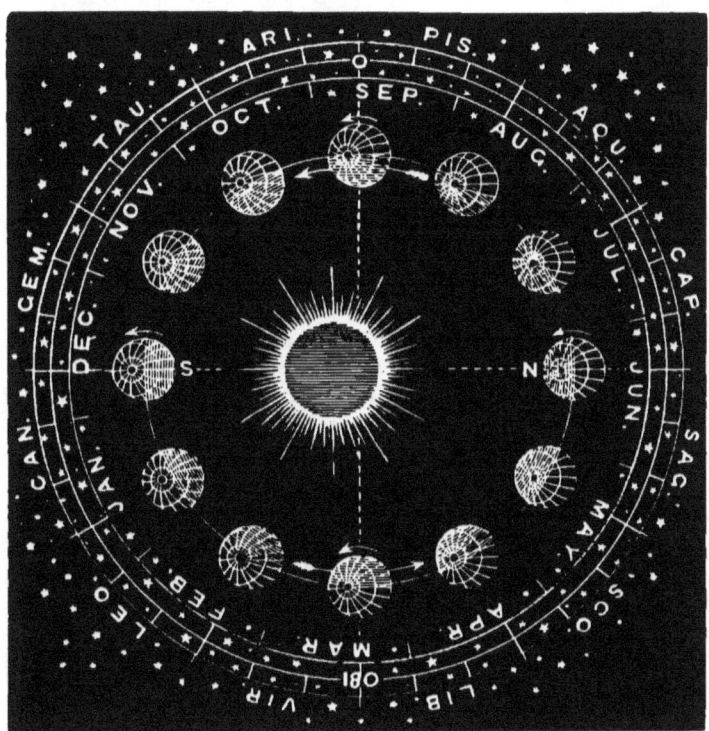

all the planets, except Ceres, Pallas, and Juno. The middle circle, in the figure, represents the ecliptic, and the space included between the other two circles represents the *zodiac*. The name *zodiac*, signifying *an animal*, is given to this belt because each of the 12 signs formerly represented some animal.

866. **The signs or constellations of the zodiac** (Fig. 1).—
The zodiac is divided into 12 equal parts, called *signs* or *constellations*; shown by the division lines crossing the circles. Each of these signs or divisions contains, of course, 30 degrees, each degree 60 minutes, and each minute 60 seconds.

The names, order, and symbols of the twelve signs of the zodiac, are as follows:

Aries, or the Ram	♈	Libra, the Balance	♎
Taurus, the Bull	♉	Scorpio, the Scorpion	♏
Gemini, the Twins	♊	Sagittarius, the Archer	♐
Cancer, the Crab	♋	Capricornus, the Goat	♑
Leo, the Lion	♌	Aquarius, the Waterman	♒
Virgo, the Virgin	♍	Pisces, the Fishes	♓

Philosophy of the Seasons.

867. **Day and night** (Fig. 1).—Day and night are due to the rotation of the earth on its axis. The sun is continually *rising* to places in the *west*, and continually *setting* to places in the *east*. But days and nights differ in length in different places at the same time, and in the same places at different times. The causes of these variations will be explained presently.

868. **Causes of the seasons** (Fig. 1).—The seasons, and unequal lengths of the days and nights, are caused by the earth's revolution around the sun, with its own axis inclined to the plane of its own orbit.

The earth, in the figure, is represented in its several positions, as regards the zodiac and its own orbit, in which it will be found, respectively, on the 20th of each month, and as it is just entering each sign of the zodiac; as shown by the names of the months and constellations. Its north pole is turned toward the observer, and its axis inclined 23° 28' to the plane of its orbit, which is represented by the surface of the paper (or chart). The direction of its motions, on its axis and around the sun, is indicated by the arrows.

The centre of the sun is to the left of the vertical dotted line 1,618,000 miles, which is the eccentricity of the earth's orbit.

869. **The earth at the solstitial points** (Fig. 1).—On the extreme right the earth is seen in the position of its north pole, N, inclined directly *toward*, and its south pole directly *from*, the sun. In this position, its northern hemisphere is more directly exposed to the sun, and, consequently, is favored with summer, and the longest days and shortest nights of the year; while the southern hemisphere, being partially turned from the sun, is subjected to winter, and the longest nights and shortest days. Yet, in this position, the earth is in its aphelion, and, consequently, at its greatest distance from the sun, being 3,236,000 miles (or twice its eccentricity) further from the sun than when it is at its perihelion. The earth is in this position on the 21st of June, called the *summer solstice.*

In the progress of the earth, for six months, from this point around to its perihelion, on the extreme left, the days of the northern hemisphere grow shorter and the nights longer; while in the southern hemisphere the days grow longer and the nights shorter. In this position, the south pole, S, being inclined directly *toward* and the north pole directly *from* the sun, it is *winter* in the northern hemisphere, and the days are shortest and the nights longest of any in the year; while in the southern hemisphere it is summer, and the days are longest and the nights shortest. The earth is in this position on the 22d of December, called the *winter solstice.*

As the earth passes on in its orbit from the winter solstice back to the summer solstice again, the same changes occur, but in the reversed order.

When the sun reaches its greatest northern or southern declination, it seems to stand for several days without any change in declination; hence, these are called *solstitial points* of the ecliptic; solstitial signifying, *the sun standing still.*

870. **The earth at the equinoctial points** (Fig. 1).—During the three months, from June 21st to September 22d, the earth passes from the summer solstice to the *autumnal equinox ;* and during the three months, from December 22d to March 21st, the earth passes from the winter solstice to the *vernal equinox.* At the equinoctial points the sun is directly over the equator, and consequently the days and nights are of equal length, in both the northern and southern hemisphere; hence the term *equinox,* which signifies *equal days and nights.*

871. **The sun's declination.**—The apparent distance of the sun north or south of the equator, is called its *declination.* When north of the equator, it is called *northern declination ;* when south of the equator, it is called *southern declination.* The amount of the declination is $23\frac{1}{2}$ degrees; that is, $23\frac{1}{2}$ degrees north, and $23\frac{1}{2}$ degrees south. This subject will be referred to when describing Fig. 22 (931).

872. **Constellations of the zodiac** (Fig. 1).—A sign is merely the twelfth part of a circle. Along the zodiac, and on both sides of it, are seen many stars. The ancients imagined that some of these stars along in the zodiac, taken together, resembled certain objects, and, consequently, gave such clusters or groupings of them corresponding names, as, the Goat, the Lion, the Bull, etc. Thus, each sign of the zodiac came to be designated by a particular constellation. The names of the signs, by these constellations, have already been given (866).

873. **The sun's apparent motion in the ecliptic** (Fig. 1).— When the earth is in the sign Libra, the sun will *appear* to be in the sign Aries; and as the earth moves on to Scorpio, the sun will *appear* to move to Taurus; and so on. Hence, as the earth moves around in its orbit every year, from west to east, the sun will *appear* to pass, in the same direction and time, through all the signs of the zodiac. Or, all the constellations of the zodiac seem to pass by the sun *westward* once a year.

874. **Division of the signs.**—The signs are divided into four divisions, corresponding to the seasons. The *Spring* signs are Aries, Taurus, Gemini; the *Summer* signs are Cancer, Leo, Virgo; the *Autumnal* signs are Libra, Scorpio, Sagittarius; the *Winter* signs are Capricornus, Aquarius, Pisces. While the sun passes through these signs, of course, the earth passes through the corresponding opposite signs.

875. **The recession of the equinoxes or precession of the constellations** (Fig. 1).—The plane of the equinoctial passes through the earth's equator, or, rather, the equinoctial is the equator of the earth, passing off into the heavens in every direction. Therefore, the equinoxes are the two opposite points in the earth's orbit where the plane of the ecliptic intersects the plane of the equinoctial. Now this intersection of these two planes does not always take place in the same point. That is, the plane of the equinoctial is revolving backward, at a rate that would complete an entire rotation in from 25,000 to 26,000 years. Consequently, the two points where these two planes intersect on the earth's orbit (which are the points of the two equinoxes, 877) are moving backward at the same rate. Therefore, the equinoxes, each year, will fall a little behind. This annual falling back of the equinoctial points is called the *precession of the equinoxes;* but it would be better to say *recession of the equinoxes* and *precession of the constellations.* The equinoxes thus *recede* to the west upon the ecliptic at the rate of 50¼ seconds of a degree every year.

Hence, the months and signs, in the diagram, do not agree, the earth entering each sign about the 21st of each month. This subject will be referred to again when describing Fig. 23 (939).

876. **Longitude in the heavens** (Fig. 1) is reckoned on the ecliptic eastward from the vernal equinox, or beginning with the first degree of the sign Aries. When the sun enters Aries, its longitude is nothing, and that of the earth is 180°; or when the earth enters Aries, its longitude is nothing, and that of the sun is 180°. When the earth enters Cancer, its longitude is 90°, and that of the sun, 270°, and so on; as will appear by observing the diagram.

877. **Figure 2.—Intersection of the ecliptic and equinoctial.**—The intersection of the plane of the ecliptic with the plane of the equinoctial forms an angle of 23° 28′, called the obliquity of the ecliptic. S represents the earth at its summer solstice; N, at its winter

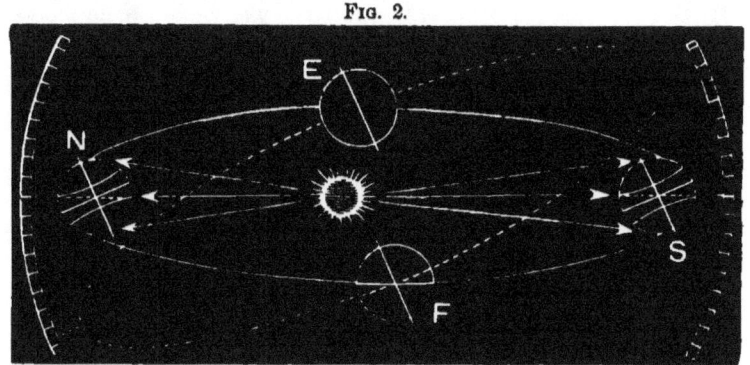

FIG. 2.

solstice; E, at its vernal equinox; and F, at its autumnal equinox. The dotted ellipse lies in the plane of the equinoctial; and the other ellipse in the plane of the ecliptic. The equinoctial points are where these two planes intersect on the earth's orbit.

It will be noticed, that, at the summer solstice, S, the sun shines upon the north pole of the earth; and at the winter solstice, upon the south pole, as indicated by the arrows. It will be observed, also, that the central arrow points to the earth over the tropic of Cancer, at the summer solstice, and over the tropic of Capricorn at the winter solstice, both of which are 23° 28′ from the equator of the earth; hence the torrid zone of the earth is 46° 56′ in width.

878. **Polar inclination and seasons of the different planets.**—From what has been said respecting the seasons, it will be seen that any planet whose axis is not perpendicular to the plane of its orbit, is subject to all the variations of seasons, difference in length of days and nights, etc., same as the earth. The extent of these variations, however, depends upon the amount of the polar inclination. If the axis be much inclined, as in the case of Venus, the variations will be correspondingly great; but if the axis is only slightly inclined, as in the case of Jupiter, the variations will be correspondingly limited; and if the axis were perpendicular to the plane of the orbit, the length of days and nights would be equal in all parts of the planet, and the climate at any given latitude would always be the same.

The following table exhibits the *polar inclination, greatest declination,* and *width* of *torrid zone* of different planets:

	INC. OF AXIS.	DECLINATION.	TORRID ZONE.
Venus	75° 00'	75° 00'	150° 00'
Earth	23 28	23 28	46 56
Mars	28 40	28 40	57 20
Jupiter	3 5	3 5	6 10
Saturn	30 00	30 00	60 00
The Sun	7 20		

It will be observed that the *inclination* equals the *declination,* and that the *torrid zone* is double the *declination.*

Philosophy of Transits.

879. **Transits.**—*Nodes* are two points where the orbit of the moon or of a planet intersects the plane of the ecliptic.

The passage of Mercury or Venus directly between the earth and the sun, and apparently over the disk of the sun, is called a *transit.* A transit, therefore, can never occur except when the interior planet is in or very near the ecliptic. The earth and planet must be on the same side of the ecliptic; the planet being at one of its nodes, and the earth on the line of its nodes. Mercury and Venus, being the only interior planets, are the only ones that can make transits visible to us; but the earth may make transits visible from Mars, the Asteroids, Jupiter, and so on.

880. **Figure 3.—Transits of Mercury.**—The figure represents the ecliptic and zodiac, with the orbit of the interior planet, Mercury. The line of his nodes, ST, as shown, is in the 16th degree of Taurus, and 16th degree of Scorpion. Now, if the earth is in Taurus, on the line, TS, when Mercury is at his *ascending node,* T, he will seem to pass upward over the sun's disk, like a dark spot, as represented in the figure in the line of the arrow drawn through the sun.

If Mercury is at his *descending node*, S, when the earth is in the 16th degree of Scorpion, he will seem to pass *downward* across the face of

FIG. 3.

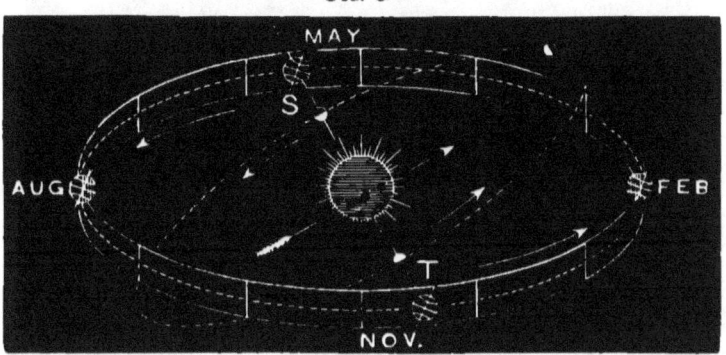

the sun. As shown in the diagram, the earth passes the ascending node of Mercury in November, and the descending node in May. The last transit of Mercury took place Nov. 4, 1868. There will be four more during the present century; two in May, and two in November.

881. **The calculation of transits.**—*To calculate transits,* at any one node, it is only necessary to find what number of revolutions of the interior planet are equal to one, or any number of revolutions of the earth; or when the earth and the planet will again meet on the line of the planet's nodes.

In the case of Mercury, this ratio is as 87,969 is to 365,256; from which it is found that,

7 revolutions of the Earth are equal to 29 of Mercury.
13 " " " 54 "
33 " " " 137 "
46 " " " 191 "

Hence, transits of Mercury, *at the same node*, may happen at intervals of 7, 13, 33, 46 years, and so on.

Upon these principles all transits and eclipses are calculated.

The following is a list of the Transits of Mercury which have occurred during the present century.

Nov. 8, 1802.   May 5, 1832.   Nov. 9, 1848.
Nov. 11, 1815.   Nov. 7, 1835.   Nov. 11, 1861.
Nov. 4, 1822.   May 8, 1845.   Nov. 4, 1868.

882. **Figure 4.—Mercury's oscillation.**—Let the straight line, joining the earth and the sun, represent the plane of the ecliptic. Now, when an interior planet is in this plane, as represented at N, it

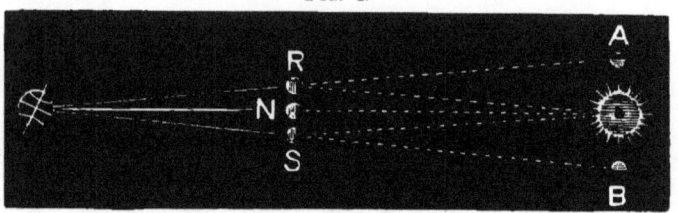

FIG. 4.

may appear to be on the sun's disk, shown by the dark spot on the sun; but if it is either above or below the ecliptic, as shown at R and S, it will appear to pass either above or below the sun, as represented at A and B. If Mercury were at R, it would *appear* to be at A, and in 44 days (that is, half the time of its periodic revolution) it would be as much below the sun as, at A, it appears to be above it; and, therefore, it would *appear* to be at B; and so on. This apparent motion of an interior planet, from west to east and from east to west, is called *oscillation*.

These oscillations do not take place in half the time of the planet's periodic revolution, because the earth, in the meantime, follows the sun in the same direction. Hence, instead of occurring (in the case of Mercury) in 44 days, the time will be prolonged to between 55 and 65 days.

FIG. 5.

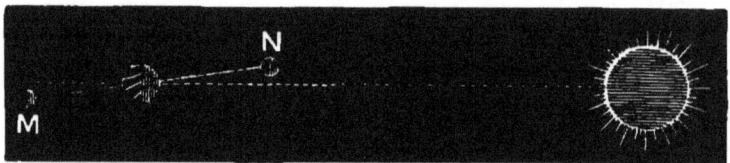

883. **Figure 5. Inclination of the moon's orbit to the plane of the ecliptic.**—The plane of the moon's orbit is very near that of the ecliptic. It departs from the latter only 5° 8' 48".

Let the dotted line represent the plane of the earth's orbit (which, of course, coincides with the plane of the ecliptic), and the line joining the moon at M and N would represent the inclination of the moon's orbit to that of the earth. At N the moon would be *within* the earth's orbit, and at M exterior; and it would be *full moon* at M, and *new moon* at N.

884. **View of the moon at the poles and at the equator of the earth.**—As the full moon always happens when the moon is directly opposite to the sun, all the full moons in our *winter* must happen when the moon is on the *north* side of the equinoctial; because *then* the sun is on the *south* of it. Consequently, at the north pole of the earth, there will be alternately a fortnight's moonlight and a fortnight's darkness, for a period of six months; and the same will be true at the *south* pole, during the six months that the sun is *north* of the equinoctial.

About the equator of the earth, the moon rises throughout the year with nearly equal intervals of delay, from one day to another, of 48 minutes and 44 seconds. But in places of considerable latitude a deviation from this rule occurs, especially about the time of harvest, when the full moon rises, for several nights together, only 18 to 25 minutes later each day, when it is called *harvest-moon ;* as it affords the farmer extra light for gathering crops.

Parallax of the Heavenly Bodies.

885. **Figure 6.—Annual parallax, or parallax of the stars.**—The change in the apparent position of the fixed stars, caused by the change of the earth's place in her revolution around the sun, is called the *annual parallax.*

Let L represent the place of the earth on the 1st of January, and A, a star observed at that time. Its *apparent* place, in the more *distant* heavens, will be at H. In six months the earth will have revolved around to the position of N, and the star, A, will appear to be at F. The angle LAN will constitute the *angle of parallax.*

Although the distance between L and N is 190,000,000 miles, yet the parallax of the star, A, is less than $\frac{1}{80}$ of one degree, and the lines LA and NA, therefore, are almost parallel. Hence, if the earth's orbit were

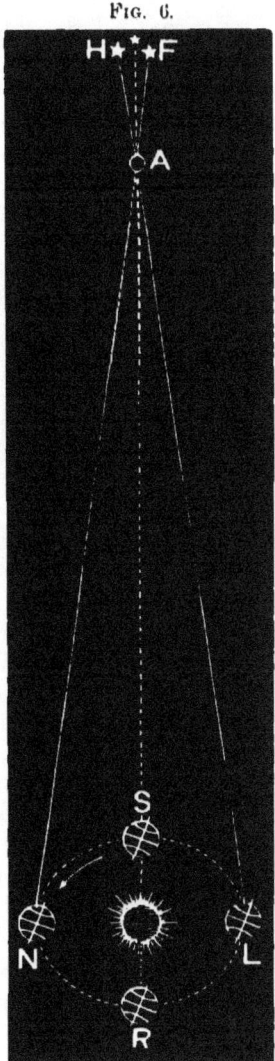

Fig. 6.

filled with a globe of fire, 190,000,000 miles in diameter, and viewed from the fixed star, A, it would appear but a point of light one minute (1') in diameter. Therefore, how distant and immense must be the stars.

Another evidence of the immense distance and magnitude of the stars is, that they appear no nearer, brighter, or larger, when viewed from the earth at S, than when viewed from the earth at R; although at S the observer is 190,000,000 miles nearer a given star than when he is at R.

886. **Figure 7.—Diurnal parallax.**—This applies to the planets and other solar bodies. It is the difference between the altitude of a solar body seen from the earth's surface and the altitude of the same body seen at the same time from the earth's centre. Or it is the difference between the true and apparent place of a solar body. The *apparent place* is that in which the body seems to be when viewed from the surface of the earth, the *true place* being that in which it would appear if seen from the centre of the earth.

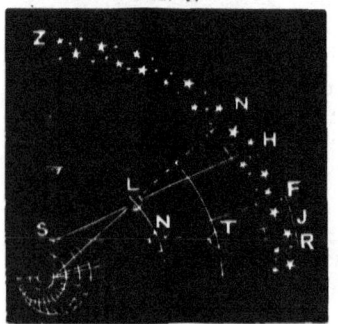

FIG. 7.

If an observer were stationed at the centre of the earth, and could see the moon at N, it would seem to be situated among the stars at F; whereas, if it were seen from the surface of the earth at S, it would appear among the stars at R. Therefore, F is the *true* and R the *apparent* place of the moon; the space between F and R being the arc which measures the moon's parallax.

The greater the distance the less the parallax. If the moon, N, were removed to T, the arc which would then measure its parallax would be included between J and R.

The horizontal parallax is the greatest. That is, the parallax is greatest when the body is on the sensible horizon; from which point it diminishes, until it reaches the zenith, Z, where its parallax ceases, or becomes nothing. Thus it will be seen that the arc NH is less than that of FR; hence, the parallax of the moon is less at L than it was at N.

Diurnal parallax applies only to bodies of the solar system. The stars are too far off, of course, to show any difference in position when viewed from points so near together as the centre and surface of the earth.

887. **The effect of parallax on bodies** is to depress them below their true place. On this account, the parallax of the sun and moon must be added to their *apparent* altitude, in order to obtain their *true* altitude.

888. **The principles of parallax are of great importance,** as by them the distance of the solar bodies from the earth, the magnitude of the planets, and the dimensions of their orbits, may all be determined. Having thus found the distance of the earth from the sun, that of all the planets may be known also; because, according to the *third* law of Kepler, the *squares of the times of their sidereal periodic revolutions are proportional to the cubes of their mean distances.*

889. **Figure 8.—Convexity of the earth's surface.**—This is shown, 1st. By the manner in which a ship disappears from sight, as she sails in any direction from the coast: The hull or body of the vessel first disappears, then the rigging, and lastly the tops of the masts vanish from sight.

2d. Navigators have sailed around the earth, and thus proved its convexity.

3d. The form of the earth's shadow, as seen upon the moon in an eclipse, proves the globular figure of the earth, and so the convexity of its surface.

4th. *Latitude found by the north star.* The convexity of the earth, north and south, is proved by the variation in the altitude of the *north star*, which is found to uniformly increase as we approach it, and to diminish as we recede from it.

Suppose an observer were standing upon the earth (Fig. 8), and viewing the pole-star from the 45th degree of north latitude; it would, of course, appear elevated 45° above his visible horizon, represented by the arrow H. But let him recede southward, over one degree of latitude, and the pole-star will settle one degree toward the horizon; or, rather, his northern horizon would be elevated one degree toward the star; till at length, as he crossed the equator, his horizon, shown by the arrow, S, would rise above the star, when it would become wholly invisible.

FIG. 8.

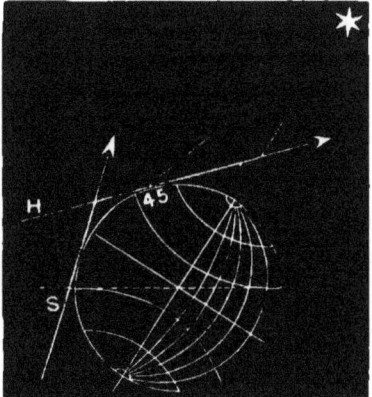

Hence the general rule, that *the altitude of one pole, or the depression of the other at any place on the earth's surface, is equal to the latitude of that place.*

890. **Figure 9.—Conjunction and opposition of planets.**
—Conjunctions are called *inferior* and *superior*. When Mercury or Venus is nearest to the earth, that is, between the earth and sun, as at D, it is in *inferior* conjunction; and when furthest from the earth, as at N, it is in *superior* conjunction, in which case the sun is between the earth and the planet.

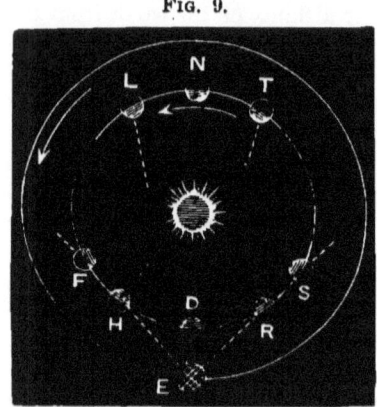

Fig. 9.

The exterior planets, namely, those whose orbits are exterior to that of the earth, have alternately a *superior* conjunction and an opposition. An exterior planet is in *superior conjunction* when the sun is between the planet and the earth; and it is said to be in *opposition* when the earth is between the sun and the planet.

Hence, when a planet is in conjunction, it rises and sets nearly with the sun; but in opposition, it rises nearly when the sun sets, and sets when the sun rises.

When at her superior conjunction, Venus is 154,000,000 miles from the earth, but when at her inferior conjunction she is only 26,000,000 miles distant. The reason of this is apparent.

Venus presents all the phases of the moon in passing around the sun.

891. **Direct, stationary, and retrograde motion of the planets** (Fig. 9).—The planets, if seen from the sun, would appear to pass from star to star, through the constellations, in a uniform and regular manner. But as seen from the earth, they *apparently* move irregularly. Sometimes they appear to go *forward;* at other times, to remain stationary, and then to recede.

When Venus, for example (Fig. 9), is at T, her motion is said to be *direct*, passing from west to east toward L. When at F, she would be coming directly toward the earth at E; therefore, while moving from F to H, she would seem to be *stationary*. In passing from H to R (travelling faster than the earth) she will pass the earth, and so *seem* to move from east to west, or to *retrograde*. From R to S she would be moving directly away from the earth, when she would again seem to be *stationary*.

Of course, the earth has been moving along in *her* orbit, which is not represented in the diagram, but the principle sought to be illustrated will be understood.

892. **The transit of Venus an important event.**—If the orbit of Venus lay exactly in the plane of the earth's orbit, she would cross the sun's disk, like a dark spot, at every inferior conjunction. But her orbit cutting the ecliptic at an angle of $3\frac{1}{4}°$, she will pass the sun a little above or below it, except when her inferior conjunction happens in or near one of her nodes; in which case she will make a transit, which can happen only twice in a century.

Progress in astronomical science since Venus' last transit (in 1822) will render her next transit, in 1874, the means of demonstrating many truths, and, therefore, one of the most important events of the age.

The following is a list of all the transits of Venus, since the time the first was observed, to the year 2012:

December 4th, 1639.	December 6th, 1822.	June 7th, 2004.
June 5th, 1761.	December 8th, 1874.	June 5th, 2012.
June 3d, 1769.	December 5th, 1882.	

The Periodic Revolution of the Sun.

893. **Figure 10.—The orbit of the sun.**—The sun has three motions. 1st. It revolves around its own axis once in 25 days 9 hours 36 minutes (814). 2d. It revolves around the centre of gravity of the

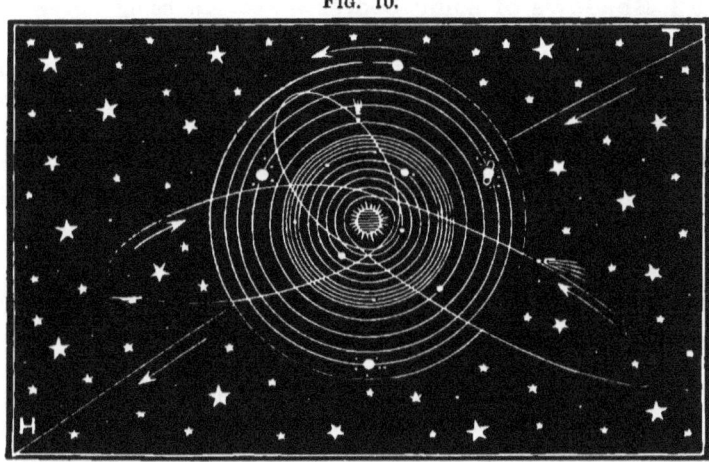

FIG. 10.

solar system (845). 3d. It has a periodic revolution, from west to east, in a vast orbit around some distant and unknown centre.

A portion of the sun's orbit is represented by the line, TH. The point of tendency is toward the constellation Hercules. The plane of this vast orbit is supposed to have an inclination of about 84° to the ecliptic. The sun is represented as surrounded by his offspring, the planets, and their offspring, the satellites, and those wandering members of the solar family, the comets.

The sun, therefore, is not stationary, but, taking with him his retinue of worlds, he is making a grand tour through the boundless Universe of God, at the rate of 20,000 miles per hour, and will return to the same point of his orbit only once in every *eighteen millions of years.*

Reader, think, for a moment, of the journey you are taking through space. We are whirling at the rate of over *a thousand miles per hour* around the earth's axis; and *sixty-eight thousand miles per hour* around the sun; and *twenty thousand miles per hour* around the sun's central orb; and at what rate we may be journeying around some other grand centre is only known by the Divine Mind.

CHAPTER XIX.

PHILOSOPHY OF ECLIPSES.

894. **Shadows of solar bodies.**—The sun being larger than the planets and satellites, the principal shadow of all solar bodies is shaped like a cone. The length of the shadow of a planet or satellite will depend upon the size of the body and its distance from the sun. In Fig. 12 (901), for instance, it will be seen that the earth on the left casts a longer shadow than the moon, while both the earth and moon on the right, being at a greater distance from the sun, throw longer shadows than the same bodies do on the left.

Respecting the umbra, penumbra, and shadows generally, see 522 and 523.

All the planets, both primaries and secondaries, cast shadows in the direction opposite to the sun (see page 412).

895. **Interest felt in eclipses.**—No phenomena of the heavens have engaged the attention of mankind more than eclipses of the sun and moon. In the early ages they were regarded as alarming deviations from the laws of nature, presaging public calamities and indicating divine displeasure. Even at the present day, to those who are unacquainted with astronomy, nothing appears more wonderful than the accuracy with which they can be predicted. They can be calculated with great precision for ages, either past or to come.

896. **Position of the sun, earth, and moon, when eclipses occur.**—Eclipses of the *sun* can happen only at *new moon*, and those of the *moon* only at *full moon ;* for the moon can never be between us and the sun, to eclipse him, except at the time of her change or new moon; and she can never pass into the earth's shadow, to be eclipsed herself, except when she is in opposition to the sun, and it is full moon.

An eclipse of the sun, or solar eclipse, is caused by the moon passing between the earth and the sun, and casting her shadow upon the *earth.*

An eclipse of the moon, or lunar eclipse, is caused by her falling into the *earth's* shadow.

897. **Eclipses are either total, partial, or annular.**—When the disk of the sun or moon is wholly obscured, the eclipse is *total;* when only partly obscured, the eclipse is *partial;* when the central part of the sun's disk is obscured, leaving a bright ring around the shadow, the eclipse is *annular* (ring-like).

The apparent diameter of the sun or moon's disk is divided into twelve equal parts, called *digits.*

FIG. 11.

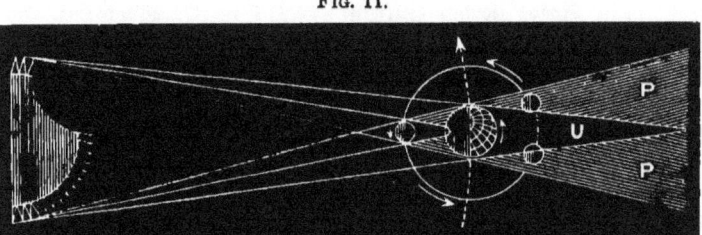

898. **Figure 11.—The direction in which eclipses come on.**—The dotted arrow represents the orbit of the earth; the other arrows, the rotation of the earth on its axis, and the revolution of the moon in its orbit. The sun is seen on the left. U represents the earth's umbra, and PP, its penumbra. The moon's umbra and penumbra are seen on the left of the earth. The upper side of the figure is the east side, and the lower side the west side.

Eclipses of the sun always come on from the *west,* and pass over eastward. On the left of the earth the moon is seen revolving eastward, throwing her shadow upon the earth, and hiding the western limb of the sun. Hence, the shadow of the moon passes over the surface of the earth from west to east.

899. **Total eclipse of the moon, and partial eclipse of the sun** (Fig. 11).—The moon, in passing through the umbra, U, of the earth, is totally eclipsed. The sun is totally eclipsed to places within the umbra of the moon (except in cases of an annular eclipse), and partially eclipsed to places outside of the umbra.

Before the moon enters the earth's umbra, U, the earth's penumbra, PP, begins to intercept the light of the sun, or to cast a faint shadow upon her. This shadow grows darker and darker, till the moon enters the umbra, or perfect shadow of the earth.

If the moon passes through the side of the shadow, instead of its centre, the eclipse will be partial instead of total.

900. **Dimensions of the earth and moon's shadows.**—As before stated, the length of the shadow of a solar body depends on the distance of the body from the sun. The diameter of a given shadow falling upon a body, will depend upon the distance between the body *casting* and the body *receiving* the shadow.

The average *length* of the earth's umbra is about 860,000 miles; and its *breadth*, at the distance of the moon, is about 6,500 miles, or three times the moon's diameter. The earth and moon revolving in elliptical orbits, will, of course, cause the above estimates to vary. The earth's umbra varies in length from 842,217 to 871,262 miles, and its diameter, where the moon passes it, varies from 5,235 to 6,365 miles.

The average length of the moon's umbra is 236,000 miles. It varies from 221,148 to 252,638 miles, according to its distance from the sun. Its greatest diameter, at the distance of the earth, is 175 miles; but the *penumbra* may cover a space on the earth of nearly 5,000 miles in diameter.

When the sun is at his *greatest* and the moon at her *least* distance from the earth, as at A (Fig. 12), her shadow will extend 19,000 miles beyond the surface of the earth. But when the sun is at his *least* and the moon at her *greatest* distance from the earth, as at P (Fig. 12), her shadow will not reach the earth by 20,000 miles.

It is owing to these variations that some central eclipses of the sun are total, while others are partial and annular.

901. **Figure 12.—Total and annular eclipses of the sun.**—At A, the earth is at her *aphelion*, or *most distant* point from the sun, consequently the shadows of the earth and moon will be of the greatest possible length. At the same time the moon, on the left of A, is in *perigee*, or its point *nearest* possible to the earth. If, therefore, under these conditions, the moon passes centrally over the sun's disk, the eclipse will be total. In order to bring the shadow of the moon to a point at the surface of the earth, the sun would require to fill the space between the points of the two long dotted arrows.

At P the conditions are reversed. The earth is at her *perihelion*, or *nearest* position to the sun, consequently the shadows of the earth and moon will be of the shortest possible length. At the same time, the moon, on the right of P, will be in *apogee*, or its point *farthest* possible from the earth. If, under these conditions, the moon passes

FIG. 12.

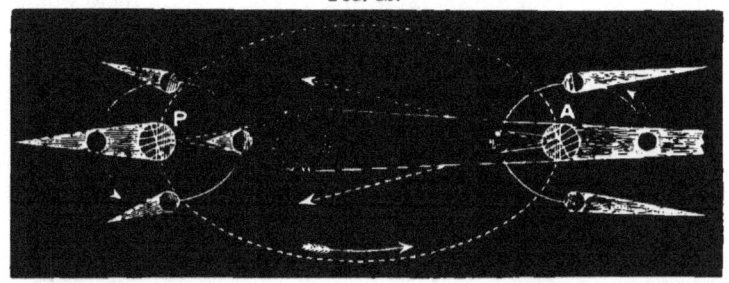

centrally over the disk of the sun, her shadow will not be sufficiently long, by 20,000 miles, to reach the earth, and so cover his whole disk or face, but will leave a ring, apparently around herself, unobscured, as shown by the appearance of the sun in the figure.

The eccentricity of the earth's orbit, in the diagram, is very much exaggerated, the better to illustrate the principles explained.

902. **The duration of eclipses.**—1. The greatest possible duration of the annular appearance of a solar eclipse is 12 minutes and 24 seconds.

2. The greatest possible time during which the sun can be totally eclipsed to any part of the earth is 7 minutes and 58 seconds.

3. The moon may continue totally eclipsed for 1 hour and 45 minutes.

903. **The general effects of a total eclipse of the sun**, is to darken the heavens at an unusual hour, and, therefore, to impress the mind with a peculiar gloom. The animal tribes also seem to be agitated by the untimely darkness. The temperature declines, and the planets and stars become visible.

904. **The number of eclipses in any one year** cannot be less than *two*, nor more than *seven*. In the former case, they will be both of the sun: and in the latter, there will be five of the sun, and two of the moon.

Eclipses, both of the sun and moon, recur in nearly the same order, and at the same intervals, at the expiration of a cycle of 223 lunations, or 18 years of 365 days and 15 hours. At the expiration of this time, the sun and moon's nodes will sustain the same relation to each other as at the beginning, and a new cycle of eclipses begins. This cycle is called the *period of the eclipses.*

905. **Figure 13.—Why eclipses are not more frequent.**
—If the moon's orbit lay in the plane of the ecliptic, instead of forming an angle of 5° 9′ with it, as represented by Fig. 5 (883), there would be two central eclipses every month; namely, one of the sun and one of the moon. But, owing to this inclination of the moon's orbit to the

FIG. 13.

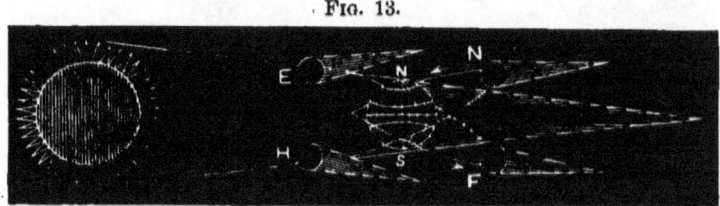

plane of the ecliptic, it is evident that she may be either *above* or *below* the ecliptic at the time of her *conjunction* with the sun, as shown at E and H, in the figure, so she will seem to *pass either above* or *below* him, and will not cause a solar eclipse. For the same reason, the moon may pass either above or below the earth's shadow, as at N and F, at the time of her *opposition*, and no lunar eclipse occur.

It is, therefore, only when the moon is *at* or *near* one of her *nodes* that either a solar or lunar eclipse can occur. Respecting nodes, see Fig. 3 (879 and 880).

906. **Retrograde motion of the moon's nodes.**—The moon's nodes do not remain in the same position, with respect to the earth and sun, but have a retrograde motion of about 19° in a year; so that she comes around to the same node in 19 days less than a year, or in 346 days, causing the eclipse to occur sooner every year by about 19 days.

In just half of 346 days, viz., 173 days, the moon passes her other node, on the opposite side of the ecliptic. It follows, therefore, that at whatever time an eclipse occurs at either node, there will occur another at the opposite node in 173 days thereafter.

907. **Figure 14.—The solar and lunar ecliptic limits.**—
It is not necessary that the earth and moon should be *exactly* on the line of the moon's nodes, in order to produce an eclipse. If she is within 17° of her node, at the time of her change or conjunction, she will eclipse the sun; and if within 12° of her node at her full, she will

strike into the earth's shadow, and be more or less eclipsed. These distances are called, respectively, the *solar and lunar ecliptic limits*.

Let the light globes represent the sun at different positions on the ecliptic, and the dark spheres, the moon; and the line running through them, the plane of her orbit. Let the point, G, represent the node of the moon's orbit. Now if the change occur when the moon is at A,

FIG. 14.

she will pass *below* the sun; if when at B, she will just touch his lower limb. At B, then, she will eclipse him a little; and so on, to G, at which point the eclipse would be central, and either total or annular.

If the moon is at H, I, J, K, or L, when the change occurs, she will eclipse the upper or northern limb of the sun; but if she is at M, she will pass above the limb, and not eclipse him at all. The points B and L represent *the solar ecliptic limits*.

The mean ecliptic limit for the sun is $16\frac{1}{2}°$ on each side of the node. The mean ecliptic limit for the moon is $10\frac{1}{4}°$ on each side of the node.

908. **Why there are more solar than lunar eclipses.—** As just explained, there are 33° about each node of the moon, making in all 66° out of 360°, in which eclipses of the *sun* may occur; and 21 about each node, making in all 42° out of 360°, in which eclipses of the *moon* may happen. The proportion, therefore, of the solar to the lunar eclipses is as 66 to 42, or as 11 to 7. Yet, in a given time, there are more *visible* lunar than solar eclipses, which is owing to the fact that lunar eclipses are visible to a whole hemisphere, while a solar eclipse is visible to only a small portion of it.

909. **Eclipses or occultation of the stars.—**The occultation of a star is caused by the moon coming between us and the star, and so concealing it from our view. This is a frequent phenomenon, and one interesting to observe; especially at *new moon*. The star occulted may be traced to the very border of the moon's eastern limb, when, suddenly, it goes out. In a short time it reappears.

910. **Eclipses of Jupiter's moons.—**Jupiter's satellites, as a general rule, are totally eclipsed at every revolution. The average number of eclipses of his moons, altogether, amount to about *forty* per month.

464 ASTRONOMY.

911. **Eclipses of Saturn's moons.**—The satellites of Saturn are seldom eclipsed. On account of the great inclination of their orbits to the ecliptic, they are not eclipsed but twice in thirty years, when the rings of the planet are edgewise toward the sun. See Figs. 1 and 9 (852).

CHAPTER XX.

PHILOSOPHY OF THE TIDES.

912. **Motion of the water of the earth.**—Owing to the perfect mobility of water, it is influenced by heavenly bodies, and by the motions of the earth itself, in a manner different from that in which the earth is influenced as a whole.

The water of the earth, covering more than two-thirds of its surface, is in regular and ceaseless motion; alternately rising and falling at regular intervals in all parts of the globe.

The rising of the water, in some portions of the earth, and its falling, at the same time, in other portions, are called *tides.*

The rising of the waters is called *flood tide;* and their falling, *ebb tide.* There are two flood and two ebb tides every 25 hours. The highest and lowest points to which they reach are called, respectively, *high* and *low* tides.

913. **The tides are not uniform** at any given place, either as to time or amount. They occur about 50 minutes later every day, and sometimes rise much higher and sink much lower than the average. The extraordinary high and low tides are called, respectively, *spring* and *neap* tides (923).

914. **The principal cause of the tides** is the attraction of the sun and moon upon the water of the ocean.

Fig. 15.

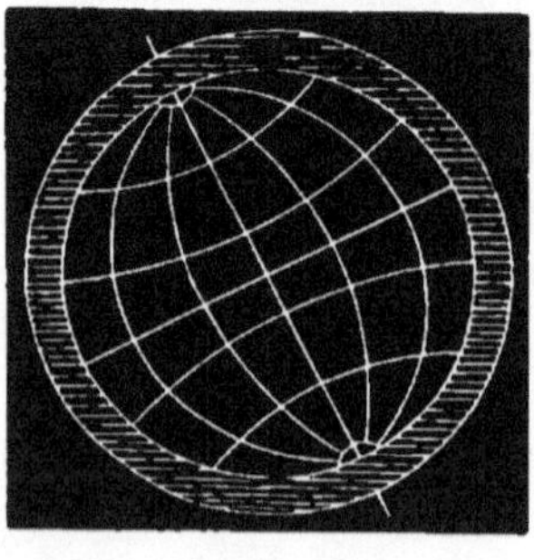

The height of the water in all the figures representing the tides, is designedly exaggerated, to better illustrate the principles to be explained.

915. **Figure 15.—Influence of the earth upon its waters.**—If the water was not influenced by the attraction of the sun and moon, it would, under the influence of the earth's own attraction and centrifugal force, come to a proper level, and, except for the disturbing influence of the wind, remain from age to age in a state of equilibrium, as represented by the diagram.

916. **Figure 16.—A single tide-wave.**—It would seem, at first thought, that the natural effect of the moon's attraction would be to produce a single tide-wave, on the side of the earth toward the moon, as represented in the figure; in which the moon is seen in its orbit on

Fig. 16.

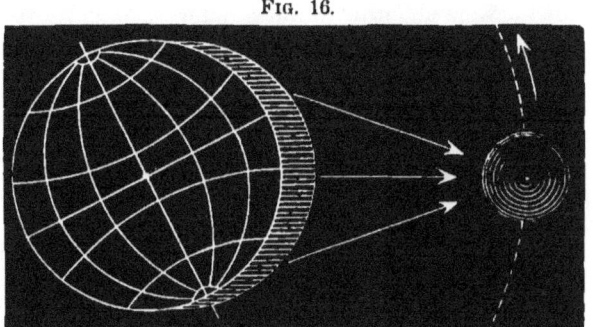

the right. The three arrows represent the attraction of the moon upon the water of the earth. If the water were thus drawn to only one side of the earth, there could be but *one* flood and *one* ebb tide in 24 hours; whereas there are *two* of each.

917. **Figure 17.—The two tide-waves.**—Instead of only one tide-wave, as illustrated in the last figure, there are two, situated directly opposite to each other, as shown in this figure. The causes of

Fig. 17.

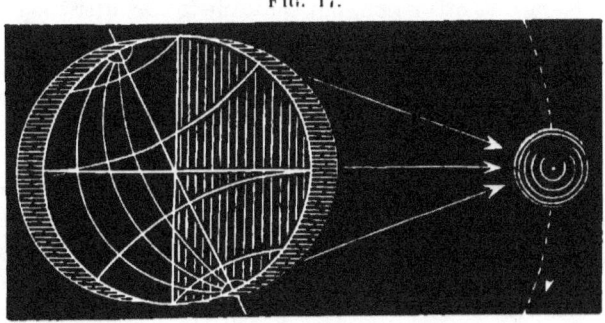

the *opposite* tide-wave will be explained hereafter. Half-way between these two *high* tides there are two *low* tides.

These four tides, viz., two high and two low, traverse the ocean from east to west every day, which accounts for a flood and ebb tide every twelve hours.

On the right is represented the moon in her orbit, the three arrows representing her attraction.

918. **Figure 18.—Lagging of the tide-wave behind the moon.**—As the moon, which is the principal cause of the tides, is revolving eastward, and comes to the meridian later and later each day, therefore the tides are about 50 minutes later each day. This makes the interval between the successive high tides 12 hours and 25 minutes.

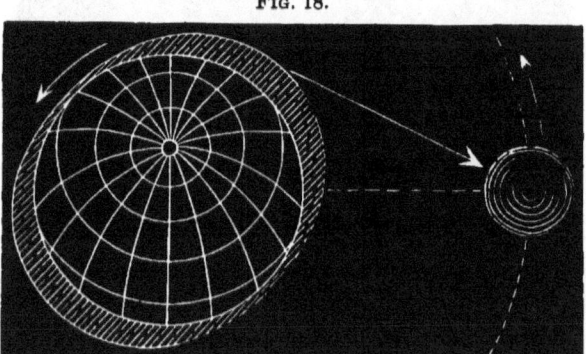

FIG. 18.

Besides this daily delay with the moon, the highest point of the tide-wave lags behind, or east of the moon, about 46°, so that the high tide does not occur till about three hours after the moon has crossed the meridian. This is because the waters do not at once yield to the impulse of the moon's attraction, but continue to rise after she has passed over.

In the figure, the moon is seen in her orbit. The arrow, pointing to the moon, represents her attraction. The dotted line between the earth and moon stands over the meridian.

919. **Figure 19.—Influence of the sun upon tides.**—Thus far, the attraction of the moon has been mentioned as the principal cause of the tides; but the sun has the same effect as the moon, only in a less degree. The relative influence of the moon and sun is about as 3 to 1.

Let the arrow M represent the attraction of the moon, and the arrow S that of the sun. Then the sun partially neutralizes the influence of the moon, and a very low tide, called the *neap tide*, is the result.

ASTRONOMY. 467

When, however, the sun and moon are either in conjunction or oppo-

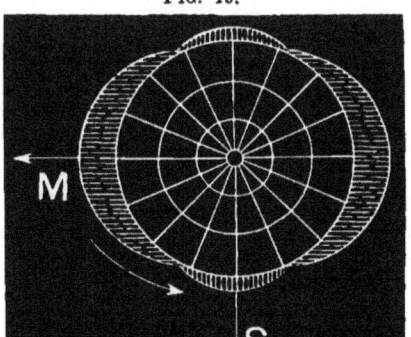

FIG. 19.

sition, as at A or P, Fig. 21 (923), their forces, being united, produce an extraordinary tide, called the *spring tide*.

Causes of the Opposite Tide-wave.

920. **Figure 20.—Causes of the opposite tide-wave.—**
The principal cause of the tide-wave on the side of the earth opposite the moon, is the *difference* of the moon's attraction on the opposite sides of the earth. The moon is represented in its orbit on the right.

The diameter of the earth being equal to about $\frac{1}{30}$ of the moon's distance, and the power of attraction being inversely as the square of the

FIG. 20.

distance, the water on the side opposite to the moon will be attracted with a force about $\frac{1}{18}$ less than that which attracts the water on the side toward the moon; while the *rigid* part of the earth would be attracted with a force commensurate with the square of the distance from its centre of gravity to the moon. The effect of this unequal attraction upon the earth, and the waters upon its opposite sides, is to elongate the general form of the water, in the direction of the moon, and thus produce the two opposite tide-waves.

921. **The secondary cause of the opposite tide-wave** (Fig. 20), is the revolution of the earth around the common centre of gravity of the earth and moon.

If the earth and moon were connected by a rod, as represented in the figure, there would be some point, as the centre of the dotted circle, where they would balance each other, which would be their common centre of gravity. This point is about 6,000 miles from the earth's centre. Therefore, every time the moon revolves around the earth, or rather around this common centre of gravity, the earth's centre will revolve around the same point, as indicated by the dotted circle, and the direction of the arrow.

By this revolution of the earth, the water on the side opposite the moon is subjected to greater centrifugal force than that on the side toward the moon; which assists, though but slightly, in the production of the opposite tide-wave.

922. **Relative influence of the sun and moon on the tides.**—The tides are not due so much to the attraction of the sun and moon, as a whole, as to the *difference* of their attraction on the opposite sides of the earth. The attraction being inversely as the square of the distance, the influence of the sun and moon, respectively, must be in the ratio of the earth's diameter to their distances.

Now, the difference, as before stated, in the distance of the two opposite sides of the earth from the moon, is $\frac{1}{30}$ of the moon's distance, as $240,000 \div 8,000 = 30$; while the difference, as compared with the distance of the sun, is only $\frac{1}{11875}$, as $95,000,000 \div 8,000 = 11,875$.

Hence, although the sun, as a whole, attracts the earth much more than the moon does; yet, because of her greater inequality of attraction on the opposite sides of the earth, the moon contributes more than the sun to the production of the tides. Their relative influence is as *three to one.* When acting together, they produce tides one-third higher than usual; when counteracting each other, the lunar tide-wave prevails, but is one-third lower than usual.

Spring and Neap Tides.

923. **Figure 21.—Spring and neap tides.**—As the tides are caused by the attraction of both the sun and moon, and as these are constantly changing their positions, with respect to the earth and to each other, therefore they sometimes *act one against the other*, and partially neutralize each other's influence; while, at other times, they combine their forces and mutually assist each other (919).

The dotted ellipse represents the earth's orbit; the small ellipses, the moon's orbit. When the moon is in quadrature, as seen in her orbit at N and T, her influence is measurably neutralized by the sun, causing low tides, called *neap tides*. These will occur at both quadratures of the moon. When the moon is in conjunction or opposition, as seen in her orbit at A and P, high tides occur, called *spring tides*. These will occur, of course, at both full and new moon.

As the moon, in revolving once around the earth, will be once in

FIG. 21.

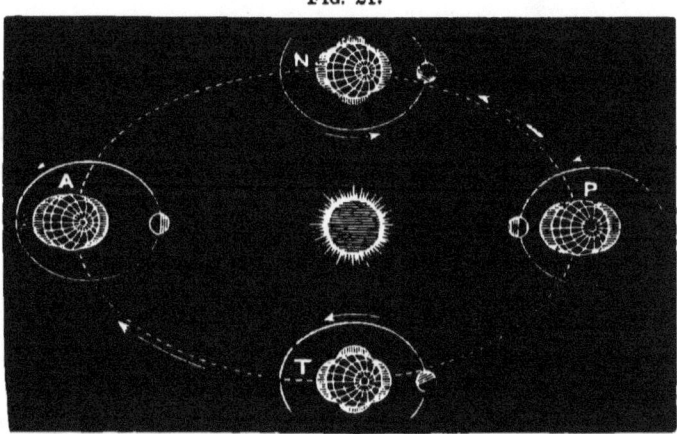

conjunction, twice in quadrature, and once in opposition, there will be two neap and two spring tides during every lunation. Thus: spring tide at conjunction, neap tide at first quarter, spring tide again at opposition, and neap tide again at second quarter.

924. **Variations in the spring tides** (Fig. 21).—The distance between the earth and sun, as also between the moon and sun, is different at different times of the year; as also the distance between the earth and moon is different at different times of the month. Therefore, the spring and neap tides are not always alike, as to their elevation and depression.

At A, the earth is in *aphelion*, its greatest possible distance from the sun; and the moon is in *apogee*, its greatest distance from the earth. Therefore, the waters of the earth are at their greatest possible distance from both the sun and moon, consequently they are the least attracted by them. Hence, the spring tides are correspondingly *low*.

At P, the earth is in *perihelion*, its least possible distance from the sun; and the moon is in *perigee*, its least distance from the earth. Therefore the waters of the earth are now at their least possible distance from both the sun and moon, consequently they are subjected to their greatest influence. Hence, the spring tides are *highest*.

925. **Tides affected by declination.**—The tide-wave tends to rise directly under the sun and moon. Hence, at the time of the equinoxes, the sun being over the equator, and the moon within $5\frac{1}{2}°$ of it, the crest of the great tide-wave will be on the equator, as represented in Fig. 19 (919).

As the sun and moon decline south, one tide-wave forms in the south, and the opposite one in the north. Suppose the moon and sun to be in the south, over or near the Tropic of Capricorn, as shown in Fig. 17 (917); then the highest wave, in the southern hemisphere, will be about 3 o'clock, P.M., and the lowest about 3 o'clock, A.M.; while at the north, over or near the Tropic of Cancer, this order is reversed. If a straight line be drawn from the crest of one wave to that of the other, it will be seen that it is highest tide in the day-time over the southern tropic, and highest tide in the night-time over the northern tropic.

It is on this account that, in high latitudes, every alternate tide is higher than the intermediate ones; the evening tides in *summer* (at the north) exceeding the morning tides; and the morning tides in *winter* exceeding those of evening.

Other Causes Affecting Tides.

926. **The winds affect the time and character of tides.**—Strong winds, according to their direction, may either retard or hasten the rise and fall of tides, or may increase or diminish their height.

927. **The conformation of the land affects the time and character of tides.**—The tide will be later or longer in rising in a large bay, with but a narrow opening into the sea or ocean. Hence, in the large Bay of New York, which has a very narrow inlet, it is not usually high tide till eight or nine hours after the moon has passed the meridian.

In the oceans, especially the Pacific, the tide rises and falls but a few feet. When pressed into narrow bays or channels it rises higher.

928. **The average elevation of tides,** at a few points on our coast, is as follows: Cumberland, at the head of the Bay of Fundy, 71 feet; Boston, $11\frac{1}{4}$ feet; New Haven, 8 feet: New York, 5 feet; Charleston. N. C., 6 feet.

929. **The different heights of water in different oceans and seas.**—As the great tide-waves proceed from east to west, they are arrested by the eastern side of the continents. For this reason, the water is 20 feet higher in the Gulf of Mexico than in the Pacific ocean, on the other side of the Isthmus. The Red Sea is 30 feet higher than the Mediterranean. Inland seas and lakes have no perceptible tides.

930. **Atmospherical tides.**—There is no doubt but that the same influences which cause tides of the sea, produce tides of the atmosphere. The air being lighter than water, and nearer to the moon, the atmospherical tides must be correspondingly higher than those of the sea. According to Herschel, these tides are, by very delicate observations, rendered not only sensible, but *measurable*.

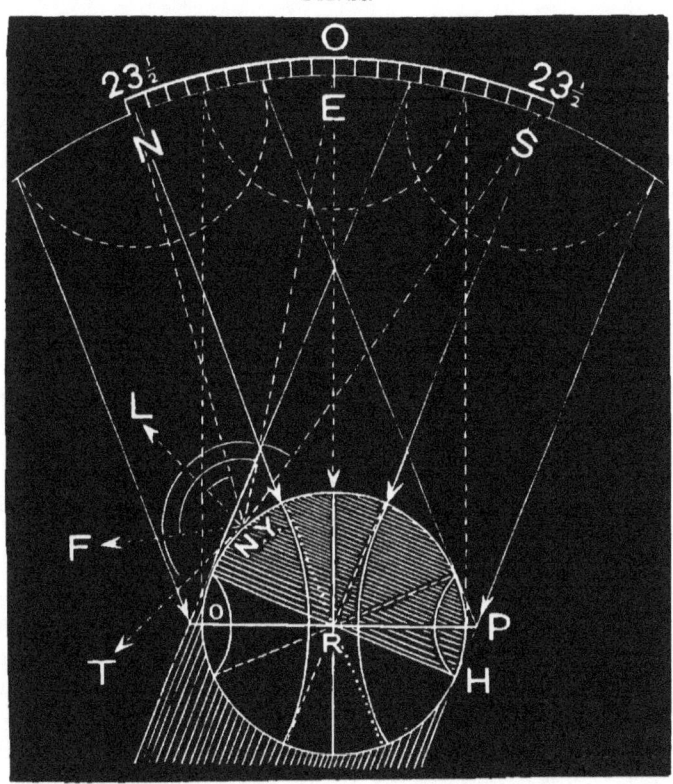

Fig. 22.

The Sun's Declination.—Zones and Temperature.

931. **Figure 22.—The declination of the sun.**—This figure represents the direction in which the rays of the sun fall upon the earth, when the latter is at her solstitial and equinoctial points.

The student should compare the following explanation with 868, 869, 870, and 871.

The dotted semicircle, N, represents the position of the sun when the earth is at her *summer solstice;* the semicircle, S, his position when the earth is at her *winter solstice;* the semicircle, E, his position when the earth is at her *equinoctial points.*

932. **The zones.—The torrid zone** (Fig. 22).—The angles, ERS and ERN, are nearly $23\frac{1}{2}$ degrees each; hence the angle, NRS, is 47 degrees; and the surface of the earth included between the lines, NR and SR, constitutes the *torrid zone,* on which the sun shines twice every year with perpendicular rays.

The frigid zones.—When the sun is at S, it shines upon the south pole, P, and the extreme rays on the right pass by the pole and are tangent to the earth at the point, H $23\frac{1}{2}$ degrees beyond the pole. When the sun is at E, he shines upon both poles; and when at N, he shines upon the north pole, O, and $23\frac{1}{2}$ degrees beyond it; while the extreme rays on the right are tangent to the earth at a point $23\frac{1}{2}$ degrees above the south pole, P; and the surface of the earth included between this point and the point H, constitutes the *south frigid zone,* which extends $23\frac{1}{2}$ degrees in every direction from the pole.

The temperate zones.—The surface of the earth included between the torrid zone and south frigid zone is the *south temperate* zone. The northern hemisphere is, of course, divided in the same manner.

933. **When the sun shines on the poles** (Fig. 22).—The sun shines on the south pole constantly while he passes from E to S and from S back to E again, which will occur while the earth passes from the autumnal to the vernal equinox, including the six months from September 23d to March 21st. During this time, which is the period of the sun's *southern declination,* the *north* pole will be in darkness. *The sun shines on the north pole* constantly while he passes from E to N and from N back to E again, which will occur while the earth passes from the vernal to the autumnal equinox, including the six months from March 21st to September 23d. During this time, which is the period of the *northern declination,* the *south* pole will be in darkness.

934. **The effect of the sun's declination on temperature** is due to the manner in which his rays strike upon the surface of the earth. Those parts of the earth upon which the rays fall *perpendicularly* are always warmest; while those portions upon which they fall *obliquely* are comparatively cold.

In the diagram (Fig. 22), the sun is supposed to be at S, which causes his rays to fall on the south pole, P, and the shadow of the earth to fall on the north pole, O. A ray of light, therefore, from the centre of S would strike at NY (New York) and glance off in the direction of T, nearly in a straight line. But if the sun were at E, a ray from his centre would fall less obliquely at New York and be reflected in the direction of F. If the sun were at N, a ray from his centre would fall upon New York still less obliquely and be reflected to L, nearly in a perpendicular direction to the earth's surface.

CHAPTER XXI.

TERRESTRIAL AND CELESTIAL GLOBES, FIXED STARS, ETC.

Latitude and Longitude.

935. **Figure 23.—Celestial and terrestrial latitude.**—*Celestial latitude* is reckoned north and south from the *ecliptic*, B, on

Fig. 23.

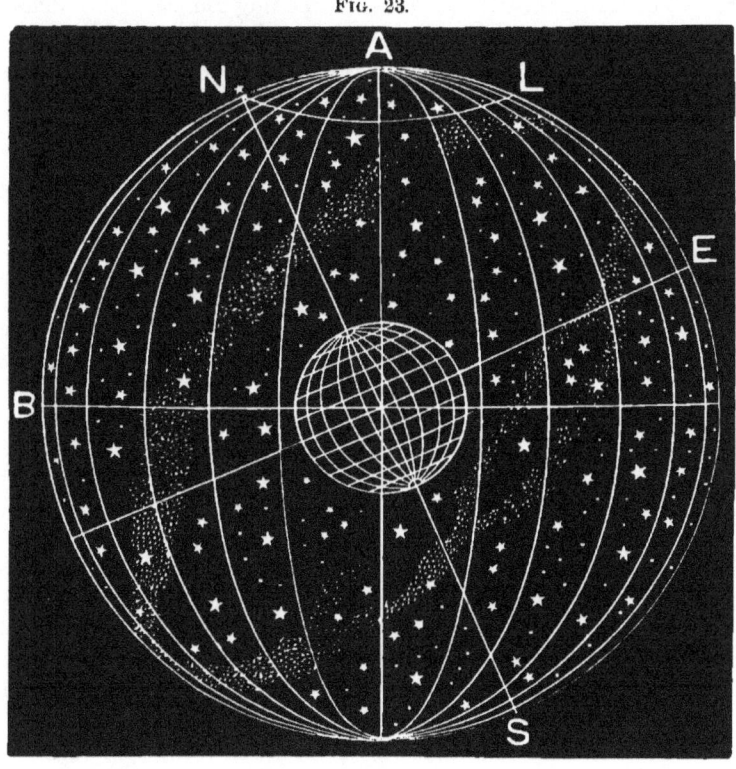

a circle of celestial latitude, and not from the equinoctial or celestial equator, E. Celestial latitude, therefore, is distance north or south of the ecliptic; and as one half of the ecliptic, B, is *south* of the equinoctial (E) and the earth's equator, it follows that a star may be in *north celestial latitude*, which is, nevertheless, *south of the equinoctial*.

Terrestrial latitude is distance on the earth's surface, reckoned in degrees and minutes, north or south from the equator to the poles, on any meridian. Hence the highest latitude, north or south, is 90°.

936. **Celestial longitude** is reckoned from the vernal equinox, or the first degree of Aries eastward, around the *ecliptic* to the same point again; therefore, the greatest number of degrees of celestial longitude is 360. See Fig. 1 (865).

Terrestrial longitude is distance on the earth's surface, reckoned east or west, from any given meridian on the equator or any parallel of latitude. The degrees of longitude diminish in length from the equator to the poles, because the earth grows smaller in circumference. The greatest number of degrees of terrestrial longitude is 180 east and 180 west. The meridian, from which the reckoning commences, is different in different countries. The English reckon from that passing through Greenwich, near London; the French from that passing through Paris; and the Americans from that passing through Washington.

937. **The terrestrial globe** represents the earth, upon which are drawn continents, islands, mountains, oceans, seas, rivers, parallels of latitude and longitude, boundaries of nations, etc.

938. **The celestial globe** (Fig. 23) represents the heavens as seen from the earth, upon which are drawn the ninety-three constellations, galaxy, or milky way, figures of various animals and objects from which the constellations are named, and circles of celestial latitude and longitude.

There are ninety-three constellations. The milky way is composed of a vast number of stars, so far away, and situated so nearly in the same direction, as to appear like a thin cloud. It extends from northeast to southwest through the whole circumference of the heavens, as represented in the figure.

The celestial poles are the points, N and S, where the earth's axis, if extended, would meet the heavens.

The plane of a meridian extends to the heavens, and forms a *celestial meridian* or *circle of declination*, upon which are measured declination and polar distance; the declination of a heavenly body being its distance from the equinoctial or celestial equator, E, north or south.

ASTRONOMY. 475

The declination and polar distance always equal 90°, or a quarter of a circle.

The right ascension of a body is its distance east of the first point of Aries, measured on the *equinoctial*, whereas celestial longitude, as before stated, is reckoned from the first point of Aries, measured on the *ecliptic*.

The angle of right ascension is included between the meridian passing through the body, and the one passing through the first point of Aries; and, like celestial longitude, is reckoned 360°.

Circles of celestial latitude pass through the poles (A) of the ecliptic, and cut its plane (B) at right angles. Upon these circles the latitude of heavenly bodies is measured, north and south, from the ecliptic.

The angle of longitude is included between the circle of latitude passing through the body, and the one passing through the first point of Aries, where they meet at the poles of the ecliptic.

The celestial horizon is a great circle, whose plane, passing through the centre of the earth, divides the heavens into two hemispheres, of which the upper one is called the *visible hemisphere*, and the lower one the *invisible hemisphere*. It is the plane of this circle which determines the rising and setting of the heavenly bodies.

The sensible horizon is the circle which terminates our view, where the earth and sky appear to meet.

A vertical circle is a great circle in the heavens, passing through the zenith and nadir, cutting the horizon at right angles.

The meridian is that vertical circle which passes through the north and south points of the horizon.

The prime vertical circle is the vertical circle which passes through the east and west points of the horizon.

Altitude and zenith distance are measured in degrees and minutes on vertical circles.

The zenith distance of a heavenly body is its distance from the zenith. The altitude and zenith distance are always equal to 90°.

The azimuth of a heavenly body is its distance, east or west, from the meridian.

The angle of azimuth is included between the meridian and vertical circle passing through the body.

The amplitude of a heavenly body is its distance, north or south, of the prime vertical circle.

The angle of amplitude is included between the prime vertical and the vertical circle passing through the body.

The angles expressing azimuth and amplitude are formed at the zenith where the vertical circles intersect each other; the measurement being made on the rational horizon.

The sums of the azimuth and amplitude are always equal to 90°.

939. **Nutation of the earth's axis** (Fig. 23).—The precession of the equinoxes (see 875) consists of a real motion of the pole of the heavens, N, among the stars, in a small circle, NL, around the pole of the ecliptic, A, as a centre, keeping constantly at its present distance of 23½ degrees from it, in a direction from east to west, and with a progress so slow as to require 25,000 years to complete one revolution, called the Platonic or great year. Hence, the bright star of the Lesser Bear, which we now call the *pole-star*, has not always been, nor will always continue to be, the polar star; for, in 12,500 years from now, the north pole of the earth will be at L, 47 degrees from its present position.

This revolution will, from age to age, cause gradual changes in the aspects of the heavens.

The Fixed Stars—Clusters—Nebulæ—Galaxy, etc.

940. **Motion of the stars.**—The stars, instead of being fixed or stationary, are found, like our sun, to be revolving around their own axes, and around some other central body, and, probably, carrying with them systems of planets, satellites, and comets.

941. **Variable or periodical stars** are those which undergo a regular periodical increase and diminution of lustre, amounting, in some cases, to a complete extinction and revival.

942. **Temporary stars, or new and lost stars,** are those which have appeared from time to time in different parts of the heavens, and, after remaining for a while apparently immovable, died away and left no trace of their existence. There are but few such stars.

943. **Double stars.**—Many stars, which to the naked eye appear single, are found, by aid of the telescope, to consist of two or more stars, situated near each other. These, as the case may be, are called *double*, *triple*, or multiple stars; or binary, ternary, etc.

944. **Binary systems.**—When two or more stars are found in a state of revolution about their common centre of gravity, as the planets revolve around our sun (845), they constitute what is called a *binary or stellar system*. These are the double and multiple stars, which to the naked eye appear single. There have been discovered about 6,000 multiple stars. Their periods of revolution about their common centre vary from a few to thousands of years. It is estimated, in some cases which have been observed, that the smaller revolve about the larger of the component stars at hundreds of billions of miles from each other, with the astounding velocity of millions of miles per hour.

Besides the revolution of these stars (which are really suns) around each other, they have a proper motion in space, like our sun, around the *great central sun* of our cluster (951).

945. **Clusters of stars.**—In a clear moonless night there can be seen, in different parts of the heavens, groups of stars which seem to be drawn together, as if by some special, mutual attraction. The Pleiades, or the Seven Stars, and Hyades, in Taurus, are instances of this kind. In the Pleiades there are seen, by aid of the telescope, over 200 stars. Such groups are called *clusters of stars*. Some of them contain ten or twenty thousand stars, apparently compacted and held together in a family, apart from other stars, under the influence of other laws of aggregation than those which have determined the scattering of stars over the general apparent surface of the heavens. Some of these clusters are of a globular form, while others have a very irregular figure.

Nebulæ.

946. **Nebulæ.**—This term is applied to those clusters of stars that are so distant as to appear only like a faint cloud or haze of light. There is probably no limit to the number of nebulæ. Prof. Mitchell concluded that some of these are so distant, that their light, travelling 192,000 miles a second, would not reach us in less than 30,000,000 of years.

Only a few nebulæ are seen with the naked eye. When seen through the telescope they appear as large as one-tenth of the moon's disk. Though they are seen in all parts of the heavens, they are most numerous in a zone of the heavens at right angles to the milky way.

947. **Classes of nebulæ.**—Nebulæ are divided into five classes, viz.:

1st. *Resolved nebulæ,* or those which have been discovered to be great clusters of stars.

2d. *Resolvable nebulæ,* or those which are considered to be composed of stars.

3d. *Stellar nebulæ,* which have an oval or round shape, increasing in density toward the centre, and, sometimes, seem to have a dim star in the centre.

4th. *Irresolvable nebulæ,* which are considered to be luminous matter in an atmospheric state, condensing into solid bodies, like the sun and planets.

5th. *Planetary nebulæ,* which resemble the disk of a planet, and are considered to be in an uncondensed state. Some of these are of enormous size. There is one situated in the head of Aquarius, computed to be of sufficient magnitude to fill the orbit of Uranus, or nearly 11,000,000 of miles in circumference. A few nebulæ are *annular* in form. There are also *double nebulæ*, or two or more near each other.

It is probable that all nebulæ might be resolved into distinct stars, had we telescopes of sufficient power.

948. **The milky way an annular nebula.**—The vast apparent extent of the milky way, as compared with other nebulæ, is owing to its comparative nearness. Could we view the galaxy or milky way from one of the other nebulæ, it would appear as an ordinary annular nebulæ, of which our sun is one of the stars. Hence, the Milky Way may be called the Great Nebula of the solar system.

949. **The number of stars.**—In the milky way, Herschel estimated that 50,000 stars passed the field of vision of his telescope in a single hour. It is safe, therefore, to estimate the number of stars in each cluster or nebula as almost numberless. Hence, when it is considered that the nebulæ themselves are also numberless, how vast must be the aggregate number of stars or suns, to say nothing of the many times as many planets, satellites, and comets.

950. **The term universe.**—Each nebula and cluster is called a Universe or Firmament. Therefore, the Universal Whole consists of Firmament upon Firmament, or an infinite series of Universes.

951. **Our cluster, or firmament.**—The single stars, visible to the naked eye, including the milky way and the solar system, constitute only one of the clusters or nebulæ of the heavens; that is, only one of the numberless Universes or Firmaments, which, under the guidance of the Divine Mind, ceaselessly, silently, and harmoniously traverse the boundless realms of space. Yet all is made up of *atoms*, inconceivably small; and the wisdom, power, and goodness of God are not less manifest in the infinitely varied combinations of the infinitesimal *molecules* of matter than in the construction, magnitude, and splendor of the heavens.

INDEX.

[THE REFERENCES ARE TO SECTIONS, NOT TO PAGES.]

A.

ABERRATION, chromatic, 437.
 of lenses, 412.
 of reflectors, 391.
Absorptive power, causes modifying, 297.
 for heat, 295.
 for light, 361.
 of colors, 295.
Accessory properties of matter, 11–18.
Accumulated electricity, 690.
Achromatic combination of lenses, 438.
Acoustics, definition, 530.
Action and reaction are equal, 65.
Action of heat on matter, 202.
 of surfaces upon heat, 290–297.
Adaptation of the eye to distance, 445.
Adhesion, 37.
 distinguished from cohesion, 37.
Affinity, 18.
Air an aërial ocean, 122.
 buoyancy of, 140.
 condensed-air fountain, 149.
 condenser, 148.
 gun, 150.
 impenetrability of, 125.
 no animal life, no flight, no combustion, etc., without it, 129.
 pump, 128.
 relation of to earth, same as glass to hot-house, 259.
 vibrating in tubes, 583. (See Atmosphere.)
Alphabet, telegraphic, 777.
Amalgam, 677.
Amalgamated zinc, 734.
Ampere's electro-magnetic theory, 766.
Amplitude of a heavenly body, 938.
 angle of, 938.
Analogy of light and heat, 358.
 of electricity and magnetism, 759.
Analysis of colors by absorption, 422.
Anemometers, 269.
Animal electricity, 789.
 heat, cause of, 213.
 respiration dependent upon atmospheric pressure, 146.
Animals, electrical, 790.
Annealing, 33.
Aphelion, 839.
Application of voltaic or galvanic electricity, 745–758.
Aqueducts, 96.
Archimedes' screw, 171.
Armature of magnets, 601.
Artesian wells, 95.
Artificial magnets, 603.
 method of making, 604.
Ascent of bodies, 55.
Astatic needle, 634, 764.
Asteroids, with table, 824.
Astronomical phenomena, early observation of, 801.
Astronomy, definition, 792.
 descriptive, physical, and practical, 793.

Atmosphere, 122.
 action of suction pumps dependent on, 132.
 action of the syphon dependent on, 188.
 an immense heating apparatus, 258.
 buoyancy of, shown by balloons, 140.
 composition of, 124.
 compression and expansion of, 127.
 density of at different altitudes, 139.
 effects of on the rising and setting of heavenly bodies, 400.
 free electricity of, 710.
 height of, 123.
 how heated, 256.
 impenetrability of, 125, 141.
 its pressure varies with altitude, 132.
 pressure of equal in all directions, 130.
 pressure of shown in various ways, 142–145.
 pressure of sustains different liquids at different heights, example and formula, 131.
 pressure of varies at the same place, 133.
 pressure of, when first understood, 139.
 tides of, 930.
 weight or pressure of, 126.
Atmospheric electricity, 709–719.
 causes of, 711.
 heat of, 209.
Atoms, 4.
Attraction, 18.
 adhesive, 37.
 capillary, 38.
 cohesive, 36.
 electrical, 656, 671.
 magnetic, laws of, 626.
 molecular, 18, 35.
 of gravitation, 39.
 of planets, with table, 822.
Attraction and repulsion, 87.
Audience rooms, 553.
Auroras borealis, 719.
 australis, 719.
 effects of, 719.
Axes of lenses, 408.
Axis, secondary, 390.
 of the ecliptic, 847.
 of the equinoctial, 847.
 optical, 446.
Azimuth, 938.
 angle of, 938.

B.

BACKGROUND, effects of, 465.
Balloons, 140.
Barker's mill, 163.
Barometer, its construction and uses, 134.
 as a weather-glass, 136.
 height of the mercury at different altitudes, 135.
 wheel form of, 138.
Barometric changes and the weather, rule for reading, 136.
 diurnal variations, 137.

Batteries, 735-740.
Battery, carbon, 739.
　　discovery of voltaic, 724.
　　effects of the voltaic, 745-758.
　　galvanic, 725.
　　Grove's nitric acid, 738.
　　of two or more couples, 740.
　　Smee's, 735.
　　sulphate of copper, 736.
　　Voltaic, 727.
Beams of light, 362.
Bellows, hydrostatic, 111.
　　pump, 178.
Bells, electrical, 686, 720.
　　diving, 141.
　　vibrations of, 562.
Belts, source of electricity, 683.
Binocular vision, 469.
Bodies, centre of gravity of, 40.
　　laws of falling and rising, 55.
　　luminous, non-luminous, transparent, translucent, and opaque, 359.
　　magnetic, and magnetised, 615.
　　method of electrifying, 661.
　　relation of to heat, 290-297.
　　relation of to light, 359.
　　stability of, 43.
　　suspended without contact, 774.
　　visible, emit light from all points, 363.
　　weight of, 39.
Body, definition of, 1.
　　electrified by induction, 668.
　　heavenly, 792. (See Heavenly Bodies.)
　　solar, 807.
Blasting under water by electricity, 706.
Boats, action of wind on sails of, 59.
Boiling by application of cold, 318.
Boiling point, 317.
　　affected by altitude, 319.
　　application in arts, 319.
　　causes modifying, 318, 320, 321.
　　nature of vessel varies, 321.
　　solids in solution varies, 320.
　　table of, at different atmospheric pressures, 334.
Bohnenberger's dry-pile electroscope, 737.
Boilers, steam, 351.
　　bursting of, 330.
Breast-wheel, 160.
Breathing dependent upon atmospheric pressure, 146.
Breezes, land and sea, 264.
Bridges, suspension, expansion of cables of, 215.
Brightness of the ocular image, 451.
Brittleness, 32.
Buckets or pots, endless chain of, 167.
Buildings, how heated, 255-257.
Buoyancy of air, 140.
　　of liquids, 113.
Burning-glasses, 301.

C.

CALCULATION of transits, 881.
Caloric, 198.
Calorimetry, 230.
Camera Lucida, 485.
　　obscura, 439, 483, 484.
　　similarity between and the eye, 440.
Candle bombs, 330.
Capillarity, 18, 38.
Carbon battery, 739.
Carbonic acid, density of, 249.
Catoptrics, 365.
Caustic curve, 391.
Celestial globe, 938.
　　horizon, 938.
　　longitude, 936.
　　meridian, 938.
　　poles, 938.
Centre of gravity, 40.
　　in man, 46.

Centre of gravity, method of finding, 41.
　　of cubes, 43.
　　of pyramids, 44.
　　of solar system, 845.
　　of vehicles, 45.
Centrifugal machine, 163.
　　pumps, 169, 170.
Centripetal and centrifugal forces, 843.
Chain-pump, 168.
Changes in matter chemical or physical, 2.
Characteristic properties of solids, 25-34.
Charging the Leyden jar, 692.
Chemistry, its relation to physics, 8.
Chemical affinity, 2.
Chord in music, 592.
Chromatic aberration, 437.
Chromatics, 419.
Circular or curvilinear motion, 842.
Circle, vertical, 938.
　　prime vertical, 938.
Climate, influence of latent heat of water on, 308.
Clothing, relations to heat, 252.
　　relation to color, 295.
Coercitive force of magnets, 627.
Co-existence of sound waves, 568.
Cohesion, 18, 36.
　　among solids, 36.
　　in solids, liquids, and gases, 87.
Cohesion and repulsion, 22.
　　relation of in the three states of matter, 23.
Cold and heat relative terms, 199.
Cold by evaporation, 335, 343.
Color blindness, 463.
Color of the electric spark, 701.
Colors, analysis of, by absorption, 422.
　　complementary, 421.
　　composition of, of the solar spectrum, 424.
　　dependent on amplitude of waves of light, 502.
　　different effects of, on vision, 464.
　　of opaque bodies, 429.
　　of transparent bodies, 430.
　　primary, 419.
　　union of two primary to produce a secondary, 423.
Combination of waves of liquids, 565.
　　of translation and rotation, 19.
　　of the five mechanical powers, example and formulæ, 86.
Combustion a source of heat, 211, 344.
　　structure of flame, 344.
Comets, 807.
　　appearance and nature of, 831.
　　direction of the motions of, 835.
　　orbits of, 832.
　　periodic times of, 833.
　　the number of, 834.
Comparison of thermometers, 273.
Compass, mariner's, 644.
　　discovery of, 644.
　　tables for correcting variations of, 644.
Compensating pendulum, 60.
Components and resultants, 58.
Compound levers, 69.
　　wheel and axle, 74.
Compressibility, 12.
　　of gases, 120.
　　of liquids, 89.
Compression a source of heat, 236.
　　of the earth at the poles, 50, 850.
Concave lenses, 405.
　　mirrors, 386.
　　foci of, 388, 389.
　　images by, 387.
Condensation, causes of, 327.
　　of steam, 332.
Condenser, air, 148.
　　electrical, 691.
　　discharge of electrical, 694, 695.
Conditions affecting terrestrial gravity, 48, 51.
Conductibility of clothing, 252.
　　of crystals, wood, etc., 244.

Conductibility of gases, 249.
  of liquids, 246-248.
  relative of moist and dry air, 250.
  relative of solids, liquids, and gases, 241.
  relative of solids liquids, and gases of the same temperature, 251.
  of solids, determination of, 242.
  table of, of solids, 249.
  varies with molecular arrangement, 244.
Conduction of electricity, 658.
  of heat, 240.
  heat in liquids not equalized by, 247.
  musical tones caused by, 243.
  the principle of Davy's safety lamp, 245.
Conductors and non-conductors of heat, 240.
  of electricity, 658.
Conjugate foci, properties of, 389.
Conjugate mirrors, reflection of heat by, 292.
Conjunction and opposition of planets, 890.
Constellations of the zodiac, 866, 872, 938.
Construction of barometers, 134.
  of thermometers, 271-283.
Copper, tempering, 33.
Convection of heat, 253.
  in liquids, 253.
  in gases, 256.
  heating buildings by, in air, 256.
  heating buildings by, in fluids, 255.
  ocean currents caused by, 254.
Conversion of thermometric scales, 273.
Convexity of the earth's surface, 889.
Convex lenses, 403.
  conjugate foci of, 409.
  spherical mirrors, 382.
  illustrated by plane mirrors, 381.
  images formed by, 384, 385.
Conveying water over hills with syphons, 191.
Cooling by radiation, 285.
Copernicus' theory of astronomy, 803.
Cords, vibration of, 570-573.
Coronas, 436.
Couples, simple voltaic, 726.
Crank, irregular action of, 354.
Cream, why rises on milk, 117.
Cryophorus, or frost-bearer, 335.
Crystallization, 310.
Crystallogenic attraction, 25.
Crystals conduct heat, 244.
  forms of, 24.
Cubical expansion, 217.
Currents, atmospheric, 258.
  in gases, 256.
  in the ocean, 254.
Curves, magnetic, 628-630.
  paraboloid, 392.
Curvilinear motion, 842.
Cyclones or hurricanes, 265.
Cylinder electrical machine, 677.

D.

DAGUERREOTYPES, how formed, 486.
  taken by electrical light, 750.
Dark lines in spectrum, 426-428.
Day and night, 867.
Day, solar, 854.
  sidereal, 854.
Davy's safety lamp, 245.
Dead centre, 354.
Declination of the needle, 638.
Declination of the sun, 871, 931.
  effect of on climate, 934.
Decomposition of light, 419.
  of salts, 756.
  of water, 755.
Defects of the eye, 458-460.
Deflagration, 751.
Density does not imply hardness, 28.
Density of air at different altitudes, 139.
  of gases and vapors, 229.
  of planets, with table, 821.
Descent on inclined planes, 55.

Descent, perpendicular, of pendulums, 61.
Depression of mercury in tubes, 58.
Determination of reflective power, 294.
Dew, 343.
Dew-point, 328.
Diamagnetism, 783.
Diathermancy, 298.
  causes which modify, 299.
  of the air, 300.
Dielectrics, 670.
Difference between musical sounds and noises, 588.
Difference between static and dynamic electricity, 744.
Differential thermometer, 283.
Diffraction, 511.
Diffraction fringes, 511.
Dioptrics, definitions, 394.
Dipping needle, 642.
  its position in different places, 643.
Direction in which objects are seen, 369.
Direction of force, 54.
  of gravity, 53.
Directive action of the earth and of magnets, 636.
Discharge, electrical, of the condenser, 693.
Discharger, electrical, 695.
  universal, 697.
Discharging-rod, 696.
Discovery of electricity, 649.
  of electro-magnetism, 760.
  of galvanism, accidental, 722.
Disguised electricity, 690.
Dispersion of light, 364.
Distance calculated by sound, 537.
  estimation of, 466.
  of distinct vision, 455.
Distance between heavenly bodies, 798.
Diving-bell, 141.
Divisibility, 11.
Double refraction, polarization by, 520.
Downward pressure of air, 126.
  of liquids, 101.
Dry-piles, voltaic, 728.
Ductility, 30.
Duration of visual impressions, 470.
Dynamical electricity, 721.
Dynamics, 54.

E.

EAR, of animals, 558.
  trumpet, 558.
Earth as a magnet, 633.
  as viewed from Mercury, 836.
  at the equinoxes, 870.
  at the solstices, 869.
  circuit, 778.
  directive action of, 763.
  drawn toward falling bodies, 52.
  figure of, 50, 850.
  the reservoir of electricity, 660.
  motion of the water of, 912.
Earth's axis, nutation of, 939.
  magnetism, action of illustrated by magnets, 641.
  cause of, 780.
  periodic revolution, 815.
  rotation, effect of upon gravity, 51.
  effect of upon winds, 262.
  satellite or moon, 826.
  surface, convexity of, 889.
Ebullition, 316.
  laws governing, 317.
  (see boiling-point.)
Echo, 547.
  tone changed by, 547.
Echoes, multiple, 548.
Eclipses, direction in which they come on, 898.
  duration of, 902.
  general effects of total of the sun, 903.
  of the stars, 909.
  position of sun, earth, and moon when they occur, 896.

Eclipses, the number of in any one year, 904.
  they are either total, partial, or annular, 897.
  total and annular of the sun, 901.
  total of the moon and partial of the sun, 899.
  why there are not more solar than lunar, 908.
  why not more frequent, 905.
  of Jupiter's moons, 910.
  of Saturn's moons, 911.
Ecliptic, 847.
  axis of, 847.
  inclination of the orbits of the planets to the plane of, with table, 849.
  its intersection with the equinoctial, 877.
  obliquity of. 848.
  poles of, 847.
Ecliptic limits, solar and lunar, 907.
Eel, electrical, 790.
Effects of accumulated electricity, 704-708.
  chemical, 708.
  heating, 706.
  mechanical, 707.
  physiological, 705.
Elastic balls transmit shocks, 65.
Elasticity, 26.
  limits of, 26.
  of air, 127.
  of cords and wires, 570.
  of flexure, tension, and torsion, 26.
  of gases, 147-150, 226.
  of liquids, 89.
Electric battery, 699.
Electric currents, action of magnets upon, 769.
  action of upon magnetic needles, 761.
  attraction of, shown by oscillating spiral, 768.
  difference between intensity and quantity of, 732.
  induced by other currents, 784.
  mutual action of, 767.
  of the pile, 730.
  resistance to, 742.
Electric light, 746.
  in a vacuum, 689.
  influences the magnet, 748.
  properties of, 750.
Electric spark, 684, 700.
  color of, 701.
  difference between positive and negative, 702.
Electric telegraph, 776-778.
Electrical animals, 790.
Electrical attraction and repulsion, 656.
  attraction and repulsion, laws of, 657.
  eel, 790.
  excitement, sources of, 650.
  pendulum, 652.
  tension, 662.
Electrical machines, 676-683.
  precautions in using, 681.
  use of, 679.
Electrical blasting, 706.
Electrical blow-pipe, 688.
  chime, 686.
  condensers, 690-694.
  egg, 689.
  experiments illustrating attraction and repulsion, 684-689.
  helix, 770, 771.
  induction, 668-671.
  puppets, 685.
  square, 703.
  wheel, 687.
Electricity, accumulated, 690-695.
  accumulated only on the surface of bodies, 663.
  atmospheric. 709-719.
  conductors of, 658.
  decomposition by, 752.
  definition of, 648.
  discharge of, 694, 695.
  discovery of, 649.

Electricity, disguised or latent, 690.
  distribution dependent on form, 665.
  dynamical, 721.
  dynamical, chemical effects of, 752-757.
  dynamical, magnetic effects of, 759.
  dynamical, physical effects of, 746-751.
  earth a reservoir of, 660.
  Franklin's experiment with, 709.
  floating currents of, 767.
  frictional, 648-653.
  from all sources identical, 744.
  from steam, 682.
  galvanic, 725.
  heating, effects of, 706-751.
  illuminating effects of, 746.
  induction of, 668-671.
  light and heat, 3.
  loss of, in excited bodies, 667.
  magneto, 781.
  measurement of quantity of, in machines, 680.
  mechanical effects of, 707.
  of animals, 790.
  of plants, 791.
  physiological effects of, 705, 758.
  positive and negative, 653.
  quantity necessary for decomposition, 757.
  relation between and magnetism, 759.
  resides on surfaces of bodies, 663.
  secondary currents of, 784.
  sources of, 650.
  statical, 648.
  statical and dynamical, difference between, 744.
  statical, chemical effects of, 708.
  theories of, 654, 655, 724, 725.
  thermo, 787.
  the two fluids of, separated and obtained, 669.
  two kinds of, 653.
  velocity of, 716.
  vitreous and resinous, 653.
  voltaic, 725.
Electrodes, 727.
  shape of carbon, 749.
Electro-chemical decomposition, 752.
  theory, 725.
Electro-dynamic force, exerted in a tangential direction, 765.
Electro-dynamic induction, 770.
Electro-dynamics, 759.
Electro-gilding and electro-plating, 754.
Electro-magnetism, 759.
  Ersted's discovery relating to, 760.
Electro-magnets, 773.
Electro-magnetic force exerted in a tangential direction, 765.
  suspension of bodies by, without contact, 774.
  theory of, Ampere's, 766.
  utilization of, 775.
Electrometers, 672.
  gold-leaf, 674.
  method of using the gold-leaf, 675.
  quadrant, 673.
Electro-motive force, 741.
Electro-positive and electro-negative, 731.
Electrophorus, 676.
Electroscope, 652.
  Bohnenberger's dry-pile, 737.
Electrotyping, 753.
  method of depositing the metal upon the mould, 753.
  preparing the mould, 753.
Elements, simple, 1.
Emission power of bodies, 296.
  causes modifying, 297.
Endless screw, 86.
Engine, fire, 186.
  high pressure steam, 349.
  low pressure steam, 354.
Eolipile, 346.
Equilibrium, 40.

INDEX. 483

Equilibrium, conditions of in liquids, 94.
  electrical, 655.
  neutral, stable, and unstable, 40.
  neutral and stable illustrated, 42.
  of heat, 203.
  of liquids in communicating vessels, 94.
  of liquids of different densities, 117.
  of the lever, 66.
  on inclined plane, 83.
Equinoctial, 875.
  intersection of with the ecliptic, 877.
Equinoxes, 870.
  precession of, 875.
Ersted's discovery, 760.
Escape of liquids through orifices, 152.
Essential properties of matter, 9, 10.
Estimation of distance and magnitude of objects, 466.
  of distance by sound, 537.
Evaporation, 322.
  causes influencing, 326.
  cold produced by, 335, 343.
  freezing by, 335.
  in a vacuum, 323.
  under pressure, 324.
Expansibility, 13.
Expansion of gases, 226.
  relation of to compressibility, 228.
  laws of, 227.
Expansion of liquids, 220.
  amount of, 221.
  beneficial effects of unequal, in water, 224.
  different in different liquids, for same heat, 222.
  table of for different liquids, 222.
  water an exception to the law, 223.
Expansion of solids, 215.
  absolute and relative, 219.
  amount of, 215.
  co-efficient of, cubical and lineal, 216.
  cubical, 217.
  cubical and lineal, relation between, 218.
  force exerted by, 215.
  linear, 215.
  ratio of increases with the temperature, 221.
  table of, for different solids, 219.
Explosion of steam-boilers, 330.
Extension, 9.
Extent of space, 795.
Extremes of temperature, 207.
Eye, adjustability of to different distances, 445.
  inversion of images in, 449.
  lachrymal or tear gland, and eyelid, 444.
  means of adjusting and holding, 442.
  optic axis of, 446.
  similarity between and camera obscura, 440.
  structure of its interior, 443.
  the pupil, method of adjusting, 441.
Eye-glasses, 474.
Eye-piece, 477, 488, 489.

F.

Fahrenheit's thermometer, 272.
Fall of light bodies, 129.
Falling bodies, accelerated velocity of, 56.
  laws of, 55.
Falling body, space described by, 55.
  table of intervals and spaces, 55.
Fire-engine, 186.
  where first employed, 186.
Firmament, 951.
Fixed lines in spectra, 426-428.
  pulley, 75.
  stars, 940-951.
Flame, structure of, 344.
Flexibility and pliability, 31.
Flotation, principles of, 118.
Fluidity, cause of, 87.
Fluids, austral and boreal, 633.

Fluids, elastic, 119.
  electrical, 669.
  magnetic, 625.
  theory of single electrical, 655.
  theory of two electrical, 654.
  the term fluid, 655.
  viscid, heating of, 253.
Flow of liquids, 153-155.
  in pipes, theoretical and actual, 153.
  through orifices at different depths, 155.
  velocity of discharge as square root of head, 155.
  of rivers, 156.
  velocity of, 157.
Fly-wheel, use of, 354.
Foci of concave mirrors, for divergent rays, 389.
  for parallel and convergent rays, 388.
  conjugate, properties of, 389.
Focus, virtual, for converging rays, 388.
Fog-bows, 496.
Force, coercitive of magnets, 627.
  directive of magnets, 636.
  distribution of, in magnets, 605.
  electro-motive, 741.
  formative in nature, 24.
  origin of, 20.
  unit of, 54.
Forces, 20.
  centrifugal and centripital, 843.
  composition of, 58.
  measure of, 54.
  molecular, 22.
  parallelogram of, 58.
  propositions in regard to, 54.
  represented by lines, 54.
  resolution of, 58.
Forces and resistances, 66.
Forcing-pumps, 180-185.
  plunger, 180.
  rotary, 75-177.
Formative force in nature, 24.
Forms of crystals, 25.
  of lenses, 405.
  of mirrors, 367.
Formulæ relating to combination of mechanical powers, 86.
  relating to compound levers, 69.
  compound wheel and axle, 74.
  conversion of thermometric scales, 273.
  falling and rising bodies, 55.
  hydrostatic press, 109.
  inclined plane, 83.
  levers, 66-68.
  pressure of liquids, 108, 133.
  pulleys, 75-82.
  the screw, 84.
  specific gravity, 115.
  velocity of discharge of liquids, 155.
  the wedge, 85.
  the wheel and axle, 71.
Fountain and vertical jets of water, 195.
Fountain, condensed air, 149.
  expansion, 131.
  Hiero's, 196.
  intermittent, 197.
  vacuum, 145.
Franklin's kite, 709.
  harmonicon, 563.
  pulse-glass, 319.
Freezing by evaporation, 335.
Freezing mixtures, 309.
Freezing point, 275.
  fixing it on thermometers, 276.
Freezing a warming process, 306.
Friction between liquids and solids, 153.
  electricity excited by, 653.
  heat produced by, 212.
  in rivers, 156.
Frictional electricity, 648.
Fringes, diffraction, caused by interference, 511.
Frost-bearer, 335.
Fulcrum, 66.
Furnaces, hot-air, 256.

INDEX.

Fusion, always gradual, 306.
  latent heat of, 303.
  laws and heat of, 304.
  peculiar in some solids, 305.

G.

GALAXY, or the milky way, 948.
Galileo's discoveries, 805.
Galvanic battery, 725.
Galvanism, 721.
  discovery of, 722.
  Galvani's explanation of, 723.
  Volta's contact theory of, 724.
Galvanometers or multipliers, 762.
Gamut, 596.
Gas, illuminating, 344.
  ignited by electricity, 683.
Gases and vapors, 119.
  capacity for heat, 236.
  compressibility of, 127.
  compression of, diminishes capacity for heat, 236.
  conductibility of, for heat, 249.
  density of, 229.
  expansion of, 120, 226.
  impenetrability of, 125.
  laws of expansion of, 227.
  Mariotte's law of elastic force of, 147.
  mechanical conditions of, 121.
  molecular force of repulsion of, 22, 23, 88, 91, 119.
  permanent, incoercible, 120.
  simple or compound, 120.
  specific heat of, 235.
  tension of, affected by temperature, 323-325.
  they transmit pressure, 121.
Gas-jets, musical notes of, 574.
Glass, burning, 301.
  night, 482.
  object-glass and eye-glass, 481.
  opera, 481.
Globes, celestial, 938.
  terrestrial, 937.
Graduation of thermometers, 276.
Gravity, 39.
  affected by the earth's rotation, 51.
  affected by the shape of the earth, 50.
  cause of weight, 39.
  centre of, 40.
  centre of, in man, 46.
  centre of, in vehicles, 45.
  centre of, of the solar system, 845.
  direction of, 53.
  law of intensity of, 47.
  tabular statement of the law, 47.
  varies with altitude, 48.
  varies with latitude, 50.
  varies with depression below level of the sea, 49.
  specific, method of finding, 115, 116.
Guage, rain, 339.
Gridiron, pendulum, 60.
Grove's battery, 738.
Gulf stream, 254.

H.

HAIL, 338.
Halos, 436.
Hand-truck, a variety of lever, 69.
Hardening, 33.
  by hammering, 33.
  by heating and cooling, 33.
Hardness, 28.
Harmonicon, 563.
Harmonies, limit of, 595.
  most pleasing, 594.
  the principal, 593.
Harmony, 592.
Heat, action of on matter, 202.

Heat and cold relative terms, 199.
  and light, analogy, 358.
  applied to warming apartments partly consumed in expanding the air, 237.
  atmospheric electricity, a source of, 209.
  cause of in animals, 213.
  causes which modify the reflective, absorbent, and emission power for, 297.
  change of state in bodies caused by, 303.
  chemical effects of, 202.
  combustion, a source of, 211.
  conduction of, 240-252.
  convection of, in gases. 256.
  convection of, in fluids, 253-255.
  definition of. 198.
  developed by solidification, 303.
  distribution of, 202.
  effects of on magnets, 608.
  equilibrium of, 203.
  expansion of gases by, 226.
  expansion of liquids by, 220.
  expansion of solids by, 215.
  general effects of, 202.
  intensity of in solar spectrum, 420.
  its effects on organic life, 202.
  latent, 303.
  light and electricity, 8.
  luminous and obscure, 204.
  mechanical sources of, 212.
  modes of communication of, 239.
  nature of, 201.
  of chemical action, 210, 211, 344.
  of compression, 212, 236.
  of friction, 212.
  of fusion, 304.
  of percussion, 212.
  of plants, 213.
  of static electricity, 706.
  of voltaic arch, 751.
  of voltaic currents, 751.
  origin of terrestrial, 208.
  physiological sources of, 213.
  polarization of, 302.
  quantity and intensity, difference between, 214.
  quantity emitted by the sun, 206.
  radiation of, 284-289.
  reflection of, 290-294.
  refraction of, 301, 419, 420.
  relation of to cold, 199.
  repellent force of, 202.
  sensible, 303, 315.
  sensible of steam, 315.
  solar radiation, 205.
  specific, 231.
  specific affected by change of state, 238.
  specific of gases, 235.
  specific of water, effect on climate, 234.
  standard of specific, 233.
  theories respecting, 201.
  transference of, 203.
  transmission of radiant, 298.
  unit of, 232.
  universal radiation of, 289.
  velocity of, 509.
Heat and light of the planets, with table, 823.
Heating buildings by hot air, 256.
  by hot water, 255.
  by steam, 257.
Heavenly bodies, different classes of, 794.
  distances between, 798.
  magnitude of, 796.
  orbital motions of, 799.
  the number of, 797, 949.
  velocity of, 800.
Height measured by barometer, 135.
Helix electrical, single, 770.
  double, 771.
  magnetizing by, 772.
Hemisphere, invisible, 938.
  visible, 938.
Hiero's fountain, 196.
High-pressure engine, 349.

INDEX. 485

High-pressure steam, 334.
Horizon, crimson appearance of, 400.
   celestial, 938.
   sensible, 938.
Horse-shoe magnets, 610.
Hot air furnaces, 256.
Hot water apparatus, 255.
House's telegraph, 777.
Humidity of the air, 343.
Hurricanes, 265.
Hydraulic and hydro-pneumatic machines, importance of, 197.
Hydraulic ram, 172.
Hydraulics, definition of, 151.
Hydro-dynamics, 151.
Hydro-electric machine, 682.
Hydrogen, density of, 229.
Hydrometers, 116.
Hydrostatic bellows, 111.
   paradox, 107.
   press, example and formulæ, 109.
   pressure in mountains, 112.
Hydrostatics, 87.
Hygrometer or moisture-bearer, 343.

I.

ICE, beneficial effects of being lighter than water, 224.
   lighting gas with, 706.
   why it does not acquire great thickness, 307.
   why lighter than water, 224.
Illumination of railways, 392.
Illumination, best materials for, 344.
   sufficiency of, 452.
Images formed by concave lenses, 418.
   by concave reflectors, 387.
   by concave reflectors, when the object is beyond the centre of curvature, 393.
   by convex lenses, when the object is twice the focal distance, 413.
   by convex lenses, when the object is at *more* or *less* than twice the focal distance, 414, 415.
   by convex reflectors, 384, 385.
   by plane reflectors, 375.
Images, inversion of in the eye, 449.
   multiplicity of, 376.
   size of on the retina, 457.
   virtual, 375.
Impenetrability, 10.
   of gases, 125.
Imponderables, 3.
Incidence, angle of, 57.
Inclination of orbits of planets to plane of ecliptic, 849.
   table of, 849.
Inclination of moon's orbit to plane of ecliptic, 883.
Inclination, polar, of the planets, 878.
Inclined plane, 83.
   conditions of equilibrium, 83.
   example and formulæ, 83.
   its combination with the other mechanical powers, 86.
   example and formulæ, 86.
   the screw, a modification of, 84.
   example and formulæ, 84.
   the wedge, a modification of, 85.
   formulæ, 85.
Indestructibility, 17.
Index of refraction, 394.
Induced currents, 784.
   different orders of, 785.
   properties of, 786.
Induction, electro-dynamic, 779.
   explanation of, electrical, 670.
   magnetic, illustrated by a series of rings, 617.
   magnetic, without contact, 620.
   of electricity, 668–671.

Induction of magnetism, 616–620.
Inductive power of the earth's magnetism, 624.
Inertia, 16.
Influence of the earth's figure on gravity, 50.
   of the earth on its waters, 915.
   relative of sun and moon on the tides, 922.
Influence of the sun, 811.
   upon tides, 919.
Insulation and insulators, 659.
Insulating stool, 684.
Intensity, conditions of, of light, 527.
   in electricity, 732, 733.
   of force, 54.
   of gravity, 47.
   of light at different distances, 528, 529.
   of light, increases with angle of incidence, 374, 527.
   of light, reflected, 374.
   of luminous, calorific, and chemical rays, 420.
   of many couples, 733.
   of radiant heat, 286.
   of sound, 555.
   of sound, causes which modify, 556.
   of sound in tubes, 557.
Interference colors, 507.
Interference of light, 503.
   demonstration of, 505.
   fringes caused by, 511.
   laws of, 506.
   non-interference, 504.
   of sound, 564.
   of sound waves, 568.
   of waves of liquid in an ellipse, 566.
Intermittent fountain, 197.
   springs, 99, 189.
Intersection of the ecliptic and equinoctial, 877.
Interstices between atoms and molecules, 35.
Iris, 441.
Iron, how made magnetic, 604.
Iron ships, the Great Eastern, 118.
Irradiation, 465.

J.

JAR, Leyden, 692.
Jets of water, 195.
Jupiter, 836.
Jupiter's belts, 836.
   length of days and nights, 878.
   seasons, 878.
Jupiter's satellites or moons, 827.
   eclipses of, 910.
   dimensions, distances, and periodic times of, 827.

K.

KALEIDOSCOPE, 377.
Keeper of a magnet, 610.
Kepler's discoveries and laws, 804.

L.

LANTERN, magic, 478.
Latent electricity, 690.
Latent heat, 303.
   and sensible, of steam, 315.
   of evaporation, 313.
   of fusion, 308.
   of steam, 314.
   of water graduates changes of temperature, 308.
Lateral pressure of fluids, to what proportioned, 101.
   total of, on walls of a vessel, 105.
Latitude found by the north star, 889.
   celestial and terrestrial, 935.
   circles of celestial, 938.
Laws of cooling by radiation, 286.

486 INDEX.

Laws of distribution of attraction in magnets, 606, 607.
  determining the force of voltaic currents, 743.
  electrical attraction and repulsion, 657.
  electrical induction, 669.
  evaporation, 323.
  expansion of gases, 227.
  falling and rising bodies, 55.
  intensity of gravity, 47.
  intensity of light, 527, 529.
  intensity of radiation of heat, 286.
  interference of light, 506.
  Kepler, 804.
  liquefaction and solidification, 304.
  magnetic attraction and repulsion, 626.
  oscillation of pendulums, 61.
  projectiles, 62.
  reflection of heat, 291.
  reflection of light, 368.
  reflected motion, 57.
  refraction of light, 395.
  refraction of sound, 582.
  the vibration of cords, 572.
Length of luminous waves 508, 509.
Lenses and prisms, 405.
  analogous effects of, 411.
Lenses, aberration of, 412.
  achromatic combination of, 438.
  conjugate foci of, 409, 410.
  convergent and divergent, 405.
  definitions relating to, 408.
  varieties of, 405.
Lenses concave, 417,
  effects of, on rays of light, 417.
  images formed by, 418.
  convex, action of on light, 408.
  images formed by, 413–415.
  magnifying power of, 476.
  optical centre of, 408.
  plano-convex, 412.
  spherical, effect of on a ray of light, 407.
Level, water, 96.
  spirit, 97.
Lever, conditions of equilibrium of, 66.
  definition of, 66.
  of the first class, 66.
  example and formulæ, 66.
  of the second class, 67.
  example, 67.
  of the third class, 68.
  example, 68.
  illustrated by limbs of animals, 70.
  compound, 69.
  example and formulæ, 69.
Leyden jar, 692.
  charging of, 693.
  discharge of, 695.
  disruptive discharge of, 694.
  electricity of resides on the glass, 698.
  limit of charge of, 694.
  slow discharge of, 720.
Libration of the moon, 858.
Light, absorption of, 361, 364.
  action of tourmaline on, 514.
  and heat, analogy of, 358.
  and heat by chemical action, 210, 211, 344.
  artificial, 357.
  cause of refraction of, 396.
  cause of waves of, 510.
  changed by polarization, 513–520.
  colors of, 419.
  color of dependent on length of waves, 502.
  definition of, 355.
  dispersion of, 364.
  direction of vibrations of, 500.
  double reflection of by mirrors, 398.
  double refraction of, 519.
  electricity a source of, 357.
  emitted from every point of visible bodies, 363.
  heat and electricity are forces in nature, 3.

Light in a homogeneous medium, 360.
  influenced by magnetism, 748.
  interference colors of, 507.
  intensity of at different distances, 529.
  intensity of dependent upon conditions, 527.
  interference and non-interference of, 503–506.
  internal reflection of, 398.
  laws of refraction of, 395.
  length of vibrations or waves of, 509.
  moves in straight lines, 363.
  nature of, 356.
  parallel rays of, how affected by a drop of water, 435.
  pencils of passing through plane glass, 397.
  polarization of, 512–521.
  properties of, 364.
  rays, pencils, and beams of, 362.
  reflection of, 370–393.
  reflection of, total, 399.
  recomposition of in several ways, 431.
  refraction of, by dense media, 401.
  refracted by parallel strata, 397.
  refraction by prisms, 406, 419.
  relation of different bodies to, 359.
  sensations of, excited by other causes, 473.
  sources of, 357.
  theories of, 356, 499.
  velocity of, 526.
  waves of, 499–510.
  white, composition of, 431.
Light and heat of planets, with table, 823.
Light-houses, 416.
  revolving, 416.
Lightning, 714.
  classes of, 715.
  Franklin's experiment with, 709.
  identity of and electricity, 709.
  liability of being struck by, 718.
  means of safety from, 718.
  return shock of, 717.
  velocity of, 716.
Lightning rods, 718.
  how to render them effective, 718.
Limbs of animals levers of the third class, 70.
Limits of elasticity, 26.
  of perceptible sounds, 590.
Linear expansion, 215.
  co-efficient of, 216.
  laws of, 215.
Liquefaction and solidification, 304.
  always gradual, 306.
  laws of, 304.
Liquids, ascent of, in capillary tubes, 38.
  cohesion in, 90.
  compressibility of, 89.
  convection of heat in, 253–255.
  direction of pressure of, 92.
  downward pressure of, 101.
  equilibrium of in communicating vessels, 94.
  equilibrium of different densities in communicating vessels, 102.
  expansion of, 220–224.
  flow of obstructed by sharp angles, 190.
  friction between and solids, 153, 156.
  heat in, not equalized by conduction, 247.
  lateral pressure of, diminished by motion, 194.
  mobility of, 88.
  mobility, cause of, 88.
  non-conductibility of, shown by experiment, 248.
  of unequal densities seek different levels in containing vessels, 117.
  practical use of transmitting pressure by, 108.
  pressure of, not in proportion to quantity, but height, 98.
  pressure of, in proportion to height and base, 100.
  pressure of, on sides of vessels, 104.

INDEX. 487

Liquids, pressure, total, on sides of vessels, 105.
  pressure, total, on sides and bottom of vessels, 106.
  spheroidal state of, 331.
  specific gravity of, 115, 116.
  tendency of to seek a level, shown by aqueducts, 98.
  transmit pressure equally in all directions, 92.
  upward pressure of, equal to downward pressure, 100.
  vary in fluidity, 88.
  velocity of discharge of, 155.
  volatile and fixed, 312.
Lodestone, 599.
  magnetic manifestations of, 600.
  method of making magnets with, 604.
  north and south poles of, 600.
Longitude in the heavens, 876.
  angle of, 938.
  celestial, 936.
Long-sightedness, 458.
  caused by defective form of eye-ball, 459.
  of old people, 460.
Looming, 403.
Low-pressure steam-engine, 354.
  illustration of the principle of, 332, 333.

M.

MACHINE, motor, power, and weight, 66.
Machines, electric, 676–683.
  for elevating water, 164–185.
  importance of hydraulic and hydro-pneumatic. 197.
Magic lantern, 478.
Magnetic attraction not intercepted, 631.
Magnetic attraction and repulsion, 625.
  at different distances, 607.
  distribution of, 606.
  laws of, 626.
Magnetic curves, 628–630.
  batteries, 610.
  dip of needle, 640.
  electricity, 781.
  fluids, 625.
  induction, 616–624.
  intensity varies, 645.
  manifestations of lodestone, 599, 600.
  meridian. 637
  needle, 635.
  polarity, 600.
Magnetic and magnetized bodies, 615.
Magnetism by contact, 616.
  by induction, 616.
  coercitive force of, 627.
  definition of, 598.
  inductive power of the earth's, 646.
  relation between and electricity, 759.
  terrestrial, 633.
  terrestrial, illustrated by action of magnets, 641.
  two-fluid theory of, 625.
  utilization of, 647.
Magnetizing, by the helix and electrical current, 772.
  method of by bent bars, 612.
  method of by straight bars, 613.
Magneto-electric machines, 782.
Magneto-electricity, 781.
Magnets, armatures of, 601.
  artificial, 603.
  bar, 609.
  both poles of must co-exist, 614.
  compound, 609.
  compound horse-shoe, 610.
  deprived of power by heat, 608.
  directive force of, 636.
  directive force of, simply rotates the needle, 636.
  distribution of force in, 605.
  do not part with their own power, 621.

magnets, electro, 773.
  force of attraction of, at different distances, 607.
  fully mounted lodestone, 602.
  law of distribution of attraction in, 606.
  method of charging, 611–613.
  method of charging horse-shoe, 612.
  method of making artificial, 604.
  natural, 599.
  preservation of, 632.
  unlike poles of neutralize each other, 622, 623.
Magnifying glasses, 476–479.
Magnifying power of lenses, 476.
Magnitude or extension, 9.
  absolute of planets, with table, 818.
  of heavenly bodies, 796.
  relative of planets, with table, 819.
Malleability, 29.
Mariner's compass, 644.
  discovery of, 644.
  variations of, corrected by table, 644.
Mariner's sextant, 380.
Matter, 1.
  accessory properties of, 11–18.
  changes in, chemical or physical, 2.
  different kinds of, 1.
  essential properties of, 9, 10.
  properties of, general or specific, 6.
  spaces between atoms of, 5, 35.
  the three states of, 23.
  ultimate constitution of, 4.
Mechanical conditions of gases, 121.
Mechanical powers, 66–86.
Medium, luminiferous, 360.
Mediums of sound, 532.
Melody, 592.
Melting a cooling process, 306.
and freezing, 304.
  always gradual, 306.
  peculiarities of in some solids, 305.
Mercurial thermometer, 272.
  limits of, 280.
Mercury, depression of, in tubes, 88.
Mercury, oscillations of, 882.
Mercury, transits of, 880.
  list of, for the present century, 881.
Meridian, magnetic, 637.
  true, 637.
Metals conduct electricity, 242.
  conduct heat, 242.
Microscopes, 476.
  compound, 477.
  object glasses of, 477.
  power of, 476, 477.
  simple, 476.
  solar, 479.
Microscopic views, 479.
Milky way, an annular nebula, 948.
Mirage, 402.
Mirrors and specula, 366.
  concave, convex, and plane, 373.
  concave reverse of convex, 386.
  conjugate foci, properties of, 389.
  convex spherical, illustrated by plane, 381.
  deception practiced by, 378.
  foci of concave, for parallel and convergent rays, 388.
  foci of concave, for divergent rays, 389.
  forms of, 367.
  objects reflected double the size of, 379.
  paraboloid, 392.
  spherical aberration of, 391.
Mobility, 15.
  of gases, 121.
  of liquids, 88.
Molecules, 5.
  spaces between, 5, 35.
Momentum, 21, 54.
Moon, as seen from the poles and equator of the earth, 884.
  dark and light spots of, 864.

Moon, eccentricity of her orbit, 864.
　her actual path, 859.
　her libration in longitude and latitude, 858.
　her light compared with the sun's, 864.
　her motion never retrograde, 859.
　her orbit always concave toward the sun, 860.
　her path around the sun, 855.
　her phases, 862.
　inclination of her orbit to plane of ecliptic, 883.
　importance of the phases and motions of, 862.
　motion of, 826.
　rotation of, on its axis, 857.
　sidereal and synodic revolution of, 856.
　size of, 864.
　view of the earth from, 861.
　weight of, 864.
　why her dark side is visible near conjunction, 863.
　when it is *new* and *full*, 855.
　why it rises later every day, 864.
Morning and evening star, Venus, 851.
Morse's telegraph, 777.
Motion and force, 54.
Motion, absolute and relative, 15.
　accelerated, retarded, and uniform, 54.
　centre of, of the solar system, 845.
　compound of the satellites, 825.
　curvilinear, 842.
　direct, stationary, and retrograde of planets, 891.
　of projectiles, 62.
　of the stars, 940.
　of the waters of the earth, 912.
　reflected, 57.
　resultant, 58.
　varieties of, 54.
Motions of the primary planets, 815-817.
　of the secondary planets, 825-830.
　of the sun, 814.
Motors, 66.
Musical scale, 596.
　formation of, 597.
Musical sounds, difference between and noises, 588.
　qualities of, 589.

N.

NATURAL PHILOSOPHY, distinction between and chemistry, 8.
Neap and spring tides, 923-925.
Near-sightedness, 458.
　caused by defective form of eye-ball, 459.
Nebulæ, 946.
　classes of, 947.
Needle, astatic, 634.
　declination of, 638.
　dipping, 642.
　diurnal and other variations of, 639.
　inclination, or dip of, 640.
　magnetic, 635.
　mariner's, 644.
　position of dipping, in different parts of the earth, 643.
Neptune's satellites, 830.
Neutral equilibrium, 40, 42.
Neutralization of magnetic poles, 622.
　shown by Y-magnets, 623.
Newton's discovery, 806.
Night-glass, 482.
Nitric acid battery, 738.
Nitrogen, density of, 229.
Nodal figures and lines, 580.
　how delineated, 579.
Nodal points, 576.
　lines of plates, 578.
Nodes, 879.
　retrograde motion of the moon's, 906.
Noise, 588

Notes, musical, absolute number of vibrations corresponding to each, 597.
Nutation of the earth's axis, 939.
Nut-cracker an example of levers, 69.

O.

OBJECT-GLASSES for the microscope, 477.
　for telescopes, 488.
Obliquity of the ecliptic, 848.
Occultation of the stars, 909.
Ocean, currents in, 254.
Octave in music, 593.
Opaque bodies, 359.
Opera-glasses, 481.
Opposition and conjunction of planets, 890.
Optic angle, 447.
Optical axis, 446.
Optical centre of a lens, 408.
Optical instruments, 474-498.
　camera obscura, 489, 483, 484.
　camera lucida, 485.
　magic lantern, 478.
　microscope, compound, 477.
　microscope, simple, 476.
　microscope, solar, 479.
　night-glasses, 482.
　opera-glasses, 481.
　spectacles, 475.
　stereomonoscope, 498.
　stereoscope, 496, 497.
　telescopes, 488-494.
　telestereoscope, 495.
　variety and principal uses of, 474.
Optical toys, 471.
Optics, definition, 355.
Orbit of the moon always concave toward the sun, 860.
Orbital motions of heavenly bodies, 799.
Orbits of comets, 832.
Orbits of heavenly bodies, elliptical, 837.
　aphelion and perihelion of, 839.
　eccentricity of, with table, 838.
　plane of, 846.
　radius vector of, 840.
Organic electricity, 789-791.
Organs of voice a reed instrument, 587.
Orifices, shape of, 152.
Oscillations of pendulums, 60, 61.
　laws of, 61.
Oscillations of the planet Mercury, 882.
Overshot wheel, 159.
Oxygen, density of, 229.

P.

PARABOLIC curve, 392.
　mirrors and reflectors, 392.
Paradox, hydrostatic, 107.
Parallax of the heavenly bodies, 885-888.
　annual of the stars, 885.
　diurnal, 886.
　effect of on bodies, 887.
　importance of the principles of, 888
Parallelogram of forces, 58.
Pencils of light, 362.
　oblique, 390.
Pendulum, compensating, 60.
　electrical, 652.
　laws of oscillation of, 61.
　scientific uses of, 61.
Penumbra, 524.
Percussion a source of heat, 212.
Perihelion, 839.
Periodic time of heavenly bodies, 815.
Perpetual revolution, 63.
Phases of undulations of light, 503-506.
　of sound, 564-568.
　of the moon, 862.
Philosophy of eclipses, 894-911.
　of seasons, 867-871.

INDEX. 489

Philosophy of tides, 912-925.
 of transits, 879-881.
Phosphorescence, 357.
Photography, 487.
Photometers, 528.
 Bunsen's, Ritchie's, Rumford's, Silliman's, 528.
Physical astronomy, 793.
Physical properties of winds, 267.
Physics, or Natural Philosophy, 8.
Physics, or Natural Philosophy and chemistry, distinction between, 8.
Physiological effects of statical or frictional electricity, 705.
 of dynamical or voltaic electricity, 758.
Pipes, rapidity of water discharged from, 155.
 reed, 585.
 sound from, 583.
 with fixed mouth-pieces, 584.
Plane glass, refraction by, 397, 398.
Plane of meridian, 938.
 of the ecliptic, inclination of orbits to, 849.
 of the equinoctial, 847.
Planes, inclined, 83-85.
 of orbits, 846.
Planets, 807.
 approximate relative distances of, 809.
 difference between equatorial and polar diameters of, 850.
 direct, stationary, and retrograde, motion of, 891.
 exterior and interior, 807.
 figure or form of, 850.
 greatest declination of, 878.
 opposition and conjunction of, 890.
 polar inclination of, 878.
 primary, 807, 815.
 relative magnitude of, 808.
 representation of the motions of, 810.
 secondary, 825-830.
 telescopic views of, 836.
 why they do not fall to the sun, 844.
 width of zones of, 878.
 (see primary planets).
Plants consume carbonic acid and supply oxygen, 124.
 electricity of, 791.
Plate electrical machine, 678.
Plates, vibration of, 577.
Pliability, 31.
Plumb-line, 53.
Pneumatics, definitions, 119.
Polar inclination and seasons of different planets, with table, 878.
Polarity of magnets, 600, 614, 619, 622, 623.
Polarity of the pile, 729.
 Œrsted's discovery of, 760.
Polarization and transfer of elements, 756.
Polariscope, 515.
Polarization of light, 513-521.
 by reflection, 515.
 by refraction, 519.
 by double refraction, 520.
 by transmission, 513.
 partial, 518.
 plane, 516.
 useful applications of, 521.
Poles, celestial, 938.
 in physics, 512.
 of magnets, 600.
 arrangement of in star-shaped bodies, 618.
 both must co-exist in every magnet, 614.
 two sets of, 619.
 unlike neutralize each other, 622.
 of the earth, when the sun shines upon them, 933.
 of the ecliptic, 847.
Polyrama, 480.
Porosity, 14.
Pores, physical and sensible, 14.
Positive and negative in electricity, 653.
 in magnetism, 605.

Power, 66.
 of points, electrical, 666.
 of steam, 202, 329, 334, 349, 354.
 relation of to weight, 66.
Press, hydrostatic, 109.
Pressure, atmospheric, 126.
 action of barometers dependent on, 134.
 action of suction pumps dependent on, 132, 173, 174.
 amount of on the human body, 126.
 animal respiration dependent on, 146.
 equal in all directions, 130.
 illustrated in a vacuum, 129.
 it varies with altitude, 132.
 shown by currents of air, 143.
 shown by hollow hemispheres, 130.
 shown by inverted tumbler of water, 142.
 shown by tubes and water, 144.
 shown by vacuum fountain, 145.
 sustains different liquids at different heights, 133.
 varied on liquids varies the boiling point, 319.
 varies at the same place, 133.
Pressure of liquids, 92.
 bursting a cask by, 110.
 downward of, 101.
 downward of independent of shape of vessel, 101.
 equal in all directions, 92.
 not in proportion to quantity, but height, 93, 107.
 on walls of vessels, 104.
 on walls of vessels, total, 105.
 on walls and bottom of vessels, total, 106.
 transmitted equally in all directions, 92.
 upward equal to downward, 100.
 use of, transmitted, 108, 109.
Primary colors, 419.
 planets, 815.
 absolute magnitude of, with table, 818.
 attraction of, with table, 822.
 density of, with table, 821.
 distance of, from Sun, with table, 820.
 diurnal revolution of, with table, 817.
 light and heat of, with table, 823.
 periodic revolution of, with table, 815.
 relative magnitude of, with table, 819.
 telescopic views of, 836.
 velocity of, with table, 816.
Printing telegraph, 777.
Prisms, 405.
 refraction by, 406, 419.
Projectiles, falling of, 64.
 greatest horizontal range of, 62.
 motion of, 62.
 thrown from horizontal guns, 64.
Proof plane, 664.
Properties, characteristic, of solids, 25-34.
 of fluids and gases, 87.
 of gases, 119-133.
 of light, 364.
 of liquids, 92-118.
 of the solar spectrum, 420.
 of matter, essential, 9, 10.
 general or specific, 6.
 physical and chemical, 7.
 secondary, 11-18.
Ptolemy's system of astronomy, 802.
Pulleys, compound, 79.
 example and formulæ, 79.
 compound, with one movable pulley, 80.
 example and formulæ, 80.
 movable and immovable, 77.
 example and formulæ, 77.
 simple fixed, 75.
 simple movable, with formulæ, 76.
 system of, with more than one cord, 78.
 example and formulæ, 78.
 system of, with more than one rope and three cords to each pulley, 81.
 example and formulæ, 81.
 the burton, 82.

Pulleys, example and formulæ, 82.
Pulse-glass, Franklin's, 319.
Pumps, centrifugal, 169.
 chain, 168.
 T-centrifugal, 170.
Pumps, rotary, double cog-wheel, 177.
 double cylinder, 175.
 single cylinder, 176.
 suction bellows, 178.
 diaphragm, 179.
 double-acting force, 183.
 double-acting, with two valves, 185.
 force, 182.
 plunger force, 180.
 principle of, 173.
 proof of atmospheric pressure in, 174.
 single acting, 184.
 single cylinder, 181.
 stomach, 187.
Pyrometers, 280.

Q.

QUALITY of musical sounds, 589.
Quantity and intensity of electricity in machines, 630.
Quantity and intensity of electricity, difference between, 732.
Quantity increases with surface, intensity with the number of pairs, 733.
Quantity of electricity required to produce chemical action enormous, 757.
Quantity and intensity of heat, difference between, 214.

R.

RADIANT heat, 284.
 intensity of, 286.
 mutual exchange of, between bodies, 289.
 partially absorbed by medium, 287.
 transmission of, 298.
Radiating power for heat, 296.
Radiation of heat, 284.
 cooling by, 285.
 in vacuo, 283.
 solar, 205.
 terrestrial, 208.
Radius vector, 840.
 passes over equal areas in equal times, 841.
Railway illumination, 392.
Rain, 336.
 annual depth of, 342.
 days of, 341.
 distribution of, 340.
 drops of, their effects on parallel rays of light, 435.
 gauge, 339.
 where most abundant, 340-343.
Rainbow, explained by effects of a drop of water on parallel rays of light, 435.
 how we see the colors of, from one position, 433.
 primary and secondary, 432.
 the arch of, 434.
 width of the arch, 434.
 width of the primary bow, 434.
 width of the secondary bow, 434.
 width of the space between the bows, 434.
Ram, hydraulic, 172.
Range of the human voice, 590.
Rays of light, 362.
 how affected by drops of water, 435.
 visual, nearly parallel, 456.
Reaction and action equal, 65.
 of escaping electricity, 687.
 of escaping liquids, 163.
Recomposition of white light, 431.
Reed pipes, 585.
 instruments, 585.
Reeds, arrangement of in pipes, 586.

Reflecting telescopes, 491-494.
Reflection of heat from concave mirrors, 292.
 incident heat absorbed and reflected, 290.
 laws which govern, 291.
 reflective power of different substances, 293.
Reflection of light at curved surfaces, 381.
 by convex spherical mirrors, 382.
 double, of mirrors, 398.
 of light at plane surfaces, 370.
 of converging rays, 371.
 of diverging rays, 370.
 of parallel rays, 372.
 polarization by, 515.
 of sound, 544-554.
Reflective power for heat, determination of, 294.
 causes modifying, 297.
Reflectors, 365.
 forms of, 367.
 paraboloid, 392.
 spherical aberration of, 391.
Refraction of heat, 301.
 of light, definitions, 394.
 by a sphere of glass, 407.
 by dense media, 401.
 by parallel strata of different media, 397.
 by plane glass, 397, 398, 406.
 by prisms, 406.
 by the atmosphere, 400.
 cause of, 396.
 depth of water rendered apparently less by, 404.
 double, 519.
 effects of, on the rising and setting of heavenly bodies, 400.
 index of, 394.
 laws of, 395.
Refraction and internal reflection, 398.
Refraction and total reflection, 399.
 of sound, 581.
 laws of, 582.
Refractory bodies, 304.
Regulator of steam-engine, 354.
Relation of bodies to light, 359.
 of cohesion and repulsion in the three states of matter, 23
 of power to weight, 66.
Relative influence of the sun and moon on the tides, 922.
Repulsion, electrical, 656, 657.
 in gases, 91.
 magnetic, 625, 626.
 of heat, 202.
Reservoir of electricity, 660.
Resistance to fracture, 27.
Resolution of forces, 58.
Resonance, 549.
Respiration, animal, dependent upon atmospheric pressure, 146.
Respiration and combustion consume oxygen and supply carbonic acid, 124.
Rest, absolute and relative, 15.
 no absolute, 15.
Resultant of forces, 58.
 of motion, 58.
Retina of the eye, 443.
 duration of impression on, 470.
 sensibility of, 462.
 size of image on, 457.
Retrograde motion of the moon's nodes, 906.
 of planets, 891.
Revolution of primary planets, 815.
 diurnal, with table, 817.
 periodic, with table, 815.
 sidereal and synodic of the moon, 856.
Revolving electro-magnets, 779.
 lights, 416.
Right ascension of a body, 938.
 angle of, 938.
Rings of Saturn, 852.
 dimensions and distances of, 852.
Rivers, flowing of, 156.
 velocity of, 157.

INDEX. 491

Rods, vibration of, 576.
Rooms for speaking, 553.
Rotary pumps, 175-177.
    steam-engines, 348.
Rotation, 19.

S.

SAFETY lamp of Davy, 245.
Satellites or moons, 807.
    compound motion of, 825.
    distance of in semi-diameters of their planets, 853.
    Earth's, 826.
    Jupiter's, with table, 827.
    Neptune's, 830.
    Saturn's, with table, 828.
    Uranus', with table, 829.
Saturated space, 323.
Saturn's rings, 852.
    dimensions and distances of, 852.
Saturn's satellites, distances and periodic times, 828.
    eclipses of, 911.
Scale, musical, 596.
    formation of, 597.
Scissors, a variety of lever, 69.
Screw, endless, 86.
    combination of with other powers, 86.
    modification of inclined plane, 84.
    example and formulæ, 84.
    of Archimedes, 171.
Seasons, 867.
    causes of, 868.
    of different planets, 878.
Secondary axis, 390.
    currents, electrical, 784, 785.
    properties of matter, 11-24.
Secondary planets, 807, 825.
    compound motion of, 825.
Self-registering thermometers, 282.
Sensible horizon, 938.
Series of elastic balls, 65.
Sextant, mariner's, 380.
Shadows, 522.
    density of, 525.
    dimensions of the earth's, 900.
    dimensions of the moon's, 900.
    of bodies larger than the illuminating body, 522.
    of bodies smaller than the illuminating body, 523.
    of solar bodies, 894.
Sidereal revolution of the moon, 856.
Signs of the zodiac, 866.
    division of, 874.
Sine of the angle of incidence, 394.
    of refraction, 394.
Size, apparent, of objects, 383.
Smee's battery, 735.
Simple microscope, 476.
    pendulum, 61.
    propositions respecting, 61.
    vision with two eyes, 467.
Snow, 337.
Solar bodies, 807.
    shadows of, 894.
Solar and lunar ecliptic limits, 907.
Solar microscope, 479.
    radiation, 205.
    spectrum, 419.
    colors of, 419.
    dark lines in, 426.
    properties of, 420.
    refraction and dispersion of, 425.
    and sidereal time, 854.
    day, 854.
    system, 807.
    centre of gravity and motion of, 845.
    impossibility of delineating, 810.
    represented by real objects, 810.
Solenoid, 770.

Solidification, 304.
Solidification, change of volume by, 304.
    liberation of heat by, 303, 304.
Solids, characteristic properties of, 25-34.
    conductibility of, for heat, 240-244.
    expansion of, 215-219.
    structure in, 24.
    undulations of, 576-580.
    velocity of sound in, 542.
Solstices, 869.
Sonometer, 573.
Sonorous or sounding bodies, 531.
    difference of bodies, 535.
    waves, length of, 590.
Sound, 533.
    a sensation, 533.
    distance calculated by, 537.
    causes which modify intensity of, 556.
    from pipes, 583.
    intensity of, 555.
    interference of, 564.
    limits of perceptible, 590.
    mediums of, 532.
    not instantaneous, 536.
    not propagated in a vacuum, 575.
    propagated by waves, 532.
    reflected, 544-554.
    refraction of, 581.
    refraction, laws of, 581.
    time required for transmission of, 536.
    velocity of, 538.
    velocity of in air, 539.
    velocity of in gases, 540.
    velocity of in liquids, 541.
    velocity of in solids, 542.
Sounding bodies vibrate, 531.
Sounds caused by burning hydrogen, 574.
    different, 534.
    qualities of musical, 589.
    time required to distinguish, 543.
    velocity the same for all, 538.
Sources of heat, 205-213.
    of heat influencing diathermancy, 299.
    of light, 357.
Space described by a falling body, 55.
Space, extent of, 795.
Spark, electrical, 684, 700, 702, 768.
    color of, 701.
Speaking, room suitable for, 553.
Speaking-trumpet, 558.
Specific gravity, 114.
    instrument for finding of liquids, 116.
    method of finding of liquids, 115.
    rule and example, 115.
    method of finding of solids, 115.
    rule and example, 115.
Specific identity of matter, 7.
    heat, 231.
    affected by change of state, 238.
    effect of, of water on climate, 234.
    of gases, 235.
    standard of, 233.
    table of, of different substances, 233.
    table of, of different states of bodies, 238.
    weight, 114.
Spectacles, 475.
Spectrum, solar, 419.
    dark lines in, 426.
    properties of, 420.
Specula, 365, 366.
Spherical aberration of lenses, 412.
    of mirrors, 391.
Spherical mirrors, concave, 386-388.
    convex, 381, 382.
Spheroidal state of liquids, 331.
    cause of, 331.
Spirit-level, 97.
    thermometer, 281.
Spring and neap tides, 923-925.
    variations in, 924.
Springs, intermittent, 99, 180.
Spy-glass, 490.
Stable equilibrium, 40.

INDEX.

Stability of bodies, 43.
Stability, dependent upon position of centre of gravity, 43.
   relative of cubes and pyramids, 44.
Stars, binary, 944.
   clusters of, 945.
   double, 943.
   motion of, 940.
   the number of, 949.
   temporary, or new, and lost, 942.
   variable and periodical, 941.
   (see nebulæ).
Statical electricity, 648.
Statics, 54.
Steam-boiler, 351.
   explosions of, 330.
Steam, electricity from, 682.
Steam-engines, 345–354.
   boilers of, 351.
   condensation in, 352.
   fly-wheels of, 354.
   governors of, 354.
   high-pressure, 349.
   illustration of principle of low pressure, 333.
   improvements in, 347.
   low-pressure, or condensing, 354.
   origin of, 345.
   parallel motion of, 354.
   reciprocating and rotary motion of, 348.
   stuffing-boxes of, 353.
   the eccentric, its importance, 350.
   the eoliplic, 346.
   valves of, 351.
   Watt's improvement, 347.
Steam heaters, 255.
Steam, high pressure of, 334.
   latent heat of, 314.
   latent and sensible heat of at different temperatures, 315.
Steelyards an example of levers, 69.
Stereomonoscope, 498.
Stereoscope, 496.
   principles of, 497.
Stomach-pump, 187.
Structure, in solids, 24.
Structure of the human eye, 440–444.
Submerged bodies displace water equal to their own bulk, 113.
   not pressed equally in all directions, 113.
Substance, defined, 1.
Suction, explained, 132.
Suction and lifting pumps, 173–185.
Sulphate of copper battery, 736.
Sun, dark spots on, 814.
   declination of, 871, 931.
   distance of, 813.
   effects of its declination on temperature, 934.
   his apparent motion in the ecliptic, 873.
   influence of, 811.
   magnitude of, 812.
   motions of, 814.
   orbit of, 893.
   periodic revolution of, 893.
   quantity of heat from, 206.
   telescopic view of, 814.
   the principal source of heat, 205.
   velocity of his motion in space, 893.
   when it shines on the poles of the earth, 933.
Synodic revolution of the moon, 856.
Syphon, 188.
   conveying water over hills with, 191.
   dependent on atmospheric pressure, 188.
   for the chemical laboratory, 192.
System, solar, 807.
   centre of gravity and motion of, 845.
Systems, binary, of stars, 944.

T.

Table of absolute number of vibrations corresponding to musical notes, 597.

Table of asteroids, 824.
   boiling point at different atmospheric pressures, 334.
   conductibility of solids, 242.
   depth of rain, 342.
   discharge of liquids, 155.
   expansion of liquids, 222.
   expansion of solids, 219.
   falling bodies, 55.
   frequency of different winds, 268.
   length of waves of light, 509.
   melting points of different substances, 304.
   specific heat of different states of bodies, 238.
   specific heat of different substances, 233.
   velocity and force of winds, 270.
Tables relating to primary planets, 815–824.
   eccentricity of orbits, 838.
   inclination of orbits to plane of ecliptic, 849.
   polar inclination, 878.
   secondary planets, 826–829.
Telegraph, first experiments in electrical, 776.
   House's printing, 777.
   Morse's recording, 777.
   the earth circuit, 778.
   Watson's, 776.
Telegraphic alphabet, 777.
Telescopes, different kinds of, 488–494.
   Galileo's, 481.
   Gregorian reflecting, 492.
   Lord Rosse's reflecting, 494.
   Newtonian reflecting, 493.
   refracting astronomical, 489.
   Sir William Herschel's reflecting, 491.
   terrestrial, 490.
Telescopic views of the primary planets, 836.
   of the sun, 814.
Telestereoscope, 495.
Temper, 33.
Temperature, 200.
   extremes of natural, 207.
   measurement of, 271.
   of climate affected by declination of the sun, 934.
   of plants, 213.
Tenacity or resistance of substances, 27.
Tenacious liquids, fall or flow of, 56.
Tension of vapors, 323.
   cold diminishes and heat increases, 323, 325.
   maximum, 323.
   electrical, 662.
Terrestrial attraction, 18.
   direction of, 53.
   globes, 937.
   heat, origin of, 208.
   magnetism, 624, 633, 638, 643.
Theoretical and actual flow, 153.
Theory, Ampère's, relating to electro-magnetism, 766.
   Copernicus', of astronomy, 803.
   electro-chemical, 725.
   of heat, emission, 201.
   of heat, undulatory, 201.
   of light, emission, 356.
   of light, undulatory, 356.
   of magnetism, 625.
   Ptolemy's, of astronomy, 802.
   single-fluid, of electricity, 655.
   two-fluid, of electricity, 654.
   wave of light, 499.
Volta's, contact of Galvanism, 724.
Thermo-electric revolving arch, 788.
Thermo-electricity, 787.
Thermometers, 271.
   Centigrade, Fahrenheit, Réaumur, 272.
   conversion of scales of, 273.
   differential, 283.
   fixing the boiling point, 277.
   fixing the freezing point, 276.
   limits of mercurial, 280.
   mercurial, 272.
   method of making, 274.

Thermometers, method of graduating, 276.
  self-registering, 282.
  sensibility of, 279.
  spirit, 281.
  standard points in, 275.
  tests of, 278.
Three states of matter, 23.
Thunder, 713.
Thunder storms, 712.
  clouds, origin of, 712.
Tides, atmospheric, 930.
  affected by winds, 926.
  affected by conformation of land, 927.
  average elevation of, 928.
  different heights of in different oceans and seas, 929.
  influence of the sun on, 919.
  lagging of the tide-wave, 918.
  not uniform, 913.
  opposite tide-wave, cause of, 920.
  principal cause of, 914.
  relative influence of the sun and moon on, 922.
  secondary cause of opposite tide-wave, 921.
  single tide-wave, 916.
  spring and neap, 923-925.
  two tide-waves, 917.
  variations in spring and neap, 924.
Time, equation of, 854.
  required for distinguishing sounds, 543.
  for transmission of sound, 536.
  for vision, 472.
  periodic, of heavenly bodies, 815.
  solar and sidereal, 854.
Tone changed by echo, 548.
Tornadoes, 266.
Torsion, 26.
Total reflection, 399.
Tourmaline, action of on ordinary light, 514.
Toys, optic, 471.
Trade-winds, 262.
Transits, 879.
  calculation of, 881.
  of Mercury, 880.
  of Venus, 892.
Translation or direct motion, 19.
Translucent bodies, 359.
Transmission of luminous waves, 513.
  of radiant heat, 298.
  of sound, time required for, 536.
Transparent bodies, 359.
Trumpet, ear. 558.
  speaking, 559.
Tubes, capillary, 38.
Tuning-fork, 564.
Turbine wheel, 162.

U.

UMBRA, 524.
Undershot wheel, 161.
Undulations, combinations of in liquids, 565.
  interference of, of liquids in an ellipse, 566.
  of elastic fluids, 567.
  of light, 499.
  of solids, 569.
Uniform motion, 54.
Unison, 591.
Unit of force, 54.
Unit of heat, 232.
Universe, 950.
Universal discharger, 697.
Unstable equilibrium, 40, 42.
Up and down, relative terms, 53.
Upward pressure of atmosphere, 126.
  of liquids, 100.
Uranus' satellites, distances and periodic times of, 829.

V.

VACUUM, evaporation in, 323.
  fountain in, 145.
  various phenomena in, 129.
Valves, operation of in steam-engine, 351.
  safety, of steam-boilers, 351.
Vaporization, definitions, 311.
Vapors and gases, identity of, 119.
  condensation of vapors, 327.
  density of, 229.
  formed in a vacuum, 323.
  tension of, 119.
  tension, maximum of, 323.
Variable motion, 54.
Variations of barometric height, 135.
  of the needle, 638-640.
Varieties of motion, 19.
Vegetables, electricity of, 791.
  temperature of, 213.
Velocity, accelerated, of falling bodies, 55, 56.
  of comets, 832.
  discharge of liquids, 155.
  electricity, 716.
  heavenly bodies, 800.
  jets, 154.
  light, 526.
  lightning, 716.
  rivers, 156.
  planets, with table, 816.
  sound in air, 538, 539.
  sound in gases, 540.
  sound in liquids, 541.
  sound in solids, 542.
Venus as morning and evening star, 851.
  transits of, 892.
  transits, list of, 892.
Vibrating cords, nodal points of, 571.
Vibration of cords, 570-573.
  laws of, 572.
  verification of laws of, 573.
Vibration of air in pipes, 583.
Vibrating rods and plates, nodal points and lines of, 578.
Vibration of plates, 577.
  of rods, 576.
Vibrations, absolute number of corresponding to musical notes, 597.
  cause of in sonorous bodies illustrated by striking a bell, 561, 562.
  of light, 499.
  of light, direction of, 500.
  of sonorous bodies, 531.
  of sonorous bodies, illustrated by Jews-harp, 560.
  transverse, of light, 500.
View of the earth from the moon, 861.
  of the moon from the poles and equator of the earth. 884.
Views, dissolving, 480.
  microscopic, 479.
  telescopic, of the planets, 836.
  of the sun, 814.
Virtual focus, 388.
Visible bodies emit light from every point, 363.
Vision, 439.
  angle of, 448.
  binocular, 460.
  brilliancy, 454.
  conditions of distinct, 461.
  double, 468.
  how we see objects close to the eye, 453.
  indistinct, 452.
  limits of distinct, 455.
  sensations of excited by other causes than light, 473.
  time required to produce, 472.
  why we see objects erect, their images being inverted, 450.
Visual rays, nearly parallel, 456.
Vocal apparatus of man, 587.
Voice, range of human, 590.
Volatile and fixed liquids, 312.
Voltaic arch, 747.
  heat of, 751.
  oval form of, 748.
Voltaic batteries, 727-740.

Voltaic circuit, 760.
  polarity of, 729, 760.
Voltaic currents, 730.
  decomposition of water by, 755.
  decomposition of salts by, 756.
Voltaic electricity, 745-758.
  chemical effects of, 752.
  heating effects of, 751.
  illuminating effects of, 746.
  physiological effects of, 758.
  quantity and intensity of, 732.
Voltaic pile or battery, 727.
  chemical effects of, 752, 753.
  chemical theory of, 725.
  electrical currents of, 730.
  grouping elements of, 727.
  heating effects of, 751.
  magnetic effects of, 761.
  physical effects of, 746.
  physiological effects of, 758.
  polarity, 729.
  theory of, 724.
  varieties of, 728.
  simple couple, 726.
Voltaic spark and arch, 747.
  oval form of, 748.
Voltaism and galvanism, 721-724.
Volta's contact theory, 724.
  discoveries, 724.

W.

Warming buildings by convection of air, 256.
  by convection of fluids in pipes, 255.
  by steam in pipes, 257.
Water as a motive power, 158.
  an exception to the laws of contraction and expansion, 223.
  beneficial effects of unequal expansion of, 224.
  boiling temperature of, 317.
  composition of, 755.
  compressibility of, 89.
  conveyed over hills by siphons, 191.
  decomposition of, 755.
  elasticity of, 89.
  expands in freezing, 223.
  its flow in rivers, 156.
  freezing of in small tubes, 225.
  freezing point, temperature of, 223.
  great capacity of for heat, 233.
  how heated, 253.
  illustrations of the pressure of, 100-113.
  importance of, 197.
  importance of elevators of, 197.
  level of, 94-98.
  loss of effective head of, 193.
  pressure of at different depths, 110-112.
  specific heat of, 233.
  standard of specific heat, 233.
  velocity of in pipes, how retarded, 190.
  velocity of in rivers, 157.
  velocity of discharge of, 155.
  vertical jets of, 195.
  why rises by suction, 132, 173, 174.
  why rises in pumps, 174.
Water elevators, Archimedes' screw, 171.
  centrifugal pump, 169.
  chain pump, 168.
  endless chain of pots, 167.
  hydraulic ram, 172.
  T-centrifugal pump, 170.
  lifting wheel, 165.
  wheel and buckets, or Persian wheel, 166.
Water level, 96.
  pumps, 173-186.
  spouts, 266.

Water wheels, 158.
  breast, 160.
  centrifugal, 163.
  overshot, 159.
  turbine, 162.
  undershot, 161.
Waves of condensation and rarefaction, 567.
Waves of light, 356, 499.
  brilliancy dependent on amplitude of, 501.
  causes of, 510.
  color dependent on length of, 502.
  determining the length of, 508.
  direction of, 500.
  in any number of planes resolved to two planes, 517.
  length of, 509.
  luminous, transmission of, 513.
  table of length of, 509.
Waves of liquids, combinations of, 565.
  from foci of an ellipse, 566.
  interference of, 565.
  interference of in an ellipse, 566.
Waves, reflection of from parabolic curves, 554.
Waves of sound, caused by striking a bell, 561.
  interference of, 568.
  sonorous, co-existence of, 568.
  tide, 916-921.
Weather indicated by barometer, 136.
  rules for judging by the barometer, 136.
Wedge, a form of inclined plane, 85.
  formulæ respecting, 85.
Weight, definition of, 39.
  different in different localities, 48-51.
  as resistance, 66.
Welding, 34.
Wells, artesian, 95.
Wheel and axle, 71.
  example and formulæ, 71.
  compound, 74.
  example and formulæ, 74.
  barometer, 138.
Whirlwind, 266.
Whispering galleries, 552.
White light, recomposition of, 431.
Windlass, simple, 72.
  differential or double, 73.
Winds, action of on sails, 59.
  cause of, 262.
  definition of, 260.
  general direction of frequency of, 268.
  hurricanes or cyclones, 265.
  kinds of, 261.
  land and sea breezes, 264.
  periodical, 261.
  physical properties of, 267.
  pressure of, 269.
  regular, 261.
  table respecting, 270.
  tornadoes or whirlwinds, 266.
  trade, 262.
  variable, 261.
  velocity of, 270.
Wood, conduction of heat by, 244.
Working point in machinery, 66.

Z.

Zero absolute, 275.
Zenith distance, 938.
Zero point of thermometers, 272.
Zodiac, 865.
  names of the signs of, 866.
  signs or constellations of, 866, 872.
Zones, 932.
  frigid, 932.
  temperate, 932.
  table of, of different planets, 878.
  torrid, 932.

www.ingramcontent.com/pod-product-compliance
Lightning Source LLC
Chambersburg PA
CBHW021415300426
44114CB00010B/502